Lord Denning:
the Judge and the Law

AUSTRALIA AND NEW ZEALAND
The Law Book Company Ltd.
Sydney : Melbourne : Perth

CANADA AND U.S.A.
The Carswell Company Ltd.
Agincourt, Ontario

INDIA
N.M. Tripathi Private Ltd.
Bombay
and
Eastern Law House Private Ltd.
Calcutta and Delhi
M.P.P. House
Bangalore

ISRAEL
Steimatzky's Agency Ltd.
Jerusalem : Tel Aviv : Haifa

MALAYSIA : SINGAPORE : BRUNEI
Malayan Law Journal (Pte.) Ltd.
Singapore

PAKISTAN
Pakistan Law House
Karachi

Lord Denning:
the Judge and the Law

J. L. Jowell
*Professor of Public Law in the University
of London (University College)*

J. P. W. B. McAuslan
Professor of Law at the University of Warwick

LONDON
SWEET & MAXWELL
1984

Published in 1984 by
Sweet & Maxwell Limited of
11 New Fetter Lane, London.
Computerset by Promenade Graphics Limited, Cheltenham.
Printed in Scotland.

British Library Cataloguing in Publication Data

Lord Denning.
1. Denning, Alfred Denning, *Baron*
2. Judgments—England
I. Jowell, J.L.   II. McAuslan, J.P.W.B.
344.207'77   KD632.D4

ISBN 0 421 28120 0

Foreword

LORD DEVLIN OF WEST WICK, P.C., F.B.A.

THERE is no precedent for so comprehensive an assessment of a judge's work to be issued almost immediately on his retirement from the Bench. Not that a lack of precedent would deeply distress Lord Denning (though I think his reputation of waywardness has become exaggerated). Indeed, I doubt if there is a precedent for any assessment at all that goes beyond a stately obituary in *The Times* or a paragraph in the D.N.B. Few judges, apart from those with a tally of famous cases, rate a biography.

Why, then, so elaborate a study of Lord Denning? I say at once that if there were no reason for it other than a whim of the authors, it would still be good value. He was an Appellate Judge for 35 years, an unprecedentedly (the word keeps intruding) long period; and to have a number of distinguished writers examining the development of the law during that period by following the activities of a central figure is a deserved honour for him and very attractive for us.

There is, however, more to it than that. How much more? That is what I hoped to find out before I wrote this Foreword. But illustrious writers are difficult to drill. They are great doers of their own thing and of doing it in their own time. Months ago I read with immense pleasure of the first essays, perhaps not yet in their final forms, and started to make a forecast of where Lord Denning's place in legal history would be. A rough forecast, I thought, whose refinement must wait until all the embroidered cloths were spread out on a field below an ivory tower from which I would meditate on them at leisure. What a hope! I find myself now in the company of the laggards being herded at a gallop towards a publication date.

The survey of the completed work, the meditation, the speculation and the draft of a judgment for posterity, I must now leave to the readers. Besides assuring them of an enjoyable occupation, I can offer them a starting point which I believe they can take as firm.

When Tom and I were young the law was stagnant. The old-fashioned judge looked to the letter of the statute and for the case on all fours. He knew that he had to do justice according to law. Either he assumed that the law when strictly applied would always do justice or else he decided that, if it did not, it was not his business to interfere. Today this is not the idea. No statement of the law, be it a precedent or a statute, is ever final: it is to be read in its context and its context can change. A judge must never assume that the law always and in all circumstances does complete justice. That would be an impossible task to put upon any lawmaker. To do justice according to law the judge must keep his eye on the justice of the case as well as on the text of the law.

A case may fall into a large or a small category. If it is small, it will be in a situation which is unlikely to be repeated, and the adaptation of the law can be thought of as a straining rather than a development. Then even the "timid soul" within the famous Denning classification can do justice while protesting that it turned on the facts of the particular case. Where the category is

large, there is no concealing the need for a major development repugnant to
conservative thought. Moreover, when the category is large, it is easy to say
that the innovation is too considerable for the court and should be made, if at
all, by Parliament. The minority speeches in *Donoghue* v. *Stevenson* [1932] A.C.
562 display the current attitude of refusing to look over the boundary wall.

In the 1920s and 1930s Lord Atkin was notable among the judges for the
vigour with which he was ready to extend a principle into unoccupied territory. After the war it was Mr. Justice Denning who led the way. It was not
the result in *High Trees* that came as a shock. That could, I think, have been
reached unobtrusively by a little twisting and blending of old authorities,
though many puisnes would have left that sort of work to the Court of
Appeal. Denning, a very recent puisne, preferred to cut a new channel from
the main stream.

In 1962 there was a turning point which made this book feasible. Denning's promotion to the Court of Appeal in 1948 when he was still under 50
after only three years as a puisne, half spent in Divorce and half in the King's
Bench, had been remarkable. Thereafter he advanced less speedily but still
fast and reached the House of Lords in 1957. His close contemporaries were
Evershed, Master of the Rolls since 1949, Radcliffe, a law Lord since 1949,
and Parker, about to become Lord Chief Justice in 1958. Thus for Denning
as a junior law Lord the offices of Chief Justice and of the Rolls, which provide the only bypass to the slow rise by seniority in the Lords, were filled by
men of his own age. In the Lords influence on the law was then heavily
dependent on seniority since the senior law Lord usually gave the leading
judgment.

In 1962 Evershed had served for 13 years as Master of the Rolls. He was
still too young to retire but he wanted less business in the law. This meant an
exchange of place with a law Lord, one who was ready to exchange the distant prospect of presiding in the Lords for being immediately the master in
his own court. This was what Denning wanted. Had he remained in the
Lords, he would have been behind not only Radcliffe but Reid. Reid was a
very great judge, progressive but not unorthodox. Though he was only just
senior to Radcliffe in appointment, he belonged to the preceding decade.
Nevertheless he outlasted Radcliffe who retired in 1965 while Reid went on
until 1974. By then 12 out of the 20 years of Tom's remaining judicial life had
passed.

If Denning had preferred in 1962 to stay where he was, this book would
not have been composed as it is. For this book is about one judge. All other
books of this sort have not been about a judge but about a period or a subject.
Had Denning remained in the Lords, his contribution would have been
great, perhaps the greatest, but it would have been a part of the whole. Even
as it is, the reader must remember that from the nature of the book the light
is focused. Who, for example, found the ultimate common law solution to the
problem of the deserted wife? Was it Lord Denning or Lord Diplock? And—
perish the thought—would it matter which? Since, as is almost bound to happen, in the end Parliament—more precisely the Government lawyers—takes
over.

Lord Denning's decision to take the Rolls was right for him because it was
coupled with the determination to seize the latent power of the office. This is
the power that a Chief Justice has always exercised, but not hitherto the
president of the Court of Appeal,—the power of choosing his own cases and

his own colleagues, the former more important than the latter since no Lord
Justice is a "yes" man.

Traditionally, the influence of the Court of Appeal is based on the fact that
over a large area of the law it is in practice the final court. Lord Denning
exercised this influence to the full. When, to the 20 years of his Presidency,
there is added the nine years from 1948 to 1957, one is enabled by that statis-
tic alone to estimate his huge contribution to the law. To be added to this
there is the novel influence exercised by the Leader of the Opposition. He has
himself given in his own books the fullest account of his opposition to the
Lords and of the decisions in which it was embodied. I look forward
especially to seeing what the eleven authors of this book make of them.

It is as the Leader of the Opposition that Lord Denning is best known to
the public. Here he has the advantage of being the monarch, albeit a constitutional monarch, of his own court: the House of Lords has only a council of
regency. The public, as well as the Press, which is avid for it, likes personifi-
cation. "Lord Denning rules that . . ." sets the pulse racing in a way that
"the Court of Appeal decides that . . ." can never do. Since 1940 when the
Lord Chancellor ceased to sit regularly, the House of Lords has been without
an active monarch. I believe that as a body they would impinge more
strongly on the public mind if they had one.

The secret of Lord Denning's attraction—for the profession as well as for
the general public—is, I think, the belief that he opens the door to the law
above the law. "I imagine that every lawyer in his heart" Lord Radcliffe has
written "sighs for some doctrine of Natural Law to bring to bear upon the
raw material of his labours. It is his escape route from the sharply delimited
areas of legislative enactment and established precedent. It is more than
that: it is his link with a more universal conception of justice than his own
municipal system is likely to seem to embrace."[1] But the natural law, he
thought, "was not likely to be more than a minor formative influence upon
the work of the judge." Lord Denning, I believe, thought differently. He
thought, as Lord Radcliffe did not, "that judges in our society could remake
the body of the law they administer into what they may approve as a shape of
greater justice."

This remaking has been done once successfully in English law, but the
enterprise took over four centuries to complete and began with a different
aim. Faced with the constrictions and inadequacies of the mediæval common
law, the Chancellor acted by threatening to imprison anyone who did not
accept instead the equitable alternative he offered. In the eighteenth century
Lord Mansfield tried his hand at direct improvement. Already the common
law courts were accepting some equitable solutions. Equity, for example, had
introduced the rules permitting secondary evidence of a deed to overcome the
common law rule that the plaintiff who could not produce his bond was para-
lysed. These and other similar relaxations came to be applied by the common
law courts themselves. Lord Mansfield greatly accelerated this process which
led a century later to the fusion of law and equity. But his attempts to get the
judges to think equitably and reform the law accordingly were with one
exception, the action for money had and received, which made binding the
"ties of natural justice and equity," frustrated.

In the United States what Lord Mansfield and Lord Denning (the latter

---

[1] *The Law and its Compass*, (Faber & Faber, 1960), p. 25.

more greatly handicapped) attempted, has been achieved by a simple manipulation of the Constitution. In the phrase "due process of law" in the Fifth and Fourteenth Amendments, the "law" is not the law as it is but the law as it ought to be, what Justice Frankfurter described as "those canons of decency and fairness which express the notions of justice of English-speaking peoples."[2] In this way equity, as static in the United States as in England and merged with the common law in 1938, has been given new life.

Has Lord Denning succeeded in giving practical effect to his conception that justice is above the law? That he has made a great impact on the law is unquestionable. But is his achievement in this respect merely a matter for comparison with the senior Law Lords of his time, Reid, Wilberforce and Diplock? Or is it something unique? The multitude who applauded his judgments and put his books into the bestseller lists, believe that it is unique. What is the verdict of the discerning? This book, I trust, provides the material for their answer.

August 1983

---

[2] *Adamson* v. *California*, 332 U.S. 46, 67 (1947).

Preface

ENGLISH legal scholarship, though much enriched over the last decade or so through the infusion of a socio-legal approach, is still rather limited in format; the textbook, monograph or an article on a specific topic or area of law is still the norm, examination of the contribution of individuals to the development of the law the exception. The genesis of this book bears witness to this statement. On or around Lord Denning's eightieth birthday in 1979, we were struck by the absence of any attempt in books or law journals to assess his contribution to the development of English law since his appointment to the Bench in 1944; in America, the leading journals would have been vying with each other to produce special issues on an American equivalent of Lord Denning. It was typical both of the man and the state of legal scholarship that the only publication celebrating Lord Denning's eightieth birthday was a book written by himself—*The Discipline of Law*.

We resolved to do something about what we saw as a gap in the literature of the law and put a proposal for this book to the publishers. Meanwhile Lord Denning produced another book—*The Due Process of Law*. The publishers did agree to the proposal, and since then Lord Denning has produced another three books—*The Family Story, What Next in the Law*, and *The Closing Chapter*—yet the combined forces of well over a thousand legal academics in the United Kingdom have between them come up with just one book of essays—*Justice, Lord Denning and the Constitution*, edited by P. Robson and P. Watchman, written entirely by Scottish legal scholars who receive all credit for a pioneering work—and two articles on Lord Denning's contribution to English Law.

This book is offered then not just as an attempt to assess Lord Denning's contribution to the development of English law over all or part of five decades during his 38 years on the Bench, but in the hope of pointing in the direction of a new field of legal scholarship in which the contribution of other noted judges with long service on the Bench might be critically assessed—in the period since 1945, Lord Reid (1949–1975, all spent in the House of Lords), Lord Diplock (1956–1984), and Lord Wilberforce (1961–1982) come to mind as obvious candidates for such treatment. While we would not suggest that the history of the development of English law can or should be rewritten purely in terms of the contribution individual judges made to the law, we think that the present position, where practically no assessment is made in these terms, presents a lop-sided picture which badly needs to be rectified. In the world of practical law individuals influence both particular decisions and the general development of the law.

We were very fortunate in being able to have as our co-authors in this venture persons of such distinction in their respective fields and we are very grateful to them for their contributions. We did not lay down in advance any ground-rules for writing the chapters or attempt to dictate what conclusions should be arrived at on Lord Denning's judicial career. We considered that each author should have a free hand in planning and writing the chapter subject only to the general principle that as definitive and rounded an assessment as possible should be attempted. In one respect the tardiness in producing this book—a tardiness for which we would like to apologise to those of our contributors and co-authors who must have begun to despair of ever seeing their contributions in print—has allowed the work to be more complete, as Lord Denning's retirement in 1982 gave us the opportunity to assess his full judicial career (although some of his cases were only reported after most chapters were complete). Yet even now we are aware that, in the fullness of time, this book will be seen as no more than an interim assessment of Lord Denning—a fuller assessment having to wait for a "Life and Times" written we would hope by an historian and a lawyer. Nevertheless, we would like to think that this book will have value both as a record of a remarkable judicial career and as a critical assessment of the judicial role in modern society.

We would particularly like to thank Lord Devlin, P.C. for his Foreword and the Lord Hailsham of St. Marylebone, Lord Chancellor, for permission to reprint his valedictory speech made on the occasion of Lord Denning's retirement.

We had hoped to print as an appendix to this book details of all Lord Denning's reported cases—over 2,000 of them—including not merely names and references but with whom he sat, whether the decision was a majority one or whether he dissented, whether the decision was appealed and if so the result on appeal. We considered that this would be an invaluable statistical record of Lord Denning's career. In the event, the information would have taken over 300 pages of print and we reluctantly acceded to the reasonable request of the publishers that this appendix be held over and possibly published later as a separate volume. It would be interesting too to publish an equivalent table of Lord Denning's unreported cases but we suspect that that would take a further volume. One incidental fact which emerges from this book and the compilation of these tables is how incredibly hard-working and productive Lord Denning was; given the number of judgments he had to write during terms it is not too surprising that he could knock off a book in his long vacation ("This book was my 'holiday task' for the long vacation" *The Discipline of Law*, p. 315). We academics have more to learn from Lord Denning than just a study of his judgments.

The task of gathering and ordering of cases was much eased by a grant from the Nuffield Foundation which enabled us to employ research assistance for that. We would like to thank the Foundation for their generous assistance and Robert Pullen, Sarah Ricketts and Carolyn Thomas for their work on the cases for us. We would like too to thank our secretaries, Vivien Fairley and Margaret Wright, for their invaluable contributions in typing our Chapters and maintaining liaison between us, our contributors and publishers. In particular, the latter deserve great thanks for their patience, encouragement and assistance.

Hampstead   J. L. Jowell
Leamington Spa   J. P. W. B. McAuslan

June 1984

Contents

Table of Cases

xiii

Table of Statutes

CHAPTER 1

Lord Denning: The Man and his Times

R.F.V. HEUSTON

"A shilling life will give you all the facts,"[1] and certainly the main facts in the life of Alfred Thompson Denning can be stated shortly. He was born on January 23, 1899 at Whitchurch in Hampshire, and was educated at Andover Grammar School and Magdalen College, Oxford, with a period of service in France in 1917–1918. He was called to the Bar in 1921, taking silk in 1938, and in 1944 was appointed a judge of the High Court. In 1949 he was promoted to the Court of Appeal, and in 1957 to the House of Lords. In 1962 he was appointed Master of the Rolls, a position from which he resigned in 1982 in his eighty-fourth year.

But, as the poet hints, more is required to understand the significance of all the facts. One must start with the home background, which has been described by Lord Denning himself[2] with a simplicity and piety which defy criticism or perhaps even comment. The paternal grandfather, William Denning, taught music at Cheltenham. His son Charles moved to Whitchurch, a small town in Hampshire on the road between Winchester and Newbury, where he owned a draper's shop. "He was not in the least suited for it."[3] In 1886 Charles Denning married Clara Thompson, whose father was a coal merchant at Lincoln.

> "Mother was a different temperament from father. She got it from her father. Like him, she was handsome with fine features. Very intelligent. Very hard-working. Determined to succeed whatever she undertook. She was the driving-force. Ambitious for her children."[4]

There were five children. The eldest, the only girl, Marjorie, married Joseph Haynes, and later both returned to live at Whitchurch. The eldest son, John Edward Newdigate Poyntz (Jack), was killed on the Somme in 1916 at the age of 23. The third son, Gordon, served at Jutland as a Midshipman, but died two years later of tuberculosis. The second and fifth sons, Reginald and Norman, became respectively a lieutenant-general and a vice-admiral, and both lived to see the extraordinary career of the fourth son, Alfred Thompson—Tom he was always called by the family, then by the legal profession, and now (it seems) by the world. Only a full quotation can do justice to Lord Denning's description of his family home.[5]

> "Although it looked attractive, our household would have been condemned today as totally unfit for human habitation. It had no indoor sanitation . . . No water from the mains. No water at all except that

---

[1] W.H. Auden, *Collected Shorter Poems* (1950), p. 31.
[2] *The Family Story* (Butterworths, 1970), Book One (hereinafter *TFS*).
[3] *TFS*, p. 13.
[4] *TFS*, p. 15.
[5] *TFS*, p. 17.

1

which we pumped up from a well just outside the back door beside the drain. To fill the iron kettle to put on the kitchen range—to fill the jugs with water to drink or to wash in—or to clean the floors.

No electric light, no gas except in two of the downstairs rooms a few flickering gas mantles which continually gave out. A paraffin oil lamp as a stand-by. Only candles to take up the stairs and into bed.

No daylight in the kitchen. No light got into it at all except through a glass panel in the door—or when the door was left open. Mother had to cook the meals for us children in that dark kitchen. It wore her out. Bath night was on Fridays. In a small zinc bath. In front of the kitchen range.

No livingroom except for a makeshift affair, a long narrow slit of a room, with no window—only a skylight in the roof and a glass door at the end. We boys sat on a long bench screwed on to the wall—for our meals—and our homework. Mother sat there every afternoon making up the books of the business.

After the elementary school at Whitchurch there was a daily journey by train to Andover Grammar School for three of the boys. Gordon and Tom were awarded free places. "An Elizabethan grammar school. What could you have better?"[6] School prizes for English literature were kept and read throughout life.

Mathematics (as distinct from English) were self-taught. There was no difficulty about this in the days before educational theorists were known. A clever boy was then allowed to exercise his natural talents. So Tom came top in English and mathematics in the entrance examination for University College, Southampton (not yet an independent university). This achievement was followed by a greater one—an entrance exhibition of £30 per annum to Magdalen College, Oxford. With the aid of the President of Magdalen, Sir Herbert Warren, this became a demyship of £80 per annum, which enabled Tom to go up to Oxford in October 1916, aged 17¾. In the summer of 1917 he was conscripted, and after service on the Western Front returned to Magdalen in February 1919.

It is difficult today to realise the position which Magdalen, together with Christ Church and New College, then occupied in Oxford and in England. Magdalen was old, rich and proud. If its members did not clearly possess social position, they achieved it by their membership of the College. It was thought that just as the undergraduates of Magdalen looked down on those from other Colleges so within Magdalen men from schools like Eton and Winchester looked down on those from other schools.[7]

Even Tom Denning's own self-confidence appears to have been shaken.

"Often freshmen ask one another, 'What school were you at?' Most men in my day were apt to name a famous public school. I turned the question on one side or prevaricated in one way or another. I felt

---

[6] *TFS*, p. vi. Blom-Cooper and Drewry, *Final Appeal*, p. 182, refer to the grammar-school backgrounds of Denning and Donovan as "lone palm-trees in a desert of educational class privilege."

[7] All this is described in a well-known novel by Compton Mackenzie (*Sinister Street*), and a less well-known one by C.E. Montague (*Rough Justice*).

ashamed at having been at a grammar school. But I need not have worried. Everyone was very understanding and when I took a First Class in 1920, they were proud of my achievement and I of theirs. Magdalen has the reputation of being a rich man's college—a college of all play and no work. The College had not had a single First for years. It is different now. It leads the field. My son is the Senior Dean of Arts."[8]

After his "First in Mathematics" Denning taught that subject at Winchester for a year. But he was ambitious and desired to be a man amongst men. With encouragement from Sir Herbert Warren he decided to return to Oxford to read for the Final Honour School of jurisprudence with a view to becoming a barrister. Financially this was possible by his election to the Eldon Scholarship. Founded in memory of the Lord Chancellor, it was awarded to "a Protestant of the Church of England" who had obtained a First. It was not required that the First should have been in Law, so Tom Denning was qualified. But there was competition for such a prize. Sir Herbert Warren went to London to recommend Denning to the trustees (a mixed body of dignitaries who met annually in the Lord Chancellor's room in the House of Lords). When Warren returned to Magdalen he sent him a note from High Table with the good news, adding "You are a marked man. Perhaps you will be a Lord of Appeal some day."[9] Sir Herbert Warren had then been President of Magdalen since 1885, and he might have been excused for being a little distant from the financial problems of a young man with a Hampshire accent. But in those days the head of an Oxford College thought it his duty to stay in Oxford and get to know his undergraduates.

Today the Oxford Law School is highly organised. Pupils receive reading lists and work-sheets and are given mock final examinations. Since 1945 Magdalen has taken a leading part in this educational effort. In 1921 it was different. "My law tutor was Robert Segar—who had been an unsuccessful barrister on the Northern Circuit. He knew no law except on the Statute of Frauds—on which he had once had a case."[10] But again a really able man can look after himself, and Denning was duly placed in the First Class in the Law School in 1922. Years later one of the examiners, G.C. Cheshire, later to be Vinerian Professor, became a personal friend. He showed Denning his marks: there was a wide range of alphas—but for jurisprudence only gamma minus. "Jurisprudence was too abstract a subject for my liking. All about ideologies, legal norms and basic norms, 'ought' and 'is', realism and behaviourism, and goodness knows what else."[11] In later life Lord Denning repeated that "the jargon of the philosophers of law has always been beyond

---

[8] *TFS*, p. 37. (Dr. Robert Denning (b. 1941), was elected a Fellow of Magdalen and Lecturer in Inorganic Chemistry in 1968). Is there a similarity between Lord Denning and his near contemporary at Christ Church, Dr. A.L. Rowse? Both like to contemplate their rise to eminence from simple backgrounds; both like to express in dogmatic language their distaste for much in contemporary England.

[9] *The Discipline of Law*, p. 200 (hereinafter *TDL*).

[10] *TFS*, p. 38. Segar is not mentioned in F.H. Lawson's *History of the Oxford Law School* (Oxford, 1968).

[11] Although this may be true of Oxford jurisprudence today, it can hardly be true of 1921, when the terminology of Kelsen was unknown west of the Landstrasse.

me,"[12] though he also devoted some effort to describing the "philosophy of my own"[13] which he developed in the Court of Appeal.

Denning did not stay up at Magdalen to do the B.C.L., though he did return for a few days in the autumn of 1923 to sit for the All Souls examination. His lack of success in that testing competition did not apparently induce the feelings of bitterness which have been noticeable in other unsuccessful candidates.[14] Anxious as ever to press on in life, he concentrated on pupillage and call to the Bar. So Denning joined Lincoln's Inn—apparently for no better reason than that the Under-Treasurer was a Magdalen man. Later he transferred to the Middle Temple. He became a pupil of Henry O'Hagan, a junior with a commercial practice, at 4 Brick Court, Temple. It was a small set of chambers. There was no silk and only one other junior—Stephen Henn-Collins, a son of Lord Collins (M.R., 1901–07), and himself to be a High Court judge from 1937–48. But Denning stayed in Brick Court until he became a judge. In 1923 he was called to the Bar, adding a Prize Studentship of £100 per annum to his Eldon Scholarship. So he survived until his practice grew. At first it was mainly small civil work—cases arising out of disputes between landlord and tenant, and traffic accidents. (His defeat at the hands of an old-style "runner king" led Theo Mathew to produce one of his best Forensic Fables—"The Double First and the Old Hand").[15] After seven years Denning was making £1,000 per annum.

He also did some writing. Two articles in the *Law Quarterly Review*[16] were followed by an invitation to bring out, with C.P. Harvey, a new edition of Smith's *Leading Cases in the Common Law*. The previous editors had included Willes J. and Collins M.R., the latter being responsible for the seventh, eighth and ninth editions. "It was an immense task involving much research. But it taught me most of the law I ever knew."[17] In particular it led down the path which eventually resulted in the famous *High Trees* case in 1947.[18]

In 1932 Tom Denning married Mary Harvey, daughter of the Vicar of Whitchurch. One child, Robert, was born before the mother died in 1941. In 1945 the widower re-married. His second wife was Joan, daughter of V. Elliott, and widow of J.M.B. Stuart by whom she had had one son and two daughters, of whom one married (Sir) Michael Fox of the Chancery Bar, promoted from the High Court to the Court of Appeal in 1981.

In 1938 Denning, with 14 others, was granted silk by Lord Maugham L.C. The others included the future Lord Jenkins, Sachs L.J., and Streatfield and Barry JJ. The war came before Denning had really established himself as a K.C., and he volunteered to act as legal adviser to the Regional

[12] *TFS*, p. 240.
[13] *TFS*, pp. 172–183.
[14] But see *What Next in the Law*, p. 14 (the college that turned me down). Sir Lawrence Jones (Eton and Balliol) remembered that "for long years I could not think or hear of All Souls without that little, private, fleeting moment of misery that Adam must have felt . . . at some tactless mention of Eden": *An Edwardian Youth* (1956), p. 100. Even successful candidates have had doubts. Lord Denning's exact contemporary Cyril Radcliffe was elected in 1922, but never voluntarily re-entered the College after his Fellowship expired, and his memories of it have a wry flavour: *Censors*, (Cambridge, 1961), pp. 26–27.
[15] *TFS*, p. 97.
[16] "Quantum Meruit" (1925) 41 L.Q.R. 79; "Repentry for Forfeiture" (1927) 43 L.Q.R. 53: One may add another article on Quantum Meruit (1939) 55 L.Q.R. 54.
[17] *TFS*, p. 94.
[18] *TDL*, p. 202.

Commissioner for the North-East Region. This involved much travelling on war-time trains to Leeds, but was a necessary war service.

One incident does attract attention, partly because Lord Denning himself referred twice to it, over an interval of 30 years,[19] but also because it illustrates a side of his mind which others have noticed—an ability to hold two contradictory views at the same time, or to distort an opposing argument into a way favourable to himself. The facts were simple. One of his duties was to advise on the exercise of the power of internment under the war-time Regulation 18B. Suspicion fell on a clergyman who had expressed pro-Nazi views. "Although there was no case against him, no proof at all, I detained him under '18B'. The Bishop of Ripon protested, but we took no notice." The clergyman remained in prison for nearly three years. "Yet he had done nothing wrong." So far the only comment might be one of surprise at the emphasis placed on the role of the legal adviser rather than of his constitutional superior, the Secretary of State, to whom parliament had entrusted a power held by the majority of the House of Lords in *Liversidge* v. *Anderson*[20] not to be capable of judicial review. What is surprising, and difficult to explain, is that Lord Denning then refers to Lord Atkin's famous dissent as being "after my own heart." It is also hard to see how approval of Lord Atkin's views can be reconciled with an emphatic judgment in 1977 that questions of security are not reviewable by the courts.[21]

In 1943 Lord Simon L.C. asked Denning to go as Commissioner of Assize to Manchester. In those days such an appointment was often regarded as a "trial run" for the Bench itself,[22] if favourable reports were received from—for example—the Leader of the Circuit. Presumably this happened in Denning's case, for on March 6, 1944, during the hearing of an appeal, Lord Simon offered him an appointment in the Probate, Divorce and Admiralty Division. Denning had never done any divorce work, because it "was considered inferior and unpleasant."[23] But he was ambitious, and it was believed at the Bar that anyone who had refused such an offer was not approached again. Also, "I have never refused any appointment requested by a Lord Chancellor of me. (Save when in 1968 Lord Gardiner asked me to return to the Lords)."[24] So the appointment was made on March 7, 1944.[25] Also appointed were two silks from the Divorce Court, H. Wallington and H. Barnard. All three were needed to cope with the expected post-war flood of matrimonial litigation.

---

[19] *Freedom Under the Law* (1949), pp. 12–13; *TFS*, p. 130. The two accounts are in substance the same, although the earlier one does not identify Denning's own part in it, and perhaps for that reason seems to have attracted no attention.

[20] [1942] A.C. 206. It is now settled that the decision of the majority was correct as a matter of statutory interpretation, though the rousing rhetoric of Lord Atkin has a certain appeal for what are called "civil libertarians": see Heuston, *Liversidge* v. *Anderson in Retrospect* (1970) 86 L.Q.R. 33.

[21] *R.* v. *Secretary of State for Home Affairs, ex p. Hosenball* [1977] 1 W.L.R. 776, 783.

[22] But not always: when Walter Monckton went as Commissioner in April 1943 he explained that he was doing as as his war work, "and it does not mean that I am leaving the Bar or aiming at the Bench": Birkenhead, *Walter Monckton* (1969), p. 206.

[23] *The Due Process of Law* (hereinafter *DPL*) p. 187. The appeal was *Reville* v. *Prudential Assurance Co. Ltd.* [1944] A.C. 135.

[24] *DPL*, p. 188.

[25] *DPL*, p. 188; [1950] A.C., p. viii. *The Law List* for 1945 gives March 9 as the date.

At the date of his appointment Denning was aged 45 years and two months. He himself later stated that he was "the youngest judge (since Lord Hodson) for 150 years."[26] This statement can hardly be supported. Francis Buller was certainly the youngest man ever appointed (in 1778 at the age of 32) to the English Bench who died after 22 years service at an age when it is usual today to be made a judge,[27] and presumably it is to him that Lord Denning refers. But both in the nineteenth and twentieth centuries men have been made judges at a younger age than Denning. So James Shaw Willes was aged 41 when he was appointed to the Common Pleas in 1885, and Gorell Barnes, Q.C. was aged 44 when he was appointed to the Probate, Divorce and Admiralty in 1892. In this century Atkin was 44 and Devlin 43 when appointed to the King's Bench Division in 1913 and 1948 respectively. Sir John Donaldson, Denning's successor as Master of the Rolls, was one week short of his forty-sixth birthday when appointed in 1966.

This may be the appropriate point at which to deal with the related questions of the length of period for which, and the age at which, Denning has exercised judicial functions. In March 1980 Lord Denning surpassed the English record for length of judicial service (claimants from Ireland such as Lefroy C.J. and Palles C.B. are not here considered) of just over 36 years achieved by Lord Bramwell, who, appointed in 1856, had resigned in 1882 but had then sat constantly in the Lords until his death in May 1892. On March 5, 1891 he delivered a judgment, at the age of 82, in the leading case of *Bank of England* v. *Vagliano*.[28]

Amongst those who have sat in old age must be mentioned Lord Mansfield, who refrained from attending court when 81, although he did not resign for another two years. When Pollock C.B. (b., September 23, 1783) resigned on July 13, 1866 it was recorded that he had "sat on the Bench at a more advanced age than any common law judge before him."[29] This fails to consider Sir Salathiel Lovell (1619–1715) who was appointed to the Court of Exchequer at the age of 88, and died in office nearly five years later. "But Lovell's years on the Bench seem to have been years of survival rather than vitality."[30] It also fails to consider an equity judge, Vice-Chancellor Bacon (1798–1895), who was in his eighty-ninth year when he retired from the Bench. In any event, records are made to be broken. Kelly C.B. (1796–1880) sat in his eighty-fourth year, as did Avory J. (1851–1935), and Lord Goddard[31] (1877–1971).

By stretching a little the concepts of a judge and a judicial function, we can include Sir James Parker Deane (1812–1902), who officiated as Dean of Arches within a few days of his eighty-ninth birthday, and Lord Maenan (1854–1951), who was created a peer in 1948 when he retired as Presiding Judge of the Liverpool Court of Passage.

But all these are clearly surpassed by Lord Halsbury, who, born on September 3, 1823, sat in the House of Lords in his ninety-third year on four

---

[26] *DPL*, p. 188. F.L.C. (Lord) Hodson (b. Sept. 17, 1895) was made a Judge of the P.D. & A. on December 14, 1937.

[27] He was a good common lawyer, but "knew no more equity than a horse": Campbell, *Lives of the Chancellors*, vol. 5, p. 252.

[28] [1891] A.C. 107.

[29] Foss, *The Judges of England* (1870), p. 525.

[30] R.E. Megarry, *The Vice-Chancellors* (1982) 98 L.Q.R. 370, 388n.

[31] He came out of retirement to sit on the appeal in *D.P.P.* v. *Smith* [1960] A.C. 290.

days in February 1916 to hear the appeal in *Continental Tyre and Rubber* v. *Daimler Co. Ltd.*,[32] and, unlike Lord Goddard in *D.P.P.* v. *Smith*, in June delivered a separate reserved judgment. (It may be noted that when Halsbury died on December 11, 1921 he had achieved the greatest age of any peer, 98 years and 99 days, in the history of England. But this record has also since been surpassed by the fifth Lord Penryhn, who died in 1967, having lived for 101 years and 40 days).

For the sake of completeness, the tenure of the Mastership of the Rolls must also be considered. Lord Denning held the post for 20 years and five months, from April 1962 to September 1982. This period is long but not unique. In the nineteenth century Sir John Romilly held it for 22 years (1851–1873) and in the eighteenth century Sir Joseph Jekyll for 21 years (1717–1738). In the seventeenth century Sir Julius Caesar obtained a reversionary grant of the office on January 16, 1611, but it did not fall into possession until September 13, 1614, when he held it until his death on April 18, 1636—a period of just under 22 years. He was clearly surpassed by Sir Harbottle Grimston, who gave the Lord Chancellor £6,000 to obtain the post, which he held from November 3, 1660 until his death ("from natural decay") on January 2, 1685—a span of 24 years and 60 days. It is true that all these are surpassed by Sir John Trevor, who held the post of Master of the Rolls for no less than 27 years (1685–1688; 1693–1717). But he can be excluded on the ground that he did not hold the post continuously—a cousin of Jeffreys, he supported the wrong side in 1688, and so was dismissed, although after some years of toadying to the new régime he was re-appointed. His visage was marred by "a vile squint," and his rapacity was notorious even in that age.

It would have been necessary for Lord Denning to have held office until June 20, 1986 to have surpassed Sir Harbottle's record span. But if he sits in the House of Lords in July 1991 he will have exercised judicial functions at an older age than Halsbury, and if he survives until March 5, 2000 he will be the longest-lived peer in the history of England.

The chronological narrative will now be taken up again. While in the Divorce Court Denning J. did not reserve judgment once in his first year, but in the early months of 1945 a number of reported judgments appear.[33] A few months later he dealt with the topic of presumptions and burdens in the law of evidence,[34] and even wrote an article on it for the *Law Quarterly Review*.[35] But he was not happy in his work, and was thankful to Jowitt, Lord Chancellor in the Labour Government, for transferring him to the King's Bench Division on October 24, 1945. "Thank goodness I only did Divorce for eighteen months."[36] But after his transfer he was Chairman of the Committee on Procedure in Matrimonial Causes, which reported in July 1946, recommending, *inter alia*, that the period between decree *nisi* and decree absolute should be reduced from six to three months. "We worked quickly. No Committee has ever worked so quickly or so well." But unhappily such speed offended Lord Merriman, the President of the Division, and he called

---

[32] [1916] 2 A.C. 307.
[33] *Fletcher* v. *Fletcher* [1945] 1 All E.R. 582; *Smith* v. *Smith* [1945] 1 All E.R. 584; *Norton* v. *Norton* [1945] P. 56.
[34] *Emanuel* v. *Emanuel* [1946] P. 115.
[35] (1945) 60 L.Q.R. 235.
[36] *DPL*, p. 189.

Denning "a blackguard" to his face. "I have never been so treated in my life."[37]

The position of a King's Bench Judge in 1945 was an enviable one. England was no longer a great power but it was still a great nation, and the common law was regarded as a great national possession. Its superiority over foreign systems of law and their practitioners was convincingly demonstrated at the Nuremberg trials of the Nazi leaders. The American team seemed inept and had to be rescued by Maxwell Fyfe from a humiliating defeat at the hands of Goering. Nobody took the French or the Russians seriously. Over all presided with wonderful serenity and authority Lawrence L.J. and Birkett J. At home there was a new Lord Chancellor (Jowitt) and a new Lord Chief Justice (Goddard). Together with the Master of the Rolls (Greene, appointed in 1937) they presided over a judicial establishment of seven Law Lords, nine Lord Justices and 47 High Court Judges. (In 1981 there were nine Law Lords, 18 Lord Justices and 80 High Court Judges.)

Jowitt, Goddard and Greene each came from an orthodox upper-middle-class background and had been to one of the better Oxford colleges (New College, Trinity and Christ Church respectively). Greene, a sensitive and scholarly Chancery lawyer, was to retire from the Mastership of the Rolls in 1949. So Denning had little contact with him. Jowitt's significance has not so far been properly recognised by the legal profession. He was not a jurist but he had been a superb advocate and was to be a very satisfactory judge. He used his great position to achieve some fundamental legal reforms—not least in the area of legal aid. Later the significance of Lord Scarman's dictum in 1977 that the previous 20 years had been the age of legal aid, law reform and Lord Denning will be considered; now it is enough to mark Jowitt's contribution.

Goddard was known to the public in a way in which Jowitt was not. Nobody doubted that a formidable figure occupied the position of Lord Chief Justice of England. A master of the common law and its history (he had risen to be a Law Lord on his professional merits), it was generally conceded that he was the right man to deal with the problems of the post-war period. His appearance on the Bench was remarkable. The stocky figure and the square clean-shaved face with its long upper lip[38] displayed a strong personality.

> "An appearance before Lord Goddard was more troublesome to the stomach than a dawn attack on a heavily defended enemy position. When Sir Walter Monckton rose to move that the editor of the *Daily Mirror* be committed to prison for contempt, he was one of the most distinguished leaders at the Bar and one of the foremost men in the country. His hands were shaking uncontrollably behind his back. Was this just ordinary nerves, or possibly the consequence of a hang-over? A glance at Lord Goddard put those thoughts out of one's mind. A gleam of light shone directly upon the hunched figure of the Lord Chief Justice.

---

[37] *DPL*, pp. 191–192.

[38] "A judicial air is given to a man by the set of his mouth and upper lip, and when these are invisible not even the wig can save a face from insignificance. Consider the long line of seventeenth-century portraits of lawyers and divines, the Coles and the Lauds, how feeble and characterless they appear with their small, trim beards and no upper lips or mouths or chins to record and communicate the lines that belong to ripe and proven men, masters of their chosen calling": L.E. Jones, *An Edwardian Youth* (1956), pp. 182–183.

The large court seemed to be quaking under the impact of his personality. Not only the assembled directors of the *Daily Mirror* but everyone else held their breath. When called upon to stand up, the editor sat immobile with fear and had to be pushed to his feet by his counsel, Valentine Holmes. The crisp prison sentence and equally crisp warning to the newspaper's directors followed. One left the court in no doubt of the majesty of the law."[39]

The change in social habits and beliefs since 1945 can also be seen if one mentions some of the terms and concepts which were then—happily— unknown: civil liberties, demonstrations, police harassment, racial and sex discrimination, one-parent families, legal action groups, neighbourhood law centres. The meaning of all these must be considered elsewhere. Lord Denning has adapted to some but not all of them, or has had an ambiguous attitude. So in relation to protest groups there is one (dissenting) judgment suggesting there was a general right to picket premises,[40] but in extra-judicial writings there are references to "trouble-makers."

Lord Denning enjoyed his life in the King's Bench Division. He was too simple a man to deny the pleasure he took in the traditional splendour which then accompanied the progress of a Judge of Assize.[41] In London he sat occasionally with Lord Goddard C.J. in the Divisional Court or in the Court of Criminal Appeal.[42]

"He was so much in command that his colleagues on either side did not venture to take much part in the discussion . . . the chief would, as often as not, whisper to his colleagues, 'There's nothing in this, is there?' Then, on getting their murmured assents, he would straightway give judgment. I have known him not to bother to ask them, but to take their assent for granted and deliver judgment forthwith."[43]

On July 18, 1946 Denning delivered judgment in one case on the law of contract[44] which quickly became known to students and practitioners and showed that a new judicial mind was at work—questioning, creative, unusual. News of it reached Australia and there was correspondence with the immensely learned Sir Owen Dixon.[45]

In 1946 Denning was specially assigned to act as Judge for Pensions Appeals. There was, exceptionally, no statutory right of appeal from his decisions, and the Ministry of Pensions (usually the unsuccessful party) does not seem to have thought of applying for judicial review by certiorari—a branch of the law later much developed by Denning himself.[46] He certainly

---

[39] See Furnival, *Law Society's Gazette*, December 17, 1980, and F. Bresler, *Lord Goddard* (1977), p. 201.

[40] *Hubbard* v. *Pitt* [1976] Q.B. 142.

[41] There is a good picture of judicial life on circuit in the 1940s ("a great company of masterful beings in scarlet and white") in Cyril Hare, *Tragedy at Law* (1942).

[42] In *R.* v. *Sims* [1946] K.B. 531 the judgment of the C.C.A. (Lord Goddard C.J., Byrne and Denning JJ.) was prepared by Denning J. Byrne J. apparently disagreed emphatically: see *The Times*, July 31, 1982.

[43] F. Bresler, *Lord Goddard*, pp. vi–vii.

[44] *Central London Property Trust Ltd.* v. *High Trees House Ltd.* [1946] K.B. 130.

[45] *Moorgate Mercantile Co. Ltd.* v. *Twitchings Ltd.* [1976] Q.B. 225, 241.

[46] If the law in 1946 had been as Lord Denning held it to be in *Re Racal Communications Ltd.* [1980] Ch. 138, he would have been controllable.

claimed for himself a freedom which he did not later permit to other judges. It was "the most rewarding series of cases in my career. . . . Never before or since have I been entrusted with such absolute power."[47]

Almost exactly three years after he had been transferred to the K.B.D., Denning was promoted to the Court of Appeal, on October 14, 1946, together with Singleton J., to fill the vacancies caused by the retirements of Scott and Wrottesley L.JJ. Some years later Lord Denning said that "some judges, when invited to go to the Court of Appeal, refuse the invitation and no-one thinks it strange. . . . Those who like dry points of law accept the invitation, whereas those who like the human side of life refuse it."[48] As is often the case, Lord Denning seems an exception to his own rule.

In 1948 the Court of Appeal was composed of the Master of the Rolls (in the next year Evershed succeeded Greene) and eight Lord Justices. Its jurisdiction then was entirely civil, as appeals in criminal cases did not come to it until 1967. But it was interesting work. What Denning said of Goddard's period in the Court of Appeal (1938–1944) was true of himself:

> "He liked the variety of cases—on every subject of law there ever was. He liked the pressure of work and companionship of minds as quick and alert as his own. In contrast, he did not like the slow pace of the House of Lords. There was not enough scope for his abundant vitality and energy."[49]

If the reader of the law reports had not already realised it, there were now many signs of a powerful new mind at work. In many ways the judgments of the Fifties are classic Denning; there is still enough respect for precedent for the analysis of the cases to be full and careful, and the style, clear and vivid, is not yet marred by the self-conscious tricks of the Seventies. Everyone who remembers those days will have his own recollections of how he reacted to the masterly line of judgments. Perhaps three cases may be mentioned—In re *Wingham*,[50] *Cassidy* v. *Ministry of Health*[51] and *Candler* v. *Crane, Christmas & Co.*[52]

In the first case the issue was whether a testamentary document made during the Second World War by an airman training in Sasketchewan was made "on actual military service" within the Wills Act 1837, s.11 so as to be exempt from the statutory formalities for execution. Pilcher J. held that a document executed 3,000 miles from the scene of hostilities could not be so described. He was reversed by a unanimous Court of Appeal.

> "If I were to inquire into the Roman Law, I could perhaps after some research say how Roman Law would have dealt with its soldiers on Hadrian's Wall or in the Camp at Chester. . . . Rid of this Roman test, this court has to decide what is the proper test."[53]

This the Court laid down in words which have always since been followed.[54]

---

[47] *TFS*, p. 165.
[48] (1954) 71 S.A.L.J. 345, 351.
[49] Foreword, p. vi, to Bresler, *Lord Goddard*.
[50] [1949] P. 187.
[51] [1951] 2 K.B. 343.
[52] [1951] 2 K.B. 164.
[53] [1949] P. 187, 195. The use of the past participle here has been much admired.
[54] See *in Re Jones* [1981] Fam. 7.

Cassidy and *Candler* are major developments in the law of torts, whose significance is explained elsewhere.[55]

In three appeals argued in the summer of 1951 the House of Lords refused to approve the views of Denning L.J., and the refusal was expressed in language markedly different from the elaborately polite phrases normally used by the Law Lords to correct errors in lower courts. In *Howell* v. *Falmouth Boat Construction Co. Ltd.*[56] the issue was whether an illegality committed under war-time legislation could be cured by an oral permission given by an official. The Court of Appeal had held that it could, either because the legislation contemplated an oral as well as a written licence, or because a public servant who gave an assurance to a citizen would be estopped from going back on it. The presiding Law Lord, Lord Simonds, said that he knew of no such principle. (In the following thirty years the courts have shown an increasing tendency to follow the Denning view). The House of Lords also held that a licence must be written and not oral. But it managed to do justice by holding that the legislation permitted a written licence to be retrospective, even though the licence in that case was expressed in "elliptical" language. An elliptical retrospective written licence is a curious concept, and a more simple way of doing justice might have been to agree with the view of Denning L.J. (which is supported by most dictionaries) that a licence can be oral as well as written.

On July 26, 1951, a month after the conclusion of argument, the House of Lords delivered judgment in *British Movietonews Ltd.* v. *London & District Cinemas Ltd.*[57] Lord Simon delivered the leading opinion, in which Lord Simonds expressly concurred. The Court of Appeal had suggested that parties were no longer bound by a contract if there had been an unexpected turn of events which might fall within the literal meaning of the words used but outside the true intention of the parties. Lord Simon repudiated Denning's judgment, in which, he said "phrases occur which give us some concern." Lord Simon wrote a letter to Denning "to soften the blow."[58]

No such letter was written by Lord Simonds when, on October 25, he delivered the leading opinion of a tribunal which also included Lords Goddard, Radcliffe, Morton and Tucker on a question of local government law which was of such little general importance that the Editor of the Law Reports stated, exceptionally, that "It is unnecessary to report the case save as relates to their Lordships' observations as to the construction of statutes."[59] Denning, in what Lord Morton called "a vigorous judgment," had said that

> "We sit here to find out the intention of Parliament and of Ministers and carry it out, and we do this better by filling in the gaps and making sense of the enactment than by opening it up to destructive analysis."

Lord Simonds retorted that

> "This proposition . . . cannot be supported. It appears to me to be a

---

[55] See Salmond & Heuston, *Law of Torts*, Chaps. 9 and 20.
[56] [1951] A.C. 837, 845.
[57] [1952] A.C. 166.
[58] *TDL*, p. 43.
[59] *Magor & St. Mellons R.D.C.* v. *Newport Corporation* [1952] A.C. 189.

naked usurpation of the legislative function under the thin guise of interpretation."

Nearly 30 years later Denning was unrepentant: "So injustice was done."[60]

At the time there was some surprise not only at the tone of these rebukes but also that Lord Simonds should have felt himself entitled to administer them. Lord Simon's qualifications to do so could not be questioned—he had been at the top of the legal profession for 40 years, and had refused the Woolsack as far back as 1915. Lord Simonds was different. A self-confident man of striking appearance from a prosperous Hampshire background he had had a successful career at the Chancery Bar before being appointed to the High Court in 1937 and promoted direct to the House of Lords in 1944. But in the summer of 1951 he was hardly known outside Lincoln's Inn. It is true that a week after the judgment in the *British Movietonews* case he was appointed Lord Chancellor by Churchill although, as his successor said, "as innocent of politics as a newly baptized babe."[61] After October 30, 1951 his position might have entitled him to say what he did: but his mysterious, if successful elevation, cannot explain or justify statements before that date.[62]

News of this tension circulated quickly in the common law world. An Oxford law teacher visiting Australia in 1953 was asked, seriously, by a senior judge whether there was a possibility that Denning might be removed from office under the procedure established by the Act of Settlement. But to younger lawyers he was something to admire. Mr. Alex Lyon M.P. recorded that

> "Denning was my great hero when I was a law student. I used to go to sit in the court just to listen to him. He has a beautiful voice and a beautiful delivery, but I was also enthralled by what he was doing to the law to advance it into the twentieth century."[63]

Many others who were students in the Fifties would say the same.

Early in 1957 the resignation of Lord Oaksey (1900–1971) opened up a vacancy among the Law Lords, to which Denning was appointed on April 24. "I was aged 58. As active as ever. No shrunk shank. No childish treble."[64] Denning wondered whether acceptance would prejudice his chances of becoming either Lord Chief Justice or Master of Rolls but after discussion with Parker L.J. decided to accept. The reduced work-load and the easier pace of life had some compensations—the House did not sit on Fridays, so in the intervals of writing judgments Denning could play golf in Sussex.[65] He also took an exceptionally active part in the legislative business of the House, although not a constant attender at debates.[66] He spoke on average six times a year, but was careful to observe the convention that Law

---

[60] *TDL*, p. 14. But the rebuke in *Magor* "no longer hurts": [1982] 2 W.L.R. 474. 482.

[61] Kilmuir, *Political Adventure* (1964), p. 194.

[62] Simonds may have been under some pressure in 1951. One of his twin sons died in March of that year; the other had been killed at Arnhem. But as late as 1960 Simonds referred to Denning's account of the issues in an important chancery case as "completely unwarrantable": H.L. Deb., Vol. 222, cols. 530–532, (1960).

[63] *The Listener*, September 27, 1979.

[64] *TFS*, p. 185. Is it necessary to add that the reference is to Jaques' sixth age of man?

[65] *TFS*, p. 145. (This is the only known reference to sports or games).

[66] *Final Appeal*, pp. 205–206, 211.

Lords should not speak on purely political matters. His speeches were always carefully prepared.

But the House of Lords did not prove as enjoyable as the Court of Appeal. The judicial work was less satisfying. There seems also to have been some tension of a personal character, perhaps not unrelated to doctrinal disputes, with Lord Simonds.

> "I, too, was ambitious. I, too, was accused of heresy—and verbally beheaded—by Lord Simonds. You can read it in *Midland Silicones Ltd.* v. *Scruttons Ltd.* [1962] A.C. 446."[67]

Lord Simonds had already criticised Denning when he was in the Court of Appeal. It was another matter to "behead" him when he was a colleague in the House of Lords, but this was done on at least three reported occasions.

How far do the Law Reports bear out the belief that he was too often in dissent? (It must be recalled that until 1966 the House held itself bound by its own previous decisions). The Appeal Cases for 1957 record no participation in any appeal in the House of Lords as distinct from the Privy Council—and in the latter tribunal the disclosure of dissenting opinions was not at that date permitted. So next year, *Re Parliamentary Privilege Act 1770*[68] a Board composed of seven Law Lords held, apparently unanimously, that the issue of a writ against a M.P. might be treated as a breach of privilege by the House of Commons. The rest of the Board refused to permit the publication of Denning's dissent—or even mention its existence.[69] The Crown could not receive contradictory advice.

The same volume of the Appeal Cases reports his first judgment in the House of Lords—and it is a dissent.[70] Lord Denning held that a sovereign state could not plead immunity from suit if the transaction in question was a commercial one. He admitted that he had considered some questions and authorities not mentioned in the argument of counsel. This produced a rebuke by Lord Simonds which was concurred in by the other Law Lords (*Per alios* as the headnote puts it). "In spite of that rebuke it was, I think, worthwhile that I did all that work on the *Rahimtoola* case."[71] For the substance of that dissent has been accepted not only by Parliament (in the State Immunity Act 1978) but also by the House of Lords itself (on pre-1978 facts).[72] A dissent is also recorded in an important case on the construction of the Factories Act—*Close* v. *Steel Co. of Wales Ltd.*[73] (it is interesting to note that here Lord Denning presided over a tribunal of which the other members were Lords Goddard, Morton, Morris and Evershed—the turnover of Law Lords at the end of the Fifties had been exceptionally rapid).

But it may be unhelpful to concentrate too much on the number of dissents. So earnest researchers have calculated that Lord Keith of

---

[67] *TFS*, p. 202. For the respondents Ashton Roskill, Q.C. had argued that "It is more important that the law should be certain than that it should be clever": [1957] A.C. 458.

[68] [1958] A.C. 331.

[69] It is deposited with the library of Lincoln's Inn: *TFS*, p. 148.

[70] *Rahimtoola* v. *Nizam of Hyderabad* [1958] A.C. 379.

[71] *DPL*, p. 289.

[72] *I Congreso del Partido, The* [1981] 3 W.L.R. 328. (At p. 325 Lord Wilberforce referred to Lord Denning's "admired judgment" in the *Trendtex* case ([1977] Q.B. 529), in which many of his arguments in *Rahimtoola* are developed further).

[73] [1962] A.C. 367.

Avonholm (Law Lord, 1953–1961) dissented in 22 per cent. of his "full opinions," and Denning only in 16 per cent.[74] But the dissents of Keith have left little mark on legal history.

Indeed, the most severe criticism of Lord Denning in those years is that he joined in the unanimous decision of the House of Lords in *D.P.P.* v. *Smith*[75] on the meaning of *mens rea* in murder. ("I would have liked to have delivered a separate judgment but was discouraged from doing so.[76]") The House[77] is generally taken to have held that it was enough for the Crown to prove that, in the words of the trial judge, "If in doing what he did, he must as a reasonable man have contemplated that serious harm was likely to occur, then he was guilty of murder." Critics fastened on the words "as a reasonable man" to suggest that the House had made a fundamental change in the criminal law by introducing an objective rest of *mens rea*. The critics included not only academics and practitioners but also Sir Owen Dixon C.J., who stated that the propositions in *Smith* were fundamentally misconceived and wrong. "They are propositions which I could never bring myself to accept."[78]

Lord Denning, perhaps unwisely, attempted to answer his critics.[79] He did so in two ways. First, he emphasised the words "he must" in the quoted passage, stating that these meant that the requisite intention must be brought home to him subjectively. Secondly, 20 years later, Lord Denning poured scorn on his academic critics "none of whom had ever tried a criminal case in their lives."[80] The tone was unusual for a public statement by a Law Lord, but there can be no doubt about the feeling behind it.

> "Smith was reprieved. But the academics persisted in their criticism. They succeeded. An Act was passed to take account of their criticism. It is section 8 of the Criminal Justice Act 1967. Moral for judges: Don't despise the academics."[81]

Almost exactly five years after his promotion to the House of Lords an opportunity of escape appeared. Lord Evershed had been finding the administrative burden of his office as Master of the Rolls too great, and was himself appointed a Lord of Appeal.

> "Who was to succeed him? We all wondered. Then at lunch one day in the Lords, the Lord Chancellor, Lord Kilmuir, (when the others had left the table) said to me: 'I hear that you would like to be Master of the Rolls yourself. Is that so?' Now I had mentioned this to no-one—unless it were to Lord Parker in 1957—five years before. I said at once that I would. It was the opportunity I wanted."[82]

---

[74] Blom-Cooper and Drewry, *Final Appeal* (1963), p. 179.

[75] *Paal Wilson & Co.* v. *Blumenthal* [1982] 3 W.L.R. 49, 57.

[76] [1961] A.C. 290.

[77] Lord Kilmuir L.C., Lord Parker of Waddington C.J., and Lords Goddard, Tucker and Denning ("The strongest team that could be gathered together to hear a criminal appeal": *TFS*, p. 195). In no other reported case have a Lord Chief Justice and his predecessor (who had come out of retirement in his 84th year) sat together.

[78] *Parker* v. *R.* (1963) 111 C.L.R. 610, 632.

[79] *Responsibility Before the Law* (Jerusalem, 1961); *TFS*, pp. 195–197.

[80] *TFS*, p. 195.

[81] *TFS*, p. 197.

[82] *TFS*, p. 197.

So on April 19, 1962 Lord Denning returned to the Court of Appeal as Master of the Rolls. (Only three months later it was his official duty to swear in a new Lord Chancellor—Dilhorne—in succession to Kilmuir.) "Some would say that I moved down."[83] Elsewhere he revealed a little more. When after asked why he had done so, he replied: "I was too often in a minority. In the Lords it is no good to dissent."[84]

Remarks like these were repeated publicly or privately on various occasions and naturally did not pass unnoticed. In general the Law Lords maintained a dignified silence. Once some feeling was discernible. In a legislative debate in 1966 on the topic of the property rights of married women (something on which Lord Denning had spoken much, both in and out of court), Lord Hodson said[85]:

> "(I was) one of the wicked men who was a member of that section of your Lordships' House which made the decision (*National Provincial Bank* v. *Ainsworth* [1965] A.C. 1175) which my noble and learned friend Lord Denning dislikes so much . . . Lord Denning moves us to tears every time he mentions a deserted wife, the poor woman he has been protecting in the Court of Appeal for years. But there are not many of them. Then he comes to this House and in sepulchral tones, says 'When the House of Lords got the case of a bank, what did they do? They protected the bank.' But let us not get our feet off the ground."

It was Lord Hodson who presided in *Pettitt* v. *Pettitt*[86] in which Lord Denning's views about the division of the matrimonial home were disapproved.

Almost exactly one year after he had returned to the Court of Appeal, Lord Denning was asked by the Prime Minister, Harold Macmillan, to undertake an inquiry into the security aspects of what was known as the Profumo Affair. Denning sat through most of the summer in a room in Whitehall, interviewing the witnesses himself. After an unprecedented build-up of anticipation in the media the Report was published in September.[87] As the author himself said, "It was a best-seller."[88] The then Warden of All Souls described it as "surely the raciest and most readable Blue Book ever published."[89] But other views were held. A critic from the media, who defended Dr. Stephen Ward, an enigmatic figure at the centre of the affair, while conceding it was very readable described it as, in parts, a "rather nasty document."[90] The nastiness was said to consist, not in the detailed factual description of life in the Ward/Astor/Profumo social circles, but in Denning's inability to "resist the temptation to regale his readers with gossipy tit-bits of the women's magazine variety which had no bearing on his brief at all." The force of this criticism is not diminished by the fact that Denning later cited some of the passages in the Report as good examples of his own prose style.[91]

---

[83] *TFS*, p. 197.
[84] *TDL*, p. 287.
[85] H.C. Deb., Vol. 275, col. 649.
[86] [1970] A.C. 777.
[87] Cmnd. 2152.
[88] *DPL*, p. 68.
[89] J. Sparrow, *Controversial Essays* (1966), p. 33.
[90] L. Kennedy, *The Trial of Stephen Ward* (1965), p. 33.
[91] *TFS*, p. 217.

The choice of Denning to conduct the inquiry was curious. At the Bar he had had almost no experience of criminal work (apart from prosecuting for the Southern Railway in magistrates' courts), and his private life was utterly remote from that of the people whose conduct he had to investigate—by himself, without the benefit of legal representation.[92] On the Bench Denning's criminal experience was equally limited—three years as King's Bench Judge, and a period as Deputy Chairman of East Sussex Quarter Sessions.[93] It is true that he had had some experience of security work during the war, but there were others at the Bar or on the Bench whose qualifications, legal and otherwise, to conduct such an investigation were superior. Perhaps Macmillan took all this into account—the Report was in any case a great relief to his hard-pressed Government. The public were assured that however odd the happenings in high places, the security of the state had not been endangered.

The publication of the *Profumo Report* had a wider significance, in the long run, for Lord Denning. His name became known to the media and so to the ordinary citizen.[94] If Denning had died in 1962 his achievements would have been commemorated by full obituaries in *The Times* and the legal journals, and, in due course, by an entry in the Dictionary of National Biography.[95] But his name and fame would have been utterly unknown to the public. It is almost impossible to write a biography of a man who has made his reputation entirely by publishing judgments in the law reports. So there is no good life of Willes or Atkin. To many this is satisfactory. So MacKinnon L.J. once wrote[96] that "he is the best judge whose name is known to fewest readers of the *Daily Mail*." In 1981, after unprecedented exposure to the media, the comment could be made that "Denning fails the MacKinnon test hands down."[97]

But the story, like the subject, must now return to Appeal Court 1 in 1962. Lord Denning has always shown a certain lack of interest in persons or cases which have not been through that court. So when there was a discussion at the Whitchurch dinner table about the merits of one newly-appointed by Lord Gardiner to the Law Commission, the words "Never saw him in my court" put an end to the conversation. Equally Lord Denning has shown little interest in the many developments in English criminal law in the past 30 years, which has now become an elaborate (perhaps over-elaborate) body of doctrine. Criminal appeals do not go through his court.

The assessment of the flow of judgments in tort, contracts, family law—and indeed all aspects of English law except criminal—must be left to other authors. Here it is enough to note that their impact was such that by

---

[92] It is not surprising that the (Salmon) Royal Commission on Tribunals of Inquiry recommended that no such body should ever again be established. Although Denning has referred to himself as "sophisticated" (*DPL*, p. 68), some of the parties involved might not have thought this. Also Denning had never been in the House of Commons (though Lord Hailsham thinks he would have gained "enormously" from this (Guardian Gazette, February 28, 1979), and so might not have appreciated some of the pressures on Profumo.

[93] *TFS*, p. 146.

[94] At the time several in Fleet Street commented that Lord Denning did not seem displeased at the amount of personal publicity which he was receiving.

[95] Then ordinary puisne judges of the High Court could expect to be noticed in the DNB; now rigorous selection is needed.

[96] *On Circuit* (Cambridge, 1940), p. 27.

[97] G. Drewry, *New Law Journal*, April 9, 1981.

the mid-1970s the Master of the Rolls had become an international as well as a national figure. Lord Scarman went so far as to say that it was "the age of legal aid, law reform,—and Lord Denning."[98] (Though Denning is cool towards law reform conducted by agencies other than Appeal Court 1, and even cooler towards legal aid both in civil and criminal cases.)[99] *The Times* once had the sub-heading "Thank God for Lord Denning" across its leading article,[1] and these words were echoed by a former Conservative Cabinet Minister in another context.[2] By 1981 no fewer than 17 universities throughout the world had awarded him honorary doctorates.[3]

On January 23, 1979 Lord Denning's eightieth birthday was marked by family and professional celebrations. These included a reception at Butterworths to mark the publication of *The Discipline of Law*. Denning signed copies on the following day at the bookshop beside the courts. It was a "sort of *festschrift* composed entirely by himself," as Lord Hailsham L.C. said in a percipient review.[4] Within two years the atmosphere had changed markedly. Early in 1980 Denning's second book, *The Due Process of Law* was published by Butterworths. It was proposed that the author should sign copies at Blackwell's bookshop in Oxford. But ugly posters appeared in the city: "Mass picket Denning." The police and proctors of a great university city evidently felt unable to protect an 81 year old judge, for the event was cancelled.

On the national scene, Members of the House of Commons, who in January 1979, had had on its Order Paper an unprecedented motion of congratulations,[5] began to criticise Lord Denning using the strident, personalised tones which had become customary in the 1970s.[6] Published commentary took on a sharper tone. Sometimes this was done in a carefully argued way,[7] sometimes in language which seemed muddled[8] and sometimes in language which was bitter.[9] When Lord Denning suggested that those accused of riot in Bristol had been acquitted because the jury contained some coloured people, the Secretary of the Society of Black Lawyers, who was a practising member of the Bar, issued a press statement alleging that "His remarks are racist and slanderous of black jurors."[10]

---

[98] *The Times*, January 5, 1977.

[99] See his dicta in *The Times*, May 20, 1975, and *Thew (R. & T.) Ltd.* v. *Reeves* [1981] 3 W.L.R. 190, 205.

[1] *The Times*, May 20, 1975 (on his judgment in the Crossman Diaries case). "Carry on, Denning" was a sub-heading in *The Economist* on April 7, 1979.

[2] Lord Boyd-Carpenter, *Way of Life* (1980), p. 240 (on the judgment in the Laker Airways Case).

[3] It is interesting to note the number of honorary degrees achieved by two other English worthies—Sir Peter Medawar, 17, and Sir Isaiah Berlin, 14.

[4] *Guardian Gazette*, February 28, 1979.

[5] But Hansard does not record the passage of this resolution.

[6] Even peers began to criticise: 416 H.L. Deb. col. 346 (January 20, 1981) records some critical remarks by Lord Gifford (himself a practising barrister, and a descendant of a Master of the Rolls).

[7] As in the volume of essays by Robson and Watchman, *Justice, Lord Denning and the Constitution* (Farnborough, 1981).

[8] So on December 9, 1979 *The Observer* assured its readers that "It is quite conceivable that Lord Denning and his fellow libertarians in the Court of Appeal could wreck existing union customs and practices." What meaning can be given to the word "libertarian" here?

[9] See Blake and Rajak, *Wig and Worker: A History of the Haldane Society* (1981).

[10] *Daily Telegraph*, July 11, 1981. On May 26, 1982, Mr. R. Narayan wrote to *The Times* to claim that "I was then the first and only one to call for his resignation."

What had happened? It is a complex story, involving such basic legal problems as the limits of judicial law-making,' and such basic political problems as the role of the media and the role of trade unions in a democratic society. Within an essay rather than a volume only an outline can be given. The starting point is the dissatisfaction which Denning had felt while in the Lords with the strict approach of the supreme tribunal to the doctrine of precedent. In 1966 the House stated that it would no longer regard itself as strictly bound by its own previous decisions. It was not clear whether this relaxation also applied to the Court of Appeal, which since 1944 had also regarded itself as so bound, with three exceptions. Lord Denning began a "one-man crusade"[11] to free the Court of Appeal from its obligation to follow its own decisions. He was conspicuously unsuccessful. "I embarked on my most extravagant dissent and met my most humiliating defeat."[12] The case was *Cassell & Co. Ltd.* v. *Broome*[13] in which he invited the Court of Appeal (and trial judges) not to follow a clear decision of the House of Lords[14] on the proper scope of exemplary damages. He asserted that the decision had been given *per incuriam*. "I am sorry that I ever said it. It earned for me a severe rebuke by the House of Lords."[15] Another rebuke, of a different kind for a different error, was delivered in *Gouriet* v. *Union of Post Office Workers*.[16] The majority of the Court of Appeal, Lord Denning dissenting, held that the courts could not control the decision of the Attorney-General to lend his name to relator proceedings.[17] The arguments to the contrary were, Lord Diplock cuttingly observed, marked by "some confusion and an unaccustomed degree of rhetoric." The majority of the Court of Appeal were emphatically and unanimously upheld by the Lords.

The "unaccustomed degree of rhetoric" may have been a reference to the passage in which Lord Denning declared that the Attorney-General was subject to the law.[18] Denning's style had always been unusual: by the mid-seventies it was not quite so admired as it had been. The structure of the judgment was as clear and sound as ever, and often praised by his fellow judges, but a certain striving after effect had become noticeable in the style rather than in the arrangement. There were few or no subordinate clauses, and sometimes no verb in the sentences. So the style was lacking in cadences. Also the terse vivid opening sentence, to which he himself attached so much importance for gripping the reader's attention,[19] often seemed inappropriate, especially in cases of severe personal injuries.[20] Parodies began to appear— sometimes quite amusing.[21]

The media now began to turn its attention to Lord Denning. It is worth speculating about the reasons for this—apart from the superficial resemblance in style between a late Denning judgment and an editorial in a popular

[11] The phrase used by Lord Diplock in *Davis* v. *Johnston* [1979] A.C. 264, 325.
[12] *TDL*, p. 298.
[13] [1972] A.C. 1027.
[14] *Rookes* v. *Barnard* [1964] A.C. 1129.
[15] *TDL*, p. 310. The "severe rebuke" can be found in [1972] A.C. 1027, 1054.
[16] [1978] A.C. 435, 496.
[17] "It was quite by chance that I sat on that case": *TDL*, p. 137.
[18] "To every subject in this land, no matter how powerful, I would use Thomas Fuller's words over 300 years ago: 'Be you never so high, the law is above you' ": [1977] Q.B. 729, 761–762.
[19] *TFS*, p. 307.
[20] "A man's head got caught in a propeller": *Allen* v. *Jambo Ltd.* [1980] 1 W.L.R. 1254.
[21] See *TFS*, pp. 219–220.

newspaper.[22] It can be suggested that there are two reasons related to Denning as a man (or as a judge), and one related to the subject-matter with which he dealt. First, in an age obsessed with the desire to abolish all barriers of race or creed or class, Lord Denning was a natural figure for admiration. In appearance and manner and voice he was the antithesis of the English legal establishment.[23] The face was round and rosy; the eyes were bright. The voice, with its Hampshire burr stressing the consonants was reassuringly unlike the clipped consonants and swallowed vowels of the public schools and the Inns of Court. It is true that Denning believed in or admired many things which the modern Englishman is reputed to dislike, *e.g.* the Christian religion,[24] his native country,[25] and the defence forces and police,[26]—but the English, like the Chinese, have always been ready to accept unfashionable statements from very old men.

Secondly, the media, especially television, thrive on confrontation. In legal matters, until the 1970s, this took the form of re-telling famous murder trials. (The English appetite for the hackneyed dramas of Crippen or Bywaters is insatiable). Then the increasingly anti-authoritarian atmosphere produced a flourishing new light industry—attacks on particular convictions to prove them unjust. But the possibility that civil cases might be treated or investigated in such a spirit does not appear to have occurred to anyone until the famous Denning dissents of the seventies.[27] By the beginning of the Eighties the mere fact that Lord Denning had expressed an opinion was news in itself, even though that opinion was not novel. So practitioners had long been familiar with Denning's view, first clearly expressed in 1954,[28] that an error of judgment by a professional man was not equivalent to negligence. But when he repeated it in 1981[29] national publicity followed. Equally the public were given the impression that the Court of Appeal was composed of only one judge. Even in *The Times*, July 30, 1982 the headline over a report of Lord Denning's last, and by no means least controversial, judgment, ran "Head entitled to refuse Sikh, Denning rules."[30]

Thirdly, the accidents of litigation brought before Denning a subject which is at the centre of English economic problems—the position of trade unions in society. His views on this were expressed with exceptional vigour, and were at once repudiated by the House of Lords. So a confrontation in an exceptionally explosive area was brought about. This may well explain why "there is something qualitatively special about the media publicity accorded to Lord Denning."[31] Certainly the media concentration on Denning was so

---

[22] See the Daily Mirror *Handbook on Style* (1981).

[23] Although 20 years have passed since Lord Radcliffe expressed the hope that nobody by pen or typewriter would again use this word (*Censors*, p. 22), it is too convenient to be abandoned completely.

[24] A view consistently asserted since 1949 (*The Changing Law*, p. 99).

[25] "It is a proud thing to be a British subject": *R.* v. *Home Secretary* [1982] 3 W.L.R. 754, 755. It is better to live in England than to have a tax-free income in Jersey: *Re Weston* [1969] Ch. 233, 241. It is also good to keep "all things bright, beautiful and British": *Hayward* v. *Thompson* [1982] Q.B. 47, 55.

[26] See *McIlkenny* v. *Chief Constable of the West Midlands* [1980] Q.B. 283.

[27] Perhaps the publicity given to the dissenting judgments has encouraged those anti-authoritarian attitudes which Lord Denning has elsewhere deplored.

[28] *Roe* v. *Minister of Health* [1954] 2 Q.B. 66.   [29] *Whitehouse* v. *Jordan* [1981] 1 W.L.R. 246.

[30] The decision was subsequently reversed by the House of Lords: *Mandla* v. *Lee* [1983] 1 All E.R. 1062.

[31] G. Drewry, *New Law Journal*, April 9, 1981.

great that in the *Duport Steel* case[32] even the Law Lords seem not to have noticed that Denning's judgment was not a dissent but was supported by closely reasoned judgments by Lawton and Ackner L.JJ. The House of Lords in this case stated in emphatic language[33] that the Court of Appeal should have followed the decision in the previous year in the *McShane* case[34] to the effect that the courts should not review the issue whether acts had been done in the course or furtherance of a trade dispute. Parliament had not intended to make the judge a back-seat driver in industrial disputes.[35]

These rebukes received great publicity. Lord Denning appeared to be unrepentant. In a judgment on a different question of statutory interpretation[36] he said:

> "The word 'furtherance' was capable of two interpretations. One that it was objective. The other that it was subjective. Five judges held that it was objective. Four that it was subjective. The choice between them was not a linguistic or semantic exercise. It was one of the policy of the law—or of public policy, or you might say—which the judges had perforce to decide. As between the two interpretations, which of the judges made the right choice and which the wrong? Subsequent events[37] and subsequent comments have shown convincingly that the four in the majority in the House of Lords made the wrong decision. Yet, as they had the last word, no-one can gainsay it."

Apart from the three trade union appeals, Lord Denning has been reversed or his dissenting judgments not approved, by a (not always unanimous) House of Lords in at least 12 appeals within two years of his eightieth birthday. Four of these cases were in the area of administrative law[38]; one dealt with the statutory functions of ACAS in industrial disputes[39] one dealt with the assessment of VAT[40]; one was on the borderline between company and administrative law[41]; three dealt with the proper interpretation of Acts of Parliament[42]; and one with a plaintiff who wished to discontinue proceedings in England in order to obtain higher damages in Texas.[43]

---

[32] [1980] 1 W.L.R. 142.

[33] The tone of Lord Diplock's remarks was, some thought, too reminiscent of Lord Simonds' rebukes 30 years before. For tart Denning comments on Diplock judgments, see *André et Compagnie S.A.* v. *Marine Transocean Ltd.* [1981] 3 W.L.R. 43, 48, and the *Paal Wilson* case [1982] 3 W.L.R. 49, 57.

[34] *Express Newspapers Ltd.* v. *McShane* [1980] A.C. 672, 694.

[35] Lord Scarman in *McShane* at p. 694.

[36] *R.* v. *Sheffield Crown Court, ex p. Brownlow* [1980] 2 Q.B. 530, 539.

[37] This seems to be a reference to the Employment Act 1980, which Denning thought had reversed *McShane*—wrongly, according to the H.L., which also reproved him for using Hansard to interpret a statute: *Hadmor Productions Ltd.* v. *Hamilton* [1982] 3 W.L.R. 322, 327.

[38] *R.* v. *Inland Revenue Commissioners, ex parte Rossminster Ltd.* [1980] A.C. 952; *Bushell* v. *Secretary of State for the Environment* [1981] A.C. 75; *Newbury B.C.* v. *Secretary of State for the Environment* [1981] A.C. 578; *R.* v. *Inland Revenue Commissioners, ex parte National Federation of Self-Employed* [1981] 2 W.L.R. 722.

[39] *U.K. Association of Professional Engineers* v. *ACAS* [1981] A.C. 374.

[40] *Customs & Excise Commissioners* v. *J.H. Corbitt Ltd.* [1981] A.C. 22.

[41] *In Re Racal Communications Ltd.* [1981] A.C. 374.

[42] *Fothergill* v. *Monarch Airlines Ltd.* [1981] A.C. 251; *Allen* v. *Gulf Oil Refining Ltd.* [1981] 2 W.L.R. 188; *Midland Bank Trust Co.* v. *Green* [1981] A.C. 513.

[43] *Castanho* v. *Brown and Root U.K. Ltd.* [1981] A.C. 557. ("I would therefore dismiss the appeal and let the plaintiff be compensated here and now by the payment of £200,000. But as Shaw and Brandon L.JJ. think otherwise he will have to wait until the proceedings end in the United States: and that may be a very long time. He may be dead by then": [1980] 1 W.L.R. 833, 858).

Another of these appeals was in an area of private law which Lord Denning has made specially his own over a period of many years—the interpretation of exemption clauses in contracts. He has always asserted that a fundamental breach of contract disentitled the contract-breaker as a matter of law from relying on an exemption clause. In *Photo Productions Ltd.* v. *Securicor Ltd.*[44] the House of Lords held that its previous decision in the *Suisse Atlantique*[45] had made it clear that there was no such rule of law; instead it was a question of construction in each case, Denning, it was said, ought to have recognised the true meaning of the *Suisse Atlantique* case, and not insisted on his own views.

The resentment against the House of Lords had always simmered beneath the surface, and it sometimes erupted in those years. After it had been emphatically stated and re-stated[46] that it was the duty of the Court of Appeal to follow its own decisions, Lord Denning retaliated by using the analogy of examiners marking scripts. In *Bremer* v. *Mackprong*[47] he said: "The House of Lords are fortunate in that there is no-one to examine them or mark their papers." A year later, after the trade union appeals, there was reported a case in which Mr. Raymond Blackburn, a private citizen, applied in person, unsuccessfully, for an order of mandamus against the Attorney-General to oblige him to enforce the law on obscenity. *The Times* reported[48] that "Mr. Blackburn, while addressing the Court on costs and leave to appeal, referred to Lord Denning as the greatest living Englishman." Lord Denning retorted: "Tell that to the House of Lords." Lord Hailsham made a charitable comment on such statements when he wrote that "Until judges become, like Lord Denning, a national institution, they cannot answer back."[49]

It may be unwise to deduce too much from the fate of a dozen appeals.[50] For within the same period there are reported cases in which Lord Denning had been upheld, *e.g. British Steel Corporation* v. *Granada*[51]; *Lonrho* v. *Shell Petroleum Co.*[52]; *Att.-Gen.* v. *BBC*[53]; and *I. Congreso*.[54] In each of the last two appeals one of the Law Lords deliberately expressed admiration for a Denning judgment.[55] In another appeal, *Lim Poh Choo* v. *Camden and Islington Area Health Authority*,[56] four Law Lords, speaking through Lord Scarman, agreed with Lord Denning's (dissenting) judgment that the law relating to assessment of

---

[44] [1980] A.C. 827. But Denning has sometimes tried to have the last word: "Incidentally, I no longer mind their decision in this case; because the legislature has intervened . . . by the Unfair Contract Terms Act 1977" (*TFS*, p. 175). See also [1982] 2 W.L.R. 745, 776; and [1982] 3 W.L.R. 462, 467.

[45] [1967] 1 A.C. 361.

[46] *Cassell & Co. Ltd.* v. *Broome* [1972] A.C. 1072; *Davis* v. *Johnson* [1979] A.C. 264.

[47] [1979] 1 Lloyd's Rep. 219, 222.

[48] March 7, 1980.

[49] (1980) Cambrian Law Review 46.

[50] As Lord Hailsham himself emphasised in H.L. Deb., Vol. 416, col. 368.

[51] [1981] A.C. 1096 (discovery). Another case in this area in which the H.L. upheld Denning was *Science Research Council* v. *Nassé* [1980] A.C. 1028.

[52] [1982] A.C. 173 (with reservations about Denning's views on breaches of statutory duty).

[53] [1981] A.C. 303.

[54] [1981] 3 W.L.R. 328.

[55] See Lord Edmund-Davies in the *B.B.C.* case ([1981] A.C. 303, 345); Lord Wilberforce in *I Congreso* (cited above, n. 71); and Lord Diplock in *Hunter* v. *Chief Constable of the West Midlands Police* [1982] A.C. 529, 537.

[56] [1980] A.C. 174.

damages was in urgent need of reform, but emphatically disagreed with his assertion that this could be done by the courts without waiting for Parliament. Lord Denning has never accepted the view that the courts should wait for the legislature to reform the law after receiving advice from the Law Commission.[57]

Many watched these developments with alarm, not least those who had been admirers of Denning. A contributor to one academic journal[58] referred to

> "the clear and ominous fact that the presiding judge in the Court of Appeal has alienated a substantial section of society. We are witnessing the tragic drama of a great judge whose acute sense of rightness has become a conviction of righteousness, whose consciousness of the need for justice has led him to become a self-appointed arbiter in the politics of society and whose desire to draw attention to defects in our law has more noticeably drawn attention to himself. Aided and abetted by the media, whose motives are not coincident with the interests of justice, of the legal system nor of the noble judge himself, the process has accelerated and the Master of the Rolls now takes his daily place alongside the good and the bad in the nation's headlines."

Even the media reacted against Lord Denning when it felt that its own interests were subject to the control of the Court of Appeal. In *Home Office* v. *Harman*[59] it was held that a solicitor had committed a serious contempt of court by showing a journalist documents which had been obtained under an order of discovery and then read out in open court. Lord Denning's judgment was described as "almost the most perverted analysis of the relationship between public interest in the administration of justice and the private interest of the individual in freedom of speech that we have ever encountered."[60]

Another academic made a perceptive comparison with Lord Mountbatten of Burma.[61] "What Lord Mountbatten was to the Royals, Lord Denning is to the judiciary: unorthodox, larger than life, a great performer, eager to emphasise his own considerable contributions to public life." To this list of shared qualities might be added a certain absence of humour about self. Neither Mountbatten nor Denning was anxious to discover the footsteps of anyone else in the sands of history.

But whatever criticisms were made of the substance or style of the judgments of the Master of the Rolls, nobody doubted that his physical capacities to preside over his court were unaffected by his years. Sight and hearing were unimpaired, and there was no sign that, to use his own phrase, "His mind had become addled by age."[62]

All these events combined to bring the question of Lord Denning's resignation into the area of public discussion. First, the law did not require Denning's resignation at any age. When he was appointed in 1944 there was

---

[57] See *Liverpool City Council* v. *Irwin* [1976] Q.B. 319, 332.
[58] (1980) Cambrian Law Journal 113, 114.
[59] [1982] 2 W.L.R. 310.
[60] *New Law Journal*, February 19, 1981.
[61] J.P.W.B. McAuslan, (1980) 44 M.L.R. 244, 246.
[62] *Re Brocklehurst* (*dec'd.*) [1978] Ch. 14, 32.

no retiring age, and when one was introduced (75 for Judges of the Superior Courts) by the Judicial Pensions Act 1959, s.2, it was specifically provided by section 3 that it did not apply to judges already in post unless they so desired. Denning had not expressed any such desire.

Secondly, many years before resignation became an issue, Lord Denning had told an audience that "A man who accepts the office of judge in England must reckon that he will stay in that position always. He has taken it on as his life work and must stand by it."[63] The judge belongs to a priesthood for ever. It is therefore not surprising to find a certain note of contempt for those who have resigned, whether on reaching the retiring age as with Barnard J.,[64] or prematurely, as with Devlin.[65]

Thirdly, Lord Denning himself publicly stated that he had no present intention to resign—or, more positively, that he had no intention to resign at present. Sometimes this was done in a way which showed his innocent weakness for repeating the same (never very good) joke. "I repeat the outworn quip about having 'Every Christian virtue except resignation.' "[66] Sometimes this was done in a way which defies classification (as with some other of his utterances). So in one judgment he said[67]: "This case will be of interest to those in the Civil Service—and elsewhere—who are approaching retiring age. Unlike me!" Hints of various kinds were dropped. A former parliamentary draftsman wrote to *The Times*[68] to suggest that Lord Denning should retire, but had little support. A more weighty statement was made by Buckley L.J. when bidding farewell in open court on his retirement in February 1981. Retirement, he said, was a beneficial institution.[69] The weight of this dictum was however, greatly lessened when the Law Reports revealed that within two months Sir Denys Buckley had come out of retirement to sit (with Lord Denning M.R.) in Appeal Court 1.[70]

The important point about resignation, or rather non-resignation, which made Lord Denning unique, was the extent of his seniority over all other judges. In 1981 the next senior judge to him was Lord Diplock, who was born in 1907, and appointed to the High Court in 1956, being promoted to the Court of Appeal in 1961 and the House of Lords in 1968. But of the 18 Lord Justices of Appeal over whom the Master of the Rolls presided in 1981, not one had been appointed to the Court of Appeal before 1971, and only nine had been called to the Bar before 1944. To put it in another way, nine of the 18 members of the Court of Appeal had not even become law students when Denning started his judicial career. It is true that the careers of some of these had been interrupted by war service, but the figures are still remarkable, as also are those relating to the Queen's Bench Division Judges in 1981. These were 48 in all, but no less than 18 of them had not even been born when

---

[63] (1954) 71 S.A.L.J. 345, 351.

[64] "He has lived on his pension for the last 20 years and is now 88. I have gone on. It is because I like the work": *DPL*, p. 188. (Barnard died in 1981).

[65] The references to Lord Devlin are somewhat muted, and there are none to Sir Henry Fisher, who retired early from the Q.B.D. to enter the City.

[66] *TFS*, p. 249.

[67] *Howard* v. *Dept. of National Savings* [1981] 1 W.L.R. 542, 543.

[68] January 20, 1981, citing the advice of Lord Brampton, "Tarry not too long upon the scene of your old labours" (*Reminiscences* (1904), vol. ii, p. 255).

[69] *New Law Journal*, May 28, 1981.

[70] *R.* v. *Hillingdon B.C.* [1981] 3 W.L.R. 109.

Denning obtained his First in law at Oxford in 1922. The striking age-gap between Lord Denning and other members of the Bench inevitably increased with each passing year and, in the nature of things, rendered it less and less likely that he would pay much attention to what was thought by people so much his junior in age and experience. Lord Denning therefore seemed to be in a state of some intellectual and social isolation. He read few newspapers, and outside his home and family circle seemed to have no close friend, male or female, legal or non-legal. In particular there was no younger judge who could act as friend and adviser, as Willes did with Parke and Hodson with Goddard. Although there was constant travelling to address audiences and conferences these were naturally composed of supporters rather than critics. There was also membership of many committees, but these seemed to reflect not so much a distinctive intellectual or social interest as the natural responsibilities of a busy professional man. All his public activities and interests seem to date from 1944.

The end of this extraordinary career came with great rapidity. In the spring of 1982, Butterworths issued a leaflet advertising a new book by Lord Denning—his fourth in three years. The leaflet had on its face the prophetic statement: What Next From Lord Denning. On Thursday, May 20, the book (entitled *What Next in the Law*) was published. On the previous day there had been the usual speeches at the usual party. Lord Denning himself had given a new turn to an old jest by quoting Tennyson's *The Brook*: "But men may come and men may go But I go on for ever."

On Saturday, May 22, it was announced that the Society of Black Lawyers had objected to some passages in the book which dealt with the capacity of black or coloured persons for jury service. On Monday 24, in a leading article entitled "A Judgment Too Far," *The Times* referred to "Lord Denning's ill-considered judgments on the unsuitability of many blacks for jury service." It also objected to the book's revelation that the Master of the Rolls had changed his mind about his judgment in *British Steel Corporation* v. *Granada* since he had delivered it. It was stated in *The Observer* of May 23, that a firm of solicitors had issued, or threatened to issue, writs for libel on behalf of two blacks who had been jurors in the Bristol riots trial in 1981. Early in the following week the publishers announced that the book had been temporarily withdrawn, and Lord Denning himself issued a statement which "deeply regretted that any of it should have given offence."

On Friday, May 28, half an hour after the courts had risen at the end of Easter Term for the Whitsun Vacation, a statement was issued by Mr. P. Post, the Clerk to the Master of the Rolls. It said that Lord Denning had intended for some time to retire at the end of the current legal year (*i.e.* September 30, 1982), "because of his advanced age," and that in the ordinary course of events this would have been announced in the middle of June.

> "In the light of recent controversy which has arisen over his latest book, which it is hoped will shortly be resolved, it has been decided to bring the announcement forward. Lord Denning will continue to sit as Master of the Rolls until the end of July."

There is a shade of ambiguity in this announcement. In fact what was brought forward was the announcement of the resignation and not the resignation itself: Lord Denning sat as Master of the Rolls for the last time on

Wednesday, September 29, with Oliver and Kerr L.JJ., to deliver the reserved judgment of the Court of Appeal in a case concerning the validity of an exemption clause—*George Mitchell (Chesterhall) Ltd.* v. *Finney Lock Seeds Ltd.*[71] On Thursday, September 30, Sir John Donaldson was sworn in as Master of the Rolls in succession to Lord Denning.

But the effective farewells had been said on Friday, July 30, at the end of Trinity Term and before the start of the Long Vacation. On that day over 300 judges, barristers and solicitors came into Appeal Court 3 to hear speeches by the Lord Chancellor, the Attorney-General and other lawyers, and a reply by Lord Denning himself. In a leading article that morning *The Times* remarked that "Lord Denning has legal genius and he has had a laudable mission to make the law accord with justice." Looking to the future, it observed that "There is much to be said for a period of quiet judicial activity now, and the predictability that is afforded by a stricter regard for precedent. Lord Denning's reign was glorious, often spectacular, occasionally wayward. English law has earned a few years' rest." That judgment will not quickly be displaced.

The conclusion is that in the 900 years of the common law Lord Denning is a phenomenon.[72] A phenomenon is a highly unusual fact or occurrence: it is distinct from a noumenon, which is a purely intellectual construction. Lord Denning is certainly not that. The attempt made here to describe and explain the main events in a phenomenal career must be provisional: each age must interpret for itself the great men of its own and previous generations.

---

[71] [1983] 1 All E.R. 708 aff'd. [1983] 2 All E.R. 797.
[72] The O.E.D. definition, cited by Lord Devlin in *The Spectator*, May 16, 1981.

Part I
LORD DENNING AND ENGLISH LAW

CHAPTER 2

Contract and Tort

P.S. ATIYAH

Introduction

Any attempt to survey Lord Denning's contribution to the law of contract and tort must virtually become an account of the development of the common law throughout the whole of the period since the end of the second world war. In every significant area of the common law Lord Denning's judgments can be found to illustrate modern trends and ideas. Further, a survey of these judgments will dispel any belief that, in this area at least, Lord Denning's views have been constantly rejected by his colleagues or overridden on appeal. Certainly, this has occurred in some instances; but what is most striking about his contribution to the common law is the number of times in which his views, while originally being received with doubt or rejection, have ultimately been vindicated. This vindication has sometimes come through the judicial process, while in other cases it has come from legislation; in some of the latter cases it is, of course, arguable whether the process truly amounts to vindication. In some instances legislative support for Lord Denning's views may have amounted to a repudiation of his views of the proper extent of judicial power, although it may have represented a confirmation of his views on the appropriate policy to be adopted; but there are other instances in which it seems quite clear, in retrospect, that Lord Denning has been conducting a temporary staying operation, pending statutory intervention, and a respectable case can be made for saying that such operations are perfectly acceptable uses of the judicial power. In yet other instances, it seems clear in hindsight, that Lord Denning's approach to the permissible extent of judicial development of the common law was more sensible and realistic than that of his colleagues.

One other common illusion ought to be dispelled by the following survey of Lord Denning's common law cases, especially his contract cases. A widespread criticism of his technique is based on the belief that Lord Denning's stress on doing justice in the circumstances of individual cases has destroyed what certainty the law possessed, especially in commercial matters. In fact, Lord Denning has almost always distinguished, in his contract judgments, between commercial and consumer transactions, and he has not infrequently adopted a fairly tough, freedom-of-contract, stand in commercial transactions which contrasts markedly with his approach to consumer cases. Where he has departed from this approach, it will often be found that his views accord closer with those of the mercantile community than do those of his colleagues.

All this is not to say that Lord Denning's work in the law of contract and tort is not open to criticism. Given the extent to which he relies on policy arguments, his views on policy issues have often seemed simplistic. In particular, his views on the impact of insurance in tort cases (such as his

29

suggestion that where both parties are insured, the insurance factor "cancels out")[1] often seems to lack sophistication. But two mitigating factors emerge from a survey of his judgments as a whole. First, his own views have not stood still: there is often sign of an increasing sophistication in relation to such matters as insurance and tort law; and second, if Lord Denning's views on policy issues often seem simplistic, the fault lies as much with the Bar as it does with him. Despite increasing recognition from the highest courts that policy issues are relevant to legal decision-making, the·arguments of counsel have not, in general, shown much sign of serious research into the policy issues in contract and tort cases. Where these issues are complex as they often are, it is unreasonable to expect judges to be able to probe their depths by the light of nature.

Another criticism which may be levelled against many of Lord Denning's judgments in contract and tort is that (especially, perhaps in the first part of his career) his use of doctrine and black-letter law to justify his conclusions has often seemed implausible and unconvincing. That many judges feel their way intuitively to their conclusions, and then articulate their justification in terms of legal principle afterwards, is now a commonplace of legal theory. But in Lord Denning's case, the articulated reasons often seem forced and unacceptable; indeed, they are often so couched as to enable him to depart from them almost at will in subsequent cases. His decisions, therefore, sometimes give the impression of being based on principles valid for the case in hand only, and therefore lacking permanence or even real generality. Part of the explanation for this must lie in the fact that Lord Denning has often been much more influenced by considerations of policy and justice than his colleagues, and in order to make his decisions more acceptable to other lawyers, he has had to couch his judgments in terms of legal concepts and doctrines in which he has little faith. For this reason, the account of his common law judgments in the following pages lays little stress on the doctrinal reasons given by Lord Denning for his decisions; equally, little attention is paid to the numerous occasions on which these reasons have been, to a greater or lesser degree, rejected by other judges, even where Lord Denning's actual conclusions have been approved or upheld on appeal. But Lord Denning cannot altogether escape criticism for his apparent lack of interest in the formulation of genuine principles, applicable beyond the case in hand; this is, and must always be an important part of the judicial role, and it cannot be enough for judges merely to attempt to do justice in the particular circumstances of each case without regard to the longer term effects of their decisions.

A survey of Lord Denning's cases in contract and tort will best convey the extraordinary impact which his judgments have had across the entire range of the law if we adopt a basically conventional framework, and analyse his leading cases under the traditional headings.

---

[1] See *post*, p. 44.

1. CONTRACT

Offer and Acceptance

Every law student knows Lord Denning's judgment in *Entores Ltd.* v. *Miles Far East Corpn.*[2] in which the Court of Appeal declined to apply the traditional posting rule to communications by telex. What is, perhaps, less obvious to the modern student is that it was not nearly so apparent at the time of the *Entores* case, as the Court made it appear, that the posting rule was an anomalous exception to a general principle. The general principle, insisted Lord Denning, was that communication of acceptance had to be received; that principle applies to communications *inter praesentes*, or even to telephonic communication. The reason for it is that, if the acceptance is not received, the offeree will normally be aware of this fact; that may not, admitted Lord Denning, be the case with a telex message, because the sender of the message may be quite unaware whether it is received or not, but (he says) the offeror will normally send an immediate message to indicate that the offeree's message has not been received. In the unlikely event of the offeree's message of acceptance not being received, while he remains under the (reasonable) belief that it has been received, there will be no contract, and the offeror will not be bound, unless it is the offeror's fault in which case he may be estopped from saying that he has not received the acceptance.

A more radical attempt to depart from traditional offer and acceptance law was rebuffed by the House of Lords in *Gibson* v. *Manchester City Council.*[3] A few years earlier the Court of Appeal had been faced, in *Storer* v. *Manchester City Council,*[4] with a simpler version of the *Gibson* case. The plaintiff had been negotiating with the Manchester Corporation to buy his council house from them. They sent him, first, an application form, which he duly completed, and then an Agreement for Sale, which they instructed him to sign, saying that it would then be signed on behalf of the Corporation and returned to him. This last step had not been completed when a new Council was elected, pledged to end the sale of houses, and the Corporation refused to complete. It was argued that, as the Agreement for Sale had not been signed on behalf of the Council, there was no binding contract. The Court of Appeal unanimously rejected this argument; the Council in sending the Agreement for Sale to the plaintiff was making an offer, which he had accepted by signing and returning it to the Council. This seems clearly right. But in the *Gibson* case, matters had not reached such an advanced stage. The plaintiff had merely completed an application form in response to a letter which stated the price at which the Corporation "may" be prepared to sell the property; and the Council had then taken the house off the list of Council-maintained properties. On this somewhat scanty basis a majority of the Court of Appeal held that a contract had been made. It was unnecessary, suggested Lord Denning, to find a precise offer and acceptance in every case. The real question was whether the parties were *ad idem*, and here they were. The price had been agreed, and the parties intended to carry through a sale.

[2] [1955] 2 Q.B. 327.
[3] [1978] 1 W.L.R. 520 (C.A.) and [1979] 1 W.L.R. 294 (H.L.). See also the brief discussion of this and the next case in Chap. 5 *infra*, pp. 202–203.
[4] [1974] 1 W.L.R. 1403.

Of course this is correct; but it is also established law (and practice) that informal agreements for the sale of houses are not lightly to be held binding contracts, because otherwise buyers may find themselves committed to buy before they have assured themselves of finance. In the *Gibson* case the Council had intimated that a mortgage might be available but had quite plainly avoided committing themselves to providing mortgage finance. A decision for the buyer in this case, if treated as a serious precedent, could have had real dangers for other buyers; and the reversal of the decision by the House of Lords was surely fully warranted. Lord Denning's judgment in this case is a good illustration of what many lawyers find unacceptable in his judicial technique—an unwillingness to explain clearly how a decision for the buyer could be reconciled with a policy (which Lord Denning would surely subscribe to if occasion arose) of protecting house buyers who have not yet secured their financial position.

Another recent offer and acceptance case is, perhaps, more controversial. This is *Butler Machine Tool Co. Ltd.* v. *Ex-Cell-O Corporation*[5] which raised in classic fashion a "battle of the forms." In response to an inquiry from the buyers, the sellers sent the buyers a quotation for the supply of a substantial machine at a price of some £75,000 on terms set out on their form. These terms included a price variation clause, and provided for delivery in 10 months. The buyers, in response, sent an order for the machine on their own terms and conditions, (which did not, of course, include a price variation clause) but they took the precaution of attaching a tear-off slip to their order form, requiring the sellers to sign and return it, which acknowledged that the order was accepted on the buyer's terms. The sellers completed and returned the slip, but sent it under cover of a letter stating that the machine would be supplied in accordance with their quotation. The machine was made and delivered, but some months late, and the dispute was over the applicability of the price-variation clause. Although Lord Denning rejected any mechanical application of the offer and acceptance rules, he did in substance, apply the traditional rules to find in favour of the buyers. The buyers' order was (said the Court) a counter-offer. The seller accepted that by signing and returning the tear-off slip. The accompanying letter was immaterial because it only reaffirmed the price, and not the rest of the sellers' terms and conditions. This may be unconvincing to some, because it seems plain that the sellers did intend to re-import their terms and conditions into the bargain. But if that had been the proper construction of the sellers' letter, traditional law would have said there was no contract at all, because the parties would not have been *ad idem*. Yet the machine had been made and delivered. So it would have been absurd to suggest there was no contract. The reality is that traditional contract rules just do not answer the sort of question that arose here because the traditional rules are based on a false assumption about business behaviour—namely the assumption that parties do not perform a contract until they have agreed on terms. The clue to Lord Denning's judgment may, perhaps, lie in the fact that the machine was several months late in being delivered—he may have felt that this delay ("the important thing" in Lord Denning's words)[6] made it unjust that the sellers should be entitled to rely upon the price variation clause. Perhaps costs had increased

---

[5] [1979] 1 W.L.R. 401.
[6] At p. 404.

only as a result of the delay. But if this was the real ground of Lord Denning's decision, he did not make it clear; and it is, in any event, an arguable point. Even if the seller's delay was the cause of the increased costs, the fact remains that the buyers paid for the machine in depreciated currency, so it is not evident that it would have been unfair to make them pay the extra.

Consideration and Estoppel

One of Lord Denning's major successes in contract law was the discovery and development of the principle of promissory estoppel as a way of modifying the strict letter of the doctrine of consideration. His judgment in the famous *High Trees*[7] case was what first propelled Lord Denning into prominence among lawyers. It undoubtedly required courage to challenge the established doctrine of consideration in 1946, for the prevalent legal attitude was that this was one doctrine so hardened by centuries of case law that further development was a matter for the legislature. Furthermore, the generally accepted conceptual apparatus of lawyers at that time (and indeed, for many years afterwards) was such that lawyers did not perceive the close relationship between the idea of detrimental reliance as a consideration, and the idea of acting to one's detriment on a promise as a ground for estoppel or promissory estoppel. Indeed, Lord Denning's own approach has tended to obscure this relationship because he has never regarded promissory estoppel as being a reliance-based doctrine, but a promise-based one.

The history of the *High Trees* principle is too well known to bear repetition here. It will be enough to make a few points. The first is that, although the *High Trees* case was itself looked at somewhat dubiously by most lawyers in 1946, the principle of promissory estoppel is now so well established that it is unthinkable that it could today be uprooted even by the most conservative House of Lords. But it is illustrative of the importance of accidents of litigation in the development of the common law that the success of the *High Trees* principle may well have depended on the fact that it did not reach the House of Lords while Lord Simonds held sway. Although he himself was responsible for one of the decisions relied upon by Lord Denning in *High Trees*,[8] his remarks in the *Tool Metal Manufacturing* case,[9] where the principle had to be assumed to be sound, and did not arise for decision, suggest that he did not find it very palatable. Since then, the doctrine has still not been fully considered by the House of Lords, though Lord Hailsham has suggested that the cases may need to be reviewed by the House[10]; however, he went on to add that he did not mean to say that any of them were "to be regarded with suspicion." The case in which Lord Hailsham made these remarks is also of some significance in suggesting that promissory estoppel is closer to integration with general contract doctrine than seemed likely at one time. Lord Denning here, in the Court of Appeal,[11] had rejected the views of the

---

[7] [1947] K.B. 130.
[8] *Re William Porter* [1937] 2 All E.R. 361.
[9] [1955] 1 W.L.R. 761.
[10] *Woodhouse A.C. Israel Ltd.* v. *Nigerian Produce Marketing Co. Ltd.* [1972] A.C. 741.
[11] [1971] 2 Q.B. 23, 59–60.

trial judge that a letter from one contracting party could be relied upon as raising a defence of promissory estoppel, where it could not be relied upon as a contractual variation; and Lord Hailsham, in the House of Lords, went out of his way to say that he shared Lord Denning's incredulity at the curious result reached by the trial judge on this point.

The second point worth making about the *High Trees* principle is that its subsequent history has helped to show how and why the doctrine of consideration itself has served useful purposes. The *High Trees* principle, if pushed to its logical conclusion, would (as indeed Lord Denning has insisted) lead to the view that *Foakes* v. *Beer*[12] is obsolete. In many circumstances this would no doubt be welcomed by lawyers; but not always. Creditors sometimes agree to accept part-payment in full satisfaction of a debt in circumstances in which it seems quite unfair that they should be held to the agreement. Such a case was *D. & C. Builders Ltd.* v. *Rees*[13] in which the debtor extracted a receipt in full satisfaction from his creditor, on paying only part of the debt. The creditor here was hard pressed for money, and was faced with either giving the receipt or getting nothing. The majority of the Court of Appeal were content to reject the agreement as not binding on the authority of *Foakes* v. *Beer*. But this route was not open to Lord Denning who wished to be able to hold that a freely given waiver of a debt or part of a debt was binding; consequently he was constrained to stress here that the *High Trees* principle is only binding where it would be inequitable for the promisor to go back on his undertaking. This is just the kind of judicial technique that irritates other lawyers: they are apt to feel that Lord Denning is inventing exceptions to his own principles just because the principle appears to lead to hard results in some cases. Moreover, they find it worrying that the application of such rules should depend on vague ideas about when it is "equitable" to hold a promisor to his promise. It is perhaps unfortunate that Lord Denning has such a predilection for qualifying his principles with vague ideas about what is equitable; in this particular instance, recent developments in the law relating to economic duress suggest that it was unnecessary to rely on such vague notions in the *D. & C. Builders* case. This was just one of those cases in which the legal remedy open to the creditor was inadequate as a matter of practical reality, and the agreement to accept the part payment in full satisfaction would therefore seem to fall squarely within the newly expanded concept of duress.[14]

The third point to be made about the *High Trees* principle has already been touched on above. While many judges have accepted the principle itself, most have rested it on the idea that a person who has led another to act to his prejudice on a promise or other conduct should not be able to go back on his word or conduct. This means that the principle is normally seen as reliance-based, and to that extent one could argue that the development of the principle falls into place as a further instance of the movement away from the promise-based principles of classical contract law. Certainly, in the United States, the parallel principle of promissory estoppel (enshrined in the

---

[12] (1884) 9 App. Cas. 605.

[13] [1966] 2 Q.B. 617.

[14] See *Occidental Worldwide Investment Corp.* v. *Skibs A/S Avanti* [1976] 1 Lloyd's Rep. 293; *North Ocean Shipping Co. Ltd.* v. *Hyundai Construction Co. Ltd.* [1979] Q.B. 705; *Pao On* v. *Lau Yiu* [1980] A.C. 614.

famous *Restatement*, para. 90) is clearly reliance-based. But Lord Denning will have none of this. It is enough, he insists, that the promise was intended to be acted upon, and has in fact been acted upon.[15] There is no need to show that the promisee has acted to his detriment. It is just possible that this difference arises from some misunderstanding of the whole concept of acting to one's detriment. To most lawyers, what it means is that the promisee must have acted in such a way that *he would be prejudiced* if the promisor resiled from his promise; perhaps Lord Denning is merely objecting to the notion that it must be shown that the promisee has acted to his detriment in a less conditional way than this. But this seems improbable. For the fact is that Lord Denning's own values suggest that he is sufficiently old fashioned to have a greater faith in the traditional promissory basis of classical contract law. To him, therefore, promissory estoppel is promise-based, not reliance-based. The promisor is bound because he has promised, not because he has led the promisee to commit himself to a change of position. On this point, Lord Denning's views seem open to challenge, not merely as a matter of positive law, but also on more general grounds. If the liability is truly promissory, why does Lord Denning insist that the promisee must have acted upon it? And if he has acted upon it, but not in such a way as to worsen his position, why should he thereby acquire greater rights than he had before?

Terms and Representations

Lord Denning has taken part in a large number of cases in which the courts have grappled with the distinction between terms and representations, with the implication of terms, and similar issues. One group of cases upholds the efficacy of oral warranties to override printed conditions in catalogues or other documents.[16] In another group of cases Lord Denning has several times attempted to explain the distinction between a mere representation and a warranty. In *Routledge* v. *McKay*[17] the Court of Appeal held that a seller of a motor cycle who repeated to the buyer information from the log book concerning the age of the cycle was only guilty of a misrepresentation and not a breach of warranty. Both parties were innocent, and the seller had no means of knowledge that the log book was incorrect. In this case Lord Denning relied on *Heilbut* v. *Buckleton*[18] to support the inference that the statement was not a warranty. In the very similar, but better known case of *Oscar Chess Ltd.* v. *Williams*[19] a majority of the Court of Appeal, including Lord Denning, reached the same result, though Morris L.J. dissented, and would have distinguished *Routledge* v. *McKay* on the ground that in that case the sale agreement had been written, and the agreement made no mention of the age of the motor cycle. In *Oscar Chess*, however, the agreement was wholly oral. It seems clear that for Lord Denning the decisive fact in *Oscar Chess* was that the seller of the vehicle had used the price as a trade-in allowance on another car which he bought from the buyers, who were dealers. Clearly if

[15] See, *e.g. Alan* v. *El Nasr* [1972] 2 Q.B. 189.
[16] *Harling* v. *Eddy* [1951] 2 K.B. 739; *J. Evans & Son* v. *Andrea Merzario* [1976] 1 W.L.R. 1078.
[17] [1954] 1 W.L.R. 615.
[18] [1913] A.C. 30.
[19] [1957] 1 W.L.R. 370.

the seller had known that he was not entitled to the price in fact paid by the buyers, he might well not have bought such an expensive car. Although this seems a very relevant fact, it does not dispose of the real issue, which was whether the seller or the buyer was responsible for ascertaining the truth of the statement about the age of the car. As to this, Lord Denning seems to have been quite right to suggest that a private seller disposing of a vehicle to a dealer should not be held to warrant the truth of statements taken from the log book. In this case Lord Denning began to indicate some dissatisfaction with the much cited judgment of Lord Moulton in *Heilbut* v. *Buckleton*. It was not, he insisted the actual intention of the parties which determined whether a statement was a warranty or not, it was a matter of inference from the behaviour of the parties, not a matter of what they thought. "If an intelligent bystander would reasonably infer that a warranty was intended, that will suffice."[20]

In *Dick Bentley Productions Ltd.* v. *Harold Smith (Motors) Ltd.*[21] Lord Denning made it clear that his sympathy for the innocent private seller did not extend to dealers. Here it was the dealer who had made an innocent misrepresentation—about the mileage of a Bentley car he sold to the plaintiff—and the Court of Appeal had no difficulty in holding that that amounted to a warranty. A statement by a person in the course of business who had the means of knowledge was not to be equated with a statement by a private buyer or seller. Given these decisions it is a little surprising that Lord Denning found it necessary to dissent in the more recent *Howard Marine* case.[22] The plaintiffs here misrepresented the carrying capacity of two barges which were hired out to the defendants for the purpose of carrying out some waste material to sea and dumping it. The size of the barges was clearly a vital matter to the defendants, and as the plaintiffs were acting in the course of business, it is difficult to see why it was in any way unreasonable for them to be held responsible for their statements. The majority of the Court of Appeal held the plaintiffs liable either under the Misrepresentation Act 1967, or on the ground of breach of warranty, but Lord Denning would have exonerated them altogether.

A more interesting case is *Esso Petroleum Ltd.* v. *Mardon*[23] where the Court of Appeal, under Lord Denning, came very close to integrating the law of misrepresentation and the law of warranties and negligence. The plaintiffs in this case had negligently estimated the likely sales capacity of a petrol filling station, on the basis of which they persuaded the defendant to take a lease of the station. It was clear almost from the outset that the estimate was excessive and that the defendant, although a competent and hardworking tenant, could not hope to sell sufficient petrol to make the filling station economically viable: in fact he could not pay the rent and lost his own working capital into the bargain. It was held that the plaintiffs were liable, either on the *Hedley Byrne* principle,[24] or on the ground that they had warranted that their estimate was "soundly" (*i.e.* competently) made. They did not, of course, *guarantee* that the estimate would be fulfilled, so no

[20] At p. 375.
[21] [1965] 1 W.L.R. 623.
[22] [1978] Q.B. 574.
[23] [1975] Q.B. 819.
[24] [1964] A.C. 465.

damages for loss of the defendant's bargain could be obtained. He was confined to reliance damages, designed to put him into the position he would have been in (so far as practicable) if he had never taken the lease at all.

Implied Terms and Implied Contracts

The process of "construction" in the law of contract, and the implication of terms, are flexible means by which much justice is done; but there is scarcely any subject in this branch of the law which provokes more judicial disagreement than the implication of appropriate terms. The most interesting case involving this question in recent times is *Liverpool City Council* v. *Irwin*[25] which looks, at first sight, like a serious judicial defeat for Lord Denning, but turns out, on closer examination, to be one of his successes. The question at issue was whether a local authority was under any, and if so, what obligations in respect of the stairways, lifts and rubbish chutes in a high rise block of flats let to tenants. The stairway lights and the lifts and rubbish chutes were repeatedly vandalised and put out of order, but in the Court of Appeal a majority held that the landlords were under no liability to repair or maintain them because there was no express duty to do so, and none could be implied. A term can only be implied, insisted the majority with strict orthodoxy, if it is *necessary* to give business efficacy to the contract. Here it was not necessary to make any implications other than that the tenants were entitled to *use* the common facilities and the rubbish chutes. Lord Denning dissented on the main issue. He was prepared to hold that it was permissible to imply a term in a contract wherever it was reasonable to do so, and that some obligation to repair and maintain lifts and stairways must be placed on the landlords; but he also held that their duty was only to take reasonable steps to maintain and repair, and this duty had been discharged. In the House of Lords, Lord Denning's novel attempt to argue that it is always permissible to imply "reasonable" terms into a contract was rejected as unwarranted by authority and unsound in principle. But, on the main issue in the case, the House overruled the majority decision of the Court of Appeal and substantially upheld Lord Denning's judgment. Construing the contract in its context, they insisted that it was indeed necessary to imply some obligation as to maintenance and repair. Lord Wilberforce went out of his way to say that he had reached exactly the same conclusions as Lord Denning with most of whose thinking he agreed. Although he was not prepared to concede a judicial power to imply any "reasonable" term into a contract, the disagreement seems to have been more about the label to be attached, than about the substantive issues. If a court is free to imply "reasonable" terms, provided only that it calls them "necessary," then the disagreement between Lord Denning and the House of Lords disappears almost entirely. Not that the Lords would (presumably) have agreed that any "reasonable" term can be said to be "necessary" simply to justify the implication; but the fact is that their own decision puts such a broad construction on the concept of a "necessary" term that it seems to mean

---

[25] [1976] Q.B. 319 (C.A.) and [1977] A.C. 239 (H.L.). See Chap. 5, p. 201 where Professor McAuslan in discussing this case adopts a more critical approach from a housing law perspective.

"reasonably necessary," and there is not much difference between that and a "reasonable" term.

This case illustrates in a fascinating way three different judicial techniques or styles. The majority of the Court of Appeal, on the one side, adopted a rather wooden attitude to the legal rules governing the interpretation of contractual terms, taking the precedents too seriously, and applying the concept of "necessity" almost literally. Lord Denning, for his part, totally discarded all fiction and restraint, and claimed the power to imply any "reasonable" term. Then the House of Lords had the final say, adopting the substance of Lord Denning's views, but wrapping them in the more traditional and orthodox coverings favoured by the majority of the Court of Appeal. There is a lot to be said for Lord Denning's complete candidness. Why do the courts, so free in their willingness to impose "reasonable" obligations in tort law, shy away from admitting that they exercise a like power in contract cases—subject always to recognition that what is reasonable in a contract case must depend on the terms of the contract?

Shell U.K. Ltd. v. *Lostock Garages*[26] provides a postscript to the above case which may afford some wry amusement. The plaintiffs supplied petrol to the defendant garage under a *solus* agreement, and the defendant was bound to take supplies from the plaintiffs to the exclusion of all other petrol suppliers. As a result of a "price war" the plaintiffs began supplying petrol to some of the defendant's nearby competitors at substantially lower prices. The defendant simply could not compete with these competitors' prices unless he lowered his own to levels which were actually below the prices he was paying to Shell. He therefore began to buy petrol elsewhere at lower prices, and Shell sued for an injunction. The defendant argued that it was an implied term of the *solus* agreement that Shell would not undercut him in this way, though great difficulty was found in formulating an implied term with sufficient precision. Bridge L.J. accepted this argument but the majority of the Court, including Lord Denning, rejected it. However, they held that an injunction, being an equitable remedy, could be refused having regard to Shell's unreasonable behaviour. Lord Denning's judgment may, perhaps, have been prompted by tactical speculations, for at first sight it seems most surprising that he did not concur with Bridge L.J. But he may have reasoned that a holding in favour of the implied term argument would lead to an appeal to the House of Lords; for such a holding would affect all of Shell's *solus* agreements and would have long term implications. A mere discretionary refusal to grant an injunction, however, could scarcely have justified an appeal, and indeed, leave to appeal would probably have been refused.

Two other cases concerning implied contracts, rather than implied terms, are worth a passing glance, although they are likely to be better known to property lawyers and family lawyers than to contract lawyers. In *Eves* v. *Eves*[27] and *Tanner* v. *Tanner*,[28] two cases which came almost simultaneously before the Court of Appeal, redress was provided to women who had been living with unmarried partners and who had children by them, with regard to the homes in which they had been living. In the former case, it was done

---

[26] [1976] 1 W.L.R. 612.

[27] [1975] 1 W.L.R. 1338. See Chaps. 3 and 4 *infra* where this case is discussed in more detail, pp. 87 and 117.

[28] [1975] 1 W.L.R. 1346. See Chap. 4 *infra* where this case is discussed in more detail and the same view taken of Lord Denning's "Heresy," pp. 153–154.

by way of implied trust, and in the latter, by way of implied contract; in the former, the woman was held entitled to an actual share in the equity, as a result of her work in improving the house, in the latter, she was held entitled to a licence to occupy the house while her children were of school age, but as she had in fact been turned out after the county court judge had denied her any relief she was awarded damages in lieu of an injunction. In this latter case Lord Denning said that the court "should imply a contract by the defendant or if need be, impose the equivalent of a contract by him . . . ." The notion of the court "imposing" a contract on the parties may seem, at first sight to be bordering on downright heresy, for is it not standard contract doctrine that the courts do not make contracts for the parties?[29] But in saying this Lord Denning is only, once again, openly recognising what the courts have in fact been doing, though under cover of various disguises. In the more recent *Panalpina*[30] case, where the House of Lords upheld the applicability of the doctrine of frustration to leases, Lord Wilberforce, no revolutionary, virtually admitted this: "I think [he said] that the movement of the law of contract is away from a rigid theory of autonomy towards the discovery, *or I do not hesitate to say imposition,*[31] by the courts of just solutions, which can be ascribed to reasonable men in the position of the parties." Lord Wilberforce was, of course, referring here to the imposition of a result which terminates a contractual relationship, not one which creates such a relationship; but there cannot in principle be any reason why the courts should be able to exercise the one, but not the other of these powers.

Undue Influence and Inequality of Bargaining Power

One of Lord Denning's most adventurous, and (perhaps) potentially significant, judgments in the law of contract is to be found in *Lloyd's Bank* v. *Bundy.*[32] The Court of Appeal here unanimously held that, in the particular circumstances of the case, the plaintiff bank had failed in its duty to a client, and that a contract of guarantee given by him to the bank was consequently unenforceable. The actual holding is seen by most lawyers to fall under the traditional heading of "undue influence," although the terminology of undue influence is most misleading in relation to a case of this nature. But the main interest of the case lies in the apparently far ranging suggestions of Lord Denning as to a possible doctrine of inequality of bargaining power. Lord Denning referred in his judgment to a variety of different cases, such as those concerning duress of goods, unconscionable transactions with expectant heirs, cases of undue influence, and undue pressure, and salvage agreements, and then went on to say:

> "Gathering all together, I would suggest that through all these instances there runs a single thread. They rest on 'inequality of bargaining power'. By virtue of it, the English law gives relief to one who, without independent advice, enters into a contract on terms which are very

---

[29] But see my *Introduction to the Law of Contract*, (Oxford, 3rd ed., 1981), Chap. IV for a rather different view.
[30] [1981] 2 W.L.R. 45, 60.
[31] My italics.
[32] [1975] Q.B. 326.

unfair or transfers property for a consideration which is grossly inadequate, when his bargaining power is grievously impaired by reason of his own needs or desires, or by his own ignorance or infancy, coupled with undue influences or pressures brought to bear on him by or for the benefit of the other."[33]

Although these remarks were wildly *obiter*, and the other members of the court found it unnecessary to express a concluded view on them, Sachs L.J. expressed "some sympathy" with them, and they may also be thought to derive some support from the dicta of Lord Diplock in *Schroeder Music Publishing Co.* v. *Macaulay*.[34] Furthermore, although the House of Lords has, since these cases, reaffirmed the basic principles of freedom of contract, and (for the second time) rejected the idea that these principles can be undermined by the use of the doctrine of "fundamental breach," it has done so in language which appears guarded enough to leave open the door to a development of a doctrine of inequality of bargaining power.[35] It will, no doubt, seem heretical to many traditional lawyers to suggest that a contract may be impeached because it was entered into by parties of unequal bargaining power and is, in consequence, grossly unfair. But any such doctrine is unlikely to go far beyond the effect of existing authorities, as a matter of fact. What is involved in Lord Denning's judgment is a more open acceptance of what is already largely acknowledged law.

Exemption Clauses

Lord Denning's name will long be associated with the exemption clause problem, and the prolonged battle waged by the courts against the unreasonable exemption clause prior to the passing of the Unfair Contract Terms Act 1977.

From the late 1940s onwards, Lord Denning was exercising his ingenuity to strike down, or avoid the application of what he took to be unreasonably wide exemption clauses. One of the earliest of these decisions was *Olley* v. *Marlborough Court*,[36] where the Court of Appeal held that a hotel customer was not bound by terms contained in a printed notice posted up in the bedroom, on the ground that the contract was made at the reception desk, before she ever entered the bedroom. Lord Denning, at this time the junior judge in the court, stressed in a brief concurring judgment that people who want to rely on exemption clauses "must prove the contract strictly." Many years later, Lord Denning, now presiding in the Court of Appeal, attempted to use the same argument in *Thornton* v. *Shoe Lane Parking*,[37] holding that a car parking contract was completed when the customer took the ticket from an automatic machine, and that notices brought to his attention later were too

---

[33] At p. 339. See also Lord Denning's judgments in *Gillespie Bros. & Co. Ltd.* v. *Roy Bowles Transport Ltd.* [1973] Q.B. 400, 415–6 and *Levison* v. *Patent Steam Carpet Cleaning Co.* [1978] Q.B. 69.

[34] [1974] 1 W.L.R. 1308, 1315.

[35] See *Photo Productions Ltd.* v. *Securicor* [1980] A.C. 827, 843, 851.

[36] [1949] 1 K.B. 432.

[37] [1971] 2 Q.B. 163.

late.[38] This was a controversial application of the argument, however, and other more acceptable arguments were also available, namely that the defendants had not done what was reasonable to bring the very unusual exemption clause to the public's attention.

In *Curtis* v. *Chemical Cleaning Co.*[39] Lord Denning took part in a decision holding that a cleaning company could not rely on an exemption clause where the customer had been misled as to the extent of the exemption. The only problem in the case was that this looked like granting relief for innocent misrepresentation of an executed contract, and moreover, relief of an unconventional kind. The objection was brushed aside by Lord Denning. Executed contracts could (he said) be rescinded for innocent misrepresentation "in a proper case" (thus laying the foundation for future cases in which he might have wanted to depart from the rule in *Seddon* v. *N.E. Salt Co.*[40]). In any event, it was too long after the Judicature Acts to worry about whether this sort of relief was legal or equitable in its nature.

Another technique for the avoidance of unreasonable exemption clauses was discovered, or rather reaffirmed, in *Adler* v. *Dickson*[41] where the plaintiff, a passenger on a ship captained by the defendant, sued him personally to avoid the effect of an exemption clause in her ticket with the shipping company. The defendants argued that if the plaintiff could thus sue the defendants' servants, a "way round" the exemption clause would have been discovered. Lord Denning's argument in rebuttal gave little comfort to counsel for the defendants:

> "I pause to say that, if a way round has been found, it would not shock me in the least. I am much more shocked by the extreme width of this exemption clause which exempts the company from all liability whatsoever to the passenger. It exempts the company from liability for any acts, defaults or negligence of their servants in any circumstances whatsoever, which includes, I suppose their wilful misconduct. And this exemption is imposed on the passenger by a ticket which is said to constitute a contract but which she has no real opportunity of accepting or rejecting. It is a standard printed form on which the company insist and from which they would not depart, I suppose, in favour of any individual passenger. The effect of it is that, if the passenger is to travel at all, she must travel at her own risk. She is not even given the option of travelling at the company's risk on paying a higher fare. She pays the highest fare, first class, and yet has no remedy against the company for negligence."[42]

Other more traditional modes of limiting the effect of exemption clauses, such as by narrow construction,[43] or by holding that the clause only affected liability in contract but not in tort,[44] were enthusiastically pursued by Lord

---

[38] But Lord Denning misstated the facts in this part of his judgment, implying that the customer paid his money into the machine on entry: in fact he paid on exit from the car park.
[39] [1951] 1 K.B. 805.
[40] [1905] 1 Ch. 326.
[41] [1955] 1 Q.B. 158.
[42] At p. 180.
[43] *e.g. John Lee & Son (Grantham) Ltd.* v. *Railway Executive* [1949] 2 All E.R. 581.
[44] *e.g. White* v. *John Warwick & Co. Ltd.* [1953] 1 W.L.R. 1285.

Denning in a variety of cases. However, it would be a great mistake to suppose that Lord Denning has never been prepared to uphold the validity of an exemption clause. There are, indeed, some early decisions of his which appear to reflect a point of view which he subsequently rejected. For instance, in *James Archdale & Co. Ltd.* v. *Comservices*,[45] the defendants were employed to decorate some premises owned by the plaintiffs, under a contract which imposed liability on them for damage generally, but not for damage done by fire. It was held that the defendants were not liable for a fire caused by their negligence. This was not, said Lord Denning, an ordinary clause as to which party was to bear the liability, but was really directed to the responsibility of the parties for insurance. The owners of the premises should insure them against fire. The facts are surprisingly similar to those of the much more famous *Photo Production* case, (of which more later) in which, of course, the Court of Appeal's judgment in a contrary sense was overturned by the House of Lords. Similarly, there are some early decisions in which Lord Denning clearly showed his belief that clauses exempting a party from liability for loss of a vehicle were not unreasonable, having regard to the strong possibility that the owner was insured. In *Halbauer* v. *Brighton Corpn.*[46] Lord Denning concurred in a decision applying an exemption clause whereby the defendants protected themselves from liability for theft of a caravan parked on their premises. The owner should insure, said Lord Denning. Stronger still was Lord Denning's judgment in *Williams* v. *Linnett*.[47] Here the majority of the Court of Appeal applied the old law of innkeepers' liability so as to impose liability on a publican for theft of a car from the pub car park. Lord Denning dissented in a vigorous judgment from what (it must now be agreed) seems a preposterous decision. "The risk of loss by theft should [said Lord Denning] fall on the owner of the car who can, and usually does, insure against it, whether it be stolen in the street, or from a car park, or anywhere else." The legislature agreed, and this form of liability was abrogated by the Hotel Proprietors Act 1956.

So also, in a variety of commercial contexts, Lord Denning was often prepared to uphold the validity of exemption clauses, sometimes more so than his colleagues. In *J. Spurling* v. *Bradshaw*,[48] Lord Denning (though castigating the extreme width of an exemption clause) actually used the construction process so as to read down the exemption clause in order to uphold it, rather than to evade it. And again in *British Crane Hire Corpn.* v. *Ipswich Plant Hire Ltd.*[49] (though strictly this case concerned an indemnity rather than an exemption clause) the Court of Appeal went out of its way to incorporate into an oral contract for the hire of a crane, written terms from the plaintiff's usual conditions of hire. Lord Denning insisted that this was entirely different from a consumer transaction, and Sir Eric Sachs indicated agreement on this point. But perhaps Lord Denning's greatest triumph in this area was his judgment in *Scruttons Ltd.* v. *Midland Silicones Ltd.*[50] This case concerned the exemptions in a bill of lading, and the right of a stevedore to

[45] [1954] 1 W.L.R. 459.
[46] [1954] 1 W.L.R. 1161.
[47] [1951] 1 K.B. 565.
[48] [1956] 1 W.L.R. 461.
[49] [1975] Q.B. 703.
[50] [1962] A.C. 446.

shelter under those exemptions. The context was, and is, of course, a purely commercial one, in which the whole question is in reality, about the incidence of insurance. Yet in that case Diplock J., a unanimous Court of Appeal and four members of the House of Lords, used the doctrine of privity of contract to reject the stevedores' right to rely on the exemptions contained in the bill of lading. Lord Denning dissented in splendid isolation, suffering, in addition to such a crushing defeat by weight of numbers, the very pointed rebukes of Lord Simonds against judicial reformers and heretics. But for most practical purposes the *Midland Silicones* case has been completely by-passed by the Privy Council decision in *The Eurymedon*,[51] in which Lord Wilberforce, delivering the majority judgment, expressed his views on the policy issues in language very close to that used by Lord Denning in *Midland Silicones*. Strictly speaking, of course, *The Eurymedon* does not depart from the law laid down in *Midland Silicones*, but merely exploits a loop-hole suggested by Lord Reid in that case; but this is to look at forms and to miss the reality. Lord Denning must be well pleased with modern developments in this area.

But the best known of Lord Denning's attempts (though they were never his alone) to control the use of unreasonable exemption clauses was, of course, the doctrine of fundamental breach. Starting from the perfectly orthodox position that exemption clauses must not normally be construed so widely as to cover fundamental breaches because this could not be in the contemplation of reasonable parties, Lord Denning gradually transmuted the doctrine into one of substantive law. The decisive case, perhaps, was *Karsales (Harrow) Ltd.* v. *Wallis*[52] in which the doctrine of fundamental breach was said to be applicable however widely the exemption clause was drafted. Even language of this kind, read against the factual background of the case in hand, could have been justified in the circumstances as going no farther than orthodox theory, but Lord Denning later made it perfectly clear that he was trying to fashion a tool with which to strike down unreasonable exemption clauses, no matter that they were plainly designed to cover the circumstances which actually occurred.

It needs to be remembered that many of the cases dealt with by the Court of Appeal during this period were hire-purchase contracts which, prior to the operation of the Act of 1964, were largely unregulated by statute. During the 1950s and early 1960s a large number of such cases came before the courts in which the widest imaginable exemption clauses were inserted, and in which hirers of second-hand motor vehicles were regularly being sued after the failure to pay instalments on the grounds that their vehicles were seriously defective. The widespread use of the doctrine of fundamental breach during this period must be seen as a response to this particular problem, and, in broad terms, it cannot be said that this was an unjustified use of judicial power. Indeed, Lord Wilberforce, in giving the doctrine its *coup de grace* in the *Photo Productions* case,[53] conceded that the doctrine had originally served a useful purpose.

The controversy that subsequently developed between the Court of Appeal and the House of Lords really revolved round the question whether that

---

[51] [1975] A.C. 154, reaffirmed in *Port Jackson Stevedoring Pty. Ltd.* v. *Salmon & Spraggon* [1981] 1 W.L.R. 138.

[52] [1956] 1 W.L.R. 936.

[53] [1980] A.C. 827, 843.

useful purpose had come to an end. In the *Suisse Atlantique*[54] case, as is well known, the House of Lords attempted to demote the doctrine from a rule of law to a rule of construction. By this time, the Hire-Purchase Acts of 1964–1965 had been passed, and the immediate need for the doctrine of fundamental breach had, perhaps, passed. But unreasonably wide exemption clauses were still to be found in other contracts, and the Court of Appeal revived the doctrine in *Harbutt's Plasticine Ltd.* v. *Wayne Tank & Pump Co.*[55] and again in *Photo Productions Ltd.* v. *Securicor.*[56] Lord Denning was able to justify his decisions here by relying on two short extracts from the judgments of Lord Reid and Lord Upjohn in *Suisse Atlantique* which lent some countenance to the notion that if the whole contract was terminated by the breach, the exemption clauses would fall with the termination.[57] These unfortunate dicta clearly ran counter to the general tenor of the speeches in the House, but they were seized upon by Lord Denning to justify holding that where the whole contract came to an end as a result of the breach the exemption clause must come to an end too, as a matter of law. In the *Photo Production* case Lord Denning was bolder still, and was prepared to reject the possibilities of strict construction, and the use of the fundamental breach doctrine, and simply to ask himself whether the exemption clause was fair and reasonable, in effect anticipating the operation of the Unfair Contract Terms Act 1977. Rather surprisingly (especially in view of his earlier decisions cited above) Lord Denning clearly thought the clause was not fair and reasonable. Both parties were insured, so the insurance factor "cancelled out." Leaving insurance on one side, the fair and reasonable result was (he thought) clearly to impose the liability on the employer of the negligent security guard.

In the House of Lords the threadbare nature of Lord Denning's attempts to explain the *Suisse Atlantique* decision were exposed; but it may well be that the really decisive difference of opinion between the two courts concerned the simple question of fairness. It seems quite clear from the speeches of Lord Wilberforce and Lord Diplock that, having regard to insurance practices, and also to the very small charges made by Securicor, they thought that there was nothing unfair about leaving the plaintiffs' fire insurers to bear the burden for which they had received full premiums. On these issues it is difficult to disagree with their lordships' decision. Lord Denning's view that the insurance factor "cancels out" is too simple: both parties may be insured but it may be more appropriate that one insurer meet the liability. The House clearly thought it more appropriate that the fire insurer should do so, and though the policy reasons suggesting this is a sound conclusion are too complex to repeat here, I, for one, would agree with that conclusion. Curiously, as we have already seen, Lord Denning's earlier decisions indicate that he might have taken that view himself at one time. Perhaps he has now reverted to it. In *Lamb* v. *London Borough of Camden*[58] Lord Denning seemed reconciled to their lordships' decision, going out of his way to say *obiter*:

---

[54] [1967] 1 A.C. 361.
[55] [1970] 1 Q.B. 447.
[56] [1978] 1 W.L.R. 526 (C.A.) and [1980] A.C. 827 (H.L.).
[57] I may be permitted to say that as soon as I saw these passages when *Suisse Atlantique* was first reported I knew they would cause trouble.
[58] [1981] 2 W.L.R. 1038.

"It is commonplace nowadays for the courts when considering policy, to take insurance into account. It played a prominent part in *Photo Productions Ltd.* v. *Securicor.* The House of Lords clearly thought that the risk of fire should be borne by the fire insurers, who had received the full premium for fire risk, and not by Securicor's insurers who had only received a tiny premium."[59]

Privity

Lord Denning has never had much love for the doctrine of privity. As we have seen already, his lone dissent in the *Midland Silicones* case, though in a practical sense vindicated by later decisions, in a more technical sense brought him into stark conflict with the doctrine of privity. In this, as in a series of other cases, Lord Denning repeated his total rejection of the generally accepted doctrine of privity. Relying on old authorities like *Dutton* v. *Poole*[60] Lord Denning repeatedly refused to accept the conventional professional explanation of *Tweddle* v. *Atkinson*[61] and *Dunlop* v. *Selfridge.*[62] Historically there is much to be said for Lord Denning's viewpoint, since it is quite plain that the modern version of privity—the rule that only a party can sue on, or rely on a contract—is of relatively recent origins. Indeed, even *Tweddle* v. *Atkinson*, which is usually treated as the source of this rule, quite plainly did not proceed on these grounds: the modern rule seems to owe its origins to writers (Anson is probably the leading culprit) rather than to explicit decisions. But it cannot be denied that after Lord Haldane's categorical pronouncements in *Dunlop* v. *Selfridge* the professional, and academic, view was that the doctrine of privity was far too firmly established in the law to be tampered with by judges. So it required considerable courage to mount the attack on it which Lord Denning persevered in over several decades. Basically, Lord Denning's argument was that the common law recognised a third party as having a right to rely upon a contract if he had a sufficient interest to enforce it[63]; this was a view which could well have been an acceptable basis for a new development of the law, but his colleagues would have none of it. His early forays were always *obiter*, and escaped appellate condemnation; but in *Beswick* v. *Beswick*[64] his frontal challenge was rebuffed by the House of Lords. Here he had not only repeated his earlier arguments about the third party's "interest" being sufficient to justify enforcement of the contract but had also prayed in aid section 56 of the Law of Property Act 1925, arguing that a broad enough construction of this section would justify elimination of the doctrine. Rather surprisingly he persuaded Danckwerts L.J. to agree with him in the Court of Appeal, but the House of Lords unanimously rejected both arguments. Nevertheless they

---

[59] At p. 1046. Not that this can be a sufficient reason for choosing to leave the fire insurers to pay. The size of the premiums should be commensurate with the risk. Here again we see a certain lack of sophistication on policy issues.

[60] (1677) 2 Lev. 211.

[61] (1861) 1 B. & S. 393.

[62] [1915] A.C. 847.

[63] See, *e.g. Smith and Snipes Hall Farm* v. *River Douglas Catchment Board* [1949] 2 K.B. 500; *Drive Yourself Hire Co. Ltd.* v. *Strutt* [1954] 1 Q.B. 250; *White* v. *John Warwick, supra.,* n. 44.

[64] [1966] Ch. 538 (C.A.) and [1968] A.C. (H.L.).

upheld the Court of Appeal's decision to grant specific performance of the contract at the suit of the promisee (herself, in this case, the third party beneficiary in a different capacity). So once again, Lord Denning, in a practical sense saw his decision survive. Moreover, there are encouraging signs that further vindication may yet lie in store. In *Beswick* v. *Beswick* Lord Denning relied on the analogy of the law relating to assignments, and suggested that a third party beneficiary could always sue in the name of the promisee to enforce the promise, if the promisee himself declined to sue. He further insisted that full (and not merely nominal) damages could be recovered in the promisee's name, and the doctrine of privity would thereby become nothing but a procedural rule, akin to those governing joinder of parties when an assignee claims enforcement of a debt or contract. Although this still remains controversial, the suggestion undoubtedly gains support from the later decision in *Snelling* v. *John Snelling Ltd.* [65] in which it was held that a promise by the members of a company to waive their claims against the company could be relied upon by the company itself, all parties being before the court.

Further evidence that Lord Denning's view are still gaining ground, though often by their fingertips, as it were, is to be found in *Jackson* v. *Horizon Holidays*[66] and *Woodar Investments Development Ltd.* v. *Wimpey Construction U.K. Ltd.*[67] In the former case Lord Denning carried the Court of Appeal with him in holding that a plaintiff suing for breach of contract to supply a family holiday, was entitled to damages for the inconvenience and disappointment suffered by his family as well as himself. This decision was approved by the House of Lords in the *Woodar* case, where, however, doubts were expressed as to how far the principle of the *Jackson* case could be taken. In particular, there were still doubts whether a promisee could recover substantial damages for breach of contract where a third party was the beneficiary of the promise. Nevertheless, it is confidently suggested that no court would tolerate the manifest injustice which would arise if it were held that an executed contract could not be enforced by either third party or by promisee. Further still, Lord Scarman made it quite clear that in his view the whole principle of *Tweddle* v. *Atkinson* was still open for review in the House of Lords. So Lord Denning may yet be vindicated here too; and if he is, the Lords will find much in his judgments to sustain them.

Illegality and Restraint of Trade

Lord Denning's judgments in cases involving illegality reflect his policy orientations very clearly. Where he finds serious illegality, a deliberate attempt to breach the law, real moral turpitude, he has no sympathy with the offenders, and is perfectly willing to refuse them all assistance. So, for instance, in *Napier* v. *National Business Agency*[68] Lord Denning was quite emphatic that a dismissed employee could not sue for breach of contract where it was shown that he had been regularly paid fictitious "expenses" to

[65] [1973] Q.B. 87.
[66] [1975] 1 W.L.R. 1468.
[67] [1980] 1 W.L.R. 277.
[68] [1951] 2 All E.R. 264.

defraud the Inland Revenue. Similarly, in *Gray* v. *Barr*[69] he insisted that an indemnity insurance contract could not be enforced if the insured had wilfully committed serious breaches of the criminal law. In *Regazzoni* v. *K. C. Sethia Ltd.*[70] he extended this approach to a case where breach of a foreign law was in question; though he went on to criticise as too widely expressed Lord Mansfield's famous dictum, "that no country ever takes notice of the revenue laws of another."[71] The true rule, he insisted, was that no country would *enforce* another country's revenue laws, not that it would never take notice of an attempt to violate them. Both the decision, and Lord Denning's views on Lord Mansfield's dictum were in substance upheld by the House of Lords.[72]

On the other hand, no judge has been more willing to find a remedy in cases where he considers that any element of illegality is merely technical (as in *Falmouth Boat Construction Ltd.* v. *Howell*)[73] or where one of the parties is entirely innocent of any moral wrongdoing (as in *Shaw* v. *Shaw,*[74] *Strongman (1945) Ltd.* v. *Sincock*[75] and *Shelley* v. *Paddock*[76]). Lord Denning has also repeatedly insisted that realities must be looked at even in illegal contracts, so that if the contract is executed, property in goods transferred must be held to pass to the transferee.[77] Generally Lord Denning has succeeded in carrying his colleagues with him in these cases[78] though there were serious disagreements as to the grounds for decision between the Court of Appeal and the House of Lords in the *Falmouth Boat Construction* case. In that case Lord Denning had argued that work done on ship repairs with the *oral* permission of the official authorised to grant licences was not illegal and the oral permission was itself a sufficient licence; he further held that citizens dealing with government officials were entitled to rely upon their exercise of authority thus in effect suggesting (as he has often done in other cases) that an estoppel might operate against the Crown in situations of this nature. Both these arguments were rejected in the Lords, though the actual decision was upheld on the ground that the subsequent issue of a written licence could be taken to have retrospective effect. The leading judgment was delivered by Lord Simonds who never attempted to conceal the distaste which he felt for anything savouring of the unorthodox in Lord Denning's judgments. Indeed, so great was the animosity between them that one feels that if in the Court of Appeal it had been held that the written licence had retrospective effect, Lord Simonds might have pointed out the impossible difficulties to which this would lead (*e.g. ex post facto* legalisation of the criminal acts of the accused) and have opted for the alternative solution of treating an oral licence as acceptable.

---

[69] [1971] 2 Q.B. 554.
[70] [1965] 2 Q.B. 490.
[71] In *Holman* v. *Johnson* (1775) 1 Cowp. 343.
[72] [1958] A.C. 301.
[73] [1950] 2 K.B. 16 (C.A.) and [1951] A.C. 837 (H.L.).
[74] [1954] 2 Q.B. 429.
[75] [1955] 2 Q.B. 525.
[76] [1979] Q.B. 120.
[77] *Sajar Singh* v. *Sardora Ali* [1960] A.C. 167; *Belvoir Finance Co. Ltd.* v. *Stapleton* [1971] 1 Q.B. 210.
[78] Though Hodson L.J. dissented in *Marles* v. *Philip Trant & Sons Ltd.* [1954] 1 Q.B. 29.

Lord Denning also played a major role in the series of restraint of trade cases in the 1960s in which it was held that *solus* agreements were subject to the doctrine of restraint of trade. In the first of these cases, *Petrofina Ltd.* v. *Martin*[79] Lord Denning declared, "The categories of restraint of trade are not closed," and went on to add that there was no reason why *solus* agreements should escape scrutiny under the restraint of trade doctrine. In the *Esso Petroleum* case[80] he went on to hold, with the rest of the Court of Appeal, that there was equally no reason why a different result should be arrived at because the covenantee was also a mortgagee. Most of these remarks were upheld in the House of Lords[81] though there was some disagreement about the permissible length of a reasonable tie: the Lords accepted that five years was not unreasonable (though they had the benefit of a Monopolies Commission Report which said as much) while in the Court of Appeal a lower limit of two to three years had been preferred. The Lords also devoted a good deal more attention to a question which the Court of Appeal had not seriously tackled, namely, if the categories of restraint of trade are not closed, how does one distinguish between any ordinary contract (which imposes restrictions on the use of labour or property) and a contract which falls within the restraint of trade category?

Other important decisions in the restraint of trade field, which there is no space to do more than glance at, are *Nagle* v. *Feilden*[82] where the court accepted the possibility of arguing that a private body which controls entry into a trade or profession must not act contrary to restraint of trade principles; and *Littlewoods Organisation* v. *Harris*[83] where, in a traditional employer-employee case, Lord Denning was prepared to go a good way in rewriting the covenant to make it reasonable, departing somewhat from the approach of, if not the decision in, *Commercial Plastics* v. *Vincent*.[84]

Mistake and Frustration

Lord Denning has for many years attempted to re-formulate the principles governing cases in which the parties labour under some fundamental, shared, mistake. Rejecting *Bell* v. *Lever Bros.*,[85] held by most lawyers to be the leading case, as having been decided on "common law" grounds only, Lord Denning has argued that a mutual fundamental mistake does not affect the validity of a contract unless there is a failure of consideration, or some element of fraud or misrepresentation which may render it voidable, or some implied condition affecting its operation. The "perished goods" cases he explained as resting on implied conditions. But he then asserted an equitable power to set aside a contract entered into by the parties on some fundamentally erroneous basis, either as to the facts or as to their rights. This doctrine was set forth in *Solle* v. *Butcher*[86] and repeated *obiter* in a number of

---

[79] [1966] Ch. 146.
[80] [1966] 2 Q.B. 514 (C.A.).
[81] [1968] A.C. 269 (H.L.).
[82] [1966] 2 Q.B. 633.
[83] [1977] 1 W.L.R. 1472.
[84] [1965] 1 Q.B. 623.
[85] [1932] A.C. 161.
[86] [1950] 1 K.B. 671.

later cases, such as *Leaf* v. *International Galleries*.[87] *Solle* v. *Butcher* concerned the lease of a flat, believed by both parties to have been so extensively altered as to have changed its identity and so to have been taken out of the control of the Rent Restriction Acts. The case for the landlord was strengthened by the fact that the tenant was his own surveyor who was at least equally responsible for the mistake, and also by the fact that, as a result of the mistake the landlord did not take the necessary steps to have the rent increased under the Rent Acts. The tenant, having gone into possession under a seven year lease, claimed that he was only liable for the controlled rent. Lord Denning argued that if the lease was void at common law, the whole lease would go, and the tenant would have no right of possession at all: consequently tenants in this situation would be reluctant to raise the argument, and would effectively lose the protection of the Rent Acts. In these circumstances he invoked the idea of equitable relief, and held that the tenant should be given the alternative of surrendering the lease altogether, or taking a new one at the contractual rent. Bucknill L.J. concurred in the result, though his reasoning differed from Lord Denning's: he regarded the contract as void on the principles of *Bell* v. *Lever Bros.* Jenkins L.J. dissented, holding the mistake to be one of law, a somewhat idiosyncratic decision, having regard to the almost universal judicial tendency to avoid ever putting anything into the category of mistake (or representation) of law.

The subsequent fate of Lord Denning's doctrine has been muted. It has been followed occasionally at first instance.[88] It was applied by Lord Denning himself in another Court of Appeal decision in which the judges split three ways, *Magee* v. *Pennine Insurance*,[89] but it must be admitted that the profession as a whole probably remain unconvinced of the existence of this equitable power to set contracts aside for mistake. Yet there is not a great deal of difference between dealing with these mistake cases by means of "implied conditions" or as questions of construction, and dealing with them on equitable grounds. It is an inescapable fact that problems of risk-allocation where the facts turn out to be wholly different from what they were believed to be, raise exceptionally delicate issues. On any view, justice sometimes requires that the literal effect of the contract should be departed from, and it is unrealistic to think that in imposing its solution the court is giving effect to the parties' own intentions. Naturally, in deciding whether a mistake has this extreme result, the court must be guided by the precedents and general principles of law, as well as by business ideas about normal and proper risk-allocations. If Lord Denning had said something like this, it is doubtful whether his judgment in *Solle* v. *Butcher* would still be regarded as so controversial, although even then it might well have incurred the disapproval of the House of Lords in 1949, had appeal been then taken.

---

[87] [1950] 2 K.B. 86.

[88] *Grist* v. *Bailey* [1967] Ch. 532; *Laurence* v. *Lexcourt Holdings* [1978] 1 W.L.R. 1128. Neither seems a very persuasive authority, and Lord Denning would probably have disagreed with the former. Having regard to *Campbell* v. *Edwards* [1976] 1 W.L.R. 403, *Baber* v. *Kenwood* [1978] 1 Lloyd's Rep. 175, and Lord Denning's strongly expressed view in *Arenson* v. *Arenson* [1973] Ch. 346 (as to which see *post*, pp. 57–58) it seems probable that he would have held the contract binding and left the seller to sue his solicitor for the loss.

[89] Fenton Atkinson L.J. found the contract void at common law, while Winn L.J. dissented.

For this is, indeed, largely what happened to the very analogous frustration, or construction case, of *British Movietonews Ltd.* v. *London & District Cinemas*[90] only a few months later. In this case the parties had made a contract for the distribution of newsreels, which was amended during the war, after the making of a statutory Order restricting supplies and then expressed to last so long as the Order itself lasted. Nobody anticipated that the Order would be retained long after the end of the war, when newsreels had ceased to be about the war and completely changed their character. The case did not strictly speaking involve an issue of frustration, but counsel argued that on the analogy of the frustration cases, the change of circumstances was so great that the contract should be regarded as terminable on notice; alternatively he argued, that as a matter of construction, the contract should not literally be held to continue throughout the new lifetime of the relevant statutory Order. In the Court of Appeal Lord Denning delivered a single judgment in which he said that courts should not always slavishly follow the literal meaning of the words in a contract but must construe the words in the commercial and indeed total context in which the contract operated. As to the analogy of frustration, he relied upon Lord Wright's well know views, several times repeated in the House of Lords, that the doctrine of frustration was based on a judicial power to qualify the literal words of the contract when justice so required. Looking back on this judgment, thirty years later, it is really difficult to see why so much objection was taken to it. The other members of the Court of Appeal concurred without a word, evidently thinking the case to be a simple matter of construction. In the House of Lords, however, the decision was reversed, and the literal construction of the contract insisted upon. Furthermore, Lords Simon and Simonds went out of their way to criticise and reject what Lord Denning had said about frustration and the power of the court to qualify the literal terms of a contract. It is difficult today to see what all the furore was about, and the suspicion must remain that personal animosities explain the extreme tone of disapproval adopted in the House of Lords. Any lawyer of the 1980s who reads Lord Denning's judgment today for the first time would probably find himself agreeing with every word of it. But even if it is conceded that on the issue of construction itself two reasonable views are possible, the dogmatic assertions of the law lords about the nature of the judicial role in construction and frustration cases look today outdated, and frankly absurd.

Any suggestion that Lord Denning's judgment in this case showed him to be over willing to hold a contract to be frustrated and to relieve a party of his strict contractual obligations in an ordinary commercial context, is surely rebutted by his decisions in *Davis Contractors* v. *Fareham U.D.C.*[91] (in which the Lords upheld the Court of Appeal, and adopted a more realistic view of the nature of the judicial role in frustration cases)[92] and also in *The Eugenia*[93] in which he held that the closure of the Suez Canal did not operate to frustrate a charter of a vessel from Genoa to India. Lord Denning may here have taken some satisfaction in citing Lord Simonds' judgment in the *Tsakirogolou* case[94] for the proposition that a finding of frustration was a

---

[90] [1951] 1 K.B. 190 (C.A.) and [1952] A.C. 166 (H.L.).
[91] [1955] 1 Q.B. 302 (C.A.) and [1956] A.C. 696 (H.L.).
[92] See also Lord Wilberforce in the *Panalpina* case, cited above, p. 39.
[93] [1964] 2 Q.B. 226.
[94] [1962] A.C. 93, 116, 119.

question of law for the court and not a matter of fact for an arbitrator. So (Lord Denning seemed to say) if it is a question of law for the court, is it not clear that it is the judge who decides whether a contract is frustrated, and not the parties?

Damages

Throughout his years on the Court of Appeal Lord Denning has been responsible for many decisions on damages in contract cases. Some are relatively straightforward, though often innovative in one respect or another. For instance, in *Anglia TV Ltd.* v. *Reed*[95] Lord Denning led the way to a decision that pre-contractual expenditure could be recovered as damages in a case where the plaintiffs were unable to quantify any loss of bargain damages. In *Trans Trust* v. *Danubian Trading Co.*[96] Lord Denning rejected the conventional belief that damages could never be awarded for a failure to pay money: here he held that a buyer who failed to provide a banker's credit as agreed when he knew that the seller himself was depending on the credit to obtain the goods, was liable for the seller's loss of profit. The buyer could not limit the damages to the difference between market and contract price because that assumed that the seller could resell the goods on breach, but here he had no goods to resell. In *Jarvis* v. *Swan Tours Ltd.*[97] Lord Denning gave his approval to the award of damages for mental upset and inconvenience in a holiday contract. This rather casual decision has opened what may prove to be a large door to damages for mental distress for breach of contract; and it is a little curious that this development should come at a time when tort lawyers are so unhappy about damages for pain and suffering in personal injury cases. If ever there was a case in which policy issues needed to be explored, this was it, but there is so far no sign that the Court of Appeal is going to do the exploring. *Lazenby Garages* v. *Wright*[98] is another interesting decision in which the mitigation rule was applied so as to acquit of all liability a person who had agreed to buy a second hand car, but who had changed his mind before delivery and decided not to proceed. The seller-dealer resold the same car without loss, but argued that he had still lost his profit on the sale. The court rejected this argument, holding that a second hand car was a unique chattel and that only one lot of profit could be made from its sale. The reasoning is unconvincing and one suspects that the court felt doubts about enforcing this wholly executory contract against a consumer who had simply changed his mind about a purchase. One wonders whether Lord Denning's apparently simple faith in the moral duty to keep a promise is beginning to waver.

More adventurous judgments are to found in the *Schorsch Meier* case[99] and in *Parsons* v. *Uttley Ingham & Co.*[1] In the former, Lord Denning persuaded his colleagues in the Court of Appeal (Lawton L.J. dissenting on one point) to depart from the rule affirmed by the House of Lords (including Lord

---

[95] [1972] 1 Q.B. 60.
[96] [1952] 1 K.B. 285.
[97] [1973] Q.B. 233.
[98] [1976] 1 W.L.R. 459.
[99] [1975] Q.B. 416.
[1] [1978] Q.B. 791.

Denning himself) in the *Havana Railways* case,[2] that judgment in English courts must be given in sterling. Relying partly on the EEC Treaty and partly on the old maxim *cessante ratione, cessat ipsa lex*, the Court of Appeal found overpowering reasons for giving a foreign creditor judgment for a debt in his own currency. Reliance on the EEC Treaty proved a mistake; and the House of Lords also subsequently disapproved the facile use of the Latin maxim to justify departure from a decision of the House itself; but the substance of the decision, and the policy reasons for it were once again largely upheld.[3]

In the *Uttley Ingham* case Lord Denning grappled with the difficult problem of remoteness of damages. Attempting to bring some order to the subject, and unwilling to accept different principles as appropriate in contract and tort actions (especially as so many actions these days can be brought in either contract or tort) Lord Denning argued that a difference must be drawn between damages for physical injury and damages for purely pecuniary loss. In the first case, the injury must only be foreseeable as a serious possibility, in the latter case a higher degree of foreseeability is required. Doubts may be felt about this suggestion (as Lord Scarman indeed did), and it may well turn out no easier to apply than some of the tests suggested by the House of Lords in *The Heron II*.[4] But sympathy must be felt for Lord Denning's criticisms of the desperate attempts of the law lords in that case to reduce the whole law to a verbal formula, as well as with his unhappiness at Lord Reid's suggested distinction between contract and tort principles of remoteness. No doubt the decision in the *Uttley Ingham* case is controversial, but there seems an element of unreality about the holding that the suppliers of the hopper ought to have foreseen that leaving the ventilator closed would cause serious injury and death to the plaintiff's pigs. One would have thought it obvious that farmers ought to be responsible for looking after and preventing injury to their pigs, and they should not be able to pass this risk so readily to the suppliers of equipment which, on the surface of things, could not be expected to involve such risks.

Penalties and Forfeitures

In accordance with his general predilection for traditional equitable doctrines, Lord Denning has always argued for an extensive use of equitable relief in relation to penalties and forfeitures. But the area has been very controversial, and many of Lord Denning's judgments have provoked dissent or appellate disagreement. In *Stockloser* v. *Johnson*[5] Lord Denning and Somervell L.J. (Romer L.J. dissenting) were prepared, *obiter*, to hold that equitable relief could be available to a seller who paid instalments on a contract but defaulted before the final payment. In *Bridge* v. *Campbell Discount Co.*[6] Lord Denning and Lord Devlin in the House of Lords held that a minimum payments clause in a hire-purchase contract was void as a penalty clause, whether the hirer defaulted, or whether he voluntarily returned the goods to the owner. Lords Simonds and Morton disagreed, and Lord

---

[2] [1961] A.C. 1007.
[3] *Miliangos* v. *George Frank Textiles Ltd.* [1976] A.C. 443.
[4] [1969] 1 A.C. 350.
[5] [1954] 1 Q.B. 476.
[6] [1962] A.C. 600.

Radcliffe reserved his opinion. This point thus remains undecided by the House of Lords and the Court of Appeal decision remains binding in the sense argued for by Lords Simonds and Morton. The result is conceded on all hands to be an absurdity—the hirer who acts in good faith and returns the goods is penalised, and the hirer who defaults and breaks his contract is relieved. Fortunately the practical implications of the question are of little importance in hire purchase contracts since the Consumer Credit Act, but the question of principle remains a potential source of trouble in the law.

More recently Lord Denning has several times attempted to provide some redress—though not by way of equitable relief against forfeiture—for charterers of vessels who are late in paying hire. In *The Laconia*[7] and again in *The Chikuma*[8] decisions of the Court of Appeal have been reversed by the House of Lords who have insisted that clauses requiring prompt payment of hire must be observed with absolute strictness if the owner is not to be entitled to exercise his right to withdraw the vessel. The first of these decisions is perhaps controversial but in the second the House of Lords seems to have been guilty of pure pedantry. In this case charter hire of over $68,000 was paid into the owner's Italian bank account on the due date, but because of some technicality of Italian banking law, the owners would have lost some $70 to $100 in interest if they had drawn the money out on the same day. This was held to amount to default on the part of the charterers, entitling the owners to put an end to the hire, with loss to the charterers (as alleged by them, at least) of some $3 million. The decision seems an outrage to common sense, and must run totally counter to all reasonable business expectations. Far from promoting certainty, one would imagine such decisions are almost bound to provoke litigation.[9]

Agency

There is only space here for a brief mention of a number of Lord Denning's decisions in the law of agency. He has played a particularly prominent role in the many modern cases dealing with estate agents. In *Dennis Read Ltd.* v. *Goody*[10] Lord Denning stressed that the common understanding of men was that an estate agent's commission was payable out of the proceeds of sale, so that there was a strong presumption that if the sale fell through, no commission was payable. In *John Meacock & Co.* v. *Abrahams*,[11] though this was not a case concerning an estate agent, Lord Denning pointed out that agents paid by commission normally receive a high return when they are successful, and for that reason are willing to forego any claim when they are not. "They take their chance on it." So no sympathy is due to the agent who, having failed to secure a sale, then claims payment on the basis of a *quantum meruit*. No doubt in pursuit of this policy Lord Denning dissented from the majority of the Court of Appeal in *Scheggia* v. *Gradwell*[12] which was a claim by

---

[7] [1976] 2 W.L.R. 668 (C.A.) and [1977] A.C. 850 (H.L.).
[8] [1981] 1 W.L.R. 314.
[9] See F.A. Mann in (1981) 97 L.Q.R. 379.
[10] [1950] 2 K.B. 277. See too for a discussion of this and other cases involving estate agents Chap. 5, *infra* pp. 170–171.
[11] [1956] 1 W.L.R. 1463.
[12] [1963] 1 W.L.R. 1049.

an estate agent for commission, on the wording of a particular agreement, where a purchaser had signed a contract to buy but had later withdrawn and forfeited his deposit. Lord Salmon has subsequently indicated serious dissatisfaction with the majority decision in this case.[13]

Another series of cases concerning estate agents involved a different question, namely whether a vendor was liable to a purchaser who paid a deposit to an estate agent, where subsequently the estate agent defaulted in accounting for the money. In a series of cases commencing with *Ryan* v. *Pilkington* in 1959[14] the Court of Appeal (not including Lord Denning) had held, rather surprisingly, that the vendor was liable for the agent's defalcations, and (stranger still) that the deposit was recoverable by the purchaser from the vendor alone, and not directly from the agent. The decisions were clearly wrong: the agent is a mere stakeholder, the purchaser can recover his money from the agent at any moment, and there is no reason to hold the vendor liable for the agent's acts any more than there is to hold the purchaser liable to the vendor. The decisions also overlooked earlier authority, as well as much Commonwealth authority. In *Burt* v. *Claude Cousins*[15] battle was well and truly joined on all these issues in the Court of Appeal, this time including Lord Denning. The majority repeated their earlier decision, holding the vendor liable for the acts of the agent. Lord Denning dissented. He insisted that at any moment prior to the formal contract, the purchaser could demand his deposit back from the agent, and the vendor had no right to demand payment of the deposit from the agent. In *Sorrell* v. *Finch*,[16] on barely distinguishable facts (except that this time there were five purchasers who had been defrauded by the agent, so that the vendor's responsibility for the agent's acts would have been costly indeed) Lord Denning once again dissented. This time the case was carried to the House of Lords where Lord Denning's judgment was upheld, and the earlier decisions of the Court of Appeal were overruled.

One final agency decision may be mentioned. In *Pearson* v. *Rose & Young*[17] the Court of Appeal, with Lord Denning delivering a powerful and very convincing judgment, finally disposed of earlier dicta which had bedevilled the interpretation of section 2 of the Factors Act 1889. Goods entrusted to a mercantile agent to be disposed of by him might be in his possession with the consent of the owner despite the fact that the agent could be guilty, under the old law, of larceny by a trick. Since that case this problem seems finally to have been put to rest.

2. TORT

Negligence

Some of Lord Denning's greatest triumphs are to be found in the modern development of the law of negligence. In this area his willingness to innovate has, at least in recent years, struck a responsive chord with most of his

[13] In *A.L. Wilkinson Ltd.* v. *Brown* [1966] 1 W.L.R. 194.
[14] [1959] 1 W.L.R. 403.
[15] [1971] 2 Q.B. 426.
[16] [1977] A.C. 728 (H.L.). The C.A.'s judgment does not seem to have been reported.
[17] [1951] 1 K.B. 275.

colleagues who have found the conceptual apparatus of tort law less constricting than that of contract law. Indeed, it is not going to far to say that a large part of the modern law of negligence owes its origins to Lord Denning's judgments.

It is appropriate to begin with the demise of trespass in modern times. In *Letang* v. *Cooper*[18] the Court of Appeal approved the decision of Diplock J. in *Fowler* v. *Lanning*[19] that negligence must be proved in all personal injury actions, whether they are framed in trespass or in negligence. Indeed, Lord Denning went further: there is, he said, in truth only one cause of action, and in this also, he was at one with Diplock J. "The truth is that the distinction between trespass and case is obsolete."[20]

On questions of negligence in fact, and the application of the various factors entering into decisions on negligence in fact, Lord Denning's common-sense has always shown through strongly. In *Watt* v. *Herts County Council*.[21] Lord Denning stated the principles involved: "It is well settled that in measuring due care one must balance the risk against the measures necessary to eliminate the risk. To that proposition ought to be added this. One must balance the risk against the end to be achieved." So it was held that a fireman could not complain of negligence when he was injured as a result of being required to travel in a lorry with a large unsecured machine, intended for lifting a vehicle which had trapped a woman in an accident, and the journey was a matter of a few hundred yards only.

In *Lewis* v. *Carmarthenshire County Council*[22] a lorry driver was killed in an accident caused by his attempt to avoid a small child who had escaped from a nearby nursery school. The mere statement of the facts was sufficient to raise a powerful prima facie of negligence against those responsible for the school. Lord Denning held that the inference of negligence had not been rebutted by any adequate explanation. In the House of Lords[23] the judgment was upheld, though perhaps on slightly different grounds. But a minute analysis of the facts is hardly necessary: Lord Denning was surely right in regarding the prima facie need for an adequate explanation as never having been met.

Nettleship v. *Weston*[24] is one of the few modern cases on the standard of care required in the law of negligence by those who are, for one reason or another, unable to exercise the care and skill of the normal, reasonable man: here it was a learner driver who had injured her instructor. The Court of Appeal insisted that the learner must show the normal care and skill of a qualified driver. Compulsory third party insurance, said Lord Denning, was the reason for maintaining these high standards. We are, he suggested, beginning to ask, "On whom would the risk fall?" and we are moving away from the principle of "No liability without fault." This kind of language is, perhaps, dangerous but it is clear in its context that Lord Denning was

[18] [1965] 1 Q.B. 232.
[19] [1959] 1 Q.B. 426.
[20] At p. 239.
[21] [1954] 1 W.L.R. 208.
[22] [1953] 1 W.L.R. 1439.
[23] [1955] A.C. 549.
[24] [1971] 2 Q.B. 691.

talking of moral fault which was, in this case, singularly absent. With the agreement of Megaw L.J., though the disagreement of Lord Salmon, Lord Denning also rejected the notion which had found favour in Australia,[25] that a passenger in a vehicle who knows that the driver has only one eye or one hand, can only expect the standard of care of a one-eyed or a one-handed driver. What seems to have weighed most with Lord Denning was on the one hand, the extreme difficulty of formulating the standard of care required of persons so handicapped, if it was to depart from that of the reasonable man, and on the other hand, his dislike of the idea that differing standards of care might be applicable to passengers and pedestrians as a result of one and the same incident. Once again, Lord Denning's instincts seem sound: Australian courts have had much difficulty with the view here rejected by Lord Denning.

Negligent Misstatement

What many will remember as Lord Denning's greatest single achievement in the common law is his contribution to the opening up of the law of negligent misstatement. In 1951, general principles of liability for negligence were still hemmed in on all sides by doctrines and precedents dating back to the pre-*Donoghue* v. *Stevenson*[26] days. Liability to trespassers and even licensees, liability in relation to negligent work done to a building, and above all, liability for negligent misstatement, were all confined by the effect of nineteenth and early twentieth century authorities. Today, when most of these authorities have been swept out of existence by the onward march of the tort of negligence, it may be difficult for lawyers to recall how piecemeal the law of negligence still seemed in 1950, or even in 1960. Indeed, not until the *Dorset Yacht* case[27] was it possible to affirm that English law recognised a general principle of liability for negligently caused physical damage, at least where the negligence consisted of affirmative conduct and not a mere omission.

In *Candler* v. *Crane Christmas & Co.*[28] the Court of Appeal was given the opportunity to re-examine the law relating to negligent misstatement in a case of great simplicity, and, from the plaintiff's point of view, very strong facts. The plaintiff had been invited to invest in a small private company, but before doing so, he had insisted on seeing the company's accounts. The accounts were shown to the plaintiff at a meeting at which the auditors' representative was there, and at which it was perfectly clear why the plaintiff wanted to see them. The accounts had been prepared with gross negligence, and the plaintiff, who invested £2,000 in reliance on them, lost the whole of it. On these facts Lord Denning was prepared to find for the plaintiff. He started his examination of the main issue by making it clear that he thought the law ought to provide a remedy on these facts:

> "If the matter were free from authority, I should have said that the defendants clearly did owe a duty of care to the plaintiff. They were

---

[25] See *Insurance Commissioner* v. *Joyce* (1948) 77 C.L.R. 39, 56–57.
[26] [1932] A.C. 562.
[27] [1970] A.C. 1004, see *post*, p. 61.
[28] [1951] 2 K.B. 164.

professional accountants who prepared and put before him these accounts, knowing that he was going to be guided by them in making an investment in the company. On the faith of these accounts, he did make the investment, whereas if the accounts had been carefully prepared, he would not have made the investments at all. The result is that he has lost his money."[29]

When Lord Denning begins like this, one can be sure that he will then analyse the authorities in order to come out where he wants to, and this case was no exception. Skilful examination of the cases showed them to be either distinguishable, or else inconsistent with the principles of *Donoghue* v. *Stevenson*. Nothing remained in the way of recognising this liability. Lord Denning went on to add some words about the proper judicial role in novel cases:

"If one reads *Ashby* v. *White*,[30] *Pasley* v. *Freeman*[31] and *Donoghue* v. *Stevenson* one finds that in each of them the judges were divided in opinion. On the one side there were the timorous souls who were fearful of allowing a new cause of action. On the other side there were the bold spirits who were ready to allow it if justice so required. It was fortunate for the common law that the progressive view prevailed."[32]

However, the majority of the Court of Appeal decided to be "timorous souls." Their analysis of the cases was, unlike Lord Denning's, not designed to lead to a pre-determined conclusion, but to see what the cases had originally stood for. But Lord Denning was right, and they were wrong. It is usually the bold spirits who win in the end, and the timorous souls whose judgments are eventually set aside. Lord Denning's judgment in this case is one of the great dissenting judgments in the history of the common law. It was fully and triumphantly vindicated in the *Hedley Byrne* case[33] when the House of Lords in substance adopted Lord Denning's views in preference to those of the majority.

Nor was this the last such success Lord Denning was to enjoy in the area of negligent misstatement. In *Arenson* v. *Arenson*[34] an action was brought against an accountant of a company in respect of his valuation of some shares, which the plaintiff was required to sell to another defendant at a price to be settled by the accountant. A majority of the Court of Appeal dismissed the action on the ground that the accountant was immune from liability as he had acted in a quasi-arbitral capacity; and this, even though the contract specifically stated that the accountant was to act as an expert and not an arbitrator. Lord Denning once again dissented, and by the time the appeal reached the House of Lords the issue had been all but determined in favour of the plaintiff by their lordships' decision in the closely analogous case of *Sutcliffe* v. *Thackrah*[35] where an architect had been held liable for negligently certifying excessive sums as due to a builder. In the *Arenson* case[36] Lord Denning's judgment was,

[29] At p. 176.
[30] (1703) 2 Ld. Ray. 938.
[31] (1789) 3 T.R. 51.
[32] [1951] 2 K.B. at p. 178.
[33] [1964] A.C. 465.
[34] [1973] Ch. 346 (C.A.) and [1977] A.C. 405 (H.L.).
[35] [1974] A.C. 727.
[36] *Supra*.

in substance, upheld, and it was insisted that the arbitrator's immunity from suit rested on special principles and should not be extended to valuers and other professional persons acting in a professional capacity. Some sympathy may nevertheless be felt for Lord Kilbrandon's view that the decision ought logically to render arbitrators liable for negligence as well, and that it was unreal to distinguish between a valuation made by accountants, whether as experts or as arbitrators.

The *Hedley Byrne* decision was not only concerned with liability for misstatements, of course: it also opened up the possibility of liability in tort for purely economic loss. This aspect of the decision at first received much less attention, both in the judgments in *Hedley Byrne* itself, and in the subsequent comments on the case. When legal actions began to be brought claiming recovery for purely economic loss, the policy and indeed, the doctrinal issues, were at first difficult and controversial. The typical case involved negligent damage to electrical, or telephone wires, with resultant interruption of supplies to consumers, some of whom suffered loss in consequence. But as the wires and other installations normally belong to the authorities and not to the consumers, the consumer is usually able to show only economic loss. In *S.C.M. (United Kingdom) Ltd.* v. *Whittal*,[37] and in *Spartan Steel & Alloys Ltd.* v. *Martin & Co. (Contractors) Ltd.*[38] Lord Denning rejected the possibility of such a claim, in the first case with the support of the whole Court of Appeal, and in the second case, with the support of one of the other two members of the Court. Lord Denning conceded that the plaintiff in such a situation could recover for any physical damage following the interruption of power, and in addition for any loss of profit consequential on the physical damage; but he denied that damages could be recovered for any economic loss which was due to the loss of power alone and did not itself flow from the physical damage. Lord Denning argued that the reason for denying recovery was fundamentally one of public policy. He rejected the idea that the issue turned on the absence of a duty of care—there was always a duty to be careful in such cases, he insisted—or on the distinction between direct and indirect damage. If a doctrinal heading was needed, the cases were basically ones of remoteness of damage. As to that, it was not sensible, he argued, to saddle the contractor who caused the damage with the enormous potential economic losses to which they may give rise; as I had previously made the same point myself,[39] it is not for me to disagree with it, but the argument is a highly controversial one, and it must be conceded that the denial of recovery has often been applied even where there is only one potential plaintiff who has suffered loss.[40] In the *Spartan Steel* case Lord Denning repeated the substance of these arguments. The cutting of electrical supply, he urged,

> "is a hazard which we all run. It may be due to a short circuit, to a flash of lightning, to a tree falling on the wires, to an accidental cutting of the cable, or even to the negligence of someone or other. And when it does happen, it affects a multitude of persons; not as a rule by way of physical

[37] [1971] 1 Q.B. 337.
[38] [1973] Q.B. 27.
[39] See (1967) 83 L.Q.R. 248 cited by Lord Edmund-Davies only to disagree with it.
[40] As, *e.g.* in *I.R.C.* v. *Hambrook* [1956] 2 Q.B. 641 in which Lord Denning and the C.A. had greatly restricted the availability of the *actio per quod* as an "anomaly." But at this time, claims of this kind were not characterised as claims for pure "economic loss."

damage to them or their property, but by putting them to inconvenience, and sometimes to economic loss. The supply is usually restored in a few hours so the economic loss is not very large. Such a hazard is regarded by most people as a thing they must put up with—without seeking compensation from anyone. Some there are who install a stand-by system. Others seek refuge by taking out an insurance policy against breakdown in the supply. But most people are content to take the risk on themselves. When the supply is cut off they do not go running to their solicitor. They do not try to find out whether it was anyone's fault. They just put up with it. They try to make up the economic loss by doing more work the next day. This is a healthy attitude which the law should encourage."[41]

He goes on to add that the number of claims might be very large and that it would be difficult to distinguish between the genuine and the bogus claims. Basically, it seems to me that Lord Denning is here recognising that, as one of the main functions of tort law is to distribute the cost of accidents, it makes no sense to invoke tort liability where these costs are already well distributed, and where legal liability, far from distributing the costs, may actually concentrate them. But the issues are undoubtedly difficult. In *Spartan Steel* Lord Denning had to suffer the discomfort of hearing Lord Edmund-Davies citing his own dicta in the *Candler* case against him, to the effect that the nature of the damage may sometimes affect the existence of a duty of care, but once a duty exists liability cannot depend on the nature of the damage. But that dictum dated from a time when Lord Denning treated doctrinal issues more seriously: by now he had little time for arguments based on distinctions between duty of care, remoteness of damage and so on.

Still, the difficulties of the economic loss problem are illustrated by *Ministry of Housing and Local Government* v. *Sharp*[42] in which Lord Denning concurred in a judgment imposing liability on a local authority for negligently issuing a clear certificate to a land developer as a result of which the developer obtained a title clear from any liability for a land charge, and the Ministry suffered, in consequence, loss of the value of the charge. Although the loss was only financial here, Lord Denning relied on the fact that the defendants ought to have foreseen the precise loss suffered.

Another group of important cases, which border on the economic loss question, are those involving liability of local authorities in respect of negligence in the inspection of houses in the course of construction. *Dutton* v. *Bognor Regis U.D.C.*[43] is one of the most adventurous judgments given even by Lord Denning. Had the case come before the courts even a decade earlier it would have seemed almost unarguable. Mrs. Dutton claimed damages in respect of serious defects in her house which had been built on inadequate foundations, which she contended the local authority had negligently passed by their building inspector. The first difficulty concerned the liability of the builder himself (who had gone out of business in this case). If the council was to be liable, ought they not to have redress against the builder? The obstacle was that in *Bottomley* v. *Bannister*[44] the Court of Appeal had held that a

---

[41] [1973] Q.B. 38.
[42] [1970] 2 Q.B. 223.
[43] [1972] 1 Q.B. 373.
[44] [1932] 1 K.B. 458.

builder is not liable to a purchaser for negligent design or construction, and
had confined *Donoghue* v. *Stevenson* to a rule about chattels. Lord Denning
would have none of that. *Bottomley* v. *Bannister* was swept out of the way, and
Donoghue v. *Stevenson* could not be limited in such an arbitrary way. The
second difficulty in the *Dutton* case arose from the fact that the claim was
based largely on an omission: the council had not built the house, but had
negligently failed to prevent it being built. And here there loomed up the
House of Lords decision in *East Suffolk Catchment Board* v. *Kent*.[45] This case
seemed to say that if a statutory body had a mere power (as opposed to a
duty) which it negligently failed to exercise, or exercised improperly, it
could not be sued for negligence. Lord Denning sensed that this decision was
out of line with contemporary legal developments, and deftly by-passed it.
The decision, he said, overlooked a third possibility, mid-way between a
power and a duty, namely the possibility of control. Five years later the
Dutton case was upheld by the House of Lords in *Anns* v. *Merton London B.C.*,[46]
and most, though not all, of Lord Denning's reasoning in *Dutton* was
approved. *Bottomley* v. *Bannister* was overruled, the *East Suffolk* case
distinguished, if not on the same ground as Lord Denning had suggested.
Less stress, perhaps, was placed on policy arguments, but they seem to have
weighed clearly enough, all the same.

   Lord Denning's earlier decisions in negligence actions had often relied on
traditional doctrinal arguments about duty of care, foresight of consequences, remoteness of damage, and so on. In the area of nervous shock, as in
that of economic loss, Lord Denning was inclined to restrict liability, and in
King v. *Phillips*[47] he did so by stressing that the test of liability for shock was
foreseeability of injury by shock. At the same time, Lord Denning was clearly
unhappy about the suggestion that a driver of a vehicle owed no duty to take
care to avoid actual injury to those who might be outside the limits of any
particular physical area. That proposition might have been derived from
Bourhill v. *Young*,[48] but Lord Denning insisted that a driver always owed a
duty of care to anyone who might be in the vicinity and who suffered physical
injury. What Lord Denning was evidently trying to do here was to limit
liability for nervous shock without limiting liability for physical injury. Later,
the nature of the limits which he was contending for became clearer in *Hinz*
v. *Berry*[49] in which Lord Denning also, for the first time, attempted to give
some more scientific meaning to the absurd phrase "nervous shock" by
defining it as "any recognisable psychiatric illness." Very recently, in a
case[50] in which Lord Denning was not sitting, the Court of Appeal has
largely accepted his view, that liability for shock, even if foreseeable, is
limited by public policy. For if all foreseeable illness was compensable in
negligence, it would be impossible to maintain the distinction between a
person who suffers injury through *seeing* an accident and one who merely *hears*

[45] [1941] A.C. 74.
[46] [1978] A.C. 728.
[47] [1953] 1 Q.B. 429.
[48] [1943] A.C. 92.
[49] [1970] 2 Q.B. 40. This case also illustrates Lord Denning's superb gift for words, and his
    ability to describe tragic events with great simplicity. His judgment opens, "It happened on
    19th April 1964. It was bluebell time in Kent."
[50] *McLoughlin* v. *O'Brian* [1981] 2 W.L.R. 1014; but see *post*, p. 76, n. 43.

of it later; yet if liability extended to this latter case, every spouse, parent, or child might be able to claim damages for shock in respect of an accident in which he was not involved.

As the years went by Lord Denning increasingly relied on policy arguments in these negligence cases, and began to see the issues much more clearly in policy terms. As we have seen, this was particularly in evidence in the economic loss cases. It was also very much in evidence in *Dorset Yacht Co.* v. *Home Office*,[51] although there is a sense in which this case illustrates the severe limits on the uses of policy arguments in modern law. If the case is approached in the traditional manner as a claim by a wronged property owner against a tortfeasor for damages in respect of physical damage done to his property, then it may make sense to insist that talk of duties of care, foresight of consequences and so on, merely obscure the real issues. "It is, I think, [said Lord Denning] at bottom a matter of public policy which we, as judges, must resolve. This talk of 'duty' or of 'no duty' is simply a way of limiting the range of liability for negligence."[52] On the other hand, no attention at all was paid to the fact that the real issue in this case was not between a property owner and a negligent tortfeasor, but between the property owner's insurers, suing as subrogees, and the Home Office, sued as vicariously responsible for the Borstal officials. Thus the ultimate policy issue in this case, whether such damage ought to be paid for by property owners' insurers and their premium payers, on the one hand, or by the Home Office, and the taxpayers, on the other hand, was never faced at all, even by Lord Denning. Another respect in which Lord Denning's (and the whole Court of Appeal's) judgment in this case was less than satisfactory was that it really gave no guidance as to how far the liability extended. Escaping Borstal boys and prisoners are, after all, only too common. When they escape, they may steal things, and do other damage, sometimes in the vicinity of the Borstal or prison, sometimes miles away and days or weeks later. The Court of Appeal simply ignored these problems, and even the House of Lords made little attempt to address them.[53] But apart from this point, the case is, once more, an example of Lord Denning blazing the trail, and the House of Lords subsequently giving their approval.

Professional Negligence

One area of the law of negligence in which Lord Denning has tended to be more defendant-minded than his colleagues is that of professional negligence. Lord Denning has frequently shown his sympathy for professional persons in negligence actions, insisting repeatedly that negligence must not be found against them too readily. In *Roe* v. *Minister of Health*,[54] for instance, Lord Denning acquitted the doctors concerned of any negligence, and insisted:

---

[51] [1969] 2 Q.B. 412 (C.A.) and [1970] A.C. 1004 (H.L.).

[52] [1969] 2 Q.B. 426, approved by Lord Diplock at [1970] A.C. 1058.

[53] Lord Denning now seems to have appreciated these difficulties more than he did in 1969. In *Lamb* v. *London Borough of Camden* [1981] 2 W.L.R. 1038, 1043–4, he argued that householders should generally recover on their insurance policies for property damage and theft committed by escaping prisoners, and should not claim from the Home Office. This may illustrate growing awareness of the differing policies which affect personal injury and property damage cases.

[54] [1954] 2 Q.B. 66.

"We should be doing a disservice to the community at large if we were to impose liability on hospitals and doctors for everything that happens to go wrong. Doctors would be led to think more of their own safety than of the good of their patients . . . ."[55]

More recently in *Whitehouse* v. *Jordan*[56] Lord Denning suggested that a doctor should not be held to have been negligent for a mere "error of judgment," but the House of Lords, in upholding the decision on its facts, with greater orthodoxy insisted that all depended on whether the error of judgment would have been committed by a reasonably skilful and competent doctor. Insofar as an error of judgment was consistent either with negligence or with a lack of negligence, such a phrase was to be avoided. It seems clear that Lord Denning really did mean to restrict liability even where there was a failure to exercise the sort of skill which a reasonable doctor ought to show, and the case shows again his great reluctance to impose liability on professional persons.

A very similar attitude can be found in the cases concerning the liability of barristers for negligence. In *Rondel* v. *Worsley*,[57] for instance, Lord Denning argued that public policy demanded that a barrister be totally immune from liability for all his advisory as well as court work. In answer to the argument that a barrister who put his duty to the court before his duty to his client would anyhow not be found guilty of negligence, Lord Denning responded that that was too simple a view:

"It is a fearsome thing for a barrister to have an action brought against him. To have his reputation besmirched by a charge of negligence. To have the case tried all over again but this time with himself, the counsel, as the defendant. To be put to all the anxiety, and I would add, all the cost of defending himself."

In *Saif Ali* v. *Sydney Mitchell & Co.*[58] Lord Denning was prepared, in response to some of the dicta in the House of Lords in *Rondel* v. *Worsley*, to limit the barrister's immunity slightly, and he now accepted that a barrister could be liable for "pure paperwork." In both these cases most of the other judges took a narrower view of the desirable limits on a barrister's immunity. Moreover, Lord Denning was unwilling to extend the barrister's immunity to solicitors,[59] although in the upshot the House of Lords could find no justification for distinguishing between barristers and solicitors in *Saif Ali*.

To some, Lord Denning's views on professional negligence will suggest a curious inconsistency in his value system. Why should the barrister be immune from liability which faces others? Why should so much concern be shown for the unfortunate barrister whose reputation is threatened, who has to defend himself in court? Why should a doctor be allowed to get away with an "error of judgment" when (say) an employer, or a driver is not? The difference cannot lie in the fact of insurance, because it can be assumed today

---

[55] At pp. 86–87.
[56] [1980] 1 All E.R. 650 (C.A.) and [1981] 1 All E.R. 267 (H.L.).
[57] [1967] 1 Q.B. 443 (C.A.) and [1969] 1 A.C. 191 (H.L.).
[58] [1978] Q.B. 95 (C.A.) and [1980] A.C. 198 (H.L.).
[59] Indeed, in *Griffiths* v. *Evans* [1953] 1 W.L.R. 1424 Lord Denning dissented from a majority decision acquitting a solicitor of negligence: his judgment looks more convincing than that of his colleagues.

that professional indemnity insurance is almost as common as employers' liability insurance or motorists' third party insurance. To some, the explanation may lie in a touch of elitism or even of class distinction; there is no evidence to support a charge of class bias elsewhere in Lord Denning's judgments though some may find evidence that there is occasionally a tinge of elitism in his value system, a belief that authority should always be observed and accorded due respect.[60] But there is one point to be made in defence of Lord Denning's attitude to allegations of professional negligence. The fact is that the present legal system, taking account of the way in which liability insurance works, does in practice draw a distinction, which has no legal basis, between professional and other forms of negligence. In road traffic cases, and even in most employers' liability cases, the negligent party is usually quite indifferent to allegations of negligence. Indeed there are many anecdotes to illustrate the point that the negligent driver, or even the employer sued for the negligence of another employee, may know virtually nothing about the insurance company's conduct of his defence. But a professional man's reputation is publicly on trial when he is sued for negligence, and the presence of insurance does not alter this fact. So if it is the case that the ordinary law of negligence leans heavily in favour of plaintiffs (especially in personal injury actions) because sympathy for the injured accident victim is so strong, this has come about partly at least because there is no countervailing sympathy for the defendant. In professional negligence cases the interests of the defendant are much more important, and perhaps, therefore, they should be allowed to enter the scales against too ready a willingness to find negligence.

Employers' Liability

It is not possible, in a survey of this kind, to study the full range of Lord Denning's decisions in particular areas of the law of negligence, but a flavour of his technique and values can be obtained by looking at some of the cases dealing with employers' liability, including cases of breach of statutory duty here as well as cases of common law negligence.

In the early 1950s a number of "window cleaning" cases came before the courts in which window cleaners sued their employers as a result of suffering accidental injury from the obvious risks of their employment. In *Christmas* v. *General Cleaning Contractors*[61] the plaintiff was injured when his fingers were caught by a defective sash window slipping down, as a result of which he fell from the sill on which he was standing 29 feet above the ground. Lord Denning's starting point was virtually that someone ought to be liable for the injury, and since the occupier was not (under the decision in *London Graving Dock* v. *Horton*)[62] the employer ought to be. Lord Denning distinguished the position of the self-employed person who sees the risks of the job, and accepts them, and the employee who is just told to get on with them. The employee

---

[60] Confirmation of this elitism or authoritarianism is to be found in Lord Denning's strong opposition to actions for malicious prosecution and other abuse of process, as illustrated by his dissent in *Leibo* v. *D. Buckman Ltd.* [1952] 2 All E.R. 1057, and the C.A. decision in *Roy* v. *Prior* [1970] 1 Q.B. 283 which was reversed in the H.L. [1971] A.C. 470.

[61] [1952] 1 K.B. 141 (C.A.) and [1953] A.C. 180 (H.L.).

[62] [1951] A.C. 737.

has no real choice, said Lord Denning, and must be protected. Unfortunately, it appeared in evidence that it was customary to clean windows by standing on the sills, and the use of ladders or belts was usually impracticable, ladders because they were not long enough and belts because there were rarely any hooks to act as anchor points. So the employers (or their insurers) were, in effect, arguing that for a window cleaner to fall from the sill was simply an inherent risk of the job, and not proof of negligence. But Lord Denning was not impressed by these arguments of practical difficulty. He was far more impressed by the evidently dangerous nature of the work.

> "If employers employ men on this dangerous work for their own profit they must take proper steps to protect them, even if they are expensive. If they cannot afford to provide adequate safeguards, then they should not ask them do it at all."[63]

In the House of Lords the judgment was upheld, but on slightly different grounds, namely that the window in question was defective and that the employers should have guarded against the risk of defective sash windows, for instance by providing chocks which could be used to wedge them.

Another case of similar nature was *Drummond* v. *British Cleaners Ltd.*[64] where evidence was given of the very serious accident history of the defendant firm. In this small firm, employing some 20 men, there had been over a 15 to 20 year period, two fatal accidents, two broken legs, and several less serious injuries. Lord Denning was clearly shocked by these figures and again the Court of Appeal held the employers liable, this time in respect of a fatal accident. The employers could, it was said, have provided a belt in this case because the window in question had a transom to which it could have been attached. It will be seen that, in effect, both these cases were ultimately decided on their particular facts, and provide no support for any argument that a mere fall from a window sill is sufficient evidence of negligence; but one wonders whether in fact insurers did not conclude, from these cases, that the courts would always find liability for such injuries.

In the *Drummond* case it was argued by the employers that even if belts had been provided the men would not have used them. This drew the response from Lord Denning that it was the employers' duty to instruct and exhort their workmen to take adequate precautions for their own safety. He had invoked a similar argument in *Clifford* v. *Charles H. Challen & Son Ltd.*,[65] a few years earlier, where a workman contracted dermatitis from using synthetic glue. The employers provided barrier cream for the men to use, but they had not instructed or pressed the men to use it, it was not available in the particular room in which they worked, and the foreman clearly did not believe in the use of the cream himself. Lord Denning again found for the plaintiff (though subject to a deduction for contributory negligence) and insisted that the employer "must remember that men doing a routine task are often heedless for their safety and may become careless about taking precautions."[66]

---

[63] [1952] 1 K.B. 149.
[64] [1954] 1 W.L.R. 1434.
[65] [1951] 1 K.B. 495.
[66] At p. 498.

Similar sympathy for injured workmen led Lord Denning in *Jones* v. *Stavely Iron & Chemical Co. Ltd.*[67] to suggest that the standard of care required of a workman is lower on a plea of contributory negligence than in a claim based on negligence itself. These remarks were disapproved of, *obiter*, by two of the law lords when the case went on appeal,[68] and the issue has remained unresolved as a matter of law since that date. But nobody familiar with employers' liability cases can doubt that in practice judges do use differing standards of care for findings of negligence, on the one hand, and contributory negligence, on the other.

One of Lord Denning's unsuccessful forays on behalf of injured workmen concerned the responsibility of employers to fence dangerous machinery under the Factories Act 1937. In a series of cases the courts had gradually restricted the protection accorded to injured workmen by holding that the requirement to fence was designed to keep the employee out, and not to keep the machinery in. Consequently, where dangerous bits of machinery were liable to shatter and fly out, it was held that a breach of the Act gave no redress, though, of course, common law negligence always remained open. In *Close* v. *Steel Company of Wales*,[69] which reached the House of Lords during Lord Denning's time as a Lord of Appeal, he vigorously dissented from a decision that the issue was foreclosed by previous decisions of the House. In a "lecturing" tone which may well have antagonised some of his colleagues in the House, he ended his judgment with the words:

> "I would remind your lordships that the statute says that 'every dangerous part of any machinery' shall be securely fenced. I fail to see how any speeches in this House can bind your lordships to hold that a dangerous part of machinery need not be fenced, when the statute expressly says it shall be."[70]

But this was disingenuous. Nobody denied that the duty to fence existed. What was in issue was the right of a workman to claim damages for an injury suffered from unfenced machinery. As to that, it was, and remains, an accepted part of the law that a breach of statutory duty is only actionable if it leads to injury of the kind the statute is designed to prevent. But it may well be, of course, that Lord Denning was right in thinking that there was no good reason for assuming that the statute here was only designed to prevent injury of the one kind and not the other.

Occupier's Liability

The liability of an occupier to a lawful visitor was, of course, radically overhauled by the Occupiers' Liability Act 1957, but there were many leading cases before that date in which Lord Denning had protested at the unsatisfactory state of the law,[71] and attempted gradually to whittle away at the distinction between an invitee and a licensee.[72] No useful purpose would

---

[67] [1955] 1 Q.B. 474.
[68] [1956] A.C. 627.
[69] [1962] A.C. 367.
[70] At p. 389.
[71] See, *e.g. Dunster* v. *Abbott* [1954] 1 W.L.R. 58; *Slater* v. *Clay Cross Co. Ltd.* [1956] 2 Q.B. 264.
[72] *Hawkins* v. *Coulsdon & Purley U.D.C.* [1954] 1 Q.B. 310.

be served by an analysis of these cases today, but they do serve to illustrate how Lord Denning could, when he wanted to, play the doctrinal game as well as anyone else.

More important was *Riden* v. *A.C. Billings & Sons Ltd.*[73] in which Lord Denning insisted that a contractor working on a site was under the ordinary duty of care with regard to visitors on the premises, and that it was of no concern to him whether they were invitees or licensees. The majority of the Court of Appeal, which included Lord Denning, overruled the judgment of Hallett J. at first instance, and also rejected *Malone* v. *Laskey*[74] and *Ball* v. *L.C.C.*[75] insofar as they denied the liability of a contractor for negligent works of construction or maintenance leading to personal injury to lawful visitors on the premises. The House of Lords concurred, and several law lords went out of their way to indicate their substantial agreement with Lord Denning's judgment.

Liability to trespassers has remained more difficult and it seems clear that the common law has not yet finally resolved this troublesome area. Lord Denning, in several of his earlier decisions in cases not involving trespassers, had held that occupiers' liability only concerned the "static condition" of the premises, and did not apply to "current operations" carried on by the occupier, as to which his liability was the same as that of any other person. In *Videan* v. *B.T.C.*[76] this argument gave Lord Denning some trouble. This was the tragic case of the stationmaster's young child who had toddled onto the railway line at the station, and been saved from a trolley only by the stationmaster hurling himself on top of his son and thereby sacrificing his own life. The court found that the trolley driver had been negligent—he was going too fast, he failed to keep an adequate look out, and he failed in sufficient time to appreciate the stationmaster's warnings to him of the danger ahead. But the child was clearly a trespasser on the lines. The Court of Appeal rejected the child's claim to damages, but upheld that of the stationmaster's widow. Students often have difficulty with this case, because they find it difficult to see how it can be said that the presence of the child was not foreseeable while the stationmaster's actions were. Yet the decision of the Court does seem clearly right. A stationmaster clearly has a duty to take emergency action such as he did take, and although the particular incident was not foreseeable, the trolley driver ought to have been on his guard against the presence of station officials on the line. Rather more difficult is Lord Denning's suggestion that the presence of any rescuer ought to have been foreseeable, although any other rescuer would doubtless have recovered because of the special tenderness which courts have for rescuers. But it is also somewhat difficult to understand why Lord Denning's distinction between "static conditions" and "current operations" was not invoked to assist the child trespasser. One would have thought this was a clear case of the child being injured by operations, not the condition of the land. Lord Denning, however, argued that the normal conduct of railway operations on railway lines was part of the "static conditions" of the land itself. This will seem unconvincing to many. Lord Denning also began to

---

[73] [1957] 1 Q.B. 46 (C.A.) and [1958] A.C. 240 (H.L.).
[74] [1907] 2 K.B. 141.
[75] [1949] 2 K.B. 159.
[76] [1963] 2 Q.B. 650.

show increasing dissatisfaction with the general rule barring all trespassers from recovering for negligence, and was willing to contemplate bringing them within the ordinary duty of care. "This [the existing] rule seems fair enough if you put all trespassers in the same bag as burglars or poachers and treat them all alike," he said, but it seemed absurd to apply it to the case of an infant of two years' of age. He added that he did not understand the suggestion that an occupier owed a duty to treat a trespasser "with common humanity."

That, however, roughly speaking, was the duty which the House of Lords decided to adopt in *Herrington* v. *British Railways*[77] when they finally jettisoned the old *Addie* v. *Dumbreck*[78] rule rejecting any duty at all to trespassers (other than a duty not wilfully to injure them). Many of the points made in *Videan* about the "static conditions/current operations" distinction, as also about the scope of the duty owed to trespassers, were rejected. But this has not been one of the more successful House of Lords' decisions in the common law in recent years. Their decisions leaves the law in a state of considerable doubt and obscurity. Very soon after the *Herrington* case, another trespasser case[79] reached the Court of Appeal, and Lord Denning seized the opportunity to "interpret" the decision. Three consequences followed from it, he asserted. First, *Addie* itself must now be taken to have been wrongly decided on its facts: all the law lords agreed that *Addie* should now be differently decided. Second, the use of fictitious "implied licences" and the like must also go. Along with these, Lord Denning discarded his "static conditions/current operations" distinction as a device to do justice which could now be done more openly. Third, the test of liability was not that of intentional conduct or subjective recklessness: it extended beyond that, though how far was not clear. Wavering somewhat between the standard of common humanity and that of reasonable care according to all the circumstances, Lord Denning found for the plaintiff. So did the other members of the Court of Appeal.

Contributory Negligence

Since the Contributory Negligence Act of 1945 the law on this subject has given rise to few legal problems, but in those areas in which it has done so, Lord Denning has once again played a prominent role. But before it became clear that the Act was indeed going to give rise to few problems, one tiresome question had to be resolved. Before the Act was passed, it is clear enough that the judges often used strained causation arguments to arrive at what they felt to be equitable results. So, for instance, even when realistically speaking both parties had been to blame, a court might well hold that the defendant's conduct was the "sole" or "effective" cause in order to give a right to damages. This was sometimes dignified by the name of "last opportunity rule" and was especially applicable where the plaintiff had been responsible for leaving some stationary obstruction in the highway and the defendant had then driven into it. It was easy in these circumstances, as in the original and famous case of the donkey, *Davies* v. *Mann*,[80] to say that the conduct of

[77] [1972] A.C. 877.
[78] [1929] A.C. 358.
[79] *Pannett* v. *P. McGuinness & Co. Ltd.* [1972] 2 Q.B. 599.
[80] (1842) 10 M. & W. 546.

the plaintiff had ceased to be an effective cause and that the defendant was
wholly responsible for the accident. After the passing of the 1945 Act, the first
question that naturally arose was whether the Act had altered the rules of
causation, so that in such circumstances it now became possible to hold that
both parties' conduct was part cause of the accident. If this was not the effect
of the Act, the many difficulties which the court had previously grappled
with would have continued to plague the law, and the Act would only have
applied in those limited circumstances in which prior to 1945 both parties
would have been held partly responsible.

In *Davies* v. *Swan Motor Co.*[81] Bucknill L.J. said that he did not think the
Act of 1945 had any effect on the rules as to causation but Lord Denning
disagreed:

> "The legal effect of the Act of 1945 is simple enough. If the plaintiff's
> negligence was one of the causes of the damage, he is no longer defeated
> altogether. He gets reduced damages. But the practical effect of the Act
> is wider than its legal effect. Previously, in order to mitigate the
> harshness of the doctrine of contributory negligence, the courts in
> practice sought to select, from a number of competing causes, which was
> *the* cause—the effective or predominant cause—of the damage and to
> reject the rest. Now the courts have regard to all the causes and
> apportion the damages accordingly."

There can be no doubt that Lord Denning was absolutely correct in his
analysis as well as in his prognosis. This is indeed partly confirmed by the
fact that Bucknill L.J. concurred in a finding of contributory negligence in a
case in which the plaintiff might well have recovered full damages before the
Act. Later cases have put the point beyond doubt, not so much by any legal
decisions on causation, but by simple *de facto* findings of contributory
negligence, often in circumstances in which one or other party would clearly
have been held solely responsible prior to the Act. In particular, there are
several instances of "subsequent and severable negligence" which, according
to the classical formulations of the old doctrines, should have been held the
sole cause of an accident, in which damages have been apportioned.[82]

Two other important points of law in the area of contributory negligence
have been resolved by recent Courts of Appeal presided over by Lord
Denning. In *Froom* v. *Butcher*[83] the Court settled an issue which had caused a
great deal of disagreement amongst judges of first instance, namely whether
the failure to wear a seat belt could amount to contributory negligence.
Strictly speaking this may not be contributory negligence according to the
old rules, because the plaintiff's "fault" in such cases does not contribute to
the accident, though it does contribute to the damage. Conceding this
distinction, Lord Denning nevertheless held that in such circumstances
apportionment under the 1945 Act is permissible, and the Court proceeded
to offer guidance to judges, and insurers, by suggesting that where the
injuries would have been altogether prevented by a seat belt the damages in

[81] [1949] 2 K.B. 291.
[82] See, *e.g. Cork* v. *Kirby Maclean Ltd.* [1952] 2 All E.R. 402; *Hill-Venning* v. *Bezant* [1950] 2 All
    E.R. 1151; *Harvey* v. *Road Haulage Executive* [1952] 1 K.B. 120. Of course these cases do not
    decide that in extreme circumstances it is not still possible to attribute the whole blame to one
    party for an accident.
[83] [1976] Q.B. 268.

respect of those injuries ought generally to be reduced by 25 per cent., while where the injuries would have been lessened but not prevented, the reduction should be of the order of 15 per cent.

Two decisions on the application of contributory negligence to cases of intentional assault appear to have involved Lord Denning in some change of mind. In *Lane* v. *Holloway*[84] the (elderly) plaintiff was struck a savage blow by a much younger man as a result of a trivial verbal altercation, and Lord Denning had refused to reduce the damages for contributory negligence, using language which seemed to imply that this could not be done in cases of intentional assault. However, in *Murphy* v. *Culhane*[85] this case was confined within narrow limits, it being said that the assault was out of all proportion to the provocation; where, as in the instant case, an assault was the result of an affray actually initiated by the plaintiff, the court held that the damages could be reduced, or even refused altogether.

Vicarious Liability

This is yet one more area in which Lord Denning has left his mark stamped firmly on the law. He played a leading part in the hospital cases in which it was first clearly established that a doctor can be an employee for the purposes of the law relating to vicarious liability. Traditional old dogmas, such as the notion that a doctor could not be employed under a contract of service because he could not be told how to do his job, were swept aside in *Cassidy* v. *Minister of Health*.[86] What possible difference, asked Lord Denning, can there be between a hospital authority accepting a patient for treatment, and a railway or shipping company who accepts a passenger for carriage? None whatever. Both were plainly liable for the negligence of their employees: indeed, Lord Denning wanted to go further and argue that they were really liable for breach of their own duties, to treat or to carry, just as though there was a contract. As for the old cases holding that charitable hospitals were not liable for the negligence of their nurses or doctors, these were "due to a desire to relieve the charitable hospitals from liabilities which they could not afford." Today, this kind of explanation of older decisions is readily accepted by academics and students without raising an eyebrow; but it must be remembered that in 1951 (or perhaps even today) it was not generally regarded as an acceptable way of distinguishing binding precedents. Nevertheless, the other members of the Court found their own way to distinguish the older cases, and the law was established on a modern footing.

In *Broom* v. *Morgan*,[87] Lord Denning pursued a suggestion he had made in the *Cassidy* case about the nature of vicarious liability. He argued here that such liability was not truly vicarious at all: the employer is liable for the act, not the tort, of the servant. The act of the employee is attributed to the employer, and his liability adjudged accordingly. This theory nicely helped to justify the decision to hold liable an employer for the negligence of a husband which caused injury to his own wife, who was a fellow-employee of his. At that time, of course, husbands and wives could not sue each other in

---

[84] [1968] 1 Q.B. 379.
[85] [1977] Q.B. 94.
[86] [1951] 2 K.B. 343.
[87] [1953] 1 Q.B. 597.

tort, so the decision involved some sleight of hand. The other members of the Court followed a slightly different line of reasoning, holding that the inter-spousal immunity was procedural only, and did not mean that the husband could not in substance be guilty of committing a tort against his wife.

Lord Denning has also attempted to expand the doctrine of vicarious liability by special rules applicable to motor vehicles. In *Ormrod* v. *Crosville Motor Services*[88] the Court of Appeal followed a considerable body of earlier authority in holding that an owner of a car could be vicariously liable for the negligent driving of someone who was not the owner's employee but merely a friend, driving his (the owner's car) on the owner's business or for his purposes. The friend was driving as the owner's agent, said the Court. The difficulty with this line of reasoning is that vicarious liability in the ordinary way does not extend to mere agents, if the agent is an independent contractor,[89] but the courts have avoided this very serious obstacle to their reasoning by simply assuming away the difficulty. So long as the label "agent" is applied, the courts seem happy to impose vicarious liability: but what they have never done is to explain how it is possible to reconcile a liability-for-agents rule with a no-liability-for-independent-contractors rule. After all, an independent contractor is a form of agent in most circumstances, if not all, and if he is not, some explanation seems called for. There is thus much to be said for the view that the liability of the vehicle owner was based on special principles applicable to motor vehicles, and not on any general rule of liability for the acts of an agent.

But when Lord Denning attempted to follow this line of reasoning in *Launchbury* v. *Morgans*,[90] he was rebuffed by the House of Lords.[91] The most difficult thing about this case is to understand what the real issues actually were, and who were the substantially interested parties. Mrs. Morgans was the appellant, having been sued by the plaintiffs in respect of injuries received in her car, while it was being driven by a friend of her husband, with her husband in a drunken stupor in the back seat. As the action was brought before the passage of the Act which introduced compulsory insurance for passengers, it might be thought that Mrs. Morgans' insurance did not cover injury to passengers, and that the action was therefore an attempt to make her personally liable. But this does not seem the true explanation: Mrs. Morgans' counsel refused to explain the insurance situation to the Court (which he would surely have done if she had been uninsured). Lord Denning speculated that the insurers wanted to challenge their liability on the ground that the driver did not have Mrs. Morgans' permission to drive the car; but this seems untenable since the evidence showed quite clearly that the husband was authorised to invite his friends to drive when he had too much to drink, and the insurers did not challenge this finding on appeal. So, it would seem that the insurers could anyhow have been reached by the action against the negligent driver's executor, who was a co-defendant with Mrs. Morgans. All this mystery makes it very hard to evaluate the decision, since one simply does not know what the issues really were—nor, I think, did the

---

[88] [1953] 1 W.L.R. 120.
[89] See my *Vicarious Liability* (1967), Chap. 9.
[90] [1971] 2 Q.B. 245 (C.A.).
[91] [1973] A.C. 127 (H.L.).

courts. They just assumed (except for Lord Denning's speculation, which was accepted by Lord Salmon) that the question was a genuine one about the liability of the owner of a vehicle to an injured plaintiff for the negligence of his driver. As to this, Lord Denning tried to establish a broad principle that the owner was liable so long as the vehicle was being driven on an occasion or purpose in which he had some interest. The Lords rejected this in favour of the traditional agency test: was it being driven on the owner's business or for his purpose? Lord Wilberforce was less sympathetic to Lord Denning's law-making attempts here than he has been in other cases, arguing that the issues were too complex for judicial solution, especially having regard to the insurance factor. There were, he suggested, at least three ways of dealing with the problem, but since in fact the legislature promptly adopted a fourth (that of making passenger insurance compulsory) this perhaps confirms Lord Wilberforce's point about the limits of the judicial role.

One other major issue in the law relating to vicarious liability found Lord Denning involved in conflict yet again with his severest judicial critic, Lord Simonds. This was the problem of the employer's indemnity. Does an employer who has to pay damages as a result of his employee's negligence, have a right to be indemnified by the employee? In *Jones* v. *Manchester Corpn.*[92] a majority of the Court of Appeal held that a hospital had no right to an indemnity from a young, newly qualified surgeon who had so negligently performed the task of giving an anaesthetic to a patient being prepared for an operation, that the patient died. It was held that the hospital should not have left such a young and inexperienced surgeon to perform this task without proper supervision. But of the majority, only Lord Denning rejected the argument that the hospital would have been entitled to an indemnity if they had not themselves been partly to blame for the accident. Singleton L.J. accepted that an indemnity would otherwise have been available, and Hodson L.J. dissented and thought the hospital not to blame and were entitled to their indemnity.

The question arose again, though in a totally different context, in *Romford Ice & Cold Storage Co. Ltd.* v. *Lister*[93] where an employer's insurer, having been called upon to pay damages to a workman injured by the negligent driving of a fellow-workman (his own son, as it happened) sought an indemnity from the son by claiming against him in the name of the employers. Except for Lord Denning, it was held by all the judges in this case that prima facie an employer has a right to an indemnity which may be pursued by his insurers as subrogees; but there was much more controversy over the applicability of this principle to the case of negligent driving. For it was argued that a term ought to be implied in the contract of employment to the effect that the employer would look after the question of insurance and that the employee would not be called to account for any negligent driving. Lord Denning put the case for such an implied term with great cogency, as even Lord Simonds acknowledged, yet a majority of the Court of Appeal, and of the House of Lords, rejected it. Looking back on the case today it seems amazingly unreal that the decision should have gone as it did. If counsel had appreciated that the case would hinge on the application of an implied term more evidence might have been adduced as to what the parties thought

[92] [1952] 2 Q.B. 852.
[93] [1956] 2 Q.B. 180 (C.A.) and [1957] A.C. 555 (H.L.).

about the insurance question. For as a matter of practical reality, Lord Denning seems unquestionably right—*of course* it goes without saying that a person employed as a driver expects his employers to look after the insurance, and would be astounded to be told that the insurers could sue him for any damages they had to pay as a result of his negligence. As Lord Radcliffe, dissenting, said in the *Lister* case, it is not possible to escape the force of Lord Denning's reasoning. In one subsequent decision[94] to raise similar issues, where rather more evidence was brought about the parties' attitude to insurance, it was held by a majority of the Court of Appeal, that the insurers could not pursue their subrogation rights against an employee, because of an implied term in the contract of employment, or (another innovation from Lord Denning) because subrogation being an equitable right, could not be used where it would be inequitable to do so.

Once again, it seems clear that Lord Denning is broadly right in his assessment of what policy requires, and of the proper extent of the judicial role. Of course, as he insists, it is right that the enterprise as a whole should be, and is, expected to carry the costs of the negligence of its employees; and surely it is not unreasonable in what is almost wholly an area of judge made law to expect the judges to pursue what is obviously and necessarily the only appropriate course. In fact, as is generally known, the *Lister* case led to a departmental inquiry which recommended no action only because none was necessary: it transpired that the insurance industry had adopted a gentleman's agreement not to pursue these subrogation rights save in exceptional cases. It is a little curious that, in the result we have a quasi-legislative solution to the problem, imposed on us by a private industry; while the judges apparently think that they have no right to fashion their own solution. In the long run, Lord Denning will surely be vindicated on this issue, as on so many others.

Nuisance

Passing over two minor, though not unimportant decisions relating to the distinction between public and private nuisance,[95] and the liability of a landlord for nuisance through defective premises,[96] one comes to something of a battle royal in which Lord Denning has recently been engaged. In *Miller* v. *Jackson*[97] the Court of Appeal was faced with a claim in nuisance by the owners of a new house adjoining an old cricket ground. The claim arose out of the fact that, from time to time, cricket balls were hit into the plaintiff's garden, with the risk of damage to the garden and house, and even of possible personal injury. The club had taken every practicable step to prevent the trouble, such as by the erection of fences, but they conceded that it was impossible for them to play cricket on the ground without the occasional ball falling into one of the adjoining gardens. The houses were new, the club old and well established. Lord Denning rejected the apparently established rule that it is no defence to "come to the nuisance." The developers who built the house must have appreciated the risk involved, and indeed so must the

[94] *Morris* v. *Ford Motor Co.* [1973] Q.B. 792.
[95] *Attorney-General* v. *P.Y.A. Quarries Ltd.* [1957] 2 Q.B. 169.
[96] *Mint* v. *Good* [1951] 1 K.B. 517.
[97] [1977] Q.B. 966.

purchasers who bought the house in midsummer. Lord Denning's judgment is an excellent example of the art of persuasion. It is difficult to read it without agreeing with it. It may be that for once Lord Denning departed from the high standards of the judge and adopted the mantle of the advocate, for the statement of facts in his judgment omits some not irrelevant material to be found in the dissenting judgment of Geoffrey Lane L.J. But perhaps what was decisive for Lord Denning in this case was his belief that the plaintiffs' complaints were unreasonable and that some balance had to be struck between the "public interest" of the villagers in having cricket on their ground, and the private interests of the plaintiffs. In the result he would have refused the plaintiffs all remedy, though in fact the defendants were willing to pay £400 towards all past and future damage, and this was incorporated in the court's order. Cumming-Bruce L.J. agreed with Lord Denning in rejecting the claim to an injunction and in thinking that some regard must be had to the public interest in deciding whether an injunction was appropriate. But he rejected the view that "coming to the nuisance" could be a defence—that was concluded by the binding decision in *Sturges* v. *Bridgman*.[98] On the other hand, in his view there had clearly been a tort (though curiously he seems to have thought it was negligence and not nuisance) and his was the decisive vote in favour of an award of damages. Geoffrey Lane L.J. dissented altogether and would have granted an injunction. In his view there had been and was a continuing interference with the plaintiffs' right to the enjoyment of their house and garden: the risk of actual injury was real. Perhaps in the end, the difference of opinion centred mainly on the judges' evaluation of the reality of the risk of injury, though even Geoffrey Lane L.J. thought the interference with the plaintiffs' land was not "unreasonable" and would have rejected their complaint had it not been for *Sturges* v. *Bridgman*.

Not long after this decision another Court of Appeal, in *Kennaway* v. *Thompson*[99] rejected the argument that the public interest had to be weighed against the plaintiff's private rights in a nuisance action, as well as Lord Denning's departure from *Sturges* v. *Bridgman*. But even in this case the Court of Appeal seems to have thought that the plaintiff had to put up with the level of noise and activity which existed on the defendants' premises at the time when she began to build her house, and it was only the subsequent expansion of the defendants' activities which gave ground for complaint. There is thus some inconsistency in this latest pronouncement. The issues are undoubtedly difficult, and curiously enough, recent economic discussion about nuisance does not help much because economic arguments really point both ways in relation to the facts in *Miller* v. *Jackson*. On the one hand, the fact that Mrs. Miller was clearly a very sensitive woman would suggest that the economically efficient solution was for her to move elsewhere, and sell the house to someone less sensitive. On the other hand, the defence of "coming to the nuisance" is rejected by economists on the ground that it would permit a prior and more inefficient use of land resources to perpetuate itself at the expense of later more efficient uses. As to the suggestion that the public interest deserves to be weighed in such cases, this is perhaps more suspect as it may just be a vehicle whereby the judges' private values are introduced into the case. In what sense is it really a matter of *public* interest that cricket

[98] (1879) 11 Ch.D. 852.
[99] [1981] Q.B. 88.

be played on a particular field? Surely the conflict here was between two sets
of private interests: the plaintiffs and the cricket club's and cricket players'.
The only relevance of the public interest is that the benefit of having village
cricket may have enured to spectators and some regard ought to be had to
that benefit. Lord Denning's judgment gives some sign of being swayed by a
sentimental attachment to traditional village cricket.

Damages and Personal Injuries

One of Lord Denning's most serious clashes with the House of Lords arose
out of the controversy concerning the place of exemplary damages in the law
of torts. Lord Denning had taken part in the decision in *Loudon* v. *Ryder*[1] in
1953 in which a jury had awarded £1,000 damages for a relatively minor
assault, an additional £1,500 for trespass (as the assault was committed in
the plaintiff's own home) and a further £3,000 by way of exemplary damages.
Although the plaintiff had not suffered serious injury, the assault was
committed in circumstances of extreme aggravation and the jury was plainly
outraged by the defendant's behaviour, as their verdict showed. Devlin J.
gave judgment in accordance with the jury's verdict and this was upheld by
the Court of Appeal. But in *Rookes* v. *Barnard*[2] Lord Devlin repudiated this
decision, and indeed much else in the law relating to exemplary damages. He
drew a distinction here between aggravated damages (intended to compensate for hurt feelings, and such like) and exemplary damages (intended to
punish). For the future, exemplary damages were to be confined to three
situations only: cases of oppressive and unconstitutional action by officers of
government, cases where the defendant had sought to make a profit from his
wrong, and cases authorised by statute. No particular attention was paid to
the question of damages in defamation actions.

In *Cassell* v. *Broome*,[3] a hotly contested libel action had led to a judicial
direction in accordance with the law as laid down in *Rookes* v. *Barnard*,
notwithstanding which the jury awarded the plaintiff £15,000 compensatory
damages and a further £25,000 by way of punitive or exemplary damages. In
the Court of Appeal counsel for the defendants, appealing against the
verdict, sought to argue that the case did not fall within any of Lord Devlin's
three categories in which exemplary damages could be awarded. Counsel for
the plaintiff could, and did argue, that on the contrary the case fell squarely
within the second category, and indeed all the judges in the Court of Appeal
and the House of Lords agreed that this was so. The appeal could therefore
have been dismissed on narrow grounds, to the great benefit of the parties.
But Lord Denning raised the question whether *Rookes* v. *Barnard* was rightly
decided on the question of damages, and invited counsel to argue that the
Court of Appeal should depart from that decision. So the case was launched
on a massive new issue, the bill for which had ultimately to be paid by the
unfortunate parties. The Court of Appeal ended by rejecting Lord Devlin's
judgment in *Rookes*: it overlooked, they said, decisions of the House of Lords
allowing exemplary damages in libel actions, apart from the three categories
of Lord Devlin. In any event, the distinction between exemplary and

[1] [1953] 2 Q.B. 202.
[2] [1964] A.C. 1129.
[3] [1971] 2 Q.B. 354 (C.A.) and [1972] A.C. 1027 (H.L.).

aggravated damages was unclear and unworkable. Juries lumped everything together where the damages were "at large" and there was nothing wrong in that. Furthermore, *Rookes* had received a distinctly frosty reception in the Commonwealth, and in the United States exemplary damages were awarded far more extensively than was envisaged by *Rookes*.

When the case reached the House of Lords, an unusually large panel of seven law lords was convened to hear the appeal. The Court of Appeal was magisterially rebuked for departing from a decision of the House of Lords—an unconstitutional procedure, it was said. But on the narrower issue, of the appropriate role of exemplary damages in the law of tort, there was more disagreement, and Lords Wilberforce and Dilhorne agreed with Lord Denning that at least in libel actions, exemplary damages could always be awarded. On the narrower issue still, of whether an adequate direction to the jury had been given, the jury's verdict was only upheld by a majority of four judges to three.

The outcome was, in a sense, a massive defeat for Lord Denning. Further, insofar as it was his actions which led to the incurring of huge additional costs by the parties, he cannot be acquitted of having acted in a way which was seriously neglectful of the interests of the parties to the litigation. On the other hand, it cannot be denied that his actions led to a reconsideration of a very important question of law and policy at a level it had not previously received. Nor, on this issue itself—should exemplary damages be more widely available in tort actions?—is it apparent that the majority had the better of the intellectual argument. They appear to have been unduly swayed by the question-begging assumption that the function of tort law is purely compensatory and not deterrent. The arguments to the contrary are, perhaps, most incisively put by Lord Wilberforce, but they do not differ much from those of Lord Denning himself.

Lord Denning has also played a not inconspicuous role in cases dealing with damages for personal injuries. On the whole, he has generally been seen advocating moderation in the award and assessment of such damages. He was in the Court of Appeal which decided *Parry* v. *Cleaver*[4] (that a disability pension should be deducted from the value of damages) which was overruled by a bare majority in the House of Lords. I have given my reasons elsewhere for preferring the Court of Appeal view in this case.[5] In *Jefford* v. *Gee*[6] Lord Denning was responsible for a decision which required judges of first instance to itemise the damages in a personal injury action; but in subsequent cases he has several times stressed that, at the end of the day, the total figure must be looked at to make sure that it is not too large and that no element of duplication is involved.[7] In *Fletcher* v. *Autocar*[8] this approach led to a clash in the Court of Appeal where record damages of £66,000 had been awarded. Lord Denning secured the agreement of Lord Diplock in reducing the figure to £51,000 (Lord Salmon dissenting) on a variety of grounds, the chief of which seems to have been the argument that severely injured persons ought not to receive full lost earnings in compensation as they will be cared

---

[4] [1968] 1 Q.B. 195 (C.A.) and [1970] A.C. 1 (H.L.).
[5] 32 M.L.R. 397 (1969).
[6] [1970] 2 Q.B. 130.
[7] See, *e.g. Taylor* v. *Bristol Omnibus Co.* [1975] 1 W.L.R. 1054.
[8] [1968] 2 Q.B. 322.

for by other components of the award, such as damages for medical and nursing treatment. But in *Lim Poh Choo* v. *Camden and Islington Area Health Authority*[9] which was substantially a rerun of the last-mentioned case, Lord Denning's plea for moderation was rejected by the House of Lords, and an award of around a quarter of a million pounds was largely upheld. In substance Lord Denning has been arguing for a re-opening of the issue settled by the House of Lords in *W. West & Sons Ltd.* v. *Shephard*,[10] that plaintiffs who are substantially unconscious of their own injuries should be compensated as though their losses were "objective" phenomena. But it is also true that more broadly Lord Denning seems to have thought (and perhaps correctly) that the itemisation of damages has led to a steady increase in the total sums awarded. More broadly still, Lord Denning pointed out here that it was wrong to think of the defendants as "wrongdoers." They were vicariously liable for the real tortfeasor, and in the end the taxpayer would be paying the damages. Many will sympathise with his statement that in cases of such catastrophic injuries, the plaintiff should be kept "in as much comfort and tended with as much care as compassion for her so rightfully demanded, and that she should not want for anything that money can buy," but that there was no justification for piling large additional sums onto the award which would probably end up passing to the plaintiff's estate. However, this is one area where the reforms required go beyond even Lord Denning's powers of legislation.

Conclusion

It seems clear that contract and tort were two fields in which Lord Denning's idiosyncratic judicial style was, in the result, at its most successful. Perhaps his two greatest contributions to particular areas of the law were his rediscovery of promissory estoppel in the *High Trees* case,[11] and his path breaking dissent in *Candler* v. *Crane, Christmas and Co.*[12] which helped to open up the law of negligence.[13] It may be worth concluding this chapter by asking why Lord Denning's innovations seem to have proved more successful in contract and tort than they often did in other areas of the law.

Three factors may, perhaps, have been partly responsible for this result. First, these two areas have continued to be predominantly common law fields in which legislation has not intruded to any great degree. It is true, of course, that many specific types of contract are in practice no longer governed purely by common law doctrines, but in those areas in which the general principles of contract law still operate, and still more in the law of tort, Lord Denning has been able to use the "grand style" of judging. He has been able to give full rein to his policy-orientations without having to contend with the often different policy-orientation of Parliament.

---

[9] [1979] Q.B. 196 (C.A.) and [1980] A.C. 174 (H.L.).
[10] [1964] A.C. 326.
[11] [1947] K.B. 130.
[12] [1951] 2 K.B. 164.
[13] Since this chapter was written, the House of Lords has indeed pushed the boundaries of tort law in two major areas beyond the points to which Lord Denning had taken it: *McLoughlin* v. *O'Brian* [1982] 2 W.L.R. 982 and *Junior Books Ltd* v. *Veitchi Co. Ltd.* [1982] 3 W.L.R. 477. I am myself far from convinced that Lord Denning was not right to stop short of these developments; but an innovative judge who sets new trends in motion can hardly complain if they carry the law even further than he would himself.

Secondly, both contract and tort law have been areas in which Lord Denning has been fundamentally in sympathy with the underlying trends in the law, trends indeed for which he was in no small measure personally responsible. In contract, the development of promissory estoppel though seen by some (including the present writer) as a reliance-based development, has always been seen by Lord Denning himself as promise-based—and respect for promises is a tradition which has not lacked friends. On the other hand, growing sympathy with the consumer, and the contractual "underdog" was also a modern movement in which Lord Denning's views soon found a ready response among other judges. And in tort law, the basic ideal that negligent parties should be required to pay compensation—however unreal this may be seen by some in the light of modern insurance practice—is also a principle whose moral appeal has been powerful in the last few decades.

Thirdly, and relatedly, the absence of much statutory activity in contract and tort, combined with the intuitive appeal of the fundamental principles underlying these bodies of the law, enabled Lord Denning to range widely and freely over large bodies of law and theory. These have been fields of law which have lent themselves to development by broad statements of principle, which is the kind of thing Lord Denning always enjoyed doing, and often did supremely well.

CHAPTER 3

Equity and Trusts

D.J. HAYTON

Introduction

Lord Denning, although in practice at common law Bar, was when on the Bench quite ready to take advantage of less familiar Chancery law to come to a just decision. Equitable principles by their nature often afford more scope for a just decision. Moreover, as Sir George Jessel M.R. remarked,[1] "The rules of Courts of Equity are not supposed to have been established from time immemorial. It is perfectly well known that they have been established from time to time—altered, improved and refined from time to time. The doctrines are progressive, refined and improved."

There are dangers in this approach, however, for as Harman, L.J. said in 1961,[2]

> "Equitable principles are, I think, perhaps rather too often bandied about in common law courts as though the Chancellor still had only the length of his own foot to measure when coming to a conclusion. Since the time of Lord Eldon the system of equity for good or evil has been a very precise one, and equitable jurisdiction is exercised only on well-known principles."

Harman L.J.'s generation of Chancery lawyers was probably a little too hidebound in its approach to equitable principles. Since then, equitable principles have had to come to terms with the much changed social and economic circumstances of our society or legislation has had to be enacted, where this has been the only means of achieving a comprehensive and satisfactory solution to a problem.

Lord Denning has been to the fore in trying to extend equitable principles—often beyond their legitimate ambit—and in pointing the way for subsequent legislative intervention. At times, in trying to develop a broader general approach, his generalised statements of principle have gone much further than strictly necessary to decide the instant case.[3] At times, he has taken a very cavalier attitude to authorities, citing sentences of Law Lords without adding their vital qualifying clauses or even citing a passage from a Law Lord, without mentioning that the very same Law Lord 18 months'

---

[1] *Re Hallett's Estate* (1880) 13 Ch.D. 696, 710.
[2] *Campbell Discount Co. Ltd.* v. *Bridge* [1961] 1 Q.B. 445, 459.
[3] *e.g. Errington* v. *Errington and Woods* [1952] 1 K.B. 290, *Quennell* v. *Maltby* [1979] 1 W.L.R. 318, *Lloyds Bank* v. *Bundy* [1975] 1 Q.B. 326, *Chief Constable of Kent* v. *Verdon-Roe* [1982] 3 All E.R. 36, *Amalgamated Investment Ltd.* v. *Texas Commerce Bank* [1981] 3 W.L.R. 565. *Ex p. Island Records Ltd.* [1978] Ch. 122.

later had admitted that his earlier passage represented a minority view which was not good law.[4]

It seems that this has all been done in the cause of affording greater scope for justice to be done between the parties before the court. Lord Denning himself states,

> "My root belief is that the proper role of the judge is to do justice between the parties before him. If there is any rule of law which impairs the doing of justice, then it is in the province of the judge to do all that he legitimately can to avoid that rule—or even to change it—so as to do justice in the instant case before him. He need not wait for legislation to intervene because that can never be of any help in the instant case. I would emphasise, however, the word 'legitimately': the judge is himself subject to the law and must abide by it."[5]

Whether the word "legitimately" really has any significance must be considered doubtful when Lord Denning also states,

> "I never say 'I regret having to come to this conclusion but I have no option.' There is always a way round. There is always an option—in my philosophy—by which justice can be done."[6]

Doing justice between the parties is obviously a good thing. But what is justice? No doubt, even fascist and communist judges consider they are doing justice between the parties before them. Was Lord Denning doing justice to the bankrupt husband's creditors in creating the deserted wife's equity? Parliament did not think so since Class F charges are void against the trustee in bankruptcy? Was Lord Denning doing justice to the proprietor of the small garage in *Re Brocklehurst*[7] when prepared to stigmatise him in setting aside a gift to him in the absence of undue influence? His highly respected colleagues, Lawton and Bridge L.JJ., did not think so. Was Lord Denning doing justice in *B.S.C.* v. *Granada Television*[8] in ordering Granada to disclose their source of confidential information? Later, Lord Denning himself did not think so.[9] If Lord Denning himself cannot be sure of what justice requires, how can lesser lawyers in trying to provide a proper service for their clients?

Furthermore, in striving to achieve justice in the face of legal difficulties it

---

[4] See *per* Lord Diplock in *Gissing* v. *Gissing* [1971] A.C. 886, 905 as cited by Lord Denning in *Heseltine* v. *Heseltine* [1971] 1 All E.R. 952, 955 and in *Binions* v. *Evans* [1972] 2 All E.R. 70, 76; and *per* Lord Diplock in *American Cyanamid Ltd.* v. *Ethicon Ltd.* [1975] A.C. 396, 409 as cited by Lord Denning in *Fellowes* v. *Fisher* [1976] Q.B. 122, 134; and *per* Lord Diplock in *Pettitt* v. *Pettitt* [1970] A.C. 777, 823 cited by Lord Denning in *Hardwick* v. *Johnson* [1978] 2 All E.R. 935, 938 despite *per* Lord Diplock in *Gissing* v. *Gissing* [1971] A.C. 886, 904.

[5] *The Family Story*, p. 174. These views go well beyond the orthodox conception of the judicial role, *e.g.* Lord Simonds in *Magor & St. Mellons R.D.C.* v. *Newport Corporation* [1952] A.C. 189, 191 and *Midland Silicones Ltd.* v. *Scruttons Ltd.* [1962] A.C. 446, 467–468; Lord Hailsham in *Cassell* v. *Broome* [1972] A.C. 1027, 1054 and *The Siskina* [1979] A.C. 210, 261; Lord Scarman in *Lim Poh Choo* v. *Camden and Islington Area Health Authority* [1980] A.C. 174, 183; Lord Diplock in *Duport Steels Ltd.* v. *Sirs* [1980] 1 All E.R. 529, 541, 545.

[6] *The Family Story*, p. 208.

[7] [1978] Fam 14.

[8] [1981] A.C. 1096.

[9] *What Next in the Law*, p. 251.

is possible that injustice may be done. In *Goldsmith* v. *Sperrings*[10] Bridge L.J. was forced to protest,

> "What Lord Denning M.R. says is unacceptable for four reasons. First, it amends the grounds of the appellant's summonses. They claim to have the actions dismissed or stayed as an abuse of process, not as disclosing no reasonable cause of action. No one but the Master of the Rolls has ever suggested or considered this latter ground. Secondly, it claims, in effect, that the Master of the Rolls' private researches demonstrate the law, as stated in the leading text book to be not only wrong but unarguable. Such a claim is untenable. Thirdly, whatever virtue there may be in private judicial researches in other circumstances, they can have no place in interlocutory proceedings for a summary remedy. But the fourth and most important reason is that this part of the Master of the Rolls' judgment decides against the plaintiff on a ground on which Mr. Hawser for the plaintiff has not been heard. This is because Mr. Comyn for the defendant never took the point, and the court did not put the point to Mr. Hawser during the argument. Hence, there is a breach of the rule of *audi alterem partem*. In a court of inferior jurisdiction this would be a ground for *certiorari*".

It must be said that, in concentrating on doing justice between the parties before him, Lord Denning has considerably diminished the coherence and consistency of Chancery law which enables justice to be done according to law, *viz.* the justice that flows from the application of sure and settled principles to proved or admitted facts. This is particularly unsatisfactory when so much of Chancery law concerns property rights, rights which are capable of binding third parties and which should be clearly definable and identifiable and have some degree of stability. In this context Lord Denning has failed to do justice to the many thousands of people who do not want to go to court, but expect their lawyers to be able to tell them exactly what their rights are so that no dispute will arise or so that any dispute that has arisen can speedily be resolved without litigation. Furthermore, in over-emphasising value judgments at the expense of the coherence and consistency of the law he is undermining the impartiality of the law which generates so much respect for the rule of law amongst laymen.

If statutory provisions provoked by Lord Denning are left out of account, the judgment of posterity may well turn out to be that Lord Denning stirred and muddied the waters but when the waters settled the bedrock of Chancery law remained as before. Time alone will tell. It does however, already seem clear that Lord Denning's development of the injunction in a commercial law context will be of lasting significance.

The Deserted Wife's Equity

Lord Denning's most well-known attempt to develop the rules of equity was his creation of the deserted wife's equity. He recognised that there was a social need to protect a wife who had been deserted by her husband in whom was vested the whole legal and equitable interest in the matrimonial home.

[10] [1977] 1 W.L.R. 478, 508. Also see *per* Lord Diplock, *Hadnor Productions Ltd.* v. *Hamilton* [1982] 1 All E.R. 1042, 1056.

On procedural grounds, now ousted by the Law Reform (Husband and Wife) Act 1962 enabling spouses to sue each other in tort, he held[11] that a husband could not evict his wife except in discretionary proceedings under the Married Women's Property Act 1882, s.17. On the substantive ground that the wife obtained an irrevocable matrimonial licence, determinable only at the discretion of the court, he also held that a husband could not evict his wife.[12]

What if the husband became bankrupt or sold the house to a purchaser? In *Bendall* v. *McWhirter*[13] the majority[14] of the Court of Appeal held that the husband's trustee in bankruptcy, by virtue of his special statutory position, was no better placed than the husband to evict the wife. Denning L.J. accepted this but further held that the wife had an irrevocable licence, giving her an equity good against successors in title with notice of her status as a deserted wife. This view was followed in first instance decisions[15] (subsequently affirmed by Denning L.J.[16] but not without some reservations from other Lords Justices[17]) which held that a purchaser of the house from the husband was bound by the deserted wife's equity to occupy the house until a court ordered otherwise, so long as the purchaser had actual or constructive notice of the wife's equity.

However, in *National Provincial Bank* v. *Ainsworth*[18] the House of Lords unanimously rejected Lord Denning's views and held that a deserted wife had no equity to occupy the matrimonial home. To allow this against the husband's trustee in bankruptcy would be to prefer the wife above the husband's creditors and place the wife in a better position *vis-à-vis* such creditors than she had had before desertion. To allow this against a purchaser from the husband would ignore the purely personal nature of a wife's rights, flowing solely from her status as wife and entitling her as wife (not as licensee) to live in the matrimonial home; it would also involve embarrassing and difficult inquiries that would be unreasonable for a purchaser to make.

Subsequently, the Matrimonial Homes Act 1967 tried to reconcile the interests of wives and purchasers. A wife, whether or not deserted, can register a Class F charge which will be revealed when a purchaser makes the standard conveyancing searches. A registered Class F charge will bind the purchaser but not the husband's trustee in bankruptcy.[19] The view was taken that Lord Denning's attempt to do justice to the deserted wife had done injustice to the husband's creditors. The wife had married for better or for worse and since she benefited from her husband's property and credit she should not expect to be untouched by her husband's bankruptcy.

---

[11] *H.* v. *H.* (1947) 63 T.L.R. 645; *Lee* v. *Lee* [1952] 2 Q.B. 489.

[12] *Bendall* v. *McWhirter* [1952] 2 Q.B. 466; *National Provincial Bank* v. *Hastings Car Mart Ltd.* [1964] Ch. 665.

[13] [1952] 2 Q.B. 466.

[14] Romer L.J. with whom Somervell L.J. concurred.

[15] *Street* v. *Densham* [1954] 1 All E.R. 532; *Westminster Bank* v. *Lee* [1956] Ch. 7; *Churcher* v. *Street* [1959] Ch. 251.

[16] *Jess B. Woodcock & Son Ltd.* v. *Hobbs* [1955] 1 All E.R. 445; *N.P.B.* v. *Hastings Car Mart Ltd.* [1964] Ch. 665.

[17] *Hole* v. *Cuzen* [1953] 1 Q.B. 300, 306 *per* Jenkins L.J.; *Jess B. Woodcock & Son Ltd.* v. *Hobbs* [1955] 1 All E.R. 445, 451 *per* Parker L.J.; *N.P.B.* v. *Hastings Car Mart Ltd.* [1964] Ch. 665, 699, *per* Russell L.J.

[18] [1965] A.C. 1175.

[19] Matrimonial Homes Act 1967, s.2(5).

Resulting and Constructive Trusts and Shares in the Matrimonial Home

Originally, Lord Denning made much of section 17 of the Married Women's Property Act 1882:

> "In any question between husband and wife as to the title to or to possession of property . . . the judge . . . may make such order with respect to the property in dispute . . . *as he thinks fit.*"

In *Hine* v. *Hine*[20] he stated it meant that

> "the jurisdiction of the Court over family assets is entirely discretionary. Its discretion transcends all rights, legal or equitable, and enables the Court to make such order as it thinks fit. This means that the Court is entitled to make such order as may be fair and just in all the circumstances of the case."

This heresy was scotched in *Pettitt* v. *Pettitt*[21] where the House of Lords unanimously held that section 17 is procedural only and does not permit questions of title to be decided except in accordance with the strict legal and equitable rights of the spouses: the Court's discretion relates only to the enforcement of proprietary or possessory rights. The concept of "family assets" was also rejected.

In *Gissing* v. *Gissing*,[22] in reversing Lord Denning in a Court of Appeal judgment[23] delivered before the Lords' decision in *Pettitt* v. *Pettitt*, the Lords reaffirmed *Pettitt* v. *Pettitt*. The Lords made the point that a claim to an equitable interest in land must be based on the legal owner holding the land on an express, implied, resulting or constructive trust. Furthermore (Lord Reid dissenting) such trust must depend upon an express or implied common intention that an interest in the land was being acquired, but a court could not impose upon or ascribe to the parties, as fair in all the circumstances, a common intention that they would probably have formed as reasonable persons if they had actually thought about the matter. Lord Diplock in a passage, oft cited by Lord Denning, sometimes with the last vital sentence omitted,[24] stated[25]:

> "A resulting, implied or constructive trust—and it is unnecessary for present purposes to distinguish between these three classes of trust—is created by a transaction between the trustee and the *cestui que trust* in connection with the acquisition by the trustee of a legal estate in land, whenever the trustee has so conducted himself that it would be inequitable to allow him to deny to the *cestui que trust* a beneficial interest in the land acquired. And he will be held so to have conducted himself if by his words or conduct he has induced the *cestui que trust* to act to his own detriment in the reasonable belief that by so acting he was acquiring a beneficial interest in the land."

[20] [1962] 1 W.L.R. 1124, 1127. See also *Rimmer* v. *Rimmer* [1953] 1 Q.B. 63; *Fribance* v. *Fribance* [1957] 1 W.L.R. 384.
[21] [1970] A.C. 777 though there were clear indications of this in *N.P.B.* v. *Ainsworth* [1965] A.C. 1175.
[22] [1971] A.C. 886.
[23] [1969] 1 All E.R. 1043.
[24] *Heseltine* v. *Heseltine* [1971] 1 All E.R. 952; 955 *Binions* v. *Evans* [1972] 1 All E.R. 70, 76.
[25] [1971] A.C. 886, 905.

Lord Diplock was probably referring to the common characteristic of resulting trusts and some[26] constructive trusts in that it is inequitable to allow the legal owner to repudiate either his express or implied agreement that his partner is to obtain a beneficial interest proportionate to his partner's contribution to the purchase price (a resulting trust in favour of the partner qua purchaser) or his express or implied agreement that his partner is to obtain a beneficial interest, such agreement leading his partner to act to her detriment (a constructive trust in favour of the partner which may be a voluntary settlement liable to be avoided under Bankruptcy Act 1914, s.42).[27]

Lord Denning however, relied upon Lord Diplock's dicta to create "a constructive trust of a new model"[28] and to treat the question whether a trust is resulting or constructive as

> "more a matter of words than anything else. The two run together: it is a trust imposed whenever justice and good conscience require it. It is a liberal process, founded on large principles of equity, to be applied in cases where the defendant cannot conscientiously keep the property for himself alone, but ought to allow another to have the property or a share in it. The trust may arise at the outset when the property is acquired or later as the circumstances may require. It is an equitable remedy by which the Court can enable an aggrieved party to obtain restitution."[29]

Lord Denning seems to have been quite ready to impose a trust on a defendant even where no evidence was present of any common intention that the plaintiff was acquiring an interest in the home.[30] Since this was in direct conflict with *Gissing* v. *Gissing*[31] it has led judges of first instance[32] to go to the lengths of saying that Lord Denning could not really have meant what he said but must have been proceeding on a basis of implied common intention!

Since the Matrimonial Proceedings and Property Act 1970, s.5, replaced by Matrimonial Causes Act 1973, s.25, the Court has had ample statutory discretion in divorce or separation proceedings to make orders as to the property of husband or wife without the need first to ascertain exactly the nature and extent of their property rights. Lord Denning has thus developed

---

[26] Many constructive trusts are imposed where the parties have no common intention, *e.g.* in the case of fiduciaries' profits and the wrongful acts of agents.

[27] *Re Densham* [1975] 1 W.L.R. 1519. Such trust may also be regarded as an express trust exempted from the requirement of writing by the principle which prevents a statute being used as an instrument of fraud: *Rochefoucauld* v. *Boustead* [1897] 1 Ch. 196; *Allen* v. *Snyder* [1977] 2 N.S.W.L.R. 685, 692.

[28] *Eves* v.*Eves* [1975] 3 All E.R. 769, 771, *per* Lord Denning.

[29] *Hussey* v. *Palmer* [1972] 3 All E.R. 744, 747.

[30] *Falconer* v. *Falconer* [1970] 3 All E.R. 449; *Heseltine* v. *Heseltine* [1971] All E.R. 952; *Davis* v. *Vale* [1971] 2 All E.R. 1021; *Hargrave* v. *Newton* [1971] 3 All E.R. 866; *Cooke* v. *Head* [1972] 2 All E.R. 38; *Hazell* v. *Hazell* [1972] 1 All E.R. 923. For deprecation of this see MacDermott L.C.J. and Lowry J. in *Macfarlane* v. *Macfarlane* [1972] N.I. 59.

[31] [1971] A.C. 886, Lord Denning has continually relied on Lord Reid's minority view. See *Allen* v. *Snyder* [1977] 2 N.S.W.L.R. 685, 694.

[32] Bagnall J. in *Cowcher* v. *Cowcher* [1972] 1 All E.R. 943, 956–957; Goff J. in *Re Densham* [1975] 3 All E.R. 726, 737 "the language of Lord Denning and Karminski L.J. might be construed as saying we will make an agreement for the parties though the evidence is there was none, but that cannot be what they were intending to say since it would be in direct conflict with *Gissing* v. *Gissing*."

the use of his form of constructive trust in other co-habitation cases, but the constructive trust may still prove useful for a wife where no matrimonial proceedings are pending, *e.g.* on the husband's death or where the wife claims to have an interest binding a mortgagee of the legal estate from the husband.[33]

Co-habitees and the Home

In matrimonial cases, whilst Lord Denning was prepared to ignore *Gissing* and allow a wife's substantial contribution in money or money's worth to family expenses to establish a trust in her favour despite any such express or implied common intention, even he was not prepared to take into account the wife's "contributions in looking after and bringing up the family, and in looking after the house, buying the food and so forth. Such contributions can be considered under the 1970 Matrimonial Proceedings and Property Act, s.5(1)(*f*) [now Matrimonial Causes Act 1973, s.25(1)(*f*)] but not under the 1882 Married Women's Property Act, s.17"[34] which leaves ordinary trust principles to govern the position as held in *Pettitt.*

However, in *Eves* v. *Eves*[35] Lord Denning held a cohabitee entitled to a one quarter share in the home, being

> "such share as was fair in view of all she had done for him and the children. . . . She did not make any financial contribution but she contributed in many other ways. She did much work in the house and garden. She looked after him and cared for the children."

In *Hall* v. *Hall*[36] Lord Denning stated,

> "If a man and a woman have been living together as husband and wife and the woman has been contributing towards the establishment of the joint household there is a resulting trust as a matter of ordinary common justice for her. Her share depends on the circumstances and how much she has contributed—not merely in money—but also in keeping up the house: and, if there are children, in looking after them."

How can this be reconciled with *Pettitt* which, in the words of Viscount Dilhorne in *Gissing*,[37] "established that there is not one law of property applicable where a dispute as to property is between spouses or former spouses and another law of property where the dispute is between others"? Moreover, Lord Denning held that Miss Hall's one fifth share in the house ceased when she separated from Mr. Hall, so that she was only entitled to a sum corresponding to one fifth of the value of the house at the date of separation! However, in husband and wife cases, shares are valued at the date of sale of the house or the date of the court hearing when the parties invite the court to value the house so that one party can be ordered to assign

---

[33] As in *Williams & Glyn's Bank* v. *Boland* [1981] A.C. 487. If the wife knows of the husband's intended mortgage then the mortgagee may be able to rely on the husband's implied authority or an estoppel: *Spiro* v. *Lintern* [1973] 3 All E.R. 319.

[34] *Kowalczuk* v. *Kowalczuk* [1973] 2 All E.R. 1042, 1045.

[35] [1975] 3 All E.R. 768, 772.

[36] [1981] C.A. Transcript 223, *The Times*, April 4, 1981.

[37] [1971] A.C. 886, 899.

his share to the other for an appropriate sum.[38] It is difficult to see how, without her agreement, Miss Hall's entitlement to a one fifth share in the house suddenly, on separation, became an entitlement to a charge on the house for a sum corresponding to one fifth of its then value or an entitlement to a mere personal claim against Mr. Hall for such sum.

In dealing with family arrangements Lord Denning's credo probably emerged in *Hardwick* v. *Johnson*[39] where he stated,

> "In most of these cases the question cannot be solved by looking to the intention of the parties because the situation which arises is one which they never envisaged. So many things are undecided, undiscussed and unprovided for that the task of the courts is to fill in the blanks. The court has to look at all the circumstances and spell out the legal relationship. The court will pronounce in favour of a tenancy or a licence, a loan or a gift, or a trust, according to which of these legal relationships is most fitting in the situation which has arisen; and will find the terms of that relationship according to what reason and justice require. In the words of Lord Diplock in *Pettitt* v. *Pettitt* "the court imputes to the parties a common intention which in fact they never formed and it does so by forming its own opinion as to what could have been the common intention of reasonable men as to the effect of the unforeseen event if it had been present to their minds' . . . .""

This citation of Lord Diplock ignores the fact that in *Gissing* Lord Diplock himself stated,

> "I did differ from the majority of the members of your Lordships' House in *Pettitt* v. *Pettitt* in that I saw no reason in law why the fact that the spouses had not applied their minds at all to the question of how the beneficial interest should be held should prevent the court from giving effect to a common intention on this matter which it was satisfied that they would have formed as reasonable persons if they had actually thought about it. I must now accept that this is not the law."[40]

The effect of *Gissing*, which Lord Denning persistently ignored, is best summarised by Goff J. in *Re Densham*:

> "If the parties have not in fact agreed about the ownership the court cannot make an agreement for them and given them such interest as it feels they would have determined had they thought about it or which the court thinks fair in all circumstances. On the other hand, the court may infer from the circumstances and the conduct of the parties, including subsequent conduct, that there was an agreement, and if it does the court will give effect to that agreement under a resulting or constructive trust."[41]

[38] *Falconer* v. *Falconer* [1970] 1 W.L.R. 1333; *Cracknell* v. *Cracknell* [1971] P. 356; *Hazell* v. *Hazell* [1972] 1 W.L.R. 301; *Bothe* v. *Amos* [1976] Fam. 46.
[39] [1978] 2 All E.R. 935, 938.
[40] [1971] A.C. 886, 904. As recently as *Bernard* v. *Josephs* [1982] 2 W.L.R. 1052, 1057 Lord Denning was still citing the discredited dicta of Pearson L.J. in *Hine* v. *Hine* [1962] 1 W.L.R. 1124, 1132 to the effect that the court can artificially impose a solution upon the parties regardless of any common intention of the parties.
[41] [1975] 3 All E.R. 726, 731 endorsed by *Allen* v. *Snyder* [1977] 2 N.S.W.L.R. 685.

Lord Denning's view that he could impose a trust "whenever justice and good conscience require it" leads to such uncertainty and unpredictability.[42] Consider *Heseltine* v. *Heseltine*[43] where the wife gave the husband £40,000 to save estate duty and £20,000 so that he could become a Lloyd's Name, intending the husband to take beneficially so that these purposes could be achieved. Lord Denning (without requiring the presence of undue influence) imposed a constructive trust on the husband to hold the £20,000 and £40,000, traced into securities purchased therewith, on trust for the wife! In *Eves* v. *Eves*[44] the man and woman found a dilapidated house which the man purchased in his own name, having falsely told the woman she was too young to take the conveyance jointly with him. She did a lot of work on the house and Lord Denning imposed a constructive trust of a quarter share in her favour. Why did she not have a half share when if the house had been put in joint names there would have been the standard declaration of beneficial joint tenancy and that would have been conclusive?

There is much to be said for the view expressed in the New Zealand Supreme Court[45] that Lord Denning had invented

> "a supposed rule of equity which is not only vague in its outline but which must disqualify itself from acceptance as a valid principle of jurisprudence by its total uncertainty of application and result. It cannot be sufficient to say that wide and varying notions of fairness and conscience shall be the legal determinant. No stable system of jurisprudence could permit a litigant's claim to justice to be consigned to the formless void of individual moral opinion."

In dealing out instant justice *inter partes* Lord Denning overlooked the fact that the imposition of a constructive trust has far-reaching ramifications for third parties, whether purchasers or donees from, or creditors of the alleged constructive trustee. The beneficiary under a constructive trust has an equitable proprietary interest in the property enabling him to trace the property, in whatever form, into the hands of any transferee, subject to the defence of bona fide purchase for value without notice. He also has priority to recover his full share in the property before the general creditors of the constructive trustee: they only have the rest of the trustee's assets available to them, except to the extent they may be able to set aside the constructive trust under section 42 of the Bankruptcy Act 1914. Moreover, in the case of land held on constructive trust for the trustee and the beneficiary a statutory trust for sale arises[46] so that a purchaser should pay his purchase money over to two trustees to obtain a good title.[47]

Furthermore, it can be argued that a person alleged to be a constructive trustee should not forfeit his property (which is one way of regarding what

---

[42] See criticisms in Hanbury and Maudsley, *Modern Equity* (11th ed.) p. 398; Oakley, *Constructive Trusts*, pp. 3–8, 19–28; Pettit, *Equity* (4th ed.) pp. 47–48; Nathan & Marshall, *Cases & Commentary on Trusts* (7th ed.) pp. 383–388.

[43] [1971] 1 All E.R. 952.

[44] [1975] 3 All E.R. 768.

[45] *Carley* v. *Farrelly* [1975] 1 N.Z.L.R. 356, 357 *per* Mahon J. Also see Lord MacDermott in *Re McKeown* [1974] N.I. 226, 232.

[46] L.P.A. 1925, ss. 34–36.

[47] L.P.A. 1925, s.27(2).

happens if he is held to be a constructive trustee of it) unless he knows distinctly and precisely what is to occasion such forfeiture.[48] As Bagnall J. said in *Cowcher* v. *Cowcher*[49]

> "In any individual case the application of established principles of property or trust law may produce a result which appears unfair. So be it: in my view that is not an injustice. I am convinced that in determining property rights the only justice that can be attained by mortals, who are fallible and are not omniscient, is justice according to law; the justice that flows from the application of sure and settled principles to proved or admitted facts. So in the field of property law the length of the Chancellor's foot has been measured or is capable of measurement. This does not mean that equity is past child-bearing; simply that its progeny must be legitimate—by precedent out of principle. It is as well that this should be so; otherwise no lawyer could safely advise his client and every quarrel would lead to a law suit."

Contractual Licences

It is trite law that the benefit of a contract can pass but the burden cannot (except in the case of an estate contract, *i.e.* a specifically enforceable contract for the purchase of an estate in land). Thus, one might expect that, whilst the benefit of a contractual licence might pass (unless creating merely personal non-assignable rights) the burden would not,[50] even though, where a licence is irrevocable for a period, any revocation may be restrained by an injunction[51] or specific performance may be ordered,[52] equity supplementing the common law where the remedy of damages is inadequate. After all, as Lord Wilberforce has stated,

> "the fact that a contractual right can be specifically performed or its breach prevented by injunction does not mean that the right is any the less of a person character or that a purchaser with notice is bound by it: what is relevant is the nature of the right, not the remedy which exists for its enforcement."[53]

However, Lord Denning in *Errington* v. *Errington and Woods*,[54] instead of dealing with the case on the straightforward basis of a volunteer being bound by an estate contract or on the basis of equitable proprietary estoppel, stated

> "this infusion of equity means that contractual licences now have a force and validity of their own and cannot be revoked in breach of contract. Neither the licensor nor anyone who claims through him can disregard the contract except a purchaser for value without notice."[55]

---

[48] *Cf. Clayton* v. *Ramsden* [1943] A.C. 320, 726.

[49] [1972] 1 W.L.R. 425, 430. These remarks are particularly apt in a conveyancing context though even here Lord Denning in *Brikom Investments Ltd.* v. *Carr* [1979] 2 All E.R. 753, 760 states, "I prefer to see justice is done; and let the conveyancers look after themselves." In the end it is the clients who foot the bill for extra conveyancing problems.

[50] *Clore* v. *Theatrical Properties Ltd.* [1936] 3 All E.R. 483, 490.

[51] *Winter Gardens Theatre Ltd.* v. *Millenium Productions Ltd.* [1948] A.C. 173.

[52] *Verrall* v. *Great Yarmouth B.C.* [1980] All E.R. 839, *Tanner* v. *Tanner* [1975] 3 All E.R. 776, 780.

[53] *N.P.B.* v. *Ainsworth* [1965] A.C. 1175, 1251.

[54] [1952] 1 K.B. 290.

[55] *Ibid.* p. 299.

Lord Denning endorsed this in a minority judgment in *Binions* v. *Evans*[56] and in *D.H.N. Food Distributors Ltd.* v. *Tower Hamlets*,[57] where he was supported by Goff L.J. who overlooked his view (as Goff J.) to the contrary.[58]

In *Binions* v. *Evans* Lord Denning developed his position in holding that if P contracts with V to purchase land from V, subject to the rights of L in exclusive possession under an irrevocable contractual licence, then, on completion of the purchase, P holds the legal estate on constructive trust for L. He went on to state that the position would be the same if P had not so expressly agreed with V but merely had notice of L's rights from L's occupation.

This seems a revival of the "fallacy that because an obligation binds a man's conscience it therefore becomes binding on the consciences of those who take from him with notice of the obligation."[59] After all, a purchaser of a freehold takes free from known positive covenants affecting the land and entered into by his predecessor[60] and also free from known restrictive covenants affecting the land and entered into by his predecessor if the covenantee has no adjacent dominant land benefiting from the covenant.[61] Thus, one would expect a purchaser of land with actual knowledge of a contractual licensee in occupation of the land to take free from the contractual licence.

Indeed, *King* v. *David Allen & Sons Ltd.*[62] was a House of Lords case which, in the words of Russell L.J., "necessarily involved a decision that a contractual licence to post advertisements on a wall for a period of years was not binding upon a purchaser from the licensor with actual notice of the licence because it created a mere personal obligation on the licensor and not an interest in land."[63] In *Clore* v. *Theatrical Properties Ltd.*[64] the Court of Appeal held that a purchaser with actual knowledge of "front of house" rights under a contractual licence (dressed up in the form of a lease) was not bound by the licence since "this is not a document which creates an interest in land but merely one which is a personal contract between the parties named therein and is only enforceable among parties between whom there is privity of contract."[65]

Lord Denning suggests that it is absence of actual occupation that distinguishes these two weighty cases.[66] However, actual occupation is merely one form of notice of the right justifying the occupation and in *King* and in *Clore* there was actual notice of the right. Notice is notice, no matter how it arises.[67] Notice of a right does not itself affect the nature of the right: the nature of the right must be sought elsewhere. *King* and *Clore* make it clear

---

[56] [1972] Ch. 359.
[57] [1976] 1 W.L.R. 852.
[58] *Re Solomon* [1967] Ch. 573, 582–586.
[59] *N.P.B.* v. *Ainsworth* [1965] A.C. 1175, 1253, *per* Lord Wilberforce and see *L.C.C.* v. *Allen* [1914] 3 K.B. 642, 655.
[60] *Austerberry* v. *Oldham Corporation* (1885) 29 Ch. D. 750, 781–785.
[61] *Sefton* v. *Tophams Ltd.* [1965] Ch. 1140, 1157, 1183, 1191, 1199, 1202.
[62] [1916] 2 A.C. 54.
[63] *N.P.B.* v. *Hastings Car Mart Ltd.* [1964] Ch. 665, 697.
[64] [1936] 3 All E.R. 483.
[65] *Ibid.* p. 490, *per* Lord Wright.
[66] *N.P.B.* v. *Hastings Car Mart Ltd.* [1964] Ch. 665, 688.
[67] *Ibid.* p. 698, *per* Russell L.J.

that the nature of a contractual licence is not proprietary so that notice cannot itself elevate such licence into a proprietary interest.

In *Re Sharpe*,[68] however, Browne-Wilkinson J. felt himself obliged, by virtue of *D.H.N. Food Distributors* v. *Tower Hamlets*, to hold that the licensor's trustee in bankruptcy is bound by the contractual licence on the basis that it is more than a mere contractual interest capable of disclaimer by the trustee in bankruptcy. He did not have to deal with the position of the purchaser from the trustee in bankruptcy but expressed

> "the hope that in the near future the whole question can receive full consideration from the Court of Appeal so that in order to do justice to the many thousands of people who never come into court at all but who wish to know with certainty what their proprietary rights are, the extent to which these irrevocable licences bind third parties may be defined with certainty. Doing justice to the litigant who appears in the court ought not to involve injustice to other persons who are not litigants before the court but whose rights are fundamentally affected by the new principles."[69]

The treatment of contractual licences in all their varieties if they are to become more than purely personal contractual interests is more likely to be satisfactory if dealt with by legislation. Such legislation might then provide for registration of contractual licences, as currently for estate contracts, and for a purchaser to have the defence of justification to any tortious claim for interference with contractual relations made by an estate contract owner or a contractual licensee, who had failed to register his interest.[70]

Lord Denning's view in *Binions* v. *Evans*[71] that if P contracts with V to purchase land from V, subject to X's contractual rights, then P holds the land on constructive trust to give effect to X's rights has recently been followed by Dillon J. in *Lyus* v. *Prowsa Developments Ltd.*[72] Here the A Co. mortgaged land to the Bank and later contracted with the plaintiff to build a house on part of the land and convey that part to him. The A Co. became insolvent leaving the house unfinished. The Bank then sold the mortgaged land to the B Co. "subject to and with the benefit of" the plaintiff's contract, although the Bank's mortgage, of course, had not been subject to the plaintiff's contract. The B Co. sold the land on to the C. Co. subject to the plaintiff's contract so far, if at all, as it might be enforceable. The transfers of the registered land made to the B Co. and to the C. Co. made no reference to the plaintiff's contract. It was only after the C Co. had become registered proprietor that the plaintiff entered a caution against its title.

In the plaintiff's action against the B Co. and the C Co. Dillon J. held that the B Co. on taking the land subject to the Bank's stipulations in favour of the plaintiff's contract became subject to a constructive trust to complete the plaintiff's contract, and the C Co., therefore, was bound by a constructive trust to complete the plaintiff's contract. Specific performance was decreed so

---

[68] [1980] 1 W.L.R. 219.
[69] *Ibid.* p. 226.
[70] Such legislation should also deal with the *Snelling* v. *Snelling* principle mentioned *post*, p. 91.
[71] [1972] Ch. 359, 368–369.
[72] (1982) 79 L.S. Gaz. 369.

that the C Co. had to finish the plaintiff's house in accordance with the plaintiff's contract with the A Co.

This is difficult to reconcile with the line of cases[73] preventing the trust from being utilised as a device to evade the privity of contract doctrine. In a property context this is difficult to reconcile with the line of cases[74] establishing that where statute prescribes registration provisions, which make it perfectly clear how the plaintiff's interest is to be protected, it is not for the court (in the absence of some personal dealing between the plaintiff and the defendant or the defendant's predecessor in title, so misleading the plaintiff that it would be a fraud on the plaintiff to allow the purchaser to invoke the statute) to say that Parliament did not mean what it said and had not provided adequate protection, and to introduce equitable doctrines for the purpose of extending protection to those who have not protected themselves by taking the prescribed statutory steps. Since the Bank was willing to look after the plaintiff, though not bound so to do, nothing would have been simpler then for it to have the B Co. directly contract with the plaintiff, who should then have entered a notice on the register to protect his interest.[75]

Lyus goes beyond Lord Denning's dicta in requiring positive action on the part of the defendant rather than negatively preventing him from evicting the contractual licensee. Whilst, for the reasons discussed above, the latter ought not to be justifiable on property or constructive trust grounds, it may, at least, be justifiable on the *Snelling* v. *Snelling*[76] principle *if* the vendor intervenes on behalf of the contractual licensee. By this principle if A agrees with B not to sue C or, presumably not to evict C, then, if A brings an action against C B can intervene to have the proceedings against C stayed or dismissed.[77]

Equitable Proprietary Estoppel

If A, under belief or an expectation acquiesced in or encouraged by O that A has or shall have a certain interest in land, thereafter by reason of such belief or expectation and with the knowledge of O and without objection by him acts to his detriment in connection with such land, a court of equity will

[73] *Vandepitte* v. *Preferred Accident Assurance* [1933] A.C. 70; *Re Schebsman* [1944] Ch. 83; *Green* v. *Russell* [1959] 2 Q.B. 226.
[74] *Hollington Bros. Ltd.* v. *Rhodes* [1951] 2 All E.R. 578; *Miles* v. *Bull* (*No. 2*) [1969] 3 All E.R. 1585, 1590; *De Lusignan* v. *Johnson* (1973) 230 E.G. 499; *Midland Bank Trust Co.* v. *Green* [1981] A.C. 513.
[75] By Land Registration Act 1925, s.20 a registered proprietor for value takes the land subject only to overriding interests and entries on the register but free from all other interests whatsoever.
[76] [1973] 1 Q.B. 87.
[77] Much will depend on how far the court is prepared to find an implied agreement not to evict the contractual licensee where the defendant agreed with the vendor to take subject to the plaintiff's licence. In *Clore* v. *Theatrical Properties* [1936] 3 All E.R. 483, 486 it appears in Lord Wright's judgment that the instrument of sale stated that the property comprising the theatre excluded X's right to manage the bars and the front of house rights but the purchaser was allowed to take free of such rights. In *Binions* v. *Evans* [1972] Ch. 359, 369, Lord Denning, however, stated if the purchaser "had acquired the theatre 'subject to the rights of the licensees' I cannot suppose that this court would have allowed him to disregard those rights."

compel O to satisfy A's reliance or expectation claim since he will be estopped from denying A's claim.[78] The relief granted to A will depend upon the circumstances, *e.g.* the conveyance of O's fee simple[79] or the grant of a lease[80] or of an easement[81] or, to satisfy a reliance claim, the grant of an equitable lien for expenditure[82] or for the value of improvements.[83]

A's claim against O has long been recognised but Lord Denning made it clear that A's claim will also bind successors in title to O unless they are bona fide purchasers of a legal estate for value without notice.[84] A thus has an equitable proprietary estoppel interest that binds third parties.

It is necessary that A has expended money or otherwise acted to his detriment. However, Lord Denning suggested in *Greasley* v. *Cooke*,[85]

> "I do not think that that is necessary. It is sufficient if the party to whom the assurance is given, acts on the faith of it, in such circumstances that it would be unjust and inequitable for the party making the assurance to go back on it. . . . It can be seen that the assurances given by Kenneth and Hedley to the defendant leading her to believe that she would be allowed to stay in the house as long as she wished raised an equity in her favour. There was no need for her to prove that she acted on the faith of these assurances. It is to be presumed that she did so. There is no need for her to prove that she acted to her detriment or to her prejudice. Suffice it that she stayed on in the house, looking after Kenneth and [his mentally handicapped sister] Clarice, when otherwise she might have left and got a job elsewhere."

In context, where the defendant had been a paid housekeeper, who had become K's *de facto* wife and so unpaid, it was easy to presume that she had acted to her detriment without the need for her to prove it. However, Dunn L.J. stated "There is no doubt that for proprietary estoppel to arise the person claiming must have incurred expenditure or otherwise have prejudiced himself or acted to his detriment."[86] In *Christian* v. *Christian*[87] another division of the Court of Appeal has held that detriment is a necessary requirement of proprietary estoppel.

Lord Denning also suggested[88] that detriment is not a necessary requirement of promissory estoppel of the *High Trees*[89] variety. Indeed, he endeavoured to fudge the distinctions between the different types of estoppel so as to develop a very broad flexible discretion in the Court as he also suggested in *Lloyds Bank* v. *Bundy*[90] where inequality of bargaining power is

---

[78] *Taylor Fashions Ltd.* v. *Liverpool Victoria Trustees Co.* [1981] 1 All E.R. 897, 912. *Ramsden* v. *Dyson* (1886) L.R. 1 H.L. 121. *Amalgamated Investment Ltd.* v. *Texas Commerce Bank* [1981] 1 All E.R. 923, 936.

[79] *Fowkes* v. *Pascoe* [1979] 2 All E.R. 945.

[80] *Stiles* v. *Cowper* (1748) 3 Atk. 692, *Gregory* v. *Mighell* (1811) 18 Ves. 328.

[81] *Crabb* v. *Arun D.C.* [1976] Ch. 179.

[82] *Unity Joint Stock Mutual Banking Assoc.* v. *King* (1858) 25 Beav. 72

[83] *Raffaele* v. *Raffaele* [1962] W.A.R.; (1963) 79 L.Q.R. 238.

[84] *Inwards* v. *Baker* [1965] 2 Q.B. 29, 37, (*E.R.*) *Ives Investments Ltd.* v. *High* [1967] 2 Q.B. 379.

[85] [1980] 3 All E.R. 710, 713.

[86] [1980] 3 All E.R. 710, 715.

[87] [1980] C.A. Transcript 838.

[88] *Alan* v. *El Nasr* [1972] 2 Q.B. 189, 213; 15 M.L.R. 1, 6–8.

[89] [1947] K.B. 130.

[90] [1975] Q.B. 326, 339.

concerned. In *Amalgamated Investment Ltd.* v. *Texas Commerce Bank Ltd.* he stated

> "All these various estoppel principles can now be seen to merge into one general principle shorn of limitations. When the parties to a transaction proceed on the basis of an underlying assumption (whether of fact or of law, and whether due to misrepresentation or mistake makes no difference) on which they have conducted the dealings between them, neither of them will be allowed to go back on that assumption when it would be unjust or unfair to allow him to do so. If one of them does seek to go back on it the courts will give the other such remedy as the equity of the case demands."[91]

In making such generalisation Lord Denning did not cite, let alone analyse, any of the cases dealing with proprietary estoppel (whether arising from acquiescence or from encouragement) estoppel by convention, estoppel by representation of fact or promissory estoppel, nor did he consider any of the implications for the doctrine of consideration or for the rules for perfecting gifts. Such a general approach makes it easier to do justice between a plaintiff and a defendant but makes it much harder for lawyers to advise and assist clients who do not want to go to court to find—at great expense—what is just or fair.

Certainty of Objects of Powers and Trusts

In *Re Gulbenkian's S.T.*[92] Lord Denning expressed the view that the test for certainty of objects of discretionary trusts should be brought into line with the test for powers though, on appeal,[93] Lord Upjohn could not see how this could be done consistently with principle. However, less than two years later in *McPhail* v. *Doulton*[94] the House of Lords (Lords Hodson and Guest dissenting), deriving support from very old cases, held that the test for discretionary trusts should be similar to that for powers, namely, that a trust or power is valid if it can be said with certainty that any given individual is or is not a member of the class benefiting under the trust or power. It follows that a discretionary trust or power will be void if the class is conceptually uncertain so that borderline cases can be envisaged where it cannot be said whether a given individual is or is not a member of the class, *e.g.* "old friends."

Such assimilation of the tests for discretionary trusts and powers is sensible as reflecting the similar substance of the position of the object of a discretionary trust and the object of a power.

Lord Denning would prefer the test to be that a discretionary trust or power is valid so long as there is even one given person who is clearly within

[91] [1981] 3 All E.R. 577, 584. Other judges have been moving towards such a broad position; *Crabb* v. *Arun D.C.* [1976] Ch. 179, 193, *per* Scarman L.J.; *Taylor Fashions Ltd.* v. *Liverpool Victoria Trustees Co.* [1981] 1 All E.R. 897, 915, *per* Oliver J.; *Amalgamated Investments Ltd.* v. *Texas Commerce Bank* [1981] 1 All E.R. 923, 936, 938, *per* Robert Goff J.
[92] [1968] Ch. 126, 133.
[93] [1970] A.C. 508, 525.
[94] [1971] A.C. 424 (Lord Upjohn did not sit).

the class, even though there may be borderline cases where it cannot be said whether or not a person is within the class.[95] This suggested test has, however, been rejected by the House of Lords for powers and for trusts since it would mean that the trustees would be selecting donees of the settlor's bounty from a narrower class than that intended by the settlor.[96] On the other hand, the suggested test at least ensures that one or more persons clearly intended to benefit do benefit rather than none at all.

For this reason in *Re Tuck's S.T.*[97] Lord Denning opined that if a conceptually uncertain class were specified by a settlor, who then provided that a third party could resolve any doubt or difficulty, this would cure any conceptual uncertainty. However, if the class were "tall relations" or "old friends" or "good business associates" and the testator's widow were given power to resolve any difficulties as to whether or not persons qualified as class members, then, since the court cannot resolve the conceptual uncertainty it is difficult to see how the widow can.[98] There are no clear conceptual criteria to guide the widow or, indeed, to guide the court if the widow's exercise of the power is challenged.

Lord Denning's suggestion thus seems heretical and unsupportable. However, equity does distinguish between fiduciary powers vested in trustees qua trustees and personal powers vested in a particular individual qua individual.[99] The latter individual is under no obligation to consider exercising the personal power and under no obligations in exercising the power except that the power can only be exercised in favour of the objects of the power.[1] Further, equity allows even a fidiciary power to be valid where it is a power to add anyone in the world to a class of discretionary trust beneficiaries.

What then if a testator leaves his residuary estate to trustees upon discretionary trusts "for my old friends A, B, C, D and E and for my good business associates V, W, X, Y and Z, with power for my widow to add as beneficiaries any one else (apart from herself) but particularly any of my other old friends or good business associates as she sees fit from time to time." If this is valid, as seems the case, then is it so clear that the court should invalidate discretionary trusts "for my old friends and for my good business associates providing always that if any doubts arise my widow shall have power to determine conclusively who are my old friends and my good business associates." Should equity really elevate form over substance? Perhaps Lord Denning's desired result may be achieved, though on different grounds.

---

[95] *Re Gulbenkian's S.T.* [1968] Ch. 126, 134. In *Re Barlow's W.T.* [1979] 1 W.L.R. 278 Browne-Wilkinson J. surprisingly applied this test to individual gifts (as opposed to class gifts) for persons qualifying under some condition precedent, *e.g.* £1,000 to each of my old friends and £500 to each of my tall relatives. But if there are 12 living relatives all male and between five feet eight inches and six feet two inches in half inch steps can the court or the executors or the residuary beneficiary ascertain precisely when the executors have carried out their duty to pay qualifying beneficiaries?

[96] See Lord Upjohn in *Re Gulbenkian's S.T.* [1970] A.C. 508, 524.

[97] [1978] Ch. 49, 61.

[98] See *Re Coxen* [1948] 1 Ch. 747; *Re Jones* [1953] Ch. 125.

[99] *Re Wills' Trust Deed* [1964] Ch. 219.

[1] *Re Manisty's S.T.* [1974] Ch. 17, *Re Hay's S.T.* [1982] 1 W.L.R. 202.

Formalities

Lord Denning himself was not always above putting form before substance. In *Grey* v. *I.R.C.*[2] H transferred shares to T as nominee on trust for himself, and a fortnight later orally directed T to hold the shares on trust for X. The House of Lords unanimously held that the oral direction was not effective to create a trust of the shares in favour of X since such direction by H was a disposition by H of his subsisting equitable interest, which required writing under Law of Property Act 1925, s.53(1)(c). By virtue of this oral direction T was supposed to hold the shares not on trust for H but, instead, on trust for X, so H was really disposing of his equitable interest to X.

In *Re Vandervell's Trusts* (*No. 2*)[3] V transferred a share option to T on such trusts as might thereafter be declared by V or T. Thus, until such trusts were declared T held the option on resulting trust for V himself. Lord Denning took the view that if either V or T declared new trusts, then the new trust filling the previous gap in the beneficial ownership, the resulting trust would automatically terminate and be replaced by the newly declared trusts without the need for any writing satisfying section 53(1)(c). However, if V himself declares the new trusts in favour of Z then surely V is disposing of his subsisting equitable interest to Z within section 53(1)(c), since T is now to hold on trust not for V but, instead, on trust for Z.

To distinguish the express trust situation in *Grey* from the resulting trust situation is surely unjustifiable.[4] It is fortuitous whether the settlor on transferring property to T expressly tells T to hold on trust for the settlor or says nothing and leaves it to the implication under a resulting trust that T is to hold on trust for the settlor. Furthermore, an express trust for A, like a resulting trust for A, automatically terminates if a new trust for B instead is validly created, *e.g.* under a special power vested in T[5] to appoint new trusts. From *Grey* v. *I.R.C.* it seems clear that if A, the equitable interest owner, himself purports to declare or create new trusts in favour of B, then A is disposing of his subsisting equitable interest and so writing within section 53(1)(c) is vital if the new trusts are to be valid.

Mitigating the Rigour of the Law

In *Re Vandervell's Trusts* (*No. 2*) Lord Denning stated,

> "Every unjust decision is a reproach to the law or the judge who administers it. If the law should be in danger of doing injustice then equity should be called in to remedy it. Equity was introduced to mitigate the rigour of the law."[6]

---

[2] [1960] A.C. 1.

[3] [1974] Ch. 269.

[4] Although L.P.A., s.53(2) states, "This section does not affect the *creation* or *operation* of resulting or constructive trusts," it is not considered that this exemption covers the disposition of equitable interests subsisting under such trusts. In *Oughtred* v. *I.R.C.* [1960] A.C. 206, 233 Lord Denning himself stated, "I should have thought that the wording of s.53(1)(c) clearly made a writing necessary to effect a transfer of an interest under a constructive trust and s.53(2) does not do away with that necessity."

[5] The ratio of *Re Vandervell's Trust* (*No.* 2) seems to be that it was the trustee company (and not Vandervell) which orally created a valid new trust of personal property.

[6] [1974] Ch. 269, 322.

Quennell v. *Maltby*[7] was a case where Lord Denning developed his idea of equity to mitigate the rigour of the law. He held,

> "In modern times equity can step in so as to prevent a mortgagee, or a transferee from him, from getting possession of a house contrary to the justice of the case. A mortgagee will be restrained from getting possession except when it is sought bona fide and reasonably for the purpose of enforcing the security, and then only subject to such conditions as the court thinks fit to impose. When the bank itself or a building society lends the money, then it may well be right to allow the mortgagee to obtain possession when the borrower is in default. But so long as the interest is paid and there is nothing outstanding equity has ample power to restrain any unjust use of the right to possession."[8]

This is heady stuff—and novel. After all, only two years earlier in *Western Bank Ltd.* v. *Schindler*[9] the Court of Appeal had emphasised the absolute nature of a mortgagee's right to possession by virtue of the mortgage operating as a 3,000 year lease. As Goff L.J. stated,

> "It has for a very long time been established law that a mortgagee has a proprietary right at common law as owner of the legal estate to go into possession of the mortgaged property. This right has been unequivocally recognised in a number of modern cases: see, for example, *Fourmaids Ltd.* v. *Dudley Marshall (Properties) Ltd.*[10] and *Birmingham Citizens P.B.S.* v. *Caunt.*[11] It has nothing to do with default: see per Harman J. in the *Fourmaids* case.[12] As he there expressed it, 'The mortgagee may to into possession before the ink is dry on the mortgage unless by a term expressly or necessarily implied in the contract he has contracted himself out of that right.' This is incontrovertible."[13]

For this very reason Parliament in the Administration of Justice Act 1970 and 1973 expressly had to confer on the courts in the case of mortgages of dwelling-houses powers to adjourn possession proceedings or to postpone the giving up of possession.

What injustice provoked Lord Denning to attempt to invent a new equity? Quennell had mortgaged his house (worth well over £30,000) to the bank to secure a £2,500 overdraft. The mortgage deed prohibited the creation of tenancies without the bank's consent. Quennell did lease the home to Maltby without the bank's consent. Later, he sought to sell with vacant possession and so asked the bank to claim possession, as mortgagee, from Maltby, whose Rent Act protected tenancy did not bind the mortgagee. The bank refused. Mrs. Quennell than paid off the overdraft and took a transfer of the mortgage and sought possession as mortgagee.

The judge gave effect to her absolute right to possession as mortgagee. Lord Denning was worried that this was unjust to Maltby and could open

---

[7] [1979] 1 W.L.R. 318.
[8] *Ibid.* p. 322.
[9] [1977] Ch. 1.
[10] [1957] Ch. 317.
[11] [1962] Ch. 883.
[12] [1957] Ch. 317, 320.
[13] [1977] Ch. 1, 20.

the way to widespread evasion of the Rent Act. Thus, he created an equity to defeat Mrs. Quennell's claim as mortgagee. As appears from the judgments of Bridge and Templeman L.JJ. the rejection of Mrs. Quennell's claim is better based on the ground that the action, though in form brought by Mrs. Quennell as mortgagee, was in substance brought by Mrs. Quennell as agent on behalf of her mortgagor husband: an action by him against his own tenant would clearly have failed.

In *Re Brocklehurst*[14] Lord Denning was prepared to hold that, although a 99 year lease of shooting rights by an eccentric old baronet over his fee simple in Swythamley Hall Estate could not be set aside in equity under the doctrine of undue influence by the baronet's devisee, the transaction could not "stand so as to work the destruction of an estate of which he was morally only a life tenant. It was his duty to preserve the estate in the interests of his family, the neighbourhood and the country at large. To my mind he had no right in equity whatever to do what he did."[15] He regarded the gift of shooting rights as "a gift which is so unreasonable and in which the donor is so affected by age and eccentricity that the transaction cannot stand unless it is shown that it was entered into by him with the benefit of independent advice."[16]

Lawton and Bridge L.JJ. disagreed and upheld the gift, Bridge L.J. stating,

> "I know of no principle of law or equity which would entitle the court to condemn this transaction as 'unconscionable' or to interfere on the grounds that the baronet was 'morally only a life tenant.' He was an absolute owner, of sound mind, entitled to dispose of his property as he chose."[17]

Interlocutory Injunctions

In his openly hostile approach to the *American Cyanamid Co.* v. *Ethicon Ltd.*[18] principles for the granting of interlocutory injunctions Lord Denning also had little support from his colleagues.

Before *Cyanamid* the grant of interlocutory injunctions depended upon the plaintiff showing a strong prima facie case that his rights had been infringed so that the merits of the case were looked into by the court.[19] *Cyanamid* now merely requires the plaintiff to show that there is a serious question to be tried so that there is no need for a proper investigation of the merits of the case at this stage. If the plaintiff clears the first low hurdle then the court considers where the balance of convenience lies.[20] In determining the balance of convenience various specified factors are to be taken into account[21] including, as a last resort, the relative strength of each party's case, except that there may be "other special factors to be taken into consideration in the particular circumstances of individual cases."

[14] [1978] Ch. 14.
[15] *Ibid.* p. 32.
[16] *Ibid.* p. 31.
[17] *Ibid.* p. 48.
[18] [1975] A.C. 396.
[19] *Stratford & Sons Ltd.* v. *Lindley* [1965] A.C. 269, 338–339; *Hoffman La Roche* v. *Secretary of State* [1975] A.C. 295, 360.
[20] [1975] A.C. 396, 407–408.
[21] *Ibid.* pp. 408–409.

Lord Denning in *Fellowes* v. *Fisher*[22] took this last quotation of Lord Diplock out of context to hold that there are numerous "individual cases" where special factors require the court only to grant an interlocutory injunction if, on examining the merits of the parties' cases, the plaintiff makes out a prima facie case. His colleagues disagreed with this and in *Hubbard* v. *Pitt*[23] where Lord Denning reaffirmed his views Stamp L.J. (with whom Orr L.J. agreed) stated,

> "I can only say that reading the latter passage [in *Cyanamid* about special factors] in the context in which it appears, it appears to me clear beyond peradventure that Lord Diplock was there referring to special factors affecting the balance of convenience and not to special factors enabling the court to ignore the general principles there laid down, or more particularly, the admonition not to require of a party seeking an interlocutory injunction that he should have made out 'a prima facie case' or 'a strong prima facie case'. It is in my view the duty of the Court of Appeal to follow and apply the practice laid down in the *American Cyanamid* case."[24]

Lord Denning, in his eagerness to examine the merits of the parties' cases so that justice could be done, also took advantage of Lord Diplock's statement,

> "If the extent of the uncompensatable disadvantage to each party would not differ widely, it may not be improper to take into account in tipping the balance the relative strength of each party's case."[25]

Lord Denning therefore stated,

> "There are many cases in which either party could suffer great disadvantages which could not be adequately compensated in damages. In all these it is permissible to consider the relative strength of each party's case."[26]

However, in quoting Lord Diplock, Lord Denning conveniently omitted the two following sentences by which Lord Diplock restricted the right to examine the merits of the case:

> "This should be done only where it is apparent on the facts, disclosed by evidence as to which there is no credible dispute, that the strength of one party's case is disproportionate to that of the other party. The court is not justified in embarking on anything resembling a trial of the action on conflicting affidavits in order to evaluate the strength of either party's case."[27]

Lord Denning ignored these restrictions.

Lord Denning, supported by many of his colleagues, was worried about applying *Cyanamid* principles in cases where the interlocutory proceedings

---

[22] [1976] Q.B. 126, 133.
[23] [1976] Q.B. 142.
[24] *Ibid.* p. 185.
[25] [1975] A.C. 396, 409.
[26] [1976] Q.B. 122, 134.
[27] [1975] A.C. 396, 409.

were likely to settle the issue, the case not proceeding to trial.[28] Lord Diplock in *N.W.L. Ltd.* v. *Woods*[29] has subsequently indicated that in such cases it is proper to treat the relative strengths of the parties' cases as a significant factor in the balancing process rather than only taking such factors into account if other factors had not already pre-empted the decision.

In *Cyanamid* the first requirement for an interlocutory injunction is stated in three ways: is the action not frivolous or vexatious; is there a serious question to be tried; is there a real prospect of success at the trial? As Browne L.J. has said[30] the third question cannot have been meant to state a test different from that embodied in the other two questions.

However, if the court asks whether the plaintiff has shown a real prospect of succeeding at the trial it does appear a little easier for there to be an interlocutory mini-trial on the merits of the case. It may be that the court is only considering whether the plaintiff has shown a real possibility of success (rather than a real probability of success as required pre-*Cyanamid*) but some examination of the merits is clearly required and it is all too easy for that examination to become fuller in the face of the court than is theoretically allowable on *Cyanamid* principles.[31] It has thus become possible for Lord Denning and other judges to pay lip-service to *Cyanamid* whilst probably actually deciding cases in the same way they would have been decided pre-*Cyanamid*. The *Cyanamid* principles are really a little artificial and elaborate for pragmatic judges to be controlled by them.[32]

Anton Piller Orders

Lord Denning was to the fore in developing the use of the interlocutory injunction and ancillary orders in a commercial context to meet current needs. The development of modern technology has inevitably led to major problems in areas involving confidential information, patents and copyright and allied matters. In some cases it has been clear that merely claiming an interlocutory injunction is not sufficient. It has been necessary for the plaintiff and his solicitor to seek an *ex parte* order authorising them, with the defendant's permission, to visit the defendant's premises and inspect and take away documents or articles specified in the order. The defendant is ordered to give his permission and if he refuses, then he will need to show cause why he should not be imprisoned for contempt of court, and adverse inferences may be drawn against him. The order needs to be *ex parte* so that the defendant is not forewarned and so able to ensure that vital evidence disappears.

The first reported decision granting such an order was one of Templeman J. in *E.M.I.* v. *Pandit*[33] but *Anton Piller KG* v. *Manufacturing Processes Ltd.*[34] was

---

[28] *Fellowes & Sons* v. *Fisher* [1976] Q.B. 122; *Thomas Marshall (Exports) Ltd.* v. *Guinle* [1979] Ch. 227.

[29] [1979] 1 W.L.R. 1294, 1306–1307.

[30] *Smith* v. *I.L.E.A.* [1978] 1 All E.R. 411; see also Megarry V.-C. in *Mothercare Ltd.* v. *Robson Books Ltd.* [1979] F.S.R. 466.

[31] *Re Lord Cable* [1977] 1 W.L.R. 7, 19; *Smith* v. *I.L.E.A.* [1978] 1 All E.R. 411, 418; *Revlon Inc.* v. *Cripps & Lee Ltd.* [1980] F.S.R. 85; *Thomas Marshall (Exports) Ltd.* v. *Guinle* [1979] Ch. 227.

[32] Generally, see C. Gray [1981] C.L.J. 307.

[33] [1975] 1 W.L.R. 302.

[34] [1976] Ch. 55.

the first occasion on which the Court of Appeal had to determine the legitimacy of such orders. Lord Denning and his colleagues firmly upheld the court's inherent jurisdiction to grant such *ex parte* orders subject to certain safeguards. Many such orders have been made, particularly to deal with video pirates.

A further difficulty arose in *Rank Film Distributors Ltd.* v. *Video Information Centre*.[35] The plaintiffs obtained in *Anton Piller* order to enable them to inspect the defendants' premises and to remove unauthorised films and ordering the defendants, vendors of pirate cassettes, to disclose the names and addresses of their suppliers and customers and the whereabouts of pirate cassettes and master copies known to the defendants. The defendants claimed to avail themselves of the privilege against self-incrimination to avoid having to make disclosures as ordered.

If such a claim were to succeed then the paradox emerges that the worse (*i.e.* the more criminal) the defendants' activities, the less effective is the civil remedy that can be granted. Not surprisingly, Lord Denning rejected such claim. He held "the court will not allow the defendant the benefit of the privilege when to do so would enable him to take advantage of his own fraud or other wrongdoing so as to defeat the just claims of the plaintiff in a civil suit."[36] However, such a broad principle could be envoked by a plaintiff in every civil case as Bridge and Templeman L.JJ. pointed out.

Lord Denning took an alternative view that equity should develop the law by analogy to section 31 of the Theft Act 1968, which in certain cases forces a person to answer questions that may incriminate him but, correspondingly, provides that such answers may not be admissible against him in criminal proceedings.[37] Thus, the defendants should disclose what was ordered but their answers should not be admissible against them in criminal proceedings. However, it is implicit in section 31 that Parliament recognised that in the absence of an express exception the rule against self-incrimination applies. Moreover, it would be revolutionary for a civil court in all civil proceedings to have power to bind a criminal court to find that certain evidence is inadmissible.

The House of Lords and Bridge and Templeman L.JJ. thus rejected Lord Denning's views reluctantly and allowed the defendants to claim the privilege against self-incrimination. However, Parliament in section 72 of the Supreme Court Act 1981 supported Lord Denning's policy view. In proceedings involving infringement of rights pertaining to any intellectual property or passing off a defendant may be forced to answer questions but his answers may not be used against him in criminal proceedings.

Anton Piller orders have become common against video pirates but there are also bootleggers who make their own unauthorised recordings of live performances and so do not infringe the copyright laws. They are guilty of a crime under the Dramatic and Musical Performers' Protection Act 1958. However, it is the civil remedies of damages and injunctions that are of crucial importance to recording companies and performers.

---

[35] [1981] 2 W.L.R. 668.
[36] [1980] 2 All E.R. 273, 281.
[37] *Ibid.*

In *Ex p. Island Records Ltd.*[38] Lord Denning left open the issue whether the criminal statute should be treated as enabling a private civil action to be brought for breach of statutory duty: "the dividing line between the pro-cases and the contra-cases is so blurred and so ill-defined that you might as well toss a coin to decide it. I decline to indulge in such a game of chance." He preferred to enunciate a broad general rule, which does not depend on the scope and language of the criminal statute, that whenever a person's lawful business in fact suffers damage as the result of a contravention by another person of any statutory prohibition the former has a civil claim against the latter for the damage caused beyond that suffered by the public at large. He (and Waller L.J.) thought an injunction and an *Anton Piller* order could be granted.

Shaw L.J. dissented. Since then, Lord Diplock,[39] in a speech concurred in by the other Law Lords, has rejected Lord Denning's broad rule. Lord Diplock stressed that if a plaintiff has no private civil right then, if he relies on the fact that the defendant's acts have caused him special damage beyond that suffered by the public at large, he cannot found a civil action unless he shows that the criminal statute created a legal right to be enjoyed by all the Queen's subjects who wish to avail themselves of it.

Lord Diplock, however, did consider that the Performers' Protection Act conferred upon performers, but not recording companies, private civil rights of action for breach of statutory duty. Vinelott J.[40] has recently indicated that recording companies may be able to proceed against bootleggers and dealers in bootlegged records and cassettes on the basis that the defendants' acts constitute the tort of unlawful interference with the plaintiffs' rights of property under their exclusive contracts with the performing artistes.

The approach of Lord Diplock and Vinelott J. to developing the law to cope with new problems seems preferable to the broader approach of Lord Denning. A broad statement of law, like public policy, is a very unruly horse: it is difficult to ride when you have mounted it, you never know where it will carry you, and it is prone to wander into places where it ought not to be.

Mareva Injunctions

Lord Denning's development of Mareva injunctions has been of tremendous significance. Take the case of foreign charterers of a ship. They are liable for £200,000 hire under the charterparty. They have £200,000 in an English bank account. If the English charterers bring an action for the £200,000 the foreign defendants can, in a trice, transfer the funds by telegraphic transfer to Switzerland, for example, and render the action fruitless. Can the plaintiffs therefore obtain an *ex parte* injunction to freeze the defendants' bank account? The traditional answer was that of Cotton L.J. in *Lister* v. *Stubbs*,[41] "You cannot get an injunction to restrain a man who is alleged to be a debtor from

---

[38] [1978] Ch. 122, 134–135. See also his views in *Nagle* v. *Fielden* [1966] 2 Q.B. 633 where he was prepared to protect a woman's right to work so that she was not automatically refused a trainer's licence by the Jockey Club on the grounds of her sex. The Australian High Court has taken advantage of these views in *Buckley* v. *Tutty* (1971) 125 C.L.R. 353.

[39] *Lonrho* v. *Shell Petroleum Co.* [1982] A.C. 173.

[40] *R.C.A. Corp.* v. *Pollard* [1982] 2 All E.R. 468.

[41] (1890) 45 Ch.D. 1, 14..ql[42] [1975] 1 W.L.R. 1093

parting with his property." A plaintiff beneficiary can get an injunction to restrain his trustee from parting with property alleged to belong to the trust, but a mere alleged debtor cannot be restrained from dealing freely with his own property until he is bankrupted.

However, in *Nippon Yusen Kaisha* v. *Karageorgis*[42] Lord Denning, supported by his two colleagues, did make an *ex parte* order freezing the English bank account of a foreign defendant. No cases were considered, reliance being placed upon section 45 of the Supreme Court of Judicature (Consolidation) Act 1925. This, like section 23(8) of the Supreme Court of Judicature Act 1873 in force when the *Lister* v. *Stubbs* line of authority was created, empowers the court to grant an interlocutory injunction "in all cases in which it appears to the court to be just and convenient to do so."

Lord Denning applied this at its bare face value, though, traditionally, it had been considered as procedural only and as not enlarging the jurisdiction or power of the court to grant interlocutory injunctions.[43] It was "just and convenient" to freeze the foreigner's English bank account.

Lord Denning endorsed this approach in *Mareva* v. *International Bulkcarriers*,[44] though having the *Lister* v. *Stubbs* line of authority cited by counsel in his *ex parte* application. Full *inter partes* argument was heard in *The Pertamina*.[45] Lord Denning (with whom Orr L.J. agreed in a court of two judges) stated,

> "So far as concerns defendants who are within the jurisdiction and have assets here, it is well-established that the court should not, in advance of any order or judgment allow the creditor to seize any of the money or goods of the debtor or to use any legal process to do so. . . . I do not think the *Lister* v. *Stubbs* line of authority should be applied to cases where a defendant is out of the jurisdiction but has assets in this country."[46]

To these cases the ancient customary courts' old process of foreign attachment should be applied via the modern procedure of an interlocutory injunction. Furthermore, to obtain such an injunction, freezing the English assets (whether money or goods) of the foreign defendant, it was not necessary for the case to be so plain that the plaintiff could obtain summary judgment under R.S.C. Order 14. It was only necessary for the plaintiff to show that he had a good arguable case "in conformity with the test as to the granting of injunctions whenever it is just and convenient as laid down by the House of Lords in *American Cyanamid* v. *Ethicon Ltd.*"[47]

Shortly afterwards, Lord Denning applied the *Mareva* principle in *The Siskina*[48] and an appeal was heard by the House of Lords.[49] However, counsel

---

[42] [1975] 1 W.L.R. 1093
[43] See *North London Ry. Co.* v. *Great Northern Ry. Co.* (1883) 11 Q.B.D. 30 and also *Pivovaroff* v. *Chernbaeff* (1978) 16 S.A.S.R. 329 where a similar South Australian provision was held procedural only.
[44] [1975] 2 Lloyd's Rep. 509.
[45] [1978] Q.B. 644.
[46] *Ibid.* p. 659.
[47] *Ibid.* p. 661.
[48] [1977] 3 All E.R. 806.
[49] [1979] A.C. 210.

for the appellants, perhaps mindful of how useful the *Mareva* injunction was
for those practising commercial law, did not seek to challenge the broad
Mareva principle (and draw an analogy with the House of Lords decision in
Pettitt v. *Pettitt*[50] which had rejected Lord Denning's use of section 17 of the
Married Women's Property Act at its bare face value[51]). Instead, he
persuaded the House of Lords to allow the appeal on the narrow ground that
a *Mareva* injunction cannot be granted if an English Court has no jurisdiction
to give final judgment on the substantive issue between the parties. In *The
Siskina* all parties were foreigners and leave to serve the writ out of the
jurisdiction under R.S.C., Order 11 was not then possible.[52]

Lord Hailsham emphasised the anomaly that a plaintiff under *Mareva* had
greater rights against a foreign defendant than against an English defendant
so that "sooner or later the courts or the legislature will have to choose
between two alternatives. Either the position of a plaintiff making a claim
against an English-based defendant will have to be altered or the principle of
the *Mareva* cases will have to be modified."[53]

Lord Denning responded in *Chartered Bank* v. *Daklouche*[54] by granting an
injunction freezing the English assets of a Lebanese defendant for the time
being based in England: "if there is a danger that he may abscond or that the
assets or moneys may disappear and be taken out of the reach of creditors, a
Mareva injunction can be granted." Thus Megarry V.-C. in *Barclay-Johnson* v.
Yuill[55] felt bound to hold that[56] "the essence of the jurisdiction is the risk of
assets being removed from the jurisdiction . . . [57] with the consequent danger
of the plaintiff being deprived of the fruits of the judgment he is seeking."
Thus, an injunction could be granted against an English defendant if there
were a danger of him absconding with his assets and not honouring any
judgment against him. However, for English defendants, Megarry V.-C.
emphasised,[58] "I would regard the *Lister* principle as remaining the rule, and
the *Mareva* doctrine as constituting a limited exception to it."

In *Prince Abdul Rahman* v. *Abu-Taha*[59] Lord Denning approved *Barclay-
Johnson* stating,

> "I would hold that a *Mareva* injunction can be granted against a man
> even though he is based in this country if the circumstances are such
> that there is a danger of his absconding, or a danger of the assets being
> removed out of the jurisdiction or disposed of within the jurisdiction or

---

[50] [1970] A.C. 777.
[51] In *Bremer Vulkan* [1981] A.C. 909, 995 Lord Scarman stated "The Court of Appeal [in *North
London Ry. Co.* v. *Great Northern Ry. Co.* (1883) 11 Q.B.D. 30] decided that the section [in the
Judicature Act] was to be construed as procedural in its purpose and effect. The section does
not extend the power of the court to cases where there is no legal or equitable right to be
protected." In view of *Lister* v. *Stubbs* can a plaintiff creditor have some special right over and
above other creditors?
[52] Now the Civil Jurisdiction and Judgments Act 1982, s.25 gives effect to Lord Denning's
policy views and enables interim relief to be granted in the absence of substantive
proceedings in England.
[53] [1979] A.C. 210, 261.
[54] [1980] 1 All E.R. 205, 210.
[55] [1980] 3 All E.R. 190.
[56] *Ibid.* p. 194.
[57] *Ibid.* p. 197.
[58] *Ibid.* p. 195.
[59] [1980] 3 All E.R. 409, 412.

otherwise dealt with so that there is a danger that the plaintiff if he gets judgment will not be able to get it satisfied."

Waller and Dunn L.JJ. agreed.

The customary form of order restrains the defendant from

"removing from the jurisdiction or otherwise disposing of or dealing with any of his assets within the jurisdiction including and in particular [certain specified asset(s)] save in so far as such assets do not exceed in value the sum of [the amount of the plaintiff's liquidated or unliquidated claim.]"[60]

The clause "or otherwise disposing of or dealing with any of his assets within the jurisdiction" is to guard against the possibility of a disposal to a friend or a collaborator within the jurisdiction such that the asset is unavailable to satisfy any judgment because the friend takes the asset outside the jurisdiction.[61]

Parliament in section 37(3) of the Supreme Court Act 1981 has now enacted

"The power under subsection (1) to grant an injunction ['in all cases in which it appears to the court to be just and convenient to do so'] restraining a party to any proceedings from removing from the jurisdiction, or otherwise dealing with, assets located within that jurisdiction shall be exercisable in cases where that party is, as well as in cases where he is not, domiciled, resident or present within that jurisdiction."

This statutory recognition[62] of the jurisdiction to grant *Mareva* injunctions leaves some matters still to be clarified. Lord Denning treated the words "or otherwise dealing with" as having a very wide meaning so that "the *Mareva* jurisdiction extends to cases where there is a danger that the assets will be dissipated in this country as well as by removal out of the jurisdiction."[63]

Other judges, such as Ackner L.J.,[64] Megarry V.-C.[65] and Robert Goff J.[66] considered that the jurisdiction is designed just to prevent judgments from being rendered ineffective by the removal of the defendant's assets from the jurisdiction; the words "or otherwise dealing with" are inserted in the court order merely to prevent the defendant from transferring the assets to a collaborator who would then remove them from the jurisdiction. If the assets are not likely to be spirited out of the jurisdiction,

"then the plaintiff, like all others with claims against the defendant, must run the risk common to all, that the defendant may dissipate his

---

[60] [1981] 2 All E.R. 565, 573.
[61] *Iraqi M.O.D.* v. *Arcepey* [1981] Q.B. 65, 71; *Barclay-Johnson* v. *Yuill* [1980] 3 All E.R. 190, 194. It will also have the effect of preventing disposals which might not be capable of being set aside under the proper law of insolvency.
[62] See Ackner and Stephenson L.JJ. in *Bekhor* v. *Bilton* [1981] 2 All E.R. 565, 576, 586, Lord Denning in *Z. Ltd.* v. *A.* [1982] 1 All E.R. 556, 561.
[63] *Z. Ltd.* v. *A.* [1982] 1 All E.R. 556, 561.
[64] *Beckhor* v. *Bilton* [1981] 2 All E.R. 565, 577.
[65] *Barclay-Johnson* v. *Yuill* [1980] Q.B. 65, 72.
[66] *Iraqi M.O.D.* v. *Arcepey* [1981] Q.B. 65, 72.

assets, or consume them in discharging other liabilities, and so leave nothing with which to satisfy any judgment."[67]

"The plaintiff, like other creditors must obtain his judgment and then enforce it. He cannot prevent the defendant from disposing of his assets *pendente lite* merely because he fears that by the time he obtains judgment the defendant will have no assets against which the judgment can be enforced . . . .The *Mareva* jurisdiction was not intended to rewrite the English law of insolvency. The purpose of the jurisdiction was not to improve the position of claimants in an insolvency but simply to prevent the injustice of a defendant removing his assets from the jurisdiction which might otherwise have been available to satisfy a judgment."[68]

However, Eveleigh and Kerr L.JJ.[69] have supported Lord Denning's view that the *Mareva* jurisdiction extends to cases where assets are in danger of dissipation within the jurisdiction so that,

"the jurisdiction may properly be exercisable in many cases which are not limited to situations where the defendant is foreign or only has some tenuous connection with this country. . . . On the other hand, it would not be properly exercisable against the majority of defendants. . . . Defendants are generally persons or concerns who are established within the jurisdiction in the sense of having assets here which they could not, or would not wish to dissipate merely in order to avoid some judgment which seems likely to be given against them; either because they have property here, such as a house or flat on which their ordinary way of life depends, or because they have an established business, or other assets which they would be unlikely to liquidate simply in order to avoid a judgment. . . . In each case the court will have to form a view on which side of the line each particular case falls, but bearing in mind that the great value of this jurisdiction must not be debased by allowing it to become something which is invoked simply to obtain security for a judgment in advance, and still less as a means of pressurising defendants into settlements."[70]

The fact that a defendant with a bank account subject to a *Mareva* injunction can obtain leave from the court to make payments thereout in the ordinary course of business or of living[71] should not encourage the grant of such injunction in the first place. It thus seems that the *Lister* v. *Stubbs* principle should still govern the vast majority of cases involving English defendants who are not likely to remove themselves from England with their assets.

Injunctions and Supreme Court Act 1981, s.37(1)

Section 45(1) of the Supreme Court of Judicature (Consolidation) Act 1925 states, "The High Court may grant a mandamus or an injunction or appoint a receiver by an interlocutory order in all cases in which it appears to the

---

[67] *Barclay-Johnson* v. *Yuill* [1980] 3 All E.R. 190, 194, *per* Megarry V.-C.
[68] *Bekhor* v. *Bilton* [1981] 2 All E.R. 565, 577, *per* Ackner L.J.
[69] In *Z. Ltd.* v. *A.* [1982] 1 All E.R. 565.
[70] *Ibid.* p. 572.
[71] *Iraqi M.O.D.* v. *Arcepey* [1981] Q.B. 65; *Z. Ltd.* v. *A.* (*supra*).

court to be just and convenient so to do." This has been replaced by section
37(1) of the Supreme Court Act 1981 which states, "The High Court may by
order (whether interlocutory or final) grant an injunction or appoint a
receiver in all cases in which it appears to be just and convenient to do so."

It is well established by House of Lords authority (such as *The Siskina*[72]) on
section 45 that

> "a right to obtain an interlocutory injunction is not a cause of action. It
> cannot stand on its own. It is dependent on there being a pre-existing
> cause of action against the defendant arising out of an invasion, actual
> or threatened, by him of a legal or equitable right of the plaintiff."[73]

Lord Denning in *Chief Constable of Kent* v. *Verdon-Roe*,[74] however, held that
section 37 plainly confers a new and extensive jurisdiction far wider than
anything known before; it is no longer necessary that the injunction should
be ancillary to an action claiming a legal or equitable right; the claim can
stand on its own; the claimant need only have sufficient interest to warrant
asking for an injunction and does not need to have a legal or equitable right
or interest; *The Siskina* would be decided differently today.

Such a surprising view was, unsurprisingly, rejected by his colleagues,
Donaldson and Slade L. JJ., who still require a claimant to have a legal or
equitable right. The problem was whether the Chief Constable had such a
right to enable him to obtain an injunction freezing the proceeds of forgeries
in the defendant's bank account. He had a legal right to seize and detain
stolen goods as held by the Court of Appeal in *Chic Fashions Ltd.* v. *Jones*.[75]
Did he have an analogous right in relation to intangible property? Donaldson
L.J. was, but Slade L.J. was not, prepared to go to the lengths of holding that
where the Chief Constable believed, on reasonable grounds, that moneys in a
bank account were traceable to property, which had been obtained from
another in breach of the criminal law, he had a right to demand that such
moneys be paid to him. The fact that the victim of such crime had such a
right capable of protection by injunction should not be decisive since the
victim might well not be in a position to take such action, *e.g.* a frail old lady
who had lost most of her money or one of many victims who, singly, had not
lost great sums of money.

Conclusion

As this last case shows, Lord Denning was too eager to develop the
flexibility of judicial discretion and too ready to develop the law in great
leaps and bounds when small steady steps are normally all that is required.
Development of the law where necessary seems better assured in the hands of
his successor as Master of the Rolls, Sir John Donaldson, if the above case is
anything to go by.[76] It is also to be hoped that the stint of any Master of the
Rolls should not exceed eight to ten years before elevation to the tranquillity
of the House of Lords in accordance with past practice. The prestige and

---

[72] [1979] A.C. 210. It now suffices if there is a substantive action justiciable abroad: Civil
Jurisdiction and Judgments Act 1982, s.25.
[73] *Ibid.* p. 256.
[74] [1982] 3 All E.R. 36.
[75] [1968] 2 Q.B. 299.
[76] See also *Evans Construction Co. Ltd.* v. *Charrington & Co.* [1983] 1 All E.R. 310.

burdens of the post are such that, as the years pass by, it must become easier and easier to become too self-assured and too ready to leap to what is regarded as a self-evident conclusion. It must become easier and easier to give way to the temptation of giving shorter judgments based on generalised principles and to dispensing with a thorough researched analysis of the authorities. Indeed, Lord Denning's attitude to earlier inconvenient authorities became more and more cavalier as the years passed by. He would be in no position to complain if future Masters of the Rolls treated his decisions equally cavalierly. It is to be hoped that they will not do so.

CHAPTER 4

Family Matters

M.D.A. FREEMAN

The Enigma of Lord Denning

Lord Denning is a bundle of contradictions. In *The Due Process of Law*, he expresses his contempt for "divorce work." "Thank Goodness," he writes there, "I only did Divorce for 18 months."[1] Despite these feelings there is no doubting the impact that Lord Denning has made on every feature of the law relating to the family, nor the pleasure that fashioning a generation's family law has given him. He professes to believe in women's equality yet he has been responsible for some of the most sexist and backward-looking rulings of any of the post-war judiciary. These are contradictions that demand an explanation. One answer is to try to show the paradoxes to be illusory: that the reforming zeal in matrimonial affairs springs directly from his perception of the old law as "sordid in the extreme"[2]; that his views about women's equality are at best unsophisticated and at worst not genuinely held. Another putative explanation would locate the various contradictory opinions at different points in his career. There is some truth in both these answers. It is also true, and this I think is rather more important, that Lord Denning has held no consistent theory as such about the family or family law. He believes in some rudimentary form of justice in which the protection of the weak is a dominant theme and his decisions are attempts, as he sees it, to dispense such justice. The result is that sometimes it is easy to agree with him and at other times virulently to take objection either to his conclusions or methods or both.

Moral Fundamentalism

Lord Denning may lack a full-blown philosophy but he certainly has a world-view (to call it an ideology may be to overplay it). It is important to say something about this because the family is central to it. Lord Denning is a moral fundamentalist. Moral fundamentalism[3] is part of the ethos of conservatism. It is a world-view firmly located within the traditional middle-classes.[4] It has been suggested that commitment to such values is sustained by a "sense of Englishness."[5] "Englishness" is built around a

---

[1] *The Due Process of Law* (Butterworths, London, 1980), p. 189.
[2] *Ibid.*
[3] See R. Wallis, "Moral Indignation and The Media: An Analysis of The National Viewers' and Listeners' Association" (Sociology, Vol. 10), pp. 271–295.
[4] See S. Ranulf, *Moral Indignation and Middle Class Psychology* (Copenhagen, Munskgaard, 1938).
[5] See S. Hall *et al*, *Policing The Crisis: Mugging, the State and Law and Order* (Macmillan, London, 1978).

cluster of core beliefs, perhaps best summarised as the "Protestant Ethic."[6]
These beliefs, about the value of hard work, delayed gratification, honesty,
social discipline, respectability, etc., are inextricably bound up with the
family, for it is there that these constraints are taught and generated. We live
in an age which is seeing the erosion of some of these traditional values.
Traditionalists are anxious about what they dub "permissiveness" and their
anxiety tends to be focussed on the activities of the young, their perceived
delinquency, promiscuity, disrespect for authority, etc., and on the family
which is the primary institution concerned with the socialisation of the
young. They see the Women's Movement as a distinct moral and political
challenge. Its rise has reinforced fears about the destruction of traditional
values and disintegration of the family. There is, accordingly, a concern with
pornography, abortion, divorce, genetic engineering which has spawned a
myriad of populist protest movements.[7] These movements find support and
political expression in the writings and speeches of the New Right. The New
Right expresses "the interests of small business-shopkeepers, small entrep-
reneurs, the family firms."[8] In economic terms the New Right stands for an
expanded role for the market and greater economic freedom.[9] Yet it is only
an illusory paradox that at the same time it should call for less social
freedom, since freedom of the market place pre-supposes a re-establishment
of traditional values and hence of the centrality of the family.

Lord Denning by background and temperament is a natural ally. He has
never disguised his admiration of Raymond Blackburn and his moral
crusades or his affection for "our Prime Minister."[10] He oozes traditional
Englishness, as a reading of his *Family Story*[11] amply testifies. His opinions on
matters relating to personal life, to women, to the family are very much those
of the traditional middle-classes. His views about the equality of women have
mellowed, though they have not matured, since he gave the Eleanor
Rathbone Memorial lecture in 1960. What he said on that occasion
encapsulates so much of his basic ideology that it merits quotation at length.

> "We ought to remember that there has been one time previously in the
> history of the world when women achieved a considerable measure of
> equality. It was in the Roman Empire, and it should serve as a warning
> of the dangers to which equality may give rise. . . . This freedom . . .
> proved to be disastrous to the Roman society. Morals decayed. The
> marital tie became the laxest the Western World has seen. Bertrand
> Russell has expressed the position in a sentence: 'Women, who had been
> virtuous slaves, became free and dissolute; divorce became common; the
> rich ceased to have children.' This decay of morality was indeed one of
> the factors in the fall of the Roman Empire. Let us look upon this and
> take heed."[12]

[6] See Max Weber, *The Protestant Ethic and The Spirit of Capitalism* (translated by Talcott Parsons, 1930).
[7] See D. Cliff, "Religion, Morality and the Middle Class" in R. King and N. Nugent, *Respectable Rebels* (Hodder & Stoughton, London, 1979).
[8] *Per* A. Gamble, *The Conservative Nation* (Routledge, Kegan Paul, London, 1974), p. 130.
[9] See M. Friedman, *Capitalism and Freedom* (University of Chicago Press, Chicago, 1962).
[10] *The Due Process of Law* p. 201.
[11] Lord Denning, *The Family Story* (Butterworths, London, 1981). His choice of music and literature (*ibid*. pp. 249–50) is quintessentially English.
[12] *The Equality of Women* (University of Liverpool Press, Liverpool, 1960), pp. 3–4.

His pronouncements on sexual morality, prudish yet sometimes almost prurient, betray, in Robert Stevens's words,[13] "a strong streak of nineteenth-century morality," but this is a morality still firmly embedded within the moral centre of society. A few examples will assist. On the artificial insemination of married women Lord Denning had the following warning:

> " . . . if this practice became widespread it would strike at the stability and security of family life; it would strike at the roots of our civilisation. I would say to the doctors 'Where by your science are you leading us? Seek to relieve suffering by all means, but do not do it by secrecy and deception.' 'For what is a man profited if he shall gain the whole world and lose his own soul?' "[14]

As ever, Lord Denning is fond of hyperbole as well as of adorning his arguments with biblical lines.

A second illustration is to be found in his judgment in the 1973 *Blackburn* case. He quotes Blackburn on pornography: "powerful propaganda for promiscuity" and he continues:

> "So it is for perversions. To those who come under its influence, it is altogether bad. We have been shown examples of it. The court below declined to look at them. We felt it our duty to do so, distasteful as it is. They are disgusting in the extreme. Prominent are the pictures. As examples of art of coloured photography they would earn the highest praise. As examples of the sordid side of life, they are deplorable."[15]

The language is not unreminiscent of the legal moralism which permeates Lord Devlin's writings on the enforcement of morals.[16]

Of the two examples I have used thus far one comes from a speech in a House of Lords debate and the second from a case which was concerned with police accountability for discretionary decision-making. But the same concern for traditional values is to be found in many of Lord Denning's decisions in the family law area. A good example is his judgment in *Bravery* v. *Bravery* in 1954. The case concerned a husband who had himself sterilised; Lord Denning thought that this was without his wife's consent though the majority found that there was no evidence that the operation was performed against her wishes. The wife petitioned for divorce on the grounds of cruelty. Lord Denning's response took him on a frolic of his own far outside what was necessary for the case. Having described sterilisation as "a shocking thing"[17] he adds:

> "When it is done with the man's consent for a just cause, it is quite

---

[13] *Law And Politics: The House of Lords As A Judicial Body, 1800–1976* (Weidenfeld & Nicolson, London, 1979), p. 500.

[14] Hansard, H.L., Vol. 206, col.943. See also his view in homosexuality: "it strikes at the integrity of the human race": *ibid.* col. 807.

[15] [1973] 1 Q.B. 241, 248.

[16] *The Enforcement of Morals* (Oxford U.P., London, 1965). Lord Devlin's views on judicial creativity are, however, very different from Lord Denning's. He wrote: "It is quite wrong for the judiciary to think they are responsible for the moral health of the community in some way." Judges, he thought, should be "impartial narrators of what the law is saying." See *The Times*, June 28, 1972 and *The Judge* (London, Oxford U.P., 1979) Chap. 1.

[17] [1954] 3 All E.R. 59.

lawful, for instance, when it is done to prevent transmission of a hereditary disease: but when it is done without just cause or excuse, it is unlawful, even though the man consents to it. Take a case where a sterilisation operation is done so as to enable a man to have the pleasure of sexual intercourse without shouldering the responsibilities attaching to it. The operation then is plainly injurious to the public interest."[18]

Lord Denning had clearly concluded that a voluntary sterilisation was criminal before he sought any support in legal authorities. It is a common criticism of judges that their so-called reasoning is more accurately characterised as rationalisation.[19] This is a criticism to which Lord Denning is particularly susceptible and his judgment in *Bravery's* case is, I think, a rather good illustration of this process at work. He appeals to analogies: an 1882 case on prize-fighting[20] and *Donovan's* case in 1934 holding that a girl of seventeen could not consent to a caning by a man for his gratification.[21] Neither case he relies upon is without its difficulties and neither is a helpful analogy, as both the other judges[22] in *Bravery* v. *Bravery* recognised. Lord Denning thought they were apposite because, he noted, in both criminal law and family law regard had to be had to the "public interest."[23] A husband who underwent an operation for sterilisation without just cause or excuse was striking "at the very root of the marriage relationship,"[24] and divorce courts should no more countenance such behaviour than, he argued, criminal courts did.

Cleary v. *Cleary* may be a less colourful example but once more it shows Lord Denning's views on sexual morality most clearly. At the centre of the case was the statutory construction of the word "and" in section 2(1)(a) of the Divorce Reform Act 1969: one of the facts which raises a presumption that a marriage has broken down irretrievably is that the respondent has committed adultery *and*[25] the petitioner finds it intolerable to live with the respondent. One first instance judge had interpreted "and" disjunctively,[26] another conjunctively.[27] The Court of Appeal in *Cleary* thought the disjunctive interpretation the right one. Whether this is the right view is considered later in this chapter. What concerns me here is Lord Denning's *obiter* comment

> "In *Rayden on Divorce* it is suggested (referring to an extra-judicial lecture by Sir Jocelyn Simon) '. . . it may even be his own adultery which leads him to find it intolerable to live with the respondent.' I cannot accept that suggestion. . . . "[28]

He then goes on to give an illustration of what he means. He poses a

---

[18] *Ibid.* He returned to the subject and the case in a debate in the House of Lords. See Hansard, H.L., Vol. 206, col. 807.
[19] See Hutcheson, *14 Cornell Law Q. 274.* See also K. Llewellyn, *Jurisprudence* (1962), p. 58.
[20] *R.* v. *Coney* [1882] Q.B.D. 534.
[21] [1934] 2 K.B. 498.
[22] Evershed M.R. and Hodson L.J.
[23] [1954] 3 All E.R. 59, 68.
[24] *Ibid.*
[25] My emphasis.
[26] Lloyd-Jones J. in *Goodrich* v. *Goodrich* [1971] 1 W.L.R. 1142.
[27] Faulks J. in *Roper* v. *Roper* [1972] 1 W.L.R. 1314.
[28] [1974] 1 All E.R. 498, 501.

hypothetical case which on examination does not stand up to scrutiny. It is of an adultery committed five years previously by a wife whose husband has forgiven and reinstated her. He then commits adultery. "He may say," says Lord Denning, "that he finds it intolerable to live with his wife, but that is palpably untrue."[29] A husband in these circumstances could not rely on his wife's adultery: that much is clear from the statute which allows for six months' post-adultery cohabitation only.[30] But that is why his divorce petition would fail. Lord Denning has in fact invoked a red herring. It is certainly arguable that a man could successfully petition for divorce where his wife had committed adultery (say) three months previously and he now found it intolerable to live with her because he preferred someone else. Although Lord Denning was favourable to the passing of the divorce reform legislation in 1969 and 1970,[31] he clearly resiles from some of its implications. It offends his code of morality that a man can divorce his adulterous wife not because he finds the adultery intolerable but because he would prefer to live with another woman. It is accordingly surprising that he found the two limbs of section 2(1)(a) to be "independent." But that is another matter. The *obiter* remark already quoted is an example of a gratuitous Denning remark which fits neither the letter nor the spirit of the legislation, but which is perfectly consonant with a rather puritanical stance on sexual morality.

Lord Denning and Women

Lord Denning clearly sees himself as a champion of the cause of women. That much is clear from *The Due Process of Law*[32] as well as from various radio interviews given by him in the last few years. He believes women have now attained complete equality; that they are no longer dependent on their husbands. He believes "Plato's ideal is substantially attained."[33] However, he accepts totally sex-role stereotyping. "The principal task in life of women is to bear and rear children." Men "of necessity" cannot devote as much time to child-rearing. Men and women have different "spheres." "She in her sphere does work as useful as man does in his." "Of all women's responsibilities, the chief is to maintain a social and healthy family life in the land. To this chief responsibility all other interests must be subordinated." These statements were written in 1979.[34] It is galling that Lord Denning must treat a particular ideological view of relationships between the sexes as some kind of unproblematic, transcultural, transhistorical concept. Lord Denning would agree with a view dominant amongst lawyers that the law plays a "minor role in creating conditions which are hoped to be conducive to the successful creation of families."[35]

This view I would argue is a complete distortion of reality. Not only does

---

[29] *Ibid.*
[30] Matrimonial Causes Act 1973, s.2(1).
[31] See *The Times*, October 1, 1971. Earlier views are found in *The Changing Law* (Stevens, London, 1953), pp. 120–122 and Hansard, H.L., Vol. 250, cols. 405–407 (May 22, 1963) when he warmly welcomed the Matrimonial Causes and Reconciliation Bill.
[32] *The Due Process of Law* p. 205.
[33] *Ibid.* p. 201.
[34] *Ibid.* pp. 194, 201.
[35] Per J. Eekelaar, *Family Law and Social Policy* (Weidenfeld and Nicolson, London, 1978), p. xxvii.

the law serve to reproduce social order but it actually constitutes and defines that order. The legal form is one of the main forms of social practice through which actual relationships embodying sexual stratification have been expressed. Law defines the character and creates the institutions and social relationships within which the family operates. The legal system is a cultural underpinning of patriarchy.[36] Looked at in this light, is Lord Denning the great reformer or rather an obstacle to reform? The significance of some of his reforms must be considered in due course. What I consider now are some of Lord Denning's judicial remarks which have helped to constitute and bolster up the patriarchy.

In *Peake* v. *Automative Products Ltd.*[37] in 1977 he had to consider a factory arrangement by which, when work stopped at 4.25 p.m., women were allowed to start leaving (as were handicapped men) but men had to wait until 4.30 p.m. A man complained that this was an infringement of the Sex Discrimination Act 1975. The Employment Appeal Tribunal had held it was. The Court of Appeal reversed this ruling. Lord Denning thought it very wrong if the statute were thought to obliterate the differences between men and women or to do away with all the chivalry and courtesy which mankind were expected to give to womankind. *The Times* headed its report: "Chivalry Not Ousted by Sex Discrimination Act."[38] Lord Denning thought it right to take account of what he called, "natural differences of sex"[39] in interpreting an Act of Parliament. In a later case *Ministry of Defence* v. *Jeremiah*[40] Lord Denning departed from this view (as noted already his very personal sense of justice often requires inconsistency) and ruled that chivalry and good administration could not be a defence against alleged discrimination. But, by then, Judge Ruttle in *Gray* v. *El Vino and Mitchell* had used Lord Denning's chivalry doctrine to hold that a wine bar which forces "ladies" to drink only while sitting down and not therefore at the bar treats men differently but not less favourably.[41] The press trivialised this: "El Vino Levitas" thundered *The Times*.[42] Even its news report took the matter as a joke. But it is decisions like these, putting women firmly in their place, which legitimate other discriminatory practices against them. Sir James Fitzjames Stephen recognised that protection and submission were correlatives.[43] It may be doubted whether Lord Denning does.

Lord Denning's judgment in *Wachtel* v. *Wachtel* is of such overwhelming significance that judges in subsequent cases have had to warn that certain of the statements of the Master of the Rolls are not legislative formulations.[44] I am not here concerned with the substantive law issues of *Wachtel*: reference is made to them later in this chapter. It may be, however, that Lord Denning's justification of the one-third rule will be remembered and quoted long after

---

[36] See M.D.A. Freeman, "Violence Against Women: Does The Legal System Provide Solutions Or Itself Constitute the Problem?" (1980) 7 Br. J. of Law and Soc. 215.

[37] [1978] Q.B. 233.

[38] *The Times*, July 5, 1977.

[39] [1978] 1 All E.R. 106 at p. 108.

[40] [1980] I.C.R. 13, 25 ("the only sound ground" for *Peake* was "de minimis").

[41] *The Times*, May 27, 1978.

[42] *Ibid.*

[43] *Liberty, Equality, Fraternity* (Smith, Elder, London, 1873), p. 286.

[44] See, for example, *Chamberlain* v. *Chamberlain* [1973] 1 W.L.R. 1557 *Robinson* v. *Robinson* (1981) 2 F.L.R. 1 (decided in 1973); *Evans* v. *Evans* (1981) 2 F.L.R. 33; *Sharp* v. *Sharp* (1981) 11 Fam. Law 121.

the substance of *Wachtel* has been eroded or torpedoed. He saw "much good sense" in the "one-third rule."

> "When a marriage breaks up, there will thenceforward be two households instead of one. The husband will have to go out to work all day and must get some woman to look after the house—either a wife, if he remarries, or a housekeeper, if he does not. He will also have to provide maintenance for the children. The wife will not usually have so much expense. She may go out to work herself, but she will not usually employ a housekeeper. She will do most of the housework herself, perhaps with some help. Or she may remarry, in which case her new husband will provide for her. In any case, when there are two households, the greater expense will, in most cases, fall on the husband rather than the wife. As a start has to be made somewhere, it seems to us that in the past it was quite fair to start with one-third."[45]

He says "in the past" (it was in fact ecclesiastical court practice) but he went on to argue that for the future one third for the ex-wife was to be the starting point, if not the end of calculations.

It is worth examining his reasoning. It is totally unrealistic. Most men whose marriages break up do not employ housekeepers. And, even if this argument were relevant, it would not explain why wives are not allowed the value of their housekeeping services. The fact that women do not employ housekeepers hardly seems a justification for cutting down the share of an ex-wife. Lord Denning makes a number of assumptions. It is doubtful whether any of them is right. First, that all women perform household duties and that no men do housework. Secondly, that only fathers maintain their children.[46] Implicit is the idea that mothers do not undertake remunerative employment.[47] Thirdly, Lord Denning is making the assumption that housework is not real work.[48] None of these assumptions is anything other than outdated, incorrect and patently chauvinist.

On a number of occasions Lord Denning has made it clear what he regards as the role and responsibilities which women are expected to fulfil. They are expected to be wives and mothers. Their place is in the matrimonial home looking after their husbands and bringing up their children. He has been in the forefront of judicial movements to treat cohabiting couples as if they were married.[49] The rhetoric used is of protection but it looks very much as if the judges, with Lord Denning very much in the vanguard, are trying to prevent women escaping from the consequences of marriage.[50] Those who do not marry must have marriage thrust upon them.[51] Nor is Lord Denning unwilling to penalise women who do not satisfy his standards of what being a

---

[45] [1973] Fam. 72, 94.
[46] In 1980 the state paid out £419 million to support the families of divorced and separated women.
[47] 49.6 *per cent.* of married females were in remunerative employment in 1979 (*Social Trends* no. 13, Table 4.3 (1983) London, H.M.S.O.)
[48] A myth effectively demolished by C. Delphy, *The Main Enemy* (Women's Research and Resources Centre Publications, London, 1977).
[49] See M.D.A. Freeman and C.M. Lyon, *Cohabitation Without Marriage: An Essay In Law and Social Policy* (Gower Press, Aldershot, 1983).
[50] See D.L. Barker, "The Regulation of Marriage: Repressive Benevolence" in G. Littlejohn *et al* (eds.), *Power And The State* (Croom Helm, London, 1978), p. 239.
[51] When their living arrangements and attitudes conform to stereotypes of married couples.

good wife involves. Thus, in *Re L (Infants)* in 1962 he reversed the decision of Plowman J. to give care and control of two small girls who were wards of court to the mother who was solely responsible for the breakdown of the marriage and was committing adultery. Care and control was transferred to the father. Lord Denning reasoned that if the girls were committed to the mother's care there was "no chance of reconciliation, whereas if they remain with their father, there may be some hope . . . that she will return for the sake of the children themselves: and if only that would happen, their welfare would be ensured in the best way of all."[52] In effect he was holding out an inducement to the mother: if you want your children you must return to your husband. It was common to use the law of child custody for deterrent purposes in the nineteenth century but, with concepts of matrimonial fault already on the wane and those of the paramountcy of child welfare increasingly dominant, Lord Denning's reasoning in 1962 was not acceptable. He clearly saw his decision as having a deterrent effect on other women, if not on this particular mother for he continued,

> "It would be an exceedingly bad example if it were thought that a mother could go off with another man and then claim as of right to say: 'Oh well, they are my two little girls and I am entitled to take them with me. I can not only leave my home and break it up and leave their father, but I can take the children with me and the law will not say me nay.' It seems to me that a mother must realise that if she leaves and breaks up her home in this way she cannot as of right demand to take the children from the father."[53]

It is significant that twice in this judgment he used the expression "as of right" and he went on to refer to the case as "a matter of simple justice" between mother and father: "the claims of justice," he insisted, "cannot be overlooked."[54] The matter should have been characterised, as it is now,[55] as one concerned with children's welfare. Lord Denning's determination to punish a loose woman got the better of him rather as it was to do in the notorious Bradford Teachers' Training College case.[56]

He has then a clear idea of what sexual morals are appropriate to good mothers. He is equally clear on what work tasks can be expected of women in marriage in the normal course of events. A good example of his thinking is found in the case of *Button* v. *Button*.[57] The husband had purchased a cottage in bad repair in his name alone. Both spouses did a lot of work on the cottage. The wife helped with painting and decorating and with the garden. The cottage was eventually sold and a profit of £1,000 was made. A divorce had taken place and the ex-wife now sought to establish under section 17 of the Married Women's Property Act 1882 that she was entitled to a half-share in property purchased in the ex-husband's name alone with the proceeds of the

---

[52] [1962] 3 All E.R. 1, 3.
[53] *Ibid.* pp. 3–4.
[54] *Ibid.* p. 4.
[55] See *S.(B.D.)* v. *S.(D.J.)* [1977] Fam. 109 and *Re K* [1977] Fam. 179.
[56] *Ward* v. *Bradford Corporation* (1972) 70 L.G.R. 27, 35. This is discussed by J.A.G. Griffith, *The Politics of The Judiciary* (Fontana, London, 2nd ed. 1981), pp. 178–179, 196–197, and by Ray Geary, "Lord Denning and Morality" in (eds.) P. Robson and P. Watchman, *Justice, Lord Denning and the Constitution* (Gower, Farnborough, 1981), p. 79.
[57] [1968] 1 All E.R. 1064.

sale of the cottage. The Court of Appeal held that she was not entitled to any property interest in the house. Lord Denning argued:

> "A wife does not get a share in the house simply because she cleans the walls or works in the garden or helps her husband with the painting or decorating. Those are the sort of things which a wife does for the benefit of the family without altering the title to or interests in the property."[58]

Women's work in other words, was seen as contributing no value and, therefore, could not be rewarded economically. These words were quoted with approval by the House of Lords in *Pettitt* v. *Pettitt*[59] where they were applied to the "do-it-yourself" activities of a husband.

It is instructive to compare Lord Denning's reasoning in *Button* and that in *Cooke* v. *Head*,[60] four years later. The case concerned cohabitants, not a married couple. Ms. Cooke did "quite an unusual amount of work for a woman,"[61] in helping Mr. Head to build a bungalow which was to be a home for both of them. In Lord Denning's words:

> "She used a sledgehammer to demolish some old buildings. She filled the wheelbarrow with rubble and hard core and wheeled it up the bank. She worked the cement mixer which was out of order and difficult to work. She did painting and so forth. Miss Cooke did much more than most women would do.";[62]

She had, it seems, the skills of a crafts*man*.[63] That is surely the point of distinction between the two cases. What women normally do, or are expected to do, has, in Lord Denning's eyes, no economic value. But "real" work must be compensated. The Court of Appeal increased Ms. Cooke's share in the proceeds of sale from one-twelfth to one-third.

The Court of Appeal's decision in *Eves* v. *Eves*[64] has troubled some commentators. For example Bissett-Johnson says that "it is difficult to see very much difference between the facts of *Button* . . . and the facts of *Eves*."[65] On one level this is right but Janet Eves (she took her cohabitant's surname though they were not married to each other) was rather like Jacqueline Cooke. She wielded a 14lb. sledgehammer to break up a large area of concrete, filled a skip, stripped wallpaper, painted woodwork and cabinets and demolished a garden shed and constructed another. As in *Cooke* v. *Head*, Lord Denning was prepared to impose a constructive trust this time to the value of one quarter of the equity. On a true understanding of Lord Denning's reasoning processes, his decisions in *Button* and *Eves* are not inconsistent. One must read Lord Denning not just for what he holds[66] but for his values and these in both cases are perfectly plain. The legal distinction may not be tenable but that is another matter.

---

[58] *Ibid.* p. 1067.
[59] [1970] A.C. 777.
[60] [1972] 2 All E.R. 38.
[61] *Ibid.* p. 40.
[62] *Ibid.*
[63] My emphasis.
[64] [1975] 1 W.L.R. 1338. See the brief discussion of this case above.
[65] 125 New L.J. 614.
[66] *Cf.* Karl Llewellyn's instructions in *The Common Law Tradition* (Little Brown, Boston, 1960).

To Lord Denning's way of thinking women ought only to acquire rights in the matrimonial home when they have done something to merit them. *Button* v. *Button* illustrates this. So, in a rather different way, does *Gurasz* v. *Gurasz*.[67] The husband and wife jointly owned the matrimonial home, but the wife left with the four children because of her husband's repulsive conduct. The wife sought an order under the Matrimonial Homes Act 1967 that her husband should leave the home. It was granted. The Court of Appeal, however, rightly held that the order could not be supported on the ground that it was made. As Lord Denning said, the 1967 Act[68] only protected a wife who had "no proprietary, contractual or statutory right to remain in the matrimonial home," what he called, rather pruriently, a "bare" wife.[69] The judge's order was, however, supported on the ground that an innocent wife has a personal right to remain in the matrimonial home. Thus, if in occupation, she has a right not to be evicted by the other spouse and if out of occupation she has a right to enter and occupy the house. Lord Denning reasoned:

> "Some features of family life are elemental in our society. One is that it is the husband's duty to provide his wife with a roof over her head: and the children too. So long as the wife behaves herself, she is entitled to remain in the matrimonial home. . . . This is a personal right which belongs to her as a wife. It is not a proprietary right. . . . So long as she had done nothing to forfeit that right, the court will enforce it."[70]

What Lord Denning says here follows what the House of Lords ruled in *National Provincial Bank* v. *Ainsworth*[71] and cannot be faulted on that ground. He is not, of course, averse to departing from precedent where he finds it distasteful. Instead, here, he proclaims the doctrine with vigour and rhetorical flourish. He is quite clear in his mind that protection of the law should be conditional upon moral worth. He could have written "so long as she has not committed a matrimonial offence." I venture to suggest that "so long as [she] behaves herself" is language suggestive of some kind of inferior status. We talk of children behaving but not, I think, of wives. The group of property cases considered in this section are thus all of a piece. They demonstrate the conditional nature of the rights Lord Denning is prepared to bestow on women. His is the sort of reform which improves the position of some women while at the same time perpetuating the view that domestic labour has no economic value and rights generally are dependent on moral proprieties. It is as well to remind ourselves of this for Lord Denning has often been seen, and has seen himself, as a harbinger of reform. There has been legislative reform to recognise the value of domestic labour[72] and to preserve maintenance and accommodation rights after matrimonial misconduct,[73] but these, it must be stressed, were reforms to reverse trends effectuated by Lord Denning.

---

[67] [1969] 3 All E.R. 822.
[68] The Act now protects joint owners. See s.1(9) of the 1967 Act, inserted by the Matrimonial Proceedings and Property Act 1970, s.38.
[69] [1969] 3 All E.R. 822, 824.
[70] *Ibid.* p. 823.
[71] 1965] A.C. 1175.
[72] The Matrimonial Proceedings and Property Act 1970, s.5(1)(*f*) (now s.25(1)(*f*) of the Matrimonial Causes Act 1973).
[73] Domestic Proceedings and Magistrates' Courts Act 1978.

Lord Denning's Contribution to Family Law

There is hardly a facet of modern family law upon which Lord Denning has not pronounced at some time or other. He sat as a judge in the Probate, Divorce and Admiralty Division for 18 months in 1944 and 1945.[74] Very few of his judgments of this period are reported. Most, he tells us, were extempore.[75] He seems to have been reversed only once.[76] His reported judgments of the period do not throw much light on his values or his methodology. But they show him to be homely and down-to-earth (sex is described as a "natural and healthy way of living"[77]); prepared to dispose of seemingly binding cases where they appear to him to lack any rationale[78]; with an eye for law reform.[79] He also demonstrated that he was prepared and able to research difficult points of law that interested him. Indeed, as a result of one such exercise in a case which demanded that the principles of collusion be stated,[80] he wrote an article on the subject of presumptions and burdens which was published in the *Law Quarterly Review*.[81] There are glimpses also of his pragmatic approach to problems. Thus, in *Cruh* v. *Cruh*,[82] where the husband was to be deported as soon as it was practicable and there was nothing left to the marriage, he formed the opinion that the "best thing" was to end the marriage, even if it meant bending the law a little to do so. These early cases show Lord Denning to have a mind of his own but I do not think they anticipate the contribution he was to make to family law or law more generally nor is there more than a hint of the controversy he was subsequently to raise.

Lord Denning disliked divorce work and was soon transferred to the King's Bench Division.[83] Within ten months, however, he was appointed chairman of a committee to inquire into divorce procedure. This worked expeditiously[84] and produced three reports (two interim and one final). The recommendations were accepted and implemented. The Denning committee was responsible for reducing the period between decree nisi and decree absolute from six months to six weeks,[85] for the establishment of commissioners to try divorces (hitherto divorce cases had been tried only by High Court judges)[86] and for a strengthening of welfare services in the divorce process.[87]

---

[74] *Op. cit.* n. 1, pp. 187–90.

[75] *Ibid.* p. 190.

[76] *Churchman* v. *Churchman* [1945] P. 44.

[77] *Fletcher* v. *Fletcher* [1945] 1 All E.R. 582.

[78] In *Norton* v. *Norton* [1945] P. 56 he disposes of cases because changes of practice mean they "cease to be binding authorities." Is this the germ of *Schorsch Meir GmbH* v. *Hennin* [1975] Q.B. 416: "Seeing that the reasons no longer exist, we are at liberty to discard the rule itself. *Cessante ratione legis cessat ipso lex?*"

[79] See *Norton* v. *Norton* [1945] P. 56. He disapproves of the way the respondent and corespondent have denied adultery solely in order to dispute damages. "I think the practice should be changed," he comments.

[80] *Emanuel* v. *Emanuel* [1946] P. 115.

[81] "Presumptions and Burdens," 61 L.Q.R. 379.

[82] [1945] 2 All E.R. 545.

[83] *Op. cit.* n. 1, pp. 189–190.

[84] According to Lord Denning: "No committee has ever worked so quickly or so well." *Ibid.* p. 191.

[85] Cmd. 6881.

[86] Cmd. 6945.

[87] Cmd. 7024.

Of these reforms the first was a response to war, the second a recognition that the number of divorces had and would increase beyond the capacity of High Court judges. The third, the Marriage Welfare Service to afford help and guidance to couples in difficulties and welfare officers to assist in sorting out custody and access arrangements, is perhaps the most significant of the reforms engineered by the Denning Committee. It looks forward to the Family Court, an as yet unattained ideal which has figured prominently in the proposals of recent commissions and reform groups.[88] Lord Denning, a great believer in the sanctity of marriage, was to emphasise the importance of reconciliation many times in later cases.[89] Emphasis on it was to become a keynote of the divorce reform legislation of the late 1960s.[90]

Work on divorce procedure being completed, Lord Denning phases out of family law for a couple of years. In 1948 he was promoted to the Court of Appeal and between then and 1957 when he moved to the House of Lords he sat on a large number of appeals on family matters. This is the period when the deserted wife's equity emerged,[91] the notion of "family assets" is born,[92] when the courts begin to liberalise the bars to divorce.[93] Lord Denning is the progenitor of the first two of these concepts and played a major role in the third. He sat at first mainly with Bucknill L.J. and Parker L.J. Sometimes the Master of the Rolls, Lord Evershed, presided. One of Lord Denning's earliest reported forays into family law in the Court of Appeal is *Hopes* v. *Hopes*.[94] He recognised the social realities of the housing shortage. Desertion, the Court of Appeal held, could take place where the couple were living under the same roof. Such a decision did not involve any departure from existing precedent: desertion is, after all, withdrawal from a state of things not a place.[95] But it involved an intelligent and socially aware application of precedent in the circumstances of post-war England.

I have stressed the Court of Appeal, rather than Lord Denning, for, though it was he who saw the decision as rendered necessary by social circumstances,[96] there was no division of opinion between Lord Denning and the other judges. Lord Denning is seen as the great dissenter but in fact it was some six years before he dissented in a Court of Appeal case concerned with family matters. By then he had *Bendall* v. *McWhirter*[97] and *Rimmer* v. *Rimmer*,[98] the two breakthrough family property cases, behind him and in both, as in all family law cases he sat in until *Bravery* v. *Bravery*,[99] the court was unanimous. Indeed, it was 1956 before he dissented again. The case[1] concerned the meaning of "free of tax" in a £1 a week maintenance award. Lord Denning's approach was the common-sense one of applying the logic of a statutory

---

[88] Most notably the Finer report on one-parent families. Cmnd. 5629 (July 1974), ss.13 and 14.
[89] *McTaggart* v. *McTaggart* [1948] P. 94; *Simpson* v. *Simpson* [1954] 1 W.L.R. 994; *Richardson* v. *Richardson* [1949] P. 16.
[90] Law Commission, *Divorce: The Field of Choice*, Cmnd. 3123, para. 15.
[91] See *Bendall* v. *McWhirter* [1952] 2 Q.B. 466.
[92] See *Rimmer* v. *Rimmer* [1953] 1 Q.B. 63.
[93] See, *e.g. Douglas* v. *Douglas* [1950] P. 85.
[94] [1949] P. 227.
[95] See *Pulford* v. *Pulford* [1923] P. 18, 21, *per* Sir Henry Duke.
[96] [1949] P. 227, 235.
[97] See above, n. 91.
[98] See above, n. 92.
[99] [1954] 1 W.L.R. 1169.
[1] *Jefferson* v. *Jefferson* [1956] P. 136.

provision on large maintenance payments to this small one as well. His dissent does not appear to have been controversial.[2] In every other family case in which Lord Denning took part in his first coming in the Court of Appeal the court was unanimous. In the absence of any behaviouralistic studies, such as exist in the United States, we have no evidence of how these blocs,[3] if that is the correct way to describe them, were formed. But there is no reason to suspect that Lord Denning, in this stage of his career, was able to exercise any disproportionate influence over his colleagues. His judgments at this time still show a respect for precedent with the result that the legal analysis is usually clear, cogent and full.

In his five years in the House of Lords from 1957 to 1962 Lord Denning had no opportunity to pronounce in a judicial capacity upon any family law matters. He became, and has remained, an active member of the legislative branch of the House of Lords and has spoken on a variety of topics.[4] Often his speeches have been reaffirmation of traditional values including matters relating to family life and sexual morality.[5]

By the time he returned to the Court of Appeal as Master of the Rolls he had established something of a reputation for dissent and controversy.[6] Soon afterwards he chaired the Profumo enquiry[7] and became a household name. Lord Denning of the 1960s and 1970s was not the same Lord Denning as the man who left the Court of Appeal in 1957. He became less cautious, less concerned with precedent and logical development. He cultivated a particular narrative style.[8] Though a conservative through and through, he committed himself to change, to right injustice. The paradox is more apparent than real for reform required the re-establishment of traditional values. He became impatient with the constraints imposed upon him by precedent.[9] A dominant theme running through Lord Denning's crusades in this period has been to protect the small man against large organisations, bureaucracies and government bodies.[10] In family law the small man has often been the small woman. *Williams and Glyn's Bank* v. *Boland*[11] is a good illustration of the way Lord Denning's concern to protect the individual's interests against the power of large organisations has reflected itself in his family law thinking. The husband had raised money for his business on the

---

[2] It is not criticised in any contemporary literature.

[3] Particularly associated with the work of Glendon Schubert. See also the popular study by B. Woodward and S. Armstrong, *The Brethren* (Secker and Warburg, London, 1980) and *cf.* A Patterson, *The Law Lords* (Macmillan, London, 1982) (there is an interesting review of this by Lord Denning in *The Listener* (October 7, 1982).

[4] See L. Blom-Cooper and G. Drewry, *Final Appeal* (Clarendon Press, 1972), p. 205, showing Lord Denning to be the most active participant in House of Lords' debates of all eligible judges.

[5] See particularly his speech at Hansard, H.L., Vol. 206, col. 943.

[6] Though Lord Keith was the leading dissenter in the period 22 per cent. of his judgments (1954–1963) were dissents. Only 16 per cent. of Lord Denning's were. See *op. cit.* n. 4, p. 179.

[7] Cmnd. 2152 (1963).

[8] His judgments are "short stories" *per* Lord Denning, *The Family Story* (London, Butterworths, 1981), p. 208.

[9] He became particularly restless after the 1966 House of Lords Practice Statement. His efforts to remove the shackles imposed by *Young* v. *Bristol Aeroplane Co.* culminated in *Davis* v. *Johnson* [1978] 2 W.L.R. 182, and must now be adjudged a failure.

[10] But there is no consistency in this. See, *e.g. R.* v. *Preston S.B.A.T., ex parte Moore* [1975] 1 W.L.R. 624, *cf. McPhail* v. *Persons Unknown* [1973] Ch. 447.

[11] [1979] 2 W.L.R. 550.

security of the matrimonial home. The wife had made substantial contributions to the purchase of the house and was, it was clear, entitled to a share in it. The business failed and the bank sought to enforce their charges. The case turned on whether the wife was in 'actual occupation' of the house. Templeman J. held she was not: "when a mortgagor is in actual occupation of the matrimonial home, it cannot be said that his wife also is in occupation."[12] He thought any other view would "lead to chaos."[13] The Court of Appeal, Lord Denning very much to the fore, disagreed and the House of Lords upheld the Court of Appeal decision. Lord Denning was concerned that: "we should not give monied might priority over social justice." He reasoned:

> "Anyone who lends money on the security of a matrimonial home nowadays ought to realise that the wife may have a share in it . . . It seems to me utterly wrong that a lender should turn a blind eye to the wife's interest or the possibility of it—and afterwards seek to turn her and the family out—on the plea that he did not know that she was in actual occupation. If a bank is to do its duty, in the society in which we live, it should recognise the integrity of the matrimonial home."[14]

Boland was the 1970s counterpart to the deserted wife's equity of the 1950s and early 1960s which the House of Lords scotched in *National Provincial Bank* v. *Ainsworth*.[15] But protection of the wife in *Boland* required statutory construction not judicial invention. It was not surprising that the House of Lords upheld *Boland*.[16]

Boland is a good illustration of Lord Denning's recent concerns. It is, however, not an especially good illustration of his reasoning processes. It is to other family law decisions, particularly those of the 1960s and early 1970s, that one must go to seek these. After the early 1970s Lord Denning has made only occasional forays into family matters. *Boland* is one example[17]; *Davis* v. *Johnson*[18] another. But his real interests have lain elsewhere, in administrative law,[19] industrial relations[20] and, as ever, in the common law.[21] He made his major impact in a series of cases about the ownership of matrimonial homes in the years immediately after *Ainsworth*.[22] It would be reading too much into these decisions to say that they were a direct reaction to the House of Lords' demolition of the deserted wife's equity he created but such might be a plausible interpretation. The passage of legislation giving judges discretion to transfer property and vary property interests[23] may have taken the sting out of Lord Denning's campaign and encouraged him to innovate in other fields. Certainly, after establishing precedents on financial provision and

---

[12] *Per* Templeman J. in *Bird* v. *Syme-Thompson* [1979] 1 W.L.R. 440, 444.
[13] *Ibid.*
[14] [1979] 2 W.L.R. 550, 560.
[15] [1965] A.C. 1175.
[16] [1981] A.C. 487.
[17] [1979] 2 W.L.R. 550.
[18] [1978] 1 All E.R. 841.
[19] See Chap. 6.
[20] See Chap. 8.
[21] See Chap. 2.
[22] See below, p. 139.
[23] Matrimonial Proceedings and Property Act 1970, s.4 (now s.24 of Matrimonial Causes Act 1973).

property adjustment on divorce, in the light of Acts which had, in his language, "revolutionised the law,"[24] he sought other pastures. *Boland* excepted, his main interest in the family, as the 1970s developed, really lay in assimilating wherever possible the consequences of cohabitation to those of marriage.[25]

Throughout the whole period as Master of the Rolls Lord Denning has taken a fairly cavalier approach to the doctrine of precedent. He has often expressed his impatience with the fetters the Court of Appeal imposed upon itself in *Young* v. *Bristol Aeroplane Co.*,[26] never more forthrightly than he did in *Davis* v. *Johnson*.[27] His more insidious attacks are those which he disguises as observances of the practice. He has a knack, close at times to deceit, of paying lip-service to precedent, while not really complying with it. A good illustration is found in Lord Denning's judgments in *Heseltine* v. *Heseltine*[28] and *Binions* v. *Evans*.[29] In both cases Lord Denning cites in support a remark by Lord Diplock in *Gissing* v. *Gissing*[30]:

> "a resulting, implied or constructive trust—and it is unnecessary for present purposes to distinguish between these three classes of trust—is created by a transaction between the trustee and the *cestui que trust* in connection with the acquisition by the trustee of a legal estate in land, whenever the trustee has so conducted himself that it would be inequitable to deny to the *cestui que trust* a beneficial interest in the land acquired."

This statement, isolated from its context, supports the proposition for which Lord Denning has cited it as authority: *viz.* that the courts will impose a constructive trust to do justice between parties wherever the result would otherwise be inequitable. However, Lord Diplock limited the principle in the sentence immediately following those quoted:

> "And he will be held so to have conducted himself if by his words or conduct he has induced the *cestui que trust* to act to his own detriment in the reasonable belief that by so acting he was acquiring a beneficial interest in the land."

Lord Denning ignores this limitation. Indeed, he treats it as if it was not there.

Throughout the 1970s Lord Denning waged war with the House of Lords. His judgments are replete with righteous indignation at the way the House of Lords treats his decisions. His glee when legislation held him to be right was clear for all to see.[31] Nor was there any longer any guarantee that he would take his Court of Appeal's judges with him. It became common for different judges in the Court of Appeal to use different lines of reasoning, even if the

---

[24] *Trippas* v. *Trippas* [1973] 2 All E.R. 1, 4.
[25] See *Cooke* v. *Head* [1972] 1 W.L.R. 518, *Eves* v. *Eves* [1975] 1 W.L.R. 1338, *Tanner* v. *Tanner* [1975] 1 W.L.R. 1346.
[26] [1944] K.B. 718.
[27] [1978] 1 All E.R. 841, 852–857.
[28] [1971] 1 All E.R. 952, 955.
[29] [1972] Ch. 359, 368.
[30] [1971] A.C. 886, 895. Lord Denning also adopted this dictum in *Hussey* v. *Palmer* [1972] 3 All E.R. 744, 747 and in *Falconer, Davis* v. *Vale, Re Cummins, Hargrave* v. *Newton, Hazell,* and *Cooke* v. *Head.*
[31] As, for example, in *Davis* v. *Vale* [1971] 1 W.L.R. 1022.

conclusion to which they came is of a piece. The reasoning of Lord Denning, Davies and Russell L.JJ. in *Bedson* v. *Bedson*[32] is a striking illustration of the conflicts. Husband and wife were joint tenants on trust for sale of a shop (the husband's business) and a flat (the matrimonial home). The wife deserted and applied under section 17 of the Married Women's Property Act 1882 for an order that the property be sold and the proceeds divided in equal shares. The county court judge had ordered that the wife should vest the freehold property in the husband upon the payment by him of a certain sum of money. The Court of Appeal, however, held that the wife was entitled to a half share in the property. The three judges reached this conclusion by different routes. To Lord Denning there was solid ground for believing that the parties intended the proceeds of sale should be divided equally. He referred to the form of the latest accounts. Davies L.J. argued that there was no agreement that the property should be owned otherwise than as stated in the conveyance. Russell L.J. believed that the wife was entitled to sever the beneficial joint tenancy, thereby becoming entitled in equity to an equal share in the proceeds of sale as a tenant in common. None of the three would order a sale. Lord Denning because, he said, the court would look at the purposes for which the property was acquired and finding that a sale would defeat those purposes would refuse to order it. Justice demanded that a sale be refused. Davies and Russell L.JJ., on the other hand, said the court should not make an order which would result in the husband being turned out of the premises or giving the wife any security which in the hands of an assignee might have the same result.

Bedson also illustrates another facet of Lord Denning. He had a tendency to make statements of the law which could not be supported. Thus, in *Bedson* he claimed that a joint tenant could not sever the tenancy.[33] Russell L.J. rightly said of this that it was "without the slightest foundation in law or equity."[34] Lord Denning's assertion has been consistently repudiated by other judges,[35] ever since, though he himself reiterated his view in *Jackson* v. *Jackson* in 1971.[36] Reference has already been made to *Bravery* v. *Bravery*[37] where his thinking was clouded by a near obsession. A third illustration is the case of *Kenward* v. *Kenward*,[38] where à propos of nothing, he made the startling *obiter* remark that an English domiciliary may marry polygamously in a country whose laws permit polygamy and that such a marriage is valid in the eyes of English law. He added that both substantial and formal validity of marriage depend on the personal law though he qualified this by saying that when an English woman domiciled in England marries a man of a polygamous "race"[39] in his homeland, the substantial validity of that marriage depends on the personal law of the husband and not on the personal law of the wife. A comment on these statements is not, I think, necessary.[40]

[32] [1965] 3 All E.R. 307.

[33] *Ibid.* p. 315.

[34] *Ibid.* p. 319.

[35] See *Re Draper's Conveyance* [1969] 1 Ch. 486; *Cowcher* v. *Cowcher* [1972] 1 All E.R. 943, 949, *per* Bagnall J. See also R.E.M., 82 L.Q.R. 29.

[36] [1971] 3 All E.R. 774, 777. See also *Ulrich* v. *Ulrich* [1968] 1 All E.R. 67, 70.

[37] [1954] 1 W.L.R. 1169.

[38] [1950] 2 All E.R. 297.

[39] *Ibid.* p. 310.

[40] But see *Radwan* v. *Radwan (No. 2)* [1973] Fam. 35 which is generally assumed to have been wrongly decided and *Hussain* v. *Hussain* [1982] 3 W.L.R. 679 (as to which see Pearl 42 C.L.J. 30). Lord Denning's remarks in *Kenward* are universally regarded as suspect.

As indicated earlier in this chapter, there are few areas of contemporary family law upon which Lord Denning has not left his mark. In the remainder of this chapter his contribution to a few selected areas is commented upon and assessed.

Divorce

The law of divorce and its administration have undergone a profound transformation since Lord Denning first tried divorce actions in 1944. The watershed is the Divorce Reform Act of 1969. The introduction of the special procedure for undefended divorces in 1973[41] may, however, ultimately prove more significant. Change was in the air long before 1969. A relaxed attitude towards collusion begins with *Blunt* v. *Blunt* in 1943.[42] A more liberal attitude towards the bars sets in in the 1950s and 1960s. The cases of *Gollins* v. *Gollins*[43] and *Williams* v. *Williams*[44] in 1964 facilitated divorce on the ground of cruelty. The judges were looking to breakdown of relationship[45] for several years before the Divorce Reform Act.

Lord Denning's attitude towards divorce has always been somewhat ambivalent. He favoured divorce reform both in 1963[46] and in 1969.[47] In his judicial capacity he enthusiastically embraced the new irretrievable breakdown concept. Thus, in *Fuller (orse Penfold)* v. *Fuller*[48] in 1973 he referred to the 1969 Act as a "reforming Act"[49] and formed the opinion as a result that old cases on desertion did not "help much." He interpreted "living with each other in the same household" purposively, very much in the spirit of the new legislation:

> "In this case the parties were not living with each other in that sense. The wife was living with Mr. Penfold as his wife. The husband was living in the house as a lodger. It is impossible to say that husband and wife were or are living with each other in the same household."[50]

On the other hand Lord Denning was clearly fearful of what divorce reform might mean for the family. Speaking to the Nottingham branch of the Marriage Guidance Council in 1971 he warned: "It is a time for all good folk to take a stand, else the permissive society will soon become the decadent society."[51]

Such views permeated many of his judgments as he administered the old divorce law. Thus, in *Moor* v. *Moor*[52] in 1954, a case on discretion statements,

---

[41] Extended in stages until by 1977 it covered all undefended divorces even where there are children.
[42] [1943] A.C. 517.
[43] [1964] A.C. 644.
[44] [1964] A.C. 698.
[45] *Masarati* v. *Masarati* [1969] 1 W.L.R. 393 is one example.
[46] See Hansard, H.L., Vol. 250, cols. 405–7 (May 22, 1963), supporting Matrimonial Causes and Reconciliation Bill.
[47] See B.H. Lee, *Divorce Law Reform In England* (Peter Owen, London, 1974), pp. 179–80. But *cf.* his foreword to W. Latey, *The Tide of Divorce* (Longman, London, 1970), p. vii.
[48] [1973] 2 All E.R. 650.
[49] *Ibid.* p. 651.
[50] *Ibid.* p. 652.
[51] Quoted in *The Times*, October 1, 1971.
[52] [1954] 2 All E.R. 458.

Lord Denning referred to Lord Simon's ruling in *Blunt* v. *Blunt* and continued:

> "In applying the ruling in recent years I am afraid that the fact that the marriage "has utterly broken down" has weighed heavily, whereas sanctity of marriage has weighed lightly, in the scale. That is not the correct method of approach. A true balance must be kept. It is most important that the court should emphasise the sanctity of marriage."[53]

He also had occasion to warn against the concepts of cruelty,[54] desertion[55] and constructive desertion[56] being stretched so far as to admit divorce where no serious misconduct was alleged. Thus, in *Kaslefsky* v. *Kaslefsky*[57] in 1950 he stressed, as he had done in *Hopes* v. *Hopes*[58] a year earlier, that gross neglect and chronic discord were not yet grounds for divorce,

> "If the door of cruelty were opened too wide, we should soon find ourselves granting divorce for incompatibility of temperament. That is an easy path to tread . . . The temptation must be resisted lest we slip into a state of affairs where the institution of marriage itself is imperilled."[59]

In *Pike* v. *Pike*[60] he was concerned lest constructive desertion be allowed to "run wild."[61] His fears that divorces would be granted for incompatibility of temperament have now been realised,[62] though I do not think those who passed divorce reform legislation intended this to happen. Lord Denning also hoped to put a brake on divorce by stressing the importance of intention in cruelty. In *Kaslefsky* v. *Kaslefsky* he said that the acts complained of must be "aimed at" the petitioner,[63] so that intentional acts might be cruel even though there was no intention to be cruel. These doctrines survived until they were uprooted by the House of Lords in 1964. After *Gollins*[64] and *Williams*[65] he was still concerned to keep cruelty "within bounds."[66] He did not however, think that regarding refusal of sexual intercourse as cruelty would be to open "too wide a door to divorce."[67]

Lord Denning never liked divorce and always wanted to keep it firmly within bounds. Despite this, from his earliest cases onwards he took a fairly realistic approach to it. His attitude in *Cruh* v. *Cruh*,[68] already referred to, was essentially pragmatic. This was echoed in *Kaslefsky*[69]: it would be a good

---

[53] *Ibid.* p. 461.
[54] *Kaslefsky* v. *Kaslefsky* [1950] P. 38; *Bartholomew* v. *Bartholomew* [1952] W.N. 535.
[55] *Hopes* v. *Hopes* [1949] P. 227.
[56] *Pike* v. *Pike* [1953] P. 81.
[57] [1950] P. 38.
[58] [1949] P. 227.
[59] *Kaslefsky* v. *Kaslefsky* [1950] 2 All E.R. 398, 403.
[60] [1953] P. 81.
[61] *Ibid.* p. 235.
[62] See *Livingstone-Stallard* v. *Livingstone-Stallard* [1974] Fam. 47 and *O'Neill* v. *O'Neill* [1975] 1 W.L.R. 118.
[63] *Kaslefsky* v. *Kaslefsky* [1950] 2 All E.R. 398, 402.
[64] [1964] A.C. 644.
[65] [1964] A.C. 698.
[66] *Sheldon* v. *Sheldon* [1966] 2 All E.R. 257, 261.
[67] *Ibid.*
[68] [1945] 2 All E.R. 545.
[69] [1951] P. 38.

thing if this marriage were ended, he stated. In *Davis* v. *Davis*[70] in 1950 he stressed that the divorce court was concerned not to punish anyone, but to give relief from a marriage that had broken down.[71] Both the sentiment and the language were ahead of their time. Lord Denning found the concept of mutual desertion acceptable for much the same reason. Thus, in *Beigan* v. *Beigan* he stated:

> "In many of these cases both are equally to blame for the breakdown of the marriage and the only just solution is a decree of divorce on the ground of desertion by each without drawing any distinction between them."[72]

Some may find the logic unacceptable (is there anything of which the other can complain?)[73] but in 1956, the year of the Morton Royal Commission report,[74] this was enlightenment. The importance of reconciliation has figured prominently in recent thinking.[75] Lord Denning's judgments of the 1950s constantly stress its importance.[76] Thus, in *Richardson* v. *Richardson*[77] in 1949 his view on what conduct could revive condoned adultery was influenced by considering what would foster and what hamper attempts at reconciliation. In *Simpson* v. *Simpson*[78] in 1954 (an application for leave to petition for divorce within three years of marriage) he stressed the importance of looking at the respondent's answer as well as the petitioner's allegations. Without so doing, it was difficult to assess the possibility of a reconciliation between the parties.

Whatever the importance of the decisions considered thus far in this section, there is little doubt that Lord Denning's major contribution to divorce law in the pre-reform days was the establishment of the civil law test in relation to the proof of matrimonial offences. In a series of cases in the early 1950s[79] he established that cruelty did not have to be proved beyond reasonable doubt and in *Gower* v. *Gower*,[80] faced with *Ginesi* v. *Ginesi*,[81] a binding Court of Appeal authority holding that adultery required a criminal standard of proof, he opined:

> "I do not think that this court is irrevocably committed to the view that a charge of adultery must be regarded as a criminal charge, to be proved beyond all reasonable doubt."[82]

---

[70] [1950] P. 125.
[71] This was echoed in many other cases.
[72] [1956] 2 All E.R. 630, 632.
[73] *Cf.* A. Irvine (1967) 30 M.L.R. 46.
[74] Cmd. 9678.
[75] See J.M. Whetton and A.H. Manchester, "Marital Conciliation in England and Wales" (1974) 23 I.C.L.Q. 339.
[76] Two examples are *Bartram* v. *Bartram* [1950] P. 1, 6–7; *Mackrell* v. *Mackrell* [1948] 2 All E.R. 858, 860.
[77] [1949] P. 16.
[78] [1954] 1 W.L.R. 994.
[79] *Davis* v. *Davis* [1950] P. 125; *White* v. *White* [1950] P. 39. (In this case Lord Denning criticised the M'Naghten rules as unscientific and urged that they should not be extended in their operation).
[80] [1950] W.N. 156.
[81] [1948] P. 179.
[82] [1950] 1 All E.R. 804, 805.

When the opportunity to reconsider *Ginesi* arose in the House of Lords in 1966 Lord Denning sat in the Lords to put the seal on the work he had commenced 16 years earlier. In *Blyth* v. *Blyth*[83] he repudiated the idea that "analogies and precedents" of the criminal law had any authority in the divorce court. It was "wrong," he stressed, to apply the analogy of the criminal law.[84] Had he remembered, I wonder, his strong words some 12 years earlier in *Bravery* v. *Bravery*[85] and, if so, would he have distinguished the two situations? They can, it is true, be distinguished: one is concerned with a ground of divorce, the other with a matter of evidence. But language as strong as that employed in *Bravery* is not readily forgotten or forgiven. It remains to haunt Lord Denning.

To each of the old grounds of divorce, the new "facts," Lord Denning has made some contribution of significance. He expressed his opinion of adultery and its significance in picturesque language in 1950:

> "The first act of adultery marks a turning point in the relationship of the guilty pair. It means that they have swept aside all scruples and committed themselves beyond recall. Thereafter repetition becomes easy, and I fear, likely."[86]

Lord Denning was part of the first Court of Appeal[87] to hear a divorce action centring on adultery under the reformed law. Reference has already been made to an *obiter* comment of Lord Denning.[88] The decision of the court that the two limbs of section 1(2)(*a*) of the Matrimonial Causes Act 1973 were "independent,"[89] "separated and unrelated"[90] is not convincing. Indeed, a differently constituted Court of Appeal some little while later in *Carr* v. *Carr*[91] expressed some doubt as to whether *Cleary* v. *Cleary* was correctly decided. It says something for the reputation of Lord Denning and Scarman L.J., as he then was, that the Court of Appeal in *Carr* was not disposed to believe that a Court of Appeal with Denning and Scarman present could have failed to take account of section 2(2) of the 1973 Act so as to render *Cleary* susceptible to the invocation of the *per incuriam* doctrine.[92] It looks however, as if they did just that. There is logical inconsistence between a disjunctive interpretation of section 1(2)(*a*) and the language of section 2(2).[93] Should the matter ever get to the House of Lords it is distinctly possible that a conjunctive test would be substituted.

References have already been made to a number of decisions on cruelty to which Lord Denning was a party. He only heard one reported appeal on "unreasonable behaviour."[94] The case, *Bradley* v. *Bradley*,[95] is one of

[83] [1966] A.C. 643.
[84] *Ibid.* p. 669.
[85] [1954] 1 W.L.R. 1169.
[86] *Douglas* v. *Douglas* [1950] 2 All E.R. 748, 753.
[87] In *Cleary* v. *Cleary* [1974] 1 All E.R. 498.
[88] Above, pp. 112–113.
[89] [1974] 1 All E.R. 498, 501.
[90] *Ibid.* p. 502.
[91] [1974] 3 All E.R. 1193.
[92] [1974] 3 All E.R. 1193, 1199, *per* Stephenson L.J.
[93] See M.D.A. Freeman, "Adultery and Intolerability" (1972) 35 M.L.R. 98.
[94] Of course, this expression is inaccurate, since reasonable(ly) qualifies "be expected to live with" and not the behaviour (see *Carew-Hunt* v. *Carew-Hunt, The Times,* June 28, 1972), but it is in common use.
[95] [1973] 1 W.L.R. 1291.

considerable importance. A woman continued to live with her husband because she had a large number of children and nowhere else to go. There was no doubt that his behaviour, which included violence, was such that she could not reasonably be expected to live with him. She was in a "Catch-22" situation: the council would rehouse her if she secured a divorce but to secure a divorce did she have to separate from her husband? The judge at first instance took the view that there was no possibility of divorce under section 1(2)(*b*). Lord Denning had seen a dilemma like this before. In *Mackrell* v. *Mackrell*[96] in 1948 he had refused to find that a wife condoned her husband's cruelty (also violence) when she stayed with him because she had nowhere else to go. In *Bradley* v. *Bradley* Lord Denning interpreted section 1(2)(*b*) so as to facilitate divorces in situations such as these. He reasoned:

> " . . . the wife is in fact living with the husband. How can she say that she 'cannot reasonably be expected to live with her husband' when she is in fact living with him? I think she can say so. The section does not go on to provide that she must have left him and be 'living apart' from him. It simply says that she 'cannot reasonably be expected to live with him.' I think she satisfies that requirement, even though she is in the same house with him—and in fact living with him—if it be the case that she has no alternative open to her—nowhere else to go. It is not reasonable to expect her to live there, but albeit unreasonable, she has no option but to be there."[97]

This is a liberal and most sensitive interpretation of the statutory provision. It is Lord Denning at his best.

On the concept of desertion Lord Denning has made a major contribution. Until *Dunn* v. *Dunn*[98] in 1948, it was the law that the husband had an overriding right to determine the location of the matrimonial home.[99] A wife who refused to join him there was said to be in desertion. This was rejected by Lord Denning in *Dunn*'s case. He said:

> "The decision where the home should be is a decision which affects both parties and their children. It is their duty to decide it by agreement, by give and take, and not by the imposition of the will of one over the other. Each is entitled to an equal voice in the ordering of the affairs which are their common concern. Neither has a casting vote. . . . They should try so to arrange their affairs that they spend their time together as a family and not apart. If such an arrangement is frustrated by the unreasonableness of one or the other, and this leads to a separation between them, then the party who has produced the separation by reason of his or her unreasonable behaviour is guilty of desertion. . . . If a wife refuses to join her husband at a place when he is ready to receive her, that is, . . . a factor of great weight, but it is not necessarily decisive."[1]

Shortly afterwards in *Walter* v. *Walter*, Willmer J. held that where both were unreasonable, neither could allege that the other was in desertion and

---

[96] [1948] 2 All E.R. 858, 860.
[97] [1973] 3 All E.R. 750, 752.
[98] [1949] P. 98.
[99] *Mansey* v. *Mansey* [1940] P. 139; *King* v. *King* [1942] P. 1, 8.
[1] [1948] 2 All E.R. 822, 823.

neither was awarded a decree.[2] But in *Hosegood* v. *Hosegood*, a year later, Lord Denning formed the opinion that in such a case both might be in desertion. He reasoned:

> "Each must know full well that, if he or she does not give way, the married life will be brought to an end; and if each unreasonably persists each may be presumed to bring it to an end."[3]

These remarks were *obiter* but he adhered to them in the later case of *Beigan* v. *Beigan*[4] "more strongly than ever."[5] Lord Denning's views have been both doubted[6] and accepted[7] and the matter has not been determined beyond doubt. Nor in a climate of opinion in which desertion is seldom alleged[8] (parties relying on two years separation instead) is it likely to be. The conceptual problem remains: Lord Denning's solution is essentially a pragmatic one. His remarks on the location of the matrimonial home remain highly significant. Their implication is far wider than their subject-matter. Can the marital rape exemption for example, survive the force of Lord Denning's arguments in *Dunn* v. *Dunn*?[9]

Lord Denning's other principal contribution to the law of desertion is his judgment in *Hopes* v. *Hopes*,[10] to which brief reference has been made. Although it did not fall to him to give the main judgment in *Hopes* (Bucknill L.J. gave it), the test of what constituted separation for the purposes of desertion was formulated more clearly in his judgment than anywhere else. The line between desertion on the one hand and gross neglect and chronic discord on the other is, he said:

> "drawn at the point where the parties are living separately and apart. In cases where they are living under the same roof, that point is reached when they cease to be one household and become two households . . ."[11]

The "one household or two" test has been consistently invoked ever since.[12] Two other decisions of Lord Denning on desertion remain authorities 30 years after they were decided, *viz.*: *Richards* v. *Richards*[13] and *Crabtree* v. *Crabtree*[14] but neither requires any further consideration.

Lord Denning's impact on the separation provisions of the new divorce law has not been great. His intelligent and expansive interpretation of what is now section 2(6) of the Matrimonial Causes Act 1973 in *Fuller* (*orse Penfold*) v. *Fuller*[15] has been commented upon. It undoubtedly gave effect to the policy

---

[2] (1949) 65 T.L.R. 680.
[3] (1950) 66 T.L.R. 735, 740.
[4] [1956] 2 All E.R. 630.
[5] *Ibid.* p. 632.
[6] In *Simpson* v. *Simpson* [1951] P. 320, 330, *per* Lord Merriman P.
[7] In *Price* v. *Price* [1968] 1 W.L.R. 1735 *per* Wrangham J.
[8] In 1981 desertion alone was alleged in only 3,745 divorce petitions out of a total of 176,162 petitions. See *Judicial Statistics*, Annual Report 1981, Cmnd. 8770, p. 65.
[9] See M.D.A. Freeman, "But If You Can't Rape Your Wife, Who[m] Can You Rape? The Marital Rape Exemption Re-examined" (1981) 15 Family Law Quarterly 1.
[10] [1949] P. 227.
[11] *Ibid.* p. 236.
[12] Most recently in *Mouncer* v. *Mouncer* [1972] 1 W.L.R. 321.
[13] [1952] P. 307.
[14] [1953] 1 W.L.R. 708.
[15] Above.

underlying the five years separation provision. So also did Lord Denning's judgment in *Chapman* v. *Chapman*.[16] The wife petitioned for divorce basing her petition on five years separation. But in her petition she alleged that the husband was responsible for the separation. Lord Denning quite rightly asserted that it was "altogether wrong"[17] for a petition based on section 1(2)(*e*) to charge the respondent with a matrimonial offence. He justified his conclusion in two ways: (i) by examining the form of the decree and (ii) by considering the likely effect of any other conclusion ("We shall be back to the bad old days of mutual recrimination in open court"[18]). He was quick to realise that once fault was alleged, more suits would be defended "to decide merely the question who should pay the costs." He stated unequivocally:

> "It would be contrary to the policy of the legislature that the court should hold a post mortem simply to make an award of costs."[19]

Lord Denning's remarks in *Chapman* nipped in the bud a practice that, had it persisted, could have frustrated the objective of burying empty shells of marriage with the minimum amount of fuss and recrimination. In the course of his judgment in *Chapman* he also gave guidance on paying for "five years separation" divorces. He ruled that the petitioner, whether husband or wife (and more wives petition on five years' separation than husbands), should pay his or her own costs. Furthermore, the husband should not be ordered to pay costs simply because the wife is legally aided.

On the three years bar Lord Denning offered guidance in *Bowman* v. *Bowman* which today is apt to provoke ribald laughter. *Inter alia* he stated:

> "The husband who commits adultery within a few weeks of marriage, or who commits adultery promiscuously with more than one woman or with his wife's sister, or with a servant in the house, may probably be labelled as exceptionally depraved."[20]

Cruelty *simpliciter* also would not do. But

> " . . . if coupled with aggravating circumstances, as, for instance, drunkenness and neglect, or if it is exceptionally brutal or dangerous to health, then, even if it does not evidence exceptional depravity on the part of the respondent, it does, at least, cause exceptional hardship to the applicant. If it is coupled with perverted lust, it shows exceptional depravity on the part of the proposed respondent."[21]

Recently, in *Blackwell* v. *Blackwell*[22] doubt was cast by Lawton L.J. on the value of guidelines such as these. He thought the words "exceptional hardship" and "exceptional depravity" should be given their ordinary meaning. It is now stressed that in the majority of cases it is unnecessary to rely on depravity anyway, with its unpleasant overtones and difficulties, since hardship can arise from the conduct of the other spouse.[23] Lord Denning's remarks have thus not really survived a change in climate of

---

[16] [1972] 3 All E.R. 1089.
[17] *Ibid.* p. 1091.
[18] *Ibid.* p. 1090.
[19] *Ibid.*
[20] [1949] 2 All E.R. 127, 128.
[21] *Ibid.* p. 129.
[22] (1973) 117 S.J. 939.
[23] *C.* v. *C.* [1980] Fam. 23.

opinion. But even in 1949 they revealed rather more of Lord Denning's own temperament and disposition than anything else.

The Economic Consequences of Marital Breakdown

In Lord Denning's time as a judge the law relating to financial provision and property adjustment has undergone profound changes and remains in a state of flux today.[24] Lord Denning played a part in most of the major changes: indeed, he can justifiably be described as a trend-setter in this area of law.

Decisions of his are some of the earliest to recognise that a wife might ask for maintenance even if she was "guilty," to use the language of those days, of matrimonial misconduct. In several cases he developed the notion of the "compassionate allowance."[25] To our eyes today this is crude and riddled with sexism. But cases such as *Sydenham* v. *Sydenham*[26] and *Trestain* v. *Trestain*[27] have to be placed in the context of 1949 and 1950 when they were respectively decided.

Increasing recognition is given today to the ex-wife's need to support herself after divorce.[28] The changed economic role of women has rendered the principle of life-long support out of date: or so at least it is commonly and persuasively argued.[29] One of the earliest cases to recognise that a wife's earning capacity ought to be taken into account in assessing financial provision is *Rose* v. *Rose* in 1950. Lord Denning said:

> "If she is a young woman with no children and obviously ought to go out to work in her own interest, but does not, her personal earning capacity ought to be taken into account."[30]

He also made the point that if a wife had worked regularly, her potential earnings should be considered. This apart, the decision embodies the notions of dependence firmly entrenched then.

> "It does not as a rule lie in the mouth of a wrongdoing husband to say that his wife ought to go out to work simply in order to relieve him from paying maintenance."[31]

That the law still has not entirely moved away from dependence and all that it entails is in part attributable to judgments like this one of Lord Denning.

Nevertheless, many today favour what is known as the "clean break" on divorce.[32] Lord Scarman explained the rationale of this in *Minton* v. *Minton*:

> "The law now encourages spouses to avoid bitterness after family breakdown and to settle their money and property problems. An object of the modern law is to encourage each to put the past behind them and

---

[24] See the two recent Law Commission reports, nos. 103 and 112.
[25] *Sydenham* v. *Sydenham* [1949] 2 All E.R. 196; *Trestain* v. *Trestain* [1950] P. 198. See also *Williams* v. *Williams* [1957] 1 W.L.R. 148 (right to maintenance suspended, not forfeited, by desertion).
[26] [1949] L.J.R. 1424.
[27] [1950] P. 198.
[28] K. Gray, *Reallocation of Property on Divorce* (Professional Books, 1977).
[29] R. Deech, (1977) 7 Fam. Law 229 and *The Times*, February 14, 1980.
[30] [1950] 2 All E.R. 311, 313.
[31] *Ibid.*
[32] See Law Com. No. 103, Cmnd. 8041 (1980), pp. 47–49.

to begin a new life which is not overshadowed by the relationship which has broken down."[33]

Though not generally recognised as such, Lord Denning is one of the earliest judicial advocates of the "clean break" principle. An early example is found in the case of *Smith* v. *Smith* in 1970.[34] There was an application to vary a post-nuptial settlement of the former matrimonial home (the ex-husband having deserted and emigrated to New Zealand) in lieu of maintenance, so as to extinguish his interest in it and to make the house entirely hers. The first instance judge refused the application but the Court of Appeal decided he had exercised his discretion wrongly. It ordered that the settlement be varied by extinguishing the husband's interest in the house as if he were dead. Lord Denning said:

> "She should have the whole interest in this house, but we should recognise that it would be very difficult for her to obtain anything further from him. So she should forgo any claim to future maintenance, lump sum or secured provision."[35]

What the court did in *Smith* v. *Smith* was tantamount to the imposition of a "clean break."

In *Minton* v. *Minton*, generally regarded as the first case and certainly the first "modern" case, Lord Scarman used words suggesting that the court has the power to dismiss an application for periodical payments without the applicant's consent so as to preclude any further application.[36] In *Dunford* v. *Dunford*,[37] Lord Denning gave unequivocal support to the "clean break" principle. He stressed that it enabled parties to "know exactly where they stood with regard to the future."[38] Disapproving of the order of the County Court judge that the husband pay his wife 5p. a year, he struck it out of the order.

> "In that way we have the 'clean break.' The wife knows exactly where she stands. The house is vested in her. She has the property in it, and she can keep the family together. She can keep it as a home for the family as they grow up. She can keep it going indefinitely, knowing exactly where she stands."[39]

Lord Scarman's remarks about the imposition of a clean break are *obiter*, since the wife in *Minton* agreed to the dismissal of her claim for periodical payments. It is accordingly arguable that Lord Denning, in his enthusiasm for the "clean break," has gone too far. There was a Court of Appeal decision[40] which held that the court could not impose a "clean break" against the will of the wife but this was not brought to the court's attention in *Dunford*. Later Court of Appeal decisions[41] have refused to follow *Dunford*. To

---

[33] [1979] A.C. 593.
[34] [1970] 1 W.L.R. 155.
[35] *Ibid*. p. 158.
[36] [1979] A.C. 593, 608.
[37] [1980] 1 All E.R. 122.
[38] *Ibid*. p. 124.
[39] *Ibid*. p. 125.
[40] *Carpenter* v. *Carpenter* (1976) 6 Fam. Law 110.
[41] *Dipper* v. *Dipper* [1980] 2 All E.R. 722, 728–729. *per* Roskill L.J. and *Carter* v. *Carter* [1980] 1 W.L.R. 390.

dismiss a claim of its own motion, as the Court of Appeal did in *Dunford*, is inconsistent with the wording of the Matrimonial Causes Act 1973.[42] Lord Denning himself accepted in the earlier case of *Jessel* v. *Jessel*[43] that *Minton* be confined to the situation where either an application has been dismissed, or a nominal order has come to an end. He emphasised the fact that on the face of the order there was continuing provision for periodical payments and that it included the words "or until further notice." He said:

> "It is as plain as can be that [these words] keep the position alive so that an application can be made at any time for a further order to vary the periodical payments upwards or downwards as the situation changes in regard to them."[44]

Lord Denning's ambivalence about the "clean break" may in part spring from the fact that the idea itself is in conflict with the direction in section 25 of the Matrimonial Causes Act 1973 to "place the parties so far as it is practicable and, having regard to their conduct, just to do so, in the financial position in which they would have been if the marriage had not broken down. . . . "The "clean break" may have a greater air of reality than this direction but it is statutory and the "clean break" as yet is not. Not that Lord Denning has in the past been unwilling to introduce ideas before they are formulated in statute or put into effect.[45]

The 1970 Matrimonial Proceedings and Property Act was the first legislation in this country to treat financial provision and property adjustment on divorce as all of one piece. Lord Denning was saying as much well before 1970. Thus, in *Button* v. *Button* he said:

> " . . . I think it would be an advantage if all financial questions between husband and wife could be settled at one and the same time. Maintenance is linked with the property. If the wife stays in the house, her maintenance may be reduced on that account. If she gets a substantial capital sum out of the house, it may affect her maintenance. So it would be a good thing if applications as to maintenance and property were heard together."[46]

He repeated these remarks in *Gissing* v. *Gissing*.[47] He contrasted the "Divorce Division" with Chancery. The former had "ample power to do what is fair and reasonable"; the latter is "asked only to answer the cold legal question: what interest has the wife in the house?"[48] That the House of Lords[49] disagreed with him as to this specific point does not concern us here.

It is Lord Denning's analysis in *Wachtel* v. *Wachtel*[50] which provides the starting point of most if not all, contemporary legal reasoning on financial

---

[42] s.31.
[43] [1979] 3 All E.R. 645.
[44] *Ibid.* p. 648.
[45] See, *e.g. Re L* [1968] 1 All E.R. 20, 23 (anticipating Family Law Reform Act 1969, s.26) and *Levison* v. *Patent Carpet Cleaning Co.* [1977] 3 W.L.R. 90, 95 (anticipating Unfair Contract Terms Act 1977).
[46] [1968] 1 All E.R. 1064, 1067.
[47] [1969] 2 Ch. 85.
[48] *Ibid.* p. 1046.
[49] [1970] A.C. 777.
[50] [1973] 1 All E.R. 829, 835–841.

provision and property adjustment. Lord Denning expressed his own view on previous case law in *Trippas* v. *Trippas*:

> "The Divorce Reform Act 1969 and the Matrimonial Proceedings and Property Act 1970 have revolutionised the law on all these matters. There is no point in going back to the cases on the earlier Act. They are now out of date. The proper approach now is to take the new Acts and build on those."[51]

Lord Denning's judgment in *Wachtel* has taken on the dimensions of a statutory pronouncement, though in fact many of the ideas were not new at all. It was Ormrod J. at first instance in *Wachtel* who coined the phrase "obvious and gross" misconduct[52]; it was Phillimore L.J. in *Ackerman* v. *Ackerman*[53] who re-introduced the one-third rule and he who stressed that it was not a rule. Nevertheless, it would be foolhardy to ignore the significance of Lord Denning's carefully reasoned judgment in *Wachtel*.

The 1970 Act had stated that conduct was a relevant matter to take into account in assessing financial provision and in reallocating capital assets.[54] The earliest decisions after the Act's implementation saw judges applying a "discount" for matrimonial misconduct.[55] *Wachtel* v. *Wachtel* puts an end to that. Ormrod J. deserves much of the credit but, had Lord Denning not picked up his remarks,[56] they might have been consigned to oblivion. As it was, the phrase "obvious and gross" has become part of the divorce vocabulary. Lord Denning was sure that judges were not expected to hear "mutual recriminations" and go into "petty squabbles for days on end."[57] He believed: "in most cases both parties are to blame—or, as we would prefer to say—both parties have contributed to the breakdown." He continued:

> "There will no doubt be a residue of cases where the conduct of one of the parties is . . . 'both obvious and gross' so much so that to order one party to support another whose conduct falls into this category is repugnant to anyone's sense of justice. In such a case the court remains free to decline to afford financial support or to reduce the support . . . But, short of cases falling into this category, the court should not reduce its order for financial provision merely because of what was formerly regarded as guilt or blame. To do so would be to impose a fine for supposed misconduct in the course of an unhappy married life . . . "[58]

The test is not clear-cut but then short of a black-and-white rule it could not be. Different judges have different perceptions of what is obvious and gross misconduct.[59] Lord Denning's own views are well-known. One wonders

---

[51] [1973] Fam. 134.
[52] [1973] 1 All E.R. 113, 119.
[53] [1972] Fam. 225, 234.
[54] s.5 (now s.25 of the Matrimonial Causes Act 1973).
[55] See *Ackerman* v. *Ackerman* [1972] P. 1, 5, *per* Sir George Baker P. *Cf.* the Court of Appeal at pp. 225, 232, *per* Phillimore L.J.
[56] [1973] 1 All E.R. 829, 835.
[57] *Ibid.*
[58] *Ibid.* pp. 835–836.
[59] See K. Gray, *Reallocation of Property on Divorce*, pp. 203 *et seq.*; M.D.A. Freeman (1978) C.L.P. 109, 124–127. See also Lawton L.J. in *Blezard* v. *Blezard* (1980) 1 F.L.R. 253, 257.

what he would have made of *Harnett* v. *Harnett*.[60] Bagnall J. was not prepared
to characterise as "gross and obvious" the behaviour of a wife who had an
affair with a youth half her age at a time when her husband was getting over
an operation. Lord Denning did not sit in the appeal in this case.[61] Would his
populism have induced him to find such conduct "repugnant to anyone's
sense of justice"? The test is such that predictability is a hazardous activity.
The subject has provoked correspondence to, and a leader in, *The Times*[62]
and, though many favour greater account being taken of conduct, informed
opinion would see this as a retrogressive measure.[63]

A second major directive in Lord Denning's judgment in *Wachtel* concerns
lump sum payments. The concept dates from 1963[64] but judges had evinced
a reluctance to order lump sum payments.[65] Lord Denning stressed that: "In
every case the court should consider whether to order a lump sum to be
paid . . . " He stressed:

> "No order should be made for a lump sum unless the husband has
> capital assets out of which to pay it—without crippling his earning
> power.
>   When the husband has available capital assets sufficient for the
> purpose, the court should not hesitate to order a lump sum."[66]

He saw it as helping to remove the bitterness so often attendant on
periodical payments. The Law Commission[67] had expressed a hope that
wider use might be made of lump sums: *Wachtel* ensured that lump sums
became common even if the number of orders is still comparatively small.
But the greater willingness on the part of judges to make lump sum orders is
illustrated by recent cases where an unemployed man was ordered to make
one[68] and where a 69-year-old homeless man was awarded £4,000 (the Court
of Appeal was critical of this since it achieved nothing).[69] A major concern
today seems to be not whether to make a lump sum order but whether there
are limits on the amount that can be ordered where the potential payer is
exceptionally wealthy.[70] Lord Denning himself has only returned to the
question once since *Wachtel*. In *Trippas* v. *Trippas*,[71] he rejected the
"suggestion that a lump sum is simply another way of quantifying
maintenance."[72] It was, he said, "a separate provision on its own." A
divorce had taken place and the husband had subsequently sold his business.
There was evidence that had the marriage survived the husband would have
settled a sum of money on the wife out of the proceeds of the sale. "Paying off
an old retainer" was how she had described it.[73] Lord Denning looked to the

---

[60] [1973] Fam. 156.
[61] [1974] 1 W.L.R. 219.
[62] See leader in *The Times*, "Family Law and Common Justice," June 22, 1978.
[63] See J. Eekelaar, 95 L.Q.R. 253; Law Com. No. 112 (1981), pp. 13–14.
[64] Matrimonial Causes Act 1963, s.5(1).
[65] See, *e.g. Davis* v. *Davis* [1967] P. 185.
[66] [1973] 1 All E.R. 829, 840.
[67] Law Com. No. 25, para. 9.
[68] *Burridge* v. *Burridge* (1983) 4 F.L.R. 170.
[69] *Curtis* v. *Curtis* (1981) 11 Fam. Law 55.
[70] *Preston* v. *Preston* [1981] 3 W.L.R. 619 and cases cited therein.
[71] [1973] Fam. 134.
[72] *Ibid.* p. 140.
[73] *Ibid.* p. 241.

language of the statute. It "tells the court to do what it can to put them both in the same position as if the marriage had not broken down." He continued:

> "It is also to do what is just considering that she looked after the home and brought up the family over these 27 years. It seems to me only just that, having regard to the capital sum received by the husband, he should provide a lump sum for her."[74]

Lord Denning's remarks in *Wachtel* on the lump sum are of significance not merely because he supported the concept and initiated a trend but also because of his thinking on the relationship between lump sums and the matrimonial home. As he realised, the home is often the only asset of any value and its disposition is the most important question of all. Lord Denning distinguished cases where the wife had left from those in which she had stayed and he had gone. When the wife leaves, he thought:

> " . . . arrangements should be made whereby it is vested in him absolutely, free of any share in the wife, and he alone is liable for mortgage instalments. But the wife should be compensated for the loss of her share by being awarded a lump sum. It should be a sum sufficient to enable her to get settled in a place of her own. . . . It should be such as the husband can raise by further mortgage on the house without crippling him."

On the other hand, where the husband leaves:

> " . . . arrangements should be made whereby it is vested in her absolutely, free of any share in the husband: or, if there are children, settled on her and the children. . . . If there is a mortgage, some provision should be made for the mortgage instalments to be paid by the husband, or guaranteed by him. If this is done, there may be no necessity for a lump sum as well. Furthermore, seeing that she has the house, the periodic payments will be much less than they otherwise would be."[75]

Lord Denning's reasoning is superficially attractive but it is also rather simplistic. He has a tendency to pat solutions and this is a good illustration. In a period of inflation it can rarely be appropriate to deny a husband any share in the former matrimonial home, particularly where he has financed it.[76] On the other hand, to vest the house in the spouse who remains does not take account of the need for homes, especially homes for children.[77] Lord Denning's judgment in *Wachtel* can be criticised for underplaying both of these matters and subsequent case law has developed a number of techniques and solutions to inject a necessary realism into the question: who gets the matrimonial home and on what terms and conditions?[78]

Lord Denning's observations on matrimonial misconduct and his espousal of lump sum payments did much to chart the future, at least the immediate

[74] *Ibid.*
[75] [1973] 1 All E.R. 829, 840–841.
[76] See *Harvey* v. *Harvey* [1982] 1 All E.R. 693.
[77] See *Browne* v. *Pritchard* [1975] 1 W.L.R. 1366; *Hanlon* v. *Hanlon* [1978] 1 W.L.R. 592; *Martin* v. *Martin* [1978] Fam. 12.
[78] See *Harvey* v. *Harvey* [1982] 1 All E.R. 693.

future, of financial provision and "equitable redistribution" of property[79] on divorce. The same cannot be said of his reactivation of the discredited[80] notion of the "one-third rule." Phillimore L.J.'s remarks in *Ackerman* v. *Ackerman*[81] on the one-third rule would be no more remembered today than remarks in that case about discounts for misconduct, had not Lord Denning approved them in *Wachtel* v. *Wachtel*. I have earlier in this chapter criticised Lord Denning's justification of the one-third rule.[82] They show Lord Denning at his most chauvinist. He saw one-third as being as

> "good and rational a starting point as any other, remembering that the essence of the legislation is to secure flexibility to meet the justice of particular cases, and not rigidity, forcing particular cases to be fitted into some so-called principle within which they do not easily lie."[83]

He placed emphasis on the flexibility of the principle. It was only a starting point.

> "It will serve in cases where the marriage has lasted for many years and the wife has been in the home bringing up the children. It may not be applicable when the marriage has lasted only a short time, or where there are no children and she can go out to work."[84]

Even where the rule is inapplicable, one effect of *Wachtel* is that "arithemetical fractions have something of a mesmeric effect in the courts."[85] Whether mathematical formulae should help to solve human problems, there is no doubting that their principal advantage lies in facilitating out-of-court settlements. This was recently recognised by the President of the Family Division.[86]

This assumes that it can readily be predicted in which cases the one-third ratio[87] will apply. But twice in 1982[88] Ormrod L.J. said that the application of section 25 of the 1973 Act in the existing economic climate made the one-third calculation on gross income wholly inappropriate. He thought the provisions of the Act, which do not mention any mathematical division, should be applied "without superimposed judicial glosses."[89] The one-third rule has not been found very helpful in cases involving very large[90] or very small sums of money.[91] It is not usually applied to short marriages.[92] It has been said that the one-third starting point is inappropriate in applications by husbands for, though they "come to the judgment seat in matters of money

---

[79] The term is Ormrod L.J.'s. See *O'Donnell* v. *O'Donnell* [1976] Fam. 83.
[80] *Per* Sir Jocelyn Simon P. in *Kershaw* v. *Kershaw* [1966] P.13, 17. See, generally, S. Maidment (1974) 4 Fam. Law 172.
[81] [1972] Fam. 225, 234.
[82] Above.
[83] [1973] Fam. 72, 94.
[84] *Ibid.* p. 95.
[85] *Per* S. Cretney, *Principles of Family Law* (Sweet & Maxwell, 3rd ed., 1979), p. 312.
[86] In *Slater* v. *Slater* (1982) 3 F.L.R. 364.
[87] *Per* Ormrod L.J. in *O'Donnell* v. *O'Donnell* [1976] Fam. 83.
[88] *Furniss* v. *Furniss* (1982) 3 F.L.R. 58, *Stockford* v. *Stockford* (1982) 3 F.L.R. 46.
[89] In *Stockford* v. *Stockford*.
[90] *O'Donnell* v. *O'Donnell* (n. 79); *Preston* v. *Preston* (n. 70).
[91] *Scott* v. *Scott* [1978] 1 W.L.R. 723; *Cann* v. *Cann* [1977] 1 W.L.R. 938; *Furniss* v. *Furniss* (above n. 88), *Stockford* v. *Stockford* (above n. 88).
[92] *S.* v. *S.* [1977] Fam. 127.

and property upon a basis of complete equality,"[93] "there is no ordinary or usual case in which the wife is in a position to provide a lump sum for the husband."[94] A number of question marks accordingly remain over the one-third rule. Lord Denning's lead may ultimately have something of the blind alley or cul-de-sac about it.

The Matrimonial Home[95]

Anyone who reads *The Due Process of Law* will be left in no doubt that Lord Denning himself thinks his most substantial ventures into family law have been in connection with the matrimonial home.[96] His first reserved judgment concerned the variation of a post-nuptial settlement. He defined a settlement in characteristically wide terms and in language which was but a foretaste of much to come.

> "That principle, as I understand it, is that where a husband makes a continuing provision for the future needs of his wife in her character as a wife, which is still continuing when the marriage is dissolved, the provision is a 'settlement' which can be brought before the court to see whether the provision should continue now that she has ceased to be a wife. The same applies to a provision by a wife for her husband or by each or either for both."[97]

By 1947 he was already protecting deserted wives in the occupation of the matrimonial home and claiming that the discretion vested in the judge by section 17 of the Married Women's Property Act 1882 was "in no way fettered, though it must be exercised judicially."[98] Many of the cases for which Lord Denning will be remembered, whether as *enfant terrible*, judicial maverick or law reformer, are concerned with the ownership or occupation of the matrimonial home.

It was he who invented the "compendious phrase"[99] "family assets." In *The Due Process of Law*[1] he says he did so in the case of *Rimmer* v. *Rimmer*[2] in 1952. The notion is certainly there but the phrase itself was not used until 1955 in the case of *Cobb* v. *Cobb*.[3] He wrote:

> "In the case of the family assets, if I may so describe them, such as the matrimonial home and furniture, when both husband and wife contribute to the cost and the property is intended to be a continuing provision for them during their joint lives, the court leans towards the view that the property belongs to them jointly in equal shares."[4]

---

[93] *Calderbank* v. *Calderbank* [1976] Fam. 93, 102, *per* Scarman L.J.
[94] *Ibid.* p. 103, *per* Cairns L.J.
[95] See too the discussion of this topic from an equity and trust angle in Chap. 3.
[96] *Op. cit.* part 6.
[97] *Smith* v. *Smith* [1945] 1 All E.R. 584, 586.
[98] In *H.* v. *H.* (1947) 63 T.L.R. 645; *sub nom. Hutchinson* v. *Hutchinson* [1947] 2 All E.R. 792.
[99] His term. See *Nixon* v. *Nixon* [1969] 3 All E.R. 1133, 1137.
[1] *Op. cit.* p. 232.
[2] [1953] 1 Q.B. 63.
[3] [1955] 1 W.L.R. 731.
[4] [1955] 2 All E.R. 696, 698.

He was to repeat this many times: in *Fribance* v. *Fribance*[5] in 1957, in *Ulrich* v. *Ulrich*,[6] in *Chapman* v. *Chapman*[7] and in *Gissing* v. *Gissing*.[8] The House of Lords were subsequently to hold first in *Pettitt* v. *Pettitt*[9] in 1969 and then in *Gissing* v. *Gissing*[10] a year later that the ordinary rules of property law are applied to determine the ownership of the matrimonial home or, for that matter, any other property, and that the expression "family assets" had no legal meaning.

Lord Denning's response in a series of cases[11] in the early 1970s was to construct a beneficial interest in the matrimonial home by imposing a trust. The problem centred on indirect[12] contributions by the wife to the family budget. In *Gissing* v. *Gissing* Viscount Dilhorne said that proof of expenditure for the benefit of the family was not sufficient.[13] Lord Pearson thought this would be enough to establish an interest "if by arrangement between the spouses one of them by payment of the household expenses enables the other to pay the mortgage instalments."[14] In *Cowcher* v. *Cowcher* Bagnall J. thought that an indirect contribution might suffice if it was directly referable to acquisition costs.[15]

Lord Denning however, rejected the need to find such a causal relationship. In *Hazell* v. *Hazell*[16] he said he hoped that less would be heard of the phrase "referable to the acquisition of the house" in the future. He added:

> "It is sufficient if the contributions made by the wife are such as to relieve the husband from expenditure which he would otherwise have had to bear."[17]

The reasoning is that by helping in this way she has placed at her husband's disposal more money with which to pay the mortgage instalments.

> "It may be that he does not strictly need her help . . . but it he accepts it (and thus is enabled to save more of his own money) she becomes entitled to a share."[18]

This comes close to the invocation of the equitable estoppel doctrine: several judges have accepted that the rights of the parties can be affected by estoppel.[19]

---

[5] [1957] 1 W.L.R. 384.

[6] [1968] 1 W.L.R. 180.

[7] [1969] 1 W.L.R. 1367.

[8] [1968] 2 Ch. 85.

[9] [1970] A.C. 777.

[10] [1971] A.C. 885.

[11] *Heseltine* v. *Heseltine* [1971] 1 W.L.R. 342; *Hazell* v. *Hazell* [1972] 1 W.L.R. 301; *Davis* v. *Vale* [1971] 1 W.L.R. 1022; *Cooke* v. *Head* [1972] 1 W.L.R. 518.

[12] See *Hazell* v. *Hazell*, above, n. 11; *Falconer* v. *Falconer* [1970] 1 W.L.R. 1333; *Hargrave* v. *Newton* [1971] 1 W.L.R. 1611; *Davis* v. *Vale*, above, n. 11.

[13] [1971] A.C. 886, 901.

[14] T.*Ibid.* p. 903.

[15] [1972] 1 W.L.R. 425.

[16] See above, n. 11.

[17] *Ibid.* p. 304.

[18] *Ibid.* This has been criticised by J. Eekelaar, *"The Matrimonial Home in The Court of Appeal"* (1972) 88 L.Q.R. 333.

[19] For example, Lord Upjohn in *Pettitt* v. *Pettitt* [1970] A.C. 777; Lord Reid in *Gissing* v. *Gissing* [1971] A.C. 885 and Megaw L.J. in *Hazell* v. *Hazell*, above, n. 11.

In *Hazell* v. *Hazell* no mention was made by Lord Denning of the need for the contribution to be substantial but in *Falconer* v. *Falconer*[20] he had said that the only question was whether there had been a substantial financial contribution in money or money's worth to family expenses. He reiterated this in *Hargrave* v. *Newton*[21] and *Davis* v. *Vale*.[22] In *Hargrave* v. *Newton* the house had been purchased in the husband's name. The wife used her salary for family expenses. Some two years later she received £5,045 as a reward for finding money stolen by the Great Train Robbers. She used this money and her earnings for holidays, to pay telephone bills, for clothes for her husband and on the family car. Lord Denning applied the "simple test.":

> "did the wife make a substantial contribution direct or indirect, to the acquisition of the house or the repayment of the mortgage or the loan? If her efforts or her contributions relieved him of other expenses which he would otherwise have had to bear—so that he would not have been able to meet the mortgage instalments or the loan without her help—then she does make an indirect contribution."[23]

He cites in support Lord Reid's speech in *Gissing* v. *Gissing*,[24] but neglects to mention that Lord Reid was in the minority in that case. In *Hargrave* v. *Newton* Lord Denning would appear to have gone rather far even for him. The reward money did not make the purchase of the house possible. It was a windfall totally unrelated to the acquisition of the home. It is difficult to see how money spent on a holiday in Spain and respraying a car can relate to a house already acquired. Is it a proper inference that the wife, when she provided the money, expected to acquire an interest in the matrimonial home as a result? The logical extension of Lord Denning's rejection of direct referability is that a wife ought to be able to claim a share in any property purchased by the husband,[25] and not just the home. The question has not yet arisen in any reported case. Can *Hargrave* v. *Newton* and the other cases (*Hazell, Falconer, Davis* v. *Vale*) be reconciled with what the House of Lords ruled in *Gissing* v. *Gissing*? It is possible to argue that the wife in *Gissing*'s case relieved the husband of expenditure he would otherwise have had to bear. This fact was not, however, regarded as material by the House of Lords in *Gissing*. It is, therefore, just possible to argue that *Hargrave* v. *Newton* is good law or at least can stand with *Gissing*. The other Denning decisions just referred to cause less problems since they could be decided the same way on narrower grounds.

But if there is some doubt about the authority of *Hargrave* v. *Newton* there can be none about another line of decisions inspired by Lord Denning which hold that the wife may acquire an interest in the matrimonial home by working gratuitously in her husband's business. There are three cases. In *Nixon* v. *Nixon*[26] the wife helped to run the husband's market stall. At various

---

[20] [1970] 1 W.L.R. 1333.
[21] [1971] 1 W.L.R. 1611.
[22] [1971] 1 W.L.R. 1022.
[23] See n. 21 at p. 1613.
[24] [1971] A.C. 866, 896.
[25] See J. Eekelaar, "The Matrimonial Home in The Court of Appeal" (1972) 88 L.Q.R. 333, 335.
[26] [1969] 3 All E.R. 1133.

times she also helped in his shop and on his farm. She received no wages. To Lord Denning the case raised a "point of principle":

> "Up and down the country, a man's wife helps her husband in the business. She serves in the shop. He does the travelling around. If the shop and business belonged to him *before* they married, no doubt it will remain his after they marry. But she by her work afterwards should get some interest in it. Not perhaps an equal share, but some share. If they acquire the shop and business *after* they marry—and acquire it by their joint efforts—then it is their joint property, no matter that it is taken in the husband's name . . . if the wife had gone out to work and had earned wages which she brought into the family pool—out of which the shop and business were bought—she would certainly be in just as good a position when she serves in the shop and receives no wages, but the profits go into the business. The wife's services are equivalent to a financial contribution."[27]

In *Muetzel* v. *Muetzel*[28] the Court of Appeal held, Lord Denning again giving the main judgment, that a wife's beneficial interest in the matrimonial home was not restricted to the proportion that her initial financial contribution bore to the original purchase price. The court looked at all the contributions, direct and indirect, that she made and these included non-remunerated partnership work which helped to establish a profitable business. In *Re Cummins*,[29] the *Nixon* principle was held to apply after the death of the spouses so that the title to the business assets or their proceeds was to be dealt with after death as when husband and wife were both alive. It was said by Lord Denning that *Gissing* v. *Gissing* had not thrown "the slightest doubt"[30] on the principles laid down in *Nixon* v. *Nixon*. Rather disingenuously he added that *Gissing* showed the "legal basis" of *Nixon* v. *Nixon, viz.*:

> "The court imposes or imputes a trust whereby the husband holds the assets of the business—or their proceeds—on trust for both jointly, and, in the absence of any evidence sufficient to enable the court to distinguish between them, for them both equally."[31]

Lord Denning must have realised that *Gissing* v. *Gissing* decided no such thing. He is prepared to impose a trust: the House of Lords only to infer an agreement. Furthermore, the "equality is equity" maxim, upheld by Lord Denning in *Nixon* v. *Nixon*,[32] though not applied to the facts of that case, and supported by him in the Court of Appeal in *Gissing* v. *Gissing* was held by the House of Lords in *Gissing* to be the wrong approach where the fair estimate of the intended share was some fraction other than one-half.[33]

Prior to *Pettitt* v. *Pettitt*[34] Lord Denning had not found it necessary to impose trusts. His path to a just solution lay along section 17 of the 1882

---

[27] *Ibid.* p. 1136.
[28] [1970] 1 W.L.R. 188.
[29] [1971] 3 All E.R. 782.
[30] *Ibid.* p. 786.
[31] *Ibid.*
[32] [1969] 3 All E.R. 1133, 1137.
[33] [1971] A.C. 886, 908, *per* Lord Diplock.
[34] [1970] A.C. 777.

Married Women's Property Act. Lord Denning believed that this gave him "a free hand to do what is just,"[35] and to ignore strict legal rules governing title to property. In *Jansen* v. *Jansen* he said that "it gives rights where none existed before."[36] But others deprecated, what they called, "palm-tree justice,"[37] and the House of Lords in *Pettitt* v. *Pettitt* in 1969 ruled that the provision was procedural only, giving the court power to declare property rights but not to vary them.[38] With the sting removed from section 17, Lord Denning began in *Heseltine* v. *Heseltine*[39] to develop a new equitable doctrine, *viz.* the court may impose a trust wherever it would be inequitable for the estate owner to claim the property as his own, that is, to impose a trust wherever the circumstances made it just (in his eyes) to do so.

In *Heseltine* v. *Heseltine*, the wife had contributed four-fifths of the purchase price of the matrimonial home but this had been conveyed into the name of the husband. She also had transferred to her husband money totalling £40,000, relying on his advice that this would save estate duty if she predeceased him. She also transferred a further £20,000 to him for the sole purpose of enabling him to raise the securities necessary to become a "name" at Lloyd's. During the marriage four houses were purchased, all of which had been conveyed into the name of the husband.

As far as the matrimonial home was concerned Lord Denning said:

> "In the usual way the court imputes a trust under which the husband is to hold it for them both jointly in equal shares. But half-and-half is not an invariable division. If some other division is more fair, the court will adopt it."[40]

He cited as authority *Gissing* v. *Gissing*.[41] He then decided that the division of the proceeds of sale should be three-quarters to the wife and one-quarter to the husband. Had Lord Denning really applied *Gissing* v. *Gissing* he would have decided the matter by considering the principles of resulting trusts. The wife would then have got 80 per cent. of the proceeds of sale, and not 75 per cent. The result may not be very different but, as Oakley[42] has written, "the advantages of such an approach, apart from the fact that the House of Lords has decided it alone should be used, is that it is certain—parties can be safely advised as to their position, something which is totally impossible, when the courts impute trusts according to their view of what is fair or just."

Lord Denning went on to hold that the £40,000 was held by the husband on trust for the wife: his "conduct" was such that it would be "inequitable" for him to claim the property beneficially as his own.[43] The same principles were held to apply to the £20,000 and the four houses. Had Lord Denning

---

[35] In *Hine* v. *Hine* [1962] 1 W.L.R. 1124.
[36] [1965] P. 478.
[37] Bucknill L.J. in *Newgrosh* v. *Newgrosh* (unreported), cited by Evershed M.R. in *Rimmer* v. *Rimmer* [1953] 1 Q.B. 63, 72.
[38] [1970] A.C. 777.
[39] [1971] 1 All E.R. 952.
[40] *Ibid.* p. 954.
[41] [1971] A.C. 886, 896, (*per* Lord Reid), 900 (*per* Viscount Dilhorne), 902 (*per* Lord Pearson) and 904–905 (*per* Lord Diplock).
[42] "Has the Constructive Trust Become a General Equitable Remedy?" (1973) 26 Current Legal Problems 17, 28–29.
[43] [1971] 1 All E.R. 952, 955.

applied the principles of resulting trusts to the houses, he would have come to the same result. But this is not so with the £20,000 and the £40,000. The wife intended to transfer both these sums to her husband absolutely: otherwise she would not have been able to avoid estate duty[44] and he could not have become a "name" at Lloyds. There was no evidence of undue influence[45] in this case. Similar reasoning was employed in *Hazell* v. *Hazell*,[46] *Davis* v. *Vale*[47] as well as outside the context of marriage, to cohabitants in *Cooke* v. *Head*[48] and to the widow of a person formerly employed by an owner's predecessors in title in *Binions* v. *Evans*[49] and in other situations as well. One further point is worthy of note. Lord Denning has also implied that the court may look at the circumstances as they exist at the time of the marriage breakdown and do what seems just in the circumstances as they then exist. It is not, in his view, necessary to go back to the time of the transaction.[50]

Another strategy adopted by Lord Denning to enable a non-estate owner to acquire a beneficial interest in the matrimonial home is through effecting improvements to it. The process began with *Appleton* v. *Appleton*.[51] The husband, the wife and the 15-year-old son did substantial work to renovate a cottage in the wife's name. Lord Denning held:

> "Inasmuch as the registrar found that the husband had done up to about one-half of the work of renovation, the husband should get something. He should be entitled to so much of the enhanced value . . . as was due to his work and materials that he supplied . . . A percentage of the proceeds ought to go to him commensurate to the enhancement due to his work in improving the property . . . , and getting a better price on that account . . . "[52]

What was decided was not clear. Did the husband acquire an equitable interest in the property itself, or merely a charge against the proceeds of sale? Did the son also acquire an equitable interest and, if not, why not?[53]

In *National Provincial Bank* v. *Ainsworth*[54] Lord Upjohn stated that, since *Appleton* depended on a "too wide construction of section 17" of the 1882 Act, it was not correctly decided.[55] But in *Jansen* v. *Jansen* Lord Denning insisted it was.[56] In that case the husband, a student, gave up his studies to convert his wife's house into flats. A profit was eventually made and he claimed to be entitled to a share either because of the parties' agreement or because of his work. Lord Denning could find nothing approximating to a contractual agreement[57] but there was, he held, "a joint enterprise akin to a

[44] *Cf. Tinker* v. *Tinker* [1970] P. 136 (also a decision of Lord Denning's).
[45] See *Inche Noriah* v. *Shaik Allie Bin Omar* [1929] A.C. 127, 135, (*per* Lord Hailsham).
[46] [1972] 1 W.L.R. 342.
[47] [1971] 1 W.L.R. 1022.
[48] [1972] 1 W.L.R. 518.
[49] [1972] Ch. 359.
[50] *Cracknell* v. *Cracknell* [1971] P. 356, 362–363; applied by the Court of Appeal (Denning not sitting) in *Bothe* v. *Amos* [1976] Fam. 46. See also *Hall* v. *Hall* (1982) 3 F.L.R. 379 (a case of cohabitation).
[51] [1965] 1 All E.R. 44.
[52] *Ibid.* p. 46.
[53] See P. Seago and A. Bissett-Johnson, *Cases and Materials on Family Law*, (Sweet & Maxwell, London, 1976), p. 240.
[54] [1965] A.C. 1175.
[55] *Ibid.* p. 1236.
[56] [1965] P.478, 488.
[57] *Cf.* Davies L.J. at pp. 489–90.

partnership."[58] He argued that if the two had not been husband and wife "the law would readily infer a provision that he should have some part of the profit. So should equity say today, seeing that the marriage has broken up."[59]

In both *Appleton* and *Jansen* major work had been undertaken of a type "which a contractor is normally employed to do."[60] This was not so in *Button* v. *Button*[61] where the work done was "the ordinary kind of work,"[62] which spouses do without acquiring an interest in the property as a result. A day earlier *Pettitt* v. *Pettitt*[63] had been decided in the Court of Appeal. (Lord Denning did not hear this appeal). When it got to the House of Lords[64] the majority approved what Lord Denning said in *Button* v. *Button*. Though the husband had done rather a lot, building in wardrobes, building an ornamental wall in the garden and a side wall, he was refused an interest in the matrimonial home. The work was, it was said, too ephemeral or insubstantial. It was merely the sort of "do-it-yourself job" which husbands often do.[65] Lord Denning thought that the House of Lords in *Pettitt* had "unsettled" the law,[66] though in an earlier case he had said that it had not altered the law to any material extent.[67]

Parliament's response was to pass section 37 of the Matrimonial Proceedings and Property Act 1970.[68] This was a great victory for Lord Denning's school of thought and he did not disguise his pleasure.[69]

> "Note that section 37 is not an *alteration* of the previous law. It is a *declaration* of the law—a declaration of what the law was before the Act. It affirms, therefore, the decision of this court in *Jansen* v. *Jansen* and the principles adopted by the equitable school."

Lord Denning has done much also to protect the occupation in the matrimonial home of the deserted wife. The wife's right to stay in the matrimonial home as against her husband had been established before Lord Denning became a judge.[70] It was a right he enthusiastically embraced in *Hutchinson* v. *Hutchinson*,[71] *Lee* v. *Lee*[72] and *Halden* v. *Halden*.[73] In the last of these cases he said:

> "Whatever the position may be as to a subsequent purchaser, it seems to me quite plain that as between husband and wife, if the husband deserts his wife, leaving her in the house, he has not a right to turn her out. She

---

[58] *Ibid*. p. 489.
[59] *Ibid*.
[60] *Per* Lord Denning in *Button* v. *Button* [1968] 1 All E.R. 1064, 1066.
[61] [1968] 1 All E.R. 1064.
[62] *Ibid*. p. 1067.
[63] [1968] 1 W.L.R. 443.
[64] [1970] A.C. 777.
[65] [1968] 1 All E.R. 1064, 1066.
[66] See *Davis* v. *Vale* [1971] 2 All E.R. 1021, 1024.
[67] *Smith* v. *Baker* [1970] 2 All E.R. 826, 828.
[68] On the recommendation of the Law Commission, Law Com. No. 25, para. 56.
[69] *Davis* v. *Vale* [1971] 2 All E.R. 1021, 1025.
[70] *Bramwell* v. *Bramwell* [1942] 1 K.B. 370. But see Lord Upjohn in *National Provincial Bank* v. *Ainsworth* [1965] A.C. 1175, 1234–1235.
[71] (1947) 63 T.L.R. 645.
[72] [1952] 2 Q.B. 489, 492.
[73] [1966] 3 All E.R. 412, 413.

has not to show a legal or equitable interest in herself. It is sufficient for
her to say: 'I am his wife and I am under the roof which he provided.'
He is not entitled to turn her out except by order of the court; and that
will not be given in the ordinary way unless he provides alternative
accommodation for her."[74]

Section 1 of the Matrimonial Homes Act 1967 is statutory confirmation of
this common law right.[75]

In a series of cases beginning with *Bendall* v. *McWhirter*[76] in 1952 the
courts, with Lord Denning very much in the vanguard, went even further
and created, what was known as, the "deserted wife's equity." The equity
was one of the boldest creations of the judiciary this century. The wife's right
to remain in the matrimonial home being "purely personal to her,"[77] it was
assumed as late as *Thompson* v. *Earthy*[78] in 1951 that it could not be enforced
against a purchaser from the husband. But in *Errington* v. *Errington and
Woods*[79] Lord Denning foreshadowed what he developed fully in *Bendall* v.
McWhirter. In *Bendall* v. *McWhirter* the defendant wife was deserted by her
husband who told her she could have the house and the furniture. He was
later adjudicated bankrupt and the plaintiff, as his trustee in bankruptcy,
brought an action for possession of the house and mesne profits. It was held
that, since the husband could not revoke his wife's authority to stay in the
house, his trustee took subject to the same right and so was not entitled to
possession. Lord Denning argued:

> "The right of a deserted wife to stay in the matrimonial home proceeds
> out of an irrevocable authority which the husband is presumed in law to
> have conferred on her. . . . This authority flows from the status of
> marriage, coupled with the fact of separation owing to the husband's
> misconduct."[80]

In other words the wife's right was analogous to that of a contractual licensee
with an irrevocable authority.[81] In Lord Denning's view the wife had an
"equity": to Somervell and Romer L.JJ. the case turned on the special
position of a trustee in bankruptcy. In *Jess B. Woodcock & Sons Ltd.* v. *Hobbs*[82]
the wife's right was described by Lord Denning once again as an "equity." It
was held to prevail against a subsequent purchaser with knowledge or notice
of the facts. Lord Denning's view was followed in other cases at first
instance.[83]

The deserted wife's equity provoked a torrent of criticism and not just
among "purists,"[84] as Lord Denning himself says. One of the earliest was
Megarry. He thought that legislation rather than litigation was the "only

---

[74] *Ibid.* p. 413.
[75] Though the right was extended to husbands.
[76] [1952] 2 Q.B. 466.
[77] *Ibid.* p. 477.
[78] [1951] 2 K.B. 596.
[79] [1952] 1 K.B. 290, 298.
[80] [1952] 2 Q.B. 466, 477.
[81] See *Errington* v. *Errington and Woods* [1952] 1 K.B. 290.
[82] [1955] 1 W.L.R. 152.
[83] *Barclays Bank* v. *Bird* [1954] Ch. 274; *Street* v. *Densham* [1954] 1 W.L.R. 624.
[84] *The Due Process of Law*, p. 214.

satisfactory way of delimiting the bounds of so complex a subject."[85] In *Campbell Discount* v. *Bridge*, Harman L.J. remarked that the deserted wife's condition "has really not been improved at all now that this so-called equity has been analysed."[86] In *Westminster Bank* v. *Lee*,[87] Upjohn J.'s concern was that every intending purchaser or lender would have to inquire into the relationship of husband and wife. The concept always remained problematic. What of the wife constructively deserted by her husband?[88] What of the husband deserted by an estate-owning wife? Why should the wife's rights have only been enforceable when the marriage had broken up? A husband who knew he was about to go bankrupt did his wife a favour if he deserted her first. As Lord Hodson put it in *National Provincial Bank* v. *Ainsworth*: "there is no reason why the wife should be in a better position if her husband becomes bankrupt after leaving her than she would have been if his bankruptcy had taken place while they were living together."[89]

The deserted wife's equity survived until 1965. In *National Provincial Bank* v. *Ainsworth* "social considerations of humanity"[90] were ceded to justice to third parties and sound principles of real property law. The House of Lords held that a wife had no right of property entitling her to remain in the former matrimonial home as against the bank as mortgagee. Her rights in relation to occupation of the matrimonial home, in her name, were personal rights against her husband, flowing from her status as wife, and did not confer on her any equitable interest or right of property in the land. Nor was she, if she lived in the matrimonial home, there as licensee of her husband. Consequently, if a deserted wife remained in occupation of the matrimonial home that belonged to her husband, she had no right, good against third parties such as a purchaser or mortgagee from him, to continue in occupation of the matrimonial home.

Michael Beloff has pointed out that Lord Denning defeated is but as a prelude to Lord Denning triumphant.[91] And so it was here. His boldest invention had been blown to "smithereens"[92] by the House of Lords but this was but a catalyst to reform. The Matrimonial Homes Act 1967 gave a deserted wife, indeed any non-estate owner spouse, the opportunity to register a charge or place a caution or notice[93] against the title of the estate-owning spouse and this would protect her (or him) against a purchaser or mortgagee, though not, ironically, against a trustee in bankruptcy.[94] Lord Denning was naturally pleased that there was to be legislation to protect non-owning spouses, but he was concerned about the limitation that protection required that a charge be registered. He writes in *The Due Process of Law*:

---

[85] "The Deserted Wife's Right to Occupy the Matrimonial Home," 68 L.Q.R. 379.
[86] [1961] 2 W.L.R. 596, 605.
[87] [1956] Ch. 7, 22.
[88] The first case to get to the Court of Appeal after the Matrimonial Homes Act 1967 concerned a constructively deserted wife. See *Baynham* v. *Baynham* discussed below.
[89] [1965] A.C. 1175, 1222.
[90] *Ibid.* p. 1242, *per* Lord Wilberforce.
[91] "Reforming Judge," New Society, February 7, 1980, p. 300.
[92] *Per* Lord Denning in *The Due Process of Law*, p. 215.
[93] See Matrimonial Homes Act 1967, s.2(7). See now new s.2(7A), inserted by Matrimonial Homes and Property Act 1981, s.4(2) (cautions no longer permissible). The law has now been consolidated in the Matrimonial Homes Act 1983.
[94] See Matrimonial Homes Act 1983, s.2(7).

" . . . When a wife is deserted, she does not go at once and register a charge. She has no solicitor to advise her. She knows nothing of the Land Register. She stays weeping at home waiting for her husband to return."[95]

He spoke[96] against registration of a charge as a pre-requisite to protection. He returned to, what he saw as, the unreality of the charge notion in *Williams and Glyn's Bank* v. *Boland*.[97] In the Parliamentary debate in 1966 he went so far as to recommend strongly:

" . . . that in future all wives, whenever their matrimonial home is bought in the husband's name, immediately, without waiting for any trouble to arise, should go and register their right in case in the future something should go wrong with the marriage."[98]

Registration is fairly widespread,[99] though whether this is to be attributed to Lord Denning's advocacy is dubious.

Lord Denning's battles to protect the wife's occupation of the matrimonial home do not end with the passing of the 1967 Act. He heard, and gave the leading judgment in, the first case under the Act to reach the Court of Appeal.[1] Interestingly, it was a case which involved the constructive desertion of a wife. The deserted wife's equity would not have protected her. She had left the matrimonial home and subsequently registered a Class F charge when she learned that her husband was proposing to sell up and emigrate. The commissioner ordered that the husband leave the home and that the wife should be allowed to come back. Lord Denning agreed with this order. It was "the only effective means whereby she could be secured. It was the only way in which the Class F charge could be perfected."[2] The wife had "a conditional right to occupy, which is conditional on leave being obtained, and is complete when leave is given by the court."[3] But can the charge be registered, even before leave is obtained? This difficult point was glossed over by Lord Denning perhaps because the wife had registered in this case. Davies L.J. sensibly was more guarded.[4] It was subsequently held that a spouse not in occupation could register a charge before leave of the court was obtained.[5]

The case of *Gurasz* v. *Gurasz*,[6] to which reference was made earlier in this chapter, also exposed a difficulty, and in this case a lacuna, in the 1967 Act. That Act only protected, what Lord Denning called, "a bare wife"[7] and not one who is a joint owner with her husband. This limitation did not concern Lord Denning unduly. He said:

---

[95] See *The Due Process of Law*, p. 220.
[96] 275 H.L. Official Report (5th Series) Col. 44.
[97] [1981] A.C. 487.
[98] [1980] 2 All E.R. 408.
[99] In 1977–1978 there were 10,687 applications to register Class F charges and a further 6,300 or so applications in respect of registered land. (Report on H.M. Land Registry, 1977–8, para. 34).
[1] *Baynham* v. *Baynham* [1968] 1 W.L.R. 1890.
[2] *Ibid.* p. 1896.
[3] *Ibid.*
[4] *Ibid.*
[5] *Watts* v. *Waller* [1973] Q.B. 153. *Cf. Rutherford* v. *Rutherford* [1970] 1 W.L.R. 1479.
[6] [1970] P. 11.
[7] *Ibid.* p. 17.

"By virtue of her joint ownership, she has a right to occupy the house by herself and her children. The courts can certainly enforce that right by allowing her to re-enter the house and by preventing her husband from interfering with her exercise of that right. It is true, of course, that the husband is also a joint owner, and by virtue thereof, the husband has a right to occupy it. But that is a right which the courts, for the protection of the wife, can restrict: just as it can restrict his right, if he were sole owner. Such a power to restrict arises out of her personal right, as a wife, to occupy the house. If his conduct is so outrageous as to make it impossible for them to live together, the court can restrain him from using the house even though he is a joint owner."[8]

The gap in the statute was plugged by amending legislation the following year.[9] Often today the regulation of housing is sought in cases of domestic violence. Lord Denning has not been prominently involved in these cases, with the exception of *Davis* v. *Johnson*,[10] where his concern was predominantly with the proper construction of a statute designed to tackle such violence.

However, and following on from *Gurasz*, in *Hall* v. *Hall*[11] in 1971 he laid down a test for orders excluding a husband from the matrimonial home which came to circumscribe judicial discretion for about four years. He said: "an order to exclude one spouse or the other from the matrimonial home is a drastic order. It ought not to be made unless it is proved to be impossible for them to live together in the same house."[12] Sachs L.J. made a similar remark.[13] It was, however, a subsidiary remark of Lord Denning's in this case which anticipated the test that would come to dominate appellate thinking. His view that it was important "to have regard to the interests of the children,"[14] did not influence the Court of Appeal in *Bassett* v. *Bassett*,[15] *Walker* v. *Walker*[16] or *Samson* v. *Samson*,[17] but it showed that despite the restrictive test in *Hall* v. *Hall* his thinking was not far out of line with contemporary judicial attitudes.[18]

Another Lord Denning decision on the occupation of the matrimonial home of the same vintage as *Hall* is *Tarr* v. *Tarr*.[19] The case turned on the meaning of "regulating the exercise . . . of the right to occupy the dwelling house" in section 1(2) of the Matrimonial Homes Act.[20] Lord Denning gave the word "regulation" a "liberal meaning,"[21] thus enabling the court to make an order which in the context the court required. He held that the court could make an order excluding the husband from a council house in his name

---

[8] *Ibid.*
[9] Matrimonial Proceedings and Property Act 1970, s.38.
[10] [1978] 2 W.L.R. 182.
[11] [1971] 1 All E.R. 762.
[12] *Ibid.* p. 764.
[13] *Ibid.* p. 765.
[14] *Ibid.* p. 764.
[15] [1975] Fam. 76.
[16] [1978] 1 W.L.R. 533.
[17] [1982] 1 W.L.R. 252, or *Richards* v. *Richards* [1983] 3 W.L.R. 173.
[18] There is, however, another line of thought, in retreat until *Richards* v. *Richards*, represented in *Elsworth* v. *Elsworth* [1980] 1 Fam. L.R. 245, *Myers* v. *Myers* [1982] 1 W.L.R. 247 and most significantly in *Richards* v. *Richards*.
[19] [1971] 1 All E.R. 817.
[20] Edmund Davies L.J. described the language as "unnecessarily obscure," *ibid.* p. 819.
[21] *Ibid.* p. 819.

"for a limited period or until further order."[22] He may have been influenced by his assumption that the husband had been particularly cruel.[23] Unfortunately, as in *Halden* v. *Halden*,[24] Lord Denning made the error of assuming that a non-cohabitation clause was only inserted in bad cases of cruelty. In fact they were often automatic, even if not requested.[25] The House of Lords reversed the Court of Appeal[26] in *Tarr* v. *Tarr*.[27] It took the view that if Parliament had wished the courts to have the power to exclude it would have said so in express terms.[28] The Finer committee on one-parent families pressed for this gap in the legislation to be closed[29] and it was in 1976.[30] Thus, once again, legislation followed to reassert an interpretation of the law for which Lord Denning had previously argued.

In *Davis* v. *Johnson*[31] the Court of Appeal's interpretation of the Domestic Violence and Matrimonial Proceedings Act 1976 was upheld by the House of Lords,[32] though the Lords was critical of the attitude taken to precedent and *travaux préparatoires* by Lord Denning. These matters are outside the province of this chapter and are commented upon elsewhere.[33] The case concerned a battered cohabitant and the question which arose was whether she could exclude her violent partner from the council flat of which the parties were joint tenants. To Lord Denning the Act was "perfectly clear."[34] He thought the reasoning in two previous Court of Appeal decisions[35] bad. Though agreeing with him, it must be said that the reasoning was not unorthodox. In essence it stressed property rights. Lord Denning's riposte was to say that if any effect was to be given to the section at all the court must be allowed to override property rights and so to exclude a man, whatever property rights he had. He continued:

> "Social justice requires that personal rights should, in a proper case, be given priority over rights of property."[36]

He referred to *Tarr* v. *Tarr*[37] and *National Provincial Bank* v. *Ainsworth*[38] and continued:

> "I know that in those two cases the House of Lords reversed the decisions of this court and gave priority to property rights. But Parliament in each case afterwards passed laws so as to restore the decisions of this court. I prefer to go by the principles underlying the legislative enactments rather than the out-dated notions of the past."[39]

---

[22] *Ibid.*

[23] *Ibid.* p. 818.

[24] [1966] 1 W.L.R. 1481.

[25] See C. Gibson, "The Separation Order: A Study In Textbook Law and Practice" (1970) 33 M.L.R. 63.

[26] It was a unanimous Court of Appeal but Edmund Davies L.J. was not completely convinced that their interpretation was right. See [1971] 1 All E.R. 817, 820.

[27] [1973] A.C. 254.

[28] See Lord Pearson's speech, *ibid.* pp. 267–268.

[29] Cmnd. 5629, para. 6.44, 1974.

[30] By the Domestic Violence and Matrimonial Proceedings Act 1976, s.3.

[31] [1978] 1 All E.R. 841.

[32] [1979] A.C. 264.

[33] See Chap. 1, pp. 13, 18.

[34] [1978] 1 All E.R. 841, 847.

[35] *B.* v. *B.* [1978] Fam. 26; *Cantliff* v. *Jenkins* [1978] 1 All E.R. 836.

[36] [1978] 1 All E.R. 841, 849.   [38] [1965] A.C. 1175.

[37] [1973] A.C. 254.   [39] [1978] 1 All E.R. 841, 847.

On this occasion the House of Lords upheld the Court of Appeal. Lord Scarman, indeed, picked up Lord Denning's point: he noted that "the restriction or suspension for a time of property rights is a familiar aspect of much of our social legislation"[40] and quoted as an example the Rent Acts. One other aspect of Lord Denning's judgment in *Davis* v. *Johnson* merits comment. The 1976 Act defines cohabitation in terms of "living with each other in the same household." Literally interpreted this would deprive a person of relief if she were to leave as a result of the violence. And so the Court of Appeal in *B.* v. *B.*,[41] interpreted it. Lord Denning, rightly it is submitted, had no truck with such formalism. As far as he was concerned, the words presented no difficulty: "They are used to denote the relationship between the parties before the incident which gives rise to the application."[42] This is so obvious and so sensible that it is astonishing that it could have been interpreted any other way. Lord Denning's interpretation has been followed since.[43]

Lord Denning's most recent foray into matters relating to protection of occupation of the matrimonial home was in the case of *Williams and Glyn's Bank* v. *Boland*[44] and once again the House of Lords upheld him.[45] Both courts held that a wife with a beneficial interest in the matrimonial home who was physically present in it was in "actual occupation"[46] and so had an overriding interest which took priority over the bank's interest as mortgagee. In retrospect the Lords' decisions in *Davis* v. *Johnson* and *Boland* are more interesting than the Court of Appeal's. Would the House of Lords twenty years ago have allowed the physical protection of an unmarried woman to prevail over a property interest; would they not, as in *National Provincial Bank* v. *Ainsworth*, have favoured a purchaser or mortgagee rather than a wife? That the Court of Appeal is now being upheld is a reflection of a change in ideology and emphasis in the final court of appeal. In no small part this change is the result of Lord Denning's campaigns, wrong-headed though some of them may have been.

Cohabitation

In the most recently reported cohabitation case,[47] Lord Denning regretted that, as he put it, the concept of marriage was being "eroded." His statement did not disguise his own sadness. "Many couples lived together as if they were husband and wife when they were not married."[48] In *The Due Process of Law* he wrote: "The only basis for a sound family life is a Christian marriage . . . "[49] These expressions are perfectly consonant with Lord

---

[40] [1979] A.C. 264.
[41] [1978] 1 All E.R. 821, 828, *per* Bridge L.J.; p. 832, *per* Waller L.J.; p. 834, *per* Megaw L.J.
[42] [1978] 1 All E.R. 841, 850.
[43] *McLean* v. *Nugent* (1979) 123 S.J. 521; *Adeoso* v. *Adeoso* [1980] 1 W.L.R. 1535.
[44] [1979] Ch. 312.
[45] [1980] 2 All E.R. 409.
[46] Within s.70(1)(g) of the Land Registration Act 1925. The case is thus authority only for registered land but it seems that it would be followed in the case of unregistered land too. *Caunce* v. *Caunce* [1969] 1 W.L.R. 286 is thus of dubious authority today. See, further, M.D.A. Freeman, "Monied Might and the Matrimonial Home" (1981) 11 Fam. Law 37, and Law Commission, Law Com. 115, para. 17 (1982).
[47] *Bernard* v. *Josephs* [1982] 3 All E.R. 162, 165.
[48] *Ibid.* p. 165.
[49] *The Due Process of Law*, p. 201.

Denning's moral fundamentalism, depicted earlier in this chapter.[50] With this in mind, his response to situations where cohabitation has broken down may surprise some. They might expect him to adopt the view that the law should only afford protection and relief to those lawfully married. Lord Denning's response, by contrast, indeed the response of the judiciary generally, has been to treat cohabiting couples like married couples wherever possible.[51] There is a legal framework governing the personal relationships of married couples. Running through it, is the notion of female dependence and concomitantly of the need to protect women. The judges, Lord Denning very much to the vanguard, have tried to impose upon cohabiting couples a relationship which approximates to that constructed for marriage. It is almost as if the judiciary's riposte to those who do not marry is to thrust marriage upon them willy-nilly. They do not do this with any relationship outside marriage: rather with those that conform stereotypically to norms associated with marriage. Thus the retaining of separate names or separate bank accounts may induce the courts to treat a relationship as contractual and not to impose upon it consequences that flow from status.[52] The female cohabitant's behaviour is scrutinised. Has she done the sort of things that a married woman might be expected to do or has she exceeded expectations in some way, for example, by her building activities.[53] Her sexual fidelity is also examined rather as a married woman's was under the old fault-based law of divorce.[54] What superficially looks progressive, on closer examination is more suspect.

In *Cooke* v. *Head*[55] Lord Denning treated an unmarried couple in the same way as he treated the married in such cases as *Hazell* v. *Hazell*,[56] *Cracknell* v. *Cracknell*[57] and *Hargrave* v. *Newton*.[58]

> "It is now held that, whenever two parties by their joint efforts acquire property to be used for their joint benefit, the courts may impose or impute a constructive or resulting trust. The legal owner is bound to hold the property on trust for them both. This trust does not need any writing. It can be enforced by an order for sale. . . . It applies to husband and wife, to engaged couples, and to man and mistress, and maybe to other relationships too."[59]

Karminski L.J. purported to agree with Lord Denning but in fact limited his principle to cases where a man and a woman set up home together "and intend also to marry when they are free."[60] Lord Denning's test may lack this qualification but it was not a reserved judgment and he may well have agreed

---

[50] Above.
[51] See, generally, M.D.A. Freeman and C.M. Lyon, *Cohabitation Without Marriage, An Essay In Law and Social Policy* (Gower Press, 1983), Chaps. 4 and 6.
[52] See, *e.g. Helby* v. *Rafferty* [1979] 1 W.L.R. 13, not a decision of Lord Denning's.
[53] As in *Cooke* v. *Head, Eves* v. *Eves*. See also, as regards married couples, *Smith* v. *Baker* [1970] 2 All E.R. 826 ("she even helped dig the foundations herself," *per* Lord Denning at p. 827).
[54] See Ruth Deech's "The Case Against The Legal Recognition of Cohabitation" (1980) 29 I.C.L.Q. 480.
[55] [1972] 1 W.L.R. 518.
[56] [1972] 1 W.L.R. 301.
[57] [1971] P. 356.
[58] [1971] 1 W.L.R. 1611.
[59] [1972] 2 All E.R. 38, 41.
[60] *Ibid.* p. 43.

with Karminski L.J.'s sentiments. Indeed, remarks he made in *Tanner* v. *Tanner* suggest that he did.[61]

In *Eves* v. *Eves*[62] the Court of Appeal, Lord Denning once again giving the leading judgment, followed *Cooke* v. *Head*. Lord Denning quoted his remarks in *Cooke* v. *Head*. He referred particularly to the male cohabitant's conduct. How he gained her confidence; how she trusted him. He had gained her compliance by a statement that he intended to put the property into their joint names as soon as it was legally possible. Lord Denning thought that "he should be judged by what he told her—by what he had led her to believe—and not by his own intent which he kept to himself."[63] He also remarked:

> "It is clear that her contribution was such that if she had been a wife she would have had a good claim to have a share in [the house] on a divorce."[64]

He cited *Wachtel* v. *Wachtel*[65] in support. In both *Cooke* v. *Head* and *Eves* v. *Eves* the female cohabitant was held to have acquired an interest by way of trust (one-third in *Cooke* v. *Head*, one-quarter in *Eves* v. *Eves*). The two cases[66] show the way the courts, but especially Lord Denning, are developing principles for drawing inferences from the relationships of cohabitants in roughly the same way as they have done in the case of husband and wife. In *Eves* v. *Eves* a trust was implied.

In *Tanner* v. *Tanner*,[67] a few days later, a contract was implied. The male partner had purchased a house for the defendant and their twin baby daughters. She had left her rent-controlled flat. The relationship broke down and the plaintiff claimed possession of the house on the basis that the defendant had only a bare licence which he had revoked. Lord Denning's response was:

> "I cannot believe that this is the law. This man had a moral duty to provide for the babies of whom he was the father. I would go further. I think he had a legal duty towards them. Not only towards the babies. But also towards their mother. She was looking after them and bringing them up. In order to fulfil this duty towards the babies, he was under a duty to provide for the mother too."[68]

A contractual licence was inferred. Consideration was found in the defendant giving up her rent-controlled flat. The terms of the licence were that she should have accommodation in the house for herself and the children so long as they were of school age and the accommodation was reasonably required. Lord Denning went further than was strictly necessary to hold that the court could not only imply a contract but "if need be, impose the equivalent of a

---

[61] [1975] 1 W.L.R. 1346.
[62] [1975] 1 W.L.R. 1338.
[63] *Ibid.* p. 772. She was under-age at the time of the conveyance: hence could not be an estate owner.
[64] *Ibid.* p. 772.
[65] [1973] Fam. 72.
[66] See also *Bernard* v. *Josephs* [1982] 3 All E.R. 162.
[67] [1975] 3 All E.R. 776. See the brief discussion of this case in Chap. 3 above.
[68] *Ibid.* p. 779.

contract."[69] Cretney is so astonished by this statement that he puts the word [*sic*] after "impose."[70] But is what Lord Denning saying so out of line with contemporary opinion? Lord Wilberforce said in a recent case that "the movement of the law of contract is away from a rigid theory of autonomy towards the discovery—or I do not hesitate to say imposition—by the courts of just solutions, which can be ascribed to reasonable men in the position of the parties."[71] It is true that he was referring, in the context of frustration, to the imposition of a result which terminated rather than created a relationship, but it shows, I believe, Lord Denning's prescience rather than his unorthodoxy. Lord Denning in a subsequent case imposed a contract. Later cases[72] demonstrate that the courts are treading warily with the notion of an implied licence.

In *Cooke* v. *Head* the Court of Appeal refused to follow a previous Court of Appeal decision. They did not say they were doing so: they simply decided the instant case as if the earlier one were not there. Lord Denning admitted this in *Dyson Holdings* v. *Fox*,[73] another case on cohabitation, in which he refused to follow *Gammans* v. *Ekins*.[74] The previous decision, he said, was "not in accord with modern thinking."[75] Lord Denning's judgment in *Dyson Holdings* v. *Fox* is a good illustration of his thinking. The question which arose was whether a 74 year old woman who had lived with a man for 21 years, the cohabitation having terminated on his death some 14 years earlier, could be turned out of a house she had occupied for 35 years, by a property company. There was no doubt where Lord Denning's sympathy lay. She could stay if she were a member of her former cohabitant's family. Existing case law would have allowed the court so to hold had they had children.[76] But they had not. Lord Denning thought this "a ridiculous distinction. So ridiculous, indeed, that it should be rejected by this court."[77] So what was to be done with the previous case law? Lord Denning had two answers. First, to assert in his grand style that the Court of Appeal was not bound by previous decisions which, as a result of a change in social conditions, were not in accord with modern thinking. And, secondly, to demonstrate, in rather a devious fashion, that *Gammans* v. *Ekins* could be disposed of by one of the exceptions laid down in *Young* v. *Bristol Aeroplane Co.*[78] I do not find the latter arguments convincing. I wonder if Lord Denning himself was not being just a little disingenuous. He was, of course, covering himself. He has learnt from experience that the House of Lords is more likely to uphold his decisions when they are grounded in traditional reasoning processes.

Children

Lord Denning has been involved in a large number of reported decisions relating to children. Many of them are important decisions, even if they were

[69] *Ibid.* p. 780.
[70] *Principles of Family Law* (Sweet & Maxwell, 3rd ed., 1979), p. 247.
[71] *National Carriers Ltd.* v. *Panalpina (Northern) Ltd.* [1981] A.C. 675, 696.
[72] *Horrocks* v. *Forray* [1976] 1 W.L.R. 230; *Chandler* v. *Kerley* [1978] 1 W.L.R. 693.
[73] [1976] Q.B. 503.
[74] [1950] 2 K.B. 328.
[75] [1975] 3 All E.R. 1030, 1033.
[76] See *Hawes* v. *Evenden* [1953] 1 W.L.R. 1169.
[77] [1975] 3 All E.R. 1030, 1033.
[78] [1944] K.B. 718.

not recognised as such when they were decided. For example, the earliest case to move away from a presumption of reasonableness in withholding consent to adoption and to substitute an objective test in determining whether the parent's attitude is reasonable is *Re L. (an infant)*, a 1962 case which is reported only in the Solicitors Journal and passed relatively unnoticed at the time. Lord Denning said:

> "A reasonable mother surely gives great weight to what is better for the child. Her anguish of mind is quite understandable; but still it may be unreasonable for her to withhold consent. We must look and see whether it is reasonable or unreasonable according to what a reasonable woman in her place would do in all the circumstances of the case."[79]

These remarks were accepted as "authoritative" by Lord Hailsham in the leading case of *Re W. (an infant)* in 1971.[80] Lord Denning's 1962 test is now *the* test.

It is difficult to detect any central philosophy behind Lord Denning's decisions in cases relating to children. He has been involved in important decisions but perhaps, if it is permissible to say so, by chance rather than design.

The case of *Hewer* v. *Bryant*[81] will be remembered long after the issue at stake is forgotten. Sachs L.J.'s judgment contains the fullest judicial analysis of guardianship and custody[82] and Lord Denning's the memorable description of the parental right to physical possession of their children as a "dwindling [one] which the court will hesitate to enforce against the wishes of the child, and the more so the older he is. It starts," said Lord Denning, "with a right of control and ends with little more than advice."[83] There is here a nascent recognition of a child's autonomy. It is found also marginally in *B.(B.R.)* v. *B.(J.)*[84] in which it was held that the High Court had the power to order a child to be blood-tested whenever it was in his best interests: Lord Denning stressed that where the child was an adolescent his views should be taken into consideration though they were never decisive.[85] But Lord Denning's views on children's rights are traditional, that is to say, he emphasises child protection rather than autonomy.[86] His concern for a child's welfare comes out well in *Re S. (an infant)*.[87] He stressed that voluntary care under section 1 of the Children Act 1948 was "transient" and that if a natural parent desired to take over the care of the child the local authority had to give him up. This, he thought, could put the welfare of that child at peril. He accordingly held, following *Re K.R. (an infant)*,[88] that the jurisdiction of the Chancery Court over a child warded by foster parents to prevent his return to his parents was not ousted by the fact that the child was in section 1 care. Lord Denning went further than Pennycuick J. had in *Re*

[79] 106 S.J. 611.
[80] [1971] A.C. 682.
[81] [1970] 1 Q.B. 357.
[82] *Ibid.* p. 373.
[83] *Ibid.* p. 369.
[84] [1968] P.466.
[85] *Ibid.* p. 473.
[86] For the different views see M.D.A. Freeman, *The Rights And Wrongs of Children* (Frances Pinter, London, 1983), Chap. 2.
[87] [1965] 1 W.L.R. 865.
[88] [1964] Ch. 455.

K.R.: the mother had not actually expressed a desire to take over the care of the child but, said Lord Denning, "the imminence of such a demand is a very relevant consideration."[89]

In another case[90] where there was a possibility that a child's life might be endangered Lord Denning had no truck with the consequences of literalism and applied an expansive interpretation (invoking the golden rule) to a provision in the Children and Young Persons Act 1969. A child had died; its father had been acquitted of murder. An application was made in respect of another child of the family as to whom there was no evidence of ill-treatment. Lord Denning had no difficulty in finding that the first child had been ill-treated so as to enable a care order to be made in respect of the second child. He reasoned, quite rightly, that if the first child had been injured rather than killed, no obstacle would have been placed in the way of care proceedings: *a fortiori*, the court should have no difficulty making a care order in these circumstances. It is difficult to quarrel with this reasoning.

This robust common sense is reflected also in the case of *R. v. Bow Road Justices, ex p. Adedigba*,[91] an affiliation case with a foreign element. The Court of Appeal ruled that affiliation proceedings could be brought notwithstanding the fact that the mother was domiciled abroad and the child in question was born in Nigeria. To decide thus the court had to dispose of a line of precedents commencing 118 years earlier. The maxim *communis error facit ius*[92] may appeal to some judges but not to Lord Denning, nor his brother judges in *Adedigba*. Said Lord Denning: "[*R. v. Blane*] is the sort of precedent which we can and should overrule when it is seen to be wrong."[93] If *Blane* were followed the father would have been able to avoid paying maintenance for his child and the mother would have to rely on national assistance. Such a conclusion disturbed Lord Denning:

> "I can see no possible reason for denying the court's jurisdiction to order maintenance and every reason for giving them jurisdiction. The father ought to be made to pay for the child."[94]

Lord Denning's arguments are irresistible.

In another case involving a foreign element Lord Denning was part of a Court of Appeal which extended wardship jurisdiction. In *Re P.(G.E.) (infant)*[95] it was held that the court had jurisdiction in respect of a stateless alien minor, who though not physically present in the jurisdiction could be said to be "ordinarily resident" in England. There was some authority in the law of treason[96] for saying that an alien resident could owe allegiance even though he was outside the country but if the analogy is tenuous Lord Denning was not deterred from making law. He characteristically commented:

---

[89] 1 All E.R. 865, 868.
[90] *Surrey County Council v. S.* [1974] Q.B. 124.
[91] [1968] 2 Q.B. 572.
[92] The force of the maxim is less where people cannot have been expected to rely upon previous decisions, as here or in *Ross Smith* v. *Ross Smith* [1963] A.C. 280.
[93] [1968] 2 Q.B. 572, 579.
[94] *Ibid.* p. 578.
[95] [1965] Ch. 568.
[96] *Joyce* v. *D.P.P.* [1946] A.C. 347.

"We are not deterred by the absence of authority in the books. Our forefathers always held that the law was locked in the breasts of the judges ready to be unlocked whenever the need arose."[97]

The leading text on wardship[98] regards the decision as "a logical and justifiable development" of the law, a view I endorse. The decision has since been followed in other jurisdictions and has the support of the Law Commission.

In three other wardship cases, however, Lord Denning has been instrumental in cutting down the ambit of the protective jurisdiction of the court. In *S. v. McC.*[99] Lord Denning thought that blood-testing a particular child was in both her financial and social interests.[1] But he believed that a balance had to be struck between the interests of the child and interests of justice. "Should it come to the crunch," he added, "then the interests of justice must take first place."[2] The House of Lords agreed with him.[3] Lord Hodson said: "The infant needs protection but that is no justification for making his rights superior to those of others."[4]

In *Re A. (an infant)*[5] the Court of Appeal held that wardship could not be used to challenge an immigration decision. Lord Denning said that the policy of the statute was to place immigration control in the hands of immigration officers. The wardship process could not be invoked "to put a clog on the decisions of immigration officers or as a means of reviewing them."[6] The decision, though a disappointment to many, is consistent with the *Wednesbury*[7] principle and has been accepted in matters of child care by the House of Lords.[8] But it showed some inconsistency in Lord Denning's own thought: a reluctance to face up to bureaucratic decision-making where he agreed with the policies being carried out, as in the case of immigration control he surely does.

In *Re X (a minor)*[9] wardship jurisdiction had been invoked to stop publication of a book, the first chapter of which contained details about the ward's dead father's alleged sexual predilections and behaviour. It was contended that publication could cause the child gross psychological damage. Latey J. granted an injunction. The Court of Appeal unanimously overruled him. Lord Denning held that the interests of freedom of publication overrode any interests the child might have. He stated:

"It would be a mistake ... to give the judges a power to stop

[97] [1965] Ch. 568, 583.
[98] N. Lowe and R.A.H. White, *Wards of Court* (Butterworths, London, 1979). See pp. 14–19, at p. 17.
[99] Not in fact a wardship case, but it may be treated as such for the operative principles are identical.
[1] [1970] 1 All E.R. 1162.
[2] *Ibid.* p. 1165.
[3] [1972] A.C. 24. *sub nom. S. v. S.*
[4] *Ibid.* p. 58.
[5] [1968] 2 All E.R. 149.
[6] *Ibid.* p. 152.
[7] *Associated Provincial Picture Houses* v. *Wednesbury Corporation* [1948] 1 K.B. 223. There was no suggestion of any impropriety.
[8] *A* v. *Liverpool City Council* [1982] A.C. 363.
[9] [1975] Fam. 47.

publication of true matter whenever the judge—or any particular judge—thought that it was in the interests of the child to do so."[10]

We know from other decisions that Lord Denning is reluctant to interfere with freedom of publication. There is, nevertheless, something of a gut reaction in these remarks of his. Sir John Pennycuick,[11] on the other hand, found a sound basis for dewarding the child: the matter did not relate to "the custody or upbringing of a minor," and only where it did was the minor's welfare "first and paramount."[12]

Not surprisingly Lord Denning's views on the family and his traditionalism are reflected in decisions of his in child law matters. The case of *Re L*,[13] denying an adulterous mother custody, is an egregious example. It was discussed earlier in this Chapter.[14] Other decisions, though less striking, nourish similar notions about family life. Thus, in *W*. v. *W. and C.*[15] Lord Denning asserted the "general principle" that it was better for a boy of eight to be with his father than with his mother, even if he had been brought up by his mother up to that age. This has since been disapproved.[16] It is but the flip side of the idea that young children should be brought up by their mothers. Lord Denning, like most people, was influenced in the 1950s and beyond by Bowlby's maternal deprivation theories.[17] The implication of *Wakeham* v. *Wakeham*[18] is that mothers should have care and control even if "innocent" fathers should retain custody. Lord Denning reasoned that the father is

> "at least entitled to a voice in the bringing up of the child, and also to the consideration of the court when any question arises as to what is to be done for the child."[19]

What Lord Denning was arguing for is strictly unnecessary: a divorced parent remains a parent and accordingly retains guardianship. But he, like most judges and commentators, was at that time lost in the conceptual quagmire that passes for child law.[20]

Lord Denning's concern for children's welfare is well reflected in the case of *M.(D.)* v. *M.(S.) and G.(M.D.A.)*.[21] He refused to order a blood test where the sole purpose was to prove an adultery which had taken place 10 years earlier and where the result would be inconclusive with possible harmful and disturbing effects on the child. His remarks that "these adults should fight out their own battles without bringing the infant into it,"[22] strikes a sympathetic chord. The view was endorsed by the House of Lords in *S*. v. *McC*.[23] where blood test applications of a "fishing" nature were rejected. In

---

[10] *Ibid*. p. 58.
[11] *Ibid*. p. 62.
[12] See Guardianship of Minors Act 1971, s.1.
[13] [1962] 1 W.L.R. 886.
[14] Above.
[15] [1968] 1 W.L.R. 1310.
[16] In *Re C(A) (an infant)* [1970] 1 All E.R. 309.
[17] *Child Care and the Growth of Love* (Penguin, Harmondsworth, 1955).
[18] [1954] 1 All E.R. 434.
[19] *Ibid*. p. 436.
[20] On which see S. Maidment, "The Fragmentation of Parental Rights" (1981) C.L.J. 135.
[21] [1969] 2 All E.R. 243.
[22] *Ibid*. p. 245.
[23] [1972] A.C. 24, 48, *per* Lord MacDermott.

another case Lord Denning rejected a wife's application for a child to be blood-grouped where her purpose was solely to support her case for custody.[24] Once again, the child's interests were seen as more important.

Two further decisions of Lord Denning have been instrumental in defining the rights, or lack of rights, of natural fathers. In *Re M. (an infant)*[25] in 1955 he held that a putative father was not a parent for the purposes of adoption legislation. His consent was accordingly not required for an adoption. Lord Denning described a putative father as "too uncertain a figure for the law to take any cognisance of him."[26] In the generality of cases this may be right: in the instant case the father had lived in a stable relationship with the mother and helped to rear the child. Nevertheless, Lord Denning was right to interpret "parent" as he did. Four years later legislation[27] gave putative fathers the right to apply for custody. These powers have been used to frustrate, or attempt to frustrate adoption applications. Lord Denning was a member of the Court of Appeal which heard one of the earliest of the reported applications. In *Re O. (an infant)*[28] Lord Denning made it clear that section 3 of the Legitimacy Act 1959 did not put the putative father in the same position as the father of a legitimate child. It did not give him a substantive right to custody, merely a procedural right to apply for it. He added, as Wilberforce J. had in *Re Adoption Application No. 41/61 (No. 2)*,[29] that the father was "entitled to special consideration by the tie of blood."[30] These remarks anticipate those of Ungoed-Thomas J. and the Court of Appeal in which Lord Denning did not sit, in the notorious "blood-tie" adoption case of *Re C.(M.A.)*.[31]

Conclusion

A study of Lord Denning's family law decisions is valuable because it throws light on much besides the law itself. From it we obtain useful insights into Lord Denning's working personality as well as his thought processes. His decisions in family matters are a microcosm of his concerns elsewhere. They reveal Lord Denning, I believe, at his most typical. His populist sense of justice may lead to some outrageous decisions and to some inconsistency, but on the whole I believe the good he has done outweighs the injustices he has caused. Without Lord Denning family law today would have been more rigid and less sensitive; it would be oriented to rights more than to needs and welfare. It would also be less committed to the patriarchy. He has been both a harbinger of, and a catalyst for, reform. He has at times also been a bastion of reaction. It is unnecessary to resolve these conflicts: Lord Denning is, and will remain, a living paradox. And yet they can be resolved. The two sides of Lord Denning use two sides of his "Englishness": an innate sense of justice

---

[24] *B. v. B. and E. (B. intervening)* [1969] 3 All E.R. 1106 (C.A.).
[25] [1955] 2 Q.B. 479.
[26] *Ibid.* p. 488.
[27] Legitimacy Act 1959, s.3.
[28] [1965] Ch. 23.
[29] [1964] Ch. 48, 53.
[30] [1964] 1 All E.R. 786, 788–789.
[31] [1966] 1 W.L.R. 646.

coupled with a traditionalism that at times gives rise to moral fundamentalism. He may not be the "greatest living Englishman"[32] but he is the very
epitome of what being "English" involves.

---

[32] *Cf.* Raymond Blackburn's remark, quoted in *The Times*, March 7, 1980.

CHAPTER 5

Land, Planning and Housing

J.P.W.B. McAUSLAN

Introduction

An assessment of Lord Denning's contribution to land law—a term which embraces both public and private law—during his tenure of judicial office must be seen in the context of a period of significant and continuous legislative and administrative input into the same area. Land law over the last 40 years has moved from being largely a matter of private relations between two parties policied by the courts—the thrust of the reforms of 1925, the apogee of the free market approach to land law—towards being once again, as of old, a public matter in which whether one is concerned with relations between landlord and tenant, or with the use to which a landowner may put his land or the rights and duties of those, both public and private, who own or deal in houses, a public interest is as much involved as is any private interest. The judges have had to come to terms with a situation in which no longer are they the only or indeed the principal formative influence on the evolution of a body of law which has always occupied a special place in the English legal and constitutional system. Lord Denning has been a central figure during this period; in his early years as a judge both at first instance and in the Court of Appeal he took part in many cases in the area of landlord and tenant; from 1962, when he became Master of the Rolls, while he did not forsake that area, he became much more heavily involved in town planning and housing matters where several of his later judgments provoked considerable controversy. But in addition to these areas which are the principal ones in public or mixed public and private land law, Lord Denning has also made important contributions in more traditional areas of land law—easements, third party rights, estate agency and contracts for the sale of land—which must also be assessed.

A discussion of Lord Denning's contribution to land law over the five decades, during the whole or part of which he has been on the bench is, however, more than just a history of the judicial development of modern land law; it is also a history of intellectual development, of the development of an approach to the law which as Lord Denning's length of service has grown, has become more pronounced, less bound by precedent, and seemingly more governed by his political and moral beliefs. I will first set out the main outlines of the approach, and then discuss its evolution through, and its influence on, the cases Lord Denning was involved in during his tenure of judicial office.

Over the years of judicial office Lord Denning has evolved a doctrine of abuse of rights in the area of land law. On its own, a doctrine of abuse of rights is a rather vague notion—the doctrine as used in the U.S.S.R. would involve very different ideas to that used in the United Kingdom—so it is necessary to flesh it out. An early statement of his beliefs was contained in the Earl Grey Memorial Lecture of 1952 on "The Influence of Religion"[1]:

> "No one doubts now that it is wrong to treat rights of property as sacred. . . . There have been many people who, having amassed or inherited property, have only too often forgotten that it is only through society that they have acquired it. They have failed to realise that they are under a duty to use it for the benefit of society as a whole and not for their own material advantage. When rights of property are carried to these lengths they are contrary to all Christian teaching. . . . The preaching of many divines and notably of William Temple brought home the evils of excessive accumulation of wealth and opportunity in few hands. This has played a considerable part in great changes in the law. . . . But this new state of society has its dangers. It has brought in its train a great increase in the powers of the central government and a lessening in the powers of Parliament and of the courts, so much so that there are fears that the initiative and enterprise of the individual have been hampered too much . . . ."[2]

Certain themes are worth emphasising from this passage; the rejection of unfettered property rights; the acceptance of a relationship between rights and duties in respect of ownership of property; the concern for the maintenance of individual initiative, and the growth of state power, above all, the location of all these ideas within the framework of a strong belief in Christianity. Translated into judicial practice, these beliefs have in this area of law, been concerned with balance; it is the judges' function to preserve, or more realistically to formulate and then apply the correct balance—between landlord and tenant, buyer and seller, and their agents, neighbouring landowners, public interest and private right in respect of land use, and public authorities and their clients in respect of housing. Applying the correct balance will prevent any abuse of rights and locating the rationale for the judges' function in a Christianity which stresses in equal measure individual and social responsibility legitimates the judges' refusal to be hidebound by precedent or indeed the strict words of the statute for

> "Religion concerns the spirit in man whereby he is able to recognise what is truth and what is justice; whereas law is only the application, however imperfectly, of truth and justice in our everyday affairs."[3]

The idea of the correct balance to prevent an abuse of rights may be considered in more detail by breaking down this large area of law into three distinct categories, which more or less correspond to the three principal substantive areas of law to be considered; the balance between private and private—aspects of traditional real property law and landlord and tenant law—the balance between public and private where the dispute is between landowners and public authorities over land use and development with the public authorities seeking to restrict or take away certain property rights from landowners—town and country planning and compulsory purchase

---

[1] Reprinted in Sir Alfred Denning, *The Changing Law* (Stevens and Sons, London, 1953), pp. 99–122.
[2] *Ibid.* pp. 119, 120.
[3] *Ibid.* p. 122.

and compensation law—and finally public and private where the dispute is between public authorities and the propertyless with the public authorities conferring or regarded as conferring benefits on the propertyless and they in turn claiming that these benefits entitle them to certain rights—housing law principally. It will be seen from the ensuing discussion that these three areas involve different aspects of balance and prevention of abuse of rights.

The Balance between Public and Private

Lord Denning always accepted the necessity for statutory involvement over the relationship of landlord and tenant—indeed in one form or another these have existed throughout his life in the law and in some of his early judgments in this area he was wont to refer to his practice at the bar in landlord and tenant cases and what happened then.[4] But equally, his view was that:

> "the statutes . . . do not settle the law with any certainty. The broad principles underlying the statutes are clear enough, but the detailed application of them gives much work to the lawyers."[5]

His concern was to ensure that within the parameters laid down by the "broad principles" and generally in other cases, neither side could use the statutes or other reasons to take advantage of the other. Thus, in one of his early cases *Eyre* v. *Johnson*,[6] he declined to accept a tenant's argument that the Defence Regulations prevented him from carrying out his repairing obligations under a lease; damages in lieu of repairs could be paid. Another case at first instance is an early example of Lord Denning's balancing approach: in *Duke of Westminster* v. *Swinton*,[7] an issue of forfeiture for breach of covenant arose. An underlessee had converted a house into flats and let the flats to homeless people. The lessee was innocent, so no forfeiture should operate against him; equally one could not compel reinstatement where this would result in people being put into the street or more likely the house being requisitioned and reconverted into flats. The underlessee who had no moral claim should be subject to forfeiture and pay damages but the house was to be left as it was.

Two contrasting cases shortly after he was appointed to the Court of Appeal neatly illustrate the same approach to the Rent Restriction Acts. In the first, *Court* v. *Robinson*[8] he commented that—

> "this is another case of which we have had several lately where a tenant has sought to push to an extreme length the advantages which have been conferred on him by the Acts."[9]

The tenant had claimed that premises which consisted of a shop and flat which he had "freely" rented at £4 per week had been let at £1 per week in 1939 and that that therefore was the standard rent beyond which the landlord could not go. But the earlier let had been a business tenancy, according to the court,—a workingmen's club—so that the earlier rent did

---

[4] *e.g. Baxter* v. *Eckersley* [1950] 1 K.B. 480.
[5] "The Changing Civil Law" in *The Changing Law*, pp. 46–47.
[6] [1946] K.B. 481.
[7] [1948] 1 K.B. 422.
[8] [1951] 2 K.B. 60.
[9] *Ibid.* p. 78.

not govern the later letting. On the other hand in *Cresswell* v. *Hodgson*,[10] a few weeks later it was the landlord who was seeking to take advantage of the Acts by transferring a tenant to another house at a higher rent so that the new vacant house could be sold at a profit. Lord Denning ruled that it was permissible for the County Court judge to disallow the move as being contrary both to the interests of the parties and to the public interest—these were factors that could be taken into account. In each case, the losing party was trying to obtain a financial gain from the operation of the Acts, as indeed had the sub-lessee in *Swinton*[11] and the tenant in *Eyre* v. *Johnson*,[12] rather than protect or re-acquire rights of occupation of a home, and this was an abuse of rights which the courts were entitled to prevent.

Two further cases, both heard shortly after Lord Denning had been appointed to the House of Lords, the first in which he presided in the Court of Appeal, the second in which he dissented (along with Lord Keith of Avonholm) in the House of Lords illustrate his concern for promoting some individual responsibility in tenants notwithstanding the Rent Acts. In the first case, *Piper* v. *Harvey*,[13] a landlord claimed possession of premises from a tenant who had lived there for 17 years. The landlord had to show that it was a greater hardship for him not to obtain the premises than it would be for the tenant to be ousted. It was, said Lord Denning, a question of balance and the Court of Appeal could only interfere if the judge had misdirected himself. The landlord lived in one room with an invalid wife; the tenant had his family with him but apart from being on a council housing waiting list had done nothing to try and obtain a house for himself. The tenant had not on the evidence proved a case of greater hardship so the Court could interfere and allow the landlord to obtain possession. In the second case, *Regis Property Co.* v. *Dudley*,[14] the issue was the calculation of rent under the Rent Acts, a matter which turned on the responsibility for repairs. What standard of tenant should be taken in these circumstances? In Lord Denning's view, one should take

> "such a tenant—you may call him a perfect tenant if you like but I would call him the reasonable tenant—who does not damage the place . . . or if he does, puts it right without bothering the landlord about it."[15]

Equally, the tenant was responsible for common law damage, *i.e.* his obligation not to commit waste which did not arise from any agreement but from common law. Since the county court judge had brought into the account common law damage, the appeal of the landlords should be allowed and the tenant's rent increased. What is interesting about these cases is that Lord Denning in effect applied the old common law of landlord and tenant to the statutory responsibilities of the parties and so devalued the protection afforded to the tenants in each case; it is difficult to see the justification for this other than a pre-existing belief that unless the law were so interpreted,

[10] [1951] 2 K.B. 92.
[11] [1948] 1 K.B. 422.
[12] [1946] K.B. 481.
[13] [1958] 1 Q.B. 439.
[14] [1958] 3 All E.R. 491.
[15] *Ibid.* p. 407.

individual tenants would be too advantaged by the Rent Acts; the balance would have tipped too far in their favour.

These themes of balance, of responsibility and of prevention of abuse of rights, became more pronounced in his judgments in this area when Lord Denning returned to the Court of Appeal as Master of the Rolls in 1962, especially from the late 1960s onwards as he made a point of taking cases when abuses were particularly striking. Good examples of landlord "abuse" which produced both strong condemnation and a creative use of his powers are *Luganda* v. *Service Hotels Ltd.*,[16] *Binions* v. *Evans*[17] and *Drane* v. *Evangelou*.[18] The first and last of these cases were examples of harrassment; in *Luganda*,[19] the tenant was put out of his room, the lock changed and another tenant put in after he had indicated to his landlords that he was taking them to the Rent Tribunal over a rent increase; the tenant was applying for an injunction to prevent the landlords stopping him from having access. In *Drane*[20] the landlord had evicted the tenant from a house, put his belongings out and damaged them, and had several people in the premises when the tenant returned from work. The landlords later declined to comply with an injunction to allow the tenant back in the premises, until threatened with imprisonment for contempt of court. In the Court of Appeal the question of an award of exemplary damages made to the tenant Drane was in issue. In both cases then, the landlord was challenging, not so much the tenant's rights, as the role and power of the adjudicatory process be it tribunal or court and in so doing clearly overstepped the mark. Thus any procedural or substantive difficulties in the way of granting an injunction to put a tenant back into occupation, or awarding exemplary damages notwithstanding the restrictions apparently introduced on such damages by *Cassell & Co. Ltd.* v. *Broome*,[21] or that they had not been pleaded in the County Court were brushed aside. It is interesting indeed to contrast the latter of the two cases under discussion with *McCall* v. *Abelesz*[22] where Lord Denning denied a tenant a civil remedy arising out of the harrassment section of the Rent Act 1965 in respect of interference with services found by the County Court judge to be intentional on the part of the landlord. The section gave rise to no such right and in any event there was no harrassment in law. Owing to the rules of procedure the tenant lost out completely because on legal advice he had not alleged breaches of contract in the County Court and it was now too late to do so. The landlords were entitled on their counterclaim to the rent outstanding. The landlords in this case were not challenging the authority of any court or tribunal so apparently in Lord Denning's eyes had not abused their rights. One further point may however be mentioned: in *Drane*[23] Lord Denning noted that the tenant found "a large Greek Cypriot was barring the entrance"[24] to his house; in *McCall*[25] he stated that "the tenant Mr. McCall

---

[16] [1969] 2 Ch. 209.
[17] [1972] Ch. 359.
[18] [1978] 1 W.L.R. 455.
[19] [1969] 2 Ch. 209.
[20] [1978] 1 W.L.R. 455.
[21] [1972] A.C. 1027.
[22] [1976] Q.B. 585.
[23] [1978] 2 All E.R. 437.
[24] *Ibid.* p. 439.
[25] [1976] Q.B. 585.

comes from Dominica in the West Indies. He has been here for 17 years."[26]

In *Binions v. Evans*[27] a landlord who had bought a house from the Tredegar Estate with knowledge of an arrangement whereby Mrs. Evans, an old widow whose husband had been employed by the Estate, could live in it for the rest of her life rent free, tried to turn the tenant out on the basis that she was a tenant at will and the tenancy had been determined. Lord Denning would have none of that: she was not a tenant of any sort but a contractual licencee with an equitable interest; the purchaser took subject to that equitable interest and had imposed upon him a constructive trust for the beneficiary of that interest. The contractual licence was therefore binding on a third party, a position Lord Denning had argued for some years before[28] but had been reversed in the House of Lords.[29] When faced with, on the one hand, inconvenient decisions and views from a superior court, and on the other, a landlord abusing his strict legal rights, Lord Denning had no hesitation in preferring to check the abuse of rights rather than follow precedents strictly.[30] His attitude to such conflicts was well summed up in his judgment in *Brikom Investments* v. *Carr*,[31] a somewhat similar type of case to *Binions* v. *Evans*.[32] Tenants were seeking to rely on oral representations given by their landlord to themselves or their assignors to the effect that the landlords would repair the roofs of the tenants' flats without charge. The leases clearly and expressly stipulated that the tenants would pay a maintenance charge and a contribution towards the landlords' expenses in excess of the maintenance charge. In Lord Denning's words:

> "In all strictness of law neither the tenants nor their assignees have any answer to the claim for contribution. The covenants of the lease are clear. But the tenants and their assignees rely on various representations or promises made by the landlords before and after the leases were executed. . . .
>
> It was suggested that if assignees are able to rely on an oral or written representation (not contained in the deeds) it would cause chaos and confusion amongst conveyancers. No one buying property would know where he stood.

---

[26] *Ibid.* p. 591.

[27] [1972] Ch. 359.

[28] *National Provincial Bank Ltd.* v. *Hastings Car Mart Ltd.* [1964] Ch. 702.

[29] *National Provincial Bank Ltd.* v. *Ainsworth* [1965] A.C. 1175.

[30] His decision in *Binions* v. *Evans* has been characterised as "controversial" and attracted a good deal of learned comment. See K.J. Gray and P.D. Symes: Real Property and Real People (Butterworths, London, 1981), pp. 490–492 and footnotes thereto. See too another decision where Lord Denning was able to rescue a "widow" from a landlord property company seeking to take advantage of the fact that the "widow" living in a protected tenancy had never in fact been married to the protected tenant though living with him for 40 years and so was not a member of the tenant's family within the Rent Acts. *Dyson Holdings* v. *Fox* [1976] Q.B. 503: "The court is not absolutely bound by a previous decision when it is seen that it can no longer be supported. At any rate it is not so bound when owing to the lapse of time and the change in social conditions the previous decision is not in accord with modern thinking." (p. 509). Earlier cases which held that in such circumstances a woman was not a member of the tenant's family were thus put on one side. See further on this case, Freeman, Chap. 4.

[31] [1979] Q.B. 467.

[32] [1972] Ch. 359.

I am not disturbed by these forebodings. I prefer to see that justice is done; and let the conveyancers look after themselves."[33]

Justice here, as in *Binions* v. *Evans*,[34] meant preventing the landlords relying on and thereby abusing their strict legal rights.

A final example of Lord Denning's use of his doctrine to prevent what he considered was an abuse of his legal rights by a landlord is *Quennell* v. *Maltby*.[35] The landlord wished to obtain vacant possession of his house from secure tenants. The house was mortgaged to a bank and the tenants had been let into possession contrary to the terms of the mortgage deed. The bank, although entitled to oust the tenants, was disinclined to take any action. So the landlord's wife paid off the bank, took a transfer of the mortgage, and claimed as the successor to the bank that she could get the tenants out.

> "Is that permissible? It seems to me that this is one of those cases where equity steps in to mitigate the rigour of the law . . . equity can step in so as to prevent a mortgagee or a transferee from him, from getting possession of a house contrary to the justice of the case. A mortgagee will be restrained from getting possession except when it is sought bona fide and reasonably . . . . The legal right to possession is not to be enforced when it is sought for an ulterior motive . . . ."[36]

which in this case was to get possession contrary to the Rent Acts.

With the exception of *McCall* v. *Abelesz*[37] these post 1962 decisions are hard to cavil at. If the law cannot stop landlords from harrassing tenants, and ignoring conditions and undertakings freely entered into, then there is clearly something very wrong with the law, and correlatively very correct with a judge that moulds the law to ensure that it can give relief where common sense and justice dictates that it should. All the more reason however to criticise *McCall* v. *Abelesz*[38] where Lord Denning seemed to prefer a rigorous and narrow approach to the issues as opposed to the broad and generous approach shown in the other cases. This latter approach will also be recalled when, later in this chapter, certain cases involving public or quasi-public housing authorities and their tenants/clients are considered.[39]

If Lord Denning was prepared to come down on private landlords abusing their rights, he has been equally prepared to hold against tenants for the same reason. Where tenants "took advantage of" the law in some way that offended Lord Denning, they were liable to be given short shrift. Thus in *Public Trustee* v. *Westbrook*,[40] the defendants had bought two sub-sub-leases of a bombed site for a nominal sum "no doubt as a speculation"[41] and were seeking relief against forfeiture for non-payment of rent by offering to pay the

---

[33] [1979] 2 All E.R. 753, 756, 760. See however, *Tiverton Estates Ltd.* v. *Wearwell Ltd.* [1974] Ch. 146, where Lord Denning's concern for solicitors in their conveyancing work was more evident.

[34] [1972] Ch. 359.

[35] [1979] 1 W.L.R. 318.

[36] [1979] 1 All E.R. 568, 571. See too Chap. 3 on Equity and Trusts where a more critical view from that perspective is taken; pp. 89–90.

[37] [1976] Q.B. 565.

[38] *Ibid.*

[39] *Post*, pp. 199–205.

[40] [1965] 3 All E.R. 398.

[41] *Ibid.* p. 400.

22 years rent outstanding not only on their sub-sub-lease but on the sub-lease ahead of it. Lord Denning considered that this was an exceptional case where it was within the discretion of the court to refuse relief:

> "twenty-two years have passed without any rent being paid and . . . everyone has treated the sub-lease as gone altogether. This is an attempt to revive them by way of an application for relief . . . ."[42]

A more difficult case arose in *Bickel* v. *Duke of Westminster*[43] where an attempt to "take advantage of" the Leasehold Reform Act 1967 was prevented. The Ancient Order of Foresters Friendly Society—a "highly respectable body of trustees"[44]—were tenants on a long lease of some houses in Belgravia owned by the Grosvenor Estate. One of the houses was sub-let to a lady on a high rent, thus taking her out of the scope of the Act. The Foresters were prepared to assign their lease to the lady with the ultimate effect that she could use the Act to compel the Grosvenor Estate to sell her the freehold. The terms of the headlease allowed the Estate to withhold consent to the assignment provided such a withholding was not unreasonable. The Estate withheld consent, and offered the Foresters a greater sum for the surrender of the headlease than was being offered by all the sub-lessees combined for assignment. The Foresters claimed that the consent was being withheld unreasonably. Lord Denning considered that past cases on the unreasonableness or otherwise of a landlord's refusal of consent to an assignment could not be regarded as precedents laying down strict rules of law; the Act of 1967 created an entirely new situation. The landlords would be greatly disadvantaged in the management and development of their estate if assignment followed by enfranchisement took place, whereas the tenants were concerned only with selling their investments at a fair price; furthermore the sub-tenant was protected in her occupation by the Rent Act. In this situation it was not unreasonable to withhold consent. On the analysis adopted by Lord Denning, the result may appear reasonable but it must be said that its effect was to support the refusal of the landlords to comply with the intent and purpose of the Leasehold Reform Act. To say as Lord Denning did that "the only result on [the sub-tenant] of a refusal will be that she will not be able to buy up the freehold for a very low figure"[45] implies that such a transaction was neither very important nor very creditable, whereas in fact it was both central to the negotiations between the Foresters and the sub-tenant and a perfectly proper transaction under the Act. It was Lord Denning's assumption about the effect of the Act on large estates that caused him to conclude that it was the tenants and sub-tenants who were abusing their rights rather than the landlord.

It would not be correct however to conclude from *Bickel*[46] that Lord Denning was in general hostile to the Leasehold Reform Act. On balance the reported cases suggest that he had a fair measure of sympathy for the aims and purposes of the Act which is why *Bickel*[47] stands out. Thus in

---

[42] *Ibid.* p. 400.
[43] [1976] 3 W.L.R. 805.
[44] *Ibid.* p. 803.
[45] *Ibid.* p. 805.
[46] [1976] 3 W.L.R. 805.
[47] [1976] 3 W.L.R. 805.

Gidlow-Jackson v. *Middlegate Properties*[48] Lord Denning went out of his way, in a dissent, to hold that a house had been let at a low rent and was therefore within the Act, justifying his doing so by references to the intention of the Act and quoting the White Paper which preceded the Act. In some respects the situation of the occupier of the relevant premises in *Bickel*[49] was objectively better than that in *Gidlow-Jackson*[50]; in the former case the occupier had been resident in the house for 28 years prior to the attempted assignment; in the latter case it was twelve years and the tenant had sub-let the second floor; in each case the landlord was the owner of several properties and was concerned with their management and improvement. In what then lay the difference other than Lord Denning's sense of balance and justice?

Two further cases involving peccant tenants, one of which came before Lord Denning twice, provide further illustrations of his notion of abuse of rights. In *Central Estates (Belgravia) Ltd.* v. *Woolger*,[51] an old man was convicted of keeping a brothel in Warwick Square, Belgravia. His landlord served a notice of forfeiture which crossed in the post with an application to purchase the freehold under the Leasehold Reform Act. The Act provided that applications to purchase should take precedence over claims for forfeiture unless the court was satisfied that the application was not made in good faith. Lord Denning considered that that meant that the claim:

> "must be made by the tenant honestly in the belief that he has a lawful right to acquire the freehold or an extended lease, and it must be made without any ulterior motive such as to avoid the just consequences of his own misdeeds or failures."[52]

That was not the case here and the application was rightly rejected. The second case, decided on the same day, was *Liverpool Corporation* v. *Husan*.[53] Here too, the tenant had made an application to purchase a freehold under the Leasehold Reform Act. The landlord claimed that the application was not made in good faith as its purpose was to avoid the consequence of serious breaches of the repairing covenants in the lease. Lord Denning considered that while relief against forfeiture would normally be granted in respect of breaches of repairing covenants, that would not be the case where the tenant had not done repairs in the past and was unable to do them in the future, as was the case here. It followed therefore that the application to purchase the freehold was not made in good faith as it was designed "to avoid the just consequences of his own failure to repair"[54]; it was then on all fours with *Woolger*,[55] a case where the tenant "desired" to purchase the freehold in order to avoid the forfeiture which would follow on his conviction.

Eleven months later Woolger came before Lord Denning again in *Central Estates (Belgravia) Ltd.* v. *Woolger (No.2.)*[56]; forfeiture had been refused and

---

[48] [1974] Q.B. 361.
[49] [1976] 3 W.L.R. 805.
[50] [1974] Q.B. 361.
[51] [1971] 3 All E.R. 647.
[52] *Ibid.* p. 649.
[53] [1971] 3 All E.R. 651.
[54] *Ibid.* p. 653.
[55] [1971] 3 All E.R. 647.
[56] [1972] 3 All E.R. 610.

the landlords were appealing against that decision. Woolger cross-appealed from a finding that the landlords had not waived the forfeiture. In Lord Denning's eyes Woolger had now become:

> "a harmless and ineffectual old man . . . [who] . . . has repented of his wrongdoing."[57]

As a matter of law forfeiture had been waived, because, owing to a mistake in the office of the landlord's agents, rent had been demanded and received since knowledge of the conviction had come to the landlord's notice, but in any event this was a proper case for the court to exercise its discretion; the value of the premises had not been affected and the gains and losses consequent upon forfeiture were wholly disproportionate to the harm caused.

Looking at these three decisions together, what seems to have been at the forefront of Lord Denning's concern was the prevention of exploitation of the law, and he was helped to his decision by the broad phrasing of the statute in the first two decisions and the discretion vested in the court in the third case. Both sides of Lord Denning's approach to the task of judging come through clearly; for the good side is his concern for justice and prevention of abuse of rights, or taking advantage of the law, particularly for obvious pecuniary gain; for the bad side, is the inconsistency of approach in the *Woolgar* cases—tacitly admitted to by Lord Denning in the second case[58]—and the characterisation of the tenants in the cases which rather obviously showed where his sympathies lay.

Another area where Lord Denning's sympathies and general moral views were only too obvious is in respect of estate agents, of whose activities he clearly had the gravest of suspicions. In no reported case coming before Lord Denning did an estate agent succeed in convincing him that he should receive his commission where a client disputed the issue; in *Sheggia* v. *Gradwell*,[59] Lord Denning was in a minority, but in *McCallum* v. *Hicks*,[60] *Dennis Reed Ltd.* v. *Goody*,[64] *Dellafiora* v. *Lester*,[62] *Jaques* v. *Lloyd D. George*[63] and *John McCann* v. *Pow*[64] agents failed in their claims. In these cases Lord Denning posed what he called "the common understanding of mankind"[65] that agents only obtained commission when the property was sold against various contractual terms or practices which agents were claiming allowed or required commission to be paid notwithstanding that they had not succeeded in selling the property, and on such a basis found the terms or practices wanting:

---

[57] *Ibid.* pp. 612, 616.

[58] "It is true as I said when this case was previously before us: 'Forfeiture was the almost inevitable consequence. Relief is rarely given for such a breach. . . . ' But it may sometimes be given." [1972] 3 All E.R. 610 at p. 615.

[59] [1963] 3 All E.R. 114. For a discussion of some of the estate agents cases in the context of the law of agency see Chap. 1, *supra*, pp. 53–54.

[60] [1950] 2 K.B. 271.

[61] [1950] 2 K.B. 277.

[62] [1962] 1 W.L.R. 1208.

[63] [1968] 2 All E.R. 187.

[64] [1975] W.L.R. 1643.

[65] This phrase appears in *McCallum* v. *Hicks* [1950] 2 K.B. 271, 276; that passage was repeated in *Dennis Reed Ltd.* v. *Goody* [1950] 2 K.B. 277, 287; "the ordinary understanding of mankind" was used in *Sheggia* v. *Gradwell* [1963] 3 All E.R. 114, 117; both "common" and "ordinary" were used in *Jaques* v. *Lloyd D. George and Partners Ltd.* [1968] 2 All E.R. 187, 190; "the justice of the case" was resorted to in *John McCann* v. *Pow* [1975] 1 All E.R. 129, 132.

"the common law is vigilant to prevent any abuse of freedom of contract."[66]

On the matter of deposits, and on whom out of vendor or purchaser should the loss fall if an agent absconds with the money as in *Sorrell* v. *Finch*,[67] or goes into liquidation or becomes bankrupt as in *Burt* v. *Claude Cousins & Co. Ltd.*,[68] and *Barrington* v. *Lee*,[69] Lord Denning's view, consistently held to in the three cases that the vendor was not liable to refund the deposit to the purchaser who had paid it because the vendor, in the absence of an express contract to that effect, had no right to the deposit in the hands of the agent until the contract for the sale of the property was complete, was finally upheld in the House of Lords in *Sorrell* v. *Finch*[70] after being a minority in both *Burt* v. *Claude Cousins*[71] and *Sorrell* v. *Finch*.[72] In the former case Lord Denning ended his judgment thus:

" . . . this case should serve as a warning to people who employ or pay deposits to estate agents. To them I would say: 'Never employ or pay an estate agent unless he is of good standing and repute.' I believe that all respectable estate agents do belong to one or other of the recognised societies . . . ."[73]

But many do not and clearly these were not, in Lord Denning's eyes, respectable, and as such the courts were perfectly justified in applying the law strictly to them.

Turning now from cases where the nature or status of the parties and *a priori* assumptions about how they ought to behave, clearly played a part in Lord Denning's decisions, we can consider two further areas where those matters were of far less importance and issues of balance and abuse of rights could be and were considered in a less "political" atmosphere. The first area is that of easements, a classic part of the land law for the development of judicial ideas about how neighbouring landowners ought to behave to one another. Between 1964 and 1974, Lord Denning considered eight easement cases, and taken together his judgments are an excellent example of the use of judicial power to try to restate and modernise a branch of the law while ensuring that no-one oversteps the boundaries of what was reasonable. Thus in *Phipps* v. *Pears*[74] a right to protection from the weather was refused because to allow it would be to hinder the redevelopment of towns, while in *Wong* v. *Beaumont Trust*[75] the placing of a ventilation duct by a tenant on a landlord's wall so that the tenant could comply with public health regulations in operating a Chinese restaurant was held to be an easement of necessity which the landlord could not refuse to allow.

A perennial issue in respect of rights of way claimed as easements is that of

[66] *McCallum* v. *Hicks* [1950] 2 K.B. 271, 276.
[67] [1976] 2 W.L.R. 833 (H.L.) The Court of Appeal decision from which Lord Denning dissented is not reported.
[68] [1971] 2 Q.B. 426.
[69] [1971] 1 Q.B. 326.
[70] [1976] 2 W.L.R. 833.
[71] [1971] 2 Q.B. 426.
[72] [1976] 2 W.L.R. 833.
[73] [1971] 2 All E.R. 611, 618.
[74] [1965] 1 Q.B. 76.
[75] [1965] 1 Q.B. 173.

increased, excessive or changed user; at what point can the owner of the servient tenement lawfully object to and stop the owner of the dominant tenement from using a right of way across the servient tenement? *British Railways Board* v. *Glass*[76] and *Jelbert* v. *Davis*[77] raised this issue in connection with caravan sites. Caravan site owners, as we will see in more detail in the next section of this chapter, occupied the same place in Lord Denning's estimation as did estate agents, and in these cases farmers were using rights of ways as essential routes to caravan sites on their land with consequent inconvenience for their neighbouring and servient landowner. In each case Lord Denning considered, though in *British Railways Board* v. *Glass*[78] he was in a minority, that the caravan site owner's use had increased beyond that which was contemplated by the original grant and had become excessive; the right of way in other words was being abused. A contrary position was arrived at in *McIlrath* v. *Grady*[79] and *Davis* v. *Whitby*[80] where in each case the servient owner was held to be adopting a rather narrow and technical approach to the existence and extent of a right of way; common sense and reason pointed in the direction of allowing such a right even though in the latter of the above mentioned cases, the point at issue—whether the length of time a right of way had existed could be made up by adding together the period of use of a way and a substituted way—was a new one in the law of easements.

In some respects the most interesting case is *Crow* v. *Wood*[81] which involved the easement of fencing. Crow and Wood occupied neighbouring farms in the Yorkshire Moors which carried with them the right to stray sheep on the moors. The plaintiff did not in fact exercise this right as she used her farm for hay, corn and cows. She was told by her neighbours, however, that she was obliged to keep up her fences and walls to keep neighbouring sheep out and she duly did so for 10 years until making the erroneous assumption that a successful court action against another farmer arising out of straying sheep absolved her from that obligation. Wood's sheep thereafter got into her farm frequently and she sued Wood in cattle trespass. He set up as his defence Mrs. Crow's failure to comply with her duty to keep her fences in repair. It was found that there was a custom to keep fences in repair but that this was not sufficient to impose an obligation on the plaintiff; that could only arise by virtue of the operation of section 62 of the Law of Property Act 1925 and that in turn could only be used if the right in question was capable of being granted by law, *i.e.* had the traditional characteristics of an easement. Lord Denning brushed aside the difficulty that, unlike easements, this right required the servient owner to spend money:

> "It seems to me that it is now sufficiently established—or at any rate, if not established hitherto we should now declare—that a right to have one's neighbour keep up the fences is a right in the nature of an easement which is capable of being granted by law so as to run with the

[76] [1964] 1 W.L.R. 294.
[77] [1968] 1 W.L.R. 589.
[78] [1964] 1 W.L.R. 294.
[79] [1967] 1 Q.B. 468.
[80] [1974] Ch. 186.
[81] [1971] 1 Q.B. 77.

land and to be binding on successors. It is a right which lies in grant and is of such a nature that it can pass under s.62(1) of the Law of Property Act 1925."[82]

It passed in the instant case and as a result the plaintiff could not complain of cattle trespass.

"Such is the custom of the moor. She abided by the custom for ten years. It is a pity she ever departed from it."[83]

Lord Denning's sympathies were clearly with the defendant who had followed the customs rather than with the plaintiff who had not in two ways—she had not kept her fences up and she had not kept sheep on her farm—and in those circumstances it was fair to penalise the plaintiff—a somewhat prickly neighbour—by retrospectively turning an a-legal custom into a legal duty. In this way the proper balance of rights and duties between neighbours would be maintained, and traditional customs of a rural community enforced—both proper matters for the law to have regard to.

Lord Denning's concern for traditional rights and customs in respect of land—perhaps part of the explanation for his seeming antipathy towards caravan site owners—is evident also in one of his most famous decisions in this area, *New Windsor Corporation* v. *Mellor*,[84] the *Bachelors' Acre* case and in one of his very last decisions, *Corpus Christi College* v. *Gloucestershire County Council*.[85] Each case involved the registration of commons under the Commons Registration Act 1965; in each case his statement of the facts and the issues stressed the ancient nature of the rights in question and the importance of the practices and activities of ordinary people on the common land over the years; they might not know the origin of their rights but they knew that they had them and they could defend them against anyone who attempted to interfere with them. Thus, the Royal Borough of New Windsor could be prevented from using Batchelors' Acre as a municipal car park and school playing fields and, despite the voiding of the registration of the Rights of Commons in the Register by the decision of the Commons Commissioner— held by Lord Denning to be an erroneous decision—Corpus Christi College could not obtain a declaration that the land in question had ceased to be common land:

"The common lands scattered all about England and Wales are part of our heritage from the past. They have enabled considerable areas of

---

[82] [1970] 3 All E.R. 425, 429.

[83] *Ibid.* p. 429.

[84] [1975] Ch. 380. The opening paragraph of Lord Denning's judgment has claims to be the most lyrical in the law reports:

"Today we look back far in time to a town or village green. The turf is old. Animals have grazed there for hundreds of years. Nowadays they are pleasant stretches of grass where people sit and talk. Sometimes they play cricket or kick a ball about. But in mediaeval times it was the place where the young men mustered with their bows and arrows. They shot at the balts. There might be stocks there where offenders were put for their petty misdemeanours. In the month of May they set up a maypole and danced around it. We have no record of when it all began but the poet tells us:

'On the green they watched their sons
Playing till too dark to see,
As their fathers watched them once,
As my father once watched me. . . . ' "

[85] [1982] 3 All E.R. 995.

land to be preserved intact and unspoilt. Wherever they are registered as 'common land' they should be preserved intact—even though there is no entry against them of any particular rights of any particular commoners."[86]

It was of such importance in Lord Denning's eyes to preserve these lands and the traditional rights associated with them that previous cases which seemed to point in the opposite direction could be disregarded.

The second area to be considered is that of third party rights in land. This area crosses the boundaries of both family law[87]—the rights of the deserted wife against the creditors of the husband—and equity[88]—third party rights, notice and registration in general—but must also be considered briefly here. Three leading cases from disparate areas of land law are *E.R. Ives Investments Ltd.* v. *High*[89]—rights of way agreed to but never registered under the Land Charges Act; *Williams & Glyn Bank* v. *Boland*[90]—whether a wife's occupation of a matrimonial home was to be classed as an overriding interest so as to prevent a mortgagee evicting her and obtaining vacant possession of a house on which mortgage arrears were outstanding; and *Midland Bank Trust Co.* v. *Green*[91]—the non-registration of an option to purchase, the legal tip of an iceberg of a family quarrel. In all these cases, a strict application of the law as it was then understood, or perhaps more accurately an application of the law in the spirit in which it was intended by the reformers responsible for the 1925 property law reform—commercial marketability of land was to take priority over family and other third party rights in the land where those rights had not been protected by complying with the relatively straightforward rules of registration—pointed in one direction, whilst prevention of abuse of rights as perceived by Lord Denning pointed in the other direction.

Thus in *E.R. Ives Investments* v. *High*[92] a new class of equitable interests in land, protectable through notice rather than through registration was discovered and an equitable right of way saved for "any other view would . . . perpetrate the grossest injustice."[93] In *Boland*[94] the wife's interest in the matrimonial home was found to be an overriding interest under the Land Registration Act 1925:

> "It seems to me to be utterly wrong that a lender should turn a blind eye to the wife's interest or the possibility of it—and afterwards seek to turn her and the family out—on the plea that he did not know she was in actual occupation. If a bank is to do its duty in the society in which we live it should recognise the integrity of the matrimonial home. It should not destroy it by disregarding the wife's interest in it, simply to ensure that it is paid the husband's debt in full with the high interest rate now prevailing. We shall not give monied might priority over social justice."[95]

---

[86] *Ibid.* p. 1002.
[87] Chap. 4, pp. 121–123; 146–148.
[88] Chap. 2, pp. 91–93.
[89] [1967] 2 Q.B. 379.
[90] [1981] A.C. 487; affirming [1979] Ch. 312.
[91] [1981] A.C. 513; reversing [1980] Ch. 580.
[92] [1967] 2 Q.B. 379.
[93] *Ibid.* p. 395.
[94] [1979] Ch. 312.
[95] *Ibid.* p. 333.

In *Green*,[96] the option to purchase was saved because the transaction which seemed to avoid it—a sale and conveyance of a farm—was at a gross undervalue and so did not come within the statutory protection given to transactions "for money or money's worth."[97] There was in Lord Denning's eyes fraud involved in the sale at an undervalue:

"Fraud in this context involves any dishonest dealing done so as to deprive unwary innocents of their rightful dues. The marks of it are transactions done stealthily and speedily in secret for no sufficient consideration. All these appear in this conveyance. . . . "[98]

This last attempt to avoid the statute in the interests of justice, as perceived by Lord Denning, was too much for the House of Lords which in a judgment of Lord Wilberforce agreed to by all the other members of the house, crisply rejected Lord Denning's approach:

"Certainly there is here no argument for departing—violently—from the wording of the Act."[99]

Lord Denning's answer to that approach was given more than a quarter of a century before:

" . . . the judges are too often inclined to fold their hands and blame the legislature, when really they ought to set to work and give the words a reasonable meaning even if this does involve a departure from the letter of them. By so doing they are more likely to find the truth."[1]

In *Green*[2] however, as Lord Wilberforce pointed out, the rights and wrongs of the impugned transactions depended upon inquiry into the purchaser's state of mind and motives and these were not at all clear. In all these cases one senses that Lord Denning arrived at "the truth" long before he began to interpret the statutes, and that "truth" was designed to reflect and advance his conception of abuse of rights.

Finally on this section of the chapter, three cases on nuisance may be considered. Whereas when dealing with third party rights, equity of one kind or another was called upon to offset the rigour of the statutes, in these cases it was the traditional common law, refashioned where necessary, which was used to try and ensure that rights were not abused and a balance maintained between neighbours. In the first case, *Pride of Derby and Derbyshire Angling Association Ltd.* v. *British Celanese*,[3] the issues were fairly straightforward: it was no defence to an action for an injunction to restrain Derby Corporation from polluting the River Derwent that the Corporation could not extend their sewage works because they could not get the necessary ministerial consents under the Defence Regulations; the injunction could be suspended and in that way a proper balance could be kept between the riparian owners and other necessary users of the river.

---

[96] [1980] Ch. 580.
[97] Land Charges Act 1972, s.4(*b*).
[98] At p. 624.
[99] [1981] A.C. 513 at p. 530.
[1] "The Influence of Religion" in *The Changing Law*, p. 106.
[2] [1981] A.C. 513.
[3] [1953] Ch. 149.

In the other two cases, *Miller* v. *Jackson*[4] and *Allen* v. *Gulf Oil Refining Ltd.*,[5] Lord Denning's views did not commend themselves respectively to his colleagues in the Court of Appeal in the first case and to the House of Lords in the second.[6] In *Miller* v. *Jackson*[7] the conflicting uses of land were village cricket and residential occupation—the former a long-standing use of the land, the latter a newcomer. There were shades of Lord Denning's attitude towards the rights of commoners in his judgment; he put on one side the direct authority of *Sturges* v. *Bridgman*[8] which his colleagues declined to do and approached the issue foursquare in terms of balance:

> "In this case it is our task to balance the right of the cricket club to continue playing cricket on their cricket ground as against the right of the householder not to be interfered with. On taking the balance I would give priority to the right of the cricket club to continue playing cricket on the ground as they have done for the last 70 years. It takes precedence over the right of the newcomer to sit in his garden undisturbed . . . . There is a contest here between the interest of the public at large and the interest of a private individual . . . . As between their conflicting interest I am of opinion that the public interest should prevail over the private interest . . . ."[9]

It is clear too from his judgment that he considered the plaintiffs were being unreasonable in their opposition to village cricket "where young men play and old men watch."[10] There are few of Lord Denning's judgments in this whole area of land law in which his views on what ought to happen so obviously coloured his perception of the facts and his analysis of the issues. There is as much public interest in the tranquillity of the home as in the playing of village cricket; there is as much private interest in a cricket club and its use of land as there is in a householder and her use of land. Nor can this case very easily be seen as the upholding of the rights of the little person, as "doing justice" which on his retirement Lord Denning claimed was always his aim.[11] In the event, justice of a sort was done since there was a majority for the award of damages to the Millers and against an injunction on the cricket club, but Lord Denning on his own would have left the Millers without remedy. In truth it seems that his desire to protect the countryside against development—expressly mentioned in this case[12]—got the better of him. The problem of one worthy personal aim conflicting with another is always likely to arise where a decision-maker exercises his discretion on the basis of his own conscience and untrammelled by precedent; it is not made the less problematic because the decision-maker is a judge.

[4] [1977] Q.B. 966. See on this case, Chap. 2 pp. 72–74.
[5] [1980] Q.B. 156.
[6] [1981] 1 All E.R. 353.
[7] [1977] Q.B. 966.
[8] (1879) 11 Ch. D. 852.
[9] [1977] Q.B. 966, 981.
[10] *Ibid.* p. 976.
[11] Lord Denning, *The Times: Law Report*, July 31, 1982.
[12] "The public interest lies in protecting the environment by preserving our playing fields in the face of mounting development. . . . " p. 981. Many local authorities, faced with harsh cutbacks on their spending powers and pressure to sell off "unproductive" land holdings, have been persuaded that the public interest lies in doing precisely the opposite to that which Lord Denning urged.

Allen v. *Gulf Oil Refining Ltd.*[13] was a classic case of the little person versus "monied might." Could Elsie May Allen, an inhabitant of the village of Waterston near Milford Haven harbour succeed in her action for nuisance against Gulf Oil's operation of its refinery or could the company rely on the defence of statutory authority arising from its private act, the Gulf Oil Refining Act 1965? According to Lord Denning the Act did not provide a defence because it only expressly authorised construction of the works not their use which accordingly was governed by the common law. That approach to the interpretation of a private Act was based on nineteenth century cases but

> "I venture to suggest that modern statutes should be construed on a new principle. Wherever private undertakers seek statutory authority to construct and operate an installation which may cause damage to people living in the neighbourhood, it should not be assumed that Parliament intended that damage should be done to innocent people without redress. . . . No matter whether the undertakers use due diligence or not, they ought not to be allowed, for their own profit, to damage innocent people or property without compensation."[14]

Lord Denning's more orthodox approach to statutory interpretation in this case and his statement of a suggested new principle, which one would have thought would have been instinctively agreed to by most lawyers, proved of no avail. In one of their least justifiable reversals of his decisions, the House of Lords by a majority of four to one rejected both his interpretation of the statute and his new approach. Although not providing a blanket immunity from actions for nuisance, the House of Lords considered the statute by inference gave immunity for operations within the intendment of the statute and clearly authorised the changing of the environment from that of a peaceful unpolluted countryside to an industrial complex without any payment of compensation. It must be said that the reasoning of the majority was jejune; as if they knew that, they relied overmuch on assertion. In this case Lord Denning's instincts which could be and were eminently supportable by authority and straightforward statutory interpretation, were overturned far too readily and without regard to any of the wider issues of balance of rights which Lord Denning had rightly brought to it and which it required.

The Balance between Public and Private: Controls over Land Use

Lord Denning's judicial career began at almost exactly the same time as did the modern statutory system of land use planning and control; a Ministry of Town and Country Planning was established by statute in 1943, the first of the post-war planning statutes—the New Towns Act—was enacted in 1946, and Lord Denning was appointed to the bench in 1944. This post-war system of land use controls created a comprehensive system of public control of the development of land, covering permissions, penalties for unauthorised development, financial imposts (this last waxing and waning over Lord Denning's period on the bench) and an increased use of the powers of

[13] [1980] Q.B. 156.
[14] *Ibid.* pp. 168–169.

compulsory acquisition of land. In a sense the old traditional approach to land use control where judges exercised their discretion in nuisance, trespass, waste, easements and restrictive covenants, was downgraded in favour of a new approach where administrators exercised their discretion in terms of planning permissions, conditions, enforcement notices and the like. For some judges whose social philosophy, training and work at the Bar had been formed and undertaken in an era when such a panoply of statutory powers was no more than a gleam in an eccentric planner's eye, the new post-war regime proved hard to take and they never came to terms with it.[15] Lord Denning was never in that group and indeed in *Miller-Mead* v. *Ministry of Housing and Local Government*[16] he was strongly critical of the approach, favoured by Lord Simonds,[17] of insisting on a strict adherence to formalities of procedure in the administration of town planning because the system encroached upon private rights. Lord Denning's approach was much more subtle; he accepted the new statutory regime and then set about engrafting on to it a framework of principles derived ultimately from the same notions of balance and prevention of abuse of rights as he applied in private law and landlord-tenant relations; neither side should abuse their rights or powers, the balance should not be pushed too far to the public or the private side and it is the judges who determine where the line is to be drawn. This approach was clearly set out in his most oft-quoted judgment in this area of law in *Pyx Granite Co.* v. *Ministry of Housing and Local Government*,[18] only his third town and country planning case, and still in a sense, in his first era in the Court of Appeal:

> "The principles to be applied are not, I think, in doubt. Although the planning authorities are given very wide powers to impose such 'conditions as they think fit', nevertheless the law says that those conditions to be valid must fairly and reasonably relate to the permitted development. The planning authority are not at liberty to use their powers for an ulterior object however desirable that object may seem to them to be in the public interest."[19]

A careful analysis of this passage shows that what Lord Denning did was, in the guise of setting what appeared to be reasonable limits to the discretion of public authorities, to substitute a wide judicial discretion for a wide administrative discretion. "The law says" means "the judges say" and terms such as "fairly and reasonably relate," "ulterior object" are not self-evident in meaning but need interpretation—by the judges, who in their interpretation can import their notions of what is permissible; what in Lord Denning's view preserves the proper balance between private development and public control. An earlier foretaste of what this proper balance was is contained in one of Lord Denning's most notable early dissents in the Court of Appeal in

---

[15] See for instance Lord Simonds in *East Riding County Council* v. *Park Estate (Bridlington) Ltd.* [1957] A.C. 223, 233; Harman L.J. in *Britt* v. *Buckinghamshire County Council* [1964] 1 Q.B. 77, 87, and Lord Upjohn in *Mixnam's Properties Ltd.* v. *Chertsey Urban District Council* [1965] A.C. 735, 764–765.

[16] [1963] 2 Q.B. 196.

[17] See n. 15.

[18] [1958] 1 Q.B. 554. Lord Denning had been elevated to the House of Lords in April 1957 but sat as presiding judge in the Court of Appeal in this case which was heard in December 1957.

[19] *Ibid.* p. 572.

Earl Fitzwilliam's Wentworth Estates Co. v. *Ministry of Town and Country Planning*,[20] a case concerned with the powers of the Central Land Board, the principle agency established by the Town and Country Planning Act 1947 to collect the development charge payable on receipt of permission to develop land. Lord Denning considered that in the instant case the Board had had a further purpose in the exercise of its powers of compulsory purchase: to enforce the policy of sales of land at existing use value, the value at which sales of land should, as a matter of economic theory, have been made but rarely were. For Lord Denning this purpose was the overriding one and was impermissible: Parliament had not legislated to impose that particular economic theory on people and to allow the Board to rush in would be to allow government departments to legislate when Parliament had decided not to. Behind Lord Denning's assertion of a judicial power to examine the purposes of the Board and strike down action if necessary, is a disapproval of the fiscal element of the town and country planning legislation:

> "The . . . Act takes away the freedom of each man to do as he likes with his own land."[21]

That element tipped the balance too far in the direction of public power and at that point, it became permissible to adopt a strict approach to an analysis of that power. Twenty years later his continued reserve about the taxation aspects of town and country planning legislation showed through again in *Croft* v. *Land Commission*[22]:

> "This is a case under the Land Commission Act 1967. The first and last I am glad to say because the Land Commission is coming to an end."[23]

In this case he applied a "liberal interpretation" to the statute so as to reduce the amount of betterment levy payable by Croft.

During his second era in the Court of Appeal from 1962 to 1982 Lord Denning made a powerful contribution to the jurisprudence of town and country planning law, both in the development of ideas and concepts, and in expanding the scope and range of the judicial role in this branch of the law. In considering this contribution, one must, inevitably, be selective and four broad areas have been picked out: caravans; enforcement notices; legal concepts developed to flesh out the broad discretions of control; and estoppel and local authority responsibility for officers' statements and actions in the administration of town planning. One matter of interest which may be mentioned as a preliminary to these topics is that Lord Denning never took or never had the opportunity to contribute to the important issue of the extent to which economic and social considerations may or should be taken into account in considering planning applications—an area where his notions of balance and prevention of abuse of rights might have been sorely tested.[24]

---

[20] [1951] 2 K.B. 284, 300–314.   [21] *Ibid.* p. 301.
[22] (1971) 22 P. & C.R. 596.   [23] *Ibid.* p. 597.
[24] In *Esdell Caravan Parks Ltd.* v. *Hemel Hempstead Rural District Council* [1966] 1 Q.B. 895 he was prepared to allow social considerations to be used by justices in determining whether restrictive conditions imposed on a caravan site licence were unduly burdensome. The conditions reduced the number of caravans on the site from 78 to 24 though on public health grounds there was no objection to the larger number. Considerations of "social balance" between villagers and caravan dwellers were permissible factors to have regard to and the justices' decision was upheld.

As noted earlier, Lord Denning did not appear to have too much time for
caravan site owners. In six cases he heard between 1963 and 1966 dealing
either with enforcement notices or caravan site licences, the caravan site
owner did not win one. Even where some procedural mistake had been made
by the public authority as occurred in *Miller-Mead*,[25] *Munnich* v. *Godstone
Rural District Council*[26] and *Blow* v. *Norfolk County Council*,[27] Lord Denning was
either prepared to overlook it, or decide that, even when it was taken into
account, the public authority's decision was right. It is a fact that in many of
the cases involving caravans, there is a long history of conflict between the
site owner and the local authority, the one attempting to put agricultural
land or open space to productive commercial use with as little outlay as
possible, the other attempting to preserve the local Green Belt; and that this
history, recited to the court, rarely reflects creditably on the site owner. As
we have seen above, Lord Denning was generally concerned about the
countryside and its preservation from development, and this concern was
reflected in his attitude towards caravan development. A good example of his
attitude was contained in *James* v. *Minister of Housing and Local Government*[28]
where the appellant was attempting to develop a caravan site on his land
alongside Llangorse Common next to Llangorse Lake in the Brecon National
Park:

> "[T]he local authorities object. They say that a caravan camp would be
> an eye-sore and spoil the landscape. Time after time the appellant has
> sought to use it for more than one caravan. Time after time the
> authorities have tried to stop him. The planning authority . . . served an
> enforcement notice on him . . . On appeal to this court we were engulfed
> in a whole host of technical points. It is an unfortunate feature of the
> legislation about caravans that it is exceedingly complicated. It is very
> easy to get lost in the maze of procedure which it lays down. Even the
> most diligent of planning authorities must be discouraged from taking
> proceedings against infringers. There seems to be no end to the obstacles
> which the ingenuity of lawyers can place in their way."[29]

Here, too Lord Denning allowed a "simple amendment" to the enforcement
notice which would cause no injustice to the appellant who "has known all
the time that he has had permission for only one"[30] caravan on his land.
Apart from Lord Denning's concern to protect the countryside, he seemed
also to be vigilant not to allow the site owner to take advantage of the
imperfectly interlocking law contained in the Caravan Sites and Control of
Development Act 1960 and the town and country planning legislation; to do
so would be an example of abuse of their rights by landowners. Thus in
Loosmore v. *Bridport Rural District Council*,[31] where a farmer, whose farm was
"situate in beautiful countryside within a mile or two of the sea"[32] in Dorset,

[25] [1963] 2 Q.B. 196.
[26] [1966] 1 W.L.R. 427.
[27] [1966] 1 W.L.R. 1280.
[28] [1965] 3 All E.R. 602. The decision of the Court of Appeal was reversed by the House of
Lords. [1968] A.C. 409.
[29] [1965] 3 All E.R. 602, 604, 606.
[30] *Ibid.* p. 607.
[31] (1971) 22 P. & C.R. 1084.
[32] *Ibid.* p. 1085.

was seeking to compel a local planning authority to concede that he had a deemed planning permission under the town and country planning legislation so that he could obtain a site licence under the caravan site legislation, alleged that he had been misled by oral advice received from the planning authority's officials, Lord Denning, in other cases sympathetic to such a claim,[33] dismissed it out of hand:

> "The truth is, of course, that since the events of 1960, [when the appellant first applied for a site licence] he has wrongly used these two fields for caravans—and used them more and more—without any site licence at all. Now he wishes to go on doing so. The planning merits are all against him. It would not be good planning to allow caravan sites in these two fields. So he seeks to find some legal ground for claiming a site licence for them as of right. I can see no basis for his claim . . . . In this case there is no room for holding that the officials misled Mr. Loosmore or misrepresented the position to him in any way."[34]

Not until *Taylor* v. *Calvert*[35] in 1978, the first case under the Mobile Homes Act 1975 to reach the Court of Appeal did a site owner succeed in his appeal before Lord Denning; he had complied strictly with the requirements of the statute on the length of the term of an occupation agreement between site owner and occupier and the courts could not therefore intervene; on all other terms and conditions however the courts could intervene and settle disputes between the parties.

Turning now to enforcement notices, Lord Denning's concern to ensure that technicalities did not stand in the way of the substance of the law did not apply only to notices in respect of caravan sites. His analysis of the relevant sections of the Town and Country Planning Act 1947 and the changes introduced into it by the Caravan Sites and Control of Development Act 1960 in *Miller-Mead*[36] applied to all enforcement notice procedures and set the tone for a more flexible approach by the courts in line with the policy of the Act of 1960. He was scathing in his criticism of the pre-1960 authorities and approach:

> "As I listened to the argument and read the cases I began to wonder whether we were not in danger of returning to the formalism of earlier days. The recitals in an enforcement notice were being treated as if they were a charge against an offender and not only a charge but a record of his conviction which must be strictly accurate else it would be a nullity and void."[37]

Three examples of this more flexible approach to procedures are contained in *Iddenden* v. *Secretary of State for the Environment*,[38] *Square Meals Frozen Foods* v. *Dunstable Borough Council*[39] and *Howard* v. *Secretary of State for the Environment*.[40] In the first case Lord Denning rejected an argument that an enforcement

---

[33] *Post.* pp. 187–190.
[34] (1971) 22 P & C.R. 1084, 1088.
[35] [1978] 1 W.L.R. 899.
[36] [1963] 1 Q.B. 196.
[37] *Ibid.* p. 220.
[38] [1972] 1 W.L.R. 1433.
[39] [1974] 1 W.L.R. 59.
[40] [1975] Q.B. 235.

notice was bad because it did not require the previous building to be
re-erected in place of the illegal erection in respect of which the notice had
been served: the authority had a discretion as to what should be done to
remedy a breach of planning control. In *Square Meals*[41] the appellants sought
to restrain the local authority from taking any steps under enforcement
notices which had been served on the grounds that they, the appellants, had
already taken out an originating summons to determine the question of
development which had caused the enforcement notice to be served. Lord
Denning noted that the appellants had commenced their development
without waiting for the originating summons to be determined; that at the
time they took their summons out, they knew an enforcement notice was
imminent; and that the issue of the summons was part of a plan to challenge
the enforcement notice. That could not be done because the Act provided a
procedure for challenging an enforcement notice in which law and planning
merits could be considered together and ruled out challenges made in any
other way, and that was the better procedure. Finally, in *Howard*[42] the issue
was whether the provision in the Act that notice of appeal against an
enforcement notice had to be made in writing and indicate the grounds of the
appeal was imperative or directory; if the former, Howard's appeal was out of
time for he had only sent a letter notifying his intention to appeal within the
specified 42-day period. Lord Denning considered that the provisions were
imperative as to time and writing but directory only as to the grounds of
appeal because it was quite possible that all the grounds or facts would not
be fully known at the time the notice had to be put in.

In all these cases then, one or other party was trying to rely on
technicalities in a situation where in Lord Denning's eyes they had no merit
at all. They were in other words trying to take advantage of the law and so
abuse their rights under the law; he was concerned that the substantive
issues behind the technicalities were dealt with and interpreted the Act
accordingly. While the approach adopted in *Howard*[43] could lead to delays in
appeals on enforcement notices—and it is worth noting that the Department
of the Environment is increasingly concerned about this[44]—the approach
adopted in the other cases is more in line with the policy behind the
legislation and more apt to facilitate enforcement. Lord Denning was never
opposed to enforcement—in some respects quite the reverse, as enforcement
hit at "irresponsible" developers or landowners abusing their rights—so long
as he and his colleagues retained the ultimate decision on the question of
whose rights were being abused by whom.

In enforcement notices, Lord Denning overrode technicalities; in the next
series of cases to be considered he used or created legal concepts of an
abstract or technical nature or gave a legal veneer to planning concepts with
the result that the system of control became increasingly sophisticated and
legalistic; in this matter Lord Denning was largely in step with his judicial
colleagues in approach if not always in result. Consider first the planning
unit, probably the most significant legal concept introduced by the judges
into the system of development control, and two cases on same drawn from

[41] [1974] 1 W.L.R. 59.
[42] [1975] Q.B. 235.
[43] *Ibid.*
[44] DoE Circular 38/81: Planning and Enforcement Appeals.

early and late in Lord Denning's second era on the Court of Appeal—*G. Percy Trentham Ltd.* v. *Gloucestershire County Council*[45] and *Jennings Motors Ltd.* v. *Secretary of State for the Environment.*[46] In the first case, Lord Denning saw the issue as relatively straightforward: farm buildings were part of a farm; the fact that the farmer had used them for storage purposes in connection with the farm business did not make them a new planning unit, so a building contractor who bought them and used them for storage purposes in connection with his business could not claim that the buildings came within the relevant class of the Use Classes Order and were available for any sort of storage; they were and remained part of the farm for planning purposes so permission was needed if they were to be used for storage purposes unconnected with the farm. No theorising was needed to prevent this particular effort at despoiling the countryside.

Sixteen years later in *Jennings*[47] the situation had changed considerably. The case concerned the use of a new building on a site where mixed light industrial uses had been in operation for some time. The building had been erected without planning permission—indeed permission had in fact been refused for it—but the local planning authority decided to accept it as it was an improvement on those it had replaced but served an enforcement notice to discontinue the light industrial use within the building on the grounds that a new planning unit had come into existence which had a "nil" use so that any unauthorised use could be prevented. By now Lord Denning could point to and discuss two theories in the cases—the theory of the "new planning unit" and the theory of the "new chapter in planning history;" he preferred the latter theory and suggested that in

> "the light of experience . . . we should discard the theory of the new planning unit."[48]

His more staid brethren did not agree, considered the difference between the two theories largely a semantic one and preferred to keep the phrase "hallowed by long usage."[49] Whichever view was accepted the result and the wider implications were the same; the balancing act which local planning authorities have to perform in considering action in respect of any development of land is made that much harder; it may still be a question of fact and degree but the factors to be considered, and whether they have been properly considered is for a court to say. The process which is 1966 was one of common sense is now one of precedent, complexity and legal theories. It was typical of Lord Denning that he was trying to sort matters out in *Jennings*[50] as the men in the ministry "were much perplexed as to the right principle to adopt,"[51] but it must be doubted whether his suggested approach would in practice be any easier to apply than the one "hallowed by long usage."

The concern with balance and prevention of abuse of rights became rather lost to view in the complexities of the planning unit; they were more

[45] [1966] 1 W.L.R. 506.
[46] [1982] 1 All E.R. 471.
[47] *Ibid.*
[48] *Ibid.* p. 476.
[49] *Ibid.* p. 481, *per* Oliver L.J.
[50] [1982] 1 All E.R. 471.
[51] *Ibid.* p. 476.

obviously to the fore in two cases of change of use, *Webber* v. *Ministry of Housing and Local Government*[52] and *Hartley* v. *Ministry of Housing and Local Government*,[53] the first being a "two use" case, the second an abandonment of use case. In each case Lord Denning was concerned to allow a "fair" use of land—in *Webber*[54] indeed one of the two uses was as a camping and caravan site, but as it had continued regularly for four years and was now a normal use of the land it could not be prevented. In *Hartley*[55] the test was whether "a reasonable man might conclude that the previous use had been abandoned."[56]

Lord Denning's facility in using legal concepts in a creative way in order to achieve ends which accorded with his notions of the proper use of land are nowhere better displayed in planning law than in three cases dealing with operations on and use of land, all of which arose in areas of great scenic beauty—*Thomas David (Porthcawl) Ltd.* v. *Penybont District Council*,[57] *Parkes* v. *Secretary of State for the Environment*[58] and one of Lord Denning's last cases in this area, *Malvern Hills District Council* v. *Secretary of State for the Environment*.[59] *Thomas David*[60] concerned the excavation of sand and gravel in "an attractive coastal area of peaceful scenic beauty and of such special scientific interest."[61] The appellants had excavated outside the area for which they had been granted permission and the local planning authority had issued an enforcement notice covering a very much larger area than that being excavated. The appellants argued that the area covered by the notice was the wrong planning unit and that in any event, their excavation had started more than four years previously and so could not be prevented. Lord Denning dismissed both points: the planning unit was similar to a caravan site—the whole field was the unit not just the individual hard standings, and the four year rule did not apply as "every shovelful is a mining operation [so] . . . an enforcement notice can be served in respect of the excavations within the last four years."[62] *Parkes*[63] raised the question of the distinction between operations on and use of land. Parkes and his sister carried on a scrap heap—"an ugly heap of waste" which "spoilt" an area of "great landscape beauty"[64] in the Peak National Park. If what they did were operations on the land because they processed the scrap, then no discontinuance order could be served because such an order was applicable only to discontinuance of use. Lord Denning considered that operations involved activities which resulted in some physical alteration to the land and had some degree of permanence to the land, whereas use comprised activities done in, alongside or on the land. Parkes's activities were of the latter sort and so could be made the subject of a discontinuance order.

[52] [1968] 1 W.L.R. 29.
[53] [1970] 1 Q.B. 413.
[54] [1968] 1 W.L.R. 29.
[55] [1970] 1 Q.B. 413.
[56] *Ibid.* p. 420.
[57] [1972] 1 W.L.R. 1526.
[58] [1979] 1 W.L.R. 1308.
[59] (1983) 81 L.G.R. 13.
[60] [1972] 3 All E.R. 1092.
[61] *Ibid.* pp. 1094–1095: the inspector's report quoted by Lord Denning.
[62] *Ibid.* p. 1096.
[63] [1979] 1 All E.R. 211.
[64] *Ibid.* p. 212.

Finally in *Malvern Hills*,[65] the scene of his first notable planning case almost a quarter of a century earlier,[66] the issue was what activities constituted a "specified operation"[67] sufficient to enable a developer to claim that he had commenced development within the period required by the law; the developer had brought equipment and plant on to the site and put in pegs to mark out a new estate road, the line of which had not however been approved by the Highway Authority as was required by conditions in the planning permission. Lord Denning, in a dissenting judgment, applied *Parkes*[68] and considered that mere pegging out a road could not be a specified operation. The majority considered *Parkes* was not authority for the proposition that there could be no operation within the meaning of the section under consideration unless physical change had been achieved; very little was needed to satisfy the section and the developers had done that very little.

In each of these three cases Lord Denning supported the local planning authority and indeed in *Parkes* supported the authority against the archetypal "little man" who was not even represented before him. But in each case it was the developer who, in Lord Denning's eyes, was abusing his rights of ownership of the land; he was putting his personal commercial interests before his wider public duty to preserve the countryside and so it was justifiable to try and stop his activities.[69] In none of the cases was the answer obvious—in *Parkes*, the Court of Appeal reversed the first instance decision, in *Malvern Hills*[70] Lord Denning was in a minority and even in *Thomas David*[71] there was some hesitation on the mining operation—but the complexity of planning law—a complexity created by the judges—allowed Lord Denning to use planning factors which had been turned into legal concepts to achieve the ends he thought desirable.

This discussion in this section may be concluded by a consideration of three important cases on planning conditions that Lord Denning was concerned with, *Pyx Granite*,[72] a majority decision in the Court of Appeal reversed in the House of Lords,[73] though with no criticism of Lord Denning's formulation of the test of a valid condition, *Kingsway Investments (Kent) Ltd.* v. *Kent C.C.*[74] another majority decision of the Court of Appeal though this time with Lord Denning giving the dissenting judgment, again reversed in the House of Lords on a three to two decision,[75] and *Newbury District Council* v.

---

[65] (1983) 81 L.G.R. 13.
[66] *Pyx Granite Co.* v. *Ministry of Housing and Local Government* [1958] 1 Q.B. 554.
[67] Town and Country Planning Act 1971, s.43.
[68] [1979] 1 W.L.R. 1308.
[69] Thus his opening sentences in *Malvern Hills*:
   "The Malvern Hills look down on a very English landscape to the west. In the valley there are charming old villages dotted here and there among the woods. One of them is Cradley which gives its name to the Cradley Brook running through it. It has quite enough houses for everyone there, but developers wish to build more. . . . An inspector at a local inquiry has found that the development would be socially unacceptable. . . . "
   at pp. 14–15.
[70] (1983) 81 L.G.R. 13.
[71] [1972] 1 W.L.R. 1526.
[72] [1958] 1 Q.B. 554.
[73] [1960] A.C. 260.
[74] [1969] 2 Q.B. 332.
[75] [1971] A.C. 72.

Secretary of State for the Environment,[76] a unanimous decision of the Court of
Appeal, allowing an appeal from the Divisional Court, which was in turn
reversed in the House of Lords in a unanimous decision.[77] These twists and
turns of judicial minds give some indication that while all might agree on the
verbal formula in which the test to be applied to conditions is expressed, the
perceptions of individual judges about the proper limits of planning result in
there being very little agreement about anything else. Here then, assumptions about what ought to be are nearer the surface than in other cases
discussed in this section.

It is sometimes forgotten that Lord Denning found the conditions in *Pyx
Granite*[78] to be valid notwithstanding that they related, not to the land the
subject of the planning application, but to land and machinery at another
site in the Malvern Hills, albeit in ancillary use to the application site. Lord
Denning's concern was not so much to cut down or restrict the local planning
authority's powers as to assert the principle that they were subject to judicial
control. This approach characterised his judgments in the other two cases in
both of which he found for the local planning authority, trying to control
development in, once again, the countryside. In *Kingsway Investments*[79] the
conditions in question were time limit conditions and the two developments
were in respectively, "a small village set in very attractive countryside"[80]
and an estate in "an outstanding area of natural beauty."[81] Lord Denning
considered that:

> "a planning authority are entitled to impose a *time limit* within which
> planning permission must be acted on. It is desirable that they should
> do so in the interests of the good planning of their area. Take the county
> of Kent. It is the garden of England. It is in danger of being overgrown.
> Just as in a garden one must prune away the old shoots so as to make
> room for the new, so in controlling development in their area, the
> authority must be able to throw out the stale permissions so as to make
> room for fresh ones."[82]

He considered that the particular time limit condition in the instant case was
valid for although not expressly making allowance for the time which might
be taken by appealing to the Minister, "the condition should be construed so
as to be valid rather than invalid"[83] and words read into it accordingly.

In *Newbury District Council*[84] the case concerned the validity of a condition
imposed on a temporary planning permission that at the end of the period of
permitted use, two hangars—"huge black structures of corrugated iron
despoiling the landscape" of what was once a "stretch of land [that] was
delightfully rural"[85]—in existence before the time the permitted use began
should be removed. The users of the hangars had bought them knowing of

---

[76] [1979] 1 W.L.R. 1241.
[77] [1981] A.C. 578.
[78] [1958] 1 Q.B. 554.
[79] [1969] 2 Q.B. 332.
[80] *Ibid.* p. 344.
[81] *Ibid.* p. 345.
[82] *Ibid.* p. 347.
[83] *Ibid.* p. 350.
[84] [1979] 1 All E.R. 243.
[85] *Ibid.* p. 246.

the condition. Both the Minister and the Divisional Court considered the condition invalid because it did not fairly and reasonably relate to the permitted development—that is the need for the removal of the hangars did not arise from the use of the hangars. Lord Denning considered that the Ministry view was wrong; put too narrow a construction on his words in *Pyx Granite*,[86] and did not have sufficient regard to the development plan or section 29(1) of the Act of 1971. A condition could be used to get rid of "these hideous hangars,"[87] since it could be related to the development plan which expressly referred both to possible temporary uses of such structures and the policy of securing their removal where possible. Lord Denning also expressed considerable disapproval of the developer's subsidiary argument that planning permission was not needed at all as they could use the hangars for storage under the Use Classes Order as they were merely continuing their former use as a repository; having acted on the planning permission for ten years it was "quite contrary to equity and justice"[88] that they should be allowed to use the Use Classes Order:

> "In conclusion I will just remind you of these facts. In 1962 this rubber company were given planning permission to use these two hangars for the next ten years on condition that they removed them at the end on 31st December 1972. They did not honour that obligation. They have raised issues and fought them with much tenacity and at great expense ever since. So much so that the delays have gone beyond all bounds. Now six years later the hangars are still there. It is high time that they were removed and obliterated from the landscape. I would allow the appeal accordingly."[89]

The House of Lords was unmoved by Lord Denning's vigorous judgment, and found for the rubber company both on the planning condition and the Use Classes Order point. But from Lord Denning's perspective, here was as clear a case as one could hope to find of an abuse of rights, and his judgment reflected his strong feelings on that point. On the narrower issue of planning law, it must be said too that Lord Denning's judgment accorded with more recent trends in the judicial approach to development control—a broad approach which looks to the purposes of the law as reflected in the post 1968 legislation and planning practice, rather than the narrower approach favoured by the House of Lords which wished to tie the condition imposed directly to the permitted development. Finally, on the hidden issue—who should bear the cost of removing the hangars?—Lord Denning's view on "equity and justice" clearly told against the company while the House of Lords' decision equally clearly told against the local authority; the company however had bought the hangars after the condition had been imposed so that the decision of the House of Lords gave them a useful capital gain; it is not easy to see good sense in legal, planning or moral terms in the House of Lords' decision.

The final matters to be considered in planning law are more in the nature

---

[86] [1958] 1 Q.B. 554, 572 quoted *supra.* at p. 178.
[87] [1979] 1 All E.R. 243, 248.
[88] *Ibid.* p. 250.
[89] *Ibid.* pp. 250–251.

of "pure" administrative law but they may be considered here nonetheless. They may be subsumed under the head of local planning authority responsibility for the statements and actions of their officials—estoppel in public law. In a series of cases during his second tenure in the Court of Appeal, Lord Denning attempted to widen the ambit of liability and responsibility of local authorities on these matters. On the important issue of estoppel—whether statements of planning officers should be held to bind their authorities—there has been a retreat[90] from the high water mark of Lord Denning's judgment in *Lever (Finance) Ltd.* v. *Westminster London Borough Council.*[91] While that is significant as indicating that in those cases where Lord Denning reached the same conclusion as his colleagues but by a less orthodox route, his views may not retain their potency all that long, what is of more importance here is that all these cases aptly illustrate once again his concern with abuse of rights. In these cases the issue could be, and was by Lord Denning, seen as the individual—be he developer, architect, landowner or business—being inconvenienced and misled by an official whose employers then sought to hide behind some technical rule of law to avoid bearing the responsibilities of those wrongful actions or misstatements; a strict reading of the law might have allowed such a defence but an approach grounded in the principle of prevention of abuse of rights would produce a different result.

A good example of this is in *Crabb* v. *Arun District Council*,[92] not a planning law case but one in which the same kinds of issues arose as in *Lever (Finance)*[93] and *Wells* v. *Minister of Housing and Local Government.*[94] Crabb owned a piece of land which he wished to divide and sell in two portions. Each portion would need an access on to a new estate road being developed by the local authority. Meetings were held between Crabb and Council officials in which Crabb and his representative were given to understand that they would be given access on to the estate road, but no formal legal steps were ever taken to confirm that. The Council however acted as if access had been granted by leaving gaps in a fence it erected between Crabb's land and the road at the agreed points of access, and then putting in gates at those two points. Later however, the Council removed the gates, fenced up the gaps, claimed there was no agreement and demanded payment for the grant of an easement to Crabb. Lord Denning considered that these facts gave rise to a proprietary estoppel which could in turn be the foundation of a case by Crabb for the grant of an easement without paying anything for it, because the Council's conduct had rendered the land sterile and useless for six years, a loss which could be taken into account. It was the Council's "conduct which led him to act as he did: and this raises an equity in favour (*sic*) against them. In the circumstances it was inequitable that the Council should insist on their strict title as they did."[95] Similarly, in *Lever (Finance)*,[96] the planning officer:

> "made a mistake . . . . But it is not a mistake for which the developers should suffer. The developers put up this house on the faith of this

[90] *Western Fish Products* v. *Penwith District Council* [1981] 2 All E.R. 204; (1978) 38 P. & C.R. 7.
[91] [1971] 1 Q.B. 222.
[92] [1976] Ch. 179.
[93] [1971] 1 Q.B. 222.
[94] [1967] 1 W.L.R. 1000.
[95] [1975] 3 All E.R. 865, 872.
[96] [1971] 1 Q.B. 222.

representation made to them. I do not think that an enforcement notice should be launched against them."[97]

Where necessary, Lord Denning was prepared to use the common law rather than equity to ensure that officials and their employers were made liable for their mistakes: in *Ministry of Housing and Local Government* v. *Sharp*[98] where negligence by a Council employee in failing to record in an official certificate from a local land registry a planning charge, resulted in the Ministry losing the benefit of a claim for compensation against a land owner, Lord Denning considered that the ordinary principles of the law of negligence would be sufficient to ensure that the employee was liable, and he was also willing (being in a minority on this point) to hold the Registrar liable for loss as well on the ground that

"otherwise the injured person would be left without a remedy—which is unthinkable."[99]

In all these cases, his concern to provide a remedy or relief against the public authority took precedence over any discussion of a wider public interest in the administration of planning law, or in local authority responsibility to ratepayers of the kind that Lord Denning was quick to engage in where countryside matters were concerned or, as we shall see later,[1] where housing matters were concerned. None of these cases in fact were set in the countryside, yet the wider issues of the due administration of the planning system were relevant as was illustrated in Lord Justice Russell's (as he then was) dissent in *Wells* v. *Ministry of Housing and Local Government*[2] and the judgments in *Western Fish Products Ltd.* v. *Penwith District Council*,[3] the case which restricted the scope of Lord Denning's views expressed in *Lever (Finance)*.[4] In the case of *Co-operative Retail Services Ltd.* v. *Taff-Ely Borough Council*,[5] however, wider public issues were thought to be relevant by Lord Denning. In an extraordinary combination of circumstances compounded of ignorance and ignoring of the law, foolishness and panic, the clerk to the Taff-Ely Borough Council issued, without any authority to do so, a backdated planning permission for a hypermarket to Tesco's Ltd. with the result that Tesco's paid the owner of land on which the development was to take place, half a million pounds, which owing to the backdating of the permission, was free of development land tax. A rival stores group whose application for a hypermarket had been turned down by the Council challenged the validity of that grant of permission. Lord Denning had no doubt that the purported grant was "utterly invalid"[6] and he concluded as follows:

"Underlying this case there is an important principle of planning law. It is that a grant of planning permission is made in the public interest—so

---

[97] *Ibid.* p. 231.
[98] [1970] 1 All E.R. 1009.
[99] *Ibid.* p. 1016.
[1] *Infra*, pp. 198 *et seq.*
[2] [1967] 1 W.L.R. 1000.
[3] [1981] 2 All E.R. 204.
[4] [1971] 1 Q.B. 222.
[5] [1980] 1 W.L.R. 271.
[6] *Ibid.* p. 237.

as to ensure that the amenities of our countryside are preserved for the good of all. The protection of the public interest is entrusted to the representative bodies and to the ministers. It would be quite wrong that it should be pre-empted by a mistaken issue by a clerk of a printed form—without any authority in that behalf . . . Representative bodies . . . should not be bound by mistakes made by the clerk or people in the office—when the result would be to damage the interests of the public at large."[7]

This was the very point being made in *Wells*[8] and *Western Fish*[9] where there was even more reason to find for the local planning authority—in both cases it was oral statements of planning officers that were being relied on. No-one would disagree with Lord Denning's judgment in the instant case—the House of Lords gave very short shrift to an appeal against it[10]—but it is permissible to draw attention to his inconsistency of approach which cannot be entirely glossed over by reference to his desire to do "justice" and prevent abuse of rights. In *Lever (Finance)*[11] the neighbours and not the developers were left to "feel justly aggrieved"[12]; the developers were not to suffer for the mistakes of the official; in *Taff-Ely*,[13] the owners of the land and Tesco's "must be left"[14] to work out the consequences of the clerk's action themselves. Yet *as between Tesco's and the local planning authority*, the perspective from which Lord Denning viewed the other cases in this section, equity and justice were on the side of Tesco's so that this could have been a case where:

"a defect in procedure can be cured and an irregularity can be waived even by a public authority so as to render valid that which would otherwise be invalid."[15]

Equity and justice no doubt looked different from the Co-op's point of view which Lord Denning espoused in this case—"the just solution" was for "the Secretary of State [to] call in both applications . . . and determine them on their merits"[16]—but this only serves to highlight the difficulty of deciding cases such as these on the basis of the "just solution."

The Balance between Public and Private: Positive Public Powers

The distinction between this and the area of law considered in the second section of this chapter is that we are concerned here with public powers and duties where public authorities are permitted or required to take active steps or perform certain duties in relation to land or houses or housing and private persons are either objecting to these positive steps being taken or are arguing that they should be taken. The two areas of substantive law involved here are

---

[7] *Ibid.* pp. 239–240.
[8] [1967] 1 W.L.R. 1000.
[9] [1981] 2 All E.R. 204.
[10] *Attorney-General, ex. rel. Co-operative Retail Services Ltd.* v. *Taff-Ely Borough Council* (1981) 42 P. & C.R. 1.
[11] [1971] 1 Q.B. 222.
[12] *Ibid.* p. 231.
[13] (1980) 39 P. & C.R. 223.
[14] *Ibid.* p. 239. On that see C. Crawford, *Taff-Ely Revisited: The Negligence Aspects* (1983) 267 E.G. 579.
[15] *Wells* v. *Minister of Housing and Local Government* [1967] 2 All E.R. 1041, 1044.
[16] (1980) 39 P. & C.R. 223, 240.

compulsory purchase and compensation, and housing with a good deal of overlapping between them, particularly in the area of slum clearance. Within housing too it is necessary to make the distinction between what may be called traditional housing law—slum-clearance and compensation therefor, and new housing law—actions by council tenants against councils, and homelessness principally; the former has been present throughout Lord Denning's judicial tenure, the latter came into prominence only in his last decade and as we will see, he had some difficulty in adjusting to the nature of the issues and the parties before him. The bulk of this section of the chapter will deal with housing law and compulsory purchase law in respect of housing, but first some consideration may be given to some of Lord Denning's judgments on matters of compensation for compulsory purchase.

The measure of compensation and the factors to be taken into account in arriving at the correct measure are notoriously complex and technical, yet underlying the abstruse law is the ideal of a fair measure of compensation, fair both for the dispossessed individual and the public purse. This was a situation tailor-made for Lord Denning and he did in fact contribute some notable and clear judgments in this field, none of which were overturned in the House of Lords.[17] As might be expected his overall concern was to cut through the sets of assumptions and hypotheses which the law requires valuers to have regard to in order to ensure that substantial justice was done,[18] and cut through too, any other technicalities standing in the way of fair compensation. A good example of this latter kind of technicality is provided by *D.H.N. Food Distributors* v. *Tower Hamlets London Borough Council*[19] The appellants and another similar company were food distributors who for various tax and other financial reasons were licencees of Bronze Investments Ltd., a company having the same directors as the two appellants, which owned land compulsorily acquired by Tower Hamlets. The two appellants claimed disturbance compensation but were met by the argument that as they were licencees their disturbance must by law be limited to that suffered by a tenant from year to year, *i.e.* negligible disturbance. Lord Denning considered that D.H.N. had an irrevocable licence which gave them sufficient interest in the land to qualify them for distubance compensation but over and above that:

> "This group is virtually the same as a partnership in which all the three companies are partners. They should not be deprived of the compensa-tion which should justly be payable for compensation. The three companies should for present purposes be treated as one and the parent company D.H.N. should be treated as that one. So that D.H.N. are entitled to claim compensation accordingly. It was not necessary for them to go through a convenyancing device to get it."[20]

---

[17] Apart from those discussed in the text, the following may be mentioned: *Camrose* v. *Basingstoke Corporation* [1966] 1 W.L.R. 1100; *Jolliffe* v. *Exeter Corporation* [1967] 1 W.L.R. 993; *Jelson* v. *Minister of Housing and Local Government* [1970] 1 Q.B. 243; *Myers* v. *Milton Keynes Development Corporation* [1974] 1 W.L.R. 696. He dissented in *Margate Corporation* v. *Devotwill Investments* [1969] 2 All E.R. 97 and the decision was reversed in the House of Lords, [1970] 3 All E.R. 864.

[18] See especially his judgment in *Myers, supra.* at pp. 1100–03.

[19] [1976] 3 All E.R. 462. For a discussion of some of the issues arising out of the application of equitable principles and licences in this case see Hayton Chap. 2, pp. 89–90.

[20] *Ibid.* p. 467.

Two contrasting pairs of cases on the law of compensation may be considered to illustrate Lord Denning's conception of balance at work here. In *Harvey* v. *Crawley Development Corporation*[21] Mrs. Harvey was claiming as disturbance compensation, surveyors' and legal fees and travelling costs in connection with the purchase of a new house in place of one compulsorily acquired by the Development Corporation. The claim included costs on a house she considered buying as well as in respect of the house she did finally buy. Lord Denning considered this was a reasonable claim; the costs were directly incurred as a result of her being put out of her house; but costs not so directly incurred, *i.e.* the costs of brokerage if the compensation money were invested in stocks and shares could not be claimed. The line was drawn at the costs of an owner "who is forced out and reasonably finds a house elsewhere in which to live."[22] In contrast to this is *Wilson* v. *Liverpool City Council*.[23] The Lands Tribunal made an award of compensation to Wilson on the basis that the relevant date for valuation was the date of the notice to treat. Five days later the House of Lords decided the *West Midland Baptist*[24] case which altered the date on which valuation was to be assessed. Wilson, whose counsel, knowing of the pending appeal in the House of Lords, had sought to keep open the question of the correct date for valuation in the Lands Tribunal hearing, appealed against the award on those grounds. Lord Denning declined to allow the case to be re-opened. The claimants should have asked for alternative valuations but did not:

> "Instead of asking for an alternative award, the claimant went before the tribunal asking for one valuation on a single date, the date of the notice to treat. They conducted a long detailed hearing for twelve days at great expense on that basis. They cannot be allowed now to re-open the matter and ask for a valuation at another date."[25]

The advisers to the claimants had made a wrong decision on how to handle the appeal but this did not move Lord Denning; they had had ample opportunity and the best possible advice and had to live with the results. Mrs. Harvey was claiming what she, an owner-occupier, had in fact spent on obtaining a new home; the Wilsons were seeking an unearned and quite fortuitous capital gain for in between the date of the notice to treat and the date of entry on to the land, some 13 months "there had been a very rapid increase in land values, especially in this part of Liverpool"[26] and the Wilsons' land would have risen in value by some 20 per cent.

The second pair of cases involves inverse compulsory purchase of land not capable of reasonably beneficial use by virtue of refusal of planning permission for housing development. In *Provincial Properties (London) Ltd.* v. *Caterham and Warlingham London Borough Council*[27] developers were refused permission to build houses on a small piece of land zoned for residential development in the Surrey County Council development plan. The land was at the top of "a high ridge of land which commands a lovely countryside . . . .

[21] [1957] 1 Q.B. 485.
[22] *Ibid.* p. 494.
[23] [1971] 1 All E.R. 628.
[24] *Birmingham Corporation* v. *West Midland Baptist (Trust) Association Inc.* [1970] A.C. 874.
[25] [1971] 1 All E.R. 628, 632.
[26] *Ibid.* p. 630.
[27] [1972] 1 Q.B. 453.

The reason for the refusal was to preserve the view of the ridge from the valley."[28] A purchase notice was served on the local planning authority and confirmed by the Minister. The issue was the measure of compensation; the developer arguing for its value with assumed planning permission for residential development, the authority for agricultural value only. In answering the question certain statutory assumptions had to be made, one of which was that planning permission for the development for which the land was zoned in the development plan might reasonably have been expected to be granted. Lord Denning considered that while the land in question might be zoned for residential development, planning permission could not reasonably have been expected to be granted for same, so that compensation was to be paid on the basis of agricultural value only. In *Jelson Ltd.* v. *Blaby District Council*[29] on the other hand the reason for the piece of land in question not being granted planning permission for residential development was, originally, that it had been reserved for a highway which had never been built, while houses had been constructed on either side of the highway strip on the assumption that it would be built, and, immediately, that the residents of those houses had objected to what was now open space being built on, an objection that was upheld by the Minister. In these circumstances Lord Denning considered that full residential value compensation should be paid;

> "I would point out that if this land had been taken for a highway, there would have been full compensation. It does not seem fair that because of the change of plan rendering it sterile the owners should not get their compensation just the same."[30]

One might also add that if the residents of houses fronting on to the strip of land wanted it to remain as open space it was only reasonable that they should have to pay for it through a rate increase caused by increased compensation. It is pertinent to note that in *Provincial Properties*[31] the land in question had been re-zoned as metropolitan green belt after the case started, a fact which Lord Denning said "did not affect the present case."[32] What then is the difference between the two cases which required the developers in the first case to bear the costs of maintaining open space yet placed those costs on ratepayers in the second? In the first case there was "natural" open space, part of some lovely countryside; in the second there was "man-made" open space, undeveloped land in the middle of a housing estate. Given that the purpose of town planning is "to ensure that the amenities of our countryside are to be preserved for the good of all"[33] there would have been an abuse of rights by the landowners in the first case if they had been able to claim compensation on the basis that there was a reasonable expectation that they would have received permission to erect houses on the land, for that would have been against the public interest as perceived by Lord Denning; no such public interest was involved in *Jelson*[34] however; there was a clash of

[28] *Ibid.* p. 459.
[29] [1978] 1 All E.R. 548.
[30] *Ibid.* p. 554.
[31] [1972] 1 Q.B. 453.
[32] *Ibid.* p. 460.
[33] *Co-operative Retail Services Ltd.* v. *Taff-Ely Borough Council* (1980) 39 P. & C.R. 223, 239.
[34] [1977] 1 W.L.R. 1020.

private interests only and those of the developers were preferred, since the owner-occupiers' had arisen through the "fault" of the public authority; to support them would have been to tilt the balance the wrong way.

We may turn now to consider the broad area of housing law—clearance and compulsory purchase, repairs and improvement, council housing, squatting and homelessness. A key to understanding these cases, raising societal issues far removed from the need to protect the countryside against development, is what can best and most charitably be described as Lord Denning's old fashioned paternalism about public powers in respect of housing; local authorities are acting beneficently when engaged in the most necessary work of clearing slums and those who try to stop them or hold them up, were treated with a fair degree of suspicion. Not so those who are not challenging the fact of clearance but its application to them and their property, *e.g.* the measure of compensation for a house compulsory purchased—such persons are usually treated sympathetically if they are acting "responsibly." These notions about beneficent public authorities, responsible and irresponsible challenges to them were carried over into the new more radical housing law of the middle and late seventies' when totally new issues and a different class of person began to emerge in housing cases and Lord Denning's touch began to desert him. His rather simplistic notions about the just solution, and balance began to take on a more overt aura of social class; abuse of rights was not just abuse of the rights of ownership of property or abuse of the rights to control the use of property, but abuse of one's position in society, the abuse consisting of the attempt to claim property rights. Similarly with the notion of balance; the balance was not so much one between, *e.g.* the property rights of private landlords and tenants, as between clients seeking benefits from public authority and the public authority properly mindful of its role as the guardian of public funds. Not surprisingly the balance more often than not came down against the clients, particularly those that Lord Denning considered to be especially undeserving for reasons not in any way connected with the case before him. In short Lord Denning's approach to the new housing law of the mid 1970s was in many respects similar to the approach of some of his colleagues in the 1950s and early 1960s to planning law; they could not and he could not adjust to the new social realities behind the law; whereas they expressed their hostility to the law by adopting narrow and technical interpretations of it, he expressed his hostility more overtly and in social terms.

These strictures must now be considered in the light of the cases. Consider first clearance and compulsory purchase. One of Lord Denning's early cases at first instance was *H. E. Green and Sons* v. *Minister of Health*,[35] where the validity of a compulsory purchase order made by Bristol Corporation for housing purposes was in issue. Lord Denning declined to admit the challenge; at issue was essentially a conflict between individual developers, who were objecting to land being acquired for social facilities within a new housing estate on the grounds that the Housing Act referred to land for houses for the working classes and the social facilities might be used by others, and the community. Conflicts of social policy, said Lord Denning, were for the electors of Bristol to determine; the judge could only look to the law which had been complied with. A similar policy of judicial restraint was

[35] [1948] 1 K.B. 34.

apparent in *Ashbridge Investments Ltd.* v. *Minister of Housing and Local Government*[36] in the early years of Lord Denning's second era in the Court of Appeal: the court should not admit fresh evidence on the question of "fit or unfit" but merely content itself with asking whether the Minister had reasonable grounds for coming to the decision he did.

In what circumstances then was Lord Denning prepared to intervene and find against a local authority? We may consider various contrasting cases, *Gordondale Investments* v. *Secretary of State for the Environment*[37] contrasted with *Coleen Properties Ltd.* v. *Minister of Housing and Local Government*[38]; *Wahiwala* v. *Secretary of State for the Environment*[39] with *Hunter* v. *Manchester City Council*[40]; *Cohen* v. *Haringey London Borough Council*[41] and *George* v. *Secretary of State for the Environment*[42] with *Munton* v. *Greater London Council.*[43] In the first named of all these contrasting cases, the appellants were attempting to prevent, by various procedural subterfuges not likely to appeal to Lord Denning at the best of times, "desirable" slum clearance, the appellants themselves not being particularly worthy characters in his eyes—a speculative property company, slum landlords, immigrants alleging underhand dealings by local authorities. The second named of the cases were all very different; the owner of a new, perfectly usable block of flats and shops objecting to the Minister including it in a clearance area so as to make a better shaped area for redevelopment, when the inspector had recommended that it should be excluded; and householders not objecting to the principle of clearance but seeking to maximise their compensation. In all these cases we can see Lord Denning's notion of abuse of rights very clearly; the appellants in the first named cases were abusing their rights and holding up desirable action; the appellants in the second named cases were doing no more than protecting their rights in danger of being overborne by the public authorities.

Some of the facts in these cases must be looked at in more detail. In both *Gordondale*[44] and *Coleen,*[45] one ground of objection to the clearance order was that the official representation on which the order was based was too formal; in *Gordondale* the representation just repeated verbatim the words of the relevant section in the Housing Act; in *Coleen* the Council's official at the public local inquiry into the proposed demolition paraphrased the Act but in neither case was evidence adduced to support the opinions of the officials. In *Gordondale* Lord Denning rejected criticism of the formal representation; it was an internal document:

> "It is kept within the G.L.C. It is not shown to objectors or made for them in any way. So long as the medical officer makes it clear that he is of the opinion that the area should be dealt with as a clearance area he

[36] [1965] 1 W.L.R. 1320.
[37] (1972) 23 P. & C.R. 334.
[38] [1971] 1 W.L.R. 433.
[39] (1977) 75 L.G.R. 651.
[40] [1975] Q.B. 877.
[41] (1981) 42 P. & C.R. 6.
[42] (1979) 38 P. & C.R. 609.
[43] [1976] 1 W.L.R. 649.
[44] (1972) 23 P. & C.R. 334.
[45] [1971] 1 W.L.R. 433.

can made his representation in general terms: and the G.L.C. can act on
it . . . . So it [the form of words] has been used 30 and more years . . . .
We ought not to upset it all now."[46]

In *Coleen* on the other hand Lord Denning considered it "quite clear that
the mere *ipse dixit* of the Council is not sufficient. There must be some
evidence to support its assertion."[47] That this decision "upset" the practice
of many years is evidenced by the unusual step taken by the Department of
the Environment: it issued a special circular to all local authorities drawing
their attention to the decision and the need, in the light of the ruling that the
question of taking the 'extra' land was a question of fact not policy, to adduce
evidence to support such proposals in the future.[48]

Similar contrasts may be pointed to in *Cohen*,[49] *George*[50] and *Munton*.[51] In
both *Cohen* and *George* there were admitted council errors of procedure in
relation to the service of orders; in *Cohen*, a notice to treat and of entry were
served on the owner of a house after the local authority had entered; the
notices were back-dated. Cohen's solicitors however ignored the back-dating
and acted on the basis that the notices were good; later on, after
disagreements with the local authority, Cohen claimed that they had
occupied his land unlawfully and were guilty of a trespass; if he was right he
was entitled to have the land with newly built houses on it returned to him.
Lord Denning did not consider that he was right:

> "the notice to treat was perfectly valid at the date it was *served*. The date
> it bore at the bottom does not matter in the least . . . . Then I turn to the
> notice of entry . . . It seems to me that a notice of entry can be served
> whilst the acquiring authority is in possession . . . It may be—as in this
> case—that the possession at that time was unlawful. Nevertheless on the
> notice of entry being given it becomes lawful 14 days after service . . . If
> it had been necessary, I should have been disposed to agree . . . that
> having regard to the dealings that had taken place between the parties it
> would be inequitable to allow Mr. Cohen now to tear the whole thing up
> and claim the land and the properties that have been built on it."[52]

In *George*[53] the landlords persistently kept an overcrowded house, looked
after it badly and paid no rates. The local authority decided to compulsorily
acquire the house. Unfortunately the local authority did not check the
property register and the order was served on Mr. George only, whereas it
should have been served on his wife as well, as she was a co-owner, registered
as such. The order finally went through but on the last day of the six weeks
period allowed for challenge to the validity of the order, Mrs. George
challenged the order. The case, in truth, had little merit and Lord Denning
was not disposed to try and find any: no substantial prejudice to Mrs. George
had occurred, no breach of natural justice had taken place therefore, and

---

[46] (1972) 23 P. & C.R. 334, 339.
[47] [1971] 1 All E.R. 1049, 1053.
[48] DoE Circular No. 52/71: Housing Acts 1957–1969: Compulsory Purchase Orders and
Clearance Orders. Giving of Evidence by local authorities.
[49] (1981) 42 P. & C.R. 6.
[50] (1979) 38 P. & C.R. 609.
[51] [1976] 1 W.L.R. 649.
[52] (1981) 42 P. & C.R. 6, 15–16.
[53] (1979) 38 P. & C.R. 609.

thus although the order should have been served on her, indeed "every joint owner should be served, when he or she is known. A wife should be served as well as a husband"[54] she could not have it set aside.

In *Munton*[55] on the other hand, technical rules were used to defeat the local authority and assist the appellant. Munton's house was subject to compulsory purchase and a notice to treat had been served, thus binding "the local authority to purchase and the owner to sell at a price to be ascertained."[56] The dispute was as to the price, the authority claiming an agreement on one sum, Munton arguing that that sum was "subject to contract" and claiming a sum 50 per cent. higher, being its value as at the date of the entry into possession. Lord Denning considered that the words "subject to contract" which featured in correspondence relating to the lower sum were decisive:

> "I know that in these cases of compulsory purchase there is no contract prepared or signed, but only a conveyance. So the words 'subject to contract' have no real application. But nevertheless they have, I think, the effect of preventing there being any firm agreement on the price."[57]

A second area of "traditional" housing law to which Lord Denning has made several contributions over a 30-year period is that of repairs and improvements. While he was not opposed to the general idea of local authorities having a responsibility to see that houses were kept in good repair—a landlord who failed to do that would be in his eyes, abusing his rights—he was clearly greatly concerned at the costs to landlords of complying with repair notices. Thus a challenge to a repair notice or closing order on procedural grounds tended to invoke a less sympathetic response than one based on unreasonable costs grounds; on the latter grounds his notions of balance could be more readily applied. Two early cases may be contrasted to bring these points out. In *Rawlence* v. *Croydon Corporation*,[58] Lord Denning gave short shrift to a landlord trying to argue that as he was not receiving a rack-rent from the house owing to the operation of the Rent Acts he was not in control of the house as required by that Act and so was not the person on whom repair notices should be served. The landlord was receiving such rent as he was entitled to under the Rent Act which had to be taken into account in interpreting the Act; the landlord was the person having control; the tenant certainly wasn't and one could not get into the "absurd position"[59] where no one was in control so no notice could be served. Two years earlier in *Cochrane* v. *Chanctonbury Rural District Council*[60] the dispute was over whether a house could be repaired at reasonable expense and what was necessary for such repairs. The county court judge had preferred the owner's view and quashed the notice; Lord Denning accepted this:

> "I do not wish it to be supposed that the courts are not anxious to see defective houses repaired but it is important to keep the right balance

---

[54] *Ibid.* p. 616.
[55] [1976] 1 W.L.R. 649.
[56] *Ibid.* p. 818.
[57] *Ibid.* p. 820.
[58] [1952] 2 Q.B. 803.
[59] *Ibid.* p. 813.
[60] [1950] 2 All E.R. 1134.

between the local authority and the owner. Since 1936 the county courts have been entrusted with the task of keeping the balance. They must see that defects are made good, but they must also protect the owner from unfair burdens."[61]

This concern to protect the owner from "unfair burdens" surfaced again in *De Rothschild* v. *Wing Rural District Council*.[62] Landlords allowed an agricultural tenant to hold over in a farm cottage. The local authority served an improvement notice requiring certain repairs and improvements to be done to the cottage which had "no proper bathroom nor basin no hot water system nor indoor water closet,"[63] so as to bring it up to standard. The landlords objected on the grounds that there was no tenant in the cottage and a notice could only be served when there was. The county court judge considered that no substantial prejudice had been caused the landlord by the invalid notice as the work needed doing. Lord Denning did not agree:

"It seems to me plain that the owner's interests have been prejudiced. He has been directed to do a lot of work on this house when it is plain that the [Housing] Act of 1964 never intended that he should be liable."[64]

The contrast with *George*,[65] admittedly an urban landlord of a very different hue, and with *Cochrane*[66] where the county court judge's decision on balance was supported, is striking.

No discussion of this area of law would be complete without considering the final two repair cases Lord Denning gave judgment in *Hillbank Properties Ltd.* v. *Hackney London Borough Council*[67] and *Phillips* v. *East Ham London Borough Council*.[68] In the first case a "one house" company was challenging a repair order served on it by the local authority in respect of its tenanted house; the company claimed the repairs would cost more than the house was or would be, after repairs, worth. The alternative, that the house would ultimately be declared unfit for human habitation, closed, the tenant rehoused by the local authority and the company left with a vacant house which they could then do up and sell on the open market, was stigmatised by Lord Denning at the beginning of his judgment as:

"socially . . . most undesirable. It means that the owners are at liberty to let houses get in a state of gross disrepair and use it as a means of depriving tenants of their homes."[69]

Not surprisingly Lord Denning overturned the county court judge's decision to quash the repair notices; he had failed to give adequate consideration to the question of the value of the house when repaired; looked at in terms of value with vacant possession the repairs were well worth doing.

[61] *Ibid.* p. 1135.
[62] [1967] 1 All E.R. 597.
[63] *Ibid.* p. 598.
[64] *Ibid.* p. 600.
[65] (1979) 38 P. & C.R. 609.
[66] [1950] 2 All E.R. 1134.
[67] [1978] Q.B. 998.
[68] (1982) 43 P. & C.R. 54.
[69] [1978] Q.B. 998, 1003.

Lord Denning explicitly recognised the "great social importance"[70] of the case and the need to ensure that the policy of Parliament which was to make owners of houses keep them in good repair, and ensure that protected tenants should be able to have their houses properly kept up was enforced. He could see through the strategem of the company; it was a clear example of abuse of the rights of ownership and he was not going to allow it.

During the course of his judgment in *Hillbank*, Lord Denning said that the financial means of the owner of the house could be taken into account:

> "I can envisage a poor widow who has only one house which she lets to bring in some rent. If she could not afford to do the repairs, I think the judge could quash the notice or reduce the requirements so as to bring the cost within her means."[71]

Such a case arose in *Phillips*[72] where once again the owner of the house, considerably out of repair, challenged the repair notice and had it quashed by the county court judge, with the local authority then appealing to the Court of Appeal. Lord Denning back-tracked on his judgment in *Hillbank*[73]; it was not correct to take the value of the house as its value with vacant possession, one should consider the value of the unrepaired and then the repaired house each time with the protected tenant there. On that basis the judge was entitled to come to the decision he did. The only possible distinction between the two cases is the nature of the house-owners and judicial assumptions about their likely behaviour once the house is repaired; *Hillbank*[74] being classified along with *Gordondale*,[75] *Cohen*[76] and *George*[77] as not worthy of judicial protection, *Phillips*[78] being classified with *De Rothschild*,[79] *Hunter*[80] and *Munton*[81] as individuals for whom the law could intervene so as to "keep the right balance" between the local authority and the owner. It was not made clear how the decision in *Phillips*[82] advanced the policy of Parliament to make owners of houses keep them in proper repair and ensure that protected tenants had their houses properly kept up. Nor indeed whether this was to be regarded as an example of the just solution.

We come now to the "new" housing law of the Seventies—council tenants challenging their local authority landlords, homeless persons challenging the failure of local authorities to house them, squatters and indeed on one occasion, a local authority, challenging the very authority of law itself. These cases must be seen in the context of the increased politicisation of public housing and homelessness, as both major political parties adopted and carried out national policies and laws on the topic, and the growth of publicly funded neighbourhood and community law centres which provided advice,

---

[70] *Ibid.* p. 1009.
[71] *Ibid.* p. 1008.
[72] (1982) 43 P. & C.R. 54.
[73] [1978] Q.B. 998.
[74] *Ibid.*
[75] (1972) 23 P. & C.R. 334.
[76] (1981) 42 P. & C.R. 6.
[77] (1979) 38 P. & C.R. 609.
[78] (1982) 43 P. & C.R. 54.
[79] [1967] 1 W.L.R. 470.
[80] [1975] Q.B. 877.
[81] [1976] 1 W.L.R. 649.
[82] (1982) 43 P. & C.R. 54.

assistance and representation to council tenants and the homeless in their
disputes with local authorities. It was a context which Lord Denning found
hard to adjust to.

Two cases in this final era of Lord Denning's involvement with housing
law seemed to set the tone for his general approach—*Southwark London
Borough Council* v. *Williams*[83] and *Asher* v. *Secretary of State for the Environment*.[84]
The first case involved squatting and trespass in empty council houses, the
second the refusal of the Clay Cross Urban District Council to apply the
Housing Finance Act 1972 and raise the rents of its council houses. In
Williams[85] Lord Denning was inclined to consider that the families who had
squatted were at fault, in that they had come to London without arranging
any accommodation and must have foreseen the situation they would get
into, thus absolving the local authority from any duty to provide temporary
accommodation, but over and above that, he unambiguously ruled against
homelessness as giving rise to any defence of necessity to an action for
trespass.

> "If homelessness were once admitted as a defence to trespass, no one's
> house would be safe. Necessity would open a door which no man could
> shut . . . So the courts must for the sake of law and order take a firm
> stand."[86]

The firm stand was against trespass but as the years went on it seemed that
Lord Denning extended it also to that which had given rise to the trespass,
namely homelessness, for which there was much less justification.

In *Asher*,[87] Clay Cross councillors were arguing that the method chosen by
the Secretary of State for the Environment to deal with the problem of the
failure to charge fair rents, as prescribed by the Act of 1972—an
extra-ordinary audit of the council's accounts—was *ultra vires* as its purpose
was not to recoup rents but penalise the councillors. Lord Denning was
highly critical of the councillors' conduct.

> "they were flagrantly defying the law. They were not fit to be
> councillors. The sooner they were disqualified the better."[88]

In bringing this action they were abusing the processes of the court as they
could have attacked the validity of the extra-ordinary audit in other
proceedings earlier on but did not. One does not seek to defend the actions of
the Clay Cross councillors who knew exactly what they were doing and
deliberately courted their "martyrdom" but attention may be directed to
Lord Denning's view that:

> "the proceedings . . . are an abuse. These councillors are seeking, by one
> shift or another, to escape the consequences of their own wrongdoing.
> The time has come when they must be told quite firmly that the law
> must be obeyed."[89]

---

[83] [1971] Ch. 734.
[84] [1974] Ch. 208.
[85] [1971] Ch. 734.
[86] *Ibid.* p. 744.
[87] [1974] Ch. 208.
[88] *Ibid.* p. 221.
[89] *Ibid.* p. 222.

This notion of the disciplinary role of the law is implicit and on occasions explicit in others of Lord Denning's judgments in the new housing law.

We may consider first a series of cases in which council tenants were suing their local authority landlords—*Greater London Council* v. *Connolly*[90]; *R.* v. *Bristol Corporation, ex parte Hendy*[91]; *Liverpool Corporation* v. *Irwin*[92] and *Bristol District Council* v. *Clark*.[93] The issues were respectively the validity of a rent increase; the proper allocation of accommodation under the Land Compensation Act 1973; the council's liability for repairs in a high-rise block of flats, and eviction over rent arrears. In two of the cases, the tenants had been advised and their cases taken up by community activists and neighbourhood lawyers.[94] In none of the cases did the tenants win or indeed get much sympathy from Lord Denning. Thus in *Irwin*[95] despite the admittedly deplorable conditions that Mr. Irwin and his family had to live in, Lord Denning managed to hold that the local authority were not in breach of any duty in respect of their contractual or statutory liability for repairs, nor in respect of any tortious liability; the corporation had done its best but had been beaten by vandals and hooligans:

> "It is to be remembered too that these tower blocks are occupied by council tenants at very low rents. They are allowed in practice virtual security of tenure so long as they pay their rent. If they were to recover damages for the discomfort and inconvenience they have suffered, the amount of such damages could be offset against their rents. That does not seem to me to be right, especially when they are all, in a sense, responsible for the deplorable state of affairs."[96]

This approach to the local authority's liability was a little too much for the House of Lords. The House did not disagree with Lord Denning's decision to imply a term in the tenancy agreement to maintain and repair the lifts and stairs, or his finding that no breach of that implied obligation had occurred but it was prepared at least to find the local authority liable in respect of its statutory obligations under the Housing Act 1961.[97]

A similar attitude informed Lord Denning's judgment in *Clark*[98] when an eviction notice had been served in respect of arrears of £45.20. Although Lord Denning made plain that in exercising their management powers local authorities must exercise them in good faith, taking into account relevant and not irrelevant considerations, he did not consider Bristol D.C. had done anything wrong in this case even though the arrears had been cleared off before the action commenced:

> "they gave this man every chance to pay up the arrears . . . There was no point in seeking an attachment of earnings order since on his own

---

[90] [1970] 2 Q.B. 100.
[91] [1974] 1 W.L.R. 498.
[92] [1976] Q.B. 319.
[93] [1975] 1 W.L.R. 1443.
[94] *Irwin* and *Clark*.
[95] [1976] Q.B. 319.
[96] *Ibid.* p. 332.
[97] [1977] A.C. 239. See Chap. 2, pp. 37–38 where Professor Atiyah discusses this case, seeing it as one of Lord Denning's contract successes.
[98] [1975] 3 All E.R. 976.

showing he said he was unemployed. It now appears that he had got employment as a milkman but had not disclosed it. That goes against him."[99]

There was an assumption in the above remarks, for which there was no evidence before the court, that Clark had dishonestly withheld information and therefore was not deserving of assistance from the court; he had abused his privileges as a council tenant. So too with *Hendy*[1]; the local authority might be under a statutory duty to rehouse him and his family, a statutory duty they had initially denied being under, but they fulfilled their duty by offering them temporary accommodation, even if that meant that they had to move every three weeks from one place to another:

> "If Mr. Hendy does have frequent moves that cannot be helped. The corporation have only to do the best they can until a council house is available."[2]

They had offered him "very suitable accommodation"[3] which he should not refuse. A factor present in the corporation's initial attitude to Hendy was that he owed some money to another council, and this was mentioned by Lord Denning though it did not seem relevant to the issue before the court.

The message in all these cases is clear: council tenants do not have enforceable rights against their landlords; they have privileges—the privilege of being in a council house or flat—and duties—the duty of observing the conditions of the tenancy—and if things go wrong, then they have only themselves to blame and are abusing their privileges in trying to throw the blame on to, or impose duties on the local authority. The local authority in these cases, was in Lord Denning's view, always "doing its best," or "doing everything possible"; the appellants were always in some way at fault.

Contrast then these cases with *Storer* v. *Manchester City Council*[4]; *Gibson* v. *Manchester County Council*[5] and *Norwich County Council* v. *Secretary of State for the Environment*.[6] In the first two cases, council tenants were seeking to purchase their council houses from their local authority; a change of political control in the authority had led to a change of policy on sales of council houses. The tenants were arguing that before the change of policy took effect there were completed contracts in their cases which bound the authority to sell to them. In each case Lord Denning found for the tenant; in *Storer*[7] he decided that an actual exchange of contracts was unnecessary in the circumstances of the authority's method of handling the sales of council houses; in *Gibson*,[8] in a majority decision which was reversed by the House of Lords[9] he considered that if one looked at all the correspondence as a whole and did not make the

---

[99] *Ibid.* p. 980.
[1] [1974] 1 All E.R. 1047.
[2] *Ibid.* p. 1049.
[3] *Ibid.* p. 1048.
[4] [1974] 1 W.L.R. 1403. This and the next case are dealt with more fully in Chap. 2, *supra*, from the offer and acceptance angle.
[5] [1978] 1 W.L.R. 520.
[6] [1982] 1 All E.R. 737.
[7] [1974] 1 W.L.R. 1403.
[8] [1978] 1 W.L.R. 520.
[9] [1979] 1 All E.R. 972.

mistake of analysing the contract into the form of offer and acceptance, then there was a completed contract:

> "It seems to me . . . that Mr. Gibson ought not to have his expectations ruined by reason of a change of policy by the local government administration."[10]

In the third case *Norwich County Council*,[11] the issue was whether the Secretary of State had acted in accordance with the law, the Housing Act 1980, in intervening in Norwich's administration of the sale of council houses under the Act on the grounds that Norwich was not making fast enough progress in its sales. Once again Lord Denning found against the local authority and put his judgment explicitly in terms of the protection of the individual:

> " . . . [T]he concern of this court as always is to protect the individual from the misuse or abuse of power by those in authority. The individual here is the tenant. He has been given by Parliament the right to buy the house in which he lives. Yet in the exercise of that right he has met with intolerable delay. The responsibility for that delay is beyond doubt, the responsibility of the Norwich City Council."[12]

The change of attitude between the two sets of cases is remarkable. In the latter set of cases, the tenants were seen as individuals with rights and the local authorities as bodies abusing those rights; the court in such circumstances "naturally" came to the aid of the tenants. In the former set of cases, as remarked earlier, the tenants had no rights and it was they who were abusing their position in trying to obtain more from an authority doing its best, than they were entitled to; in those circumstances the court, again "naturally" found for the local authority. It could be that Lord Denning was adopting the view that whereas there could be no private property rights in public property, there were, by definition, such rights where the impugned transactions were aimed at turning public property into private property, but a careful reading of his judgments, both in these cases and in others in this whole area, suggests that back of the analyses in his judgments lies the notion of the deserving and undeserving poor; the former are seeking to better themselves and the balance should tip in their direction; the latter are not and until they do better, the balance is rightly tipped against them.

The contrast between the deserving and the undeserving, the former of whom are exercising their rights, the latter of whom are abusing their privileges when they seek the assistance of the courts, comes through even more clearly in Lord Denning's judgments in four important homelessness cases arising under the Housing (Homeless Persons) Act 1977, which he took part in in 1980 and 1981—cases which, it must be said with regret, did little to enhance his reputation for seeking the just solution. The cases were *De Falco* v. *Crawley Borough Council*[13]—an Italian family seeking accommodation; *R.* v. *Hillingdon London Borough Council, ex parte Streeting*,[14] an Ethiopian wife of

---

[10] [1978] 2 All E.R. 583, 588.
[11] [1982] 1 All E.R. 737.
[12] *Ibid.* p. 747.
[13] [1980] Q.B. 460.
[14] [1980] 1 W.L.R. 1430.

a deceased British subject, granted refugee status seeking accommodation in the United Kingdom; *R. v. Slough Borough Council, ex parte Ealing London Borough Council*[15] a dispute between two local authorities over their housing responsibilities towards Ms. Jack, a "coloured woman"[16] and the Lynch family; and *R. v. Hillingdon London Borough Council, ex parte Taffazul Islam,*[17] a Bangladeshi seeking accommodation for himself and his newly arrived family. Only in the case of *Streeting*[18] did Lord Denning find any primary obligation on the local authority to house the applicants; in the other cases he made only too plain his disapproval of the applicants and the unreasonable burden they were imposing on local authorities and "true born Englishmen."[19] In *De Falco*[20] he talked of the "advancing tide" and suggested that the applicants may have come to England because:

> "there are all sorts of benefits to be had whenever you are unemployed. And best of all, they will look after you if you have nowhere to live."[21]

He decided they were intentionally homeless because they voluntarily left Italy where they had accommodation and came to England where they did not; the Code of Guidance which suggested that that might be the wrong way to look at the facts of the case was not binding and did not have to be followed.

In the *Slough and Ealing* case[22] the two local authorities had taken different views on whether Ms. Jack was intentionally or unintentionally homeless—if the former, as determined by Slough Borough Council, the local authority was not under an obligation to house her; if the latter, as determined by Ealing London Borough Council, then Slough was under an obligation to house her. Lord Denning decided that on a proper interpretation of the statute, Slough had to accept Ealing's determination and rehouse Ms. Jack:

> "It is an intolerable burden to put on the Slough council and worse still on the people of the neighbourhood who have to put up with them. Yet the statute will have it so."[23]

An interesting contrast is provided by looking at Lord Lane C.J.'s statement of the facts of the case in the Divisional Court and Lord Denning's in the Court of Appeal: Lord Lane referred to Ms. Jack's rent arrears and complaints from her neighbours about her behaviour, but he also said that the arrears were disputed, as were the complaints and that there were counter allegations about racialist interference. Lord Denning referred only to the complaints of neighbours which he said Slough B.C. found to be justified. Similarly with the Lynchs; Lord Lane said the rent arrears were in dispute and Mr. Lynch suffered from a severe disability; Lord Denning

[15] [1981] 1 All E.R. 601.
[16] *Ibid.* p. 611.
[17] [1981] 3 W.L.R. 109.
[18] [1980] 1 W.L.R. 1430.
[19] *De Falco* v. *Crawley D.C.* [1980] Q.B. 460, 473.
[20] [1980] Q.B. 460 at p. 472. See too *Lambert* v. *Ealing L.B.C.* [1982] 2 All E.R. 394: "This is another housing case which shows the impact of our joining the European Community" at p. 395. Lambert was French.
[21] *Ibid.* p. 472.
[22] [1981] 1 All E.R. 601.
[23] *Ibid.* p. 614.

quoted the amount of the arrears as if there was no dispute about it and did not refer to Mr.Lynch's disability.

The least defensible of the three hostile judgments occurred in *Islam*,[24] a majority decision, the only one of the cases appealed to the House of Lords which reversed the Court of Appeal.[25] Islam had indefinite leave to stay in the United Kingdom in terms of the Immigration Act 1971; he had been in the United Kingdom for 15 years when he finally brought his family in, again in accordance with the law. He had arranged accommodation for himself and his whole family before they arrived, but after their arrival the landlord required them all to leave. Hillingdon London Borough Council considered that Islam was intentionally homeless as he had brought his family to the United Kingdom when it would have been reasonable for them to continue to live in accommodation in Bangladesh. With this finding Lord Denning agreed: the home of Islam and his family was in Bangladesh; he was only in lodgings in England; he "occupied" a home in Bangladesh through his wife and family:

> "The moral of this case is that men from overseas should not bring their wives and children here unless they have arranged permanent and suitable accommodation for them to come to. The applicant is homeless intentionally. He is not entitled to permanent accommodation. He will not take priority over young couples here who are on the waiting list for housing accommodation."[26]

The House of Lords, while expressing concern at the scope of the Act and whether it was "as well considered as it [was] undoubtedly well intentioned,"[27] firmly rejected any suggestion that the Act did not apply to immigrants or that a "strained construction" should be adopted:

> "which would frustrate the policy of the Act and would promote the object, which is not to be found there either expressly or by necessary implication of postponing the otherwise valid claims of homeless persons and families who have their origin outside Great Britain."[28]

It would be easy and not unreasonable to wax indignant about Lord Denning's judgments in these cases which rather too obviously put prejudice before law or indeed the just solutions. From the perspective adopted in this chapter however, it is sufficient to draw attention to the fact that they exhibit in a rather extreme form his views about rights, privileges and their abuse in the field of housing law—and to that extent are consistent with other cases in the field—and to the problems inherent in an approach to judging, which relies on an instinctive "feel" for justice; if the instinct goes awry or is too heavily overlaid with disapproval of a particular section of the community or course of conduct or behaviour, then it all too easily degenerates into injustice or worse.

Conclusion

A standard orthodox legal criticism of Lord Denning is that he was not

[24] [1981] 3 W.L.R. 109.   [25] [1981] 3 All E.R. 901.
[26] [1981] 2 All E.R. 1089, 1093.
[27] [1981] 3 All E.R. 901, *per* Lord Wilberforce at p. 905.
[28] *Per* Lord Lowry at p. 911.

consistent; his colleagues, the legal profession and their clients did not know
where his fancy was going to take him next. Does that criticism have validity
in this area of law? Perhaps more important, was Lord Denning consistent to
his own beliefs, ideas, and notions throughout his judicial career or did they
too change as time went on? In the analysis used in this chapter, can we see a
consistent pattern of prevention of abuse of rights, or is that overlaid too
often by personal idiosyncracies? The answer advanced here is that Lord
Denning's notion of abuse of rights was a highly personal one, which while
always developing and adjusting to new situations, as equity did of old, did
have some common themes and principles running through it. Landlords
and tenants were expected to behave responsibly and the law, whether the
rules of common law or statutes, was not be used by either side so as to get an
advantage over the other. Landowners too had to behave responsibly and
where they owned land in the country, that meant doing their best to
preserve the countryside. Similarly, with local planning authorities; their
efforts to preserve the countryside—the object of town and country
planning—were to be facilitated and supported. In towns however, which
were the proper places for development, landowners and developers were not
to be unreasonably hindered by local authorities placing procedural
obstacles in their way, or imposing onerous financial obligations on them.
Those without land should have a proper regard for the efforts of the
authorities to provide for them and should act responsibly in trying to better
themselves, or in not creating situations where onerous duties were unfairly
imposed on others. One is reminded irresistably of the Victorian hymn:

> "The rich man in his castle
> The poor man at his gate;
> God made them high or lowly
> And ordered their estate."[29]

This is no doubt a little unfair for, unlike the Victorians, Lord Denning
considered that duties should be imposed equally on the rich man in his
castle and the poor man at his gate; furthermore he clearly approved of the
poor man attempting to better himself by obtaining his own castle.[30] But
nonetheless, at the end of the day, Lord Denning's notion of abuse of rights in
land did embrace fairly pronounced views which distinguished between the
deserving and the undeserving, whether in the field of housing—owner-
occupiers and council tenants, vendors, purchasers and estate agents—or

---

[29] Mrs. Alexander: "All things bright and beautiful," (1848). *Oxford Dictionary of Quotations New
Edition* (Oxford 1979), p.3. Perhaps the best illustration of this attitude in Lord Denning's
judgments is contained in the splendid case of *Re Brocklehurst (dec'd.)* [1978] 1 All E.R. 767,
discussed in Hayton, Chap. 3, p. 97. In describing how the eccentric Sir Philip Brocklehurst
allowed the garage proprietor Roberts to shoot rabbits on "the great estate of Swythamley
Hall" Lord Denning said (at p. 772):

> "After each day's shoot, they went, as befitted them, to the backdoor of the Hall to thank
> Sir Philip for his kindness. They left any game for his larder but took the rabbits away
> with them. They were not asked into the house. At any rate not when Lady Brocklehurst
> was there."

[30] Metaphorically speaking. He did not approve of Roberts obtaining the shooting rights of the
Swythamley Estate in Sir Philip's will and dissented on the issue of whether undue influence
was involved. Once again his concern about the countryside was uppermost: "It was his [Sir
Philip Brocklehurst] duty to preserve the estate in the interests of his family, the
neighbourhood and the country at large." *Re Brocklehurst (dec'd)* [1978] 1 All E.R. 767, 777.

planning and land use—"protectors" of the countryside, and despoilers, particularly caravan site owners, or land rights generally. The picture then that emerges is that of the comfortable, reasonably well-meaning, country gentleman, with not too much understanding of, and, as he grew older, not too much sympathy for, the problems of urban life outside suburbia. His most lyrical judgments concern the countryside; his most censorious urban poverty.

Finally, a more legal issue: how long-lasting will Lord Denning's contributions in the area of land be? The question is virtually impossible to answer with either confidence or certainty. Some of his approaches have passed into the common currency of the law; one thinks of his judgments in *Ives* v. *High*,[31] *Coleen*,[32] *Pyx Granite*,[33] *Binions* v. *Evans*[34] and its forerunners, *Harvey* v. *Crawley Development Corporation*,[35] even *De Falco*[36] and the vindication of his approach to the question of estate agents and deposits in *Sorrell* v. *Finch*[37] to name but one judgment alone from each of the areas discussed in this chapter. Others of his approaches have fallen by the wayside, some almost as soon as uttered, and by no means all of them deserving of such a fate; again one can instance *Green* v. *Midland Bank*,[38] *Newbury District Council* v. *Secretary of State for the Environment*,[39] *Allen* v. *Gulf Oil*,[40] surely one of the worst decisions to come out of the House of Lords for many years, the whittling down of *Lever (Finance)*[41] in *Western Fish Products*[42] and his dissent in *Regis Property Co.* v. *Dudley*.[43] One can say that it will not be possible to ignore his contributions, that he played a vital and important role in the transition of land law from a mainly private law to a mainly public law subject over the last forty years and that even where his contributions appear now to be discarded, they remain available to be resurrected in the future by enterprising counsel and unorthodox judges. In sum whether assessed in social or legal terms, Lord Denning's contributions to land law have been significant and far-reaching and his influence is likely to continue to be felt well into the twenty-first century.

---

[31] [1967] 2 Q.B. 379.
[32] [1971] 1 W.L.R. 433.
[33] [1958] 1 Q.B. 554.
[34] [1972] Ch. 359.
[35] [1957] 1 Q.B. 485.
[36] [1980] Q.B. 460.
[37] [1976] 2 W.L.R. 833 (H.L.).
[38] [1980] Ch. 580; reversed [1981] A.C. 513.
[39] [1979] 1 All E.R. 243; reversed [1981] A.C. 578.
[40] [1980] Q.B. 156; reversed [1981] 1 All E.R. 353.
[41] [1971] 1 Q.B. 222.
[42] [1981] 2 All E.R. 204.
[43] [1959] A.C. 370.

CHAPTER 6

Administrative Law

J. L. JOWELL

Administrative law is not a discrete part of the legal system. Its existence is rooted in constitutional law, which is in turn justified and explained by constitutional theory. The philosophy of and principle behind any decision in administrative law must therefore ultimately be supplied by constitutional theory which delineates the scope of the judicial control of official action and the rights of individuals against public administration.

Lord Denning's contribution to administrative law must therefore be examined in the context of his philosophy of the constitution, and, in particular, of the role of the judiciary *vis-à-vis* the administration. I shall suggest in this chapter that Lord Denning's decisions do provide a coherent theory, and (insofar as this is possible for judges seeped in heavy caseloads often requiring *ex tempore* judgments) a theory that is relatively consistent, and one also that differs sharply, if implicitly, from the philosophy prevalent at the time of his first judicial appointment. During his time as Master of the Rolls he took the opportunity to further his own philosophy of administrative law, despite opposition from other judges with a differing philosophy. To be more explicit, I shall suggest that throughout Lord Denning's judicial career two competing philosophies of administrative law were warring in the courts. The one, which I shall call the "activist model," was espoused by Lord Denning, who, with Lord Reid in particular, succeeded in challenging the second "restraint model" espoused by other leading and persuasive judges (especially Lord Diplock). The development of an activist administrative law is surely one of Lord Denning's great contributions.

To understand Lord Denning's contribution we must begin with the state of administrative law at the outset of his judicial career, in the context of the constitutional theory of the time. The two World Wars and the growth of the welfare state greatly increased administrative powers. Dicey[1] and Hewart[2] were once powerful voices against an increasingly centralised state and the encroachment of executive power on the freedom of the individual. The constitutional debate of the 1920s and 1930s, however, effectively silenced this concern. Jennings[3] and Robson[4] were particularly influential in depicting a constitutional theory that, emphasising the sovereignty of parliament, effectively accepted strong central state power, "collectivist" solutions to social problems, and necessary executive discretion. The Donoughmore Committee on Ministers' Powers[5] further allayed anxiety

---

[1] *The Law of the Constitution* (1885).
[2] *The New Despotism* (1929).
[3] *The Law and the Constitution* (1933).
[4] *Justice and Administrative Law* (1928).
[5] Report of the Committee on Ministers' Powers, Cmd. 4060 (1932).

about these matters. British constitutional law, in its infinite flexibility, accommodated the socialist alternative in a framework contrived in an age of *laissez faire.*

The courts, contrary perhaps to current mythology, were not ever in the vanguard of challenge to the collectivist devices. On the contrary, they were conspicious in their acceptance of the constitutional principle of sovereignty of Parliament as a norm even higher than that of the rule of law. Administration was to be left free to get on with policy jobs, without judicial interference or judicialised fetters.[6]

A spate of legislation from 1906 onwards conferred wide discretionary powers on ministers in regard to a variety of subjects. Many of these powers were formulated in subjective terms, such as the phrase considered in 1942 in the case *Liversidge* v. *Anderson,*[7] "If the Secretary of State has reasonable cause to believe." The majority of the House of Lords in that case held that the mere statement by the Home Secretary of his belief in that case (that a person was of "hostile origin and associations") was conclusive, not open to challenge or examination, and entirely within the Minister's discretion. Lord Atkin's dissenting view, seeking some evidence of the reasonableness of the Home Secretary's belief, was not accepted. Indeed, we are now told that Lord Atkin was socially ostracised by his fellow Law Lords for his heretical view.[8]

The prevalent model of administrative law at the outset of Lord Denning's career was one that I call the "restraint model," to indicate its concern to be deferential to the new executive powers of the increasingly centralised state. In terms of constitutional theory, this model accepts the sovereignty of Parliament as the highest constitutional norm. Parliament, after all, possesses the mandate of the electorate and in its wisdom has allocated wide powers to administration of one form or another. These powers are thus derived from Parliament and, in accordance with the constitutional norm of the separation of powers (which is almost but not quite equal in importance to the sovereignty of Parliament) the judiciary should be slow to intervene in areas of decision allocated to other branches of government.

The restraint model is not deferential for reasons of formal allocation alone. Courts must know their place, but reasons of function dictate that courts should not deal with matters of policy; modern public administration requires wide-ranging discretion unfettered by inappropriate legal controls. If controls are to be exercised (and the restraint adherents by no means deny that they should be) then the conventions of the constitution ensure that Parliament controls the Executive through the doctrine of ministerial responsibility, and that ministers (the policy-makers) in turn control their civil servants (the policy-appliers).

This is not to say that the restraint model allows no scope for any judicial control of administrative action. Where administration is acting in a "judicial" role, judging rights rather than policy, the reviewing court, familiar with the triangular model of judge atop and advocates on each side, will apply its own procedural code to the familiar adjudicative situation.[9]

The restraint model also allows judicial intervention in substantive

---

[6] At least from about 1915. See *Local Government Board* v. *Arlidge* [1915] A.C. 120.
[7] [1942] A.C. 206.
[8] Robert Stephens, *Law and Politics* (1979), p. 287.
[9] As in *Errington* v. *Minister of Health* [1935] 1 K.B. 249.

decisions. This may be done much more cautiously, avoiding interference with policy decisions but nevertheless promoting the attainment of strict accountability. The justification for this rests on the notion that administration has powers to achieve certain objectives, but once it strays outside the "four corners" of these powers the courts may consign it to its proper place. The court's function is here one of containment, review being directed towards keeping administration within the directives that parliament has issued. Thus the courts do not challenge parliamentary supremacy, but in a sense act as guardians of parliament's intentions.

Even so, however, judicial interference in the name of accountability will be carefully and sparingly undertaken. Where wide powers are provided (such as the prerogative power, or a power to act "as the Minister thinks fit") the restraint model accepts a presumption against interference, and will intervene even against "unreasonable" action only on the so-called "objective" or "Wednesbury"[10] grounds, namely where the act is such that no reasonable authority would undertake it: a test that which allows more than what the judges consider wayward, unwise or improper.

The spirit of the restraint model is perhaps best encapsulated in the words of Lord Parker, then Lord Chief Justice, who argued in 1962 that the courts have a "positive responsibility to be the handmaidens of the administration rather than its governor" and "have a duty to facilitate the objectives of administrative action as approved and authorised by parliament."[11]

By contrast to the restraint model, the activist model is marked first by a confidence in, and willingness to assert, the courts' role in the constitutional structure. The doctrine of separation of powers is said not to exclude the courts from review of other branches of government but to ensure for the courts an equal place with the others. The doctrine of the rule of law perhaps gives a degree of primacy to the judiciary as it imposes a duty, especially on the Executive, of fidelity to legal principles, which are enunciated by the courts.[12]

While this belief in the Court's rightful place does not negate the doctrine of Parliamentary sovereignty, it does lead to a presumption, *e.g.* against the exclusion by parliament of the jurisdiction of the courts to review administrative action, and even to a denial of parliament's right to exclude the court from pronouncing upon *ultra vires* or even illegal acts.

The activists are more confident than the proponents of the restraint model about the effectiveness of legal techniques to control administrative action, and are somewhat sceptical of parliamentary techniques and the doctrine of Ministerial Responsibility as an effective controlling device. For that reason the activists are willing to impose judicial-type procedures even upon administrative settings, even when policy is in issue and in situations involving no rights but mere "interests" or "privileges." In all situations the activists would give affected persons a "fair crack of the whip,"[13] by means of judicial techniques.

[10] *Associated Provincial Picture Houses Ltd.* v. *Wednesbury Corp.* [1948] 1 K.B. 223.
[11] Quoted in G.T. Williams, "The Donoughmore Report in Retrospect," Public Admin., August 1982, 273, 291.
[12] See Lord Denning's quotation in *Gouriet* v. *Union of Post Office Workers* [1977] 1 W.L.R. 310, 331: "Be you ever so high, the Law is above you."
[13] See Lord Edmund Davies and Lord Denning in the *Bushell* case (n. 12, p. 233).

It is here that we notice a distinct difference between the two models. While both are willing to intervene to achieve *accountability* to legislative purpose, the activists would intervene for another reason as well, namely, that of achieving *responsiveness* to the public served by the relevant body. While conceding the power of administration to make decisions in the public interest, the activists are concerned that the public interest be reached by a process where all relevant private interests may be assessed. Confidence in judicial techniques of investigation and trial (the fair hearing, proofs and arguments, cross examination, full reasons) leads them to insist on this as a model also for administration. Administrative law thus becomes a device of participation, adopting what has been called a "consumer perspective"[14] to the law, insisting not only that powers are properly contained but that they are exercised in a way that allows sufficient consideration of the variety of both rights and interests affected by official decisions.

Lord Denning's contribution to administrative law can be understood in the context of his view of its purpose. Although not always explicitly stated, the assumptions behind and implications of his judgments differ strongly from those implicit in the administrative jurisprudence at the time of his appointment, and also from the competing stream of decisions from other judges right up to his retirement. It is by no means clear that Lord Denning's philosophy won the day. The battle still rages.

Proceeding now to specific issues in administrative law to which Lord Denning contributed, we shall see that certain results flow naturally from each philosophy and that certain techniques of analysis are supportive of each. for example, the activist model will be willing to accord standing to sue to those with mere "interests" in the issue whereas the restraint model will insist on confining standing to those with "rights" in the matter. If achieving responsiveness is as much a part of the purpose of administrative law as accountability, then the public to whom a duty is owed is wider, and standing more liberally construed. Similarly, with the fair hearing; if rights are in issue then fairness will not be accorded to those with "mere privileges" or expectations.

The supportive techniques are not necessarily logically necessary to the respective models, but in practice they tend to accompany them. The restraint model tends to rely on "literal" interpretation of statutes, *e.g.* those giving seemingly unlimited discretion to the decision-maker, or those excluding judicial review. The activist model in practice tends to abandon "strict constructionism" and relies instead on "purposive" interpretation, that, *e.g.* reads certain limits into discretion that the general purpose of the statute provides, or that insists upon general principles (the fair hearing, or jurisdictional limits) as limiting the words of the act. A recent device of the restraint model is the distinction between public and private law—used, as will be seen, as a justification for limiting claims against the state and encouraging judicial deference to administration. Neither of these techniques—statutory interpretation or assumption of the category of law (public or private)—are logically the preserve of either model, but in practice have been consistently employed by one or the other to achieve their purpose.

---

[14] Edmond Cahn, "Law in the Consumer Perspective," U.Penn.L. Rev. 1 (1963).

Machinery of Review and Standing to Sue

The point at which the activist can initially be distinguished from the restraint model is on the willingness to accept a case for review at all. Lord Denning addressed himself to the machinery of review as early as 1949 when he wrote in his Hamlyn Lectures,

> "Our procedure for securing our personal freedom is efficient, but our procedure for preventing the abuse of power is not. Just as the pick and shovel is no longer suitable for the winning of coal, so also the procedure of mandamus, certiorari, and actions on the case are not suitable for the winning of freedom in the new age. They must be replaced by new and up to date machinery, by declarations, injunctions, and actions for negligence."[15]

In 1952 in *R. v. Northumberland Compensation Appeal Tribunal, ex. parte Shaw*[16] the question arose whether the Court of King's Bench could intervene to quash by certiorari an error of law committed by a statutory tribunal. The error in this case, which had the effect of depriving Mr. Shaw of compensation to which he was entitled, was admitted, although not on the "face of the record." Lord Denning was in no doubt that the Courts did have power to correct the error, and gave a wide definition of what matters appeared "on the record" including the initiating documents, any pleadings and affidavits disclosing points of law decided by the tribunal. Lord Denning was adamant that the Court has an

> "inherent jurisdiction to control all inferior tribunals, not in an appellate capacity, but in a supervisory capacity. . . . When the King's Bench exercises its control over tribunals in this way, it is not usurping a jurisdiction which does not belong to it. It is only exercising a jurisdiction which it has always had."

In a comprehensive historical survey he showed convincingly what had been forgotten, namely, that the scope of certiorari was not only confined to the correction of excess of jurisdiction. This decision opened the way for a good deal of judicial review over tribunals and a variety of quasi-judicial bodies. In the end Lord Denning was allowing certiorari against officials like immigration officers because they have "a power conferred . . . by Parliament to give or refuse leave to enter."[17] In one of his last judgments, in 1982, Lord Denning wrote:

> "At one time there was a black-out of any development of administrative law. The curtains were drawn to prevent the light coming in. the remedy of certiorari was hedged about with all sorts of technical limitations. It did not give a remedy when inferior tribunals went wrong, but only when they went outside their jurisdiction altogether.[18]

He went on to cite 1952 and the *Shaw* case as a time when the darkness was

---

[15] *Freedom under the Law* (1949), p. 126.
[16] [1952] 1 K.B. 338.
[17] *R. v. Chief Immigration Officer, Gatwick Airport, ex p. Kharrazi* [1980] 1 W.L.R. 1396.
[18] *O'Reilly* v. *Mackman* [1983] 3 W.L.R. 604, 617.

relieved.[19] "While the darkness still prevailed, we let in some light by means of a declaration." Here he refers to *Barnard* v. *National Dock Labour Board*[20] and *Anisminic Ltd.* v. *Foreign Compensation Commission*[21]—cases in both of which Lord Denning sat.

In *Barnard,* dock workers sought a declaration that the Board suspended them unlawfully. The Board claimed that only certiorari was available to the courts to interfere with statutory tribunals, but the Court of Appeal disagreed. Lord Denning said that since certiorari was hedged around with limitations, and may not be available, "Why, then, should the court not intervene by declaration and injunction? If it cannot so intervene, it would mean that the tribunal could disregard the law." Furthermore discovery was available through an action for a declaration and without discovery the truth in those proceedings would never have been known.

In the *Anisminic*[22] case, a declaration was sought to challenge a decision of the Foreign Compensation Commission in the face of a statutory provision that any determination of the Commission "shall not be called in question in any court of law." Although Lord Denning's name does not appear in the Court of Appeal reports, and he did not sit on the merits of the issue, the note of Brown J[23] shows that he did sit with Harman and Diplock L.JJ on appeal from the master and judge in chambers to decide whether the question of jurisdiction should be tried on a preliminary point of law. Lord Denning and Harman L.J. allowed that important case to go forward. Diplock L.J. dissented.[24] This was the first of a number of cases where Denning and Diplock were on different sides of the issue, as we shall see. It is also one of a number of leading administrative law cases where Lord Denning's view was accepted in the House of Lords by Lord Reid. The point about the appropriateness of an action for a declaration was not much discussed in the House of Lords, but it was accepted there that if a tribunal limited by statute mistook the law applicable to the facts of a case, and thus asked itself the wrong question, it had no jurisdiction to determine the question. The "determination" was therefore a nullity.

The scope for challenge for excess of jurisdiction in the face of an ouster clause was for a time uncertain in the light of a conflicting House of Lords decision in *Smith* v. *East Elloe Rural District Council*.[25] Lord Denning faltered briefly in his quest to broaden review in *Ostler*,[26] which will be discussed below, and from which he recanted in his book *The Discipline of Law*.[27] In later cases, however, he was willing to barge through any ouster clause and to insist on judicial review, where any error of law was made "on which the

---

[19] Lord Diplock is anxious to give Lord Goddard much of the credit for *Shaw.* See *O'Reilly* v. *Mackman* [1982] 3 W.L.R. 1096, 1102.

[20] [1953] 2 Q.B. 18.

[21] [1969] 2 A.C. 147.

[22] Above.

[23] Above, at p. 231B-C.

[24] Lord Diplock takes issue with the way in which his dissent is reported, *O'Reilly* v. *Mackman* [1982] 3 All E.R. 1124, 1129.

[25] [1956] A.C. 736 (Lords Reid and Somervell dissenting).

[26] *R.* v. *Secretary of State for the Environment, ex p. Ostler* [1977] Q.B. 122.

[27] (1979) at p. 108.

decision of the case depends" on the ground that when a court tribunal made an error of law this is a "question of law for the judges to decide."[28]

Standing to sue

The concept of standing to sue implies a certain *nexus* between the person suing and the result of the action. English law has not allowed the *actio popularis* of Roman law where any person was entitled to allege unlawful action before a Court. Whether deciding if a person was "aggrieved" under a statutory definition, or had standing to apply for a prerogative order, English judges, up to Lord Denning's day, tended to take a restrictive view, confining standing to those alleging interference with their rights (not mere interests) or to those suffering special damage over and above that suffered by the general public. Exceptions had been made, particularly in applications for certiorari or prohibition, but by and large standing was narrowly construed.

Lord Denning's more liberal view of standing is significant in interpreting his view of administrative law. The restraint approach would of course be wary of widening standing to individuals with mere "interests," or to groups of individuals, pressure groups and the like, partly as a protection against a flood of claims against the state, but partly also because it is felt that the purpose of administrative law is to render public authorities accountable for unlawfulness to specific individuals to whom duties are owed. The activist model, by contrast, would see administrative law as a method of promoting a broader notion of accountability, owed not only to specific individuals but to society at large. A general public interest exists in lawful administration which can be asserted by any member of the public, except the proverbial "busybody" or "meddlesome interloper." In fact, persons who seek review of maladministration are to be encouraged, providing the courts with a welcome opportunity to keep executive action in its place and to assert the rule of law.

There is however the second aspect of accountability that emerges in the activists approach to *locus standi*, which concerns a wider notion of accountability as involving also responsiveness to the public that the authority is charged with serving. The activists recognise that public administration today is concerned not only with adjudicative or policy functions, but with managerial functions (road building, running of utilities, etc.) that affects not only rights but interests in society. Some of these interests concern amenity (a view obstructed by a new road), others are less easy to define, such as the interest in the structure of a person's community (will it be damaged by the road, or the withdrawal of a railway line?) The activist's argument from responsiveness thus recognises the duty of modern public administration towards interests as well as rights, and therefore permits interests to assert themselves against public authorities through the courts in order to hold public power to account.

Beginning with statutory remedies requiring standing of a "person aggrieved," the view predominating until very recently has been that the phrase should, with rare exceptions (for ratepayers on issues involving

---

[28] *Pearlman* v. *Harrow School Governors* [1979] Q.B. 56. In *Re A Company* [1981] A.C. 374 Lord Diplock cut down that statement for review of judicial bodies, but Lord Denning insisted on its validity for other public bodies in *Kharrazi* (above) and *A.C.T. Construction Ltd.* v. *Customs and Excise Commissioners* [1979] 1 W.L.R. 870.

public expenditure, for example) be interpreted narrowly so as to discourage the "meddlesome interloper" from invoking the jurisdiction of the courts in matters that are really not his business. Thus the phrase was interpreted to mean someone with a right—a property right in most cases in the *lis*, or, at most, someone suffering some special damage over-and-above that suffered by the general public; and this damage was considered also to relate not to a "mere interest" (such as amenity) but to a right.

This was the view that found favour in the *Buxton* case,[29] where owners of land sought planning permission for the excavating and processing of chalk. Permission was refused and the owner appealed. At the public inquiry Major Buxton and others objected (his estate, ornithological pursuits and brood mares, he said would be adversely affected by the operations). The Inspector at the inquiry recommended that the appeal be dismissed but the Minister, on the advice of the Minister of Agriculture, and without giving the local authority or any party to the inquiry an opportunity of reply, allowed the appeal. The Major then applied under the Act as a person aggrieved to challenge the legality of this decision that was in effect delegated to the Agriculture Minister. However, on the point preliminary to the merits it was held by Salmon J. that the Major had no standing to sue. While the judge "could well understand his (the plaintiff's) annoyance," the Minister's action infringed none of their common law rights. "They have no rights as individuals under the statutes." The judgment of James L.J. in *Re Sidebotham*[30] was followed, to the effect that "person aggrieved" means someone who has

> "suffered a legal grievance, a man against whom a decision has been pronounced which has wrongfully deprived him of something or wrongfully refused him something, or wrongfully affected his title to something."

Only nine months after *Buxton*, the phrase "any person aggrieved" fell to the Privy Council to determine in the case of *Attorney-General of the Gambia* v. *N'Jie*.[31] The Attorney-General sought leave to appeal a decision of the West African Court of Appeal setting aside a judicial order to strike a barrister off the roll for professional misconduct. Lord Denning examined James L.J.'s dictum in *Sidebotham* but held that it should not be regarded as exhaustive. By contrast, he preferred Lord Esher M.R.'s statement in *Re Reed, Bowen & Co., ex parte Official Receiver*[32] that

> "the words 'person aggrieved' are of wide import and should not be subjected to a restrictive interpretation. They do not include, of course, a mere busybody who is interfering in things which do not concern him; but they do include a person who has a genuine grievance because an order has been made which prejudicially affect his interests.

In this case it was held that the Attorney-General in a colony represents the Crown as guardian of the public interest, and therefore had an interest in the outcome of the decision reversing a previous decision relating to professional misconduct.

[29] *Buxton* v. *Minister of Housing and Local Government* [1961] 1 Q.B. 278.
[30] (1880) 14 Ch. 458.
[31] [1961] A.C. 617.
[32] (1887) 19 Q.B.D. 174.

Three years later Lord Denning was given the opportunity to expand on the kind of interest that might qualify as "aggrieved." In *Maurice* v. *London County Council*[33] an owner of an artist's studio had contested the building of a proposed block of flats 225 feet high less than 100 yards away. The Appeal Tribunal had restricted her evidence to anticipated loss of light and air—to any rights she may have to these, thus excluding any evidence of loss of visual amenities both to her, and to Battersea Park and to citizens of London generally. On a case stated the Divisional Court upheld the Tribunal's decision, Lord Parker C.J. holding that the statute in question, dealing with public health, rather than planning, precluded the assertion of amenity interests. The Court of Appeal however disagreed and felt that Miss Maurice's grievance, even though confined to amenity, would qualify for *locus standi*. Lord Denning confessed that the appellant's interest was "slight," as the proposal would not affect her view, and she would only see the tower if she "went out to Battersea Park for recreation and pleasure." Citing the *Gambia* case with approval, he rejected the "very narrow and restricted interpretation" of the words person aggrieved as applied in *Buxton* and made it clear that a grievance that "prejudicially affects" a person's interests could include not only legal rights but also amenities.

Lord Denning arrived at this conclusion because he considered, contrary to Lord Parker in the Court below, that amenity matters were those on which she was entitled to address the Tribunal, under the terms of a statute in which public health and housing questions overlapped. Consider here the much narrower ground on which Pearson L.J. allowed the appeal, linking standing to property rights rather than amenity interests, requiring the appellant to establish that, "by reason of the height of the intended building, (she was) likely to suffer damage in her capacity as owner or lessee of her property."[34]

Moving now to the equitable remedies of declaration and injunction we find that an injunction may be sought by the Attorney-General at the relation of a private individual without a right or special damage; the Attorney-General thus asserts the public interest. Declarations, however, have generally been held to be declarations of right and therefore not open to anyone with a mere interest. In the case of *Gregory and Another* v. *London Borough of Camden*,[35] *e.g.* the plaintiffs were the owners and occupiers of two houses at the back of which it was proposed to erect a large school. The access and the school, though not on any land owned or occupied by the plaintiffs, would nevertheless greatly affect their amenity, as many hundreds of school children would use the access and pass close to the plaintiffs' houses. Planning permission had been granted for the school in this case by the defendant Council, but without notifying the Minister (as they were required to do) that the proposal either involved a "substantial departure from the development plan" or "injuriously affected the amenity of adjoining land." Paull J. accepted that the grant of planning permission in this case was *ultra vires*, but refused the plaintiff standing to seek a declaration to that effect. He said that the declaration was a declaration of the rights of the parties involved. Since, in this case, what was affected was

---

[33] [1964] 2 Q.B. 362.
[34] Wilberforce L.J. agreed with both the judgments.
[35] [1966] 1 W.L.R. 899.

only the loss of amenity, that was not enough to grant standing. "Persons aggrieved" meant "persons with a legal grievance."

This view was first challenged by Lord Denning in 1973 in the case of the *Attorney-General, ex rel. McWhirter* v. *Independent Broadcasting Authority.*[36] Eventually in this case the Attorney-General did give his leave to the relator action seeking to restrain the I.B.A. from broadcasting a "pornographic" film by the American director, Andy Warhol. However Lord Denning said *obiter*:

"I am of opinion that, in the last resort, if the Attorney-General refuses leave in a proper case, or improperly or unreasonably delays in giving leave, or his machinery works too slowly, then a member of the public who has a sufficient interest can himself apply to the court itself. He can apply for a declaration and, in a proper case, for an injunction, joining the Attorney-General, if need be, as defendant . . . I have said so much because I regard it as a matter of high constitutional principle that if there is good ground for supposing that a government department or a public authority is transgressing the law, or is about to transgress it, in a way which offends or injures thousands of Her Majesty's subjects, then in the last resort any one of those offended or injured can draw it to the attention of the courts of law and seek to have the law enforced."

The matter was brought to a head in the case of *Gouriet* v. *Union of Post Office Workers.*[37] Mr. Gouriet, Secretary of the Association of Freedom, appeared simply as a citizen seeking the consent of the Attorney-General to his application for an injunction to restrain the Union from refusing to handle mail and other communications to South Africa as a protest against that country's laws. The Attorney-General refused consent to the relator proceedings and Mr. Gouriet then on his own sought an injunction. This was refused at first instance. On appeal, all three members of the Court of Appeal (including Lord Denning) in effect (after an amended claim) held that Mr. Gouriet was entitled to seek a declaration and interim relief[38] against the unions. The House of Lords reversed this decision, also unanimously.[39]

It is interesting to see the different reasons given by the three Appeal Court Justices in this case. Lord Denning, having cited the passage in the Bill of Rights Act 1688 prohibiting suspending or dispensing powers, said:

"Mercifully our constitution has, I believe, provided a remedy. It is what I have said already: if the Attorney-General refuses to give his consent to the enforcement of the criminal law, then any citizen in the land can come to the courts and ask that the law be enforced. This is an essential safeguard: for were it not so, the Attorney-General could, by his veto, saying 'I do not consent,' make the criminal law of no effect. Confronted with a powerful subject whom he feared to offend, he could refuse his consent time and time again. Then that subject could disregard the law with impunity. It would indeed be above the law.

---

[36] [1973] Q.B. 629. See also the *Blackburn* cases, [1968] 2 Q.B. 118; [1971] 1 W.L.R. 1037.
[37] [1977] 2 W.L.R. 310.
[38] Ormrod and Lawton L.JJ. would have granted interim injunctions but not interim declarations (which Lord Denning was willing to do).
[39] [1978] A.C. 435.

This cannot be permitted. To every subject in this land, no matter how powerful, I would use Thomas Fuller's words over 300 years ago: 'Be you ever so high, the law is above you.' "[40]

Lord Denning is clearly referring in the final quotation above to the Union as not being above the law. The popular press took the reference as being directed against the Attorney-General. However, his reason for giving standing is clear: that without it the criminal law could be broken with impunity. The rule of law requires laws not to be broken; the courts should be responsive to any person who wishes to assert the rule of law. Lord Denning did not even consider whether a right, rather than a general interest, was required to trigger judicial intervention.

By contrast, Lawton L.J. allowed standing on the ground that a right was threatened, the right to enforce the criminal law:

"The fact that every other person in the realm had it too does not make it any less a right which he could use. He has asked the courts to enforce the criminal law so that he and the rest of the public can enjoy that right."[41]

Lord Justice Ormrod's judgment was different again in style and content. Characteristically, he went back to original sources in a tight historical survey of the relator action which he found to be a "quasi legal fiction" perhaps intelligible to lawyers, but in the public mind producing nothing but confusion, and sometimes frustration. He however went further than Lawton L.J., being content to ground standing upon an interest rather than a right. Gouriet had standing because,

". . . like the rest of the public, [the plaintiff] has a very real interest in the availability of the postal and telephone services and a real interest in ensuring, . . . that these facilities are not interfered with by the illegal acts of the defendants or others."[42]

The House of Lords reversed the Court of Appeal's decision, and refused standing to Mr. Gouriet.[43] Lord Denning's dictum in *McWhirter* was roundly condemned as lacking authority and being contrary to principle. Lord Wilberforce's robust speech adopted a functional view of the Attorney-General's exclusive power to bring actions to restrain the breach of the criminal law in the public interest. He was, because of his constitutional role, better equipped than a private individual to decide whether a prosecution would be effective on policy grounds (appealing to moderation, avoiding provoking martyrdom, etc.). Nor should the courts have discretion to decide these questions which could attract political criticism and controversy and therefore were "outside the range of discretionary problems which the courts can resolve. Judges are equipped to find legal rights and administer, on well-known principles, discretionary remedies. These matters are widely outside those areas."[44]

Lord Diplock's different approach was based on the distinction between private law and public law. He said that "the failure to recognise this

[40] [1977] 2 W.L.R. 310, 331.
[41] *Ibid.* at p. 340.
[42] *Ibid.* at p. 345.
[43] [1978] A.C. 635.
[44] *Ibid.* p. 484.

distinction has in my view led to some confusion and an unaccustomed degree of rhetoric in this case." While every citizen has the "right" to enforce the criminal law once it is broken, a future breach of criminal law can be restrained, where no private damage is involved, only by a public official, the Attorney-General, "in accordance with principles of public law with which analogies may be deceptive and where different principles apply."[45]

We shall return later to the public law/private law distinction. For the moment we might note that it is here used by Lord Diplock to differentiate the rules of administrative law in a way that favours the exercise of state power. Also notable in this case is the very different approach of each judge—Lord Denning's being marked by a greater willingness than any to allow standing simply for the purpose of allowing the courts to treat unlawful action that might otherwise go unchallenged until the harm was done. His attitude towards the exclusive power of the Attorney-General, and the use of that power, will be discussed below.

Turning now to the prerogative orders, these in theory gave an opportunity for a liberal definition of standing, because of the fact that these remedies were historically brought on behalf of the Crown, their purpose initially to keep inferior courts within their legal bounds. The plaintiff is thus technically bringing an action in the public interest, on behalf of the Crown, and his own private rights are not of prime importance. Nevertheless, even in the late 1960s the Privy Council refused standing to a mayor seeking to quash by certiorari the alleged unlawful dissolution of his council.[46] With regard to mandamus, standing was more narrowly construed, requiring a direct link between the duty enforced and a person whose rights were protected by the enforcement. The Courts tended to accept the reasoning of *R. v. Lewisham Union*[47] where the applicant, as a mere member of the public was held to have no standing to seek to command the guardians of the poor to enforce the provisions of the Vaccination Acts.

Lord Denning, as early as 1957, indicated that certiorari

> "Extends to any person aggrieved, and furthermore to any stranger. . . . When application is made . . . by a party or a person aggrieved, it will intervene (as it is said) *ex debito justiciae,* in justice to the applicant. When application is made by a stranger it considers whether the public interest demands its intervention. In either case it is a matter which rests ultimately in the discretion of the Court."[48]

In 1965 (three years before *Durayappah*[49]) Lord Denning held that the prerogative orders of both certiorari and mandamus would lie to ratepayers who had themselves suffered no financial harm. In *R. v. Paddington Valuation Officer, ex. parte Peachey Property Corp. Ltd.,*[50] Lord Denning allowed the applicants standing to challenge the rating valuation list, despite the fact that their own rating valuation would not be affected by the decision. He said:

---

[45] *Ibid.* p. 501.
[46] *Durayappah* v. *Fernando* [1967] 2 A.C. 337.
[47] [1897] 1 Q.B. 498.
[48] *R.* v. *Thames Magistrate's Court, ex p. Greenbaum* (1957) 55 L.G.R. 129.
[49] [1967] 2 A.C. 337.
[50] [1966] 1 Q.B. 380.

"I do not think that grievances are to be measured in pounds, shillings and pence. If a ratepayer or other person finds his name included in a valuation list which is invalid, he is entitled to come to the court and apply to have it quashed. He is not to be put off by the plea that he has suffered no damage. . . . The court would not listen, of course, to a mere busybody who was interfering in things which did not concern him. It will listen to anyone whose interests are affected by what has been done, just as it did in *R. v. Thames Magistrates' Court, ex parte Greenbaum* and in *Att.-Gen. of Gambia v. N'Jie.* So here it will listen to any ratepayer who complains that the list is invalid."[51]

In 1968, Lord Denning dealt with an application by Raymond Blackburn who sought mandamus to require the Metropolitan Police to enforce the gaming laws.[52] Lord Denning thought it an "open question" whether Mr. Blackburn had a sufficient interest to be protected. In 1973 he considered Mr. Blackburn's standing to seek enforcement of the laws against pornography—although no mandamus was issued, standing was granted. In 1976 Lord Denning was ready to grant a prohibition to both Mr. and Mrs. Blackburn to prevent the Greater London Council, as licensing authority, from licensing premises in accordance with conditions too narrow to prohibit the showing of "indecent" films.[53] In that case Bridge and Stevenson L.JJ. found Mrs. Blackburn standing on the ground that she was a ratepayer (although no issue of unlawful expenditure of rates was in issue).[54] Lord Denning, however, eagerly granted Mr. Blackburn standing to sue on the ground that he was "a citizen of London," coupled with the fact that his wife was a ratepayer and his children could be harmed by the exhibition of pornographic films. In his book *The Discipline of Law* Lord Denning makes it clear that any of the prerogative remedies would be available to "any responsible citizen"[55] who "complains that the law is not being enforced as it should."

In 1977 Order 53 of the Rules of the Supreme Court reflected the advice of the Law Commission that *locus standi* should be widened for the new Application for Judicial Review. Rule 3(5) provided that "the court shall not grant leave (for an Application for Judicial Review) unless it considers that the applicant has a sufficient interest in the matter to which the application relates."[56] This definition appeared to allow standing to individuals and groups with a mere "interest"—even in proper law enforcement.

The new definition came before Lord Denning in *R. v. Inland Revenue Commission, ex parte National Federation of Self-Employed and Small Business Ltd.*[57] He and Ackner L.J. (Lawton L.J. dissenting) had little difficulty in granting standing to the National Federation, playing on the new rules and distinguishing the *Gouriet* case. The Federation sought an action of mandamus ordering the Commissioners to assess and collect taxes according to the law. They alleged that the Commissioners had acted unlawfully in

---

[51] *Ibid.* p. 401.
[52] [1968] 2 Q.B. 118.
[53] [1976] 1 W.L.R. 550.
[54] See (1977) M.L.R. 74.
[55] At p. 127.
[56] See now also the Supreme Court Act 1981, s.31.
[57] [1980] Q.B. 407.

granting an "amnesty" to casual workers in the printing industry who, under a practice sanctioned by their employers and unions, had for years signed on for work under false names, defrauding the Inland Revenue of about £1 million per year. An investigative television programme eventually goaded the Inland Revenue into entering into an agreement whereby the Casuals would pay up in the future, and reveal their identity, in return for an amnesty for past misdeeds. The National Federation (described by Lord Denning as "good men and true who pay their taxes") claimed that the amnesty was *ultra vires* in that it involved an abuse of the Inland Revenue's discretion, particularly since the decision was taken in response to threats of industrial action.

The applicants however had suffered no direct damage by the action over-and-above that suffered by any member of the tax-paying public whose sense of justice was offended by the alleged abuse of discretion. A few years earlier, in *Arsenal Football Club Ltd.* v. *Ende*[58] a ratepayer was considered to be a "person aggrieved" by the under-assessment of the Arsenal football ground (by Lord Denning in the Court of Appeal and then in the House of Lords), but a taxpayer had still to qualify.

Lord Denning swept aside the *Lewisham* case:

> "The time has come when we must declare that those cases were wrongly decided. They meant that public authorities could break the law with impunity: for the simple reason that no one had any locus standi. It is now clear that all the talk about 'specific legal right' was a mistake. There is only one requirement and that is simply that the applicant must have a "sufficient interest in the matter to which the application relates.' That was the test recommended in 1975 by the Law Commission in their Report on Remedies in Administrative Law . . . and adopted in the R.S.C. Ord. 53, r. 3(5). The rule committee must have thought that it represented the existing law: else the rule would have been ultra vires. I also think it represents the existing law."

He distinguished the *Gouriet* case on the ground that it dealt with relator proceedings and not the prerogative writs. He would allow the "whole body of taxpayers a *locus standi* to complain" (especially as the Attorney-General would not complain on their behalf against a government department). The statement of Professor Wade was quoted in support, that

> " . . . the court should be able to award the remedy on the application of a public-spirited citizen who has no other interest than a regard for the due observance of the law."[59]

The House of Lords disagreed, and refused standing to the Federation.[60] The majority held that it was wrong to treat standing as a preliminary or threshold matter independent of the merits of the complaint which, in this case, were considered few. Nevertheless, they did hold squarely that standing in all the prerogative remedies was subject to the same rules and they all thought that the narrow interpretation of *Lewisham* in relation to mandamus ought now to be abandoned. Even Lord Diplock (who would

[58] [1979] A.C. 1.
[59] *Administrative Law* (4th ed., 1977) p. 608.
[60] [1982] A.C. 617.

have granted standing) cited Lord Denning's *McWhirter* dictum[61] with approval (although he said it was expressed "in language more eloquent that it would be my normal style to use"), and all their Lordships agreed that even a taxpayer would be granted standing in a case of sufficient gravity—linking standing to a test of degree of illegality that is perhaps not very easy to comprehend.

Fair Hearings and Natural Justice

Two concerns prompted Lord Denning in his desire to extend the right to a fair hearing. First, an appreciation of the power of monopolistic entities (public and private) over their members, and the consequences to individuals of their membership of those entities. Second, an appreciation of the utility of public participation to promote responsiveness in decision-making, and assisting a decision that, even if not favourable to the individual concerned, was at least made with an awareness of the decision's effect on that individual.

In respect of the first, Lord Denning was instrumental in reviving the "fair hearing" for domestic tribunals, and, with Lord Reid in particular, in extending the concept from purely "judicial" situations also to the administrative and even on occasion to the legislative. In respect of the second he was willing to implant judicial procedures into tribunals and inquiries even where public policy was in issue, confident that judicialised procedures were appropriate even in administrative fora. As he said in his Hamlyn lectures as early as 1949:

> "I know of nothing which is so essential to a right decision as to have the benefit of arguments which put forward all that can be said on each side . . . every tribunal should give a reasoned decision, just as the ordinary courts do. Herein lies the whole difference between a judicial decision and an arbitrary one. A judicial decision is based on reason and is known to be so because it is supported by reasons. An arbitrary decision . . . may be based on personal feelings, or even on whims, caprice or prejudice."[62]

It is well known that the concept of natural justice was greatly restricted in the face of the growth of governmental power in the twentieth century. The belief that the rule of law ought to accommodate the effective use of official discretion was largely accepted by courts, who were reluctant, after the *Arlidge* case[63] to impose judicial procedures in essentially administrative situations. As with the cases on standing, the assertion of right was held to constitute the necessary prerequisite for judicial intervention. The courts preferred not to protect mere "privileges," even if they contained expectations, and even though their withdrawal could constitute grave personal hardship. Thus, in 1951, in *Nakkuda Ali* v. *Jarayatne*,[64] the Privy Council held that a textile trader could be deprived of a licence to trade without being given the opportunity to rebut charges of his having falsified documents, on the ground that the licence was a mere "privilege." Similarly, two years later, the Queen's Bench division[65] held that a London taxi-driver's licence

---

[61] Repeated in *Blackburn* [1976] 1 W.L.R. 550.   [62] *Freedom under the Law*, above, at pp. 91–92.
[63] *Local Government Board* v. *Arlidge* [1915] A.C. 120.
[64] [1951] A.C. 66.   [65] [1953] 1 W.L.R. 1150.

could be revoked without a hearing. In both these cases the words of the relevant statute said nothing about fair hearings, but it was also forgotten that in the past in this kind of case "the justice of the common law will supply the omission of the legislature."[66] In the taxi-driver's case Lord Goddard based his argument upon the fact that a "disciplinary authority" should be beyond judicial control, and not "be fettered by threats of orders of certiorari and so forth."

In the case of *Ridge* v. *Baldwin*[67] the House of Lords re-established the right to a fair hearing in the case of Brighton's Chief Constable who had been dismissed from office without a hearing. Although the police authority were empowered to dismiss any constable "whom they think negligent in the discharge of his duty, or otherwise unfit for the same," the "justice of the common law" was extended, or reinstated, to supply the legislature's omission, even though the decision makers were acting in an executive or administrative capacity, and even though the plaintiff's rights were not in issue. The Chief Constable's livelihood, his "freehold office" was at stake, and ought to be protected by a hearing.

While there is no doubt that Lord Reid and others confirmed in this case what Professor Wade has rightly called a return to classic authorities,[68] it should be noted that in the 16 years before *Ridge* v. *Baldwin* Lord Denning was quietly laying the groundwork for the acceptance of a number of the basic principles behind that case. He began in 1948 in *Russell* v. *Duke of Norfolk*[69]—a case usually cited for Tucker L.J.'s statement that natural justice depends on circumstances, but also containing a forceful but scarcely-cited *obiter* by Lord Denning who, while agreeing on the facts that there was no evidence of a breach of natural justice was adamant that an inquiry *ought* to be held in the circumstances of that case (which involved the withdrawal of a horse trainer's licence and the placing of his name on a public list of disqualified trainers). This and other early cases involved the power of voluntary associations, seemingly unfettered by judicialised procedures. In *Russell* Lord Denning makes points that he was to repeat for the rest of his career: first, that the power of the Jockey Club involved "a monopoly in an important field of human activity. It has great powers with corresponding responsibilities." Second, that even if there were an express stipulation permitting a man to be condemned unheard "It may be that such a stipulation would be contrary to public policy." Third, he was willing to provide a protection not only to deprivation of property in the usual sense but also to the deprivation of a person's livelihood.

Four years later, in *Abbott* v. *Sullivan*,[70] the plaintiff, a cornporter in the London Docks was struck off the Union's register by a Committee, and hence could no longer be employed in the Docks. Denning L.J. agreed with the Master of the Rolls, Sir Raymond Evershed, that the Committee acted in breach of natural justice, even though the jurisdiction of a domestic tribunal was established upon contract rather than statute. He said:

> "The right of a man to work is just as important to him as, if not more important than, his rights of property. We see in our day many

---

[66] *Cooper* v. *Wandsworth Board of Works* (1863) 14 C.B. (N.S.) 180.
[67] [1964] A.C. 40.
[68] *Administrative Law* (5th ed.), pp. 461–468.
[69] (1949) 65 T.L.R. 225.
[70] [1952] 1 K.B. 189.

powerful associations which exercise great powers over their members to work. They have a monopoly in important fields of human activity. A wrongful dismissal by them of a member of his livelihood is just as damaging, indeed more damaging, than a wrongful dismissal by an employer of his servant."

Lord Denning dissented however from the court's refusal to award the damages for the *ultra vires* action of the committee. He said:

"I should be sorry to think that, if a wrong has been done, the plaintiff is to go without a remedy simply because he has no peg to hang it on . . . where there is a right there should be a remedy."

Three months later, in *Lee* v. *Showman's Guild*,[71] Lord Justice Denning, this time with the majority, repeated a number of his assertions in *Russell* and *Abbott*. *Lee* also involved an expulsion from a trade association. He said:

"It was once said by Sir G. Jessel M.R. that the courts only intervened in these cases to protect rights of property . . . *Abbott* case shows that the power of this court to intervene is founded on its jurisdiction to protect rights of contract . . .
     Domestic tribunals which sit in judgment on the members of a trade or profession . . . can deprive a man of his livelihood . . . Is such a tribunal to be treated by these courts on the same footing as a social club? I say: 'No.' A man's right to work is just as important, if not more important, to him than his rights of property. They must also intervene to protect the right to work."

These cases were not referred to in the Lords in *Ridge* v. *Baldwin*. Being Court of Appeal decisions, and concerned with domestic tribunals, this is understandable. The principles they uphold, however, are by no means far removed from *Ridge's* seemingly radical reaffirmation of an older approach.[71a]

Two judgments that were used to support *Ridge* v. *Baldwin* were both delivered by Lord Denning for the Privy Council two and three years before. In 1961 the case of *Annamunthodo* v. *Oilfields Workers Trade Union*[72] the appellant succeeded in setting aside his expulsion from the Union in circumstances where he had been denied natural justice in knowing the charges against himself. Although no prejudice may have been suffered it was said that

"If a domestic tribunal fails to act in accordance with natural justice, the person affected by their decision can always seek redress in the courts. It is a prejudice to any man to be denied justice."

In 1962 Lord Denning was again present in the Privy Council in the case of *Kanda* v. *Government of Malaya*[73] an appeal by an inspector of police against his dismissal from the force without being given a reasonable opportunity to be heard. He said:

"If the right to be heard is to be a real right which is worth anything, it

---

[71] [1952] 2 Q.B. 329.
[71a] This is Lord Denning's view. In a private interview with the author (on January 19, 1984) he said of *Ridge* v. *Baldwin*: "We'd already got them going. . . .We were working at it all the time."
[72] [1961] A.C. 945.   [73] [1962] A.C. 322.

must carry with it a right in the accused man to know the case which is made against him. He must know what evidence has been given and what statements have been made affecting him: and then he must be given a fair opportunity to correct or contradict them. It follows, of course, that the judge or whoever has to adjudicate must not hear evidence or receive representations from one side behind the back of the other. The court will not inquire whether the evidence or representations did work to his prejudice. Sufficient that they might do so."

After *Ridge* v. *Baldwin* it was easier to insist on natural justice in non-judicial situations, Lord Parker C.J. using the phrase "duty to act fairly" in the case of *Re H.K. (An Infant)*,[74] requiring such a hearing for an immigrant refused entry into the United Kingdom on the ground that he was not under 16 years of age.

Three Denning judgments thereafter stand alone as attempts further to extend the right to a fair hearing. The first, *R.* v. *Gaming Board for Great Britain, ex parte Benaim and Khaida*[75] involved two French nationals resident in the United Kingdom who managed the gaming club Crockfords. Applying for a certificate for a licence for the premises, they were refused without being provided with information from the Board. Lord Denning thought it an error to regard Crockfords as being deprived of any "right." Nevertheless, the Board were bound by the rules of natural justice. He continued:

"At one time it was said that the principles only apply to judicial proceedings and not to administrative proceedings. That heresy was scotched in *Ridge* v. *Baldwin*. . . . At another time it was said that the principles do not apply to the grant or revocation of licences. That too is wrong. *R.* v. *Metropolitan Police Commissioner, ex parte Parker* . . . and *Nakkuda Ali* v. *Jayaratne* . . . are no longer authority for any such proposition. See what Lord Reid and Lord Hodson said about them in *Ridge* v. *Baldwin* . . .

So let us sheer away from those distinctions and consider the task of this Gaming Board and what they should do. The best guidance is, I think, to be found by reference to the cases of immigrants. They have no right to come in, but they have a right to be heard. The principle in that regard was well laid down by Lord Parker C.J. in *Re H.K. (An Infant)*."

The second case, *R.* v. *Liverpool Corporation, ex parte Liverpool Taxi Fleet Operators' Association*[76] could be referred to as the high water mark of natural justice or fairness, as it seems to extend the concept almost into a legislative situation. In this case the Liverpool Council failed to consult with the respondent (after having given an undertaking to do so) about a decision to increase the number of taxi licences. As we shall see later, the breach of an undertaking is probably determinative in this case, but Lord Denning and the full Court of Appeal held that even in this situation, about as far as it is possible to get from the "judicial," the duty to provide a fair hearing applied.

The third case, *R.* v. *Barnsley Council, ex parte Hook*[77] can best be set out in one of Lord Denning's most eloquent first paragraphs:

[74] [1967] 2 Q.B. 617.
[75] [1970] 2 Q.B. 417.
[76] [1972] 2 Q.B. 299.
[77] [1976] 1 W.L.R. 10.

"To some this may appear to be a small matter, but to Mr. Harry Hook it is very important. He is a street trader in the Barnsley market. He has been trading there for some six years without any complaint being made against him; but, nevertheless, he has now been banned from trading in the market for life. All because of a trifling incident. On Wednesday, October 16, 1974, the market closed at 5.30. So were all the lavatories, or 'toilets' as they are now called. They were locked up. Three-quarters of an hour later, at 6.20, Harry Hook had an urgent call of nature. He wanted to relieve himself. He went into a side street near the market and there made water, or 'urinated,' as it is now said. No one was about except one or two employees of the council, who were cleaning up. They rebuked him. He said: 'I can do it here if I like.' They reported him to a security officer who came up. The security officer reprimanded Harry Hook. We are not told the words used by the security officer. I expect they were in a language which street traders understand. Harry Hook made an appropriate reply. Again we are not told the actual words, but it is not difficult to guess. I expect it was an emphatic version of 'You be off.' At any rate, the security officer described them as words of abuse. Touchstone would say the security officer gave the 'reproof valiant' and Harry Hook gave the 'counter-check quarrelsome': 'As You Like It,' Act V, Scene IV."

Mr. Hook was then dismissed from the market at a hearing where the market manager who prosecuted the case was present throughout the proceedings. The Court agreed that this was a breach of the right to a fair hearing, Lord Denning holding that the applicant had a right to the stallage (Scarman L.J. willing to grant the hearing even though Hook had only been deprived of a "legitimate expectation"). Interestingly, Lord Denning would also quash this decision on the ground that the punishment (dismissal) was out of proportion to the occasion—a new concept in English administrative law, known well however to the French as the principle of "proportionalité."

Lord Denning's contribution to the reassertion and extension of natural justice was enormous. The groundwork he laid in favour of procedural protections of rights other than property, and especially the right to work, must be acknowledged, and makes *Ridge* v. *Baldwin* seem perhaps less radical a turn than it is often made out to have been. There were other cases not mentioned above: *Nagle* v. *Fielden*[78] (the refusal of the Jockey Club to admit a woman), *Edwards* v. *SOGAT*[79] (expulsion from a union without the opportunity of being heard), and the strong dissent in *Breen* v. *A.E.U.*,[80] where the district committee failed to approve Mr. Breen's appointment as a shop steward for erroneous and prejudicial reasons. Edmund Davies and Megaw L.JJ. did not think the error influenced the decision, but Lord Denning disagreed and took the opportunity to repeat many of his themes over the past twenty-three years: that domestic bodies are as powerful as statutory authorities and "control the destinies of thousands"; that they should no more be able to claim unfettered discretion than could the Minister in the *Padfield*[81] case who "was roundly rebuked by the House of

[78] [1966] 2 Q.B. 633.
[79] [1971] Ch. 354.
[80] [1971] 2 Q.B. 175. See the discussion of these and other cases in Davies and Freeland, below, Chap. 8.
[81] [1968] A.C. 997 (to be discussed below).

Lords for his impudence"; that the courts could, through their inherent jurisdiction, always review the actions of tribunals and could grant declarations and injunctions even if not the prerogative writs; that a person deprived of his right to earn a livelihood was as much entitled to procedural protection as a person deprived of property. Finally, in determining those situations in which a person was entitled to a fair hearing he refined the analysis to situations first where a person "seeks a privilege to which he has no particular claim"—such as an appointment to some post or other—in which case he could "be turned away without a word"; second, a case where property or livelihood is in issue, or some "legitimate expectation." In this last case (covering the *Breen* situation, where, having been elected to office, Breen had a legitimate expectation of approval by the district committee) a fair hearing plus the giving of reasons "is one of the fundamentals of good administration." These categories formed the basis for Megarry V.C.'s forfeiture cases, application cases and expectation cases (the first always carrying the right to fairness, the second never and the third mostly) in *McInnes* v. *Onslow-Fane*.[82]

The Scope and Limits of Natural Justice

Having seen Lord Denning's contribution to the extension of the fair hearing, and some of the motives that impelled his creative approach, we must now see more precisely where he drew the line, and to what extent he was consistent in his approach. On the latter point we may note his own confession, in *The Changing Law* of a "practical instinct."[83] He wrote: "The English distrust abstract philosophy as much as they distrust formal logic . . . The English approach is empirical."

In my view only a very stark form of empiricism could possibly justify Lord Denning's judgment (supported, it should be said, by his two fellow Lords Justices Phillimore and Orr L.JJ.) in *Ward* v. *Bradford Corporation*.[84] In this case a female student was expelled for having had a man in her room, contrary to regulations. The disciplinary board recommending this decision to the Board of Governors had been referred the case by the Governors themselves, who gave themselves the power of referral (previously vesting only in the principal herself) by a retrospective amendment to the rules. On top of all this an assistant education officer was present throughout the hearing and advised the committee of the policy they ought to adopt and apply in the particular case. In other cases one could imagine Lord Denning maintaining at least six principles, many of which he had pioneered (or re-instated): the absence of bias—or appearance of bias (through the Governors being prosecutor and judge); the absence of a fair hearing (through the education officer's interference in the case); the taking into account irrelevant considerations (the fact that the plaintiff had discussed the issue with the press); the retrospective amendment to the rules about referral and, perhaps, the failure of an opportunity to appeal, coupled with the severity of the sentence.

In the end Lord Denning was swayed by the fact that he did not think the

[82] [1978] 1 W.L.R. 1520.
[83] (1953) p. 16.
[84] (1971) 70 L.G.R. 27.

plaintiff was treated unfairly or unjustly in fact. In other cases he would no doubt have proclaimed that justice must not only be done but be seen to be done,[85] but his motives were clear for all to see:

> "She had broken the rules most flagrantly. She had invited a man to her room and lived there with him for weeks on end. I say nothing about her morals. She claims they are her own affair. So be it. If she wanted to live with this man, she could have gone into lodgings in the town and no one would have worried, except perhaps her parents. Instead of going into lodgings she had this man with her, night after night, in the hall of residence where such a thing was absolutely forbidden. This is a fine example to set to others! And she a girl training to be a teacher! I expect the governors and the staff all thought that she was quite an unsuitable person for it. She would never make a teacher. No parent would knowingly entrust their child to her care. Six members of the disciplinary committee voted decisively for her expulsion. Not a single vote was cast against it, nor for any less sentence. Three abstained for reasons best known to themselves."

In no way can this case be declared consistent with the mainstream of Lord Denning's judgments on natural justice, but it does further his strong views on family life and infidelity as expressed in his earlier writings.[86]

Another area where Lord Denning would be content to relax the rigours of natural justice is, as he freely admits in *The Due Process of Law*,[87] that involving state security. In *R. v. Secretary of State for Home Affairs, ex parte Hosenball*,[88] Mark Hosenball, an American reporter living in London, sought certiorari to quash the Home Secretary's decision to deport him. He was heard before a panel of advisers but not told the case he had to meet. Unlike other cases Lord Denning here shows a complete confidence in the actions of the Minister, who ought to be responsible to parliament, not to the courts, for national security under our constitution:

> "When the state was in danger, our own cherished freedoms, and even the rules of natural justice had to take second place. . . . The rules of natural justice have to be modified in regard to foreigners here who prove themselves unwelcome and ought to be deported."

At base the rationale of this case lies in a desire to protect information collected by the secret service. The approach shows Lord Denning willing to leave certain decisions to parliamentary rather than judicial review in cases that he considers appropriate—even to the extent of citing in support the majority speeches in *Liversidge* v. *Anderson*[89]—a case that he consistently criticises elsewhere for excessive judicial deference to executive power.[90]

In 1968 Lord Denning's attitude to the right of aliens to fair hearings was shown in a different setting in *Schmidt* v. *Secretary of State for Home Affairs*.[91]

---

[85] See, *e.g. Metropolitan Properties Co. (F.C.G.) Ltd.* v. *Lannon* [1969] 1 Q.B. 577.
[86] See *The Changing Law*, above, p. 121.
[87] (1980), see p. 85.
[88] [1977] 1 W.L.R. 766.
[89] [1942] A.C. 206.
[90] *e.g.* in the *Tameside* case—discussed below.
[91] [1969] 2 Ch. 149.

The Home Secretary had refused, without a hearing, to extend the stay of United States students who were Scientologists. The Home Secretary's action was upheld by Lord Denning and Lord Justice Widgery, Lord Denning making the point that the fair hearing could only be claimed in connection with a right, interest or "legitimate expectation." In *Re H.K.* the Commonwealth minor had a right to be admitted if under 16 years of age. Here the foreign alien had no right to be—or legitimate expectation of being—allowed to stay. He would have had however if his permit was revoked *before* his time limit expired.

Do *Hosenball* and *Schmidt* show a personal bias against foreigners? The exceptions to the rule of fairness are argued more rigourously than those in *Ward*, although it is never made quite clear why foreigners, who may not have expectation of remaining in the country, may nevertheless have expections that British justice—including the right to a fair hearing—would operate on decision-making processes irrespective of the nationality of the parties. *Hosenball* however involves particularly delicate matters of security where some secrecy could be justified even by the most open of governments. *Schmidt* could be justified more easily as falling within the "application" category (in *McInnes* v. *Onslow Fane*[92]) where no deprivation of rights or expectations are involved, thus weakening the claim to a fair hearing. A more recent case where the plaintiffs were held by Lord Denning not to have an expectation of a hearing was *Cinnamond* v. *B.A.A.*[93] where six minicab drivers had been banned from Heathrow airport without a hearing, having been successfully prosecuted for touting for passengers there on numerous previous occasions. In this case Lord Denning was alive to Professor Wade's view that a hearing, even when punitive action seemed clearly justified, could "soften the heart of the authority and alter their decision" but nevertheless makes it clear that the past convictions removed any legitimate expectations of a hearing. This is not quite as sharp a position as that of Brandon L.J. in that case, who made it clear that no prejudice was suffered by the plaintiffs by the lack of a hearing, as the opportunity "would have availed [them] nothing."[94]

What of the content of the hearing, according to Lord Denning? Here again, the "empirical" approach prevails, and depends upon the circumstances. In *Benaim*, involving an application for a licence (with an expectation of renewal), the board

> "must give the applicant an opportunity of satisfying them of the matters specified. They must let him know what their impressions are so that he can disabuse them. But I do not think that they need quote chapter and verse against him as if they were dismissing him from office . . . or depriving him of his property . . . (nor were they) bound to give reasons for their misgivings. And, when they did give some reasons, they were not bound to submit to cross-examination on them."

---

[92] Above, n. 82.
[93] [1980] 1 W.L.R. 582.
[94] *Cf. R.* v. *Secretary of State for Home Department, ex p. Santillo* [1981] 2 W.L.R. 362 (where a court has already recommended deportation, the Home Secretary can be trusted to act fairly) and *Payne* v. *Lord Harris of Greenwich* [1981] 1 W.L.R. 754 (reasons for refusal of prisoner's release on parole not required for convicted murderer).

In cases involving only a preliminary investigation, to be followed by a further inquiry, such as the investigation into Pergamon Press by Board of Trade Inspectors,[95] Lord Denning did require the inspectors to act fairly, again however not necessarily to quote "chapter and verse" of the charge. They should remain "masters of their own procedure" and not permit cross-examination as of right. In *Norwest Holst Ltd.* v. *Secretary of State for Trade*[96] however, the Minister's decision to set up an investigation into a company was held by Lord Denning with a strong Court of Appeal not to attract the right to a fair hearing at all. In his dissent in *Breen,* however,[97] he makes it clear that reasons should be given where a person's livelihood, property and also "legitimate expectations" are at stake. "The giving of reasons," he said, "is one of the fundamentals of good administration." This statement goes further than has generally been accepted, and echoes Lord Denning's statement in 1949 that reasons check the possibility of an arbitrary decision, and "if the tribunals are to command the confidence of the public they must give reasons."[98]

A final aspect of procedural fairness on which Lord Denning has been somewhat equivocal concerns the right to legal representation. In *Pett* v. *Greyhound Racing Association Ltd.*[99] legal representation was held to be part of natural justice in a case involving the possible deprivation of man's livelihood. However, in *Enderby Town Football Club* v. *Football Association Ltd.*[1] Lord Denning felt that legal representation could be excluded, in a domestic tribunal, by the Associations's rules, although he would be prepared to override rules that were against public policy, unless parliament had provided to the contrary.[2] Nor is he willing to extend legal representation to cases involving disciplinary hearings (in prisons) where speedy hearings were necessary:

> "We all know that where a man is brought up before his commanding officer . . . it has never been the practice to allow legal representation."[3]

Public Inquiries

In his Hamlyn lectures Lord Denning made it quite clear that he was waiting for an opportunity to extend the concept of a fair hearing as it related to public inquiries, despite the case of *Franklin* v. *Minister of Town and Country Planning,*[4] which was decided the previous year, where it was held that the Minister's duties in this kind of inquiry (into the designation of a New Town in Stevenage) were "purely administrative," not judicial or quasi-judicial, and so he could act on his preconceived ideas, bias and policy considerations. Lord Denning noted that it had previously been commonly understood that a Minister must "observe the elementary rules applicable to

---

[95] *Re Pergamon Press Ltd.* [1971] Ch. 388. See also *R.* v. *Commission for Racial Equality, ex p. Cottrell & Rothon* [1980] 1 W.L.R. 1580.
[96] [1978] Ch. 201.
[97] [1971] 2 Q.B. 175.
[98] *Freedom under the Law*, above, pp. 90–91.
[99] [1969] 1 Q.B. 125 (and see [1970] 1 Q.B. 46).
[1] [1971] 1 Ch. 591.
[2] See *Fraser* v. *Mudge* [1975] 1 W.L.R. 1132.
[3] *Maynard* v. *Osmond* [1976] Q.B. 240.
[4] [1948] A.C. 249.

judicial functions, such as to allow each party to deal with information adverse to him." That view, however, must, in the light of *Franklin* be "regarded as wrong." So long as the statutory procedure is complied with and, as Lord Thankerton put it, the Minister "genuinely considers" the matter, the courts will not interfere. Nevertheless, Lord Denning left the way open for some interference by latching on to the word "genuinely," and linking the French concept of "detournement de pouvoir." (Lord Denning quotes frequently in these lectures from the Anglo-French legal conference, held in 1947 and which seems greatly to have influenced his realisation of the paucity of English administrative law remedies.)[4a] He goes on to say therefore that for power to be "genuinely" exercised, the administrator must have the "proper state of mind"—that which "parliament expects him to have," of an administrator who

> "carefully investigates all the relevant considerations and rejects the irrelevant ones: who will fairly balance public interest and private right; and thereupon after due consideration comes to an honest decision as to whether to exercise the power or not for the purpose authorised by parliament. If the courts are satisfied that he did not bring that state of mind to bear on the matter—or that his action was so unreasonable that he cannot have brought it to bear—then the courts will interfere."[5]

In these words we see sketched a number of principles by which the courts—nearly 20 years later—began to intervene to check administrative action and, particularly, "subjective" discretion by the Executive. Here, however, we see Lord Denning willing to lift the veil on public inquiries to ensure that they are more than empty rituals, that they are "genuine" rather than symbolic exercises that simply allow the public to let off steam.

Lord Denning's disquiet with the procedures of the public inquiry was widely reflected in the decade following his Hamlyn lectures and taken up by the *Franks* Committee[6] which led to changes in many inquiry procedures through the Tribunals and Inquiries Act, or regulations such as those affecting planning appeal inquiries. Nevertheless, it was always possible for an inspector or minister, through inadvertence or bias, not "genuinely" to keep an open mind. Without evidence of either, however, it is difficult if not impossible for the courts to prove lack of fair consideration, and it is very rarely done.

One of the very few cases where discretion was checked for, in effect, lack of "careful investigation" was that of *Coleen Properties Ltd.* v. *Minister of Housing and Local Government.*[7] In that case a public inquiry was held into the question of a clearance area which would involve compulsory purchase of houses "unfit for human habitation." A particular house there was not unfit, but could still be brought into the area as "adjoining land reasonably necessary for the satisfactory development of the area." The Minister, disagreeing with his Inspector, thought that the land was "reasonably necessary," but he had no evidence upon which to base his disagreement. The Court of Appeal held that the Minister's decision was, for that reason, beyond the powers of the Act. Lord Denning cited the criteria for

---

[4a] Lord Denning told me that he did not attend that conference, but received the papers, probably from his friend Professor Jack Hampson of Cambridge. *Interview* n. 71a above.
[5] *Freedom Under the Law,* above, p. 121–122.
[6] Cmnd. 218 (1957).   [7] [1971] 1 W.L.R. 433.

interference that he had laid down in the *Ashbridge* case[8] (which will be considered more fully below), one of which was the absence of evidence. These are clearly pioneering decisions, not perhaps going as far as the American rule which insists that decisions must be based on the "substantial evidence" before the decision maker. They were, however, as Professor Wade points out,[9] contrary to the weight of authority of the time, but have been followed frequently since.

Another issue which may provoke judicial interference with inquiry procedure arises in connection with the issues on which a minister may base his decision. Under various statutory rules governing inquiries and under judicial principles of natural justice a minister may not disagree on questions of fact with his inspector, without notifying parties or re-opening the inquiry. In *Coleen*,[10] it was held that the "reasonable necessity" of including the additional land was a question of fact, not policy.[11]

The difference between fact and policy arose in a challenging way in the case of *Bushell* v. *Secretary of State for the Environment*.[12] The issue there related to an inquiry into a proposal for a motorway scheme. Two points were in issue. First, was the Inspector correct in holding that that which was known as the "Red Book," containing the government's basis for assessing future traffic growth, was in fact government policy and therefore exempt from cross examination by objectors at the inquiry? Second, ought the Secretary of State to have re-opened the inquiry because, after its close but before his decision (accepting his Inspector's recommendations to approve the scheme), the Red Book was revised? At the heart of these issues was the more profound question of the extent to which public local inquiries were for the purpose of examining government policy at all.

In the Court of Appeal[13] Lord Denning and Shaw L.J. (Templeton L.J. dissenting) were of no doubt that the minister's decision ought to be quashed. The House of Lords, however, Lord Edmund-Davies dissenting, reversed the Court of Appeal, with the speeches highlighting profound differences in the interpretation of the purpose of and philosophy behind administrative law. Lord Diplock's speech[14] makes it clear that "the local inquiry does not provide a suitable forum in which to debate . . . a matter of government policy." He admits that policy is a "protean word" and he defines it in a way that is functional, namely, as a "topic which is unsuitable to be the subject of an investigation as to its merits at an inquiry at which only persons with local interests affected by the scheme are entitled to be represented." The merits of the Red Book, although a "grey area" between the clearly policy question (such as whether to build a nationwide motorway network) and the purely local question (*e.g.* about the exact line of a motorway), was declared to be a policy question because it was "clearly not appropriate for investigation . . . by an inspector whose consideration of the matter is necessarily limited by the material which happens to be presented to him at the particular inquiry which he is holding."

[8] [1965] 1 W.L.R. 1320.
[9] *Wade*, above, pp. 287 *et seq.*
[10] Above, n. 7.
[11] On the difference between fact and policy see *Lord Luke of Pavenham* v. *M.H.L.G.* [1968] 1 Q.B. 172.
[12] [1981] A.C. 75.
[13] (1977) 76 L.G.R. 460.
[14] [1981] A.C. at pp. 94 *et seq.*

Lord Denning's approach had been quite different, based on fairness rather than function. He begins with a concern that recent protests about fairness at inquiries are a signal for the courts to take a hand. It was important that the inspector should not be "subject to the dictates of the Department" and conduct inquiries "free from the suspicion of departmental prejudice." He insists that "People should not go away from an inquiry saying 'I've not had a fair deal.' " Most important, "The objectors should not be brushed off with the remark 'It is Government policy'."

Although Lord Denning does clearly believe that traffic forecasts are matters of fact rather than policy "just as much . . . as the evidence of a medical man on the prognosis of a disease," he comes close to saying that the subject matter of an inquiry is policy as much as fact. At least he is not willing to concede that all policy is out of bounds at public inquiries. Certainly he must be right that objectors at inquiries (admitted both of right and at the discretion of the inspector and often representing broad public interests and not only local issues) would indeed feel a grievance if the inspector's report were based on unsound forecasts that could not be fully questioned at the inquiry. As he said, the objectors would not have had "a fair crack of the whip."[15]

On the second point in *Bushell* (alterations of the Red Book after an inquiry) the majority in the Lords held that the change in forecasts should not require a re-opening of the inquiry. The majority all indicated a concern about excessive delay, with Lord Diplock willing for these purposes to consider the minister and his department as one, to the extent that information—continually changing—in the department, was not to be regarded as extraneous and thus requiring a re-opening of the inquiry. Lord Denning, however, in the Court below, felt that "A delay . . . is preferable to leaving the objectors with a legitimate sense of grievance." In typically robust fashion, he said simply that the inspector's recommendations were out of date and if the new forecasts could have had a "probable influence" on the outcome of the minister's decision "it would seem only fair that the objectors should have an opportunity of commenting on it."

In my view it would be difficult to find any aspect of Lord Denning's reasoning in Bushell that was weaker, analytically, than Lord Diplock's. In fact, the way in which traffic forecasts are fashioned into policy by Lord Diplock, and his circular definition of policy as being intrinsically non-local displays, with respect, a certain intellectual sleight of hand. Lord Denning's position demonstrates what, with a few notable exceptions, has been his consistent position since 1949. He is alive to the abuse of monopolistic power (state or private), impatient of rules or procedures that insulate unfair decisions from attack, unwilling to leave individuals with a "sense of legitimate grievance," and, above all, confident in full judicial-type procedures (including cross-examination) as a technique of participation and an assurance of "careful investigation" whether the context involved rights or interests, administration or policy.

---

[15] A term also used by Lord Edmund Davies in the Lords, and borrowed from Lord Russell in *Fairmount Investments Ltd.* v. *Secretary of State for the Environment* [1970] 1 W.L.R. 1255, 1266.

Abuse of Discretion

A good part of *Freedom under the Law*[16] was devoted by Lord Denning to the subject of abuse of power. In *The Changing Law*[17] he continued this theme, opening with an account of the social revolution that had, this century, been accompanied by a constitutional revolution. "In legal theory," he said, "Parliament is still sovereign, and we still claim to be under the rule of law: but anxiety is raised in many quarters by the growing powers of the executive."[18] Throughout both books however he stakes a role for law and judges (sometimes called "upright" or "independent" judges) as arbiters of the constitution, and protectors of freedom against abuse of power.

Even in 1949 he was alert to uncontrolled executive power, sceptical about parliament's ability to control the executive, and willing confidently to assert the judicial role. In *Freedom under the Law* he lays down the actual principles by which executive power may be controlled—failure to carry out the purpose for which power was conferred and "unreasonableness" (a principle carefully constrained but nevertheless reasserted in the previous year by Lord Greene M.R. in the *Wednesbury* case).[19] He also searches hard for additional substantive and procedural principles to control discretionary powers and finds them in French administrative law.[19a] The French concept "detournement de pouvoir" is accepted as a worthy import and translated into terms that he uses in later cases and that now find much wider acceptance in our law. He refers, *e.g.* to power being "exercised genuinely for the purposes conferred by Parliament and not for any ulterior purpose"[20] and says that "If they take into account things which they ought not to take into account, or if they do not take into account things which they ought to take into account, so also the court will interfere." He accepts that power should not be used in a way that the French call "cynical or maladroit"[21] but uses again the term in *Franklin* that power should be "genuinely exercised" after consideration of all "relevant considerations" and rejection of the "irrelevant." He says that if these principles are applied by the courts, "we may yet find in the courts protection against undue encroachment on our liberties by the executive."[22]

This was written at a time when *Liversidge* v. *Anderson*[23] was still fresh in memories, and subjective discretion not readily regarded as open to judicial challenge. In 1957 in *Pyx Granite*[24] Lord Denning interpreted the provision of the Town and Country Planning Act 1947, which allowed conditions as the local authority "think fit." While upholding the conditions in that case, he added a judicial gloss that clearly circumscribed conditions to those that "fairly and reasonably relate" to the permitted development. The planning

---

[16] (1949).
[17] (1953).
[18] *Ibid.* p. 1.
[19] [1948] 1 K.B. 223.
[19a] See n. 4a above.
[20] *Freedom under the Law*, p. 117.
[21] *Ibid.* p. 120.
[22] *Ibid.* p. 121.
[23] Above.
[24] *Pyx Granite Co.* v. *M.H.L.G.* [1958] 1 Q.B. 554. See also *Fawcett Properties Ltd.* v. *Buckinghamshire C.C.* [1961] A.C. 636.

authority, he insisted, were "not at liberty to use their powers for an ulterior object, however desirable that object may seem to them to be in the public interest."

In 1965, in the *Ashbridge* case,[25] again upholding the minister's action (in accepting his inspector's description of a building not being a "house," without seeking further evidence) he laid down his now accepted test for judicial intervention in discretionary decisions. He said:

> "it seems to me that the court can interfere with the Minister's decision if he has acted on no evidence; or if he has come to a conclusion to which, on the evidence, he could not reasonably come; or if he has taken into consideration matters which he ought not to have taken into account, or vice versa; or has otherwise gone wrong with the decision of a lower tribunal which has erred in point of law."[26]

The *Padfield*[27] case came to the Court of Appeal in July 1966. In issue was what appeared to be an "unfettered" discretion of the Minister of Agriculture to refer a complaint to a committee of investigation (and then to take action after a report of such a committee). The Minister failed to refer the complaint on the ground that he would be expected to take action on any recommendation of the committee, and because the complaint could better be resolved through other mechanisms. The Court of Appeal refused to grant an order of mandamus commanding the Minister to refer the complaint to the committee, but Lord Denning dissented. This was the case in which to apply the principles of intervention he had long prepared. He stated that the Minister was under "a duty to consider" every complaint and to refer every genuine complaint to the committee. Not only could the Minister not refuse to refer complaints on grounds that were arbitrary or capricious, but also on other "irrelevant grounds." Again on familiar ground, Lord Denning rejected the distinction between "administrative" and "judicial" decisions. "Good administration requires that complaints should be investigated and that grievances should be remedied." Without good reason it was not for the Minister to "brush (the machinery) on one side." If asked, the Minister should give his reasons. If he does not do so "the court may infer that he has no good reasons." Echoing *Ashbridge,* he says that if the Minister was influenced by "extraneous considerations which ought not to have influenced him—or, conversely, had failed . . . to take into account considerations which ought to have influenced him—the court has power to interfere." The Minister's reasons in this case were those which "ought not to have weighed with him." He therefore had not "properly exercised his discretion."

Again in this case Diplock stood against Denning, displaying a very different philosophy of the court's role *vis-à-vis* the Executive (consistent with that shown later in *Bushell*) and upholding wide discretionary power. Diplock L.J. placed a good deal of store on the fact that the Minister's decision was "administrative, not judicial." This permitted him to take into account general policy beyond the merits of this case. The Minister need not give reasons, but if he did the courts ought to interpret them liberally, not as "lawyer's jargon but Civil Servicese." In the end the Minister's decision was

---

[25] *Ashbridge Investments Ltd.* v. *Minister of Housing and Local Government* [1963] 1 W.L.R. 1320.
[26] *Ibid.*
[27] *Padfield* v. *Minister of Agriculture, Fisheries and Food* [1968] A.C. 997.

"a policy decision" for which he was accountable only to Parliament, and the courts should not interfere.

The House of Lords, in a landmark decision, allowed the appeal. In so doing it became clear that Lord Reid, in particular, shared a good deal of Lord Denning's constitutional theory, although in this case Lord Reid's grounds for interference were narrower than Lord Denning's. Whereas Lord Denning had based his decision upon "principles of good administration" as well as statutory interpretation (principles such as the duty to give reasons, and to consider complaints), Lord Reid based this decision entirely on the ground that the Minister's action failed

> "to promote the policy and objects of the Act; the policy and objects of the Act must be determined by construing the Act as a whole and construction is always a matter of law for the court."[28]

Lord Reid held that it was plainly the intention of the Act that even the widest issues should be investigated "if the complaint is genuine and substantial, as this complaint certainly is," and if the Minister failed to investigate the complaint he would be "rendering nugatory" a safeguard provided by the Act (and a remedy which Parliament intended complainers to have).

In 1972, in the *ASLEF* case[29] Lord Denning upheld the Secretary of State for Employment's order requiring a ballot to be taken of union members on the question of industrial action, without specifying his reasons for doubting whether the workers had an opportunity of indicating their wishes. Lord Denning affirmed that the words "If it appears to the Secretary of State" did not put the Minister's decision beyond challenge, but departed to some extent from his position on the duty to give reasons expressed in *Padfield*, and from his words there about the inferences that could be drawn by the court when reasons were not given. In this case, the Minister had been concerned with "a grave threat to the national economy" and his decision would not do any harm to anyone; would not "imperil their liberty, livelihood or property," in which cases his proposition about reasons would apply. The decision here, to hold a ballot, would "ensure the freedom of each man to express his own will."

In the mid-1970s a spate of cases on ministerial discretion came before Lord Denning's court—*Tameside*,[30] *Congreve*[31] *Gouriet*[32] and *Laker*.[33] In three of the four ministerial discretion was curtailed by the court and Lord Denning's view prevailed.[34]

Tameside involved interpretation of section 68 of the Education Act 1944 which permitted the Secretary of State "if satisfied . . . that any local educational authority (had acted) unreasonably" to give appropriate directions. The Minister here sought a mandamus to give effect to his

---

[28] *Ibid.* p. 1030.

[29] *Employment Secretary* v. *ASLEF* [1972] 2 Q.B. 455.

[30] *Secretary of State for Education and Science* v. *Tameside M.B.C.* [1973] A.C. 1014.

[31] *Congreve* v. *Home Office* [1976] 1 Q.B. 629.

[32] *Gouriet* v. *U.P.O.T.W.* [1977] 2 W.L.R. 310.

[33] *Laker Airways* v. *Dept. of Trade* [1977] Q.B. 643.

[34] In *Gouriet* the Lords reversed the Court of Appeal. See also Lord Denning's judgment in *R.* v. *I.R.C., ex p. Rossminister Ltd:* [1980] 2 W.L.R. 1, 15, holding that officers of the I.R.C. had no "reasonable cause to believe" any fraud and hence no right to enter on the premises to seize material. This decision was reversed in the Lords [1980] A.C. 952.

direction that the Tameside Council had acted unreasonably in seeking to reintroduce grammar schools between May and the new school year in September. Lord Denning was not willing to grant the order, nor to accept that the Minister's discretion was as wide as was claimed. *Liversidge* v. *Anderson* and similar cases were held in relation to war time regulations, when "the decisions of the executive had to be implemented speedily and without question." The minister had to be satisfied not about opinion but about unreasonable conduct. This required a fair hearing (which had been granted). It also required evidence that the local authority had acted, not wrongly or erroneously, but unreasonably, which had not been demonstrated. This view was accepted in the House of Lords, even by Lord Diplock who, although coming close to accepting Lord Denning's "genuine consideration" test (putting the question thus: "did the Secretary of State ask himself the right question and take reasonable steps to acquaint himself with the relevant information to enable him to answer it correctly?") nevertheless preferred to rest his decision on the narrow ground of not asking the right question (namely, to what extent a policy of noncooperation by the teachers might have made selection in the time allowed impossible).

In *Congreve,* the Court of Appeal confirmed the issuance of a declaration that the Home Secretary's revocation of the plaintiff's television licence was invalid. On increasing the licence fee the Home Secretary had issued instructions that persons applying for a renewal before the date of the new fee should pay the new fee. Thousands of licence-holders managed however to receive overlapping licences and were informed that their licences would be revoked. The relevant Act gave wide discretion to the Home Secretary to revoke licences. The Parliamentary Commission for Administration had already found the Home Secretary's actions to be "maladministration." The question was whether it was also unlawful.

It was during this case that the executive started firing across Lord Denning's bows. During the course of his argument for the Home Secretary Roger Parker Q.C. said:

> It would be a very sad day if the courts were to use the power—which is undoubtedly one of the most valuable powers in English Law—to curb the executive as they are being invited to do. It would not be long before that power started to be called in question—and it is one of the most valuable powers which the courts have."[34a]

After wide press publicity of this statement, during the course of the hearing Roger Parker read out an apology (which is not contained in the reported judgment). Lord Denning's judgment ends with a reference to Mr. Parker's initial statement and then says simply: "We trust that this was not said seriously, but only as a piece of advocate's licence."

Again in this judgment Lord Denning addresses the question of reasons, endorsing his view in *Padfield* that the courts may draw inferences from the lack of reasons. The reasons given here for revoking the licences namely, want of money, were bad, as "The licence is granted for 12 months and cannot be revoked simply to enable the Minister to raise more money." It was also contrary to the Bill of Rights, which makes unlawful the levy of money for the Crown without the authority of Parliament.

In 1977 Laker Airways sought declarations against the Department of

[34a] [1976] 1 Q.B. 629, 646.

Trade that the cancellation of the designation of their aircraft as carriers to the United States would be unlawful.[35] Two main issues arose: first, could the Minister completely reverse his previous policy, and decide not to encourage competition between the state-owned and privately-owned airlines. The Court of Appeal held that he could not do so through the procedure of "guidance" under the Act, because such guidance could not alter the statutory purposes, one of which was to encourage such competition.

The second issue in *Laker* concerned the contention of the Attorney-General that the Minister could withdraw Laker's designation as a carrier under his prerogative power arising under a treaty, thus outside the cognisance of the courts. Lords Justices Roskill and Lawton dealt with this question in a different way from Lord Denning, holding that the Act in this case by necessary implication fettered the use of the prerogative. They agreed that the prerogative power could not be challenged in the courts, but held that the prerogative—being a residue of authority left in the Crown's hands—by implication cannot be used when a statute governs the situation. Lord Denning, in sharp contrast, was willing to extend the law to challenge even prerogative power just as he would challenge any other discretionary power to make sure it was used for the public good and not improperly or mistakenly. However, in this case he was not content to allow the Minister to use prerogative powers to displace a statute by a "side wind," particularly as the statute provided a number of procedural protections to the applicant.

A few weeks later Lord Denning was again confronted by the Attorney-General, asserting this time, in the *Gouriet* case,[36] that his own consent or refusal to act in relator proceedings was exempt from judicial interference since he was responsible to Parliament alone. Lord Denning agreed that the Attorney's consent was exempt from review but was adamant that his refusal could be challenged. The Attorney's contention was "a direct challenge to the rule of law." The Attorney-General claimed in the alternative that his power was a prerogative of the Crown. This, too, Lord Denning was not prepared to accept, on the ground that the Attorney would then be able to dispense with the laws and allow a breach of the law to go unpunished with impunity. Lawton L.J. was willing to go some way towards allowing review of the Attorney's discretion in cases where he revealed his reasons, but the issue was not pursued in the appeal in the Lords,[37] where it was accepted that the Attorney-General's prerogative power was immune from judicial review.

Two more cases on ministerial discretion came to Lord Denning. In 1980 he upheld an appeal from the Newbury District Council[38] to the effect that the Secretary of State for the Environment had misdirected himself in law by holding that a condition attached to a planning permission was unlawful. Planning permission had been given in this case for the change of use of aircraft hangars to a warehouse. The permission contained a condition that the building be demolished after a period of years. The Court of Appeal

---

[35] [1977] 2 W.L.R. 234.
[36] [1977] 2 W.L.R. 310.
[37] [1978] A.C. 635.
[38] *Newbury D.C.* v. *Secretary of State for the Environment* [1981] A.C. 578. See McAuslan's discussion, above, pp. 186–188.

held, unanimously, that the Minister was wrong,[39] and, using the *Pyx Granite* test[40] that the condition related "fairly and reasonably" to the permitted development. The House of Lords (also unanimously) disagreed, considering the condition extraneous to the proposed use. (It seems—though it is never made quite clear, that a condition requiring an operation was extraneous to a permission for a change of use). Hidden in their Lordships' speeches however is a subtle return to judicial deference to the executive in this kind of appeal—a retreat which Lord Denning's dictum in *Pyx Granite* by no means intends. Lord Scarman puts it thus:

> "Was it fairly and reasonably related to the permitted development? . . . This was for the Minister in the light of all the circumstances, to decide; and he decided it. I would comment only that the Minister, being the ultimate authority on planning questions arising in the enforcement of planning control, is the appropriate authority to determine whether a condition 'sufficiently,' *i.e.* fairly and reasonably, relates to the permitted development."

There is little doubt that the Denning approach would, on an appeal of this kind (not a matter of judicial review) consider the question to be a matter of law, for the courts to decide.[41]

One of the last cases on this subject Lord Denning had to decide involved the power of the Environment Secretary to intervene in the event of a local authority (the Norwich City Council) not doing sufficient to enable Council house tenants to purchase their homes under The Housing Act 1980. The Act allowed the use of these default powers "Where it appears to the Secretary of State" that tenants were experiencing difficulty in buying their homes, and he could then "do all things as appear to him necessary or expedient."[42]

Despite these "draconian" powers, Lord Denning was not willing to grant the certiorari to quash the Minister's decision sought by the Council. He did not shrink from the criteria for judicial intervention that he himself had pioneered in *Padfield*, *ASLEF* and *Tameside*—citing all of these cases, and insisting too that the Minister must afford the Council a fair hearing. In the end however he and the full court felt that the statutory powers had been properly exercised; there was evidence that the Council had acted unreasonably; the Minister had given them time to mend their ways and had given their case "careful consideration."

Local authority discretion

The principles of review of executive action have been applied equally by Lord Denning to local authorities. *Padfield* and *Breen* were cited in *Cumings* v. *Birkenhead Corporation*,[43] upholding a scheme whereby parents' choice of

---

[39] [1978] 1 W.L.R. 1241. See the discussion by Sir Patrick Browne "Judicial Reflections," (1982) C.L.P. 1, 15.

[40] Above, n. 24.

[41] Compare Lord Scarman's statement to Lord Denning's in *Kharrazi*, above, and *ACT Construction*, above, that once you have established primary facts, the question of law is for the judges to decide. The differences in Denning's and Scarman's approach at that time is highlighted in *U.K.A.P.E.* v. *ACAS.* [1980] 2 W.L.R. 254.

[42] *R.* v. *Secretary of State for the Environment, ex p. Norwich City Council* [1982] 2 W.L.R. 580.

[43] [1972] Ch. 12.

secondary school was curtailed by the religious character (Catholic or non-Catholic) of the child's primary school. The policy itself was held not to be unreasonable, capricious or irrelevant.[44]

In this case Lord Denning also dealt with the principle of "fettering" of discretion, which had just been firmly established in regard to policy considerations by Lord Reid in the *British Oxygen* case.[45] Lord Denning agreed that a policy was permissible, provided the authority were "ready to consider" an exceptional case—which, on the facts, they were in this case.

The "fettering" principle, eagerly adopted by Lord Denning in other cases, is close to his principle of "genuine consideration" and related to the fairness doctrine. Thus, a rigid policy against amusement arcades was held to be wrong in law,[46] although in *Smith* v. *Inner London Education Authority*[47] a policy of applying the comprehensive principle to education throughout the area was upheld. Lord Denning said:

> "I cannot see that there is anything *ultra vires* in an education authority having a policy by which they aim at the comprehensive principle throughout their area. Nor do I see anything unlawful to their applying that policy in the case of any individual school, provided that they listen to all the objections and consider whether or not the policy should be applied."

To these cases one should add another that in a sense stands the fettering principle on its head and *requires* equality of treatment. In *H.T.V. Ltd.* v. *Price Commission*[48] the respondents (not a local authority but a quasi-governmental organisation) changed the method by which a levy on the appellants was calculated. Lord Denning admitted that a public body should not "fetter" its discretion but a competing principle was that they should not misuse their powers in a manner that was unfair or unjust towards the private citizen. In this case they ought to have acted with "fairness and consistency," only departing from what they had held out as established practice if there was "good cause" for departing from it.

The requirement of consistency in this case is new as a substantive principle of English administrative law. In Continental systems it is very familiar as the principle of egalité (equality of treatment).[49]

The powers of local authorities came before the Court of Appeal dramatically in the case of *Bromley London Borough Council* v. *Greater London Council*.[50] Almost immediately after the local elections, the newly Labour-controlled Greater London Council moved to reduce London Transport fares by 25 per cent., which would result in a loss of over £69 million and necessitate additional rate precepts upon the London Boroughs—including the applicants, who were seeking judicial review by way of certiorari to quash the Greater London Council's actions. The case turned in good part upon the interpretation of the Transport (London) Act 1969, which required

---

[44] For Lord Denning's approach to a local authority's statutory duty to provide schools see *Meade* v. *Haringey L.B.C.* [1979] 1 W.L.R. 637. See P. Cane, [1981] P.L. 11, 17–19.

[45] [1971] A.C. 610.

[46] *Sagnata Investments Ltd.* v. *Norwich Corp.* [1971] 2 Q.B. 614.

[47] [1978] 1 All E.R. 411.

[48] [1976] I.C.R. 170.

[49] In full: "Egalité devant les services publiques."

[50] [1982] 2 W.L.R. 62.

an "integrated, efficient and economic" transport service, and required the London Transport Executive "as far as practicable" to break even from year to year.

The Court of Appeal unanimously, and the House of Lords, unanimously, upheld Bromley's application, but it was Lord Denning who received most press publicity for interference with a political decision and the attempt of the new Labour Greater London Council to implement their party's manifesto. In fact his judgment keeps very close to principles to which he has consistently adhered. Although resuscitating the cases of *Roberts* v. *Hopwood*[51] and *Prescott* v. *Birmingham Corporation*[52] (cases which require councils to act in a fiduciary relationship to their ratepayers and not to engage in excessive "philanthropy" at ratepayers' expense), Lord Denning links the fiduciary concept to his tried and tested "genuine consideration," used by him in the past to promote fair hearings, the non-fettering of discretion as well as attacks on wide ministerial discretion. As he put it in *Bromley*, "The members of the Greater London Council have to hold the balance between these conflicting interests (the travelling public and ratepayers). They have to take all relevant considerations into account on either side." In the absence of affidavit evidence from any councillor in this case, Lord Denning accepts the principal overt reason for pressing ahead with the scheme, namely, that the Greater London Council felt committed to fulfill their election promise and considered that they had a mandate so to do. They were under a misconception to give such undue weight to the manifesto. There follows in Lord Denning's judgment a closely reasoned argument as to why a manifesto should not be "taken as gospel." It may contain unworkable promises, and many electors vote not for the manifesto but other reasons. "When the party gets into power, it should consider any proposal or promise afresh, on its merits (and) . . . what is best to do in the circumstances of the case and to do it if it is practicable and fair."

Lord Denning's approach to the "fiduciary" standard is here very different from its adoption by Lord Diplock in the House of Lords. Whereas Lord Denning seizes it as another method of ensuring fair consideration of relevant considerations Lord Diplock extends it into a notion that the authority should not act in a manner that is "thriftless"—a notion that surely allows even more judicial interference with local authority policy.[53]

Lord Denning's reservations about the doctrine of the mandate is however not at all surprising. His 1953 book *The Changing Law* contains a strong section criticising the doctrine in much the same terms that he does in *Bromley*. He wrote then:

> "Some people vote for (a member) because they approve of some of the proposals in his party's manifesto, others because they approve of others of the proposals. Yet others because, while they do not really approve of the proposals, they disapprove still more of the counter-proposals of the rival party, and so forth. It is impossible to say therefore that the majority of the people approve of any particular proposal, let alone every proposal in the manifesto."[54]

[51] [1925] A.C. 578.
[52] [1955] Ch. 210.
[53] Above, pp. 100 *et seq. Cf.* the interpretation of the "fiduciary" cases by Ormrod L.J. in *Pickwell y. Camden L.B.C.* [1983] 1 All E.R. 602.
[54] Above, pp. 8–10.

He ends the section saying that elected leaders are under a constitutional duty to govern in the interests of all and not in the interests of their party. "But this is not a duty which can be enforced by law—the only real check on their power is the force of public opinion." Thirty years later Lord Denning was able to find a way of checking the unbridled use of the doctrine of the mandate—through the law.

Public Liability and Immunity

Lord Denning's treatment of public entities in respect of their liability for tortious acts or breach of contract was consistently to treat them as equivalent to private persons, and not to shield them from a remedy on behalf of an aggrieved individual. Only at the very end of his career was he prepared to assert a distinction between public law and private law. When other judges made that distinction it was usually (although not always) a preface to surrounding the public body with a protection that the law would not allow a private individual. As he wrote in 1970: "Our English law does not allow a public officer to shelter behind a droit administratif."[54a]

Misleading statements

In 1948, sitting as Denning J. in the King's Bench Division he held in *Robertson* v. *Minister of Pensions*[55] that the Crown was bound by an assurance from the War Office that the plaintiff's disability was due to military service. The assurance was intended to be acted upon and was acted upon. The Crown ought to be bound like any private person. In 1950, now in the Court of Appeal, he repeated the principle in a case where the Admiralty gave verbal permission to carry out shipbuilding work, taking it even further, saying:

> "Whenever governmental officers, in their dealings with a subject, take on themselves to assume authority in a matter with which he is concerned, the subject is entitled to rely on their having the authority which they assume."[56]

This decision was reversed by the Lords,[57] Lord Simonds responding to the above words saying: "I know of no such principle in our law nor was any authority for it cited." Those words seemed for a time to have ended the possibility of "estoppel" as a result of misleading advice from public authorities. In 1962 Lord Parker held that estoppel could not be sought to prevent the performance of either a statutory duty or a statutory discretion as a public authority could not be fettered from exercising its free discretion.[58]

Lord Denning was not to be deterred. In *Wells* v. *Minister of Housing and Local Government*[59] a letter in reply to a planning application stated that a structure was "permitted development" which did not require planning

---

[54a] *M.H.I.G.* v. *Sharp* [1970] 2 Q.B. 223, 266.
[55] [1949] 1 K.B. 227.
[56] *Howell* v. *Falmouth Boat Construction Co. Ltd.* [1951] A.C. 837, 845.
[57] *Ibid.*
[58] *Southend-on-Sea Corp.* v. *Hodgson (Wickford) Ltd.* [1962] 1 Q.B. 416.
[59] [1962] 1 W.L.R. 1000.

permission. The Minister held that the letter was not a formal "section 43 (now 53) determination" and that the authority should not be bound by the letter. The majority in the Court of Appeal rejected this view, Lord Denning saying that the defect or irregularity in procedure can be cured to render it valid, and bind the authority.[60]

In 1971 Lord Denning once again attempted to revive the estoppel concept in *Lever Finance Ltd.* v. *Westminster London Borough Council.*[61] The Westminster Council in this case had, in response to a telephone conversation, told the plaintiff's architect that variations in his plans (which had been approved) were not "material," thus not requiring planning permission. Later the authority brought enforcement action against the plaintiff, on the ground that the variations now being undertaken were indeed material, and denying that they were estopped from changing their officer's previous representations. Lord Denning held that the recent cases saying that public authorities cannot be estopped from doing their public duty "must now be taken with considerable reserve," because they were made before legislation gave the power to a Council to delegate its powers to officers.

> "So here it is their practice of the local authority . . . to allow their planning officers to tell applicants whether a variation is material or not. Are they now to be allowed to say that the practice was all wrong? I do not think so. It was a matter within the ostensible authority of the planning officer, and, being acted on, it is binding on the council."

In 1972 we have seen that the assurance by the Liverpool Council to the Taxi Operators was considered by Lord Denning to be a material factor in binding the Council at least to a fair hearing before making an essentially legislative decision to increase the taxi licences.[62] In 1981 however a Court of Appeal on which Lord Denning was not sitting considered the estoppel doctrine in a planning context,[63] Megaw L.J. (*obiter*) restricting it to two situations: first, where power has been delegated to officers for specific purposes (as, it was suggested, in *Lever Finance*) and second, where the authority waives a procedural requirement. In the same year Lord Denning himself was unwilling to allow a mistaken issue of planning permission, without any authority, from binding the Taff-Ely Borough Council[64] on the ground that "the protection of the public interest is entrusted to representative bodies and to the minister," and that the grant was *ultra vires*.

The problems of the extent to which public authorities ought to be, and can be, bound by representations acted upon by another are by no means resolved.[65] One can say, however, that without Lord Denning the concept would have been unlikely to have been considered in the context of public administration.

---

[60] But see Russell L.J.'s strong dissent.
[61] [1971] 1 Q.B. 222. See McAuslan's discussion, pp. 188–190, above.
[62] *R.* v. *Liverpool Corpn. ex p. Liverpool Taxi Fleet Operators Association* [1972] 2 Q.B. 299. And, in a different context, see the *Laker* case, above.
[63] *Western Fish Products Ltd.* v. *Penrith D.C.* [1981] 2 All E.R. 204. See A.W. Bradley (1981) 34 C.L.P. 1, 6.
[64] *Co-operative Retail Services Ltd.* v. *Taff-Ely B.C.* [1980] 39 P. C.R. 223—affirmed in the House of Lords in (1981) 42 P. & C.R. 1.
[65] See A.W. Bradley (1981) 34 C.L.P. 1, 6.

Liability for tort

Another principle put beyond doubt by Lord Denning (with Lord Evershed and Romer L.JJ.) in 1952, was that a public authority that commits an unauthorised nuisance is not to be protected by its public status, even when it had taken all reasonable action possible in the public interest. An injunction was granted (although postponed) to prevent pollution of the river Derwent by the overloaded sewage works of the Derby Corporation.[66]

The liability of a public authority for negligence—under the ordinary common law principles—was established, affirming a judgment by Thesiger J., in the Court of Appeal in *Dorset Yacht Co. Ltd.* v. *Home Office.*[67] Damages for negligence were claimed against the Home Office for damage to the plaintiff's yacht by Borstal Boys who had escaped from a camp. Although the evidence of negligence in allowing the boys to escape was strong, the Home Office asserted that no duty of care was owed to the plaintiff, and that prison authorities would be greatly hampered if it were held that there were such a duty. Lord Denning asked:

> "What then is the right policy for the judges to adopt? On whom should the risk of negligence fall? Up till now it has fallen on the innocent victim. Many, many a time has a prisoner escaped—or been let out on parole—and done damage. But there is never a case in our law books when the prison authorities have been liable for it. No householder who has been burgled, no person who has been wounded by a criminal, has ever recovered damages from the prison authorities such as to find a place in the reports."

He then asks whether this should now be altered, and comes to the conclusion that it should, "because of the people who live in the neighbourhood (whose) confidence in the law would be undermined if the judges were to declare that the authorities owed no duty of care to them."

The decision of the Court of Appeal was affirmed by the House of Lords, Lord Reid once again taking up Lord Denning's position. Lord Diplock, while agreeing, was only willing to provide a remedy where the officers had acted not only negligently but also *ultra vires*.

In 1970 Lord Denning dissented from a Court of Appeal decision that failed to hold a council registrar liable to the Ministry for wrongly issuing a certificate relating to land that failed to indicate that compensation was payable on the land.[68] He thought that the relevant statute failed to exempt the public officer. "So he is personally liable. Otherwise the injured person would be left without a remedy—which is unthinkable."

Two years later he took his Court with him in *Dutton* v. *Bognor Regis U.D.C.*[69] The Council building inspector was alleged to have been negligent in passing a house's foundations which were found by a subsequent purchaser to have been faulty. As Lord Denning said, never before had an action of that kind been brought before English courts nor, it appeared, by any common law court. He sought, therefore, an answer to "a question of

---

[66] *Pride of Derby and Derbyshire Angling Association* v. *British Celanese Ltd.* [1953] Ch. 149.
[67] [1970] A.C. 1004. According to Lord Denning, Lord Diplock had initially intended to dissent in this case. *Interview*, n. 71a above, p. 225.
[68] *M.H.L.G.* v. *Sharp* [1970] 2 Q.B. 223.
[69] [1972] 1 Q.B. 373.

policy which we, as judges, have to decide." He characterised the local authority's "function" not as a duty or a power but as a control which was exercised over building work. The control required "reasonable care." Under ordinary tort principles Mrs. Dutton, who "suffered a grievous loss" which she was in no position to bear, ought to be compensated by "those who were responsible." There was no policy reason for exempting the Council from liability. The position is put very simply:

> "(The Council) were entrusted by Parliament with the task of seeing that houses were properly built. They received public funds for that purpose. The very object was to protect purchasers and occupiers of houses. Yet they failed to protect them. Their shoulders are broad enough to bear the loss."

Dutton was applied in 1977 by the House of Lords in *Anns* v. *Merton London Borough Council*[70] again involving the lack of adequate inspection of foundations. The simplicity of Lord Denning's reasoning is not found in the speeches there. Lord Wilberforce bases his argument very much upon the fact that the authority's powers and duties "are definable in terms of public not private law." Where public powers or duties are provided the authority must give "proper consideration" to exercise them but can only be held liable for damage caused as a result of unreasonable or *ultra vires* acts. Where the power or duty has been made "operational," then ordinary negligence principles apply. So public bodies have an additional ring of protection (the negligent act must also be *ultra vires*)—at least before operational exercise of discretion—that private bodies lack. Lord Denning, achieving similar results, was unwilling to sanction any additional "public law" protection.[71]

One way in which public bodies have traditionally sought protection from the rigours of liability in tort for damage caused has been under the doctrine that exempts liability for damage that is the "inevitable consequence" of what Parliament authorised. Thus nuisance from a train running on a particular line authorised in the statute would be exempt but if the statute simply authorised a railway, without specifying further, nuisance would be actionable.

In 1979 this issue came to the Court of Appeal in *Allen* v. *Gulf Oil Refining Ltd.*[72] The defendants were authorised by statute compulsorily to acquire land for the purposes of a construction of an oil refinery. The operation of the refinery was however not expressly mentioned. Lord Denning, applying the old cases, held that "it should not be assumed that Parliament intended that damage be done to innocent people without redress," and that damages should be awarded for the nuisance caused. The House of Lords however reversed the Court of Appeal,[73] and held that, since Parliament considered it in the public interest that a refinery should be constructed on lands compulsorily purchased, and since the statute's preamble referred to "refinement," immunity for nuisance should be implied to have been conferred.

As Professor Wade writes, "this decision seems to have weakened, if not

---

[70] [1978] A.C. 728.
[71] See D. Oliver (1980) 33 C.L.P. 269.
[72] [1980] Q.B. 156.
[73] [1981] A.C. 1001.

removed, the protection which it gave to persons injured by the operations of public authorities and bodies with statutory powers."[74]

Public law and private law

In the above judgments we see that the principles applied by Lord Denning to establish public liability have always been those that apply in the common law. Those judges who wished to give additional protection to public authorities would often justify their position on a distinction between public and private law. Public bodies should not, according to them, be subject to the full rigours of private law liability.[75]

No mention has been made so far of one of Lord Denning's greatest dissents in *Conway* v. *Rimmer*,[76] where the Home Secretary claimed what, since *Duncan* v. *Cammell Laird*[77] had been perhaps the most absolute of "public law" protections, that of Crown Privilege. The House of Lords[78] (again with Lord Reid sitting) upheld Lord Denning's position that the documents sought ought not to be automatically privileged, but produced for inspection for the courts to decide. On three occasions before *Conway* v. *Rimmer* Lord Denning with a unanimous Court of Appeal had held that the court had a residual power in a proper case to override the Crown's objections. In *Grosvenor Hotel*[79] he said that

> "it is the judges who are the guardians of justice in this land: and if they are to fulfil their trusts, they must be able to call on the Minister to put forward his reasons so as to see if they outweigh the interests of justice."

I shall not in this chapter continue to examine how Lord Denning applied his powers thereafter to weigh claims of what is now known as "public interest immunity," as Palley's chapter does this in sufficient detail. Suffice it to say here that the removal of absolute public immunity was made possible largely by Lord Denning's tenacious insistance upon its injustice to litigants against public authorities.

It must be mentioned, however, that the immunity of judicial bodies for actions of negligence was carefully preserved by Lord Denning, on the ground of maintaining judicial independence.[80]

Nor should it be assumed that Lord Denning was above taking into account administrative exigencies, or inconvenience, as a justification for not interfering with a technically unlawful decision. McAuslan deals[81] with cases in relation to planning enforcement notices where Lord Denning was impatient with legal technicalities attempting to tie the hands of local authorities. In the *Ostler*[82] case he was greatly influenced in refusing the applicant's claim to quash a decision reached without a fair hearing by the

---

[74] *Wade,* above, p. 651.
[75] See C. Harlow, "Public" and "Private" Law: Definition without Distinction" (1980) M.L.R. 241. See, *e.g.* the discussion on the *Gouriet* case, above pp. 219–20.
[76] [1967] 1 W.L.R. 1031.
[77] [1942] A.C. 624.
[78] [1968] A.C. 910.
[79] [1965] Ch. 1210. The other two cases were *Merricks* v. *Nott-Bower* [1965] 1 Q.B. 57, and *Wednesbury Corp.* v. *M.H.L.G.* [1965] 1 W.L.R. 261.
[80] *Rondel* v. *Worsley* [1967] 1 Q.B. 442; *Sirros* v. *Moore* [1975] Q.B. 118.
[81] Above, pp. 78–82.
[82] See, above [1977] Q.B. 122.

fact that the authorised activities had already gone ahead. In many other instances, however, he was unwilling to bow even to the plea of chaos. In *Bradbury* v. *Enfield London Borough Council*[83] he said that "The Department of Education and the Council are subject to the rule of law and must comply with it, just like everyone else. Even if chaos should result, still the law must be obeyed."

Similarly, whereas in most cases Lord Denning would insist on claiming the court's right to check the discretion of public authorities, and indeed even to place the onus of proof against them, in some cases, by reason of function he would hesitate to intervene. Thus, in *De Falco* v. *Crawley Borough Council*[84] and *Lambert* v. *Ealing London Borough Council*[85] he held that housing of homeless persons was largely a matter for the local authorities, whose discretion should be looked upon benevolently, because of the difficulties with which they are faced. Similarly, in cases involving national security, as we have seen,[86] Parliament, rather than the courts, was held to be the more appropriate forum for control of ministerial discretion. Nor was Lord Denning ever eager to review discretion in the area of Supplementary Benefit.[87] There is little doubt, however, that these cases form the rarer exceptions to Lord Denning's confident assertion of the principle that public bodies are to receive no special dispensation from the full rigours of administrative law.

Shortly before his retirement, however, Lord Denning did accept the public law—private law distinction. In *O'Reilly* v. *Mackman*[88] he said: "Private law regulates the affairs of subjects between themselves. Public law regulates the affairs of subjects *vis-à-vis* public authorities." In this case he struck out as an abuse of process the writs and originating summonses issued by prisoners in Hull prison seeking declarations that penalties imposed upon them for breach of prison discipline were in breach of natural justice. They could not proceed by way of application for judicial review under Order 53 of the Rules of the Supreme Court as they were out of time. Lord Denning makes it clear that because of its special features, the new procedure for judicial review to determine questions against public authorities should be exclusive. He mentions the advantages to the applicant of this procedure (speed, cheapness, etc.) but also the disadvantage (leave has to be obtained, and limited discovery and cross-examination). He states that if applicants were permitted to bypass these "safeguards," "I can well see that the public authorities of this country would be harassed by all sorts of claims—long out of time—on the most flimsy grounds."

This reasoning is out of step with Lord Denning's generally consistent removal of obstacles against claims against public bodies. Ironically, at a time at the end of his career when many of his decisions were reversed by the House of Lords, *O'Reilly* v. *Mackman* was affirmed.[89]

---

[83] [1967] 1 W.L.R. 1311.

[84] [1980] Q.B. 460.

[85] [1982] 1 W.L.R. 550. See McAuslan's discussion, pp. 204–205 above.

[86] *R.* v. *Secretary of State for Home Affairs, ex p. Hosenball* [1977] 1 W.L.R. 766. See also the disciplinary cases, above p. 231.

[87] *R.* v. *Preston S.B.A.T., ex p. Moore* [1975] 1 W.L.R. 624.

[88] [1982] 3 W.L.R. 604.

[89] [1982] 3 W.L.R. 1096. Lord Diplock surveys much of administrative law in this case, admitting the errors of his own ways, and giving credit for its development largely to Lord Goddard and Lord Reid.

Conclusion

Despite Lord Denning's own distrust of "philosophy,"[90] his judgments in administrative law display a consistent approach to the role of the courts in a welfare state. At the outset of his judicial career this approach was not shared by his colleagues, who felt bound, by technical rules and constitutional role, to be deferential to the growth of strong state power.

Lord Denning's "activist" approach was based upon a constitutional theory that saw the doctrines of the rule of law and separation of powers as permitting, indeed encouraging, the confident development of principles by the courts, to be applied even against the executive. While the sovereignty of Parliament is by no means denied, this approach contains a realistic understanding that Parliament cannot today control effectively the necessary discretion allocated to a variety of public authorities.[90a] The realism extends to a sceptical view of the doctrine of the mandate, and a "consumer perspective,"[91] based on an awareness that individuals today are subjected to the control of "powerful groups" with very little opportunity to influence the direction of policy.

To further his approach Lord Denning first set about dismantling the procedural obstacles to the assertion of claims against the state, allowing certiorari and then declarations to be more easily available. His view of jurisdiction would not easily allow official action to be protected by exclusionary clauses, and throughout his career he was never willing to allow a restrictive definition of standing to block a claim of official lawlessness from reaching his court. (His courtesy and helpfulness to litigants in person should be remembered—in stark contrast to the frosty reception they mostly received in other courts of his day).

With technical obstacles removed, it was possible to develop the principles of administrative law that had been arrested by almost a century of judicial deference to official action—in an age of what Lord Denning called "darkness." The task began with the imposition of fair procedures on domestic tribunals which, though essentially private, had many features of control and unconstrained power in common with the official bodies that were then the subject of judicial attention in *Ridge* v. *Baldwin*.[92] As with his approach to standing, Lord Denning was concerned to allow fair hearings not only when individual rights were involved; he was also concerned to protect interests and expectations, and to extend procedural protections from tribunals to other official decisions where a genuine inquiry would promote responsiveness to the public the body was designed to serve. His approach differed sharply here from those who considered policy decisions outside the realm of judicial control.

Did he himself wrest the role of policy-maker from public authorities? He rarely justified a decision on social or political goals, although equally rarely masked his view of a case's merits. When controlling subjective discretion, the principles he employed were not that different from those employed in relation to the fair hearing. Even in *Padfield*[93] it was the "genuine

[90] *Freedom under the Law*, p. 32. See also Heuston, pp. 3–4 above.

[90a] In 1952 he wrote that "Parliament is much too busy to do all it should for law reform" and "does not act until the sky is heavy with complaints," "The Need for a New Equity" (1952) C.L.P. 1, p. 6–7.

[91] Cahn, above, p. 212, n. 14.

[92] [1964] A.C. 40.   [93] [1968] A.C. 910.

consideration" of complaints that was required, as well as the necessity to avoid "irrelevant considerations," although he was, with Lord Reid in particular, willing to interpret Parliament's purpose widely in his assessment of a statute's objects.[94] He was also unwilling to tolerate special immunities in discovery of documents[95] afforded to the state that were denied private individuals, and extended ordinary private law liability to a range of official actions.

A number of Lord Denning's decisions take English administrative law further than has generally been accepted and perhaps point the way ahead. For example, his willingness to review prerogative power,[96] his application of the continental concepts of equality[97] and proportionality,[98] the duty to give reasons,[98a] the substantial evidence test[99] and, recently, a requirement not only of procedural but also of substantive fairness.[1]

Some cases do exist where he shows uncharacteristic deference to official decisions. Where national security is involved,[2] he admits this. Immigrants are sometimes treated less favourably than citizens,[3] but not always.[4] Prisoners and others who may have forfeited the court's sympathy[5] by past misdeeds are often not afforded rights of fair hearing eagerly granted to others. Yet his decisions vary in their support for authorities of differing political persuasion.[6]

Lord Denning wrote in 1971 that "it may truly now be said that we have a developed system of administrative law."[7] Other judges and most administrators would not have had it so, and his application of administrative law principles in individual cases may not please us all. Without him, however, it is unlikely that the most significant of those principles would ever have been established.

---

[94] See the discussion on statutory interpretation in *Duport Steel* [1980] 1 W.L.R. 142, 157. In a recent case however the Lords reversed Lord Denning's narrow interpretation of an immigration statute. *Alexander* v. *Immigration Appeal Tribunal* [1982] 2 All E.R. 766.
[95] *Conway* v. *Rimmer*, above.
[96] In the *Gouriet* and *Laker* cases above.
[97] In *H.T.V.* v. *Price Commission*, above.
[98] In *ex p. Hook*.
[98a] In *Breen* v. *A.E.U.*
[99] In *Coleen*, above.
[1] In *Chief Constable of the North Wales Police* v. *Evans* reversed in the Lords [1982] 1 W.L.R. 1155, see Lord Brightman at p. 194.
[2] See the discussion on *Hosenball*, above.
[3] *e.g. Alexander* v. *Immmigration Appeal Tribunal* [1982] 1 All E.R. 763.
[4] *R.* v. *Chief Immigration Officer, Gatwick Airport, ex p. Kharrazi* [1980] 1 W.L.R. 1396. Cases against the Race Board also go both ways. Compare *R.* v. *Race Relations Board, ex p. Selvarajan* [1975] 1 W.L.R. 1686; *R.* v. *C.R.E., ex p. Cottrell & Rothon* [1980] 1 W.L.R. 1580 and *C.R.E.* v. *Amari Plastics* [1982] 2 W.L.R. 499.
[5] In *Ward, Cinnamond*, above. See also *Payne* v. *Lord Harris of Greenwich* [1981] 1 W.L.R. 754.
[6] *Smith* v. *ILEA*, above allows a programme of comprehensive schools: *Tameside*, above does not permit the Minister's interference with a programme of selective schools.
[7] *Breen* v. *A.E.U.* [1971] 2 Q.B. 175, 189. Lord Diplock called this "the greatest achievements of the English courts in my judicial lifetime." *R.* v. *I.R.C. ex p. N.F.S.E.S.B. Ltd.* [1981] 2 W.L.R. 722, 737.

CHAPTER 7

Lord Denning and Human Rights—Reassertion of the Right to Justice

CLAIRE PALLEY

Writing about a man who is good, great, and got on with the practical job in hand without time or inclination for introspective analysis of his activities is difficult.[1] Academic critics are seldom themselves creative. They are trained to dissect, differentiate and distance themselves. They do not have to decide pressing questions, so carp and hedge their views with reservations and wise afterthoughts in articles which are often similar to the kind of precise, unemotional, authoritative judgment against which Lord Denning so set his face. In contrast, he deliberately wrote for maximum public understanding and consumption, using his carefully cultivated style to make his judgments live, simplifying and setting out the merits "because the merits go to show where justice lies."[2] Nonetheless, Lord Denning did not despise the academics,[3] often responding in subsequent judgments to their criticisms, and accepting good humouredly penetrating criticisms of much of his judicial output.[4] Although he might well privately respond: "Oh yes. Of course, I could have told you that," the writer of this essay has therefore rashly, and necessarily subjectively and impressionistically, dared to assess the Denning contribution to the preservation and furtherance of "human rights." What must go without discussion, for purposes of this assessment, is that the general concept of "human rights" is accepted. Similarly, the individual rights enumerated in the United Nations Covenants on Civil and Political Rights and on Economic, Social and Cultural Rights and in the European Convention on Human Rights and Fundamental Freedoms are taken as providing appropriate standards for evaluating the results of Lord Denning's work. In addition, certain human rights concepts now in process of receiving general recognition are used.

The diversity and number of Denning judgments, when conjoined with the fact that "human rights" involve the whole body of law reclassified on criteria of individual interests, make it at first sight appear impossible to rationalise Lord Denning's contributions to the maintenance of "human rights." Indeed, some critics see Lord Denning in associated spheres as inconsistent, idiosyncratic, illiberal and as even merely rhetorical.[5] There is, however, a sure guide to his whole *oeuvre*. In a short burst of musing about the Common Law, its goals, methods and peculiar characteristics, Lord

---

[1] Lord Denning clearly shared the English distrust of philosophy and formal logic mentioned in *The Changing Law*, pp. 15–16. His dislike of Jurisprudence strikes sympathetic chords in many student hearts.

[2] *The Family Story*, p. 207.

[3] *Ibid.* p. 197.

[4] *Cf.* his reaction to P. Robson & P. Watchman (eds.), *Justice, Lord Denning and the Constitution*.

[5] *Justice, Lord Denning and the Constitution, passim.*

Denning worked out for himself his own homespun philosophy. His Hamlyn Lectures, published as his first book, *Freedom Under the Law* (1949), together with some adventurous judgments on contract, tort and property questions, had led to Denning L.J. becoming the "star turn" as university and law society guest lecturer.[6] His subsequent occasional lectures, put together as *The Changing Law* (1953) and *The Road to Justice* (1955), but which are really only expansions of themes already touched upon in *Freedom Under the Law*, were not long thereafter to complete the trilogy. When, 30 years later, Lord Denning produced *The Discipline of Law* (1979), the *Due Process of Law* (1980) *The Family Story* (1981) and *What Next in the Law* (1982) the same arguments and historical analogies reappeared, with the addition of summaries and extensive extracts from his judgments. These facts are here indicated not in denigration, but to indicate that the mould of his philosophy had firmly been cast, and that most of his judicial activity was prefigured in the various lectures between 1949 and 1955.[7]

At the core of Lord Denning's thought is a theory of balance—balance "between personal freedom on the one hand and social security on the other."[8]

He saw the genius of the British constitution in

> "a practical instinct leading us to balance rights with duties, and powers with safeguards so that neither rights nor powers shall be exceeded or abused."[9]

Balancing was to be crucial in his judicial decisions according or restricting individual rights.[10] Those who were to strike the balance were, for the most part,[11] the independent judiciary, which he saw as playing a crucial

---

[6] *The Family Story*, p. 178, confirms that the Hamlyn lecture series was the starting point of his extra-judicial lecturing fame.

[7] See *The Family Story*, pp. 177–183. Although Lord Denning is not egotistic enough to be introspective about his own intellectual development, *The Family Story* is revealing—it is also very moving. He says little about the influences upon him. Yet he clearly followed Hewart's basic position, while taking account of what Laski and Jennings had said about tribunals, property rights and welfare needs. It seems that Lord Goddard (whose contribution to administrative law is not generally realised) had a great influence upon him. See *Freedom Under the Law*, pp. 67–126, *passim*, and *The Changing Law*, pp. 31–35. From the Law Reports of the period it is possible to speculate that Lord Denning was a protégé of Goddard: there is a cordiality apparent when they sat together, and he would not have been made a Lord Justice without warm support from Goddard L.C.J. Lord Denning is less than generous in *The Discipline of Law*, pp. 64–66 and 81–82, in recognising Lord Goddard's contributions.

[8] *Freedom Under the Law*, p. 16. See also pp. 18 *et seq.* on balancing individual freedom from arrest and police powers.

[9] *The Changing Law*, p. 16. See also p. 11 for abuse of press power, a recurring theme. See also *The Road to Justice*, pp. 67, 81 and 87: "It is better still to strike the happy mean."

[10] Especially those concerning journalists, the press, the rights of citizens to public information, and the right to a judicial procedure ensuring justice by way of discovery of documents. These cases begin with *Att.-Gen.* v. *Mulholland* [1963] 2 Q.B. 477 and end with the controversial decisions of *British Steel Corporation* v. *Granada Television* [1980] 3 W.L.R. 774, *Schering Chemicals Ltd.* v. *Falkman Ltd.* [1981] 2 W.L.R. 848 and *Home Office* v. *Harman* [1981] 2 W.L.R. 310. Sometimes the balancing exercise is between two different individual rights, but sometimes it is put as being between two different public interests: see *What Next in the Law*, pp. 219–263, *passim*.

[11] The balance between rights of property and freedom of contract are for Parliament to ensure, as are the duties of property-owning individuals towards their neighbours and the community at large: *Freedom Under the Law*, pp. 67 *et seq.*

part in protecting freedom,[12] and which would

> "hold the scales evenly not only between man and man but also between man and the State."[13]

He asserted that

> "there must be judges in the land who are 'no respecters of persons and stand between the subject and any encroachment on his liberty by the executive.' "[14]

It is in this context that his continuous assertion of judicial power to intervene (whether or not exercised in any particular case) must be seen.[15] If the judges are guardians, then they must have power.[16] Similarly, those who work the judicial process must have protection.[17]

But the judges were hampered by the doctrine of precedent.[18] Little wonder then that within a short period he had started developing his own distinctive view of judicial role, both in regard to extensive powers of statutory interpretation,[19] and to creative handling of inconvenient judicial precedents.[20] The point made here is that, although Lord Denning has frequently been criticised for inconsistency in relation to his views on the judicial role (himself sometimes adopting a strict although usually a liberal construction) and for his disregard and even misuse of precedent, there has been insufficient emphasis on why he developed those views and felt entitled to behave judicially as he did.

The apparent inconsistency has arisen because he has at times, in reaction to reception of his approach in other judicial quarters, tended to dwell on the questions of judicial technique, and their appropriateness for a modern judge as if they were his primary concern. Consequently, his view of judicial methodology has been placed at the forefront as the criterion for examining his consistency. Judged on this standard, he is inconsistent, because, as a utilitarian for justice, he picks and chooses the techniques, being, in sociological jargon, entirely result-oriented, with his use of technical or non-technical procedures being mere means to achieve his great end, justice

---

[12] *Freedom Under the Law*, p. 32. In *The Changing Law*, p. 4, the necessity for judicial independence is emphasised.

[13] *The Changing Law*, p. 5. See also *The Road to Justice*, p. 4, where he envisages the judges as representing "the right-minded members of the community in seeking to do what is fair between man and man and between man and the State."

[14] *Freedom Under the Law*, p. 15.

[15] See *R.* v. *Newspaper Proprietors Agreement* [1963] 1 All E.R. 306, claiming extended jurisdiction for the Restrictive Practices Court, as well as the series of administrative law decisions seeking to extend jurisdiction and the grounds for intervention.

[16] In *What Next in the Law*, p. 320, Lord Denning urged that English judges should have the power to "set aside statutes which are contrary to our unwritten Constitution—in that they are contrary to reason or fundamentals."

[17] Thence the imunity of a barrister to a suit for negligence in conducting a case in court (*Rondel* v. *Worsley* [1967] 1 Q.B. 443) and the extension of immunity to all the judges of the land in respect of all acts done judicially, even if outside their jurisdiction (*Sirros* v. *Moore* [1974] 3 W.L.R. 459).

[18] *Freedom Under the Law*, p. 68.

[19] *Seaford Court Estates Ltd*. v. *Asher* [1949] 2 K.B. 481.

[20] *Robertson* v. *Ministry of Pensions* [1949] 1 K.B. 227.

(of course as he himself sees it on the particular facts). He would plead guilty to that soft impeachment.

However, applying his own overriding goal as the standard, he has been consistent in seeking to implement his intuitive views of justice. This is in accordance with what he sees as a major aspect of the spiritual heritage of the English people. That heritage is, Lord Denning thought, composed of the instinct for justice, the instinct for liberty, the practical instinct of balancing rights with duties, and

> "throughout all this runs the Christian instinct and with it a sense of the supreme importance of the individual and a refusal to allow his personality to be submerged in an omnipotent State."[21]

In his extra-judicial writing he emphasised the moral quality of law and the necessity that it corresponded with or at least did not unduly diverge from what the people of England consider to be right and just, at the same time attacking those lawyers who divorce law and justice, and think it their function merely to interpret or enforce the law irrespective of its morality or justice.[22] Although he implicitly urges that the English people should have confidence in their judges, and states that the judges hold the scales evenly,[23] he has not hesitated harshly to criticise the views of those of his brethren, who have disagreed with him.[24] Perhaps this latter inconsistency can be forgiven: Lord Denning is urging that the judges should have power to do justice, and castigating them when they fail to act in accordance with what his view of justice requires.

All Lord Denning's subsequent decisions and writings fall within the framework first set out in 1949 and finally developed by 1955. Careful readers should have foreseen the pattern of Denning decisions. For many years he was, however, perceived by academics (then mainly teachers of contract, tort, property, and equity) and law students as Sir Galahad, especially because of his chivalry towards the claims of deserted wives and his inventive coming to the rescue to save one party from the injustice of an implacable law. This came about because his judgments, where he sought justice as he saw it, mainly lay in areas of lawyer's law, and because of his constant emphasis on a creative judicial role in aid of justice. Had Lord Denning been Chief Justice, instead of Master of the Rolls, the public view of him as libertarian would have been very different. Already, by 1968 specialist practitioners and some note writers had observed that, when he moved into the criminal law (with which he had little judicial contact) or constitutional law areas, Lord Denning almost invariably brought the balance down in favour of public order, police powers, an extended criminal law and the validity of state action, especially where security was concerned.

It is worth surveying his judgments in these spheres before the academic world reacted to the first alarm signals in *Chic Fashions (West Wales) Ltd.*[25] He

---

[21] *The Changing Law*, p. 3.

[22] *The Road to Justice* (1955), pp. 2–3, repeated in *The Family Story*, pp. 181–183.

[23] *The Changing Law*, p. 5, repeated in *The Family Story*, p. 192.

[24] *e.g.* "We cannot stand idly by": *Chapman* v. *Honig* [1963] 2 Q.B. 502, discussed at pp. 23–26 of *The Due Process of Law*. Both this case and *Att.-Gen.* v. *Butterworth and Others* [1963] 1 Q.B. 696 show Lord Denning protecting the legal process and the authority of the law by treating victimisation of a witness as a contempt of court.

[25] [1968] 2 Q.B. 299.

consistently thought criminal trials must be fair to both sides—to the prosecution as well as to the defence, thus in *Sims*,[26] a sodomy case, he took an extensive view as to admissibility of evidence regarding repetitions of similar acts. This was paralled by *Selvey*, again a case involving buggery. There, deciding on a point of law of public importance, he denied there was a general rule that cross-examination of the accused as to previous convictions was not permissible when the defence necessarily (as opposed to unnecessarily) attacked prosecution witnesses. The accused alleged he had been solicited by the complainant who in pique had then implicated the accused. Lord Denning thought the jury should not be left in the dark about the accused's character.[27]

The presumption of innocence until proved guilty and the right not to be punished without a fair trial were given scant weight in *Ross-Clunis* v. *Papadopoullos*, upholding emergency regulations providing for collective fines on the inhabitants of areas in Cyprus which harboured terrorists.[28] A three man Privy Council[29] found the regulations capable of being related to the prescribed purposes of securing public safety and order. Because the District Commissioner had familiarised himself with the facts of terrorist outrages and then held an advertised public meeting to which councillors and Mukhtars were invited as well as publicising invitations for representations, the Privy Council held he had, as required, satisfied himself that the inhabitants had had an adequate opportunity of understanding the subject matter of the enquiry and of making representations thereon. His satisfaction was subjective, and only if there had been "*no* grounds" on which he could be satisfied would the court intervene. A similarly indulgent approach to Colonial Office actions was taken in his judgment in *Mungoni* v. *Attorney-General of Northern Rhodesia*, refusing to uphold a first instance award of damages for false imprisonment under a detention order by taking the view that the Governor could both delegate his *power* to make such orders and his *duty* under Emergency Regulations to be satisfied that it was necessary to exercise control over any person.[30]

A negative attitude to the English courts' jurisdiction to examine exercises of the Crown's power in protectorates was taken in *Nyali Ltd.* v. *Attorney-General*, Denning L.J. going so far as to say that the courts should not mark out the limits as the Crown's power under a treaty, instead accepting its view as to the extent of Crown jurisdiction.[31]

Lord Denning's palpable inclination to treat colonial territories differently

---

[26] *R.* v. *Sims* [1946] K.B. 531, a case subsequently subjected to much criticism in the Privy Council and ultimately heavily distinguished by the House of Lords.

[27] [1967] 3 W.L.R. 1637.

[28] [1958] 1 W.L.R. 546 (P.C.).

[29] We cannot know whether Lord Denning dissented, but he certainly shares collective responsibility. Arguably such punishment is also degrading and in breach of Art. 3 of the European Convention. The European Commission on Human Rights on June 2, 1956 declared the case of *Greece* v. *United Kingdom* (Application 176/56) admissible. Owing to a political settlement the Commission's report on the merits has never been published.

[30] [1960] A.C. 336 (P.C.).

[31] [1956] 1 Q.B. 1. *Cf.* Morris L.J. at pp. 21–23 who would have looked at the limits of jurisdiction. That Lord Denning's approach was conservative in comparison with those of his contemporaries is shown by *Re Mwenya* [1959] 1 Q.B. 241 (C.A.).

from the United Kingdom and foreshadowing his attitude towards immigrants and citizens of the United Kingdom and Colonies seeking entry (*cf.* the right to enter his own country under Article 13.4 of the International Covenant) appeared in his first reported case under the Commonwealth Immigrants Act 1962. Mauritian citizens of the United Kingdom and Colonies were issued passports by the colonial Governor of Mauritius, a colony set up under the royal prerogative and without any power over foreign affairs. Such passports were watermarked "United Kingdom of Great Britain and Northern Ireland" and stated that they remained "the property of Her Majesty's Government in the United Kingdom." It was then argued that the holders had passports "issued . . . by the government of the United Kingdom," in which event they could come into the United Kingdom without restriction.

Lord Denning's response was:

> "it would mean that the territories in like situation to Mauritius—and several were mentioned to us such as Hong Kong, Fiji, Gibraltar and St. Helena—would be in the same position. The result would be that all people coming from these countries would be entitled to come into England as of right. That cannot be correct."[32]

Lord Denning then inferred that, because the Act expressly provided that the Channel Islands and Isle of Man were to be treated as though they were part of the United Kingdom, while there was silence as to the colonial territories of the Queen which had not yet achieved independence, Parliament intended immigration controls to apply not only to independent Commonwealth countries but to non-independent colonies run by United Kingdom Colonial Office officials.

In contrast, when it was convenient to assert United Kingdom authority there was no hesitation. Thus, in *Sabally* v. *Attorney-General*[33] he held valid an Order in Council retrospectively validating the electoral register in the Gambia and resulting in a legislature in which the representatives of the Colony of Gambia were greatly outnumbered by those of Gambia Protectorate, and which was to be the legislature of a new State created by merger of colony and protectorate and shortly to be given independence. Behind the legal issue of whether a retrospective Order in Council was permissible lay the real issue, namely one of the right to self-determination (Article 1(1) of the International Covenant) of the people of the Colony.

Retrospectivity was not an issue which worried Lord Denning. In *Attorney-General* v. *Vernazza*,[34] dealing with a vexatious litigant who was abusing the judicial machinery, he interpreted the Supreme Court of Judicature (Amendment) Act 1959 to give the court power to stay proceedings which had been commenced before the Act's enactment, and went out of his way to endorse wartime decisions upholding interpretations of Acts so as retrospectively to increase penalties after the commission of an offence. Such dicta would now conflict with Article 15 of the International Covenant. So in reality would *Sykes* v. *D.P.P.*, resurrecting the offence of

---

[32] *R.* v. *Secretary of State for the Home Department, ex p. Shadeo Bhurosah* [1967] 3 All E.R. 831, 833.
[33] [1964] 1 Q.B. 273.
[34] [1960] A.C. 965 (H.L.).

misprision of felony, although it had been so little invoked that it was generally thought obsolete.[35] What is more, the right to privacy and family life received short shrift in connection with misprision. Lord Denning held that close family ties will not suffice when offences of so serious a character ought to be reported. Obviously "the merits" affected him, as it was clear that the accused was involved in receiving stolen United States Air Force arms and attempting to sell them to the I.R.A., but could not be convicted of receiving because there was no evidence that he had been in possession of such arms. Again *D.P.P.* v. *Smith*,[36] retrospectively changed the circumstances in which an accused would be guilty of murder by making the intent to some extent objective, as also did *Attorney-General for Northern Ireland* v. *Gallagher*[37] and *Bratty* v. *Attorney-General for Northern Ireland*.[38] In *Bratty* the scope for arguing non-criminality by reason of automatism was much reduced. In *Gallagher* Lord Denning cut down any possible defence based on such drunkenness that no intent could be formed. The "morality" or otherwise of the accused dictated the result for him. He thought "the law should take a clear stand." Referring to the "wickedness" of the accused's mind before he got drunk, Denning considered that this was enough to condemn him when coupled with the act that when sober he had intended to do and had done when drunk.

It becomes transparently obvious that Lord Denning had a gut reaction to criminals, especially sexual criminals[39] and fraudsters.[40] His view that wrongdoers should be punished and disciplined led him into refusing to apply the *ne bis eadem* principle and upholding subsequent suspension of certain road-haulage licences when a road-haulage firm had already been convicted, punished and "taught a lesson." He considered disciplinary bodies (such as the bar) should have such powers for subsequent exercise, this being good for the whole profession as a deterrent to others.

So far as concerns public powers of law enforcement the capacity of officers of the law to take effective action clearly outweighed, in Denning's judgments, various individual rights. The first indication came in *Southam* v. *Smout*[41] when, after a lot of bombast about the poorest man in his cottage and

---

[35] [1962] A.C. 528 (H.L.).

[36] [1960] A.C. 290. Interestingly his verbal formulation of an objective test for intent conflicts with his subjective view of intent in constructive desertion cases: see *Hosegood* v. *Hosegood* (1950) 66 T.L.R. (Pt. 1) 735, 738, views relied on by the Court of Criminal Appeal. Lord Denning was so taken aback at the unwonted criticism that in a lecture in 1961 he gave an apologia: see "Responsibility before the Law." Conscious of his image, he was still emphasising his views in *Hardy* v. *Motor Insurers Bureau* [1964] 2 Q.B. 745.

[37] [1963] A.C. 349 (H.L.).

[38] [1963] A.C. 386 (H.L.).

[39] *Cf. D.P.P.* v. *Head* [1959] A.C. 83 (H.L.) in which other Law Lords made the point that going to prison should not depend on the distinction between void and voidable. Lord Denning seemed more concerned that if the detention were void the Secretary of State would be liable for damages for 10 years of unlawful detention. *Cf.* his tenderness for the taxpayer's interest in arguing that the National Health Service should not pay large damages for pain and suffering and loss of amenities in *Lim Poo Choo* v. *Camden and Islington Area Health Authority* [1979] 1 Q.B. 196.

[40] See *Welham* v. *D.P.P.* [1960] A.C. 103 (H.L.) where he treated intent to defraud as the equivalent of intent to deceive, so that, even where no economic loss was intended, if an accused deceived a person into doing something he would not otherwise have done there was a fraud, a view that was not inherent in the wording of the Act and was contrary to the views of most modern commentators.

[41] [1964] 1 Q.B. 308.

references to *Freedom Under the Law,* Lord Denning extended an 1851 case expressly confined to a stable to a dwelling house, holding that, provided they knocked, bailiffs could open an unlocked door and enter a house, there being, by reason of leaving a door unlocked, an implied invitation for all with lawful business to come in. Such a novel ruling ("the law has not been settled until this moment") constitutes a gross breach of the right to privacy and the right of an owner or occupier to control entry to his property.

The powers of a police constable received a boost from dicta in *Dallison* v. *Caffery* when, Lord Denning held that

> "When a constable has taken into custody a person reasonably suspected of felony, he can do what is reasonable to investigate the matter ... He can for instance take the person suspected [who had been arrested elsewhere] to his own house to see whether any of the stolen property is there else it may be removed and valuable evidence lost ... So long as such measures are taken reasonably, they are an important adjunct to the administration of justice. By which I mean of course, justice not only to the man himself, but also to the community at large."[42]

The suspect was not taken immediately to a police station or taken before a magistrate, being taken for over six hours on various investigatory trips in the London area. This was not considered by Lord Denning to be a false imprisonment, although it is doubtful whether it conforms to the requirements, both under Article 9.3. of the Covenant and Article 5(3) of the European Convention, that an arrested person be brought "promptly" before a judicial officer.

In yet another action for false imprisonment Lord Denning was to extend powers of arrest without warrant. Section 6(4) of the Road Traffic Act 1960 gave powers of arrest without warrant in respect of a "person committing an offence." Pointing to the danger to the public arising from apparently drunken driving, he held persons *apparently* committing an offence could be arrested under the section provided that the facts, as they appeared to the arresting officer at the time, were such that they would have warranted his bringing the persons arrested before a court. The judge was, in such a case, to tell the jury what facts would give the officer reasonable grounds for his belief.[43]

When matters touched on the security of the state Lord Denning was in no doubt as to which way any decision should go, no matter by what grandiloquent references to freedom and the duty of courts to intervene should the facts justify it he might preface his decision. For close Denning-watchers the judgment which proved his "state-mindedness" was the *Soblen* case,[44] though an adulatory press only began to have doubts 15 years later with the *Hosenball* decision[45] and even then for full appreciation of his stance had themselves to be touched by the *Granada* case,[46] making

---

[42] [1965] 1 Q.B. 348, 367. These dicta go wider than his subsequent dicta in *Ghani* v. *Jones* [1970] 1 Q.B. 693, 706. See the discussion as to the scope of search powers in his home when a suspect is arrested elsewhere in *Jeffrey* v. *Black* [1978] Q.B. 490.

[43] *Wiltshire* v. *Barrett* [1966] 1 Q.B. 312. Criticised in *Wills* v. *Bowley* [1983] A.C. 57.

[44] *R.* v. *Secretary of State for Home Affairs, ex p. Soblen* [1963] 1 Q.B. 829.

[45] *R.* v. *Secretary of State for Home Affairs, ex p. Hosenball* [1977] 1 W.L.R. 776.

[46] *British Steel Corporation* v. *Granada Television* [1980] 3 W.L.R. 774.

investigative journalism more difficult by denying journalists an absolute right not to reveal their sources of information. The paradox is that Lord Denning's predilection for bringing down the balance in favour of the State and the principles on which he would act had been clearly set out by him in *Attorney-General* v. *Mulholland*[47]:

> "A judge is the person entrusted, on behalf of the community, to weigh these conflicting interests—to weigh on the one hand the respect due to confidence in the profession and on the other hand the ultimate interest of the community in justice being done, or in the case of a tribunal such as this, in a proper investigation being made into these serious allegations."[48]

The cases discussed are not mere random samplings of Lord Denning's pre-1968 reported judgments, but emerge from surveying all cases reported in the *All England Reports*[49] of significance in the areas of state interest, police powers and criminal law. They are not counter-balanced by noteworthy reported judgments *in the same area* striking the balance in favour of individual liberty, a fair criminal trial, non-retrospectivity, the scope of the criminal law, privacy and property rights as against official power, and rights of entry to the United Kingdom. There is one exception, but that was really the work of Lord Goddard, who directed the issue of a writ of habeas corpus when the Army authorities treated a released soldier as if he were a member of the regular forces, arrested him, transported him to Germany, and court martialed him.[50]

Only belatedly, with *Chic Fashions*,[51] reinforced by *Ghani* v. *Jones*,[52] *Schmidt*,[53] *Benaim and Khaida*,[54] and the *ASLEF* (*No.*2) case,[55] did younger academics and the profession generally begin to appreciate that Lord Denning did not always favour individual rights. That he would in many spheres bring the balance down in favour of state authority should however, have been predicted from a careful reading of *Freedom Under the Law*.[56] He believed that the executive should be trusted because of the calibre of the men who administer powers and because of a vigilant parliament.[57] He had

---

[47] [1963] 2 Q.B. 477, 488.

[48] The Vassall Tribunal involved inquiry into Navy security. Lord Denning's "statemindedness" (known to Mr. Macmillan else he would not have appointed him to inquire into the Profumo affair) was apparently ignored, as was the fact that his brother, Norman, was Director of Naval Intelligence. *The Family Story*, pp. 118–119, shows Lord Denning acquired information from Norman, and effectively explains his attitude in *Broome* v. *Cassell and Co.* [1971] 2 Q.B. 354.

[49] It is assumed that unreported judgments of significance would have been cited by the profession and subsequently reported, or would have been quoted by Lord Denning himself in his trilogy about his life's work.

[50] *R.* v. *Governor of Wormwood Scrubs Prison, ex p. Boydell* [1948] 2 Q.B. 193.

[51] *Chic Fashions (West Wales) Ltd.* v. *Jones* [1968] 2 Q.B. 299.

[52] [1970] 1 Q.B. 693.

[53] *Schmidt* v. *Secretary of State for Home Affairs* [1969] 2 Ch. 149.

[54] *R.* v. *Gaming Board for Great Britain, ex p. Benaim and Khaida* [1970] 2 Q.B. 417.

[55] *Secretary of State for Employment* v. *ASLEF* (*No. 2*) [1972] 2 Q.B. 455.

[56] See pp. 103–111 and especially p. 107 for his approval of *Elias* v. *Pasmore* [1934] 2 K.B. 164 and *Thomas* v. *Sawkins* [1935] 2 K.B. 249. Approval of such decisions by a lawyer who had lived through the 1930s would be regarded by liberal lawyers of the period as a litmus paper test for support of state authority.

[57] *Freedom Under the Law*, p. 16.

an idealised view of the police.[58] He recognised that "increasing powers of the executive . . . are an inseparable part of modern society," and then reverted to his emphasis on balance:

> "At every point, however, these powers involve interference with private rights and interests; *and granting that private rights must often be subordinated to the public good* (my emphasis) it is essential in a free community to strike a just balance in the matter."[59]

In reality he had an authoritarian approach—as is in one sense inevitable with all who are interventionist, whether of the right or the left. Why he has become increasingly controversial and criticised is because he has been so articulate about justice and individual liberty, and about his allegiance to English[60] spiritual, moral and constitutional traditions, while his judgments have clearly indicated the influence the values he has imbibed in the course of his life—namely morality, honesty, patriotism, courage and conscientiousness (in the sense of being hard-working)—have had on his choice of the appropriate place for the striking of the balance between individual right and the public interest, or as to what was just in the particular case. His perceptions as to English traditions and values obviously differ greatly from those of many other Englishmen, who have grown up or been educated in a different English tradition, or who come from a subsequent generation. As indicated earlier, some labour lawyers took a less than favourable view of Lord Denning long before his recent judgments. Professor Griffith, well within the academic tradition, although necessarily selective with his cases in so short a volume, made fair points, long known to the Inns, about Lord Denning's attitudes, *inter alia*, to immigrants (rights to freedom of entry) to squatters (right to housing) and to students (right to an effective remedy). Those in the tradition of radical dissent saw Lord Denning as reflecting the views of the English ruling class—even though his own immediate family origins were far from privileged—while a writer in *The New Statesman* suggested "how close is Denning's philosophy to that of the National

---

[58] *Ibid.* p. 24: "The police are, on the whole, such a fine body of men that they do not abuse the powers which they have."

[59] *Ibid.* p. 99. See also p. 23 dealing with police powers and individual freedom: "it is simply a question of balancing the conflicting interests."

[60] His consciousness of Englishness is not always expressed in well-chosen language. It is contrasted with foreign attitudes and "the English view of human society": *Freedom Under the Law*, p. 4. The attitudes of the English people are "born in them. We know in our bones . . . ": *The Changing Law*, p. 4. His family background is described in chauvinistic language: *The Family Story*, pp. 5–8. His judgments have often expressed implicit disapproval of foreign parts and foreigners as in *Re Weston's Settlements* [1969] 1 Ch. 234 (persons who settled in Jersey *must* be tax-evaders); *Lim Poo Choo*, above; and *De Falco* v. *Crawley Borough Council* [1980] Q.B. 460. His descriptions of parties as "of German origin" (see *The Due Process of Law*, p. 182) or as Greeks (*The Due Process of Law*, p. 141) are irrelevant and condescending. References to "the Jews" in English history and to the Jewish race (*Freedom Under the Law*, pp. 48–51) are insensitive and condescending as well as historically inaccurate in implying that England was immune from persecution and discrimination. Equally lacking understanding of the feelings of black people were some of his remarks in the withdrawn edition of *What Next in the Law*, where it was obvious that he considered that the obtaining of a jury ethnically representative of the inhabitants of an area in Bristol was "packing" and that it had led to a failure of justice. It is ironic to contrast this view with his views on the value of a jury in cases involving freedom of speech and the right of a jury to give a general verdict because "the judges . . . may not always see clearly on a question of freedom of speech because of their own predilections on the matter in hand": *Freedom Under the Law*, pp. 39–40.

Association for Freedom and the right wing of the Tory Party."[61] The younger (though now perhaps becoming middle-aged) generation of Marxist lawyers, engaging in their alternative legal discourse, would see Denning as underpinning the dominant forces within the social formation, upholding the superstructure, and as articulating "in many instances the dominance of a ruling fragment."[62] Conventional British philosophers would certainly characterise Lord Denning as a naive utilitarian.

Lest it be thought that, by referring at length to criticisms of his values and to his manifestations of "statemindedness," this essay is unbalanced, much of the rest will show that in other areas of law where either different rights (*e.g.* freedom of speech, rights to an effective remedy, a fair civil trial) or the same rights in different contexts (*e.g.* where property rights were being arbitrarily affected) or any question of abuse of power arose, Lord Denning would strike a very different balance that could be characterised as individualist. But, before examining his overall record, certain fundamental points about judicial decision-making require emphasis.

The varying perceptions of Lord Denning's attitudes as manifested in his decisions point up the inevitability of differences of opinion when the values of a decision-maker so obviously influence his choice, and when the criteria for his decision-making are so open-textured, as are the striking of a balance between competing public interests or the ensuring of justice on the merits.

Before criticising Lord Denning for adopting a trite or simplistic balancing approach, it is as well to ask what alternatives there were. After all, a judge has quickly to decide in an unending stream of cases, and to choose between competing contentions put forward on behalf of conflicting interests standing for different values: enforcing one man's right usually invades another man's rights and interests and often affronts his values. Few judges (or academics) are intellectually capable of developing coherent principles of decision-making, and they have not the time to philosophise when setting out their reasons in an often *extempore* judgment. In any event, if philosophy could provide an effective guide to good decision-making, then philosophers would long ago have been harnessed as judges. The reality is that applying principles or rules to facts is extraordinarily difficult, and, apart from pleas of guilty, there are almost no open and shut cases. Judging in appeal courts, where "the trouble cases" come, and where Lord Denning spent most of his judicial life, is even more difficult.

If it is argued that Lord Denning might have relied to a greater extent on the legal rules, applying these faithfully to the facts so as to ensure a greater degree of certainty, there are two answers. First, many of the same critics would have accused him of being non-activist and conservative. Second, more seriously, the existence of rules does not give certainty, because every rule provides pegs for spectra of more or less persuasive arguments as to interpretation, quite apart from inevitable discretion in categorising the facts and applying the rules to the categorisations. Far from there being uncertainty when appearing before Lord Denning, counsel could predict whether he would be with them; the uncertainty was whether he would sit or not. It cannot be bad for any judicial system for the profession—as well as Ministers and officials—to feel that if matters went on appeal there was a

---

[61] Jeremy Smith, *New Statesman* July 19, 1979, p. 78.
[62] *Justice, Lord Denning and the Constitution* (1981), p. 224, n. 46.

chance (and, if it was a significant case, a virtual certainty) that someone like Lord Denning would be there doing justice on the merits.

If critical emphasis is placed on the lack of complexity and refinement, *i.e.* simplicity of Lord Denning's balancing test, this implies that a more complex test or set of tests would have made answers either easier to reach, more certain, or less discretionary. It has already been argued that it is fallacious to think that any of these results could be achieved as a consequence of using different tests.

What can however be asked is whether, when applying his chosen (balancing) test and in developing the law Lord Denning was sufficiently analytical. As Robert Stevens observed:

> "Denning came through as a judge who shot from the hip and who, despite his prominence, gave scant thought either to the juristic techniques available to him or to the constitutional implications of his approach. His commitment to judicial legislation was clear, but the public nuances of judicial restraint and activism were overlooked in the hectic judicial life.[63]

Stevens is only partly right. Lord Denning thought about his methodology, but not deeply enough to realise the long term constitutional implications for the judiciary consequent upon his approach. He seized on the merits as he saw them, and chose a technique which would enable him to rationalise his desired result. One wonders whether Lord Denning was sufficiently afflicted by doubt—but then can a working judge afford to indulge in the luxury of that state of mind?

Nonetheless, there are simple questions, which, adapted to his specific functions, every decision-maker should systematically ask himself. In the case of a judge, it is suggested that they are:

(a) Whence? What was the starting point? What was the accepted state of the law and the relative relationships of the parties or interests involved before any dispute? Is it desirable that the *status quo ante* be maintained?

(b) Why? What gave rise to the dispute? What are the facts, assuming them to be determinable?

(c) Who? Who are the parties (nominal and real) and what interests and values do they represent? Would the result be different if other parties or interests were involved?

(d) When? At what time is this issue being raised and what effect should time and surrounding circumstances have upon any decision or rule to be laid down?

(e) What? What are the legal issues and the issues behind the legal façade?

(f) Where? Where should the line be drawn? Where do the merits lie?

(g) How? Which methodology is most appropriate for rationalising the decision?

(h) Whither? What will this decision do to the future state of the law, to the interests involved and to the role of the courts? Will it be exploitable?

---

[63] *Law and Politics: The House of Lords as a Judicial Body, 1800–1976* (Weidenfeld and Nicolson, 1979), p. 503.

It is of failure to ask the last set of questions that Lord Denning must be suspected. It is apparent that he impetuously characterised the merits without assessing long-term impact, perhaps appropriately for one who thought precedent discardable.

Indeed, his good record in contributing to the right to an effective remedy is marred by cases making exceptions because Lord Denning felt the applicant was opprobrious.[64] Such criticism can of course go too far. It is perverse to suggest that when he stretched the law to give family and persons not covered by the Rent Acts or enjoying contractual rights a right to housing by developing doctrine concerning licences he was reorientating the common law to emasculate the provisions of the Rent Acts.[65] To suggest that he sought to erode and virtually deprive tenants of statutory protection is turning truth on its head. In fact, the reported cases in Lord Denning's period when he sat frequently in Rent Acts and landlord and tenant cases (until mid–1957) show that this is a calumny on Lord Denning who, by more than a two to one ratio, found in favour of tenants, only finding for landlords where tenants sought to exploit their position, to claim protection well outside the scope of the Acts or had unlawfully sublet.[66] It would be far nearer the truth for landlords to complain that Denning was concerned to protect tenants at their expense—and not merely in the immediate post-war period.[67] Mixing metaphors, the reality is that the devil can quote scripture, and that ingenious lawyers can always use any peg to swing from right to left or wrong, so that it is almost impossible to see how dicta will be exploited. Thence, of course, the caution of other judges.

Perhaps the most fundamental point about judicial decision-making requires emphasis. As Professor Griffith points out:

> "The judiciary in any modern industrial society, however composed, under whatever economic system, is an essential part of the system of government and . . . its functions may be described as under-pinning the stability of that system and as protecting that system from attack by resisting attempts to change it."[68]

He continues:

> "In both capitalist and communist societies, the judiciary has naturally served the prevailing political and economic forces. Politically, judges are parasitic.
>
> That this is so is not a matter for recrimination. It is idle to criticize institutions for performing the task they were created to perform and have performed for centuries. It is possible to criticize the police if they use excessive force or illegal means in maintaining law and order, but to criticize them for fulfilling their functions is absurd. So also with the judiciary. Their principal function is to support the institutions of government as established, by law. To expect a judge to advocate

---

[64] See, *e.g. Ward* v. *Bradford Corporation* [1972] 70 L.G.R. 27 and *Cinnamond* v. *British Airports Authority* [1980] 1 W.L.R. 582.

[65] "Sabotaging the Rent Acts," in *Justice, Lord Denning and the Constitution*, above, p. 208.

[66] See further on this matter McAuslan Chap. 5, pp. 163–170.

[67] The *All England Reports* for 1955, Vol. 3, give a more characteristic snapshot of Lord Denning: see *Morcom* v. *Campbell-Johnson*, p. 264; *Sills* v. *Watkins*, p. 319; and *Wheeler* v. *Mercer*, p. 455.

[68] *The Politics of the Judiciary* (Fontana, 1977), p. 213.

radical change, albeit legally, is as absurd as it would be to expect an
anarchist to speak up in favour of authoritarian society. The confusion
arises when it is pretended that judges are somehow neutral in the
conflicts between those who challenge existing institutions and those
who control those institutions."[69]

Lord Denning's hyperbole about judicial independence has caused some
public confusion and cynicism. Yet he is a noble and sincere man, as all who
know him say, and as is transparent in *The Family Story*. Apart from the odd
doubt, when almost in his eighties and when dealing with the House of
Lords, he believed that the judges consistently stood between individuals
and the state, and he always believed in their independence in the sense of
their not being influenced by reward or penalty. If asked to define his use of
"independence" more precisely, he would have agreed with Professor
Griffith that the judges are not neutral when social order is under threat.

On one matter of profound significance to the preservation of freedoms
and to the health of British political society he and Professor Griffith agree.
The ability of the press and vigilant individuals to publicise breaches of
freedoms, taken together with the continuing vulnerability of public officials
and powerful private interests to accusations that freedoms are being
infringed, are major determinants of the continuance of civil and political
rights.[70] Freedom of speech for individuals and the press has been one of
Lord Denning's favourite themes since 1949.[71] Except in the area, always
sensitive with him, of state security, his judgments are consistent in
furthering freedom of speech and of the press to seek and impart
information. He has restricted the law of contempt of court (with some
exceptions occasioned by, inevitably, what he sees as misbehaviour),[72] in
general encouraging investigative journalism. He has extended defences in
the law of libel.[73] He has tried to stop "gagging writs."[74] He has widened the
scope of discovery orders, stopping unnecessary claims to secrecy. In general

[69] *Ibid.* p. 215.
[70] *The Politics of the Judiciary*, p. 214.
[71] *Freedom Under the Law*, pp. 35 *et seq.*; *The Changing Law*, p. 7: "The keystone of our political
liberty is freedom of discussion"; and p. 10: "The only real check on their power
[governments] is the force of public opinion. This brings me back to the importance of
freedom of discussion."
[72] *Home Office* v. *Harman* [1981] 2 W.L.R. 310: "a gross breach of the undertaking which she
impliedly gave to the court and affirmed in writing to the Treasury Solicitor." See *British Steel
Corporation* v. *Granada Television* [1980] 3 W.L.R. 774.
[73] *Slim* v. *Daily Telegraph* [1968] 2 Q.B. 157.
[74] *Wallersteiner* v. *Moir* [1974] 1 W.L.R. 991, 1004. Here Lord Denning was following the lead of
Salmon L.J., in *Thomson* v. *Times Newspapers Ltd.* [1969] 1 W.L.R. 1236. Salmon L.J. has
several times alerted Lord Denning to arguments for asserting rights. Thus the arguments for
a right to a fair trial by way of discovery were first effectively rehearsed by Salmon in *Re
Grosvenor Hotel, London (No. 2)* [1965] Ch. 1210. This raises an interesting question as to the
influence on Lord Denning of colleagues whom he respected: *e.g.* when sitting with Scarman
L.J., as in *R.* v. *Home Secretary, ex p. Phansopkar* [1976] Q.B. 606, Lord Denning, after being
caustic about "patriality" and its acquisition, did recognise that "the most precious right that
anyone can have" (abode in the United Kingdom) could be exercised by the wives of
immigrants who had acquired patriality. Similarly, under Lord Evershed M.R.'s guidance
and that of divisions of the Court of Appeal to which he allocated Denning L.J., there was, it
becomes apparent from perusing the reports, a restraining effect on Denning's waywardness,
e.g. Somervell, Denning and Romer L.JJ. worked well together, as did Singleton, Denning
and Hodson L.JJ.

he has encouraged the creation of an informed public opinion and an ability outspokenly to criticise authority.

Paradoxically, Lord Denning and Griffith agree that a judicially enforceable United Kingdom Bill of Rights is undesirable. Griffith is opposed because, if there were a Bill (Bills merely dressing up competing claims by individuals and groups in the language of rights), even more political decisions would pass out of the hands of politicians into those of judges,[75] whereas politicians are at least more vulnerable to public criticism and to dismissal.[76] Lord Denning is opposed because a Bill of Rights would tie the judges' hands by removing their virtually unfettered discretion when seeking to protect liberty. Yet he vacillated in 1979 about the desirability of incorporating the European Convention on Human Rights into domestic law. He used as cover for his change of mind the *Thalidomide* case, wherein the House of Lords had denied the *Sunday Times* a right to continue publishing articles on whether the Distiller's Company had been guilty of negligence in its production and continued marketing of thalidomide because actions were still pending, and such publicity was intended to bring pressure to bear on the Company, thereby prejudicing a fair trial.[77] He also referred to *UKAPE* v. *ACAS*, obviously expecting their Lordships' reversal of his judgment that the right of association gave a worker the rights to join a union of his choice and to have such chosen union recognised.[78]

Lord Denning publicly stated:

> "But what has changed my mind is the tendency of some judges nowadays to forget that it is their duty to protect human rights. You will find that some of them go by the literal interpretation of Acts of Parliament and allow them to operate so as to make drastic inroads into our fundamental freedoms. It is time that there was some superior law by which the judges would be bound to give effect to human rights . . .
> So in regard to human rights today, I have changed my mind. At first I was against it, but now on the whole, I am for it; because some of the judges are not strong enough, some of them. In the old days the judges could and did protect our fundamental freedoms. The judges of today do not seem inclined to do it somehow."[79]

In reality his change of mind arose out of his opposition to Parliament's extension of trade union immunities[80] and from his differences with the House of Lords about the interpretation of such immunity under the Trade Union and Labour Relations Act 1974 as amended in 1976.[81] He had since 1955 asserted the freedom of persons to go about their business in peace undisturbed by industrial confrontations,[82] and, if asked to specify the

---

[75] "The Political Constitution," (1979) 42 M.L.R. 1, 16.
[76] *Ibid.* p. 18.
[77] *Att.-Gen.* v. *Times Newspapers Ltd.* [1973] Q.B. 10, reversed in [1974] A.C. 273.
[78] [1979] 1 W.L.R. 570. The House of Lords had not given judgment, but did so shortly thereafter, reversing Lord Denning.
[79] The Lord Fletcher Lecture, delivered December 10, 1979. See *Guardian Gazette*, Vol. 76, No. 45, 19.12.79, pp. 1–2.
[80] *What Next in the Law*, p. 321. It was because of these Acts that Lord Denning wished Parliament's power to be limited by judicial review of statutes.
[81] For a detailed account see the essay by Davies and Freedland, Chap. 8.
[82] See *The Road to Justice*, pp. 104–105.

infringed freedoms, would have referred to equality before the law (no immunities), the right to an effective remedy, to property rights, to freedom of contract, and to the duty to respect the rights and freedoms of others. He was now publicly criticising the judges for affirming those competing rights (or interests) preferred by Parliament and reflected in the Acts. Ultimately Lord Denning came back to his long standing attitude of opposition to a United Kingdom Bill of Rights. Not only did he fear choking up the courts with frivolous or vexatious actions,[83] but he considered that any Bill modelled on the European Convention on Human Rights and Fundamental Freedoms would, because of the broadness of its statements of principles and of exceptions thereto, give rise to an infinity of arguments.[84] Proposing to rely for the maintenance of rights and freedoms on the prevailing political climate and traditions in England, which he saw as being an "independent" judiciary, he reverted to his old theme, "trust the judges."[85] But not, of course, if they were European.[86] He did not like the judgments of the European Commission on Human Rights, the European Court of Human Rights, and the European Court of Justice at Luxembourg.[87] Their judgments did not accord with his own sense of values and of fitness. When it came to European judges and their enforcement of Bills of Rights he would have agreed with Griffith that

> "The solution to such problems should not lie with the imprecisions of Bills of Rights or the illiberal instincts of judges."[88]

Lord Denning's attitudes prove Griffith's contentions about the political choices inherent in judging, and that for assessment of the results of judicial decisions political opinions are the determinants. References to "rights," "morality" and "justice" are then seen as useful rhetorical adjuncts to use in argument in support of particular political opinions or interest choices.[89]

His consistent broad thrust[90] towards enhanced decision-making power (*i.e.* power of choice) for the English judiciary is manifest in his attitude towards cases coming before him which touched on the European Convention on Human Rights or the rights protected in the Treaty of Rome or by directives thereunder. Manifested too are his eclecticism and idiosyncratic choices, both as to appropriate judicial techniques and as to his

---

[83] *What Next in the Law*, pp. 276, 291, 302.

[84] *Ibid.* p. 291.

[85] *Ibid.* p. 303.

[86] *Ibid.* pp. 291–292. Lord Denning refers to the European Court and Commission of Human Rights as not having the "feel" of a case and to their lack of knowledge of "our way of life" and of "our common law." His earlier remarks make it apparent that his attitude is partly based on their broad approach. This is an apparently inconsistent position for one himself happy to give quasi-legislative guidelines (*Cf. Ghani* v. *Jones* on police rights of search and seizure) and to favour teleological approaches to statutory interpretation. But, as pointed out earlier, Lord Denning's methodology was selected for the particular result he sought.

[87] *Ibid.* pp. 287–292, and 294–301. However, courtesy impelled him to pay lip-service tribute to the work of the European Court at Luxembourg. His deeper feelings as the European tide advanced across the Channel appear in the Lord Fletcher Lecture where, quoting *Shields* v. *E. Coomes (Holdings)* [1978] 1 W.L.R. 1408, 1416, he spoke of the tide of Community Law having "broken the dykes and the banks. It has submerged the surrounding land."

[88] "The Political Constitution" (1979) 42 M.L.R. 1, 14.

[89] *Cf. Ibid.* p. 17.

[90] There were the exceptional deviations occasioned by his view of particular parties.

preferred interests. Thus, in interpreting the European Convention Denning would give it a wide or a narrow interpretation as suited his purpose.[91]

Initially enthusiastic about the Convention once it was raised in litigation before him (doubtless his frequent sitting at that time with Scarman L.J. was influential) Lord Denning even held that were a Statute to conflict with the Convention it would be invalid.[92] He soon recanted this heresy, although he was still of the opinion that the courts should and would take the Convention into account whenever interpreting a statute which affects the rights and liberties of the individual. Consequently, he opined that immigration officers and the Secretary of State in exercising their duties ought to bear in mind the principles stated in the Convention.[93] However, when application of this dictum could have resulted in an immigration officer's discretion in refusing entry to a family being challenged, Denning further limited the effect of the Convention, disputing altogether that it was "part of our law," and holding that immigration officers could not be expected to know or apply the Convention, being confined simply to knowing the Secretary of State's immigration rules.[94] Only in case of "any ambiguity in our statutes or uncertainty in our law" would the Convention be an aid.[95] Nonetheless, the Convention was now, according to Denning, indigestible and so vague as to give much difficulty in application. Indeed some Articles, such as Article 8 (the right to respect for family life) were too wide to be capable of practical application.[96] Similarly, freedom to manifest religion in practice and observance (Article 9) was disregarded as being too vague, as permitting all sorts of unreasonable claims, and as provoking all sorts of litigation.[97] Yet, when the Convention accorded with Denning's view of what was appropriate, Articles would then be cited as stating basic principles of English law.[98] At other times, having to deal with counsel's argument, Lord Denning might embellish his judgment with a reference to the principle set out in the

---

[91] *R.* v. *Home Secretary, ex p. Bhajan Singh* [1975] 3 W.L.R. 225 where Lord Denning, invoking Art. 5(1)(*f*), ruled that Art. 12, recognising the right to marry, was subject to an illegal entrant's lawful detention, so that a prisoner was not entitled to demand facilities to marry at a local registry office, thus being unable to avoid deportation. Lord Denning was obviously reacting to the Home Office's contention that the marriage had been arranged to avoid deportation. In contrast, in *UKAPE* v. *ACAS* [1979] 1 W.L.R. 570, where Lord Denning's sympathy was engaged, freedom of association under Art. 11 was extended to cover a right of an employee that his employer should for negotiating purposes recognise the union of his employee's choice.

[92] *Birdi* v. *Secretary of State for Home Affairs*, February 11, 1975, Bar Library Transcript No.67B.

[93] *R.* v. *Secretary of State for the Home Department, ex p. Bhajan Singh* [1975] 3 W.L.R. 225, 231.

[94] *R.* v. *Chief Immigration Officer, Heathrow Airport, ex p. Salamat Bibi* [1976] 1 W.L.R. 979, 984–985.

[95] Must Common Law principles be applied in such fashion as to reach a result consistent with the Convention? In *Ahmad* v. *Inner London Education Authority* [1978] Q.B. 36, 41, Lord Denning stated: "We will do our best to see that our decisions are in conformity with it."

[96] *Bibi*, above, at p. 985.

[97] *Ahmad, ante*, at p. 41.

[98] See *UKAPE* v. *ACAS* [1979] 1 W.L.R. 570 at p. 582. In *Cheall* v. *APEX* [1983] Q.B. 126 at p. 137 he said: "Article 11(1) . . . is part of the law of England or at any rate the same as the law of England."

Convention and then without weighty reason decline to apply it.[99] He saw the Convention merely as a means to further his ends. In *R.* v. *Home Secretary, ex parte Hosenball*[1] he relied on Convention jurisprudence to limit common law rights, holding that the Commission's decision in the *Agee Case* (No. 7729/76) "confirmed" that the rules of natural justice should be modified where national security was at stake. In two of his last judgments, because he disapproved of English statutory provisions permitting the closed shop to operate, he incited an unsuccessful appellant to seek compensation under Article 11 of the Convention through the Strasbourg machinery.[2]

Lord Denning decided too few cases on EEC Law concerning the Treaty freedoms of movement and establishment of workers, the provision in Article 119 on equal pay for equal work and the Directive against sex discrimination in working conditions to be able to make a major contribution. His approach was somewhat less hostile to EEC Law human rights, than to the European Convention, because EEC Law was "part of our law," so that, despite some tendentious language, he applied Article 119 to hold that a woman counterhand employed in a betting shop in a rough and sometimes violent area was entitled to equal pay with a man although the man also had a protective role.[3] In *Macarthys Ltd.* v. *Smith*[4] he loyally applied EEC Article 119, again emphasising it was not supplanting English law but was "part of our law," and that consequently the Equal Pay Act was overridden to the extent that it was inconsistent with Article 119, thereby holding that employees engaged at different times and doing the same work should be paid the same. However, when he thought arrangements reasonable in themselves, he reacted adversely to his duty to implement the absolute equality dictated by Article 119.[5]

A case illustrating his habit of giving no effect to what he considered inconvenient is *De Falco* v. *Crawley Borough Council*.[6] The rights of EEC workers to freedom of establishment and to equal access to housing and social security were quoted, and then given no weight when upholding a local authority decision to refuse to provide housing to Italian immigrant families on the grounds that by leaving Italy to come to the United Kingdom

---

[99] See *Maynard* v. *Osmond* [1976] 3 W.L.R. 711, where Lord Denning (in dealing with whether a police officer accused of a disciplinary offence was entitled to legal representation at his original hearing) rather than relying on Art. 6(1), providing for minimum rights when charged with a criminal offence, relied instead on a constructional inference that this was excluded because the Police (Appeals) Rules 1965 expressly provided for legal representation on appeal. In *Allgemeine Gold-und Silberscheideanstalt* v. *Customs and Excise Commissioners* [1980] 1 Q.B. 390 he interpreted Art. 1 of the First Protocol to permit forfeiture of property by way of penalty *when such property was not owned by the offenders* but by an innocent third party.

[1] [1977] 1 W.L.R. 766, 779.

[2] See *Taylor* v. *Co-operative Retail Services Ltd.* [1982] I.C.R. 600, and *Cheall* v. *APEX* at p. 137, where Lord Denning hinted that litigants could, if they took trouble and expense, go to Strasbourg.

[3] *Shields* v. *E. Coomes (Holdings) Ltd.* [1978] 1 W.L.R. 1408. His reluctance comes through clearly in *What Next in the Law*, pp. 296–297.

[4] [1980] 3 W.L.R. 929, 948.

[5] *Worringham* v. *Lloyds Bank* [1981] 1 W.L.R. 950. The English statute permitted discrimination in respect of pensions. It worried Lord Denning that the banks had to establish new pension schemes although their original schemes had been lawful at their inception.

[6] [1980] Q.B. 460. Ironically, he refused to interfere with local authority discretion on precisely similar criteria to those invoked by the House of Lords in *UKAPE* v. *ACAS*, a decision of which he was bitterly critical.

they had made themselves "intentionally homeless," thereby disqualifying themselves from demanding local authority housing provision. This decision was combined with chauvinistic remarks about the rising tide of immigration and the burdens placed on local authorities near Gatwick Airport.[7]

All Lord Denning's prejudices manifested themselves in the case of *R.* v. *Secretary of State for the Home Department, ex parte Santillo.*[8] There Lord Denning gave the widest view to the state's power to deport criminals on grounds of *ordre public*, failed to insist on the due process standards required by EEC case law before deportation of a Community national,[9] and modified, with possible long term adverse effects, the application of the common law rules of natural justice so as to deny a fair hearing. The deportee was a sex criminal serving a long term of imprisonment.

In evaluating his contribution to the Bills of Rights debate several points must be made. First, Lord Denning's free-ranging choices are not merely manifestations of his own distinctive judicial personality, but are inherently available in any Bill of Rights. As Griffith said of the formulation of Article 10 of the European Convention (dealing with freedom of expression and the possible restrictions thereon):

> "This sounds like the statement of a political conflict pretending to be a resolution of it."[10]

Second, adoption of a bill of Rights, as Griffith has sarcastically put it, means that

> "questions . . . will be left for determination by the legal profession as they embark on the happy and fruitful exercise of interpreting woolly principles and even woollier exceptions."[11]

The point concerning professional participation must be emphasised: Lord Denning was, like other judges, much influenced by the presentation of particular counsel.[12]

More significantly, the transfer to the judges of an even greater volume of political decision-making, particularly in the most controversial and publicised cases, cannot but lead to charges of political partisanship. To

---

[7] In the Lord Fletcher Lecture Lord Denning was even more blunt. He said "Two Italian families got to know of the Common Market. They heard there was freedom of movement of workers. Each family had little babies. Take one as an example. The husband was out of work in Naples. He had been out of work for 12 months. He had a brother-in-law here at Crawley near Gatwick Airport. He told him, I expect: 'England is a good place to come to. There is social security here. There is a new Act for housing the homeless. Why not come here?' So the man, his wife and baby packed up their belongings. They came lock, stock and barrel to Gatwick Airport."

[8] [1981] 2 W.L.R. 362.

[9] *Cf. Rutili* v. *Ministry of Interior of French Republic* [1975] E.C.R. 1219, and *R.* v. *Bouchereau* [1978] 2 W.L.R. 250 (E.C.J.).

[10] "The Political Constitution," p. 14.

[11] *Ibid.*

[12] *Cf. Peake* v. *Automative Products Ltd.* [1977] I.R.L.R. 365, where the plaintiff was unrepresented, with *Ministry of Defence* v. *Jeremiah* [1979] 3 W.L.R. 857. In the latter case Anthony Lester, Q.C. provided the court with a detailed analysis of the authorities under the Sex Discrimination Act, thereby influencing Lord Denning to resile from his dicta in *Peake* that courtesy and chivalry (good motives) or safety and good administrative practice permitted of discriminatory treatment as between men and women employees.

such risks he was by and large insensitive,[13] either being blinkered by his focus on the trustworthiness of English judges, or, with a naivety scarcely credible in the holder of such high office, believing that, if he set out the issues in his story-telling fashion, he would convince the public (including those of very different political persuasions) as to the merits of his decisions.

Fourthly, middle-aged professional men are not prone to questioning or analysing their assumptions about their role or the society in which they function, or to accommodate easily to change. Lord Denning was exceptional in thinking about aspects of judging and of justice as much as he had done earlier between 1949 and 1955 when already in his late forties and fifties. By the time he was forced to deal with international human rights instruments to which the United Kingdom had adhered (and to which the profession was now bringing his attention) or with rights under the new order of EEC law, Lord Denning was in his seventies. In the relatively short period when such a political task became relevant, he was unsuccessful in adopting a new role and reconciling his longstanding perceptions of appropriate behaviour for an English judge applying common law principles with the duty now imposed on the same judge to take heed of international human rights instruments, imported from alien parts, either as interpretative guides or even, in case of EEC law, as part of municipal law. He simply saw such instruments in any particular case as a fetter or as an aid in reaching his desired result.[14]

In the context of any debates about the desirability of enacting a judicially enforceable United Kingdom Bill of Rights *as such,* or about whether human rights in English law have been enhanced by United Kingdom adherence to international human rights instruments, it is a harsh, but not unjust conclusion that Lord Denning's contribution has been that of providing negative evidence in his own person. His judicial behaviour throughout his career, let alone his last decade, and disregarding his use and misuse of human rights instruments, provides the strongest possible argument against a politically "non-responsible" judiciary, and against investing judicial decisions with the finality that follows from a Bill of Rights.

In contrast, Lord Denning's contribution to furtherance of certain individual human rights is vast. Discussion of this contribution raises methodological problems, and, in the compass of this essay, ones of compression. First, whether formulated by philosophers or lawyers, rights are inevitably set out as statements of general individualist principle, subject to equally generally phrased qualifications, limitations or restrictions, either in the interests of some competing public policy or some other individual or group. The international human rights instruments themselves conceal deep divisions about priorities and do not resolve them. All that can be done, without excessively intruding one's own preferences, is here to say whether Lord Denning has leaned towards one principle or another, or towards one

---

[13] See however *H.L. Deb.,* Vol. 369, cols. 797–798, March 25, 1976, for his opposition to a Bill of Rights because if judges could overthrow Acts of Parliament "they *would become* political, their appointments would be based on political grounds and the reputation of our judiciary would suffer acordingly." Lord Denning also referred to potential conflicts between the judges and the Legislature.

[14] *What Next in the Law,* p. 286, sums up Lord Denning's attitude to the European Convention: "We look at it for help. Sometimes we find it helpful. Sometimes not. Sometimes we think the articles are too general. Sometimes the exceptions do much to wipe out the principle. So we do not spend too much time upon it."

of the limitations, for example, by giving more weight to a fair hearing in the administration of justice than to the competing interests of privacy or confidence. Often this means stating that he has leaned more to the claims of one interest group, dressed up in human rights language, than to the competing claims of another.[15] Of course, leaning in favour of one right rather than another in particular circumstances confirms rather than depreciates the significance of rights in general.

Secondly, analysis in terms of furthering human rights in English law is problematic because of the absence of a comprehensive Bill of Rights.[16] The way around this difficulty is use of the categories of rights listed in international instruments. In this essay the broad concepts and the generalised exceptions will provide the standards, rather than the particular language of the international instruments. Such an approach is necessary because human rights are nowhere all-inclusively stated and because their scope is expanding, particularly by way of the jurisprudence of international enforcement machinery. Thus, the United Nations Committee on Human Rights has been extending Article 2(3)(*a*) and (*b*) of the Civil and Political Rights Covenant so as to confer a right to an effective remedy judicial in character.

Thirdly, confusion should not be occasioned by reason of the fact that human rights issues are infrequently litigated *as such*, instead arising in other contexts and being decided on traditional legal grounds, for example, as in the case of the right to work, on whether or not a restraint on trade exists and whether a non-party to a contract can be granted an injunction,[17] or, as in case of the right to housing, whether statutory powers, under a statute imposing duties in regard to homeless persons upon local authorities, have been reasonably exercised.[18] Human rights thinking is essentially "realist." Indeed, in this connection, Lord Denning has made a major contribution to formalising thinking about human rights in English law by his tendency to formulate issues in terms of rights such as the rights to strike, to work, to have access to information of public concern and to freedom of expression.

Practical difficulties of discussion arise from the number of Denning judgments, with many raising human rights issues because they touch on basic human needs and their satisfaction, or on individual freedom of action and limitations thereto, or on when national, group or other individual interests should prevail. Commentary has had to be minimal, so that cross-reference to other essays has been relied upon. Such reliance has made it sensible here to deal first and cursorily with Lord Denning's contributions in the sphere of economic, social and cultural rights, merely adding uncovered aspects, and then to proceed to his contributions in the sphere of

---

[15] Irony about his unfairness to classes such as squatters, students, immigrants, and taxi-drivers may be misguided. Such classes are of legal significance once they are given a status by virtue of the application to their category of distinctive rules of law.

[16] The Bill of Rights 1688 recognises a limited number of basic civil rights as well as prohibiting certain monarchical behaviour. It gives a general right that the laws be enforced, which Lord Denning once called a right to the rule of law.

[17] In *Nagle* v. *Fielden* [1966] 2 Q.B. 633, 646 Lord Denning first put forward the "right to work at his [her] trade or profession." In *Langston* v. *A.U.E.W.* [1974] 1 W.L.R. 185 the right to work at his employment was constructed by reading an implied term into the employment contract that the employer must provide work.

[18] *De Falco* v. *Crawley Borough Council* [1980] Q.B. 460.

civil and political rights. Repetition has been minimised by concentrating discussion of a case under one rubric, even if it involves several rights, for example personal liberty and fair trial, and by dealing together with rights that overlap or are related, such as equality for men and women, guarantees against discrimination, equality before the law and the equal protection of the laws.

ECONOMIC, SOCIAL AND CULTURAL RIGHTS

The Right to Work and Rights Regarding Trade Unions[19]

Lord Denning has been the leading judicial proponent in developing a right to gain a living by work freely chosen and accepted. A series of adventurous Denning decisions over three decades means that the courts will usually protect such right whether it is in issue in the context of domestic tribunals concerned with licensing, or of professional bodies seeking to impose trading restrictions on their members, or of trade unions attempting to discipline or expel their members or to limit their membership. In each case, as appropriate, the doctrine concerning the natural justice rules, the lawfulness or unreasonableness of association rules, arbitrary or capricious use of discretion, unreasonable restraints of trade, or breach of contract will be invoked.[20]

Lord Denning's perspective, since at least 1952, had been one of seeing the individual's right to work as requiring protection against group freedoms, especially where the group is a trade union which has entered into closed shop arrangements with employers.[21] His own extra-judicial account in 1978 of significant twentieth century legal developments in which he had taken part deals with the cases involving the right to work and voluntary associations' use of their powers against their members under the heading "Abuse of group powers."[22]

When disputes arising from trade union exercises of power came before him, Lord Denning naturally favoured individual freedoms, *inter alia*, the rights to work and to associate freely, and a worker's right not to be expelled from the union of his choice except for reasonable cause and in accordance with natural justice.[23] Lord Denning also asserted an implied right not to

---

[19] Art. 6 (the right to work) and Art. 8 (rights regarding trade unions) in the International Covenant on Economic, Social and Cultural Rights.

[20] *Russell* v. *Duke of Norfolk* [1949] 1 All E.R. 109; *Abbott* v. *Sullivan* [1952] 1 K.B. 189 (Lord Denning's dissent now representing the law); *Lee* v. *Showmen's Guild* [1952] 2 Q.B. 329; *Bonsor* v. *Musician's Union* [1954] Ch. 479 (Lord Denning's dissent now representing the law); *Faramus* v. *Film Artistes' Association* [1963] 2 Q.B. 527 (with Lord Denning dissenting); *Boulting* v. *ACTAT* [1963] 2 Q.B. 606 (with Lord Denning dissenting); *Nagle* v. *Fielden* [1966] 2 Q.B. 633; *Dickson* v. *Pharmaceutical Society of Great Britain* [1967] Ch. 708; *Edwards* v. *SOGAT* [1971] Ch. 354; and *Hill* v. *C.A. Parsons and Co.Ltd.* [1972] Ch. 305. See Davies and Freedland, Chap. 8, pp. 368–375.

[21] See "The Rule of Law in the Welfare State" (Haldane Memorial Lecture) in *The Changing Law* (1953), pp. 35–37, and *The Road to Justice* (1955), pp. 99–103.

[22] *The Discipline of Law*, (1979), pp. 147–174 read with the Preface.

[23] *Cheall* v. *APEX* [1982] 3 W.L.R. 685 (now overruled) is, despite its emotionalism, quite consistent with the decisions protecting union members against abuse of power by their union.

associate, derived from freedom of choice of association.[24] Obviously, in the closed shop context exercise of such right would be followed by effective denial of the right to work. However, even Lord Denning could not avoid such a result in face of the express statutory provisions making it lawful for an employer to enforce a closed shop if this was done in accordance with a union membership agreement between union and employers' association and it was the practice under such agreement for employees to belong to a specified union.[25] Lord Denning had to confine himself to the suggestion that the dismissed employee might have a remedy in Strasbourg for breach of Article 11 of the European Convention, in that his freedom to join the union of his choice was contravened by compulsion, by reason of his dismissal for refusing to join a trade union which operated the closed shop.

Earlier, when in the 1960s trade union dispute techniques had caused disruption and hardship to third parties, Lord Denning had extended the tort of inducing a breach of commercial contract although well before his extensions, rights thinking recognised the concept of a right to enjoy commercial contractual rights free from unlawful interference.[26] In the late 1970s he rhetorically asserted that there was a right to go about one's business in peace.[27] In rights parlance he could equally well have invoked the right to peaceful enjoyment of property, but, probably because in some circles "property" is regarded as an evil and the judiciary is often accused of over-protectiveness to it, he avoided such language. Similarly, awareness of the abuse to which "this catchword freedom of contract" had been put in the nineteenth century[28] precluded use of the latter concept.

Another right, emphatically asserted by Lord Denning in the context of industrial action showing solidarity and sympathy (secondary action by blacking), was the freedom of the press to express opinions free of trade union interference, subject only to such constraints as are afforded by the law regarding libel, confidential information or contempt.[29] Interference with press freedom was, he considered, so contrary to the public interest that it was *per se* unlawful and would therefore constitute the tort of interfering with a business by unlawful means.[30]

---

[24] *Cf.* Art. 22 of the UN Civil and Political Rights Covenant with Art. 20(2) of the Universal Declaration of Human Rights. The latter provision was not incorporated into the Covenant, because of the closed shop system practiced in certain Anglo-Saxon states. The UN Human Rights Committee in 1978 nonetheless raised with the United Kingdom the question whether coercion by an employer to join a labour union was covered by Art. 22.

[25] *Taylor* v. *Co-operative Retail Services Ltd.* [1982] I.C.R. 600.

[26] In *Emerald Construction Company Ltd.* v. *Lowthian* [1966] 1 W.L.R. 691 and *Torquay Hotel Co. Ltd.* v. *Cousins* [1969] 2 Ch. 106, both "blacking" cases, he extended the tort of inducing breach of commercial contract by imposing liability where a union recklessly, even if not knowingly, disregarded the terms of the contract affected, and held that unions would be liable if they hindered or interfered with the execution of contracts, it no longer being necessary to show actual breach. See *The Discipline of Law* (1979), pp. 178–180.

[27] *Express Newspapers Ltd.* v. *McShane* [1979] I.C.R. 210, 218. *Cf. Freedom Under the Law,* (1949), p. 5: "by personal freedom I mean the freedom of every law-abiding citizen to . . . go where he will on his lawful occasions without let or hindrance from other persons."

[28] *Freedom Under the Law* (1949), p. 69.

[29] *Associated Newspapers Group Ltd.* v. *Wade* [1979] 1 W.L.R. 697, 708–709. Lord Denning also invoked Art. 10 of the European Convention (freedom of expression).

[30] Interfering with a business by unlawful means was a newly developed general head of tort in the recognition of which Denning judgments had played a major part. See *Daily Mirror Newspapers Ltd.* v. *Gardner* [1968] 2 Q.B. 762, 783A and *Acrow (Automation) Ltd.* v. *Rex Chainbelt Inc.* [1971] 1 W.L.R. 1676.

Yet Lord Denning partly overcame his reluctance to see effective trade union pressures operating.[31] This he did by asserting a right to strike. His views accord with Article 8(1)(d) of the Economic Rights Covenant, which ensures "the right to strike provided that it is exercised in conformity with the laws of the particular country." He preserved the right to strike by holding that a strike notice and strike are not unlawful as breaching the contract of employment, there being an implication in the contract that, provided any strike notice is of equivalent notice to that required for termination of the employment contract, such notice is to be construed as a notice to suspend the contract.[32] Even in his impassioned judgment in *Associated Newspapers* v. *Wade*, with his peroration on the fundamental principle that "the press shall be free," Lord Denning was concerned to make the *caveat* that newspaper workers could strike for better wages or conditions.[33] Yet, in reality when it came to giving protection to the right to strike he was unwilling to do so.[34]

Overall his individualist approach prevailed, particularly in respect of the statutory trade union recognition procedures which applied in the late 1970s. Thus, where safeguards were afforded, Lord Denning explained that he would construe these in favour of the individual and not of the trade union.[35] His techniques were, as always, eclectic. Thus, in upholding refusal of recognition to a large and militant union, he ignored "the right of trade unions to function freely" and the significance of the right of any worker to join unions "for the promotion and protection of his economic and social interests."[36] The case illustrated a danger of Lord Denning's approach in general. In order to achieve his desired outcome (convenience to the statutory body as employer) he was willing to make countervailing rights formal rather than effective. Arguably his decision was in conflict with Articles 4 and 8 of the Economic Rights Covenant as the restriction (denial of recognition) was incompatible with the nature of the rights, was not "necessary," and was not "solely for the purpose of promoting the general welfare." It also justified charges that he was not principled but capricious (in the sense of being changeable, irregular and appearing to be ungoverned by law).Of course this charge can partly be mitigated by analysing the case as consistent with his overriding desire to do justice on the merits of the facts as he saw them.

---

[31] Effectiveness usually involves economic pressure, which is almost always effectuated unlawfully.

[32] *Morgan* v. *Fry* [1968] 3 All E.R. 452. The Industrial Relations Act 1971, s.143(2) subsequently provided that a strike after due notice was not to be regarded as a breach of contract for the purposes of any tort proceedings. See also Davies and Freedland, Chap. 8 below.

[33] [1979] 1 W.L.R. 697, 709. This is somewhat inconsistent because an effective strike would interfere with the business of their employers, *i.e.* the press, which interference would in itself be unlawful.

[34] *Williams and others* v. *National Theatre Board Ltd.* [1982] I.C.R. 715.

[35] *Grunwick Processing Laboratories Ltd.* v. *ACAS* [1978] A.C. 655, 662.

[36] Art. 8(1)(a) and (c) of the UN Covenant on Economic, Social and Cultural Rights. See *R.* v. *Post Office, ex p. ASTMS* [1981] I.C.R. 76, where, after repeal in 1980 of the recognition procedure supervised by ACAS, the statutory powers of the Post Office as employer were in issue.

Conditions of Work and Social Security Rights[37]

According to the Economic Rights Covenant, the right to just and favourable working conditions must, in particular, be ensured by equal remuneration for work of equal value, equal opportunity in employment and safe and healthy working conditions.

Lord Denning's attitude to just conditions of work has been analysed by Davies and Freedland under the rubric of individual employment law, and some aspects of the right in relation to safe and healthy working conditions have been dealt with under the heading Employer's Liability by Atiyah.[38] However, a comment should be added about the general themes and idiosyncracies arising in the reported cases, some of which still have effect in relation to workers' claims for injuries at work.

Lord Denning gave protection to workers carrying out their jobs on premises not belonging to their employers, a protection particularly necessary before the enactment of the Occupiers Liability Act 1957. He extended the duties of an occupier under the Factories Act to cover independent contractors (themselves in reality often workers) and such contractors' employees,[39] and imposed a duty to provide safe access to work for the employees of independent contractors[40]; he asserted employers' duties to provide a safe system of work[41] and safe access to work at premises to which they were sent.[42] He held that employers' duties under the Factory Acts, even if delegated by an apparently proper system, still remain, with the employer being liable if there is a neglect by either an independent contractor or another employee.[43] Nor will an employee's claim to be protected be lightly cut down by reason of a finding of contributory negligence (the Factories Acts aiming to protect workmen against some inattention) whereas negligent acts by co-workers will be more strictly regarded in order to ground vicarious liability of the employer.[44] Where he was most vehemently outspoken was in seeking to protect workers from unsafe machinery.[45]

In assessing damages Lord Denning sought to avoid hardships. He thus took a generous view in respect of causation of virtually total blindness

---

[37] Art. 7 (the right to just and favourable conditions of work) and Art. 9 (the right of everyone to social security).

[38] Above, Chap. 2. Safe working conditions and state compensation for injuries at work are sometimes aspects of the right to social security.

[39] *Whitby* v. *Burt, Boulton and Hayward* [1947] K.B. 918.

[40] *Lavender* v. *Diamints Ltd.* [1948] 2 All E.R. 249. On the facts he did not award damages, holding the worker, by not providing tackle and safety equipment, was the cause of the accident. He was reversed on this point by the Court of Appeal [1949] 1 K.B. 585) but his dictum that a worker who is contributorily negligent to such an extent that he is virtually the cause of the accident must be awarded no damages, was not pronounced upon.

[41] *Christmas* v. *General Cleaning Contractors Ltd.* [1952] 1 K.B. 141.

[42] *Smith* v. *Austin's Lifts Ltd.* [1959] 1 W.L.R. 100.

[43] *Braham* v. *Lyons and Co. Ltd.* [1962] 1 W.L.R. 1048.

[44] *Jones* v. *Stavely Iron and Chemical Co. Ltd.* [1955] 1 Q.B.474. The decision was affirmed, but Lord Denning's dicta were disapproved by the House of Lords: [1956] A.C. 627.

[45] See *Burns* v. *Joseph Terry and Sons Ltd.* [1950] 1 K.B. 454 (a Denning dissent); *Dickson* v. *Flack* [1953] 2 Q.B. 464 (protection given against flying broken-off pieces of machine); *Close* v. *Steel Co. of Wales* [1960] 2 Q.B. 299 (dissenting in part about the law); and *Stanbrook* v. *Waterlow and Sons Ltd.* [1964] 1 W.L.R. 825 (fencing of printing machinery—perhaps the print unions should forget grievances about the industrial disputes cases and think of this concrete contribution to their workers' safety).

where an employee with one bad eye had his good eye injured at work.[46] He was even willing to make exceptions to the once-and-for-all rule governing assessment of damages and to allow fresh evidence where, shortly, after the award, it emerged that hardship would have ensued by underestimation.[47] His attitude to extensions of the limitation period for an action for damages for personal injuries was also usually generous and non-technical.[48]

Nonetheless, other balancing themes manifested themselves. He thought so far as safety was concerned that it would be "unfortunate if little or no responsibility were to be placed on the workmen themselves."[49] This attitude dictated his factual finding in *Qualcast (Wolverhampton) Ltd.* v. *Haynes*,[50] where a worker who did not wear his protective spats was refused damages. The case is significant in manifesting another of Lord Denning's attitudes: judicial discretion to intervene must be maintained by treating precedents as relative to factual findings and not as rulings of law.[51]

Lord Denning was also sympathetic to arguments about balancing the cost or extent of safety precautions with the risk when deciding what was an appropriate standard of care and whether an employer had been negligent.[52] He was prepared to interpret the Factories Act restrictively so as to avoid imposing absolute liability.[53] Cost to the taxpayers, where public bodies were defendants, also weighed unduly with him.[54]

In concluding on this aspect of Lord Denning's work it is worth dealing with Robert Stevens' implied query whether he was really "the champion of the worker."[55] Lord Denning would never have claimed to be a protagonist—except for the cause of justice. Thus, while having sympathy for the

[46] *R.* v. *Industrial Injuries Commission, ex p. Cable* [1968] 1 Q.B. 729. *Cf. Minister of Pensions* v. *Chennell* [1946] K.B. 250, where in one of his early cases he took a similarly generous approach to causation and entitlement to a pension for injury inflicted when a bomb injured a child.

[47] *Jenkins* v. *Richard Thomas and Baldwins Ltd.* [1966] 1 W.L.R. 476.

[48] See, *e.g. Re Clark* v. *Forbes Stuart (Thames St.) Ltd.* [1964] 1 W.L.R. 836 (even if a slippery floor was involved); *Harkness* v. *Bell's Asbestos & Engineering Ltd.* [1967] 2 Q.B. 729; *Pickles* v. *National Coal Board (Intended Action)* [1968] 1 W.L.R. 997; *Harper* v. *National Coal Board* [1974] Q.B. 614. But *cf. Goodchild* v. *Greatness Timber Co. Ltd.* [1968] 2 Q.B. 372 and *Baker* v. *Bowkett's Cakes* [1966] 1 W.L.R. 861, Winn L.J. dissenting.

[49] *Norris* v. *Syndi Manufacturing Co. Ltd.* [1952] 1 All E.R. 935, 939, overruling Devlin J., placing a duty on the workmen and reducing damages by one-fifth. Adoption of a nursemaid approach (in Diplock L.J.'s words) was also rejected in *Savory* v. *Holland* [1964] 1 W.L.R. 1158. Contending that such doctrines were no longer necessary because of changes to occupiers' liability, Lord Denning did not accept that the skilled employee of an independent contractor was *pro hac vice* to be treated as an employee of the occupier so as to be entitled to absolute protection.

[50] [1959] A.C. 743 (H.L.).

[51] *Ibid.* p. 761.

[52] In *Latimer* v. *A.E.C. Ltd.* [1952] 2 Q.B. 701, where a slippery floor resulted from exceptional flooding, Lord Denning thought it would have been quite unreasonable to have sent all the men home.

[53] In *Latimer* v. *A.E.C. Ltd.* above, he held that the Factories Act only applied to the floor and not to liquids *on* the floor.

[54] See *Watt* v. *Herts. C.C.* [1954] 1 W.L.R. 835, where he indicated that in a commercial establishment he would have imposed liability, but not in case of an injury to a fireman where risks must be balanced against the end (saving life) to be achieved. *Cf. Buckoke* v. *G.L.C.* [1970] 1 W.L.R. 1092 where firemen who insisted on drivers observing road safety laws were disciplined. Why should public workers alone bear the brunt? The reluctance to impose costs on the public foreshadows *Lim Poh Choo* v. *Camden and Islington Area Health Authority* [1979] Q.B. 196.

[55] *Law and Politics*, pp. 496–497, referring to his "not entirely deserved reputation."

injured, his judgments in the area of worker protection are characteristic of his approaches elsewhere: he was reluctant to impose absolute liability without fault, unless no other way of protecting an injured worker was available; he had a rather robust view of the duties of workers to observe the procedures for their own safety, and he was aware that in most cases an action for damages was additional to social security benefits[56]; he sought to balance the costs to industry of imposing excessively high standards of care; and he was unsympathetic to those who by his lights had misconducted themselves.

Protection for the Family and Children[57]

The widest possible protection should be accorded to the family, and in addition special measures of protection and assistance must, by Article 10(3) of the Economic Rights Covenant, be taken on behalf of all children and young persons, without any discrimination for reasons of parentage or other conditions.

Freeman's survey does not differ from the writer's view that Lord Denning overcame his personal reluctance to see divorce, and realistically interpreted the grounds of divorce so as to permit divorce where the marriage had broken down, even if from time to time he warned against an opening of the flood gates.

Where children were concerned he generally gave paramountcy to their welfare, except where his predilections for other rights outweighed his concern for child and family protection, as occurred in a wardship case seeking to restrain freedom of the press and affecting the public interest in publication of the truth.[58] As elsewhere, Lord Denning's judgments were sometimes logically inconsonant because of the view he took of particular sets of facts. Thus, earlier, he would have restrained publication of an infant's memories exposing his family life as not being for his benefit by bringing disgrace upon himself and others.[59] Again, while generally willing to exercise the protective wardship jurisdiction, even extending it to stateless alien children ordinarily resident in England,[60] he would not let it be invoked "so as to put a clog on the decisions of immigration officers or as a means of reviewing them."[61] His attitude that immigration officers acted under the Commonwealth Immigrants Act honestly and fairly, and investigated claims as thoroughly as the circumstances permitted, and his unwillingness to come to a result different from their decision and their interpretations of the immigration rules was again manifested towards the end of his career.[62] However, a year earlier, doubtless aware, although there

---

[56] Even if some benefits must be taken into account in partial reduction of damages. His opposition to doubling up in "damages" was most clearly articulated in *Parry* v. *Cleaver* [1968] 1 Q.B. 195. It also explains his blind spots about floors. See *The Changing Law* (1953), p. 73.

[57] Art. 10.   [58] *Re X (A Minor)* [1975] Fam. 47.

[59] *Chaplin* v. *Leslie Frewin (Publishers) Ltd.* [1965] Ch. 71, a Denning dissent.

[60] *P. (G.E.) (An Infant)* [1965] Ch. 568.

[61] *Re A. (An Infant)* [1968] 2 All E.R. 145, 152.

[62] In *R.* v. *Immigration Appeal Tribunal ex p. Alexander* [1982] 1 W.L.R. 430, a majority Denning decision, reversed by the House of Lords ([1982] 1 W.L.R. 1076), Lord Denning strictly construed requirements of the immigration rules as imperative, in the same fashion as had the immigration officer, to hold that the officer had no discretion to admit an intending 17 year-old student, even for a short period, when not satisfied that she intended to leave the country on completion of her studies.

is no reference to this in the case, of the treatment of many wealthy Iranians in *post*-Shah Iran, he had held that an immigration officer had misconstrued the rules as to when a period of study was completed and had therefore not exercised his discretion to admit a young Iranian boy to enable him to attend a public school.[63]

Lord Denning was anxious to ensure that succession rights of all children were equal. In *Re D. (An Infant)* he permitted the mother of an illegitimate child to adopt the child, the welfare of the child being served by the fact that an adopted child was entitled to certain property rights.[64] In the academically much criticised case of *Re Jebb*[65] he treated the word "child" in a will as including an adopted child, thereby entitling it to benefits. However, within a year, in a conflicts of law case, he had taken a conservative approach to recognition of foreign adoptions and to the question whether children adopted abroad were "children" for purposes of an English settlement.[66] Later an often cited case shows Lord Denning reverting to his earlier attitude and, in a dissenting judgment, provocative to his colleagues, asserting that the term "dependant" included an illegitimate child, a ruling which commonsensical though it was, was contrary to the settled practice of draftsmen.[67] Lord Denning and his differing colleagues should all take credit for forcing subsequent reform: section 15 of the Family Law Reform Act 1969 reversed the rule of construction confining words denoting family relationships to legitimate relations, so that a gift to children, dependants, relations, etc., will now benefit the illegitimate as well as the legitimate, "unless a contrary intention appears."

In order to protect a child from illegitimacy Lord Denning was prepared to hold that a second marriage, contracted at a time when a divorce decree had been obtained on the basis of misinformation, the decree in fact subsequently being set aside, was merely voidable.[68]

In a society in which the stigma attached to illegitimacy was lessening and where scientific advances enabled serological tests assisting elimination of paternity allegations, Lord Denning gave less weight to the presumption of legitimacy. Before the Family Law Reform Act 1969, a reform anticipated in part by his decisions, he had held that the High Court in any proceedings had a discretion to order a child to be bloodgrouped whenever it was in his best interests,[69] and that the presumption of legitimacy would be rebutted on a balance of probabilities, the object being to find the truth.[70] After the Act had conferred a discretion generally to order blood tests, Lord Denning ruled that, unless there are exceptional reasons for not admitting it, the best

---

[63] R. v. *Chief Immigration Officer, Gatwick Airport, ex p. Kharrazi* [1980] 1 W.L.R. 1396, a majority Denning decision.

[64] [1959] 1 Q.B. 229. Under the Adoption Act 1976 adoption by a parent is now only permitted under exceptional circumstances.

[65] [1966] Ch. 666.

[66] *Re Valentine's Settlement* [1965] Ch. 831. Salmon L.J.'s far more protective judgment should be contrasted here with that of Lord Denning. One suspects that this is another of the cases where Lord Denning was persuaded by Professor Cheshire's views, and overreacted to criticism.

[67] *Sydall* v. *Castings* [1967] 1 Q.B. 302.

[68] *Wiseman* v. *Wiseman* [1953] P. 79.

[69] *B.(B.R.)* v. *B.(J.)* [1968] 3 W.L.R. 566.

[70] *Re L. (An Infant)* [1967] 3 W.L.R. 1645.

evidence should be available, with justice being the overriding consideration, rather than the welfare of the child, should there be any conflict
between these criteria.[71] Tilting the balance to justice, subject to the caveat
for exceptional cases (such as likelihood of affecting the child's health),
seems to be congruent with the child's best psychological if not financial best
interests: it can hardly be in the interests of the child to hold that his
mother's husband, bitterly disputing his paternity, should not have his
doubts resolved by a blood test. The outcome of the exercise of discretion
may be more cases of "illegitimacy," but it cannot be said that the welfare of
children will have suffered, and there will not have been discrimination in
favour of children as against adults, as, for example, by ordering a putative
father to support a child, who may well not be his.

Housing—Women and Property Rights[72]

Lord Denning's contribution to furtherance of the right to housing has been
dealt with obliquely in McAuslan's essay which shows that in many areas
the same themes emerge: justice, balancing of rights, responsibility, abuse of
rights and exploitation of the law.

In two spheres his attitudes have been severely criticised. The first relates
to eviction of squatters occupying vacant property, often owned by local
authorities.[73] Lord Denning upheld the legal rights of owners, rejecting any
pleas of necessity, but was lax in insisting on strict enforcement of the
procedure for eviction. The decisions limited the effectiveness of the
so-called "family squatting" movement. Perhaps they might have been less
critically received, had Lord Denning's point, that "if homelessness were
once admitted as a defence no one's house could be safe,"[74] been appreciated
in relation to the general consequences of permitting a plea of necessity, and
had his non-insistence on technicalities of procedure been considered in
relation to private owners seeking to recover possession of temporarily
empty houses from squatters. The second sphere provoking criticism relates
to exercises of local authority discretion under the Housing (Homeless
Persons) Act 1977, where his approach was generally chauvinistic and
improperly restrictive to others than "trueborn Englishmen."[75]

A category of persons given special protection by Lord Denning in the
provision of housing and of an adequate living was married women. It is
unnecessary to describe the cases (and their progeny) because Hayton and
Freeman have covered the law in this area. Yet perhaps only a woman law
teacher who lived through the era of Lord Denning's major contributions in
this area can appreciate fully the enlightened approach he showed in
practice to women. The history is impressive. Starting in 1947 with the

---

[71] *W.* v. *W.* [1970] 1 W.L.R. 682 and *S.* v. *McC.* [1970] 1 W.L.R. 672, affirmed [1970] 3 W.L.R. 366.

[72] Art. 11 (the right of everyone to an adequate standard of living, including housing).

[73] J.A.G. Griffith, *The Politics of the Judiciary*, pp. 117–119, and P. Robson and P. Watchman "Resisting the Unprivileged" in *Justice, Lord Denning and the Constitution*, pp. 117–121. The most controversial cases are *Southwark L.B.C.* v. *Williams* [1971] 1 Ch. 734; *McPhail* v. *Persons Unknown* [1973] 3 W.L.R. 71; and *Metropolitan Police Receiver* v. *Smith* (1974) 118 S.J. 583 (C.A.).

[74] *Southwark L.B.C.* v. *Williams* [1971] Ch. 734, 744.

[75] Robson and Watchman, *op. cit.* pp. 122–123. McAuslan, pp. 203–5, in measured tones, is also condemnatory of cases such as *De Falco*.

ruling that an order for possession of the family home owned by a husband would not be given where this was unjust,[76] Lord Denning proceeded to give protection to wives in property held under a husband's tenancy under the Rent Acts.[77] He held in 1950 that a husband who did not provide a proper home for his wife was in desertion.[78] He invented the deserted wife's equity to remain in the husband's property as against third parties.[79] He was responsible in part for the concept of "family assets,"[80] and wholly responsible for "palm tree justice" with its attribution of compensation for contributions to the family home by way of apportionment of ownership.[81] He gave the courts tremendous discretion in apportioning the assets between the spouses on divorce.[82] He protected wives in actual occupation of the home who had made a financial contribution towards it as against a husband's creditors.[83] With justifiable pride Lord Denning tells the story in *The Due Process of Law*.[84] He did not add, but should have, the important protection he gave in an era where many, instead of marrying, live together as man and wife on a semi-permanent basis. Not only were women living with a man on this basis accorded shares in a jointly acquired matrimonial home on the same property law principles applicable to wives,[85] but, perhaps even more significantly, were given protection under the Rent Act, such a woman being treated as a member of the original tenant's family and thus a statutory tenant by succession.[86] Subsequently, Denning extensively interpreted the Domestic Violence and Matrimonial Proceedings Act 1976, which applied to all domestic violence, to allow women already driven out of the common home to claim an injunction permitting entry.[87] It matters not that some of Lord Denning's remarks reflect his personal sadness at changing moral standards: he took firm and courageous steps to safeguard persons who needed protection. Indeed after 1975 he did not use the phrase "mistress," which offended many, to describe women in a "living together" arrangement. It was fatuous for some "alternative society" critics to have expected that the Master of the Rolls should have spoken neutrally or tactfully of extra-marital relationships, when the official policy of the legal system was and is to preserve, so far as possible, the institution of marriage.

  Subordinating his own moral views to the need for protection of the living

---

[76] *Hutchinson* v. *Hutchinson* [1947] 1 All E.R. 792.

[77] *Old Gate Estates Ltd.* v. *Alexander* [1950] 1 K.B. 311. Later, at a time of continuing housing shortage, he was to protect a wife occupying a parentally owned house against eviction: *Errington* v. *Errington and Woods* [1952] 1 K.B. 290.

[78] *Munro* v. *Munro* [1950] 1 All E.R. 832.

[79] *Bendall* v. *McWhirter* [1952] 2 Q.B. 466—with the help of Somervell and Romer L.JJ. The case was shortly preceded by *Lee* v. *Lee* [1952] 2 Q.B. 489, where a licence in the deserted wife was recognised.

[80] *Rimmer* v. *Rimmer* [1953] 1 Q.B. 63—preceded by Vaisey J.'s important judgment in *Jones* v. *Maynard* [1951] Ch. 572.

[81] *Cobb* v. *Cobb* [1955] 1 W.L.R. 731. This was too far for Romer L.J.

[82] *Wachtel* v. *Wachtel* [1973] Fam. 72.

[83] *Williams and Glynn's Bank Ltd.* v. *Boland* [1979] 2 W.L.R. 550.

[84] pp. 205–240.

[85] *Cooke* v. *Head* [1972] 1 W.L.R. 518; *Eves* v. *Eves* [1975] 1 W.L.R. 1338; *Tanner* v. *Tanner* [1975] 1 W.L.R. 1346; and *Barnard* v. *Josephs* [1982] 2 W.L.R. 1052.

[86] *Dyson Holdings Ltd.* v. *Fox* [1976] Q.B. 503.

[87] *Davis* v. *Johnson* [1978] 2 W.L.R. 182, a 3–2 decision on whether, in view of an earlier Court of Appeal decision, a property owner could be ordered out of his home. The case was affirmed by their Lordships: [1979] A.C. 264.

standards even of a "guilty" wife on dissolution of marriage, Lord Denning had more than three decades ago generously approached the then "compassionate allowance," when maintenance was related to conduct, and held a divorced wife entitled to some maintenance.[88] He recognised that through marriage a wife had contributed, and held that on its dissolution the older wife could not be turned out to work by her husband.[89]

For some, looking with hindsight, the achievement is marred by Lord Denning's emphasis on protection and courtesy and extra-judicial utterances about his moral attitudes to marriage: protectiveness can be seen as infuriating paternalism. Already in his late middle age before the astonishingly rapid changes in attitude during the 1960s to marriage, morality and the role of women, Lord Denning could not be expected to transcend the morality of a lifetime or to abandon language which appears now archaic and patriarchal to supporters of women's liberation. After all, in any final analysis it is what he did that really matters, rather than some marginal remarks. For others, his movement away from sure and settled Chancery principles, and his tendency to overlook countervailing interests such as those of creditors, in order to have a flexible judicial discretion to do justice to the spouses, was dangerous. Such criticism is founded on assumptions about the judicial role and the propriety and permissible extent of judicial law making, assumptions he would regard as timorous. For yet others, Lord Denning's patch-work law reform, at risk always from House of Lords upset, by taking off any head of steam for parliamentary intervention, pre-empted systematic law reform.[90] Lord Denning's own assessment is that without the Court of Appeal's activism in this area it might have taken over 40 years to obtain any protection for a deserted wife.[91] He is probably right. Major reform of social and economic institutions requires a long-term process of conditioning: it is doubtful whether, without the pioneering process of attrition to which Lord Denning subjected male economic legal dominance in the family, the concept of co-ownership between spouses would be as widely accepted as it is today, and have become a candidate for general statutory regulation.

Education and Parental Rights[92]

Lord Denning's judgments have been important in the few cases touching on the right to education or on parental rights to ensure that their children are educated in conformity with their own convictions, religious or moral, or, according to Article 2 of the First Protocol to the European Convention, philosophical. In legal terms most such cases have involved statutory powers or duties, turning on whether there has been unreasonableness in exercising

---

[88] *Sydenham* v. *Sydenham* [1949] 2 All E.R. 196 and *Trestain* v. *Trestain* [1950] P. 198.

[89] *Rose* v. *Rose* [1951] P. 29.

[90] This happened in respect of the deserted wife's equity (Cmnd. 9678 (1956), para. 664) and again for several years after *Wachtel* v. *Wachtel*, when the Law Commission treated the case as largely disposing of the need for reform of matrimonial property law. Words delivered to two decades of students are here being eaten by the writer, who has criticised Lord Denning for his lucky dip reforms, his making justice dependent on discretion rather than on clear right, and for risking men feeling that they were being discriminated against by a Lord Denning-headed Court of Appeal. Despite his emphasis on its flexibility, reiteration of the traditional "one-third starting point" in *Wachtel* was hardest to swallow.

[91] *The Due Process of Law*, p. 205.   [92] Art. 13.

discretion, or on whether affected persons are entitled to bring civil proceedings in event of any breach of statutory duty or are merely left with the remedy, if any, contained in the statute, which, in case of the Education Act 1944, is, in many instances, an appeal to the Minister that he exercise his default powers. Although the different results can partly be explained by the time frame, with the first case being decided when courts were reluctant to interfere with statutory discretions, and partly by the fact that in some cases the purely legal arguments for intervention were more compelling (as where duties under the Education Act had not been observed) it is impossible not to infer that Lord Denning was prepared to exercise the extensive judicial freedom of choice enjoyed in respect of administrative law issues since the mid-1960s only if he was opposed to the policy of the statutory decision-maker, or if the facts excited his indignation.

In *Meade* v. *London Borough of Haringey,* where schools were closed by a local authority because of strike action by non-teaching staff, resulting in no heating or cleaning, he held that the authority was in breach of its duty to "secure that there shall be available . . . sufficient schools for full-time education."[93] Parents, to assure the right of their children to education, were accorded standing to bring these proceedings.

In contrast, in *Ward* v. *Bradford Corporation*[94] the right to higher education, equally accessible to all, was not enforced. Here Lord Denning declined, despite a serious breach of the rules of natural justice, to set aside the expulsion from teacher training college of a student who had had a man staying for nearly two months in her room in college.

So far as concerns equal accessibility of higher education, the provision of a Local Authority Education Award is often the determinant in practice whether higher education will be available to an intending student. Lord Denning interpreted the phrase "ordinarily resident in the United Kingdom" in the Education Act 1962 and Regulations made under it "in the context of the situation brought about by the Immigration Act 1971."[95] The effect was that immigrant students, so long as they were present in the United Kingdom with immigrant status subject to conditions and without the right of (permanent) abode in the United Kingdom, and even though educated for over three years in the United Kingdom whether at school or in preliminary higher education before applying for any award, would not be eligible for awards. Lord Denning achieved this result by legislating "for a state of affairs for which Parliament has not legislated," treating it as inconceivable that Parliament could have intended to bestow awards for higher education out of public funds on persons permitted to enter the country on a temporary basis.[96] He was reversed by their Lordships, holding that the policy and impact of the Immigration Act 1971 could not be invoked, neither could any subjective judicial notions as to policy, in interpreting the Education Act 1962.[97]

It is worth contrasting two sets of cases touching on the right of parents to ensure that their children's education is in conformity with their own

---

[93] [1979] 1 W.L.R. 637. A hidden issue was the motivation of many Labour councillors in making the closure decision to show sympathy for the strikers.
[94] (1972) 70 L.G.R. 27. This case is discussed by Jowell, pp. 228–229 above.
[95] *R.* v. *Barnet L.B.C., ex p. Shah* [1982] 2 W.L.R. 474, 482.
[96] *Ibid.*
[97] *Ibid.* [1983] 2 A.C. 309 (H.L.) *per* Lord Scarman at p. 346.

convictions. In cases where administrative arrangements have been made for education at particular schools Lord Denning has given little weight to parental wishes. In *Watt* v. *Kesteven County Council*[98] the question arose whether, when a public authority, to ensure the availability of schools for secondary education, made arrangements to pay school fees at a public school within the county of its choice, it was unreasonable to refuse to accede to the wishes of parents to send their child to another public school outside the county of their own denomination (Roman Catholic), recognised as efficient and charging lower fees than those payable by the county to the school of its choice. Lord Denning held that section 76 of the Education Act which provides that

> " . . . the general principle that, so far as is compatible with the provision of efficient instruction and training and the avoidance of unreasonable public expenditure, pupils are to be educated in accordance with the wishes of their parents,"

only laid down a general principle to which the county council must have regard among other considerations, and to which it was, if it thought fit, free to make exceptions. The sole parental remedy was to make complaint to the Minister of Education in the hope that he would exercise his default powers. Denning emphasised his opinion that the case did not in the least depend on the religious views of the parents. In reality, having regard to Catholic educational philosophy that religious and other education are inseparable in shaping a child's beliefs, the parents were denied the possibility of ensuring their child's education in conformity with their own convictions. The result in *Watt* v. *Kesteven County Council* is also arguably counter to Article 18 of the Civil Rights Covenant (freedom to manifest religion or beliefs in practice and in teaching—in this case their own children) and Article 27 (the right of religious minorities in community with other members of their group to enjoy their own culture and to practise their own religion).

Subsequently, in *Cumings* v. *Birkenhead Corporation*[99] he reiterated his view that parental wishes were only one factor for consideration. Owing to a shortage of secondary school places at non-Roman Catholic Schools, the local authority had sent a circular stating that children who had attended Catholic primary schools would be allocated to Catholic secondary schools. (There was the usual safeguarding reservation that exceptional cases would be considered). Parents of both denominations challenged the lawfulness of this decision, whether for philosophical or moral reasons, or whether because they did not wish their children to be educated in a religiously segregated school system, or whether because they wished their children to receive secular rather than religious education. There were other hidden issues: the Liverpool area has a notorious history of hostility between certain sections of the Protestant and of the Roman Catholic communities, especially those of Irish origin. Such hostility has entered at times into local authority politics (there is even a hint of this in the first instance report). It also explains why parents of goodwill of both denominations objected to a criterion of allocation, effectively religious in character, and likely to perpetuate religious segregation in secondary schooling. Lord Denning, however, did not insist that the Corporation adopt another criterion for

[98] [1955] 1 Q.B. 408.
[99] [1972] Ch. 12.

selection, upholding its decision on grounds of administrative convenience. This result not only ignored the philosophically or morally based wishes of parents, but meant that, counter to Article 13(2)(*b*) of the Economic Rights Covenant, certain forms of secondary education *i.e.* non-denominational, were not made available to all. It was also arguably counter to Article 2, in refusing to make accessible such education on grounds of religious school primary education, and to Article 26 of the Civil Rights Covenant, entitling all persons without discrimination to the equal protection of the laws. That it was discriminatory was impliedly acknowledged by Lord Denning, who stated that if the criterion had been colour this would have been counter to the Race Relations Act.

This tenderness to local authority discretion and convenience in the policy area of schooling provision, with consequent outweighing of parental religious convictions, contrasts strongly with Lord Denning's willingness to intervene when local authority or central government discretions in relation to the policy of replacing grammar schools by comprehensive schools arose. Such cases, it can be argued, touch on parental philosophical convictions to the extent that parents have a set of beliefs about appropriate educational goals and methods. In litigation involving the London Borough of Enfield, he upheld actions by parents, who were ratepayers, because the local authority had failed to take the requisite procedural steps to notify proposed changes in the composition of existing schools which it was maintaining, thereby not affording parents sufficient time to object.[1] Subsequently, in the long drawn out struggle over reorganisation to turn grammar schools into comprehensives, a struggle sometimes involving the competing powers in education of central and local government authorities of different political complexions, he was willing indirectly to assist certain parents who sought the continuance of grammar school education by holding that the Secretary of State for Education had no power to direct a newly elected local education authority to implement the part-executed plans of its predecessor for comprehensivisation.[2]

Even a judge determined, as was Lord Denning, to mould the law to fit his sense of what was required, faces limits to his powers of intervention. Thus, in *Smith* v. *Inner London Education Authority* he felt compelled to set aside the interlocutory injunction restraining the local authority from ceasing to maintain a distinguished grammar school as a consequence of implementing I.L.E.A.'s policy of comprehensivisation. He said:

> "Search as I may, and it is not for want of trying, I cannot find any abuse or misuse of power by the education authority. So their proposals must take effect. It is sad to have to say so; after so much effort has been expended by so many in so good a cause. The fate of the grammar school is sealed . . . . Many will grieve 'when that which was great is passed away.' "[3]

[1] *Bradbury* v. *Enfield L.B.C.* [1967] 1 W.L.R. 1311; *Lee* v. *Enfield L.B.C.* (1967) 66 L.G.R. 195; and *Lee* v. *Department of Education and Science* (1967) 66 L.G.R. 211.

[2] *Secretary of State for Education and Science* v. *Tameside M.B.C.* [1976] 3 W.L.R. 641. Lord Denning's judgment, with which the House of Lords did not disagree, provides further dicta in support of the "no evidence" ground of judicial review and indicia as to when a discretion can be said to have been unreasonably exercised.

[3] [1978] 1 All E.R. 411, 418. See also *Re S.* (*A Minor*) (*Care Order: Education*) [1977] 3 W.L.R. 575 forestalling a father adamant against comprehensive schooling from martyrising himself by contempt.

Nonetheless, the cases indicate that for Lord Denning the criterion for his intervention was not whether parental wishes were followed, but whether he had objections to the policy being implemented. Despite his remark in *Meade* that he saw the courts as "the last resort available to the beleaguered citizen," educational administration was an area in which the rights of the individual were not the motor force behind his judgments.

Intellectual Property Rights[4]

Rights of the owner of intellectual property to protection and the countervailing right of everyone to enjoy the benefits of scientific progress and its applications are shortly set out in the Economic Rights Covenant. Only a patents specialist could write of Lord Denning's particular contributions in the area. However, some of his more general decisions touching on the moral and material interests resulting from intellectual production, especially if the notions of scientific and artistic productions are broadly treated so as to include knowledge which is the product of skill and work in business or industry, are very significant.

Lord Denning sees his work in this field in terms of the "conflicting" rights to privacy and to the freedom of the press.[5] It is of course closely connected with other aspects of the right to privacy, which will be discussed in connection with Articles 14 and 17 of the Civil Rights Covenant, aspects where there is also conflict of rights—as between the rights to privacy and to fair trial (or the interest in administration of justice) in relation to discovery and privilege cases. However, some points are appropriately made here.

First, Lord Denning gave primacy to the public interest. Starting with *Initial Services Ltd.* v. *Putterill*,[6] he held that misconduct done or contemplated, in the conduct of a business, or any design which would defeat the public welfare, could be disclosed without liability for breach of confidence. In *Fraser* v. *Evans*,[7] so as to allow publication of information in a public relations consultant's report for the Government of Greece (then under the Colonels' control) he restricted the scope of copyright to the "form" and not to the "information" in the report, and, on the separate issue of breach of confidence, held that wherever there was "just cause or excuse" (iniquity being an example of such just cause) publication of the confidence could not be restrained or sanctioned. Subsequently in *Hubbard* v. *Vosper*,[8] where a former scientologist published a book stating facts acquired by him during his membership of the movement, Lord Denning held that the public interest that "medical quackery of a dangerous kind" be disclosed, served as the defence of justification in a libel suit. Only because he thought that the press had abused its position did he take a different attitude when the British Steel Corporation brought proceedings for the disclosure of the name of an informant who had given secret British Steel documents to Granada Television, documents which contained information of concern to the public

---

[4] Art. 15 (the right of an author to protection of the moral and material interests resulting from any scientific, literary or artistic production).
[5] *What Next in the Law*, p. 219.
[6] [1968] 1 Q.B. 396.
[7] [1969] 1 Q.B. 349.
[8] [1972] 2 Q.B. 84.

as to the management of British Steel.[9] He treated the circumstances as
exceptional and ones in which, on balancing the interests, disclosure should
be ordered. Extra-judicially he subsequently changed his mind.[10] His final
contribution came in a noteworthy dissent, asserting press freedom and
dealing with the criteria for balancing the public interest in making matters
known to the public and the private interest in maintaining confidence.[11]
Apart from the deviation occasioned by his feeling that "Granada had not
behaved with due respect," Lord Denning consistently favoured press
freedom and public interest in disclosure,[12] as against private interest in
protection of private knowledge and information, thereby making investigative journalism a less hazardous activity and enabling the newspapers to act
as agents of the public in collecting and exposing information of public
concern.

A major contribution to protection of intellectual property—and one
which has already been extended to other causes of action, consequently
being classifiable as furthering the right to fair trial and administration of
justice—is Lord Denning's upholding and development of the Anton Piller
order, an *ex parte* order requiring the defendant to permit the plaintiff to
enter his premises to search for articles infringing copyright, and failing
compliance with which the defendant will be in contempt.[13] Such orders
bring the balance heavily down in favour of owners of intellectual property
as against the rights of property owners, whose property is effectively to be
subjected to search and whose privacy is diminished. He sought to extend
the procedure so as to force defendants to answer questions about their
suppliers, thus making inroads into the privilege against self-crimination.[14]
This approach was rejected by the House of Lords, but was subsequently
vindicated by legislation.[15]

Lord Denning made a final revolutionary attempt to extend protection
even further—and by a sidewind to get rid of the case law on whether an
action for damages for breach of statutory duty was available. In *Ex parte
Island Records* he ruled that whenever a person's business suffers damage over
and above that suffered by other members of the public as a result of breach
of a statutory provision by another person, the injured person then has a
civil claim for damages.[16] This principle has now been rejected by the House
of Lords.[17]

One major Denning innovation still stands and is likely to be fruitful of
further development. The decision in *Seager* v. *Copydex Ltd.* added to the

[9] *British Steel Corporation* v. *Granada Television* [1980] 3 W.L.R. 774, affirmed by the House of
Lords.
[10] *What Next in the Law*, p. 251. He had earlier vacillated (p. 249). It is interesting to note Lord
Salmon's strong dissent in the House of Lords, where he adopted Lord Denning's general
reasoning as to the principles governing refusal by a newspaper or a television company to
disclose the name of an informant, and upheld Granada's refusal.
[11] *Schering Chemicals* v. *Falkman Ltd.* [1981] 2 W.L.R. 848.
[12] *Cf. Home Office* v. *Harman* [1981] 2 W.L.R. 310, dealt with in relation to privacy and fair trial
under Art. 14 of the Civil Rights Covenant.
[13] *Anton Piller K.G.* v. *Manufacturing Process Ltd.* [1976] Ch. 55; and *Ex p. Island Records Ltd.* [1978]
Ch. 122. See *The Due Process of Law*, pp. 123–130.
[14] *Rank Film Distributors Ltd.* v. *Video Information Centre* [1981] 2 W.L.R. 668.
[15] See Hayton's chapter at pp. 99–101.
[16] See Hayton's comments at p. 101.
[17] *Lonrho Ltd.* v. *Shell Petroleum Co. Ltd.* [1982] A.C. 173.

courts' jurisdiction to restrain publication of confidential information a power to award damages calculated on the basis of reasonable compensation for use of the confidential information.[18] He relied on a broad principle of equity that he who has received information in confidence shall not take unfair advantage of it, and excluded any contractual basis. Subsequently, he and Winn L.J. indicated the basis was tortious.[19] Arguably a new tort is in process of emerging.

The Right to Property

Because international agreement would have been difficult to achieve, the Covenants do not protect the right to property, although Article 5(2) preserves rights already existing in ratifying states. Earlier, Article 17 of the Universal Declaration recognised the right of ownership, and provided that no-one should be arbitrarily deprived of his property. For purposes of discussing Lord Denning's contributions to the right of property it is useful to refer to Article 1 of the First Protocol to the European Convention, which provides for "peaceful enjoyment of . . . possessions," and for no deprivation "except in the public interest and subject to . . . the general principles of international law," the State, however, having the right to enforce such laws as it deems necessary "to control the use of property in accordance with the general interest or to secure the payment of taxes or other contributions or penalties." "Possessions" is used in the widest Civil Law sense as comprising both corporeal and incorporeal property and obligations. It will be apparent that the right to property has many aspects, and that Lord Denning's contributions to protection of the right can here merely be touched upon.

"Peaceful enjoyment" is protected in English law by various tortious causes of action—negligence, nuisance, trespass, claims for damages for breach of a right to performance of a statutory duty, interference with existing contracts and, possibly, interfering with a business by unlawful means. In all these spheres Lord Denning's activities have been considerable, and have largely been covered by Atiyah[20] and by Davies and Freedland.[21]

The traditional English judicial approach to inroads on property rights has been one of suspicion of legislative or executive intervention. This was not Lord Denning's attitude. From the beginning of his judicial career he thought that private rights must often be subordinated to the public good as, for example, by way of compulsory acquisition of land, slum clearance, town and country planning, requisitioning of houses, rent controls, duties to maintain housing and to preserve land under one's control—of course bearing always in mind the need to strike a just balance.[22]

He was also aware that the State had been put under duties and responsibilities in regard to welfare and availability to all of all the supplies and services necessary for individual well-being,[23] a notion embracing all

---

[18] [1967] 1 W.L.R. 923. In an earlier case, *Nicrotherm Electrical Co. Ltd.* v. *Percy* [1956] R.P.C. 272, Harman J. had awarded damages.

[19] [1969] 2 All E.R. 718. In *What Next in the Law*, p. 226, Lord Denning suggests breach of confidence is a tort. See also P.M. North, (1972) 12 J.S.P.T.L. 149.

[20] Chap. 2, pp. 52–55 (the economic loss aspects of negligence) and pp. 78–81 (nuisance).

[21] Chap. 8, pp. 379–411.

[22] See *Freedom Under the Law* (1949), pp. 99 *et seq.* and 67 *et seq.*

[23] *Ibid.* pp. 74–75.

aspects of the Economic Rights Covenant. Lord Denning accepted the administrative law distinction betwen duties and powers, considering that duties were largely matters for the independent tribunal system, except where errors of law were involved,[24] while powers were for the Government unless there was an excess or abuse of power. Then

> "One of the most important tasks of the courts is to see that the powers of the executive are properly used, that is, used honestly and reasonably for the purposes authorised by Parliament and not for any ulterior motive."[25]

Denning judgments in the property sphere fit the pattern of subordination of private interest to public interest and reluctance to intervene against exercises of public power, unless an abuse of power, as described in *Freedom Under the Law*, had occurred. The cases on limitations on the use by owners of their property, whether in relation to planning permissions, control of development or preservation of amenities,[26] bear this out.

Significant limitations on rights of property, and ones on which Lord Denning gave leading judgments, arise from police power to enter, search, seize, or detain property, topics which could equally be dealt with under the right to privacy and protection of correspondence set out in Article 17 of the Civil Rights Covenant.

He himself, in examining his own cases on search, seizure and detention of property, concluded in *The Due Process of Law* that:

> "Long have I associated myself with human rights . . . But looking back over the cases of the intervening 30 years, I find that I have been concerned—not so much with freedom—as with keeping the balance between freedom and security. As I said in 1949 of personal freedom: "It must be matched of course, with social security, by which I mean, the peace and good order of the community in which we live . . . "[27]

In *Chic Fashions (West Wales) Ltd.* v. *Jones* he extended police powers of seizure of goods, despite the lack of any authorisation in a search warrant, by eliminating the requirement that there be a relationship between the seized articles and the offence for which the warrant was issued. After balancing the security of the individual's home against society's interest "in finding out wrongdoers and repressing crime," he relied on a constable's power of arrest on reasonable grounds to contend that goods should not be more sacred than persons. Going out of his way to make a broad statement of principle, he said:

> " . . . when a constable enters a house by virtue of a search warrant for stolen goods, he may seize not only the goods which he reasonably believes to be covered by the warrant, but also any other goods which he believes on reasonable grounds to have been stolen and to be

---

[24] *Ibid.* pp. 86–96, *passim.*
[25] *Ibid.* p. 102. See also pp. 110–111, and 114–115 (improper purpose).
[26] See McAuslan, Chap. 5, pp. 177–190.
[27] p. 101.

material evidence on a charge of stealing or receiving against the person in possession of them or anyone associated with him."[28]

It is interesting to compare his burial of the *Six Carpenter's Case* along with the old forms of action, in *Chic Fashions* with his earlier suggestion in *Freedom Under the Law*[29] that the case might provide the key to the principle by which the courts can ensure that new powers of entry and search are not abused. The key he discerned was a limitation that such powers should not "be used oppressively or unreasonably."

Subsequently, in *Ghani v. Jones*[30] Lord Denning practically eliminated the requirement of a search warrant by a new doctrine authorising, in certain circumstances, the warrantless seizure of evidence of a serious crime, no longer confined only to theft. He stated:

"I would start by considering the law where police officers enter a man's house by virtue of a warrant, or arrest a man lawfully, with or without a warrant, for a serious offence. It take it to be settled law, without citing cases, that the officers are entitled to take any goods which they find in his possession or in his house which they reasonably believe to be material evidence in relation to the crime for which he is arrested or for which they enter. If in the course of their search they come upon any other goods which show him to be implicated in some other crime, they may take them provided they act reasonably and detain them no longer than is necessary."[31]

Then, expanding upon this dictum, and balancing the privacy of the individual and his possession with the interest of society at large in finding out wrongdoers and repressing crime, he laid down five requisites for taking an article when no man had been arrested or charged. The police officer must have reasonable grounds for belief that a serious offence had been committed, that the seized article was the fruit of the crime, the instrument of commission or material evidence of the crime, and that the person had himself committed it or been implicated in it, or that any refusal to hand over the article was quite unreasonable.[32] The article might then be kept by the police no longer than was reasonably necessary to complete their investigations or to preserve it for evidence, while the lawfulness of police conduct was to be judged at the time of seizure and not by what happened afterwards.

In fairness to Lord Denning it must be said that on the facts of *Ghani v. Jones* he did not uphold the police' assertions of a right to retain the seized property, letters and Pakistani passports belonging to the parents and sister of a murder suspect, which were effectively seized on a police visit to their house without warrant (none being permissible in case of murder—and here Lord Denning incited the police to commit trespass in their investigations if co-operation was not forthcoming). The police did not show reasonable grounds for believing either that the passports were material evidence of the

---

[28] [1968] 2 Q.B. 299, 313. Salmon L.J. did not accept the sweep of this dictum, holding that a police officer had no common law right to seize property in the possession of a person whom he had no reasonable grounds to believe to be criminally implicated.

[29] pp. 109–110.

[30] [1970] 1 Q.B. 693.

[31] *Ibid*. p. 706.

[32] Seemingly a deferential nod to Salmon L.J.'s views.

commission of the murder or that the family were implicated. In fact, Lord Denning suspected that the police motive was to prevent the family leaving the United Kingdom pending police enquiries, something not legitimate unless they were arrested. He said:

> "A man's liberty of movement is regarded so highly by the law of England that it is not to be hindered or prevented except upon the surest grounds. It must not be taken away on a suspicion which is not grave enough to warrant his arrest."[33]

Despite these libertarian words, his decision enhanced police seizure powers in broad legislative fashion—leaving other questions open,[34] because judicial decisions cannot serve as blueprints for reform. Already it has been the basis for further developments[35] and could justify yet greater extensions of powers of entry and search.

There is little doubt that Lord Denning must have been disconcerted by the academic reception and judicial reaction in some Commonwealth jurisdictions to *Ghani* v. *Jones,* particularly by the allegations of its inconsistency with *Entick* v. *Carrington.*[36] My speculation is that his judgment in *R.* v. *Inland Revenue Commissioners, ex parte Rossminster,* narrowly construing the Revenue's search powers, and referring to attempts to seize John Wilkes' papers and to *Entick* v. *Carrington,* was designed to refurbish his tarnished liberal image and to show that he was prepared to vindicate "the liberties of the people of England."[37] It was certainly not occasioned by any tenderness for taxpayers engaging in expensive games of wits with the authorities. In the event, the House of Lords accorded the search power, reversing Lord Denning.

Lord Denning was not, basically, averse to search powers. Thus, he seized the irresistible opportunity in *Re a Company*[38] to order, in a procedure under the Companies Act affording the equivalent of a search warrant, production of the books of Racal Communications, which had allegedly engaged in fraudulent accounting, to apply his new ruling in *Pearlman,*[39] and to disregard a section making a judge's order not appealable. He rushed into holding that a High Court Judge's ruling was subject to judicial review, as if he were an inferior court judge going wrong in law, whereas the jurisdiction of the Court of Appeal is wholly statutory, it having no inherent review jurisdiction, and depending always on express conferment of jurisdiction. Obviously on the ruling that judicial review was available (and on *Pearlman*) he was reversed by the House of Lords.[40]

In his last important case in the area of public interest seizure of property,

---

[33] *Ghani* v. *Jones* [1970] 1 Q.B. 693, 709.
[34] See P.G. Polyviou, *Search and Seizure* (1982), pp. 288 *et seq.,* and Bailey, Harris and Jones, *Civil Liberties* (1980), pp. 97–103.
[35] See, *e.g.* *Garfinkel* v. *Metropolitan Police Commissioner* (1972) Crim. L.R. 44 and *Frank Truman Export Ltd.* v. *Metropolitan Police Commissioner* [1977] Q.B. 952.
[36] (1765) 19 St. Tr. 1030.
[37] [1980] 2 W.L.R. 1, 19.
[38] [1980] Ch. 138, discussed (before its reversal) with relish in *The Due Process of Law,* pp. 79–81.
[39] [1979] Q.B. 56: instead of enquiring into whether error was inside or outside jurisdiction, whenever a case depended on error of law this would take the court outside jurisdiction, so that it could be put right on review.
[40] [1980] 3 W.L.R. 181.

Chief Constable of Kent v. *Verdon-Roe,* Lord Denning (with whom on this point Donaldson L.J. agreed) relying in part on *Chic Fashions* and extending it to intangible assets, was prepared to give the police power to apply for the freezing of bank accounts by way of injunction if they reasonably believed that money fraudulently taken by way of forged cheques had been paid into the defendant's account. Withdrawals could be restrained pending investigations into the source of the moneys.[41]

To complete the "seizure" or rather freezing picture, it remains to mention what Lord Denning himself described as "the greatest piece of judicial law reform in my time."[42] The reference is to the development of the *Mareva* injunction.[43] Despite a temporary rebuff at the hands of the House of Lords, his views were recognised by section 37(3) of the Supreme Court Act 1981, and Lord Denning, now basing himself on that Act, continued to develop to the end of his career the notion that any defendant about to dispose of his assets could be, if it were just and convenient, restrained from so doing.[44] Certainly, to any civil lawyer it was extraordinary that, until Lord Denning's intervention, English law had no machinery for preventing debtors effectively defeating creditors' claims by removal of assets outside the jurisdiction or by internal dealings which were only potentially voidable under the relatively ineffective law of bankruptcy.

The last aspect of the right to property dealt with in this essay is the taking by law to secure the payment of taxes or other contributions or penalties. So far as concerns penalties, Lord Denning's decision in *Allgemeine Gold und Silberscheideanstalt* v. *Customs and Excise Commissioners*[45] upheld the forfeiture of gold coins, even though the owner was not guilty of any offence.

Lord Denning was certainly not prey to any neo-Lockian assumptions about Government's duty to sustain private property or capital.[46] He does not fall within Miliband's generalisation that "the courts have always conceived it as one of their many duties to 'society' to protect the rights of property against such attempts as the State has been compelled to make to reduce their scope."[47] This is amply proven by the town planning, Rent Acts, and slum clearance cases already referred to. Miliband's generalisation is even more untrue of Lord Denning's approach to tax law, apart from the exceptional case in which he saw abuse of power, or inequity,[48] or

---

[41] [1982] 3 W.L.R. 462, criticised by Hayton at Chap. 3, p. 106, for ruling that no legal or equitable right is required to warrant asking for an injunction under the Supreme Act 1981, s.37(1). Lord Denning held the court had power to issue an injunction whenever it appeared just and convenient, provided the applicant had standing.

[42] *The Due Process of Law,* p. 134.

[43] See his own comments: *ibid.* pp. 134–151. Hayton discusses the cases at pp. 101–105.

[44] *Chief Constable of Kent* v. *Verdon-Roe,* above.

[45] [1980] 1 Q.B. 390.

[46] Would any economically literate judge have ruled as he did in *Treseder-Griffin and Another* v. *Co-operative Insurance Co.* [1956] 2 Q.B. 12, 145, concerning an attempt to fix rental under a long lease in relation to gold rather than to sterling: "What, then is to become of sterling? It would become a discredited currency unable to look its enemy inflation in the face. That should not be allowed to happen."

[47] R. Miliband, *The State in Capitalist Society* (1973), p. 129.

[48] In *I.R.C.* v. *Frere* [1964] Ch. 359, Lord Denning and Donovan L.J. (Russell L.J. dissenting) allowed certain deductions of "short-term" interest against surtax. Lord Radcliffe's reversing judgment ([1965] A.C. 402, 429) gives the background: the Revenue, by way of "extra-statutory concessions," of which he disapproved, suggesting recourse to Parliament, was recognising certain claims to tax relief as otherwise there would have been anomalies as between cases where taxpayers paid interest to different kinds of recipient.

hardship to an individual[49] or his sympathies were excited even for extraneous reasons.[50]

He did not follow older judicial traditions of interpreting tax laws in favour of the subject, or even the more modern approach of treating tax laws as an elaborate game in which it was to be decided whether the Crown had succeeded in bringing the subject within the letter of the law or whether the subject had escaped. He looked at the substance, rather than the form.

Doubtless, much to the discomfiture of tax counsel, Lord Denning sat for two major periods in tax cases. His House of Lords cases show him as generally being with their Lordships when they upheld the Revenue's contentions and higher taxes,[51] and in dissent when they did not.[52] His virulent dislike of dividend stripping and equation (using fashionable jargon) of petty bourgeois entrepreneurial activities in this respect to "burglary" began in the Lords,[53] and continued[54] in his next incarnation in the Court of Appeal, where, as Master of the Rolls, he allocated many tax cases to his own division between 1962 and 1966, having a particularly effective period in 1962 when he sat with Donovan and Pearson L.JJ., carrying for the most part his colleagues with him, and being almost appeal proof.[55] Seldom would ingenious schemes prevail in the Court of Appeal, as Lord Denning would look at the mischief which Parliament was seeking to

---

[49] *Jarrold* v. *Bousted* [1964] 1 W.L.R. 1357 (a signing on fee for a rugby league footballer on relinquishing once and for all amateur status held capital and not taxable).

[50] See *Re Downshire's Settled Estate* [1953] 2 W.L.R. 94, 137, where he was, in his attempts to introduce new equity, to hold that the court had a wide equitable trust jurisdiction to deal with property of persons under a disability and to vary settlements to their advantage, even if this would save them death duties. He was subjected to bitter sarcasm by Lord Simonds in *Chapman* v. *Chapman* [1954] A.C. 429 (H.L.) on this non-existent unlimited equitable jurisdiction.

[51] *Escoigne Properties Ltd.* v. *I.R.C.* [1958] 2 W.L.R. 336 (stamp duty liability, with some teasing provocation for Lord Simonds on statutory interpretation); *Newton* v. *Commissioner of Taxation* [1958] A.C. 450 (P.C.), a Denning judgment; *Oughtred* v. *I.R.C.* [1960] A.C. 206 (stamp duty payable); and *Barclays Bank* v. *I.R.C.* [1961] A.C. 509 (a wide view taken by Denning of "control" of a company for estate duty purposes).

[52] *Ostime (Inspector of Taxes)* v. *Australian Mutual Provident Society* [1960] A.C. 459 (limiting effect of double taxation agreement); *Hinton (Inspector of Taxes)* v. *Maden and Ireland Ltd.* [1959] 1 W.L.R. 875 (no investment allowance); *Abbott* v. *Philbin* [1961] A.C. 352 (tax on directors' share options calculated at date of exercise) one of the several dissents with Lord Keith; and *Imperial Tobacco Co.* v. *Pierson* [1961] A.C. 463 (rates on advertisement hoardings).

[53] *Griffiths (Inspector of Taxes)* v. *J.P. Harrison (Watford) Ltd.* [1963] A.C.1, a dissent with Lord Reid.

[54] *Argosam Finance Co. Ltd.* v. *Oxby* [1965] Ch. 390 (abuse of the Court's process to obtain a declaration on how to make up accounts): and *Finsbury Securities* v. *Bishop* [1965] 3 All E.R. 337, 342, a majority judgment where Lord Denning sought to discourage the discreditable trade of "forward" stripping.

[55] The third volume of the All England Reports for 1962 shows Lord Denning at his prime—and supporting the *fiscus*: *Butter* v. *Bennett* at p. 204 (tax on living expenses paid to employee); *Gilmore* v. *Baker-Carr* at p. 230 (no rating exemption). *C.H.W. (Huddersfield) Ltd.* v. *I.R.C.* at p. 243 (surtax liability); *E.Y.L. Trading Co. Ltd.* v. *I.R.C.* at p. 303 (profits tax assessment); *Henning* v. *Church of Jesus Christ of Latter Day Saints* at p. 364 (no rating exemption—but see *post* on discrimination); *I.R.C.* v. *Stafford Coal and Iron Co. Ltd.* at p. 410 (a majority judgment on profits tax liability); and *Shell-Mex and B.P. Ltd.* v. *Langley* at p. 433 (a majority judgment rateable values upheld). Typical too was the only case in which fiscal contentions were not upheld: in *Walker* v. *Wood* at p. 188, with Donovan L.J. dissenting, Lord Denning's sympathy for a disabled ratepayer led to a construction exempting his garage ("structure") housing his invalid-adapted vehicle.

remedy, so as effectively to impose tax, his attitude being broadly that the Revenue was right.[56]

In tax matters he was more in accord with other human rights concepts than were their Lordships: he wished to put the right to equality before the law into practice by allowing standing to those objecting to non-enforcement of tax, as in the case of Fleet Street printing operatives given a tax amnesty for undeclared income which was raised in *R. v. I.R.C., ex parte National Federation of Self-Employed and Small Businesses Ltd.*[57] However inconvenient it might be for the Revenue to find their extra-statutory discretion challenged by other taxpayers aggrieved by its use, there are real risks that if the tax authorities are to accord themselves discretionary exempting power (dispensing power) they may go beyond acting with administrative common sense and treat taxpayers inconsistently and unequally. This their Lordships had earlier recognised in *Vestey v. I.R.C.*[58]

CIVIL AND POLITICAL RIGHTS

Equality and Non-Discrimination Articles [59]

These rights overlap to such an extent that it is convenient to deal with nearly all Lord Denning's cases in this area together, although his case law on certain aspects of Article 2 of the Civil Rights Covenant (the right in Article 2(2) to an effective remedy) and other Articles requiring equality (Article 14 on a fair trial, which involves equality of arms, Article 16 on recognition as a person before the law, and Article 26 on equal protection of the law, implying equal access to such protection) will be dealt with separately.

Except in respect of a degree of equality between the sexes[60] and the removal of discrimination against illegitimate children,[61] areas where Lord Denning was inventive in applying common law and equitable principles, a number of his judgments lay him open to charges of inconsistency with his self-created libertarian reputation, in that he appears to have discriminated against certain categories of persons, even if there are admittedly other judgments which could be invoked to justify an egalitarian and forward-looking image. It seems to me that the explanation lies partly in his basic

[56] *Morgan and Another v. I.R.C.* [1963] Ch. 438, a Denning dissent, looking at the realities so as to make estate duties payable, with Diplock L.J. at p. 488, pointing out that "an ethical basis for its incidence is no reliable guide to the construction of the Finance Act 1894."

[57] [1980] 2 W.L.R. 579 (reversed [1982] A.C. 579.). No inference that Lord Denning supports a Poujadist philosophy should be drawn because of the identity of the applicants: with the limited legal aid system only groups or the very rich or poor can risk the costs of litigation.

[58] [1979] 3 W.L.R. 915 at pp. 926 and 946, nodding towards Parliament, which has remedied the particular defect, but has left the general problem of extra-statutory concessions untouched.

[59] Art. 2 of both Covenants (no distinctions of any kind), Art. 3 of both Covenants (equal rights of men and women), and Art. 18 (freedom to manifest religion or beliefs), Art. 26 (no discrimination in the equal protection of the law) and Art. 27 (rights of minorities) in the Civil and Political Rights Covenant.

[60] According the wife property and housing rights was not on a basis of equality, but a recognition of the social need to protect women, shares to property being calculated not equally, but on the basis of contributions, while in *Wachtel v. Wachtel* [1973] Fam. 76, the one-third starting point was enunciated for discretionary transfer of property ordered by a court on divorce.

[61] See above, pp. 278–279.

common law approach, the common law being too blunt an instrument to deal with subtleties of discrimination, even if exceptionally, by ingenious approaches such as that in *Nagle* v. *Fielden*,[62] it could be used to effect. However, once legislative intervention occurred in respect of discrimination between the sexes, as under the Equal Pay Act 1970 and the Sex Discrimination Act 1975, Lord Denning could and did interpret these in his usual manner in favour of the incorporated legislative policy,[63] unless he saw the instrumentalities involved abusing their power or the persons protected abusing their rights.[64] He was also ambivalent about having to interpret in accordance with directly applicable EEC Law,[65] if drawn to his attention.[66] Any aberrations from this pattern were occasioned by his attitudes of paternalistic courtesy or chivalry,[67] or by a residual fondness for the "reasonableness" standard of the common law, which he might apply in interpreting what the Act prohibited.[68] But he was open to persuasion, changing his mind when alerted to the consequences.[69] Lord Denning also cannot be held responsible for Parliament's carefully circumscribed prohibitions on discrimination.

[62] [1966] 2 Q.B. 633.

[63] See his dissent in *Macarthys Ltd.* v. *Smith* [1979] I.C.R. 785, taking a broader view of the provisions under the Equal Pay Act, and holding that in any event Art. 119 of the Treaty prevailed. He was pleased to be vindicated by the European Court to whom the case was referred: see [1980] 3 W.L.R. 929.

[64] In *Science Research Council* v. *Nassé* [1979] 1 Q.B. 144, with remarks about being back in the days of the general warrants, Lord Denning held that industrial tribunals should very rarely grant discovery of confidential reports (relative to appointments). Fairness to the public service and to industry were balancing public interests, and only where it was essential in the interests of justice should confidence be overridden. The same ruling applied in respect of discovery in relation to racial discrimination allegations: *Leyland Cars* v. *Vyas*, reported with *Nassé*.

[65] This is clear from his comments in *What Next in the Law*, p. 296 on "the authoritarian attitude" of the European Court in ruling that Community Law is supreme, made in relation to *Shields* v. *E. Coomes (Holdings) Ltd.* [1978] 1 W.L.R. 1408 and the comment (p. 301) on *Worringham* v. *Lloyd's Bank* [1981] 1 W.L.R. 950 and [1982] 1 W.L.R. 841.

[66] In *Garland* v. *British Rail Engineering Ltd.* [1982] 2 W.L.R. 918 the Lords thought that the attention of the Court of Appeal had not been drawn to the need to construe in accordance with Art. 119 of the Treaty. They were referring to *Roberts* v. *Cleveland Area Health Authority* [1979] 1 W.L.R. 755, where Lord Denning upheld the validity of concessionary arrangements for rail travel for families continuing after retirement of male workers, but not for families of retiring female workers, characterising this as a provision in relation to retirement and not to salary, and thus exempted from equality by the English Act. In the same case he held that a larger redundancy payment to male workers because of their duty to work till 65, whereas women retired at 60, was similarly exempted, as was the stipulation by law of different retirement ages for men and women. On this last point his result was in accordance with the subsequent ruling of the European Court in *Burton* v. *British Railways Board* [1982] 3 W.L.R. 387 (E.C.J.) because, although conditions of access to voluntary redundancy benefit must be the same, the EEC Directive on removal of discrimination as to pensionable age permitted Member States flexibility in attaining this ultimate objective.

[67] *Peake* v. *Automotive Products Ltd.* [1978] Q.B. 233, a motive of courtesy and chivalry permitting women to leave a factory 5 minutes earlier than men being justifiable—and of course infuriating home-going workmen.

[68] As in *National Vulcan Engineering Insurance Group Ltd.* v. *Wade* [1979] Q.B. 132, where he construed "material difference" as permitting a salary grading system according to ability, skill and experience, a system applied irrespective of employees' sex.

[69] *Ministry of Defence* v. *Jeremiah* [1980] I.C.R. 13, 25, explaining *Peake* as based merely on his second reason of *de minimis*; and *Clay Cross (Quarry Service) Ltd.* v. *Fletcher* [1978] 1 W.L.R. 1429, 1433, eliminating motive as a defence, and holding that pay differentials must be genuinely due to material differences. Sarcastically, he added that there was no doubt that the European Court with its liberal approach would introduce an exception on the same lines.

Lord Denning adopted a similar attitude of giving full effect to the legislative policy in construing the Race Relations Acts 1968 and 1976 in *Race Relations Board* v. *Charter* (the members of clubs case)[70] and *Dockers' Labour Club and Institute Ltd.* v. *Race Relations Board*[71] (the associated members of clubs case), both of which he treated as involving discrimination in the provision of services or facilities to a "section of the public," which he held club members to be. Again, he gave the lead to the House of Lords, which, although reversing him in the clubs' cases, now followed him in *Applin* v. *Race Relations Board*[72] in holding that the fostering of a child in care was the provision of services to a section of the public, so that incitement by a National Front member to prospective foster parents not to foster coloured children was unlawful discrimination. The courts were here ahead of legislative opinion, one consequence of their view being that foster parents could not now refuse to take into their homes children on grounds of race or colour. Accordingly, the decision in *Applin* was to some extent statutorily reversed by section 23(2) of the 1976 Act, exempting a person's arrangements for taking certain other persons into care in his home from the prohibition on discrimination in provision of facilities or services contained in section 20.

Nor did he hesitate to strike down discrimination in governmental contexts. In *Savjani* v. *I.R.C.*[73] the Revenue had been requiring from taxpayers born in the Indian sub-continent full birth certificates for their children, even if born in the United Kingdom, thereby imposing difficulties, expense and a higher level of proof on them than on other United Kingdom taxpayers, who were merely required to produce the short form. He dismissed the Revenue's technical argument that they were not providing "services," holding that they were giving a valuable service to the public in collecting revenue, or giving relief or advice about tax.

Initially, with his respect for Parliament's chosen agencies for enforcement, Lord Denning was reluctant to intervene against its instrumentality, the Race Relations Board. This led him into the extraordinary decision in *R.* v. *Race Relations Board, ex parte Selvarajan*.[74] Effectively the decision whether there had been discrimination was delegated to three of the seven members of the Board's employment committee, four members not having had all the relevant papers, merely having seen a prejudicial recommendation by an officer, and being ignorant of the full facts set out by the Board's own conciliation committee, which had seen all parties, had investigated, and had upheld the complaint of unlawful discrimination. Both improper delegation and breach of natural justice would in other contexts have been found by Lord Denning. The case was to have consequences. In *R.* v. *Commission for Racial Equality, ex parte Cottrell and Rothon*,[75] the Divisional Court, following *Selvarajan*, held that if the Commission were to function efficiently there could not be cross-examination of those complaining of discrimination, and delegation to the Commission's staff was permissible, with hearsay evidence being presented in summary to Commission

---

[70] [1972] 1 Q.B. 545, reversed [1973] A.C. 868. The 1976 Act, s.25 provided that clubs could not discriminate on racial grounds.
[71] [1974] Q.B. 503, reversed [1976] A.C. 285, also now irrelevant in view of s.25 of the 1976 Act.
[72] [1973] 1 Q.B. 815, affirmed [1975] A.C. 259.
[73] [1981] 2 W.L.R. 636.
[74] [1975] 1 W.L.R. 1686.   [75] [1980] 1 W.L.R. 1580.

members. Lord Denning approved this case in *Commission for Racial Equality v. Amari Plastics Ltd.*[76] However, while expressing sympathy for the Commission that although their cumbersome machinery might have gone through a full inquiry they might still find themselves traversing the same ground on appeal to an industrial tribunal, he pointed out that the person complained against (and effectively found "guilty" of acts of unlawful racial discrimination if a non-discrimination notice was issued) would have had no opportunity to challenge the Commission's findings of fact which in fairness and in justice they should have. The first proper opportunity in the absence of cross-examination, would come on appeal. Accordingly, he required the Commission, when it proposed to issue a non-discrimination notice, to accompany this with a statement setting out the findings of fact on which it proposed to act, so that the person complained against had an opportunity to controvert those facts on appeal.

Reluctance on appeal to upset findings of fact by the chosen instrumentality of enforcement, in this case a county court judge sitting with two assessors, explains his refusal in *Race Relations Board* v. *Associated Newspapers*[77] to set aside a ruling that publishing an advertisement for nurses to work in South Africa and stating "white patients only" was not by implication conduct indicating an intention to do an act of discrimination, *i.e.* discriminatory advertising, in Great Britain. The presence or not of such an intention was a matter of fact for the county court. The result was doubtless affected by the anomaly, pointed to by Lord Denning, that the Race Relations Act permits discrimination in engaging persons for employment outside Great Britain.

However, he became more wary of the Commission, a position to some extent brought about by its assertion in *R.* v. *Commission for Racial Equality, ex parte Hillingdon L.B.C.*[78] that the court had no jurisdiction in the absence of bad faith on the Commission's part to undertake any judicial review of the terms of reference it had drawn up for a formal investigation. His natural indignation at the Commission's high-handed attitude that it was unchallengeable temporarily blinded Lord Denning to the very real evils that the Commission was seeking to eradicate. Although there was evidence that Hillingdon Council had been responsible for three unlawful discriminatory acts concerning homeless families arriving at Heathrow Airport in November and December 1978, he held that the Commission did not have sufficient grounds for commencing a formal inquisitorial investigation, and that the terms of reference for such investigation were so wide as to enable it to act as a roving investigator without limit into the Council's housing activities. The House of Lords upheld the trial judge's quashing of the Commission's terms of reference as too wide (and the Court of Appeal's confirmation thereof) on the grounds that the Commission had, at the House of Lords' hearing, admitted that they did not have the necessary belief that the Council was discriminating generally in the provision of housing through homelessness against all black residents or immigrants (as opposed merely to those black immigrant families arriving at Heathrow and claiming to be homeless). Such a belief was a condition precedent to its very wide terms of reference.[79]

[76] [1982] 2 W.L.R. 972.
[77] [1978] 1 W.L.R. 905.
[78] [1981] 3 W.L.R. 520.
[79] [1982] 3 W.L.R. 159 and 170.

In *Mandla* v. *Lee*[80] Lord Denning was to go so far as to express regret that the Commission for Racial Equality had taken up the case of a private school headmaster who refused to admit a Sikh boy unless he had his hair cut, ceased wearing a turban and conformed to school uniform rules. Lord Denning held that the Sikhs were a religious community, not a "racial group" defined by "race . . . or . . . ethnic . . . origins," so were not entitled to protection against discrimination under the Race Relations Act. In any event, he thought that there was neither direct nor indirect discrimination under the Race Relations Act, since other Sikh and many other non-Christian or non-English children, willing to conform to the rules, were admitted. At the same time he was anxious to protect "the Jews" in England against discrimination, holding by virtue of his interpretation that they had racial characteristics.[81] His judgment was reversed by the House of Lords in a notable opinion by Lord Fraser, taking the broad view and following a New Zealand case (itself in line with UN doctrine and the teaching of sociologists) that there was an ethnic group where a distinct social and cultural entity cohered together and had, as an essential aspect, apart from its solidarity, beliefs as to its common historical origins.[82] Accordingly the Sikhs were an ethnic group. There had, Lord Fraser found, also been indirect discrimination in that a condition of entry had been applied to all intending pupils, but it was one which could conscientiously only be complied with by a smaller proportion of Sikhs than it could by non-Sikhs. Nor could such a condition be "justified" under the Act because, although the court was sympathetic to the headmaster's wish to have homogeneity in his school and to preserve its Christian character, the condition being imposed in pursuance of this aim, it was designed to prevent the manifestation of ethnicity. At the same time their Lordships regretted criticism of the Commission (far stronger from other members of the Court of Appeal), pointing to the difficult task faced by the Commission in implementing the Act.

Immigration and Deportation

Another category of cases where Lord Denning appears open to charges of "discrimination" is that of judgments on immigration and deportation matters.

Professor H.W.R. Wade, relying to a large extent on inferences drawn from Lord Denning's decisions, stated that

> "The courts have shown a marked reluctance to extend to aliens the same principles of procedural protection and fair play that apply to citizens of this country."[83]

Apparent inconsistencies in the manner of controlling executive discretion as between immigration and deportation decisions in comparison with decisions in other areas are also pointed to in *Justice, Lord Denning and the Constitution*.[84]

---

[80] [1982] 3 W.L.R. 933.
[81] *Ibid.* pp. 936–937. He obviously had not read Arthur Koestler, and would have been shocked had he been told that this part of his judgment sounded like Rosenberg.
[82] [1983] 2 W.L.R. 620, 626–627.
[83] *Administrative Law* (4th ed.), p. 483.
[84] pp. 168–170. At pp. 7–11 the examination of Lord Denning's cases in the context of "racism" in Britain, carries the innuendo that he was not immune from this.

International Law clearly distinguishes between nationals and aliens in the protections it confers. Article 12(4) of the Covenant provides that no national may be arbitrarily deprived of the right to enter his own country, whereas the international instruments are strictly circumscribed as to the rights and protections conferred on aliens' entering and remaining in states of which they are not nationals. It is consequently difficult to argue that extensive rights of entry exist. Nonetheless, once lawfully within that territory, Article 13 of the Civil Rights Covenant confers minimal procedural protections on aliens as also does the Fourth Protocol of the European Convention, which the United Kingdom did not ratify on account of her legislation preventing many nationals from entry to the United Kingdom as of right. Since January 1976 the European Convention on Establishment 1955 has conferred additional detailed rights and protections in the United Kingdom on nationals of other ratifying states, while, since her accession to the EEC, EEC workers have had rights in the United Kingdom under the EEC Treaty. These protections, other than the Covenant, do not apply to immigrants from the Commonwealth, Third World countries or the United States. In such a context, with the series of amendments since 1962 enhancing the immigration authorities' power to refuse Commonwealth citizens entry to the United Kingdom and the implicit legislative policy of keeping persons not of United Kingdom descent out of the country, it was inevitable, because of the legislative and treaty pattern, that judgments upholding governmental power to exclude persons from the United Kingdom would risk characterisation as racially motivated. With the exception of his later trade union and labour relations decisions, Lord Denning's approach has not been the anti-democratic one of seeking to frustrate Parliament's intention. Rather, it has been of extending provisions to fill in gaps inadvertently omitted, and of promoting Parliament's policy. Taken in conjunction with his normal approach of crediting public authorities with acting reasonably, and even ignoring his own authoritarian attitudes, such as respect for official policy choices in national matters, a heightened consciousness of his "Englishness," and adverse attitudes to all persons he considered to have acted unlawfully, dishonestly or improvidently, he was bound to give judgments upholding official power to exclude persons from the United Kingdom. His approach was, in the main, not dissimilar from that of his judicial contemporaries, as is shown by the fact that in so few of the cases were there dissents,[85] and that the Law Lords during the 1970s, apart from two liberal judgments,[86] in which Lord Denning had no opportunity of participating, also gave full faith and credit to immigration officials, even construing the power of exclusion pending appeal more strictly,[87] and imposing a duty of absolute candour, so that omission to notify officials of any factor which might affect the permission,

---

[85] *Cf.* Buckley L.J. in *R.* v. *Governor of Pentonville Prison, ex p. Azam* ([1973] 2 W.L.R. 949, and Lord Salmon's outstanding dissent in the Lords ([1973] 2 W.L.R. 1058, 1075–1076), leading the Labour Government to give an amnesty against removal to persons who had before January 1, 1973 unlawfully entered the United Kingdom and were no longer liable to prosecution under the Commonwealth Immigrants Act 1968.

[86] *D.P.P.* v. *Bhagwan* [1972] A.C. 60 and *Waddington* v. *Miah* [1974] 2 All E.R. 377.

[87] *Suthendran* v. *Immigration Appeal Tribunal* [1976] 3 W.L.R. 725 (H.L.).

even one supervening after permission but before entry, would turn the immigrant into an illegal entrant.[88]

Disappointment felt and charges of inconsistency by liberal lawyers at his performance in the immigration and deportation spheres is of his own making. As he himself said: "Long have I associated myself with human rights."[89] He had also associated himself with freedom of the individual, only the careful reader being able to detect that it was freedom of the "citizen" which was to prevail.[90] Above all, he had associated himself with justice.[91]

How then did Lord Denning behave in court in immigration and deportation matters? First, he promoted the legislative policy of restricting entry of "non-patrials" (the category effectively created by the Immigration Act 1971) and of deporting them by extensively interpreting the legislation, reading words into the relevant sections so as to uphold either refusal of entry or an order for removal.[92] Indeed, in one of his last reported cases, *R. v. Secretary of State for Home Department, ex parte Margueritte*,[93] this time for purposes of registration as a citizen, he relied on his earlier reading in of the word "lawfully" to alter section 5A(3) of the British Nationality Act in the context of the Immigration Act 1971, consequently disallowing for purposes of a citizenship application the early years of the applicant's residence as periods when he was "ordinarily resident" because he had "overstayed" his permission as then granted.

Secondly, he misinterpreted International Law. Thus, in *R. v. Secretary of State for the Home Department, ex parte Thakrar*, he held that the admission of British protected persons (Ugandan Asians expelled by the Amin Government from the former protectorate) was not required by International Law, and that even if it were, such a rule was excluded by the fact that the Immigration Act was a code.[94] This decision is contrary to Article 12(4) of the Civil Rights Covenant to which the United Kingdom was soon to accede, and, even more significantly, it was contrary to her international practice. Lord Denning also misinterpreted the scope of the right to marry in the European Convention (which right if exercised would have resulted in a

---

[88] *R. v. Secretary of State for the Home Department, ex p. Zamir* [1980] A.C. 930, a decision much cut down in *R. v. Secretary of State for the Home Department, ex p. Khawaja* [1983] 2 W.L.R. 321 after Lord Denning's retirement. The judgments by Lords Scarman and Bridge are hallmarked by real concern with civil liberties. "Realist" remarks on the accidents of changes in court composition and the possibility of "swinging" votes, are wholly justified here: Lord Wilberforce and Lord Fraser were now persuaded that their earlier judgments required confining. Lord Templeman was new to the Lords.

[89] *The Due Process of Law*, p. 101.

[90] *Freedom Under the Law*, p. 4—indeed not all "citizens" after the Commonwealth Immigrants Act 1962 were to be protected. But it may be, with his attention to style, that Denning thought it uneuphonious to use "individual" 3 times in 8 lines of text.

[91] *The Family Story*, p. 172. Public lectures in the early 1950s on this theme was published in 1955 as *The Road to Justice*.

[92] *R. v. Secretary of State for the Home Department, ex p. Shadeo Bhurosah* [1968] 1 Q.B. 266, referred to above at p. 256; *Re Abdul Manan* [1971] 1 W.L.R. 859, reading in "lawfully" before "ordinarily resident"; *Azam*, above, reading "is not given" as "has not been given," so as to allow removal of pre-1973 unlawful entrants, and declining to read the Act as dealing with methods of exercising the basic freedom of any British subject to move at will about the Crown's dominions, rather than as removing such right in the case of "non-patrials."

[93] [1983] Q.B. 180.

[94] [1974] Q.B. 684. M.B. Akehurst, "Ugandan Asians and the Thakrar Case" (1975) 38 M.L.R. 72, trenchantly criticises the decision.

right to remain, the prospective spouse being a patrial with the right of abode in the United Kingdom) by reading Article 12 as limited by Article 5(1)(*f*) authorising detention of a person against whom action is being taken with a view to deportation.[95] His interpretation denied the substance of the right, whereas the Convention cannot be interpreted so as to destroy the substance of a right by implied limitations, and does not preclude either the provision of facilities for celebration of a marriage in prison or temporary release for such purpose. Although in this same case Lord Denning held that Article 8 (respect for family life) could provide immigration officers with guidance as to how to exercise their discretion, he was subsequently to rule that the Article would give rise to too much uncertainty, and that the immigration officer was correct in ignoring it when declining to admit a wife and family on an allegedly short visit to the husband, who was a temporary worker and resident in the United Kingdom.[96]

Thirdly, he construed the immigration rules strictly, upholding interpretations by immigration officers,[97] unless his sympathy was specially excited so as to hold that the rules had been misconstrued and that officials had a discretion.[98]

Fourthly, he would automatically ascribe good faith to those with authority who were exercising their power to exclude.[99] Indeed, he made challenge by way of habeas corpus ineffective, by ruling that production of the relevant order for detention was prima facie good, and that the burden of

---

[95] *R.* v. *Home Secretary, ex p. Bhajan Singh* [1976] Q.B. 198. See above, p. 267, n. 91. Lord Denning, from the report, mentally characterised the marriage as one of mere convenience to avoid deportation, not giving due weight to the fact that arranged marriages are the accepted pattern for most Asians. Since 1976 the Civil Rights Covenant Art. 26 has also protected the right to marry, while Art. 10 requires persons deprived of their liberty to be treated with humanity and respect for the inherent dignity of the human person.

[96] *R.* v. *Chief Immigration Officer, ex p. Bibi* [1976] 1 W.L.R. 979. Since 1976 Art. 23 of the Civil Rights Covenant also requires protection of the family and thus of family life.

[97] See *R.* v. *Immigration Appeal Tribunal, ex p. Alexander* [1982] 1 W.L.R. 430, a majority decision, reversed by the House of Lords ([1982] 1 W.L.R. 1076) which held that the rules were not to be construed with the strictness of a statute. *Cf. R.* v. *Home Secretary, ex p. Hosenball* [1977] 1 W.L.R. 766, where Lord Denning declared the Immigration Rules were merely rules of practice to be prayed in aid. Even if conformity was required, he would broadly construe a letter refusing any particulars at all as conforming to the requirements of rule 42.

In contrast, within a year, he was construing the Rules strictly, even harshly, in *R.* v. *I.A.T. ex p. Marek* [1978] 1 W.L.R. 1190, where he overruled the Divisional Court. Para. 39 of the Immigration Rules provided that these "cover the admission for settlement of the dependents of a person who is already in the United Kingdom and settled here." He read this as meaning that a sponsor must be physically present and not merely ordinarily resident in the United Kingdom at the time when his dependents apply for permanent settlement. Consequently, when an infant son, who met all other requiremets for settlement applied while his mother was in Kenya on a business visit, he was not entitled to permision. The mother died in Kenya before permission was refused, so the matter could not be remedied by an application made on her return.

[98] *R.* v. *Chief Immigration Officer, Gatwick Airport, ex p. Kharazzi* [1980] 1 W.L.R. 1396, a majority judgment.

[99] *Schmidt* v. *Home Secretary* [1969] 2 Ch. 149 (the scientology students); *R.* v. *Home Secretary, ex p. Mughal* [1974] Q.B. 313; and *R.* v. *Chief Immigration Officer, ex p. Bibi*, above.

Lord Denning was not prepared to interfere with Home Office characterisation of non-disclosures of information by immigrants. If the Home Office thought that the non-disclosure was not so material that they should treat the immigrant as an illegal entrant (in accordance with *R.* v. *Secretary of State for the Home Department, ex p. Zamir* [1980] A.C. 930) then the immigrant would have the benefit of being treated as an overstayer entitled to remain in the United Kingdom pending appeal on the merits as to whether his leave should be extended. Otherwise, he would be removed from the United Kingdom and have to appeal,

proof on any applicant was to show that he was being unlawfully detained.[1] This decision in one sense furthered the policy of the Act and rules, as, with existing appeal procedures to a tribunal, re-investigation by the courts could be seen as duplication and interference. Yet it effectively meant that habeas corpus was defeated by production of a piece of paper, the courts intervening only in the event of bad faith or absence of any evidence on which the immigration officer could have acted being proven.

It is strange that Lord Denning as a first rate administrative lawyer should have followed Geoffrey Lane L.J.'s lead in taking a "Wednesbury approach" in *Hussein*,[2] because earlier in *Azam* he had recognised that the question whether an immigrant was illegal or not was to be fully investigated.[3] New life was however given to habeas corpus by their Lordships in *R.* v. *Secretary of State for the Home Department, ex parte Khawaja*,[4] a case overruling *obiter dicta* by Lord Wilberforce in *Zamir*[5] as to a duty of candour and positive disclosure on immigrants. On this last point Lord Denning had, before the Lords' ruling in *Zamir*, taken a typical common-sensical position, distinguishing between deception and absence of deceit, holding that where an immigrant was not asked questions and was not deliberately concealing any matter he would not be in breach of the Immigration Act.[6] On habeas corpus the position since 1818 has now been reinstated: the courts have a duty to enquire into and to be satisfied whether the applicant is an illegal entrant, with the burden of proof resting on the immigration authorities, who must discharge it to a standard, which while civil, is that appropriate to a grave matter affecting personal liberty.[7]

Similar automatic ascription of good faith to the Home Secretary occurred in *R.* v. *Governor of Brixton Prison, ex parte Soblen*.[8] Unabashedly, in *The Due Process of Law*[9] Lord Denning stated:

without facilities for fully putting his case, from abroad. In *R.* v. *Secretary of State for the Home Department, ex p. Jayakody* [1982] 1 W.L.R. 405 the Home Office looked kindly on a visitor who did not disclose that he was married when visiting his wife in the United Kingdom. In contrast, in *R.* v. *Home Secretary, ex p. Khawaja* [1982] 1 W.L.R. 625, where an entrant, married by Muslim rites, entered on a short visit and thereafter married the wife in a United Kingdom ceremony after she had obtained a final decree, this was characterised as material non-disclosure making him an illegal entrant. Lord Denning upheld both decisions, commenting on the "gross deception" in the second case. He was upheld by their Lordships ([1983] 2 W.L.R. 321).

[1] *R.* v. *Secretary of State for the Home Department, ex p. Choudhary* [1978] 1 W.L.R. 1177.
[2] [1978] 1 W.L.R. 700, a case preceding *Choudhary*, but not a binding precedent.
[3] [1974] A.C. 18, 31–32.
[4] [1983] 2 W.L.R. 321, the judgments by Lords Scarman and Bridge will prove historically significant in preserving habeas corpus as an effective remedy.
[5] *R.* v. *Secretary of State for the Home Department, ex p. Zamir* [1980] A.C. 930.
[6] *R.* v. *Secretary of State for the Home Department, ex p. Mangoo Khan* [1980] 1 W.L.R. 569, doubted in *Zamir* in the Lords.
[7] [1983] 2 W.L.R. 321 at p. 356, *per* Lord Bridge, relying on Lord Denning's dicta on the standard required to discharge the burden of proof when the "grave and weighty offence" of adultery was in issue: *Bater* v. *Bater* [1951] P.35.
[8] [1963] 2 Q.B. 243. Earlier, in *R.* v. *Secretary of State for Home Affairs, ex p. Soblen* [1963] 1 Q.B. 829, 842, Denning, dealing with refusal and "leave to land," held that "land" means "land as a free man, free to move about in this country," so that a humane necessitous allowing of Soblen into hospital in the United Kingdom, after injuries self-inflicted to ensure that he would be landed in the United Kingdom, was not permission to land. Accordingly, detention pending his removal by direction of the immigration authorities was upheld in habeas corpus proceedings.
[9] p. 160.

"The United States Government wanted him to be sent there. Now his offence was not an extraditable offence. So he could not be extradited to the United States. *In order to do what the United States wanted,* (my italics) the Home Secretary took another step. He made an order that Dr. Soblen be deported . . . ."

In 1962 Lord Denning had found there was no evidence that the Home Secretary was using the power of deportation for an ulterior purpose, although to most observers there was evidence that that was his dominant purpose. There were the admitted representations by the United States, the fact that Dr. Soblen could have been deported to other countries willing to receive him, and that the Home Secretary insisted on placing him only on an aircraft bound for the United States.

Fifthly, he would restrictively interpret the rules of natural justice,[10] even though he might purport to lay down a more liberal test generally for application of the rules.[11]

Sixthly, although there was no binding precedent as to the applicability of the rules of natural justice in so serious a matter as deportation, he declined to overrule a Divisional Court judgment given in 1920.[12] This he could well have done: administrative law and the principles of natural justice had greatly developed since then. The result is that the English Court of Appeal behaved less courageously to an American Communist sympathiser and possible spy than did the South African Appellate Division in reading into the South African Suppression of Communism Act a requirement that the Minister of Justice observe natural justice before making a banning order, rather than merely listening to any subsequent representations.[13] Once Lord Denning had given the *Soblen* ruling, the decisions in *Schmidt* and *R.* v. *Home Secretary, ex parte Hosenball*[14] were predictable. In *Soblen* Lord Denning did not rely on national security, merely stating that the purpose of the legislation would be defeated if it were necessary in advance to give aliens the right to be heard before making a deportation order. Also, if allowed to make representations, the alien, being on notice, might absent himself to avoid apprehension. In *Hosenball* Lord Denning now relied on the public interest in the security of the realm, which outweighed the public interest in the administration of justice, holding that the balance between national security and freedom of the individual is a matter for the Home Secretary, who is answerable, not to the courts, but to Parliament. In *The Due Process of Law*[15] he indicated that it was information possibly leading to the elimination by a

---

[10] In *Mughal*, above, reports contradicting an immigrant's story were not revealed to him but only an outline of the facts; and in *R.* v. *Secretary of State for the Home Department, ex p. Santillo* [1981] 2 W.L.R. 362, a prisoner proposed to be deported was given no opportunity to answer information given to the Home Secretary by the Police and prison authorities that he had been acquitted of other crimes, that there was similar fact evidence as to his criminal behaviour, and that he had been refused parole.

[11] According to *Schmidt*, above, the natural justice rules proper apply where there is a "legitimate expectation" of a benefit. It suffices, where there is a mere hope of a permit being granted, that the Home Secretary will listen to representations made subsequent to the decision.

[12] *R.* v. *Leman Street Police Station Inspector, ex p. Venicoff* [1920] 3 K.B. 72.

[13] *R.* v. *Ngwevela* (1954) 1 S.A. 123.

[14] [1977] 1 W.L.R. 766.

[15] p. 85. Did he obtain this information through Norman's intelligence contacts?

foreign power of intelligence agents which was the basis of the decision in *Hosenball*, who together with Philip Agee was deported. On that assumption there would have been conformity with Article 13 of the Civil Rights Covenant, because "compelling reasons of national security" would have justified refusal to give such particulars.

The few cases where Lord Denning found against the immigration authorities, or at least gave a ruling differing from their interpretation, are all easily explicable on the usual criteria of his decision-making. In *R.* v. *Home Secretary, ex parte Phansopkar*[16] there was a right on the part of wives of patrials to be admitted to the United Kingdom on production of a certificate of patriality. It seemed quite wrong that the Home Office's lengthy procedures, carried out in the Indian sub-continent, should stop wives and families joining husbands working in the United Kingdom. In *Mehta* v. *Home Secretary*,[17] a student was technically out of time to appeal, the fault being that of her lawyer. Lord Denning held that such technicality could not be relied upon. In *R.* v. *Immigration Appeal Tribunal, ex parte Subramanian*,[18] he ruled in law that the Home Office's administrative delays in appeal proceedings meant that an appellant could not be deported pending the appeal, even if his leave to remain had expired, but, on the facts, he found that discretion to refuse extension of leave had been properly exercised in the light of events during the appeal. Finally, in *Kharrazi*[19] the Iranian public schoolboy case, Lord Denning's sympathy led him to hold that the immigration officer had misconstrued the rules.

One cannot leave the subject without letting Lord Denning speak for himself:

> "In recent times England has been invaded—not by enemies—nor by friends—but by those who seek England as a haven. In England there is social security—a national health service and guaranteed housing—all to be had for the asking without payment and without working for it. Once here, each seeks to bring his relatives to join him. So they multiply exceedingly . . . "[20]

Later, in concluding his review of his immigration cases he says:

> "It seems to me that the immigration officers do their work efficiently and honestly and fairly. I have never known a case where they have been unfair."[21]

---

[16] [1976] Q.B. 606.

[17] [1975] 2 All E.R. 1084.

[18] [1976] 3 W.L.R. 630. His ruling as to non-removal pending appeal was not upheld in a highly technical judgment in the House of Lords: *Suthendran* v. *Immigration Appeal Tribunal* [1976] 3 W.L.R. 725. Neither Lord Denning's nor the House of Lord's judgments would accord with the requirement of Art. 13 of the Civil Rights Covenant that there must be a review either by the competent authority or by persons especially designated by that body.

[19] [1980] 1 W.L.R. 1396.

[20] *The Due Process of Law*, p. 155. A similar attitude informs his remarks in *Lim Poh Choo* v. *Camden and Islington Area Health Authority* [1979] Q.B. 196, where he made disparaging remarks about the possibility that because of the National Health Service and its facilities the plaintiff's mother and family in Singapore would inherit massive damages if these were awarded.

[21] *Ibid.* p. 176.

It is difficult not to conclude that these opinions and the imposition of burdens on the taxpayer[22] influenced his decisions. This was particularly evident in the way in which he interpreted certain legislation conferring financial and social benefits so as effectively to exclude immigrants, the two most notable categories being the criteria for eligibility for Local Education Authority awards[23] and housing on the grounds of homelessness. Indeed the combined effect in practice of his interpretation of the Housing (Homeless Persons) Act 1977 and his treatment of administrative decisions thereunder was that a local authority seriously contended that there was no duty on housing authorities to "foreigners" or to persons in any family unit which had not previously occupied a family home in Great Britain. This suggestion having been dismissed by their Lordships,[24] he then ruled that those who came to Great Britain without beforehand finding for themselves "permanent" accommodation[25] would be disentitled as "intentionally homeless." The formal basis of this judgment was of course that the courts should not interfere with the admittedly extremely difficult exercise of balancing claims to the limited housing stock, a task entrusted by Parliament to local authorities, their decisions requiring to be looked upon benevolently and only to be interfered with when so unreasonable that they cannot stand.[26]

Other Groups Less Favourably Treated

Lord Denning had jaundiced views about certain categories of person whom he believed either behaved unlawfully, or badly, or were prone to do so. The most notable species not to receive impartial treatment at his hands were convicted prisoners, especially I.R.A. men, foreign businessmen, crooks or those he considered lacking in business integrity, and those with beliefs he thought misguided or dangerous.

Prisoners

Prisoners must, by Article 10 of the Civil Rights Covenant, be treated with humanity and with respect for the inherent dignity of the human person. Except to the extent that their other rights are expressly or by necessary implication limited, prisoners still continue to have such rights.[27] Litigation by convicted prisoners asserting such rights received from Lord Denning a consistently chilly reception. In *Goody* v. *Odhams Press Ltd.*[28] a prisoner, attempting to vindicate his right to reputation by a libel action, found Lord Denning distinguishing dicta in his own House of Lords decision in *Plato*

---

[22] Some years ago, at a time of fuller employment, economists showed that immigrants, who were mainly workers, used the social services less and made greater contributions per capita to the economy than did the aging "indigenous" population.
[23] *R.* v. *Barnet L.B.C., ex p. Shah* [1982] 2 W.L.R. 474, reversed [1983] 1 All E.R. 226. (H.L.).
[24] *Cf.* Lord Lowry's remarks (on contentions derived from Lord Denning's judgments) in *R.* v. *Hillingdon Borough Council, ex p. Islam* [1981] 3 W.L.R. 942, 953c, reversing *Islam* [1981] 3 W.L.R. 109 (C.A.).
[25] *Lambert* v. *Ealing L.B.C.* [1982] 1 W.L.R. 550. See also McAuslan, pp. 203–205.
[26] *Ibid.* p. 557.
[27] *Raymond* v. *Honey* [1982] 2 W.L.R. 465, 468, *per* Lord Diplock.
[28] [1967] 1 Q.B. 333. See also *Morgan* v. *Odham's Press Ltd.* [1971] 1 W.L.R. 1239.

Films Ltd. v. *Speidel*[29] as to non-admissibility of particular instances: Lord Denning admitted in mitigation of damages evidence of previous convictions as the raw material on which a reputation is built up. In *Rondel* v. *Worsley*[30] he held a barrister sued for negligence in conducting a case was immune, the basis really being, as Lord Pearce pointed out in the House of Lords, unwillingness to allow criminal cases to be reopened.[31] That Lord Denning's motivation was to prevent convicted prisoners from having a retrial of offences for which they had been tried and convicted was made abundantly clear in *Barclays Bank Ltd.* v. *Cole,* where he denied the plaintiff a jury, even though "fraud", entitling a defendant to a civil jury, was in issue. Lord Denning said:

> "So Cole denies the robbery and is determined to have it tried again. He wishes to canvass again his guilt or innocence, but this time before a jury in a civil case. There is too much of this sort of thing going on: Hinds [July 30, 1964, *The Times*], Goody, Rondel and now Cole."[32]

He avoided the right to jury trial by characterising robbery as involving violence rather than false representations (the meaning he gave to "fraud"). He again inveighed against *Hollington* v. *F. Hewthorn and Co. Ltd.,*[33] as he had done in *Goody,* and argued that a conviction should be admissible as prima facie proof of the facts on which the conviction was based, thus in any second set of proceedings assuming the guilt of the convicted party. It was therefore unsurprising that, when the I.R.A. Birmingham bombers sought to sue the police for damages on the ground that they were assaulted in custody, Lord Denning was determined not to allow them to sue and to reopen the judge's findings that their confessions were voluntary, the confessions being the only sufficient evidence on which to charge, let alone convict the men.[34]

He said of their actions against the police:

> "It is really an attempt to set aside the convictions by a side-wind. It is a scandal that it should be allowed to continue."[35]

He did it by an enormous extension of the law of "issue estoppel" and by broad interpretation of statutory modifications to the rule in *Hollington* v. *Hewthorn.* Putting their decision on the ground of an abuse of the process of the court, and leaving aside "issue estoppel," which they thought should be a term confined to civil actions between the same parties or their privies, the House of Lords upheld Lord Denning's judgment that the statements of claim against the police should be struck out.[36] Lord Diplock also

---

[29] [1961] A.C. 1090 (H.L.). In *Speidel*, at p. 1138, he had suggested that *general* evidence as to the bad character of a notorious rogue could be given, while in *Dingle* v. *Associated Newspapers Ltd.* [1962] 3 W.L.R. 229 (H.L.) at p. 253 he had suggested that the person who gave the general evidence would know of the conviction.

[30] [1967] 1 Q.B. 443.

[31] [1969] 1 A.C. 191, 257.

[32] [1967] 2 Q.B. 738, 743. Diplock and Russell L.JJ. for reasons of administrative convenience (cheapness, speed and certainty) agreed.

[33] [1943] K.B. 587. In a quite different context, the validity of enforcement notices as against a category of person of whom he was not over fond (a caravan site owner), he had already declined to apply *Hollington* v. *Hewthorn* in relation to proof of convictions: see *Munnich* v. *Godstone R.D.C.* [1966] 1 W.L.R. 427.

[34] *McIlkenny* v. *Chief Constable of the West Midlands* [1980] 2 W.L.R. 689.

[35] Quoted by Lord Denning himself at p. 214 of *The Family Story*.

[36] *Hunter* v. *Chief Constable of the West Midlands Police and Others* [1981] 3 W.L.R. 906, 912–913.

emphasised that the action was designed to put pressure on the Home Secretary to release the Birmingham bombers from their life sentences, and pointed to the fact that the Home Office now admitted the assaults were by prison officers so that the Home Office should rather be pursued[37]—but this of course would not have affected the validity of the confessions and would not consequently be a reason for early release.

Subsequently, he restrictively interpreted the Prison Rules to hold that one of the I.R.A. prisoners, who had applied to the European Commission on the basis of "degrading treatment" in breach of Article 3, was not a "party to any legal proceedings," and was therefore not entitled to the benefit of Prison Rule 37A that the prison governor may not read correspondence with his solicitor.[38] Lord Denning delivered himself of remarks about "the audacity to complain" about a little bit of rough handling, bruising and black eyes and nothing more. Despite the horrific crime committed by the I.R.A. bombers, it is sad that Lord Denning did not remember what he had himself written in *Freedom Under the Law*, concerning "the 'passage à tabac' " and freedom from oppression while under arrest.[39] The essence of human rights thinking is that the dignity of the individual and integrity of his person is not to be sacrificed even to the national interest and the welfare of the group.

In an earlier case, alleging breach of the Prison Rules, and consequent damage following wrongful detention of a cheque (breach of a prisoner's property rights and of right to respect for his correspondence) he held the Prison Rules, dealing with what was to be done with securities for money, were merely regulatory directions and that prisoners could not initiate proceedings on the basis of an action for breach of statutory duty: "if the courts were to entertain actions by disgruntled prisoners, the governor's life would be made intolerable. The discipline of the prison would be undermined."[40]

A similar attitude that discipline must be maintained, with cases being decided quickly, led to his departing in *Fraser* v. *Mudge*[41] from his own precedent, *Pett* v. *Greyhound Racing Association Ltd.*[42] that legal representation should be permitted when a serious charge is made. Disciplinary charges can effectively lead to loss of liberty by way of loss of remission, and it seems that not only is natural justice not observed, but that the principle of equality of arms, inherent in Article 6 of the European Convention (even if, on the narrow interpretation now current, the Article does not apply to administrative tribunals) is breached because an unrepresented prisoner has not the same degree of competence in defending himself as have prison officers presenting a disciplinary case against him. Lord Denning's ruling in *Payne* v. *Lord Harris of Greenwich*[43] that the Parole Board need not give reasons even in outline for rejecting parole to a prisoner, who had more than once been rejected and was seeking the reasons so as to be able to meet them on

---

[37] *Ibid.* p. 914.
[38] *Guilfoyle* v. *Home Office* [1981] 2 W.L.R. 233. This decision should be contrasted with that of the Lords in *Raymond* v. *Honey*, above.
[39] pp. 23 and 26.
[40] *Becker* v. *Home Office* [1972] 2 Q.B. 407, 418. Mrs. Becker was imprisoned for obtaining credit as an undischarged bankrupt and was also "a vexatious litigant."
[41] [1975] 1 W.L.R. 1132.
[42] [1969] 1 Q.B. 125.
[43] [1981] 1 W.L.R. 754.

his next application, in effect denied the prisoner natural justice. He held
that at best a prisoner might possibly, if thought fit, be interviewed by a
Board member and told of a serious new factor affecting the reasons why he
should not be released—a suggestion he had made in *Santillo,* where a
prisoner had made representations against deportation.[44]

Finally, in *O'Reilly* v. *Mackman*[45] he denied Hull prison rioters (some of
whom were I.R.A. members serving terms for "terrorist" offences) the right
to proceed by declaration when judicial review was unlikely to be available
as being out of time and discretionary. It is difficult to believe that this is the
same judge who in *Pyx Granite Co. Ltd.* v. *Minister of Housing*[46] (and quoted by
him in 1979 in *The Discipline of Law*) was writing:

> "I take it to be settled law that the jurisdiction of the High Court to
> grant a declaration is not to be taken away except by clear words."

In *O'Reilly* v. *Mackman,* Lord Denning was also to make another
unprecedented extension of immunity. In *Sirros* v. *Moore*[47] he had extended
absolute immunity to Crown Court judges and to judges of courts from the
lowest to the highest, so long as the judge honestly believed that the steps he
was taking were within his jurisdiction. Police acting on the judge's
instructions would also enjoy immunity, *e.g.* against actions for trespass or
false imprisonment.[48] Now he held that the board of visitors of a prison was
in the same position as a magistrate, and was protected against actions by
prisoners.

In sum, so far as prisoners are concerned, Lord Denning effectively
limited their rights to protect their reputations by libel actions, limited their
rights to civil jury trial, conferred immunity on their barristers, conferred
immunity in suits by them against police officers who extort, or may have
extorted, confessions from them by violence, refused to uphold even those
limited rights to respect for correspondence enjoyed by them, impeded their
rights of access to the European Commission of Human Rights, denied them
the right to marry while in prison, denied them the right to enforcement of
the prison rules designed for their protection, denied them the right to legal
representation in disciplinary proceedings, conferred immunity on boards of
visitors should they in disciplinary proceedings wrongfully deny a prisoner
remission, and cut down the time and manner within which prisoners may
sue to challenge administrative decisions affecting them. This restrictive
attitude was in part occasioned by plaintiffs being I.R.A. men, as with
Guilfoyle, McIlkenny and *O'Reilly*—an attitude also influential in *Re Keenan.*[49]

[44] Above, p. 302.
[45] [1982] 3 W.L.R. 604.
[46] [1958] 1 Q.B. 554. He was also reneging on the reasoning in *Barnard* v. *National Dock Labour Board* [1953] 2 Q.B. 18 and in *Punton* v. *Ministry of Pensions (No. 2)* [1964] 1 W.L.R. 226.
[47] [1975] Q.B. 118.
[48] *Ibid.* p. 137, so long as they did not know his directions were wrong.
[49] [1972] 1 Q.B. 533, where I.R.A. detainees, had they been released by order of the courts at Westminster in habeas corpus proceedings, could not have been re-arrested (as they were to be in Northern Ireland) because the Civil Authorities (Special Powers) Acts applied only in Northern Ireland and there was then no Prevention of Terrorism (Temporary Provisions) Act applicable in the United Kingdom. By extensively interpreting a 1783 Act, he denied there was jurisdiction to issue a writ of habeas corpus in respect of events in Northern Ireland, thereby also avoiding the embarrassing necessity of ruling on controversial regulations conferring powers on H.M. Forces (subsequently held *ultra vires* by the Northern Ireland High Court and retrospectively validated by the Northern Ireland Act 1972).

Foreign Litigants

Lord Denning's judicial scepticism about foreign businessmen as litigants began in 1947 with a restrictive interpretation of the Foreign Judgments (Reciprocal Enforcement) Act 1933 and heavy distinguishing of the cases on security for costs by non-residents[50] and was implicitly admitted in *The Due Process of Law*,[51] addressing himself to the topic of absconding debtors or to a debtor who "lives in a foreign country and removes his assets outside England." Such thoughts commended to him the *Mareva* order, introduced in 1975, and eventually extended to United Kingdom debtors in 1979.[52]

Certain Business Interests

Lord Denning is similarly frank in the *Due Process of Law*, about his attitude to directors and companies[53] about whose integrity he was doubtful, and to gambling businesses.[54] In cases by such persons he was either to alter the scope of the rules of natural justice or to bend the legal rules to fit the needs of the situation.[55]

Perhaps the most apt comment, which can be applied to Lord Denning's attitude in all such cases, was made in a dissent by Diplock L.J.:

"It is not a presumption of law that a hire-purchase finance company cannot be innocent."[56]

Religious Groups

Those with beliefs Lord Denning thought dangerous or misguided, apart from the I.R.A., were scientologists. In *Hubbard* v. *Vosper* he had upheld a breach of confidence as being justified in the public interest by revealing "medical quackery of a dangerous kind."[57] There are parallels in this approach, although he was careful not to pre-judge the character of the sect,

---

[50] *Kohn* v. *Rinson and Stafford (Brod.) Ltd.* [1948] 1 K.B. 827.

[51] p. 133.

[52] See Hayton, pp. 101–105.

[53] pp. 49–51, 74–81, 155–156 and 182–183.

[54] pp. 82–84. He should perhaps have added a reference to the series of cases on contracts tainted by gaming and his negative attitude to enforcement, beginning with *William Hill (Park Lane) Ltd.* v. *Rose* [1948] 2 All E.R. 1107, where he doubted *Hyams* v. *Stuart King* [1908] 2 K.B. 696 and was upheld by the House of Lords who reversed it ([1949] A.C. 530). He continued with *MacDonald* v. *Green* [1951] 1 K.B. 594.

[55] In *R.* v. *Gaming Board of Great Britain, ex p. Benaim and Khaida* [1970] 2 W.L.R. 1009, Crockford's certificate was refused on grounds of unrevealed information regarding association of the club with certain persons of unacceptable background. This non-disclosure was upheld by Lord Denning as sources of information must be protected. If an organisation such as the Mafia had been moving into English gaming, this decision was not one at which it would have been proper to cavil. In *Re Pergamon Press* [1971] Ch. 388 and *Maxwell* v. *Department of Trade* [1974] Q.B. 523 the application of natural justice was restricted, as it also was in *Norwest Holst* v. *Secretary of State for Trade* [1978] Ch. 201. In *Wallersteiner* v. *Moir* [1974] 1 W.L.R. 991, remarks about fraud were made, even though it was not pleaded and the onus of proof is high. In *Re a Company*, above, powers of judicial review were wrongly assumed so as to order inspection of Racal Communications' books.

[56] *Snook* v. *London and West Riding Investments* [1967] 2 Q.B. 786, 800. His indignation at refinancing "shams" led in this case to injustice to the hire-purchase company.

[57] Above, p. 285.

when he dealt with an application by the Attorney-General at the instance of the Exclusive Brethren for an injunction against transmission of a television broadcast about their activities. In a dissent, he held that freedom of speech and of the press had priority over any suggested interference with fair trial of a civil action, and a *fortiori* in respect of proceedings pending in a valuation court dealing with the Exclusive Brethren's entitlement to rating exemptions on grounds that their property was a place of worship. His view was that all gagging injunctions, whether by way of contempt of court or arising in other proceedings, seeking to prevent true and fair comment on matters of public interest, should fail. In any event, he held that the law of contempt was inapplicable, being confined to courts proper and not extending to a valuation court. On this point he was upheld by the House of Lords.[58]

Lord Denning's negative attitude to scientology was also manifested in *Schmidt*,[59] where he upheld the Home Secretary's discretion to refuse an extension of scientology students' permits to stay in the United Kingdom, although, had he been minded so to do, there were legal arguments the other way, and *Soblen* could have been distinguished as applicable only to cases when national security was affected. In *R.* v. *Registrar General, ex parte Segerdal*[60] he declined to recognise scientology as a religion, rather holding it to be a philosophy, thereby disentitling it to registration as a place of worship and to rating advantages. This judgment had parallels with his earlier judgment in *Henning* v. *Church of Christ of Latter Day Saints*,[61] taking a restrictive view of what is a place of "public" religious worship, and holding that a Mormon temple, open only to Mormons of good standing with "recommends," was not exempt from rating.

These cases contrast starkly with *Attorney-General, rel. Bedfordshire County Council* v. *Trustees of the Howard United Reform Church, Bedford*[62] where a religious community to which Lord Denning was sympathetic sought entitlement to exemption under legislation, which if granted would have given it financial benefits. He construed section 56(1)(*a*) of the Town and Country Planning Act 1971 to exempt the United Reform Church from planning control, even though, as the House of Lords pointed out, reversing the Court of Appeal, the special exemption from public control was for ecclesiastical buildings being used as churches, and it was not intended to exempt them when they were demolished and church use ended.[63]

Since the question of discrimination is here under examination, it is appropriate to examine other Denning decisions impinging on the right to religious freedom and to manifest religious beliefs in practice. Mention has already been made of his insensitivity in relation to education, as shown by

---

[58] *Att.-Gen.* v. *B.B.C.* [1981] A.C. 303. Lord Salmon was far more outspoken about the nature of the sect, and considered it would have been a shocking blot on the law if it had granted an interim injunction against republishing a broadcast of great public service if it were subsequently found to be not libellous.

[59] [1969] 2 Ch. 149.

[60] [1970] 2 Q.B. 697.

[61] [1962] 1 W.L.R. 1091. The decision was affirmed by the House of Lords ([1964] A.C. 420), with Lord Evershed doubting whether "public" was not wrongly being construed as "open to the public," rather than as a place for collective worship as opposed to private worship at home. For historical reasons Church of England "closed" places of worship are differently treated and benefit from exemptions.

[62] [1975] Q.B. 41.

[63] [1976] A.C. 363.

Cumings and *Watt*[64] and in relation to the Race Relations Act and the Sikh Community in *Mandla* v. *Lee*.[65] Indeed, *Cumings* can be seen as *de facto* maintaining separate education systems as institutions for distinct groups of persons, and as contrary to the 1960 Convention Against Discrimination in Education, to which the United Kingdom is a party, the separate schooling not being exempted because of the absence of optionality.

He had been insensitive in the two other cases where attempts to assert special treatment in order to manifest religious beliefs were before the courts. In the second of these cases, *Ostreicher* v. *Secretary of State for the Environment*[66], a claim was made that a compulsory purchase order should be quashed, the hearing having been held on a festival day when the Jewish religion made it impossible for the applicant either to work or to employ anyone to work for her. The applicant had left her objection to the date on religious grounds too late to reorganise the hearing (involving many people), although some special arrangements were requested and denied. Lord Denning somewhat unfairly blamed the applicant's surveyors for not at this stage pushing the Department for a postponement. He found that under the circumstances the departmental decision to proceed with the hearing was reasonable, and that no breach of natural justice had occurred, considering that it would have been reasonable for the applicant to have sent her surveyor to the hearing.[67] It is implicit in his judgment that he thought that the religious objection was subsequently being pursued more vigorously only because the result of the hearing was in some respects adverse to the applicant, it being ruled that for certain properties she was entitled only to site value and not market value. However that may be, the case shows no awareness of the right of all persons, recognised in Article 18 of the Covenant, to manifest their religious beliefs in observance and in practice, limited by law only so far as is necessary to protect the rights of others. The same applies in respect of Article 27, requiring that, where ethnic or religious minorities exist, persons belonging to such minority shall not be denied the right to practice their own religion.

A much stronger case, showing insensitivity to the right to manifest religious beliefs in practice was *Ahmad* v. *Inner London Education Authority*.[68] Section 30 of the Education Act 1944 provided that "no person might be dismissed by reason of his attending . . . religious worship." A Muslim teacher required time off on Friday afternoon for prayers. Lord Denning held that the qualification should be read into section 30 "if the school time table so permits." He also dismissed Article 9 of the European Convention as drawn in vague terms and as unreasonable and provocative of litigation, suggesting that in his view minorities should not be given and would be unwise to claim preferential treatment.

---

[64] Above, p. 283.

[65] Above, p. 297.

[66] [1979] 37 P. & C.R. 9 (C.A.).

[67] p. 16. Very early, in Lord Denning's judicial career his attitude to religious beliefs, to whether conduct in relation to them was reasonable, and to balancing arose in *Fletcher* v. *Fletcher* [1945] 1 All E.R. 582, where he had to consider whether a husband, who had removed the matrimonial home to a religious movement in which sex was not permitted but had subsequently offered to resume co-habitation in a "community," was in desertion. He held that religious convictions and matrimonial duties and rights had to be balanced as a matter of commonsense, and that the offer was not a reasonable offer terminating the desertion.

[68] [1977] 3 W.L.R. 396.

In contrast, Scarman L.J., in dissent, construed section 30 broadly against the background of protection from discrimination, the European Convention, and international obligations, and suggested that sensible administrative arrangements could avoid such problems. Had Lord Denning wished to decide differently, he was in no way bound to follow his restrictive reading of section 30, and he could easily have invoked public policy,[69] as he had often done elsewhere, to reach a result which would have accorded the applicant rights to manifest his religion in practice. Perhaps the best comparison is his own purposive approach when sex discrimination was in issue in *Nothman* v. *Barnet Council*,[70] where he did not hesitate to read words into the unfair dismissal legislation in order to prevent discrimination in respect of unfair discrimination as between men and women workers with their different retirement ages.

The Right to an Effective Remedy in Public Law[71]

The last page of *Freedom Under the Law* (which with the addition of "Discuss" used to be a standard examination question) urged that the procedure for preventing abuse of power required reform by the judiciary and not by Parliament, the latter being unable to control the day to day activities of the many who administer the multiple activities of the State, or to award damages to those injured by any abuses. Lord Denning saw this task of reform and control as the most significant confronting the judiciary. In performing it, along initially with colleagues such as Lord Goddard and Devlin J., and later with Lords Parker, Reid, Wilberforce and Diplock in particular, Lord Denning greatly contributed to the power of the courts to intervene in executive decision-making.

This question is dealt with by Jowell,[72] so I shall not here treat its detail. My evaluative standpoint in this essay is the furtherance of individual human rights. Although with that measuring rod one can evaluate Lord Denning's work, there still remains the difficulty that his rulings, as C.K. Allen long ago said of statutory interpretation, hunt in pairs. Yet Lord Denning was consistent in that his goal was extended judicial power to do justice as he saw it: if he thought intervention necessary the rules would be enunciated so as to permit it; if not, the rules would be suitably interpreted, accorded exceptions, even limited in scope, especially in the case of natural justice, made of discretionary application, or the issue or the procedural requirements would be so characterised as to avoid intervention. On standing, however, he was always generous: that permitted judicial intervention, but did not require it. Thus, although he created the machinery which permits one to say that the possibility of an effective judicial remedy exists, one must also say that the machinery might frequently be immobilised.

---

[69] By Art. 2(3) of the Civil Rights Covenant the United Kingdom has undertaken if rights are not given effect "by existing 'legislative or other measures' to adopt such legislative or other measures." Judicial decision-making would be an appropriate "other measure."

[70] [1978] 1 W.L.R. 220.

[71] Art. 2(3) of the Civil Rights Covenant.

[72] Above, Chap. 6. Jowell's discussion of *locus standi* also makes it unnecessary here to discuss Lord Denning's furtherance of the right to recognition as a person before the law (Art. 16) and the right to equal protection of the law (Art. 26).

Effective Remedies in Private Law

Parallel to his development of effective remedies against public authorities, Lord Denning sought to confer effective remedies in respect of exercises of power by private law associations such as trade unions and domestic tribunals, applying to them similar principles, derived in part from public law and in part from contract, holding that their discretion could not be arbitrarily or capriciously exercised, and that their rules would be invalid if unreasonably in restraint of trade, being however unsuccessful in achieving judicial power to strike down rules because they were unreasonable, arbitrary or capricious.[73] He required such bodies to observe procedural fairness[74] and made all the private law remedies, including damages,[75] available against them.

A significant aspect of developing effective civil remedies is the refinement and refurbishing of causes of action, or put more modernly, extension of the grounds of liability of those infringing the interests of others. Lord Denning's contribution to this process has been covered in relation to protection of the family, especially wives, by Hayton and Freeman, in relation to bodily integrity and security of person[76] by Atiyah, in relation to property rights by Atiyah on contract and tort, by McAuslan on rights in land, by Davies and Freedland on interference with a business, and by this essay in relation to confidential information.

Just as extension of liabilities creates effective "positive" remedies, so also does the creation of new defences create effective "negative" remedies. This was an area where Lord Denning was even more inventive, with his development of the *High Trees House* line of cases, equitable proprietary estoppel, contractual licences, and other aspects of the "new equity," dealt with by Atiyah and by Hayton.

In seeking to deny that certain kinds of loss give rise to damages Lord Denning was effectively diminishing remedies by making the loss not actionable. Such cases were few, and are explicable on the basis that Lord Denning thought that no financial loss had in fact occurred, and that damages were in any event too large for persons injured so severely that they were insensible, especially when the taxpayer was paying for National Health Service negligence.[77]

Immunity, either in theory or in practice, and whether in the public or private spheres, denies those suffering at the hands of the immune party any effective remedy, and results also in inequality before the law.

Lord Denning rightly takes satisfaction at the statutory acceptance of his

---

[73] *Faramus*, above; *Nagle* v. *Fielden*, above; *Dickson* v. *Pharmaceutical Society*, above; and *Edwards* v. *SOGAT*, above. See Davies and Freedland, Chap. 8.

[74] *Breen* v. *A.E.U.*, above.

[75] *Bonsor* v. *Musicians Union* [1954] Ch. 479, his dissent being affirmed by the House of Lords ([1956] A.C. 104).

[76] His decisions in *Broom* v. *Morgan* [1953] 1 Q.B. 597 and *Ormrod* v. *Crosville Motor Services Ltd.* [1953] 1 W.L.R. 1120, in the latter case taking up Devlin J.'s first instance reasoning, were highly significant in extending liability. So was his decision in *Cassidy* v. *Ministry of Health* [1951] 2 K.B. 343. Occupiers' liability extensions were also protective of physical safety of individuals.

[77] *Lim Poh Choo*, above, and *Re C. (A Minor)* v. *Wiseman* [1982] 1 W.L.R. 71. *Cf.* Lord Scarman's comments on the inadvisability in such matters of judicial law reform, legislative consideration being more appropriate: *Lim Poh Choo* [1980] A.C. 174, 182.

views[78] about the limitation of immunity accorded foreign sovereigns by the United Kingdom courts. He had over a lengthy period urged that they should not be entitled to claim immunity when they engaged in commercial transactions.[79]

He was unwilling to see the immunity of the Crown extended by applying the principle that the Crown is not bound by statute absent express statement or necessary implication. Thus, he held public corporations bound by the Rent Restriction Acts.[80] He refused to hold a Crown servant, exercising official functions as Custodian of Enemy Property, had "Crown Status" in respect of his activities, Lord Denning's purpose being to ensure that income tax would be paid and end up in the fiscus, rather than that all sums held should be returned to their owners.[81]

His result-oriented approach was also manifest in another "immunity" issue, that of Post Office liability to businessmen who were put at risk by non-delivery of their mail following sympathetic action by Post Office workers during the Grunwick strike. He upheld the unarguable immunity of the Post Office for failure to carry out its general duties and its immunity in tort for any loss or damage under sections 9, 29 and 30 of the Post Office Act 1969. But he would not pronounce, as being "too difficult a subject matter," on whether the immunity extended to an action in bailment in respect of mail in Post Office custody.[82] In any case he would refuse relief by way of discretionary mandatory injunction, because, were the Post Office forced to reopen the Cricklewood sub-post office, it would then have to take back men it had disciplined for discriminating against Grunwick in their provision of services. This would give postal workers tremendous power to take sympathetic blacking action against any employer in dispute with his employees.

Other restrictions of immunity have been touched on already: trade unions and their officials had their immunity greatly eroded,[83] and businesses had contractual immunities derived from exemption clauses restricted by interpretative techniques and "fundamental breach."[84]

If courts lack jurisdiction either in the sense of power to entertain a suit or that of power to award particular relief, there is then immunity, so far at least as English courts are concerned. In the family law sphere Lord Denning was not prepared to see such immunity. From his early judicial days he sought to enlarge the jurisdiction of the courts to award maintenance,[85] and at a later stage successfully widened jurisdiction.[86] He insisted that the court had jurisdiction on divorce to make decisions for the welfare of all children, when their parents were married, even if the

---

[78] See *The Discipline of Law*, p. 289, referring to the State Immunity Act 1978.

[79] *Rahimtoola* v. *Nizam of Hyderabad* [1958] A.C. 379, a dissent; *Thai-Europe Tapioca Service Ltd.* v. *Government of Pakistan* [1975] 1 W.L.R. 1485; and *Trendtex Trading Corp.* v. *Bank of Nigeria* [1977] Q.B. 529.

[80] *Tamlin* v. *Hannaford* [1949] 2 All E.R. 327: the British Transport Commission was not entitled to protection of the Rent Restrictions Acts.

[81] *Bank voor Handel en Scheepvaart N.V.* v. *Administrator of Hungarian Property* [1953] 1 Q.B. 248, reversed [1954] A.C. 584.

[82] *Harold Stephen & Co. Ltd.* v. *Post Office* [1977] 1 W.L.R. 1172.

[83] See Davies and Freedland, pp. 377–411.

[84] See Atiyah, pp. 40–45.

[85] *Parks* v. *Parks* [1945] 2 All E.R. 580, reversed [1945] 2 All E.R. 491. Again he was statutorily confirmed, legislation subsequently conferring maintenance jurisdiction on the High Court.

[86] *King* v. *King* [1954] P. 55.

particular child was illegitimate and could not, because of section 1(2) of the Legitimacy Act 1926, be legitimated *per subsequens matrimonium*.[87] He extended the wardship jurisdiction,[88] covering also alien children ordinarily resident in England.[89] In private international law cases he was equally generous in extending jurisdiction whether for divorce proceedings,[90] nullity[91] a declaration of status,[92] or affiliation proceedings.[93]

Lord Denning's judgments on upholding or extending jurisdiction in private international law matters are too complex for examination here, but it is fair to generalise that although initially cautious about assuming jurisdiction,[94] subsequently he sought to apply English standards of actionability, especially in tort cases so as to secure an effective remedy for personal injury.[95] Later he was even to encourage forum-shopping in England, commenting on litigation arising out of a collision in Belgian river waters between Dutch and Belgian owned barges and a Dutch vessel, and duplicating Belgian litigation, that "if the forum is England, it is a good place to shop in, both for the quality of the goods and the speed of service," thus earning himself a rebuke from Lord Reid that his comments appeared:

> "to recall the good old days, the passing of which many regret, when inhabitants of this island felt an innate superiority over those unfortunate enough to belong to other races . . . The time is right for a re-examination of the rather insular doctrine."[96]

Reacting to this remonstration, Lord Denning in his dissent in *McShannon* v. *Rockware Glass Ltd.* delivered himself of dicta on *forum conveniens*, possibly going too far in denying all Scots plaintiffs the right to litigate in England, although his general ruling was upheld by their Lordships.[97]

Despite Lord Reid's remarks, the shipping and international commercial community, seeking to enforce their "property" rights, would pay tribute to Lord Denning for a series of significant judgments encouraging English litigation and arrestment of assets (which often at some stage pass through the City of London) and for developing the substantive legal rules.[98]

---

[87] *Packer* v. *Packer* [1954] P. 15.
[88] *Re S. (An Infant)* [1965] 1 W.L.R. 483.
[89] *Re P. (G.E.) an Infant* [1965] Ch. 568.
[90] *Cruh* v. *Cruh* [1945] 2 All E.R. 545.
[91] *Ramsay-Fairfax* v. *Ramsay-Fairfax* [1956] P. 115.
[92] *Har-Shefi* v. *Har-Shefi* [1953] P. 161.
[93] *R.* v. *Bow Road Justices, ex p. Adedigba* [1968] 2 Q.B. 572.
[94] *Korner* v. *Witkowitzer Bergbau und Eisenthütten Gewerkschaft* [1950] 1 All E.R. 558 and *Re Dulles Settlement Trusts (No. 2)* [1951] Ch. 842.
[95] In *Boys* v. *Chaplin* [1968] 2 Q.B. 1 he attempted to overrule *Machado* v. *Fontes* [1897] 2 Q.B. 231 so as to award certain heads of damage for personal injury and to develop the doctrine of the proper law of the tort. Taken together with *Phillips* v. *Eyre* (1870) L.R. 6 Q.B. 1, either a claim to such damages was not cognisable in an English court, being not actionable in Malta where the accident occurred, or damages were not claimable in terms of the relevant law to be applied by the English Court, namely Maltese Law.
[96] [1973] 2 W.L.R. 795, 800.
[97] [1977] 1 W.L.R. 376, 380, affirmed, [1978] 2 W.L.R. 362.
[98] The most cursory glance at Lloyd's Reports shows contributions by Denning on their own meriting an essay. His attempt in *The Siskina*, 2 Lloyd's Rep. 230, reversed [1979] A.C. 210 to ensure that maritime "fraud" assets could be attached, even if there was no cause of action in England, before they disappeared into "thin air", and the subsequent attempt in *Chief Constable of Kent* v. *Verdon-Roe*, above, broadly to interpret the Supreme Court Act 1981, s.37, would have given effective remedies to the international commercial community—and have had the side effects of bringing business to the United Kingdom and to the English legal profession.

That the assets of the dishonest or the bankrupt should not escape creditors' reach was so powerful a factor with Lord Denning that he was prepared to give a ruling conflicting with United Kingdom foreign policy towards the U.D.I. in Southern Rhodesia, holding in a dissent that the "High Court of Rhodesia" was a "British court" so that its orders could be enforced in England under the reciprocal provisions of the Bankruptcy Act 1914.[99]

Once English courts had jurisdiction, Lord Denning was reluctant to see it ousted,[1] even at the instance of a litigant who sought to withdraw his writ because he would get higher damages in the courts of another legal system.[2] Here, however, he disapproved of various factors: "ambulance chasing," Texas lawyers, contingency fees,[3] massive Texan damages, and insurance liability with British syndicates as well as an American insurer.[4] He took this approach even further in *Smith, Kline and French Laboratories Ltd.* v. *Bloch*,[5] enjoining a United Kingdom resident from suing an American company in the United States on the basis that it was in the public interest to have the dispute tried in England as the natural and proper forum, and that it would be an illegitimate advantage that, if not restrained, the United Kingdom resident would sue in the United States and "would there get higher damages, trial by jury, and lawyers on contingency fees."

Just as Lord Denning extended jurisdiction, there were other areas where he was to accord immunity.

His earlier reluctance to subject the Crown to liability in respect of events abroad had its culmination in his denial of jurisdiction to English courts to entertain proceedings for judicial review seeking a declaration that treaty obligations entered into by the Crown to the Indian peoples of Canada, in particular reserving lands to them, were still owed by Her Majesty in right of the Government in the United Kingdom. He held that the Crown was divisible, with its obligations to the Indian people being those of the Crown in right of Canada and not in right of the United Kingdom, in which latter case the Crown Proceedings Act 1947 would have given United Kingdom courts jurisdiction. The Canadian courts alone had jurisdiction.[6] Obviously the result was politically convenient. No United Kingdom court could be expected to intervene in so delicate an "international" issue—as was borne out by the House of Lords' refusal to permit an appeal,[7] and the subsequent

---

[99] *Re James* [1977] Ch. 41.

[1] *The Fehmarn* [1958] 1 All E.R. 333, even where there was an exclusive foreign jurisdiction clause. Diplock L.J. appears however in *Mackender* v. *Feldia A.G.* [1967] 2 Q.B. 500 to have convinced Lord Denning that the discretion to permit service of a writ outside the jurisdiction should not be exercised where there was such a clause. Later he fully accepted the *forum conveniens* doctrine, as in *Trendtex Trading Corporation* v. *Credit Suisse* [1980] 3 W.L.R. 367, with rueful references to the absence of discovery in other systems—although he objected to the excess of information required in United States pre-trial procedures in the *Westinghouse* Litigation.

[2] *Castanho* v. *Brown and Root (U.K.) Ltd.* [1980] 1 W.L.R. 833, a Denning dissent, with the House of Lords affirming the majority ([1981] A.C. 557).

[3] He regarded contingency fees as champertous and contrary to public policy: *Trendtex*, above and *Wallersteiner* v. *Moir (No. 2)* [1975] Q.B. 373.

[4] *What Next in the Law*, pp. 105–106.   [5] [1983] 1 W.L.R. 730 at p. 738.

[6] *R.* v. *Secretary of State for Foreign and Commonwealth Affairs, ex p. Indian Association of Alberta* [1982] 2 W.L.R. 641.

[7] The House of Lords, denying leave to appeal (*ibid.* p. 671), held that it was not arguable that Crown obligations in respect of the Indian people of Canada were still a United Kingdom Government responsibility, and that jurisdiction was exclusively in the Canadian courts.

striking out by a differently constituted Court of Appeal of a statement of claim challenging the validity of the Canada Act 1982, and its ruling that the Act in any event conformed with the Statute of Westminster 1931 and could not be challenged.[8] Areas such as these indicate the limits of judicial authority: the courts abdicate, otherwise political conflict becomes inevitable.

Reference has already been made to Lord Denning's view that the exercise of the royal prerogative abroad could not be questioned,[9] that the courts had no jurisdiction to issue habeas corpus in respect of arrests by the armed forces in North Ireland,[10] and that disputes involving dealings between various foreign sovereigns were not justiciable.[11] Again, a conspiracy in England to induce trespass to chattels abroad was not justiciable on policy grounds because it involved the standing of "two autonomous administrations."[12] Nor did the courts have jurisdiction to restrain publication of confidential material if done with just cause or excuse, as for example if done in the public interest, jurisdiction being based on a duty to be of good faith.[13] The extension of immunity to all inferior court judges and to magistrates[14] and to prison visitors[15] has already been mentioned, as has that to barristers,[16] the reason primarily being in the last case that criminals should not relitigate their guilt.[17] Witnesses in proceedings would also, had Lord Denning's view prevailed, have been accorded absolute immunity.[18] On the difficult question of absolute immunity when sued for injurious falsehood and libel of middle ranks of army, secret service, and visiting

---

[8] *Manuel* v. *Att.-Gen.* [1982] 2 W.L.R. 821.

[9] *Nyali Ltd.* v. *Att.-Gen.* [1956] 1 Q.B. 1 (involving property rights) and *Sabally and Njie* v. *Att.-Gen.* [1965] 1 Q.B. 273 (voting rights). In *Nissan* v. *Att.-Gen.* [1968] 1 Q.B. 286, while use of the prerogative could not be questioned, there was, if property of a British subject was damaged, a common law duty to pay compensation. See above, pp. 255–256.

[10] *Re Keenan*, above, at p. 307, n. 49.

[11] *Buttes Gas and Oil Co.* v. *Hammer (No. 3)* [1980] 3 W.L.R. 668, 679. This was inconsistent with his earlier decision reported in [1975] 1 Q.B. 557, a case reversed on appeal to the Lords on the basis that such disputes were non-justiciable, there being no manageable standards for reviewing transactions abroad of foreign sovereigns: [1981] 3 W.L.R. 787 (H.L.).

[12] *Hesperides Hotels Ltd.* v. *Aegean Turkish Holidays Ltd.* [1978] 1 Q.B. 205. Denning's ruling and findings about Cyprus were made without hearing argument or evidence on this point from the plaintiffs. As Roskill L.J. said at p. 226: "History, especially recent controversial political history, is not one-sided". *Cf.* Griffiths' comment that Denning was unhistorical and grotesquely summarised 19th century English history to suit his purpose: (1979) 42 M.L.R. 349.

[13] See *Fraser* v. *Evans* [1969] 1 Q.B. 349, above, p. 285 and *Woodward* v. *Hutchins* [1977] 1 W.L.R. 760.

[14] *Sirros* v. *Moore*, above, p. 307.

[15] *O'Reilly* v. *Mackman*, above, p. 307.

[16] *Rondel* v. *Worsley*, above. Immunity is only to their own client, not "to the court and to the other side" should they unnecessarily run up costs: *Kelly* v. *London Transport Executive* [1982] 1 W.L.R. 1055, 1065.

[17] As Denning commented in respect of *Goody*, *Rondel* and *Cole*, above, p. 305. Later, in *Saif Ali* v. *Sydney Mitchell and Co.* [1978] Q.B. 95, 103, in giving extensive immunity for negligence, he placed more emphasis on a barrister's duty to the court requiring independence, especially to ensure non-abuse of legal aid. The House of Lords by 3–2 reversed his decision, confining immunity to conduct in court: [1978] 3 W.L.R. 849. Law Lords pointed to factors for immunity: protection of those involved in court proceedings; the duty to the court; the duty to be fearless for the client; and the need to prevent re-litigation. Yet they felt that as professional men barristers should not have greater privileges than were necessary.

[18] *Roy* v. *Prior* [1970] 1 Q.B. 283, reversed [1969] 3 W.L.R. 635.

forces of a friendly foreign power, he was unwilling to order the trial of a preliminary point, leaving these questions unanswered, at the same time remarking on the undesirability of jury trial in so complex a libel suit, when several special verdicts would be required.[19]

It is also appropriate to mention the according of immunity in effect (rather than as of right). Lord Denning's reported decisions on malicious prosecution[20] and false imprisonment[21] effectively either give immunity to the police, or to those who initiate proceedings depriving others of their liberty[22] or damaging their honour and reputation, or at very least make successful litigation unlikely.[23] Nor was Lord Denning concerned, as was Somervell L.J., with the absence of any remedy, either by way of an action for malicious prosecution, an appeal, or certiorari in respect of a binding over order, Lord Denning's attitude being that by having made threats, the aggrieved person's conduct was similar to that on which a criminal prosecution, rather than *quia timet* proceedings, could have been brought, and that only if the proceedings had ended favourably would he have had a cause of action.[24]

A negative attitude was, for reasons of balancing the interests of the mentally ill and their relatives and society, taken to an applicant, who had between 1925 and 1954 been held in Rampton and subsequently sought leave under section 330(2) of the Lunacy Act 1890 to commence proceedings,[25] alleging that he had been unlawfully detained. Lord Denning construed the requirement that there be "substantial ground" for the contention that the person against whom the proceedings are sought to be brought had acted without reasonable cause as not meaning "reasonable grounds" but as "solid grounds."

The police were made immune in practice in proceedings alleging that they were condoning breaches in the law by non-enforcement,[26] while local authorities could even order breaches of the law by their employees.[27]

Although Lord Denning had made the National Health Service liable for

---

[19] *Richards* v. *Naum* [1967] 1 Q.B. 620.

[20] *Roy* v. *Prior*, above; and *Glinski* v. *McIver* [1962] A.C. 726 (H.L.) in which case, although the defendant had been actuated by malice, the plaintiff could not succeed, because there was reasonable and probable cause for prosecuting for conspiracy to defraud.

[21] *Att.-Gen. of Northern Rhodesia* v. *Mungoni*, above; *Dallison* v. *Caffery*, above; *Wiltshire* v. *Barrett*, above; and *Sirros* v. *Moore*, above. See above, pp. 255, 258 and 307.

[22] *Everett* v. *Ribbands and Another* [1952] 2 Q.B. 198.

[23] See, *e.g. Leibo* v. *D. Buckman Ltd. and Another* [1952] 2 All E.R. 1057, a dissent against a majority decision to permit a civil jury trial in an action alleging malicious prosecution.

[24] *Everett* v. *Ribbands and Another*, [1952] 2 Q.B. 198.

[25] *Richardson* v. *L.C.C.* [1957] 1 W.L.R. 751. Protection of public authorities against such litigation was much more necessary in the days when concepts of mental health care were very different and when medication enabling out-patient treatment of the mentally ill was not available.

[26] In all the *Blackburn* cases against the police, whilst standing was accorded, in no case was any abuse of discretion found to exist: see [1968] 2 Q.B. 118; (*No. 3*) [1973] 1 Q.B. 241; and (*No. 4*) *The Times*, March 7, 1980. It is a policy decision for the police whether and when to intervene: see also *R.* v. *Chief Constable of Devon and Cornwall, ex p. C.E.G.B.* [1981] 3 W.L.R. 967.

[27] In *Buckoke* v. *G.L.C.* [1971] Ch. 655, the G.L.C. was insisting that their drivers of fire engines break the law regarding red light signals and the court upheld their power to discipline crewmen who would not travel with such drivers.

doctors' negligence,[28] he subsequently exhibited reluctance to find that doctors had been negligent. In *The Discipline of Law* he states that "from articles in journals and periodicals and so forth" it became known to the Courts that the medical profession was alarmed, "so in the next case we sought to relieve the anxieties of the medical men."[29] His departure from normal negligence standards arose from several concerns: he feared defensive medicine on the American model; he feared colossal awards of damages would become common in malpractice suits; he knew such damages would generally be payable by the taxpayer who would already often have financed the litigation by way of the Legal Aid Fund[30]; he knew that doctors are subjected not only to the ordinary courts, but also to the jurisdiction of the General Medical Council.[31] The result of these concerns was that he ensured that effectively doctors were usually accorded immunity.

A last aspect of developing an effective remedy is the introduction of new or modification of existing procedures. The *Anton Piller* order, the *Mareva* injunction, subsequent developments of the interlocutory injunction under section 37(1) of the Supreme Court Act 1981, and Lord Denning's earlier attitudes to interlocutory injunctions have been examined in detail by Hayton.[32] His non-technical approach to questions of applicability of the Limitation Acts in respect of workmen has been mentioned[33] and it should be added that a generous view as to when time started running was ultimately taken by him in respect of claims arising out of badly done building work which had been covered up (such as foundations).[34] Finally, Lord Denning contributed greatly to the law governing discovery orders, a topic dealt with below in connection with the right to a fair trial.[35]

Degrading Treatment and Punishment[36]

For a man who in other aspects of his life showed compassion and sympathy, Lord Denning was remarkably impervious where the interests of national security or aliens were involved. On not dissimilar facts to those in *Soblen* the United Kingdom Government felt impelled, by reason of the European

---

[28] In *Cassidy* v. *Ministry of Health* [1951] 2 K.B. 343.
[29] p. 241. Presumably "so forth" refers to innumerable encounters between judges and the higher ranks of the medical profession in their clubs.
[30] See his remarks in *What Next in the Law*, pp. 102–104, followed 2 pages later by insistence that lawyers should not be permitted to take contingency fees.
[31] See Sheila McLean, "Negligence—a Dagger at the Doctor's Back" in *Justice, Lord Denning and the Constitution*, pp. 99–112 for a careful analysis of the cases. Two early cases, not dealt with by her, already show Lord Denning's reluctance to penalise doctors as individuals: *Burns* v. *Campbell* [1952] 1 K.B. 15, and *Jones* v. *Manchester Corporation* [1952] 2 Q.B. 852 foreshadowing his majority decision in *Romford Ice and Cold Storage Co.* v. *Lister* [1956] 2 Q.B. 180, reversed [1957] A.C. 555, protecting the worker.
[32] Hayton, Chap. 3. See also above, pp. 286 and 291.
[33] Above, p. 276.
[34] In *Sparham-Souter* v. *Town and Country Developments (Essex) Ltd.* [1976] Q.B. 858, he recanted his opinion in *Dutton* v. *Bognor Regis U.D.C.* [1972] 2 W.L.R. 299, that time began to run from the date of the negligent act, and not from the time of manifestation of the damage. However, his "discoverability" test has been repudiated, the Lords ruling in *Pirelli General Cable Works Ltd.* v. *Oscar Faber and Partners* [1983] 2 W.L.R. 6 that time starts running when the cause of action arises, namely at the time of the negligence.
[35] Below, pp. 331 *et seq.*
[36] The rights not to be subjected to inhuman or degrading treatment or punishment (Art. 7).

Commission declaring it admissible on grounds of inhuman treatment,[37] to settle a claim by the widow of a Moroccan airforce officer, who had sought asylum in Gibraltar, following flight there after an attempt to assassinate King Hassan. Refused asylum, as was Soblen, he was declared a prohibited immigrant and handed over to Moroccan representatives for return on a Moroccan Air Force plane to Morocco where he faced certain imprisonment and was actually executed.

Again, as mentioned above, in *Greece* v. *United Kingdom* the Commission had held that collective punishment imposed by Regulations on Cyprus local communities thought to have harboured terrorists was prima facie degrading punishment or treatment contrary to Article 3 of the Convention, whereas in *Ross-Clunis* v. *Papadopoullos*, Lord Denning, as part of a three man Privy Council, had, despite a Colonial Office-appointed Supreme Court in Cyprus having declared the Regulation *ultra vires* as unreasonable, held collective punishment capable of being related to the purposes of public safety and public order for which the Governor had power to make such Regulations as appeared to him necessary or expedient.[38] Yet again in *McIlkenny* and in *Guilfoyle*,[39] where he was heavily sarcastic about approaching the European Commission, Lord Denning could not conceive that mishandling of the I.R.A. Birmingham bombers, either by police or by prison officials, might constitute degrading treatment, regarding some rough handling, bruising and black eyes (the visible evidence) as all in a day's work.

Collective responsibility, to be followed by a collective sanction, was obviously in his mind in *Liverpool County Council* v. *Irwin*.[40] While theoretically finding that the Corporation had a duty to keep the common parts of its slum-like and vandalised tower blocks, known locally as "The Piggeries," reasonably fit for the use of tenants and their visitors, he declined to find the Corporation in breach of its duty or that there was any duty to keep sanitary systems in order. In any event, he would afford no damages offsettable against the small rent payable, stating that there

> "is no evidence that it is the tenants themselves or their families who actually do the wicked damage. But collectively the tenants could do much to improve the situation. They should do their part in disciplining these youngsters . . . In these circumstances I would not award the tenants any damages."

The result (for which the other judges of the Court of Appeal were even more responsible, denying any contractual liability at all) was that hundreds of council tenants had to continue living in degrading conditions without obtaining any relief from the courts.

That his decisions (and the law generally)might result in degrading treatment was apparently not present to Lord Denning's mind. Certainly in

---

[37] *Amekrane* (1973) 16 *Yearbook E.C.H.R.*, July 19, 1974. Asylum is only a right in terms of Art. 14(1) of the Universal Declaration of Human Rights and is not incorporated into the Covenants except indirectly if refusal will effectively constitute inhuman treatment.

[38] See above, p. 255. As there pointed out collective punishment was also contrary to the right to a fair trial and to the presumption of innocence.

[39] Above, pp. 305–306.

[40] [1976] Q.B. 319, 332.

respect of foreign workers in the United Kingdom who, by reason of the immigration rules and discretions in permitting or refusing entry, were separated for lengthy periods from their families, he did not appear conscious that exclusion of their families and admitting the worker on the basis that he could not bring his family with him was turning the worker into, using deliberately tendentious language, a wage slave, treating him in a degrading fashion and denying him family life, the latter point being accepted in respect of East African Asians who were United Kingdom citizens or British protected persons by the European Commission.[41] Lord Denning even implied that workers should not bring their families to England if they would need state assistance (by way of local authority housing) to accommodate them once in England. In my opinion, the Hillingdon Council's decision in conjunction with the Court of Appeal decision in *R. v. Hillingdon London Borough Council ex p. Taffazul Islam*,[42] involved degrading treatment. Islam had come from Pakistan to work in England in 1965. He had married in Bangladesh in 1968, where he five times visited his wife, with children being conceived, the wife and children being supported by money sent from England and living with Islam's father. In 1974, then being eligible to do so, Islam applied for a visa for his family, but entry certificates were granted only in February 1980 and had to be presented within six months. Until his family came to England Islam could get no priority on any council housing list. Arranging with his landlord accommodation in his single room, his family arrived in April 1980, but were subsequently evicted. Hillingdon, upheld by Lord Denning, held that he had made the family "intentionally homeless." Lord Denning went on to say:

> "the moral of the case is that men from overseas should not bring their wives and children here unless they have arranged permanent and suitable accommodation for them . . . . He will not take priority over young couples here who are on the waiting list for housing accommodation."[43]

Islam had contributed to the economy of the United Kingdom and to the services of the state by way of paying indirect or direct taxation for 15 years, and was by any standards entitled to make demands on such services without being treated as a feckless scrounger.

The Right to Life[44]

The Covenant requires the right to life to be protected by law, a function performed by the rules regarding homicide and damages surviving under the Law Reform (Miscellaneous Provisions) Act 1934 or actions for damages under the Fatal Accidents Acts.

Lord Denning, as pointed out earlier, slightly widened the scope of the crime of murder by making the required intent to some degree objective.[45]

---

[41] [1970] 13 *Yearbook E.C.H.R.* 928 at p. 1006. Various cases alleging breaches of Arts. 3, 5, 8 and 14 were declared admissible.

[42] [1981] 3 W.L.R. 109, reversed [1981] 3 W.L.R. 942.

[43] *Ibid.* p. 114. Until his family came to England Islam could not try to obtain any priority on the housing list.

[44] Art. 6 of the Civil Rights Covenant.

[45] *D.P.P.* v. *Smith, Bratty* and *Gallagher*, see above, p. 257.

In contrast, on the civil damages side, he sought to reduce the *quantum*, his aim being to spare the general public the burdens by way of insurance or taxation that would follow were massive carefully itemised damages payable to a deceased person's estate.[46] Such reductions were to apply also to a state of "living death," with damages not being recoverable for loss of expectation of life or for compensation for earnings in the lost years, or in case of unconscious patients, for pain and suffering and loss of the amenities of life.[47] This approach takes the law back to the pre-Fatal Accidents Act situation where it was cheaper to kill (and now to inflict a "living death") than merely to maim. It is only because of insurance arrangements in the modern state and the average tortfeasor's ignorance of the law that removal of the deterrent and protective factor probably does not matter.

English law no longer requires that there always be an inquiry by a coroner's jury into cases of homicide, but exceptionally such an inquiry must be held. As explained below in connection with the jury, Lord Denning ordered the coroner to summon a jury to enquire into the much publicised death of Blair Peach.[48]

Because of the absence of a Bill of Rights in England there have been few cases touching on the right to life and its possible conflict with other rights along the lines of those occurring in the United States and West Germany. Lord Denning was involved in one of the few cases which came before the courts, raising questions as to the legal position of nurses who are members of a team inducing an abortion. He construed the Abortion Act 1967 narrowly, allowing the statutory defence to apply only to the doctor terminating the pregnancy.[49] He would not read it as covering others, unless they were acting directly under the instructions of the doctor, who remained in physical control of the termination proceedings. Had this decision stood, it would have limited considerably the number of abortions, partly because of shortage of qualified doctors and partly because the method of inducing abortions was time-consuming. Their Lordships by 3–2 overruled the decision. Obviously the conscientious scruples of the various judges played a major part in their judgments, Lord Denning referring vividly to the "soul destroying task" of the nurses in being compelled, on the interpretation of the Act taken by the National Health Service, to destroy life when they were dedicated by their profession and training to do all they can to preserve life.[50]

In another case touching on life and its continuance, although he did not put it in this way, probably because in the post-war era it would have sounded too reminiscent of the science of "eugenics," Lord Denning effectively asserted that it is in the public interest of the state that its citizens remain healthy and able to procreate. Thus, he characterised a voluntary sterilisation operation, raised as constituting cruelty in a divorce suit, as unlawful and as akin to cases involving assaults upon the person, which are

---

[46] In *Watson* v. *Powles* [1968] 1 Q.B. 596 Denning had sought to end division of damages under separate heads. He was against the use of actuaries as a practice, preferring to keep the courts' global discretion.

[47] His views are summarised best in *What Next in the Law,*, pp. 133–157, and refer to his leading decisions, *inter alia, Lim Poh Choo*, above, overruled by their Lordships, and *Re C. (a minor)* v. *Wiseman* [1982] 1 W.L.R. 71, a dissent.

[48] *R.* v. *H.M. Coroner at Hammersmith, ex p. Peach* [1980] 2 W.L.R. 496. See below, p. 329.

[49] *Royal College of Nursing* v. *D.H.S.S.* [1981] 2 W.L.R. 279, reversed [1981] A.C. 800.

[50] *Ibid.* p. 282.

not capable of being validated by consent.[51] At the time, in the early 1950s, medico-legal opinion in the Anglo-American world was heatedly debating the legality of sterilisation and concerned with the flood-gates argument that it would lead to sterilisation programmes and even to euthanasia. Lord Denning's judgment, in that context, was a reassertion of the duty to continue the human species, and gave guidance to the profession that sterilisation operations should not be conducted without good medical cause. Who is confidently to say, in light of subsequent experience in India, that sterilisation, even if in over-populated countries it is thought by the elite to be necessary, should lightly be undertaken by the medical profession, and that Lord Denning's view, that it is prima facie a criminal assault, is not, from the standpoint of human rights law, much preferable.

Personal Liberty and Arbitrary Arrest[52]

Lord Denning does not emerge as a practical defender of personal liberty on the basis of the limited number of relevant published cases in which he sat.

His reputation of concern for personal liberty springs from *Freedom Under the Law*,[53] and in particular from his pride in habeas corpus, with references to *Sommersett's Case*[54] and to *R.* v. *Governor of Wandsworth Prison, ex parte Boydell*[55] in which he had sat with Lord Goddard. Lord Denning was full of liberal sentiments too in *Ex parte Chapple*,[56] suggesting, in accordance with the then prevailing opinion, that the applicant for habeas corpus could go before another differently composed or different Divisional Court, but not to the *same* Divisional Court.

Intermittently, he would make libertarian pronouncements, as in *McIlraith* v. *Grady*, that "no man's liberty is to be taken away unless every requirement of the law has been strictly complied with."[57] The case was one on contempt of court, an offence towards which he was ambivalent, wishing to preserve both the authority of courts and individual rights to personal liberty and freedom of speech. He always sought in such cases to achieve a compromise. Thus, in *McIlraith* v. *Grady*, because the matter of contempt had not been set out as required by the County Court Rules, with the Court of Appeal not knowing the facts grounding the contempt and the contemnor unable to make proper submissions on sentence on appeal, Lord Denning set aside the decision. Subsequently, he made it clear that, since contempt is a criminal offence, the principles applicable to such offences applied, such as

---

[51] *Bravery* v. *Bravery* [1954] 3 All E.R. 59.

[52] The rights to liberty, security of person, to freedom from arbitrary arrest, and to take judicial proceedings on the lawfulness of any detention (Art. 9 of the Civil Rights Covenant).

[53] The first chapter is entitled "Personal Freedom."

[54] 20 St. Tr. 1, referred to at p. 7, and still being referred to in *The Due Process of Law* (1980) pp. 157–159. F.O. Shyllon in *Black Slaves in England* (Oxford, 1974), debunks the view of Mansfield as libertarian with his oft-cited remark that "the air of England is too pure for any slave to breathe," cases of slavery *de facto* continuing in England until 1834.

[55] [1948] 2 K.B. 193. See above, p. 259.

[56] (1950) 66 (pt. 2) T.L.R. 932. This view was overruled in *Re Hastings (No. 2)* [1959] 1 Q.B. 358.

[57] [1968] 1 Q.B. 468, 477. Liberal dicta also appeared in *Ghani* v. *Jones*, above, p. 290, on freedom of movement which was only to be curtailed on arrest.

proof beyond reasonable doubt.[58] A similar attitude to strict proof had been taken when releasing the five dockers imprisoned by the National Industrial Relations Court, and whose continued imprisonment might have led to a general strike.[59] When giving such judgments Lord Denning was able to bemuse journalists so as to create an impression of great liberality, even where his ruling had harsh aspects. A notable instance was his ordering the release from prison of Welsh students who, in a demonstration for preservation of the Welsh language, had broken up the trial in *Broome* v. *Cassell,* and had been sentenced to three months' imprisonment. Subsequently, Lord Denning was at pains to point out that his ruling upheld the common law power of High Court judges to imprison for contempt, a power "not affected in the least" by the Criminal Justice Act 1967, section 39 of which seemingly required a suspended sentence for such first time offenders. Furthermore, although releasing them from prison, where they had already served one week, he had bound the students over to be of good behaviour and to keep the peace, subject to a right to recall them, should this prove necessary, to commit them for the rest of their sentences of imprisonment.[60]

Lord Denning's negative attitude to "collateral" challenge by those arrested whether by way of actions for false imprisonment, malicious prosecution, libel suits or defences by prisoners, or by way of habeas corpus proceedings by immigrants or aliens awaiting deportation has already been mentioned.[61] As he pointed out in *Freedom Under the Law,*[62] personal freedom depends on the procedure of the courts and the remedies for its enforcement, a remark which is ironical in view of his decision in *Choudhary,*[63] which was arguably contrary to Article 9. "Lawfulness" of a detention, as the concept is understood in international human rights law, does not mean "in accordance with legislation" or "on the production of an official certification of an executive act," but incorporates an international minimum standard (as does the term "arbitrary")[64] of not being unjust, consequently requiring substantive evaluation of any alleged justification, something now required by the Lords' decision in *Khawaja.*[65]

The right to security of person was, however, upheld strenuously in *Loudon* v. *Ryder,*[66] where a young woman was awarded damages, including exemplary damages for trespass and assault. Lord Denning seems to have

---

[58] *Re Bramblevale Ltd.* [1970] 1 Ch. 128; *Balogh* v. *St. Alban's Crown Court* [1975] Q.B. 73; and *Re F. (A Minor)* [1976] 3 W.L.R. 813. These remarks were not limited, appearing also to apply to contempts prejudicing the administration of justice where there was strict liability and proof of intent was thought unnecessary. See also *Heaton's Transport Ltd.* v. *T.G.W.U.* [1972] 3 W.L.R. 73.

[59] *Churchman* v. *Joint Shop Stewards Committee* [1972] 1 W.L.R. 1094. His explanation (p. 1101) of how the proceedings started shows him taking an active role in advising on the way to get the matter before the Court of Appeal. That he saw himself as emulating Lord Mansfield's subtle handling of John Wilkes is clear from *The Family Story*, p. 173.

[60] *The Due Process of Law*, pp. 7–11, telling the story of *Morris* v. *Crown Office* [1970] 2 Q.B. 114.

[61] Above, pp. 258, 300–301, 304–305 and 317.

[62] pp. 4 and 36.

[63] [1978] 1 W.L.R. 1177.

[64] The European Court of Human Rights held that no detention that is "arbitrary" can ever be lawful in the *Wintwerp Case*, Pub. Eur. Ct. H.R. Series A, October 24, 1979, when dealing with the equivalent Art. 5.

[65] [1983] 2 W.L.R. 321, where Lords Scarman and Bridge emphasised the implications for personal liberty of "a Wednesbury approach," instead of substantive evaluation.

[66] [1953] 2 Q.B. 202.

been carried away by the fact that a foreigner had behaved extremely badly and had used force against a young woman. Nearly three decades later he was mentioning the irrelevant fact that "He spoke in broken English," referring to the defendant as "Ryder, the Pole."[67]

Imprisonment for Debt[68]

Cases on imprisonment for civil debt, which had been greatly restricted in 1869 and was eventually abolished by the Administration of Justice Act 1970, seldom found their way into the law reports. Imprisonment for maintenance arrears, which can still be ordered, is more properly described as an obligation flowing from status than as a contractual obligation from the contract of marriage, but, to complete the Denning picture, his only reported judgment in the *All England Reports* should be mentioned: he cut down the length of a period of imprisonment imposed for maintenance arrears.[69]

Equality Before the Courts[70]

Most of the notions developed to protect accused persons or civil litigants come under the broad and flexible concept of a "fair hearing." Even though the Article sets out detailed requirements only in respect of criminal trials, such safeguards must, by reason of "fairness," apply *mutatis mutandis* to civil litigation. Again, since the dominant purpose of the Article is to protect human rights whenever these are determined, in spirit it applies to administrative proceedings, an approach being adopted in the developing jurisprudence of the United Nations Human Rights Committee, relying also on Article 2(2). In that latter connection, Lord Denning's contributions have already been outlined under the right to an effective remedy. Here his major reported cases touching on the "fairness" aspects of civil and criminal procedure and evidence will be sketched.[71]

Legal Aid

The equality of arms required by Article 14 is only to a limited extent met by the English Legal Aid system. Lord Denning, although having conflicting feelings about legal aid, still to some extent characterising it as maintenance,[72] was particularly concerned about the hardships to the legally unassisted[73] with only those of very modest means being eligible for aid. He emphasised hardships on the unassisted in *Wyld* v. *Silver (No. 2)*,[74]

[67] *What Next in the Law* (1982), pp. 198–199. This cannot be excused as short story-telling technique: it is writing showing his attitude to "lesser breeds without the law."
[68] The right not to be imprisoned for inability to fulfil a contractual obligation (Art. 11).
[69] *Riding* v. *Riding* [1958] 1 All E.R. 65; [1958] P. 88.
[70] The right to equality before courts and tribunals and to a fair hearing (Art. 14 of the Civil Rights Covenant).
[71] A full study of his work would require analysis of hundreds of unreported cases. I have also omitted here reference to reported cases on all the specialised procedural aspects.
[72] See *What Next in the Law*, pp. 92–116 and 101 and 111 in particular.
[73] Exceptionally his sympathies might go against an unassisted party who had law rather than morality on her side as in *Dugon* v. *Williamson* [1964] 3 Ch. 59, where a plaintiff was denied most of her costs against a defendant who had been legally aided only for a limited purpose.
[74] [1962] 1 W.L.R. 863.

where he ordered security for costs on an appeal by an assisted person, and in *Chapman* v. *Honig*, where he would otherwise have dissented on denying leave to appeal (as he had already done on the merits) because the unassisted defendant would have been liable to be saddled with a great amount of costs.[75] He was also concerned that legal aid for expert's reports did not alter the rules regarding discovery, so that a Legal Aid-funded expert's report could not be ordered to be disclosed.[76] This was only superficially unjust, because the legally-aided plaintiff was willing to disclose the report, provided that the defendant in exchange disclosed his experts' reports, which he was unwilling to do. In effect Lord Denning was seeking to put the unassisted defendant in a position of knowing what case his opponent could make out, while still holding his own cards unexposed, with privilege applying to the defendant but not to the plaintiff.

He became even more vocal about deficiencies in the Legal Aid Scheme towards the end of his career, speaking of the " 'unacceptable face' of British justice" and saying "I hang my head in shame that it should be so."[77] Because an articled clerk's and the legal aid clerk's combined errors had resulted in an omission in the legal aid certificate of any reference to a "counterclaim," the unassisted plaintiff, who took far less than was due to him (further pursuit of the litigation involving more money than it was worth) was denied even the limited rights of recourse then given against the Legal Aid Fund.[78] At first instance only if the unassisted party would suffer "severe financial hardship" from having had litigation funded against him was he entitled to claim from the fund should he win, but such a rule even though at first too strictly interpreted,[79] and only subsequently being relaxed by Lord Denning in favour of unassisted parties,[80] excluded insurance companies,[81] large businesses and public corporations.[82] Lord Denning, by administrative enjoinders to the legal profession, sought to mitigate such hardships by warning about the care needed in advising that legal aid, with its potential for harming others, be granted.[83] He also advised the Bar that on appeal the criteria for refusal were different, it merely being necessary that it be "just and equitable"[84] to award appellate costs to the unassisted party, and that they should apply for these for their clients.[85] Later he went out of his way to indicate that counsel's immunity did not protect him against the court or against other parties, if he negligently and improperly incurred large costs in litigating.[86]

---

[75] [1963] 2 Q.B. 502. He naughtily implies in *The Due Process of Law*, p. 26 that only his two colleagues took this view. See, however, p. 526 of the judgment.

[76] *Re Saxton (decd.)* [1962] 3 All E.R. 92. *What Next in the Law*, pp. 93–94 gives a one-sided account. Lord Denning could be similarly selective in his choice and emphasis of stated facts when writing judgments.

[77] *R. and T. Thew Ltd.* v. *Reeves* [1981] 3 W.L.R. 190, 205.

[78] Lord Denning, in dissent, would have rectified the verbal slip in the certificate.

[79] *Nowotnik* v. *Nowotnik (Hyatt intervening)* [1967] P. 83.

[80] *Clifford* v. *Walker* [1972] 1 W.L.R. 724.

[81] *General Accident Fire and Life Assurance Co. Ltd.* v. *Forbes* [1972] 3 W.L.R. 657.

[82] *Kelly* v. *London Transport Executive* [1982] 1 W.L.R. 1055.

[83] *Hanning* v. *Maitland (No. 2)* [1970] 1 Q.B. 580.

[84] *Parker* v. *Thompson* [1967] 1 W.L.R. 28. Seemingly "just and equitable" merely meant that the unassisted party should have won.

[85] *Clifford* v. *Walker*, above, at p. 727.

[86] *Kelly* v. *London Transport Executive*, above.

He also sought to ensure that the Legal Aid Fund did not harshly enforce its charge for legal costs secured on property recovered, so as to result in eviction of a wife who succeeded in claiming a share in the matrimonial home. There was a discretion as to time and mode of enforcement, and this should normally be exercisable only when the home was sold.[87]

Lord Denning was always anxious for the taxpayer's interest and, while denying any suggestion by him that in the case before him there had been any exploitation of the Legal Aid Fund, emphasised that there must be no blank cheques for legal aid for endless proceedings, and that the taxing master must act as a watchdog.[88] So, too, it seems must counsel and solicitors, who must draw to the court's attention any case where an assisted party declines a reasonable compromise.[89] Legal Aid funding of claims Lord Denning thought unmeritorious, in particular massive damages on allegations of medical negligence,[90] was another reason for Lord Denning urging alteration of the criteria of eligibility for legal aid. This consideration, together with the risk of oppression of the unassisted party, led him, at the end of his career, to contend that the question should be: "Is this a proper case in which the plaintiff's claim should be financed by the state?"[91] The problems that would flow from such a test are illustrated by the divergent approaches of Lord Denning and Russell L.J. in *Wyld* v. *Silver* on appeal on the merits, a case illustrating that the oratorical language of "rights" may bear little relationship to the realities. Lord Denning spoke lyrically of the rights of the inhabitants of Wraysbury to enforce their rights in the Queen's courts to hold a fair or wake on Whit Friday on waste lands of the parish, whereas Russell L.J. pointed out that a small builder had bought a piece of derelict land for erection of five bungalows after planning permission following on a public local enquiry, that the buyer's solicitors had investigated so far as possible, and that subsequently a member of one of the leading families of Wraysbury had brought up the question of an ancient and outmoded right not exercised for over one hundred years, invoking this to restrain the erection of any building or use interfering with the holding of a fair on the land on Whit Friday.[92] Having, on existing criteria, insisted

---

[87] *Hanlon* v. *Law Society* [1980] 2 W.L.R. 756 (H.L.), wherein their Lordships upheld this discretion.

[88] *Storer* v. *Wright* [1980] 2 W.L.R. 208, 212–213, described in *What Next in the Law*, pp. 97–99. It seems to me unfair that such doubt was attached to the necessity of holding a conference in *loco* when all kinds of factors affecting the causes of the accident could be appraised by lawyers and experts together.

[89] *Manley* v. *Law Society* [1981] 1 W.L.R. 335, commented on harshly in *What Next in the Law*, pp. 99–101. Had the assisted plaintiff succeeded, his award would have been far greater, while in the compromise he and his lawyers suggested the Legal Aid Fund avoided the risk of incurring massive costs in a lengthy trial. It should be added that the legal profession and litigants have very different views as to what is a reasonable compromise. Not being hardened cynics about litigation, as are practising lawyers, outsiders studying settlements see compromises as occurring after the lawyers and expert witnesses have earned large fees at the expense of the parties or if involved, the Legal Aid Fund, both sets of clients then being "cooled down" by their respective lawyers. The resulting compromise has relation to risks of litigation, rather than reflecting an adequate recompense.

[90] *e.g. Whitehouse* v. *Jordan* [1981] 1 W.L.R. 246, a case on which it is quite permissible to take very different views, merely disagreeing on whether or not there was, on the facts, negligence, the attitude adopted by their Lordships: [1981] 1 All E.R. 267.

[91] *What Next in the Law*, pp. 113 and 238. See also p. 116.

[92] [1963] 1 Q.B. 169. See Russell L.J.'s irony at p. 193.

that the legally-aided defendant give security for costs out of the small amount of disposable capital he owned, this was not a case where on policy grounds Lord Denning would have given legal aid. *A fortiori* he would not give aid for an appeal claiming "excessive" damages. Thus such a test of being "a proper case" would remit the right to legal aid to the realm of caprice and ideological approval.

Another aspect of equality of arms, the right to have legal representation, has already been mentioned in connection with disciplinary bodies, where, although initially taking the position in respect of non-statutory domestic tribunals that when a serious charge was made there was a right to legal representation, Lord Denning subsequently held that the right could be excluded by an association's rules, or by inference from other provisions in case of a statutory tribunal, or by the need for speed in case of a disciplinary body such as a prison.[93]

Access to the Courts

Lord Denning's generous views on *locus standi* have already been described.[94] In contrast, if his views on the criteria for legal aid were to prevail, access would in practice be greatly diminished. If access is genuinely to be available, the courts must effectively be open to the poor, the oppressed, those who think themselves oppressed, including those with a psychiatric history[95] and even vexatious litigants.[96] Mention has also been made of the negative attitude both of Lord Denning and the House of Lords to prisoners relitigating their innocence in civil proceedings.[97]

Jury Trial

Extra-judicially in 1949, Lord Denning delivered himself of a panegyric extolling the virtue of the jury system.[98] By 1982 he was writing that the system had been whittled away, no longer subsisting in civil cases in England save for libel, and advocating further changes, *inter alia*, to make all civil jury trials discretionary. His judgments were the principal agents in "whittling away" civil juries. Whereas Lord Denning's reasons for streamlining are ones with which most practitioners would agree, they do not sit compatibily with his earlier extra-judicially expressed views that juries could be trusted to draw the line fairly, and were the best guarantee of our freedom, admittedly before he became aware of the extent of the jury's "democritisation," from being "male, middle-aged, middle-brow, and middle-class" to representative of the local community. If jury trial is such a significant guarantee, then effectiveness and convenience of working only

---

[93] Above, p. 306, referring to *Pett* v. *Greyhound Racing Association Ltd.*; *Enderby Town Football Club Ltd.* v. *Football Association Ltd.*; *Maynard* v. *Osmond*; and *Fraser* v. *Mudge.*

[94] See Jowell Chap. 6, pp. 215–223.

[95] *Cf. Richardson* v. *L.C.C.*, above, p. 317 and *Gaskin* v. *Liverpool C.C.* [1980] 1 W.L.R. 1549.

[96] The courts' negative attitude is psychologically understandable, but, since so severe a restriction on rights is involved in requiring permission to sue, any invasion should be narrowly rather than broadly construed as it was in *Attorney-General* v. *Vernazza*, above, p. 256.

[97] *McIlkenny* and *Hunter* v. *Chief Constable of the West Midlands Police*, above, pp. 305–306.

[98] *Freedom Under the Law*, pp. 36 *et seq.*, and especially at p. 63. *Cf. What Next in the Law*, p. 33, referring to panegyrics.

with elite juries, if at all, might have to be outbalanced by the need to protect safeguards of freedom. However that may be, when put to the test of "What did he do in cases before him involving jury trial?" Lord Denning was not an advocate of the system. Beginning with *Leibo* v. *D. Buckman and Another*,[99] he dissented in respect of an order for jury trial in a malicious prosecution case because of the consequences for criminal law if a different test of what was reasonable and probable cause for institution of proceedings emerged. In *Hennell* v. *Ranaboldo*,[1] with Russell L.J. dissenting, he held that to order a jury trial in that case "would be to extend the criteria for civil jury trial." In *Sims* v. *William Howard and Sons Ltd.*[2] he held that there should be no civil jury trial unless there were exceptional circumstances, the matter being completely within the discretion of the court, effectively overruling the five-man Court of Appeal headed by Lord Wright, which had decided *Hope* v. *Great Western Railway Company*.[3] In *Watts* v. *Manning*, with Salmon L.J. strongly dissenting and holding that limitation of the right to civil jury trial was a matter for Parliament, Lord Denning, in a majority judgment, held that a civil jury was not to be ordered in running down cases, but was to be confined to cases involving honour and integrity, because, if there were a jury, liability and the extent of damages would be governed by sheer chance.[4] Calling together a full Court of Appeal of five Lord Justices, in *Ward* v. *James* he gave their collective judgment that jury trial in personal injury cases was to be stopped in all but exceptional circumstances, because juries could not be put right; there was a need for uniformity of decisions on the amounts of damages awarded; and there should be more predictability and ability to assess appropriate levels of damages likely to be awarded to assist settlements.[5] In *Barclays Bank Ltd.* v. *Cole* he again denied a civil jury to a defendant, convicted of robbery and sued by a bank for money had and received to their use, because robbery merely involved violence and not fraud, while in any event the defendant's honour and integrity was no longer at stake, having gone altogether.[6] Being a statutory right, civil jury was ordered in the libel action, *Rothermere* v. *Times Newspapers*.[7] Lord Denning at the end of his career wished however to remit "right" to judicial discretion.

Even for him jury trial did have its uses in libel actions: once a general verdict was given there was finality as there could be no question as to the grounds of the verdict.[8] Nor could issues be reopened by the jury after its discharge: they could not say that they meant something different by their verdict, and were not at liberty to explain—even where there were complex

[99] [1952] 2 All E.R. 1057.
[1] [1963] 1 W.L.R. 1391.
[2] [1964] 2 Q.B. 409.
[3] [1937] 2 K.B. 130.
[4] [1964] 1 W.L.R. 623, 627. Salmon L.J. could in no circumstances be described as a feeble or "timorous soul," the category to which Lord Denning consigns those who believe that certain reforms should be enacted by Parliament: *What Next in the Law*, p. 268.
[5] [1966] 1 Q.B. 273. There is an ironic parallel in that, now Lord Denning considers judges are awarding inflated damages, he wishes to see the heads of damage reduced, except in case of exemplary damages: *What Next in the Law*, Parts 4 and 5.
[6] [1967] 2 Q.B. 738. Diplock and Russell L.JJ. concurred on the grounds that a trial by judge alone would be quicker, cheaper and more certain, as with 2 juries it was possible that different verdicts would be reached.
[7] [1973] 1 W.L.R. 448.
[8] *Barnes* v. *Hill* [1967] 1 All E.R. 347.

special verdicts on various issues, as the court would not entertain evidence of what took place in the jury room, thus securing the finality of decision and protecting the jury against exposure to pressure or to inducement either to explain or alter their views.[9]

There are few reported Denning decisions on criminal jury trial. In one Privy Council appeal, even where a judge had virtually coerced the jury into its finding, he would not interfere with the verdict.[10] Late in his career much press publicity was given to "jury vetting." Lord Denning seized the opportunity, in his dissenting opinion in *R.* v. *Sheffield Crown Court, ex parte Brownlow,*[11] a case involving a provision ousting certiorari in respect of Crown Court orders "relating to trial on indictment," of interpreting the ouster'clause narrowly and as permitting certiorari where orders were made in connection with arrangements for the jury panel, holding that this was too preliminary a matter to relate to trial. He then described it as "unconstitutional" and an "invasion of privacy" with liability to have a "past record raked up . . . and presented on a plate to prosecuting and defending lawyers" if the police authorities engaged in jury vetting.[12] In my view what precipitated the decision was provision of the information to the defence, so that two accused policemen could challenge potential jurors armed with details as to jurymen's previous convictions. That it was really challenge by the defence which most concerned Lord Denning emerges from *What Next in the Law,* where he defended the random selection of juries, without criticising the prosecution's right to demand that a juror "stand by for the Crown," and condemned the accused person's right of peremptory challenge, especially in joint trials where multiplication of challenges by a number of accused persons could even lead to packing a jury.[13] These remarks in the now withdrawn first edition were applied to a trial in Bristol, possibly carrying the innuendo that counsel had been guilty of unprofessional conduct, and that challenges were racially motivated so as to obtain a "black" jury. Sadly, these opinions expressed in the context of a book on suggestions for law, including jury, reform occasioned reactions and events which accelerated his decision to retire.

In one significant respect he insisted on jury participation in the administration of justice. Where, for example, the police were issued with dangerous weapons, such as a heavily loaded cosh which could cause fatalities, or if policemen were undisciplined or out of control and a blind official eye was turned, or if hospitals were prescribing dangerous drugs, then any "death would have occurred in circumstances the continuance or possible recurrence of which is prejudicial to the health or safety of the public or any section of the public." Accordingly, in terms of the Coroners Act a coroner's jury was compulsory. This he held in respect of the controversial death of Mr. Blair Peach, which had occurred during the

---

[9] *Boston* v. *W.S. Bagshaw and Sons* [1967] 2 All E.R. 87. The police, at the request of auctioneers, requested a television company to transmit a notice about a theft. The broadcast apparently referred to an innocent plaintiff who sued auctioneers and T.V. company, malice being alleged against the former. The jury was obviously confused, as their subsequent inadmissible evidence showed. The trial action is reported as [1966] 1 W.L.R. 1126.

[10] *Shoukatallie* v. *R.* [1962] A.C. 81. (P.C.).

[11] [1980] 1 W.L.R. 892.

[12] *Ibid.* pp. 899–900.

[13] pp. 63–69.

suppression of a riot in West London, during which police were allegedly equipped with dangerous weapons.[14]

Protection of Witnesses, Counsel and Court

To prevent extraneous factors, pressures, or fears of consequences from threatening a fair trial, witnesses, counsel and court, including jury, must be protected. That this need for protection generally outweighs conflicting rights, such as freedom of speech or a right to vindicate honour or even personal liberty of a person who has been convicted will already have emerged. Thus, the courts at all levels and bodies exercising functions akin to courts are given immunity for all acts within jurisdiction or honestly believed to be within jurisdiction.[15]

The usual mode of protecting courts against disruption of their proceedings or defiance of their orders or obstruction of the administration of justice is by way of a charge of contempt of court, but even then, according to Lord Denning, such charge should not be heard by a judge on the spot, unless it was urgent and imperative so to act.[16] Lord Denning, as pointed out in connection with personal liberty, was anxious to pursue multiple purposes, both protecting the courts and acknowledging individual rights, especially of expression and to personal liberty.[17] When Mr. Quintin Hogg was brought before the court for contempt at Mr. Blackburn's instance for an article in *Punch*, critical of the Court of Appeal's judgment in the first *Blackburn* case seeking to enforce the gaming laws, Lord Denning ruled, with freedom of expression in mind, that the court must be sparing in the exercise of jurisdiction to punish expressions of opinion, fair comment, even if it was prejudiced and incorrect, being permissible.[18] Nor was a discourteous letter to the courts administrator about inconsiderate setting down of a case for hearing a contempt, either by way of insulting the court or by way of interfering with the course of justice.[19]

Lord Denning had accorded counsel immunity for their conduct in cases brought against them by clients alleging negligence,[20] especially when choosing between the duty as an officer of the court to further truth and justice and the duty to defend a client, although this immunity would not extend to protect them against action by the court should they improperly run up legal costs.[21]

The protection given by earlier cases to jurors was extended by Lord

---

[14] *R.* v. *H.M. Coroner at Hammersmith, ex p. Peach* [1980] 2 W.L.R. 496.

[15] *Sirros* v. *Moore*, above, the protection extending to police officers acting on a magistrate's mistaken order. The protection was extended by Lord Denning to prison visitors in *O'Reilly* v. *Mackman*, above, p. 307.

[16] *Balogh* v. *St. Alban's Crown Court* [1975] Q.B. 73.

[17] As in *Morris* v. *Crown Office*, above, and in *Balogh* v. *St. Alban's Crown Court*, above, where he held that there had as yet not been an attempt to commit a contempt as opposed merely to theft of a "laughing gas" cylinder preliminary to an intended contempt. In the latter case he reduced sentence to 14 days already served in prison, taking into account an apology purging any contempt.

[18] *R.* v. *Commissioner of Police of the Metropolis, ex p. Blackburn (No. 2)* [1968] 2 Q.B. 150.

[19] *Weston* v. *Central Criminal Court Courts Administrator* [1976] 3 W.L.R. 103.

[20] *Rondel* v. *Worsley*, above, p. 305, sought to be extended, unsuccessfully, by Lord Denning to all advice by counsel in *Saif Ali* v. *Sydney Mitchell and Co.* [1978] Q.B. 95, 103.

[21] *Kelly* v. *London Transport Executive*, above, p. 316.

Denning to witnesses, who were now to be protected against interference by the law of contempt.[22] Had his views prevailed, witnesses would also have received protection by entitlement to bring an action for damages for contempt of court and an injunction. This issue arose when a landlord served a notice to quit on a tenant who had given evidence against him, but the majority of the Court of Appeal doubted whether there was such a cause of action, holding that the fact that the giving of notice was both malicious and a contempt did not render it tortious when it was a valid exercise of contractual rights.[23] He would also have conferred absolute immunity on a witness (a solicitor) making statements in open court to obtain the issue of a warrant of arrest. The House of Lords, reversing him, held that such a ruling would make the wrong of procuring an arrest with malice not actionable, because the giving of evidence in court was the very basis for showing that the tort had been committed.[24]

Conduct prejudicing a fair trial is also punishable by the law of contempt and is more appropriately dealt with under freedom of expression, which is the context in which such conduct usually becomes relevant.

Discovery Orders and Evidential Privileges

It is impossible in discussing Lord Denning's contribution to deal separately with discovery orders (the procedural facility of having both sides in litigation ordered by the court to disclose to the other their papers) and the right of litigants to refuse to make such papers available or to answer certain questions relying on an evidential privilege given in support of public purposes, such as preserving the stability of marriage. The difficulty arises primarily from developments in the area once referred to as "Crown privilege," but now usually called "public interest immunity." Denning judgments and attempts to change the law read against multiple judgments in the House of Lords have blurred the former conceptual clarity.

Beginning his development of the law concerning discovery in his accustomed fashion of enhancing judicial power, Lord Denning, as far back as 1948, took a wide view of power under section 14 of the Crown Proceedings Act to order production of accounts so as to cover also records and documents, but was reversed by the Court of Appeal.[25] By 1954 he was taking a narrow view of what was within the scope of privilege, declining to hold that a surveyor's report coming into existence as a result of a "without prejudice" discussion was privileged.[26] To his chagrin in 1962 he was precluded by section 1(7)(b) of the Legal Aid and Advice Act 1949 from ordering discovery of experts' reports made for a legally aided plaintiff.[27] In 1963 he permitted the use of irregularly obtained documents regarding tax liability, even though the *subpoena duces tecum* had been issued without a master's or a judge's consent, while to it had been added specified

---

[22] *Att.-Gen.* v. *Butterworth* [1963] 1 Q.B. 696 and *Moore* v. *Clerk of Assize, Bristol* [1971] 1 W.L.R. 1669.

[23] *Chapman* v. *Honig* [1963] 2 Q.B. 502

[24] *Roy* v. *Prior* [1970] 1 Q.B. 283, reversed [1971] A.C. 470.

[25] *Commissioners of Customs and Excise* v. *Ingram* [1948] 1 All E.R. 927 (C.A.).

[26] *Rabin* v. *Mendoza* [1954] 1 W.L.R. 271.

[27] *Re Saxton (decd.)* [1962] 1 W.L.R. 968. In *What Next in the Law*, p. 93, he was still giving a partial version of the issues.

documents not listed before issue. He drew a parallel with unlawfully obtained evidence in criminal cases, also holding that no cause of action could arise from such irregular obtaining of a *subpoena*.[28] Then came the trilogy of cases preceding *Conway* v. *Rimmer*.[29] In *Merricks* v. *Nott-Bower*[30] Salmon L.J. took the lead, going far further than Lord Denning in distinguishing *Duncan* v. *Cammell Laird*.[31] Lord Denning subsequently adopted this approach, with Salmon L.J. leading the charge,[32] in *Re Grosvenor Hotel*[33] and in *Wednesbury Corporation* v. *Ministry of Housing and Local Government*,[34] holding that the courts had a residual power themselves to inspect documents to decide whether, on weighing the public interest in due administration of justice and candour in the public service, production should be ordered, although on the facts of these cases the court did not think it appropriate or necessary to exercise the power. Lord Denning's dissent in *Conway* v. *Rimmer*[35] was revolutionary in its direct attack on binding precedent and its ultimate substitution, with the House of Lords on the latter point basically agreeing, of absolute judicial discretion for absolute executive discretion in deciding, by a balancing process, whether documents involving public interests of the state, at that time referred to as "Crown privilege", should or should not be discovered.[36]

In parallel Lord Denning was making direct and indirect forays into "privilege" in the law of evidence, a concept to which he was opposed, "privilege" for him meaning "a right to keep things secret—to keep things back from your opponent or from the court—so that they cannot get to know of them."[37] In *McTaggart* v. *McTaggart*[38] he made it clear that no privilege attached to a priest, a medical man, a banker, or a probation officer, although in *Mole* v. *Mole*[39] while repeating that there was no privilege attaching to such persons, he held that conversations with them between a husband and a wife with a view to matrimonial reconciliation were privileged. Even so this matrimonial privilege resulting from without prejudice negotiations was easily waived.[40] His narrow view of the scope of privilege resulting from "without prejudice" discussion in relation to the making of experts' reports has already been indicated.[41]

Although denying journalists any privilege, Lord Denning, with his preferred position on Press freedom, indicated ways of effectively giving

---

[28] *Soul* v. *I.R.C.* (*Practice Note*) [1963] 1 W.L.R. 112. The case can be seen as making inroads into the privilege against self-crimination. So too can *R.* v. *Selvey* [1967] 3 W.L.R. 1637 above, p. 255 allowing cross-examination as to previous convictions.

[29] [1967] 1 W.L.R. 1031 (C.A.).

[30] [1965] Q.B. 57.

[31] [1942] A.C. 624.

[32] Thence Russell L.J.'s appellation of Lord Denning M.R. and Harman and Salmon L.JJ. as "Porthos M.R., Athos and Aramis L.JJ." In *Air Canada* v. *Secretary of State for Trade* [1983] 2 W.L.R. 494 at p. 507 Lord Denning discloses that he designedly so composed the court, and that it was mischance that by the time of *Conway* v. *Rimmer* the court was differently composed.

[33] (No. 2) [1965] Ch. 1210.

[34] [1965] 1 W.L.R. 261.

[35] Above.

[36] See S.A. de Smith's penetrating criticisms and questions in *Constitutional and Administrative Law* (3rd ed., 1977), pp. 611–613.

[37] *What Next in the Law*, p. 227.

[38] [1949] P. 94.

[39] [1951] P. 21.

[40] *McTaggart*, above.   [41] *Rabin* v. *Mendoza*, above, p. 331.

journalists a right to decline to reveal their sources, unless exceptional factors were present. In *Georgius* v. *Vice-Chancellor and Delegates of the Press of Oxford University*[42] he extended an earlier rule of "settled practice," that discovery or interrogatories would not be ordered in a libel suit against a newspaper to force it to disclose its sources of information before trial, to cover monthly, annual and quarterly reviews and even "publishers."[43] Protectiveness towards the press was less manifest in *Attorney-General* v. *Mulholland*[44] where Lord Denning emphasised that journalists had no privilege, upholding a six months' prison sentence for contempt by virtue of refusal to divulge sources of information for a press story about deficiencies in naval security to the Tribunal of Inquiry into the *Vassall* case. Nonetheless, it was in this case that he first crystallised his concept of it being the court's duty to balance the need for confidentiality and the public interest in having justice done when exercising the discretion that a court has not to compel an answer but to respect confidences entrusted to journalists (and other professional men) unless it is relevant, proper and necessary for such a question to be put and answered. The case bore fruit two decades later in *British Steel Corporation* v. *Granada Television*.[45]

The television media also received protection in his partial dissent in *Senior* v. *Holdsworth, ex parte Independent Television News*[46] where, while holding that the court had jurisdiction to order production of all film footage, he would only have permitted a *subpoena* for untransmitted film of events if it had been shown that the film had a direct and important part to play in determining the issues before the court. The court as a whole held that an order for production of all the film footage was too wide and oppressive.

While denying the police information to facilitate their prosecuting decisions, unless they were able to pinpoint a precise need for it, Lord Denning was, conversely, willing to protect information in the possession of official bodies concerned with the regulation of gaming. Thus, as already mentioned, in *Benaim and Khaida*, he had ruled that Crockfords, refused a certificate of consent, did not have to be told by the Gaming Board the source of their information leading to the refusal "if that would put their informant in peril or otherwise be contrary to the public interest."[47]

Denning judgments were to be important in developing a new "privilege."[48] In *Re D. (Infants)*[49] he held that case records kept by local authorities in respect of children in their care who are boarded out, must not without the authorisation of the Secretary of State be disclosed even to a court except in very rare cases, the basis being that if welfare officers were

---

[42] [1949] 1 K.B. 729.
[43] *Ibid.* p. 733. The protection was given to Crockford's Clerical Directory.
[44] [1963] 2 Q.B. 477.
[45] [1980] 3 W.L.R. 774.
[46] [1976] Q.B. 23.
[47] [1970] 2 W.L.R. 1009, 1017. See above, p. 308, n. 55. This case was built upon by the House of Lords in *R.* v. *Lewes JJ.* [1973] A.C. 388.
[48] "Privilege" is here used because Lord Denning himself used the term when it suited his purposes. It will be seen that sometimes he spoke of "public interest" (in accordance with the majority view of their Lordships in *D.* v. *N.S.P.C.C.* [1978] A.C. 171), but that on other occasions he referred to "privilege" (*Neilson* v. *Laugharne* [1981] 2 W.L.R. 537, 543) so that he could then contend that the "privilege" could be raised by one of the litigants as well as by a government department, and that it could be waived.
[49] [1970] 1 W.L.R. 599.

frankly and fully to report to their social service committees, fear that their notes were liable to disclosure would imperil that frankness. No discovery orders were, or should be, given in custody cases.[50] The case was later to be followed by *D.* v. *N.S.P.C.C.*[51]

Implementing his concept of a right (or duty) to confidence, mentioned in connection with intellectual property,[52] and overridable if the public interest required disclosure, Lord Denning applied the notion to situations where information was received in confidence for a limited and restricted purpose, holding that normally it might not be used for other purposes. He attempted, being however reversed as to the law on this point by their Lordships, to treat "confidentiality" as a new ground of privilege where documents were entrusted to a party to litigation by a third party.[53] Before this reversal he also refused discovery as against the customs authorities to a chemical company whose patents were being infringed by imports, information as to which would have been revealed to the Customs Commissioners. At this stage, trying to create a right to confidence, he relied on such a right, as well as on the public interest in ensuring candour by importers if the system were to work well.[54] Here too the House of Lords reversed him.[55]

An inroad into the privilege against self-crimination, which was also an invasion of personal liberty, was constituted by Lord Denning's indirect forcing of plaintiffs in personal injuries litigation to submit to a medical examination, sanctioned, in the event of refusal, by a stay of action.[56] The defendant's privilege to withhold his experts' reports was reciprocally overridden to the extent that, if asked, he must give the plaintiff a copy of the report obtained from the compulsory medical examination.[57] But, although Lord Denning in a dissent would have had it otherwise, the defendant's privilege in relation to all other medical reports in his possession remained.[58]

A statutory example of denial of the privilege of self-crimination was also pronounced upon by Lord Denning in relation to the scope of legal professional privilege. The latter in his view meant only that a solicitor must not produce or disclose in any legal proceedings any of the communications between himself and his client without the client's consent. This was backed up by a second "privilege" (Diplock L.J. saw the latter merely as a matter of a contractual duty of confidence) arising out of the confidence subsisting between solicitor and client, similar to that between doctor and patient, banker and customer, accountant and client and the like, there being an implied term that such confidences will not be disclosed other than in the

---

[50] *Ibid.* p. 1089.   [51] [1976] 3 W.L.R. 124 (C.A.).   [52] Above, pp. 285–286.

[53] *Alfred Crompton Amusement Machines Ltd.* v. *Customs and Excise Commissioners* [1972] 2 W.L.R. 835 at p. 859, reversed [1973] 3 W.L.R. 268. Their Lordships did however rule that in considering the public interest in the proper functioning of a government department confidentiality in being entrusted documents would have to be taken into account: pp. 284–285.

[54] *Norwich Pharmacal Co.* v. *Customs and Excise Commissioners* [1972] 3 W.L.R. 870, 877–878.

[55] *Norwich Pharmacal* [1973] 3 W.L.R. 164. Their Lordships' novel ruling permitting discovery against third parties and prior to proceedings was a significant law reform facilitating the enforcement of legal rights.

[56] *Edmeades* v. *Thames Board Mills Ltd.* [1969] 2 Q.B. 67. Lord Denning did not think legislation was needed to achieve this power, despite such a suggestion in Winn L.J.'s report of the Committee on Personal Injuries Litigation (1968 Cmnd. 3691. para. 312).

[57] *Clarke* v. *Martlew* [1972] 3 W.L.R. 653.

[58] *Causton* v. *Mann Egerton (Johnsons) Ltd.* [1974] 1 W.L.R. 163.

most exceptional and special circumstances and also an implication that the solicitor will obey the law. Consequently, a solicitor into whose accounts the Law Society were enquiring had to make disclosure under rule 11 of the Solicitors' Accounts Rules 1945.[59]

These cases may appear as a wilderness of single instances, but Lord Denning was now to attempt to draw the threads together to accord the court power to balance all interests, irrespective of whether privilege was involved, and to allow the court to decide whether to compel an answer or the production of documents or to deny their accessibility to the other party in the trial. He took this broad approach in *D.* v. *N.S.P.C.C.*[60] where parents, extremely upset by an inquiry into their treatment of their child by an inspector from a national society concerned to protect children, which had received information alleging ill treatment of the child, sought to obtain discovery of the report and the name of the informant. Lord Denning denied there was any privilege, instead holding that the court must balance competing public interests in deciding whether this should be disclosed, using as six of his eight stepping stones to this test his own earlier judgments.[61] Having taken the mother's desire for redress, the confidentiality in which the information was entrusted, and the interest in protecting children into account, he held that the public interest in maintaining the society's sources of information outweighed the public interest that the mother as an injured party had to obtain information enabling her to obtain legal redress. His refusal to order disclosure of the informant was upheld by their Lordships, but on the narrow ground that information as to possible child abuse given to local authorities or to the N.S.P.C.C., which had a status to bring care proceedings under the Children and Young Persons Act 1969, was immune from disclosure. Lord Hailsham went some way in generalising with Lord Denning by accepting that where an authority was charged with the enforcement and administration of the law by the initiation of court proceedings there was a public interest in maintaining confidentiality of information given to such authority.[62]

Lord Denning was undeterred. He now saw the conceptually very different issues as to the power of the courts to order discovery of documents, to call for the name of an informant, to require answers to questions, to make or refuse to make available reports to local authority members, and how the courts must deal with claims to legal, marital and child care privilege, to "public interest immunity," and to rights to confidentiality and privacy, and whether arising in ordinary civil litigation, by special interlocutory procedures, in contempt of court proceedings, or on judicial review, as

---

[59] *Parry-Jones* v. *Law Society* [1968] Ch. 1. The case also illustrated that in the investigative jurisdiction of the Law Society Lord Denning would not require the solicitor to be informed of the nature of the complaint and who was making it, the inquiry merely being whether there was prima facie evidence and not constituting an actual determination, following his own decision in *Wiseman* v. *Borneman* [1968] Ch. 429.

[60] [1976] 3 W.L.R. 124.

[61] *Ibid.* p. 132.

[62] [1977] 2 W.L.R. 201, 218. Their Lordships were divided 3–2 as to whether to adopt Lord Denning's broader conception. It has been suggested that Scarman L.J. deliberately took a very conservative approach, wholly out of character, so that a majority of the Court of Appeal would not be pushing up a radical decision to their Lordships, which would then in all likelihood be reversed. If so, the tactic worked. I do not accept this view. Scarman L.J. was a consistent opponent of secrecy and an ardent believer in justice. He foresaw that secrecy could be exploited.

simply involving the court in balancing competing public interests,[63] and of then deciding whether or not to order disclosure. Conflicts of interest arose especially in connection with the need to preserve confidential information so as to facilitate the effective and candid working of government,[64] of governmental or of administrative bodies.[65] Such conflict might, he thought, be between two specialised public interests, such as the need to preserve confidentiality in relation to child care records and the need to ensure that justice was duly administered by producing documents necessary for that purpose,[66] the latter public interest obviously coinciding with the private interest of the party seeking disclosure. At other times the conflict might be between ensuring "due administration of justice"[67] and the right of an individual to privacy in respect of his documents.

According to Lord Denning other interests also came into the balancing exercise. The interest might be a claim to honour confidence entrusted to the recipient of personal reports on workers in public bodies or in industry,[68] or it might be a journalist's claim to honour confidences and preserve sources of information[69] or it might be a claim that in litigation touching on sovereign aspects of a foreign state's dealings discovery should not, as a matter of comity and of judicial restraint, be ordered.[70] Further factors would be that a party should not be oppressed, or be put to unnecessarily great expenditure[71] or be subjected to a mere "fishing expedition."[72]

Had he not been constrained by an excess of authority, which even he could not avoid, he would have got rid of both legal professional privilege and the privilege against self-crimination,[73] substituting for these a

---

[63] See *What Next in the Law*, p. 227.

[64] The earlier cases were *Merricks* v. *Nott-Bower* [1965] 1 Q.B. 57; *Re Grosvenor Hotel, London (No. 2)* [1965] Ch. 1210; *Wednesbury Corporation* v. *M.H.L.G.* [1965] 1 W.L.R. 261. Later came *Norwich Pharmacal Co. Customs and Excise Commissioners* [1972] 3 W.L.R. 870; his dissent in *Burmah Oil Co. Ltd.* v. *Bank of England* [1979] 1 W.L.R. 473; and *Air Canada* v. *Secretary of State for Trade (No. 2)* [1983] 1 All E.R. 161.

[65] *Conway* v. *Rimmer* [1967] 1 W.L.R. 1031 (the police—a dissent upheld in the House of Lords); *D.* v. *N.S.P.C.C.* [1978] A.C. 171 (a child caring organisation—a dissent, upheld on narrow grounds by their Lordships); *Gaskin* v. *Liverpool City Council* [1979] 1 W.L.R. 1549; *Burmah Oil* v. *Bank of England*, above, (a dissent with the Lords adopting the same reasoning, but disagreeing on the result): [1980] A.C. 1090); and *Neilson* v. *Laugharne* [1981] 1 W.L.R. 537 (police).

[66] *D.* v. *N.S.P.C.C.*, above; *Gaskin*, above; and *Campbell* v. *Tameside B.C.* [1982] 3 W.L.R. 74.

[67] See below, p. 344, on the tortuous meaning Denning later gave this phrase in order to cut down the possibility of discovery of high-level state documents once he thought discovery had been abused.

[68] *S.R.C.* v. *Nassé* [1979] 1 Q.B. 144. The case, affirmed by their Lordships [1979] 3 W.L.R. 762) governs the circumstances in which industrial tribunals can, on application by the C.R.E. or the E.O.C., order disclosure of confidential reports on employees.

[69] *B.S.C.* v. *Granada Television* [1980] 3 W.L.R. 774.

[70] *Buttes Gas and Oil Co.* v. *Hammer (No. 3)* [1980] 3 W.L.R. 668. Lord Denning denied that there was a legal privilege to this effect. The House of Lords, did not pronounce on this, considering the subject of the dispute not justiciable, a contention Lord Denning had urged in the Court of Appeal as an alternative ground of his opinion that discovery should not be ordered.

[71] *Lonrho Ltd.* v. *Shell Petroleum Co. Ltd.* [1980] 2 W.L.R. 367.

[72] Above.

[73] The privilege against self-crimination was preserved in section 14 of the Civil Evidence Act 1968. Lord Denning had upheld the privilege in *Comet Products U.K. Ltd.* v. *Hawkex Plastics Ltd.* [1971] 2 Q.B. 67. He ruled (at p. 74) that where a person was accused of a civil contempt this was a criminal matter, and he was not compellable either to give evidence or to answer interrogatories to prove his guilt.

balancing of the various public interests, which would also take the parties' personal interests into account. He expressed regret that he could not scrap the privilege against self-crimination in *Rank Film Distributors Ltd.* v. *Video Information Centre*,[74] making the revolutionary suggestion that a court could get around the privilege by conferring immunity against criminal proceedings.[75]

Earlier, in *Westinghouse*,[76] he had sought to limit the privilege by requiring a witness claiming it to have reasonable grounds, by way of a real or appreciable danger of exposure to penalties for making such claim. Furthermore, he opined that, there being no real risk of criminal libel proceedings, the privilege no longer applied in civil libel suits.[77]

He would like too to have disposed of legal professional privilege, but had to content himself in his dissent in *Waugh* v. *British Railways Board* with confining legal professional privilege as much as possible, by applying a requirement that any document should have been made "wholly or mainly" for the purpose of the litigation if it were to be privileged. He was on this occasion upheld by the Lords who were unfettered by precedents.[78]

Extra-judicially in *What Next in the Law*[79] he also characterised the rule that discovered documents should only be used for authorised purposes as a balancing exercise. He saw the conflict as being between freedom of the press to deal with matters of public interest, especially when they had been ventilated in court, and of preserving the rule that discovered documents were usable only for authorised purposes, the discovery process being already an invasion of the privacy of the party whose documents were discovered. These comments referred to *Home Office* v. *Harman*.[80] From a human rights' viewpoint an analysis that various interests are concerned is correct, but it is easy to understand Lord Diplock's *cri di coeur* that the case was not about freedom of speech or the press or openness of justice or the European Convention on Human Rights, but about an aspect of the law of discovery in civil actions in the High Court.[81]

Lord Denning's balancing approach in this area, merely labelling certain contentions as an interest in confidentiality, privacy, etc., did not help choice between them. He tended to simplify so much that he omitted vital interests from his balance, such as the need for a civilised society to be informed as to prison conditions and policies. Even the sophisticated approach of Lord Scarman,[82] only facilitates choice by emphasising preferred values and reminding courts of the interests affected. In developed legal systems, other than in discretionary areas, courts must apply recognised rules. Human rights values are thus not decisive criteria, athough they endure as evaluative standards for results.

There was a legal issue in *Harman* not resolvable by reference to various freedoms. That was whether one of the several kinds of contempt of court,

---

[74] [1980] 3 W.L.R. 487, 504. Lord Denning was again dissenting.
[75] He would have done this on the basis of *Riddick* v. *Thames Board Mills* [1977] Q.B. 881, a view criticised by their Lordships when *Rank* was on appeal: [1981] 2 W.L.R. 668.
[76] [1978] A.C. 547, 574.
[77] *Ibid.* p. 573 and *Rank*, above at p. 507.
[78] [1979] 2 All E.R. 1169, cited extensively by Lord Edmund- Davies expecially at p. 1181.
[79] pp. 262–263.   [80] [1981] Q.B. 534.
[81] [1983] A.C. 280, 299.
[82] See his judgment in *Home Office* v. *Harman* [1983] A.C. 280, which is a model of human rights thinking and judging.

such as defiance of the court or prejudicing the administration of justice had been committed. The accused, a solicitor, who was full-time legal officer to the National Council for Civil Liberties (N.C.C.L.), to enable a journalist to write a feature article had given him sight of documents ordered to be discovered in litigation by her client, a prisoner, suing the Home Office for having held him in a "control unit" without having observed the requirements of the Prison Rules and for having inflicted upon him cruel and unusual punishment contrary to the Bill of Rights. The article, which appeared in *The Guardian*, angered Lord Denning,[83] particularly as there was reference to "a legal milestone" in achieving discovery of such high-level policy-making documents in the Home Office. The judge ordering discovery had based this on the implied undertaking (by solicitor and client obtaining discovery that the documents will not be used for any purpose other than the particular action) mentioned in Lord Denning's decision in *Riddick* v. *Thames Board Mills*,[84] and on a letter by Miss Harman, as the plaintiff's solicitor, to the Treasury Solicitor acknowledging her awareness of the rule that discovered documents "should not be used for any other purpose except for the case in hand," thereby also impliedly agreeing to the Home Office's stipulation, conveyed to her, that the documents should not be used for the general purposes of the N.C.C.L., or purposes other than the action. Lord Denning found that there had been a serious contempt by a solicitor of the Supreme Court, much to be regretted, and that the disclosure of the documents had been abused by Miss Harman.[85] The decision was upheld by a divided House of Lords,[86] and the matter was subsequently taken to the European Commission of Human Rights.

Immediately, in *Home Office* v. *Harman*, Lord Denning regretted that the documents had even been discovered and said "The 'legal milestone' will have to be taken up and set back a bit."[87] He made good this threat, setting it back almost to the first stage of the journey, as soon as he got the opportunity in a "public interest immunity" case involving discovery of documents by a Minister. He ruled that Harman's case

> "is a good illustration of the need for keeping high-level documents secret. Once they are let out of the bag, untold mischief may be done. It is no use relying on safeguards. The documents must not be let out of the bag at all. I trust that today we are setting back the 'legal milestone' to the place where it was before."[88]

The House of Lords were to achieve the same result by a different technique, which will be dealt with later.[89] Such a judicial reaction, endangering the facility of discovery, should have been foreseen by those who used discovered documents for extraneous, even if laudable, purposes.

---

[83] In *Home Office* v. *Harman* [1981] 2 W.L.R. 310, 329 he said that the documents had been 'exposed to the ravages of outsiders. I regard the use by the journalist in this case of these documents to be highly detrimental to the good ordering of our society. They were used so as to launch a wholly unjustified attack on Ministers of State and high level servants—who were only doing their very best to deal with a wicked criminal who had harassed society and was serving a long sentence for armed robbery."

[84] [1977] 1 Q.B. 881.

[85] [1981] 2 W.L.R. 310, 329.

[86] [1983] A.C. 280 by 3–2.

[87] [1981] 2 W.L.R. 310, 329.

[88] *Air Canada* v. *Secretary of State for Trade* [1983] 1 All E.R. 161, 180.

[89] *Air Canada* v. *Secretary of State for Trade (No. 2)* [1983] 1 All E.R. 910 (H.L.). See below, p. 345.

Lord Denning's generalised approach in this area of law of merely balancing interests can easily lead to neglect of other principles, something shown in two of his later disclosure cases. In *Hook*[90] after an Authority decision taken on counsel's advice that a report on the Lancashire Constabulary possibly contained defamatory matter and should not further be circulated, a new county councillor and member of the Police Authority was not permitted to have access to it. Disciplinary action consequent on the report had already been taken. Lord Denning held that new as well as old members had the right to see such documents, whereas the majority of the Court of Appeal considered that the Police Authority had taken a discretionary decision, and that it had not been shown that no reasonable authority could have reached that conclusion, especially in view of counsel's advice.

In *Ex p. O*[91] a councillor chairing the housing sub-committee demanded access to reports on certain foster parents as prospective adopters by the council's social workers (who took up the matter as one involving their professional confidentiality). On their solicitor's advice, the council ordered that the councillor be allowed to inspect the file. An injunction was sought restraining the council from giving such access. Lord Denning, in a majority judgment, granted the injunction after adopting what the Law Lords described as a "simple balancing approach" as between child care confidentiality and the need for councillors to be well informed to do their council duties. He was reversed on the grounds that it could not be said that the decision to give access to the councillor was so unreasonable that the council's exercise of discretion could be set aside, having regard to councillors' public duties. Lord Denning's approach, seen from a "realist" standpoint, cuts across other interests, namely the democratic principle that elected publicly responsible bodies should be able to take their own decisions without judicial intervention unless they ignore administrative law constraints. From the orthodox technical legal standpoint, it results in confusion, and *cadi* justice, even if the *cadi* was good, wise and old, as in *The Arabian Nights*.

Lord Denning's later extra-judicial comments on *Granada*[92] confirm these criticisms. In that case it was laid down by their Lordships, adopting Lord Denning's approach in the Court of Appeal, that the criterion for deciding whether a journalist, a newspaper or a television company must reveal the name of an informant was whether the public interest in protecting the free flow of information against revelation of sources and in not compelling confidence bona fide given to be broken was, exceptionally, outweighed by the public interest in favour of doing justice. Lord Denning introspected about his vacillations concerning *Granada* in *What Next in the Law*. The factor at the time of delivery of judgment which turned the scales towards disclosure was that *Granada* in his opinion, "had not behaved with due respect,"[93] obviously bringing themselves into his category of those who have abused their position or power. On reconsideration, because disclosure

[90] *R.* v. *Lancashire C.C., ex p. Hook* [1980] 3 W.L.R. 71 with Lord Denning in dissent.
[91] *R.* v. *Birmingham C.C., ex p. O* [1982] 1 W.L.R. 679, a majority Denning judgment, reversed [1983] A.C. 578.
[92] *British Steel Corporation* v. *Granada Television* [1980] 3 W.L.R. 774.
[93] p. 249.

of sources impedes the free flow of information, he divulged a change of mind.[94] Admission of fallibility and the difficulty of choice is endearing, but it also points up the fact that when there are no clear criteria governing choice it is easy to "err," and that in related areas there may be other unadmitted "errors."

Of the 20 major reported cases[95] involving discovery or disclosure since, but also including *Conway* v. *Rimmer*, Lord Denning ordered disclosure of disputed material in seven.[96] In each case where an order was made or where one was refused his well-known predilections were significant factors in the decisions. Thus, in *Conway* he felt there was possible official misbehaviour and injustice to the trainee policeman.[97] In *Waugh*, the next case, 11 years later, it was obvious that, once the hearsay rule had been abolished, the best evidence, which would be immediate post-accident inquiry reports, should be made available to the court. It appeared wrong to Lord Denning that British Rail could suit themselves and put in a report if it favoured their case, but withhold it on grounds of legal professional privilege if it did not.[98] There were also overtones of *Saxton* and *Mendoza*: with expert reports available to one party only, he would always wish to see both having access. In addition, he would have sympathised with the widow, whose husband was killed in the railway accident. In *Campbell* he sympathised with a teacher attacked by a disturbed child so severely that she had to retire in consequence of her injuries. *Granada*, *Rank* and *Hook* all showed disapproval of misbehaviour: of the television company in *Granada*; of the defendants' dishonesty and of "piracy" of film and transcription for resale on video-cassettes in *Rank*; and of the serious mismanagement of and the state of affairs in the Lancashire Constabulary in *Hook*. In his dissent in *Burmah* he would have brought to light Ministerial pressure on the Bank of England to impose conditions on the company when conducting a rescue operation (obviously in the interests of sterling), which conditions the Bank had not sought to impose and which were harsh. Lord Denning had never wished to give immunity to the state in commercial transactions, while it could be said that the Bank, at state dictation, had prescribed unconscionable conditions at a time when Burmah had been placed in a relationship with the Bank that was similar to one in which undue influence might in any ordinary relationship between borrower and lender be presumed.

---

[94] p. 251.

[95] *Conway* v. *Rimmer*; *D. (Infants)*; *Benaim and Khaida*; *Crompton*; *Norwich Pharmacal*; *D.* v. *N.S.P.C.C.*; *Westinghouse*; *S.R.C.* v. *Nassé*; *Waugh*; *Burmah*; *Lonrho*; *Granada*; *Gaskin*; *Neilson*; *Rank*; *Buttes*; *Hook*; *Ex p. O*; *Campbell*; and *Air Canada*.

[96] *Conway*; *Waugh*; *Burmah*; *Granada*; *Rank*; *Hook*; and *Campbell*. I have not counted *Westinghouse*, because Lord Denning, although giving effect to letters rogatory, would not permit the controversial documents or evidence to be given, ruling that the privilege against self-crimination could apply. Nor have I included *Crompton*, because on grounds of confidentiality he declined to make an order, or *Nassé*, because although remitting the matter to the industrial tribunal for consideration on the principles he had laid down, he clearly indicated disclosure should not be made.

[97] See *The Discipline of Law*, p. 301.

[98] See however his dicta about a case involving a suit against the police for false imprisonment and malicious prosecution, where he would have allowed the police to have claimed "public interest immunity" for statements to an inquiry into police conduct, and thereafter to use an immune document at the trial for cross-examination purposes: *Campbell* v. *Tameside B.C.* [1982] 3 W.L.R. 74 at p. 79, referring critically to *Hehir* v. *Commissioner of Police of the Metropolis* [1982] 1 W.L.R. 715.

Conversely, in the thirteen cases where disclosure was refused, a similar "realist" analysis shows Lord Denning as motivated by considerations always present in his thinking. It was Chancellor's foot justice, but the size of Lord Denning's shoe was well known. *D. (Infants), D.* v. *N.S.P.C.C., Gaskin* and *Ex p. O* all protect the system of obtaining frank reports on children, and cannot be said to have neglected the welfare of any particular child involved, any overriding of interests being in respect of adults making claims, with the former child in *Gaskin* falling into his category of persons abusing their rights by engaging in a fishing expedition, and the councillor in *Ex p. O.* being, from Lord Denning's way of telling the story, a self-appointed inquirer into the workings of other committees of the Birmingham Council.

Sources of information had to be protected in *Benaim and Khaida*, while in *Nassé*, not only did sources and efficient functioning of all employers in public and private sectors require safeguarding, but it also appeared to him that there were "presumptuous" claims by the Commissions to use inquisitorial powers taking one back to the days of the General Warrants and the Inquisition.[99] In *Crompton* preservation of confidentiality of information given by hirers of games and fruit machines to the Customs authorities was, he thought, necessary. *Norwich Pharmacal* also involved confidentiality of information to the Customs and Excise and there is a hint of disapproval, with references to the "monopoly" of a chemical company, and putting "pirate" importations in italics at a time when international pharmaceutical companies, well before the days of video-pirates and *Anton Piller* orders, were being arraigned for over-pricing. *Neilson* can be seen as protecting the working of police misconduct inquiries, influenced by his disapprobation of a litigant suspected of possessing drugs (Lord Denning well-knowing that search warrants are not sought unless trading as well as mere possession is also suspected) and made worse in his view by the obtaining of legal aid to sue the police in trespass and "to delve through . . . statements so as to make out a case—which he would not otherwise have."[1]

Air Canada, Buttes, Lonrho, and *Westinghouse* all concerned the national interest, close to his heart. *Air Canada* involved high-level policy-making, and was characterised as a "fishing expedition," but was also decisively affected by the use of discovered documents in *Harman*—in Lord Reid's words in *Conway* v. *Rimmer*[2] to "create or fan ill-informed or captious public or political criticism," or in Lord Denning's own words, "severe criticisms of ministers and of higher civil servants who could not answer back."[3] Indeed, lessons from experience had taught him to give great weight to a certificate by a Minister, and not to override it except in extreme cases.[4]

Buttes involved delicate negotiations about territorial seas, likely to contain off-shore oil, between the Foreign Office, Iran and various emirates (states) adjacent to the Straits of Hormuz. In aspects of foreign policy, Lord Denning had always been reluctant to intervene. *Lonrho*, involved a plaintiff

---

[99] *S.R.C.* v. *Nassé* [1979] 1 Q.B. 144, 172. It will be interesting to see what a generation of judges unschooled in the Whig interpretation of history and in the major constitutional cases of the 17th and 18th century cases invokes in the 21st century. Perhaps judgments by the great Lord Denning?

[1] See *What Next in the Law*, pp. 237–238, with his comments and extracts from his judgment.

[2] [1968] A.C. 910, 952.

[3] *Air Canada* [1983] 1 All E.R. 161, 180f.

[4] *Ibid.* p. 180d.

company, in respect of some of whose activities Mr. Heath had coined the phrase "the unacceptable face of British capitalism" and which had been the subject of continuous controversy in its business adventures, clashing with the established City institutions, so that it was unlikely to enjoy Lord Denning's sympathy. Far more significant was the fact that had discovery been granted in Lonrho's arbitration against Shell and B.P., a mixed enterprise, for supplying Mr. Smith's Rhodesia with oil, despite United Nations mandatory sanctions (and United Kingdom Sanctions Orders in Council) proof of United Kingdom Ministerial complicity could have resulted. This would have led to political, if not legal, claims on Her Majesty's Government by the Government of Zambia, to condemnation at the United Nations, and to possible economic reprisals by some African States. In such circumstances Lord Denning's response was effectively to decline jurisdiction, which he did by taking the technical point (disregarding his own case law on piercing the veil of corporate personality)[5] that documents in the possession of Shell's Rhodesian and South African subsidiaries were not within immediate possession or power. The House of Lords, while affirming this decision on the same grounds,[6] subsequently gave the *coup de grâce* to possibilities of Ministerial and Foreign Office exposure by ruling that Lonrho had no cause of action as a result of Shell's breach of the Sanctions Orders in Council.[7] Many international lawyers regard the breaching of United Nations oil sanctions and the British "Oilgate" as the most discreditable incident in post-war British foreign policy, flouting United Nations decisions binding on the United Kingdom, and facilitating, if not actually effectuating, the lengthy continuance of U.D.I. in Southern Rhodesia.

Westinghouse[8] had similar ramifications. Discovery of Rio Tinto Zinc's documents and evidence by its directors,[9] could have led both to triple damages in another suit in Illinois alleging violation of United States anti-trust laws and to United States attempts to assert extra-territorial jurisdiction in relation to its anti-trust legislation, which would then have sanctioned British business activities wherever in the world they were conducted. Lord Denning gave the discovery requested by the letters rogatory, but greatly cut down its scope because of lack of specificity as to which documents were required, there being in the facilitating Act no requirement that general pre-trial discovery as in English trials should be granted. Simultaneously, he declared that R.T.Z. and its directors were entitled to raise the privilege against self-crimination on grounds of potential EEC liability, and subsequently upheld actual pleas to this effect.[10] His judgments were upheld as to the privilege issue, but the House of Lords went

---

[5] *Littlewoods Mail Order Stores* v. *I.R.C.* [1969] 1 W.L.R. 1241 and *D.H.N. Foods Distributors Ltd.* v. *Tower Hamlets L.B.C.* [1976] 1 W.L.R. 852.
[6] [1980] 1 W.L.R. 627 (H.L.), upholding Denning's judgment reported in [1980] 2 W.L.R. 367 (C.A.).
[7] [1982] A.C. 173.
[8] [1978] A.C. 547.
[9] An earlier Denning judgment, *Penn-Texas Corporation* v. *Murat Anstalt and Others* (*No.* 2) [1964] 2 Q.B. 647, had ruled that an English limited company could be ordered, on request made by any foreign tribunal under the Foreign Tribunals Evidence Act 1856 (replaced when *Westinghouse* was heard by the Evidence (Proceedings in Other Jurisdictions) Act 1975) to give evidence and to produce documents specified in the order.
[10] [1978] A.C. 547, reports both Court of Appeal judgments.

further in setting aside the order to discover even a limited number of documents.[11]

Consistently with his dislike of retaining the concept of privilege he deliberately cut it down for future cases, requiring there to be a real or appreciable danger of being fined or exposed to a penalty, and that there must be reasonable ground for a witness to claim that an answer could tend to incriminate him.[12] Furthermore, he delivered himself of dicta that the privilege could no longer apply to civil libel cases, because in his view, there was no real risk of prosecution for criminal libel.[13] As mentioned earlier, he made an attempt in his dissent in *Rank* to force video pirates to answer interrogatories as to their suppliers, avoiding the privilege against self-crimination by arguing that the court could accord criminal immunity, also repeating his views regarding disappearance of the privilege in libel suits.[14] I do not believe that had *Westinghouse* been an appeal against an order by the Restrictive Trade Practices Court to answer interrogatories (rather than a request for facilities for letters rogatory by a United States Court), that Lord Denning would have upheld a plea against self-crimination on grounds of potential EEC liability.

Lord Denning contended, in order to create yet another discretionary element, that there was power to permit the use of documents coming into the "public interest immunity" category by way of waiver.[15] Where waiver was sought the court should engage in a balancing exercise as to whether public interest in the administration of justice outweighed public interest in keeping the documents confidential, permitting a document to be used for cross-examination purposes notwithstanding that it was from a class for which immunity had been claimed.[16] Had he recollected his own earlier judgment in *Burnell* v. *British Transport Commission*[17] he might not have permitted public bodies latitude to eat their cake and have it too. In *Burnell* he had ruled that it would be "unfair" for part of a document advantageous for this purpose to be used for cross-examination and then, on grounds of privilege, to deny sight of the rest of the document. Waiver in any event is inconsistent with the justification for "public interest immunity," namely that the court has "objectively" determined the public interest. Logically public authorities cannot challenge and the court cannot go back on such determination by producing a document in the immune class, even if by

[11] *Ibid* p. 609 *per* Lord Wilberforce, holding, after the Attorney-General's intervention and the commencement of a grand jury investigation, that discovery proceedings were an abuse of process.

[12] *Ibid*. p. 574.

[13] *Ibid*. p. 573.

[14] *Rank* [1980] 3 W.L.R. 501, 507. Lord Denning gave no weight to the very real threat of private prosecutions as in *Goldsmith* v. *Pressdram* [1977] Q.B. 83, and *R.* v. *Wills St. JJ.* [1978] 1 W.L.R. 1008, affirmed *sub. nom. Gleaves* v. *Deakin* [1980] A.C. 477. As *Gatley on Libel and Slander* (8th ed. 1981), by P. Lewis, at p. 646, n. 1, points out, while Lord Denning was reading his judgment in *Rank* that it was "mere moonshine" that charges of criminal libel might be brought, *The Times* was being subjected to a private prosecution lasting for two weeks.

[15] *Burmah* [1979] 1 W.L.R. 473, 487–488. This view he reiterated in *What Next in the Law*, pp. 235–236.

[16] *Campbell* v. *Tameside B.C.* [1982] 3 W.L.R. 74, 79. Although in *Burmah* he had suggested all "public interest immunity" could be waived, he now regarded this as impermissible where the vital interests of the state were at issue as in national defence, diplomatic relations and detection of crime.

[17] [1956] 1 Q.B. 187, 190.

oversight such immunity has not been raised as an issue. In *Air Canada* Lord Fraser, probably in response to *Campbell*, went out of his way to state that "public interest immunity, is not a privilege which may be waived by the Crown or by any party."[18]

It is a schoolman's game to analyse Denning decisions by reference to logic and precedent, because he was so instrumental in his approach that, if convenient, he would ignore both. Of course, the criteria for exercise of the discretion to order inspection and production are sufficiently indeterminate to permit characterisation of acts as not justifying discovery.[19] Nonetheless, he wanted even more room for manoevre, both to permit and to refuse discovery—thence his view of public bodies waiving their public interest immunity despite inconsistency with the principle that it is for the court objectively and *proprio motu* to determine the public interest.[20] He was even willing to rely on the distinction he had once discredited between "contents" cases, involving specific documents, and "class" cases, contending that "class" objections were administratively useful and that in such cases inspection should be rare.[21] Furthermore, at the end of his career, he considered that the courts should not overthrow any Ministerial objection to production in the absence of misdirection, incorrect consideration of the documents, or the giving of Ministerial reasons which did not "commend themselves to the Court." Only where the objection was not Ministerial was the task one of balancing by the Court.[22]

The balancing process was most seriously undermined by his definition in *Air Canada* of the meaning to be attached to "the due administration of justice" as a factor in the scales. Viewing *Home Office* v. *Harman* as an abuse of the discovery process and now determined to keep high-level documents secret, Lord Denning abdicated in favour of Ministers by holding that "the due administration of justice" did not require the truth to be ascertained. Instead, in the English adversarial system a party often had in accordance with legal procedure and evidential exceptions to prove his case without assistance from the other side's documents. This interpretation Lord Denning derived from a prosecutor's inability to force disclosure of an accused's documents, the absence of discovery in mandamus and certiorari[23] and from legal professional privilege.

[18] [1983] 1 All E.R. 910 (H.L.), 917g. See also *S.R.C.* v. *Nasse* [1979] 3 W.L.R. 762 (H.L.), 777 and 784; *R.* v. *Lewes JJ.* [1973] A.C. 388, 407; and *Duncan* v. *Cammell Laird* [1942] A.C. 624, 641–642, not yet oxidised away on the point that the Court should *proprio motu* exclude evidence contrary to the public interest. See his own *dictum* in *Crompton* [1972] 2 Q.B. 102, 134.

[19] As in *Gaskin*, above, and *Neilson*, above, where applications were described as merely "fishing expeditions" motivated by the hope of dredging up a cause of action.

[20] *Burmah* [1979] 1 W.L.R. 473, 487–488. In *Campbell* v. *Tameside B.C.* [1982] 3 W.L.R. 74 he apparently did not appreciate the inconsistency and possible injustice of allowing public bodies (such as the police) to claim immunity for documents and then to waive it for cross-examination purposes.

[21] In *Neilson* v. *Laugharne*, at p. 545, Lord Denning mentioned the heavy burden on the police to eliminate all documents naming informers if only "contents" claims were permitted.

[22] *Air Canada*, at p. 179.

[23] Contending that no-one had "ever doubted the justice of those proceedings" (*Air Canada* at p. 181) he overlooked the Law Commission's Working Paper No. 40 (1971) and subsequent Report "Remedies in Admnistrative Law" (Law Com. No. 73, Cmnd. 6407 (1976)) recommending discovery be available whatever the nature of the remedy sought. See now Ord. 53, r. 8. He even suggested that discovery should not be available on judicial review: at p. 181d.

Should Lord Denning's meaning prevail, "justice" in its ordinary sense of requiring justice to be done on all the facts cannot be placed in the balance against competing interests. Evidential rules thus exclude the balancing process, and governmental interests are most likely to prevail. The majority of their Lordships, while approving the Denning interpretation of "due administration of justice,"[24] however upheld the decision on the basis that no case had been made out for inspecting the documents.[25] If discovery is refused when Ministerial conduct is challenged, the practical outcome is likely to be that evidence will be insufficient to discharge the burden of proof against the Crown or to show that it was acting *ultra vires*.[26]

From the individual rights standpoint, there was a great victory when Lord Denning and his fellow musketeers seized the keys to the citadel from the executive and handed the determination of "public interest immunity" to the judiciary. Even if currently judges are cautious, hanging up the key on a hook, there have been significant effects. Large numbers of public documents are by administrative decision now made available. Public bodies are conscious that their papers are liable to discovery. When combined with judicial review developments, there is potentiality for the courts to find internal documents, revealing inadequate assessment of relevant considerations or the presence of irrelevant considerations, and to strike down numerous public decisions.

His overriding aim had been to secure judicial discretion to determine all claims for evidential exclusion or discovery rather than to further individual human rights. Indeed, his "confidentiality" cases, apart from *Seager* v. *Copydex*,[27] justify disclosure to the public or to the court of confidential information. Conversely, so as to be able to protect public bodies, as well as the central Government, he pushed the concept of "public interest" in "confidentiality." His reasoning, at first protective of "child welfare," was later extended to inquiries into police misconduct. In this context he apparently overlooked his earlier remark that "Our English law does not love tale-bearers,"[28] although Scarman L.J. in *D.* v. *N.S.P.C.C.* in

---

[24] [1983] 1 All E.R. 910 (H.L.), 921–922, 919 H–J and 916, *per* Lords Edmund Davies, Wilberforce and Fraser. Lords Scarman and Templeman repudiated it.

[25] The majority "no-win" test for inspection bolts the door to discovery by requiring the court to be satisfied that documents are likely to (or it is a reasonable probability that they will) contain material which will give substantial support to the case of the party seeking disclosure or will damage that of his opponent, and that without them he would be deprived of the means of proper presentation of his case (at pp. 917–918, 919–921, and 922–923). If the applicant must show that the documents are "very likely" (Lord Fraser at p. 917e) to contain such material, or there is "some concrete ground for belief" (Lord Wilberforce at p. 920d) he will have independent evidence as to their contents, in which event they will not be "necessary for disposing fairly of the cause" as required by R.S.C., Ord. 24, r. 13. If the applicant has no evidence as to the documents' contents, he will be unable to show it as "very likely" that disclosure will help, so that, the cards being even, the court will characterise the request as speculative. Lords Scarman and Templeman (at pp. 924–925 and 927) applied "justice" in its ordinary sense, and irrespective of advantage to either party, as the factor for deciding whether the documents were necessary for fairly disposing of the issues.

[26] *Soblen*, above, exemplifies the situation, as did the trial in *Air Canada*. *Tameside* was exceptional, with the Crown itself disclosing correspondence when seeking mandamus against the Council, while *Congreve* was a marginal case, the outcome being dictated by Lord Denning's intuition that power was being abused.

[27] [1967] 1 W.L.R. 923 and [1969] 1 W.L.R. 809.

[28] *Associated Newspapers* v. *Dingle* [1964] A.C. 371 (H.L.), 757.

Denningesque style had warned of the dangers of going back to the days of the Inquisition.

Again, except in *Burmah*, Lord Denning did not wish governmental internal decision-making to be exposed and criticised, a contention substantiated by *Lonrho, Harman* and his sarcasm in *Air Canada* about "the advocates of open government."[29] Pharmaceutical companies,[30] casinos,[31] shady business practices[32] and the misbehaviour of pop stars[33] were the proper topics for investigative journalism, rather than Home Office administration of prisons, and possible misdeeds by Ministers in breach of international obligations.[34] Refusal to facilitate litigation embarassing to national interests was not of course Lord Denning's sole prerogative.[35]

Discretion to deny disclosure was paralleled by growth of power to force disclosure. Statutory provision requiring witnesses to answer questions put by the Tribunal of Inquiry was enforced in *Mulholland* by contempt proceedings.[36] Subsequently, by an enterprising concoction, mixing in the Lords' decision in *Norwich Pharmacal* and *Nassé*, Lord Denning's judgments in *Mulholland, Initial Services* v. *Putterill* (iniquity), *Rank* (on *Anton Piller* orders), *Westinghouse* (on the limits on self-crimination) and his general balancing approach and flavoured by a refusal to apply the "newspaper rule" as being confined to libel, Megarry V.-C., the Denning-led Court of Appeal and their Lordships (except Lord Salmon) all ordered disclosure of the identity of an informant who had given British Steel Corporation documents to a television journalist.[37] Despite praising investigative journalism, Lord Denning, disturbed by Granada's failure to "act with due sense of responsibility, not so much in the use of the information but in the way they went about it," struck a blow at journalists' ability to obtain and use information of public interest.[38]

Once the turbulence and contemporary waves have settled, it will be seen that his decisions on discovery and privilege decisively affect the likelihood of enforcing individual rights against public authorities. Even if the law

---

[29] *Air Canada*, at p. 180.

[30] *Attorney-General* v. *Times Newspapers Ltd.* [1973] Q.B. 710 (the thalidomide case) and *Schering Chemicals Ltd.* v. *Falkman Ltd.* [1981] 2 W.L.R. 848 ("The Primodos Affair").

[31] *What Next in the Law*, p. 252.

[32] *Initial Services Ltd.* v. *Putterill* [1968] 1 Q.B. 396.

[33] *Woodward* v. *Hutchins* [1977] 1 W.L.R. 760 (C.A.).

[34] *Air Canada* touched on United Kingdom obligations under the Chicago Convention and the Bermuda II Agreement, and *Lonrho* involved B.P., a mixed enterprise, and possible Foreign Office complicity in breaching UN mandatory sanctions.

[35] "Oh, of course," as Lord Denning, Lord Diplock *et al.* would testily, but not suppressively, in common comment. I have only boringly sought to prove in Lord Denning's case what Griffiths elegantly asserted in *The Politics of the Judiciary*, p. 213. See above, pp. 263–264.

[36] See also *Attorney-General* v. *Clough* [1963] 1 Q.B. 773 *per* Lord Parker C.J. Lord Radcliffe, pursuant to s.1(2) of the Tribunals of Inquiry (Evidence) Act 1921, had referred a refusal by witnesses to the Inquiry to answer questions to the High Court.

[37] *British Steel Corporation* v. *Granada Television* [1981] A.C. 1096.

[38] *Ibid.* at p. 1130. The reality was that Lord Denning perceived normal journalistic behaviour to any public figure venturing onto an investigative television programme—in this case the Chairman of a nationalised corporation—as akin to an abuse of power, and therefore exercised his discretion against the company's plea that it should not be forced to disclose its informant's identity. Yet, as Lord Salmon pointed out, if information was given in the public interest, how the company went about presenting it would not alter that public interest, and should not result in their being obliged to disclose their sources: at p. 1191.

seems now to be back in the days of *The Thetis, Air Canada* should be regarded only as a temporary resurfacing occasioned by *Harman's* eddies.

Denning decisions on disclosure and confidentiality will in historical perspective also be significant. Judges may invoke them to protect individual rights in the computerised age, although the other side of Lord Denning's disk hazards a 2084 government relying on them to sustain a society of informers. Final evaluation must depend upon the assessor's attitude to according the judiciary such discretionary latitude and upon ultimate judicial choices.

The Presumption of Innocence

Although not technically breached by a rule permitting the tendering in evidence of previous convictions as probative of similar facts in issue, the presumption of innocence is in spirit rendered ineffective. Lord Denning's judgment in *R. v. Sims*,[39] now much criticised,[40] almost displaced the presumption of innocence, where there were convictions for sex offences, with an effective "presumption of guilt."

The principle of "fairness" implies an equivalent "presumption of innocence" in civil litigation. With his aversion to *Hollington* v. *Hewthorn*, his unwillingness to see duplicating litigation long after the event, and his attitude to convicted prisoners, Denning did not treat the convicted parties in *Goody* v. *Odham's Press* and *Barclay's Bank* v. *Cole* as if they could possibly be innocent and wrongly convicted.[41]

The Right to be Heard by the Court

Lord Denning never denied standing to persons potentially affected by a decision and an opportunity to be heard by the court—even if it was clear that the case would subsequently be dismissed. If notice of matters had not been given to an affected party, an opportunity to appeal would be given.[42]

In a quite exceptional case he ruled that a party's appeal would not be heard.[43] A divorced wife, appealing against a custody order, had on her remarriage taken the child to a new home in Australia. On discovering that this was contrary to a court order she had not returned the child to England. Although the common law did not know of any right not to hear a party, ecclesiastical and chancery courts had taken this concept from the canon law where the course of justice was impeded by a party's contempt. In the event, after the wife, obviously at great expense, had brought the child to England, thereby purging her contempt, her appeal was upheld.

Lord Denning was renowned for his courtesy, listening to counsel and unrepresented litigants with patience. He could not have been accused of excessive intervention, as was Hallett J. in the case tactfully handled by

---

[39] [1946] K.B. 531. The court's judgment was delivered by Lord Goddard, but prepared by Lord Denning.
[40] *R. v. Kilbourn* [1973] A.C. 729. *R. v. Boardman* [1975] A.C. 421 and *Noor Mohammed* v. *R* [1949] A.C. 182.
[41] [1967] 2 Q.B. 738. See above, pp. 304–305. I am not basing any criticism on the facts underlying such cases, but on standards of fair procedure applicable irrespective of any "truth."
[42] *S.* v. *S.*[1965] 1 W.L.R. 21 (wife's child declared not a member of the family without the wife being heard).
[43] *Hadkinson* v. *Hadkinson* [1952] P. 285.

Romer, Parker and Denning L.JJ.[44] Where he could be faulted was in taking points of law or fact as the basis of his judgment when these had not been argued, or when an opportunity had not been given to controvert the points involved.[45]

The Right to Appeal

Paradoxically one of his important criminal law judgments had side-effects, denying a right of appeal contrary to Article 14(5). If an accused raised the issue whether his acts were done during a state of non-insane automatism, the Crown, in the interests of the public, might raise the question of insanity or of diminished responsibility.[46] If the accused was found to be insane, this was a verdict from which there was, at the time, no appeal.[47]

The right not to be punished again[48]

Although the right not to be tried again applies only to criminal trials, Article 14(7) is so broadly drafted, referring to being "tried or punished again," that it can be contended that additional sanctions may contravene the Article. If so, Lord Denning's denial, by virtue of the doctrine of issue estoppel, of rights of action to convicted persons on facts dealt with at their trial is effectively another punishment for the guilty.[49] So too serious disciplinary action following a criminal conviction can constitute "punishment," as occurred with suspension of licences, although such disciplinary action may be taken for public protection or the good of certain trades and professions.[50]

Publicity on Trials

Lord Denning's judgment in *Harman*[51] did not alter the basic rule of English law that court hearings shall be open to the public, and that the press can freely and fairly report on all proceedings other than in those strictly limited circumstances where Parliament has imposed restrictions on reporting.

Before the Contempt of Court Act 1981 courts had very limited powers to restrict publicity, but, if they did so, disobedience to any order would constitute contempt. There was even authority that, although a newspaper was unaware of the order, should it publish a report there would be strict liability if the course of justice was prejudiced. By section 4(2) any court may now make an order postponing publicity if there is a risk of prejudice to the administration of justice, this being the sole criterion. In *R. v. Horsham JJ., ex*

---

[44] *Jones* v. *N.C.B.* [1957] 2 Q.B. 55.
[45] *Hesperides*, see above, p. 316, is a well-documented example. See Lord Denning's own self-deprecatory comment on gems of law reform being lost to posterity by his being stopped by his brethren from dealing with an unargued point: *The Afovos* [1982] 1 W.L.R. 848, 854.
[46] *Bratty* v. *Att.-Gen. for Northern Ireland* [1963] A.C. 386 (H.L.).
[47] See Lawton J. in *R. v. Price* [1963] 2 Q.B.1. The matter of such verdicts was satisfactorily remedied by the Criminal Procedure (Insanity) Act 1964.
[48] Art. 14(7).
[49] *McIlkenny*, above, p. 305. Lord Diplock's judgment avoids this imputation, as it does not rely on issue estoppel, and suggested the plaintiffs sue the Home Office.
[50] *Re R. Hampton and Sons* [1966] 1 Q.B. 135. See above, p. 257.
[51] Above, pp. 337–338.

parte Farquharson[52] the whole court upset a blanket order by magistrates postponing publication of proceedings as being too wide. Lord Denning in a minority judgment, maintaining that two of the most fundamental principles are "open justice" and "freedom of the Press," restrictively interpreted section 4(2). He held that the purpose of the section was to clarify, not to cut down freedom of the Press, telling it when it could not publish reports of a trial. Consequently the section created no new offence, only common law contempts still being punishable,[53] and it protected against the former strict liability rule, which would have applied had there been an innocent publication which prejudiced the course of justice. Since the sole consideration in making a postponement of publication order was risk of prejudice to the administration of justice, this could not be determined at the outset of a trial, but only when evidence suggesting a risk had been presented. He was fortified in these views by the fact that such a drastic order could be made by any court from the highest to the lowest. If his minority view prevails, the case will prove a charter for newspaper court reporters.

Retrospectivity[54]

Lord Denning's relative unconcern with retrospectivity has already been mentioned.[55] Although tax law does not come within the scope of the prohibition on retrospectivity, it is worth noting in relation to "the spirit" of the Article that Lord Denning (like many other judges) was unwilling to adopt an interpretation enabling him to avoid applying a taxing statute retrospectively to transactions in issue.[56]

Privacy[57]

Article 17 and the concept of privacy are amorphous, but two major aspects emerge: the freedom from interference aspect; and the prohibition on publication of material about the individual by way of unlawful attacks on his honour and reputation. The latter aspect constitutes a limitation on freedom of speech, so is more conveniently dealt with under Article 19.[58]

Some of the freedom from interference aspects have already arisen in relation to other rights, because, although privacy only became a matter of public debate in the United Kingdom from 1970, Lord Denning soon started

---

[52] [1982] 2 W.L.R. 430.

[53] The only circumstances when an order prohibiting publication could at Common Law be made in criminal cases, breach of which would result in contempt, were if (a) postponement was necessary for the furtherance of justice; (b) there was a trial within a trial on confessions; (c) pseudonyms were used in a blackmail case; and (d) there was a joint indictment, but separate trials.

[54] The right not to be held guilty of retrospectively created crimes and not to be subjected to heavier penalties (Art. 15).

[55] Above, pp. 256–257. The most significant cases were *D.P.P.* v. *Smith, Sykes* v. *D.P.P.* and *Att.-Gen.* v. *Vernazza*, with which case should be contrasted Lowry L.C.J.'s liberal ruling in *R.* v. *Deery* [1977] Crim. L.R. 550 (N.I. Ct. Cr. App.), declining to follow English wartime Court of Appeal cases on the retrospective imposition of heavier penalties.

[56] An example is *Shop and Store Developments* v. *I.R.C.* [1966] Ch. 108 reversed [1967] 1 A.C. 472.

[57] The right not to be subjected to arbitrary interference with privacy, family, home or correspondence or to attacks on honour and reputation (Article 17).

[58] Below, pp. 358–362. See also above, pp. 285–286.

taking an interest in the area. Much of his case law has already been discussed under such rubrics as discovery and privilege, conflicts between the right to confidentiality and to a fair trial often having to be resolved when disclosure was sought in litigation.[59] Most of the case law on clashes between confidentiality and the right of the Press to impart information in the public interest and the rights of journalists to claim confidentiality for their sources was, for convenience, also dealt with then.[60] Privacy likewise arose in connection with invasions of property rights by reason of law enforcement officers' use of their powers of entry, search and seizure,[61] and was also relevant in connection with intellectual property and information rights, an area where, in addition to the public interest in having information disclosed to it, the giving to copyright owners of an effective remedy by way of an *Anton Piller* order gave rise to conflicts and Denning case law.[62]

Another aspect of Article 17, the right to freedom from interference with family life, has been touched on, both where it arose in connection with immigration decisions, a subject dealt with under the Articles dealing with equality and absence of discrmination,[63] and where it concerned the right to protection of the family in terms of Article 10 of the Economic Rights Convenant.[64]

A case not so far discussed in connection with family life is his judgment in *Sykes* v. *D.P.P.*,[65] decided in relation to the former offence of misprison of felony, abolished by the Criminal Law Act 1967. It is still relevant in relation to the offence of failing to disclose information known to be of material assistance in preventing an act of terrorism or in securing the apprehension of any person for an offence involving the instigation, preparation or commission of an act of terrorism.[66] In *Sykes* Lord Denning thought that close family ties would not suffice as a reasonable excuse for not reporting an offence where it was of so serious a character that it ought to be reported.[67] This reasoning imposes on spouses in certain limited situations a duty to act as police informers, and would appear justifiable only in time of war or declared emergency.

Had the issue whether the right to privacy prohibits investigation of private sexual behaviour arisen directly, Lord Denning is unlikely to have taken a permissive stance. This was indicated by *Bravery* v. *Bravery*,[68] where he applied criminal law authorities on prize-fighting and flagellation, to hold that voluntary sterilisation, if done without just excuse, was unlawful, and was conduct constituting "cruelty" and thus grounding divorce. His condemnation of the student teacher in *Ward* v. *Bradford Corporation*[69] was based not on her breaching residential rules by having a second person occupying a room, which only she was licenced to occupy, but on her

---

[59] Above, pp. 331 *et seq.* See also pp. 258–259.
[60] See above, at pp. 337–339, and 345–346.
[61] Above, at pp. 288–290.
[62] Above, p. 286.
[63] Above, pp. 299–300.
[64] Above, p. 277.
[65] [1962] A.C. 528.
[66] s.11(1) of the Prevention of Terrorism (Temporary Provisions) Act 1976.
[67] p. 47.
[68] [1954] 3 All E.R. 59.
[69] (1972) 70 L.G.R. 27. See above, p. 282.

presumed sexual relationship with her male visitor. His revulsion at charges of sodomy, and strict interpretation of the rules of criminal evidence was manifested in *Sims* and *Selvey*.[70] His views on pornographic material available for purchase and on exhibitions of pornographic films were condemnatory.[71] Although on the facts considering that a documentary film about Andy Warhol was one which the Independent Broadcasting Authority could reasonably have concluded was not offensive to public feeling, not offending against good taste or decency, thus not contravening the Television Act 1964, section 3(1), Lord Denning's judgment[72] made it clear that television viewers' "privacy" must be respected by not having offensive material transmitted to them via sets in their homes (which of course required the positive act of switching on and a decision to continue watching the offensive material). Transmission of offensive material is surely rather to be characterised as a question raising appropriate limitations on freedom of expression, either or both by way of prior restraint and by criminal sanction, than as a question raising privacy and its invasion by "imposing" such material on viewers.

He did not utilise the concept of "impositions" on privacy when he was squarely faced with the issue whether there was a right to privacy. He accepted the Younger Report view that there was "no general remedy for infringment of privacy, the reason given being that on balance it is not in the public interest that there should be."[73] The issue had arisen in a case where gross psychological damage would be inflicted on a highly-strung 14 year-old girl if a book describing her late father, who was "utterly depraved in his sexual activities, who indulged in sordid and degrading conduct and who was obscene and drank to excess" were published and she learnt of this. Although the trial judge had invoked the wardship jurisdiction to restrain publication unless the offensive passages were removed, Lord Denning felt he could not create a remedy by extending the jurisdiction because of the importance the law "attaches to the freedom of the press." It would be

> "a mistake to extend [limits on press freedom] so as to give the judges a power to stop publication of true matter whenever the judges—or any particular judge—thought that it was in the interests of a child to do so."[74]

Freedom of Religion and Belief[75]

Lord Denning's somewhat restrictive attitudes to freedom to manifest religion and belief in practice, to the conferment of financial advantages by way of exemptions under legislation on some and not on other religious groups, and to parental rights to ensure education of their children in

---

[70] Above, pp. 255 and 347.
[71] See Jowell on *R.* v. *Commissioner of Police of the Metropolis, ex p. Blackburn (No. 3), Blackburn (No. 4)*, and *R.* v. *G.L.C., ex p. Blackburn*. See also *The Discipline of Law*, pp. 122–132.
[72] *Att.-Gen., ex rel. McWhirter* v. *Independent Broadcasting Authority* [1973] 1 Q.B. 629.
[73] *Re X (A Minor)* [1975] Fam. 47, 58 referring to *Report of the Committee on Privacy*, 1972, Cmnd. 5012.
[74] *Ibid.* p. 58.
[75] Art. 18.

conformity with their religious convictions or philosophical beliefs have already been discussed.[76]

Freedom of Expression[77]

Lord Denning's reputation as a defender of civil liberties[78] must largely rest, apart from his enlargement of the potentiality of remedies for individual challenge of state action,[79] on his contribution to the law governing freedom of expression and the Press. The competing rights of individuals and the Press to express themselves or to seek information and to publish it as against the right of other individuals to respect for their reputations or the right of the state to protect certain narrowly defined public interests created tailor-made opportunities for him to apply his balancing approach. It was also the one right, above all others, which Lord Denning had consistently advocated, beginning with his *Hamlyn Lectures* in 1949,[80] and continuing in 1951 with his essay in the *Canadian Bar Review* urging that

> "It is essential to political liberty that all these powerful means of influencing opinion should be free to put all relevant facts before the public and to give voice to the views of all, whether for or against the government of the day."[81]

He believed that

> "Those three great institutions, Parliament, the Press and the Judges, are safeguards of justice and liberty: and they embody the spirit of the Constitution."[82]

The theme was repeated in 1955,[83] but by now Lord Denning was becoming concerned that the Press should keep the right balance between freedom and the abuse of it. He concluded

> "It is better to have too much freedom than too much control: but it is better still to strike the happy mean."[84]

Certainly so far as the Press was concerned the overall pattern of Denning judgments was much more in favour of freedom than it was for control. How do the judgments substantiate this generalisation?

Prior Restraint

Although he did not use such terminology until late in his career, his

---

[76] Above, pp. 309–310 (manifestation in practice), 309 (exemptions) and 282 *et seq.* (education).

[77] The right to freedom of expression and to seek and impart information in conjunction with necessary restrictions to secure the reputations and rights of others or to protect *ordre public*, public health, and national security (Art. 19).

[78] As a supporter of economic rights it will probably rest on the individual right to work, on the property rights of women and on his strengthening of consumer rights.

[79] See Jowell (effective remedies in public law) and above pp. 331–347 (discovery).

[80] *Freedom Under the Law*, p. 35.

[81] "The Spirit of the British Constitution" (1951) 29 Can. B.R. 1180 p. 1192, subsequently reprinted in *The Changing Law*, (1953).

[82] *Ibid.* p. 1196.

[83] See his lecture "The Free Press" published in *The Road to Justice*, pp. 64–87.

[84] *Ibid.* p. 87.

consistent position was that freedom of expression should not be subject to prior restraint, infringement of other interests by exercise of such freedom rather being protected after the event by the appropriate sanctions in civil or criminal proceedings.

In his dissent in *Schering Chemicals* v. *Falkman* he generalised the principle that, because of the significance of Press freedom, injunctions should not be granted.[85] Earlier he had declined injunctions where confidential information was proposed to be published, if publication was in the public interest.[86] He refused to prejudice the issues in a libel suit by granting an injunction when the defence was fair comment or justification,[87] applying this also where qualified privilege was a defence,[88] although exceptionally an injunction might be granted were it clearly shown that a party was acting dishonestly or maliciously and saying what he knew to be untrue. Lord Denning declined too to enjoin intended breach of copyright.[89] He refused to restrain publication of a book by invoking extended wardship jurisdiction, although justifiable for the welfare of a child and enabling development of a right of privacy.[90] He rejected any form of "gagging writ" being given operation by way of contempt proceedings alleging that comments would prejudice pending civil litigation. Nor could writs be used to muzzle shareholders where a plaintiff in libel sought to restrain any repetition at a company meeting.[91] Similarly, he refused an injunction against intended newspaper articles on the issues in the Thalidomide tragedy, holding that a balance of the public interest must be determined as between the interest of the parties in a fair trial or a fair settlement without unfair pressure, and the public interest in being informed of matters of national concern and the freedom of the Press to make fair comment on such matters.[92]

Although pointing out that safeguarding the administration of justice might sometimes outbalance freedom of expression and result in subsequent contempt proceedings,[93] he was determined that all "gagging" injunctions seeking to prevent true and fair comment should fail.[94] In a dissent, he refused to extend the law of contempt to cover a valuation court, holding that a B.B.C. television broadcast on the activities of the Exclusive Brethren

---

[85] [1981] 2 W.L.R. 848, 859–860. Generously (at p. 862) he gave Lord Scarman credit for reintroducing the doctrine of prior restraint in the Exclusive Brethren case (*Att.-Gen.* v. *B.B.C.* [1981] A.C. 303).

[86] *Fraser v. Evans* [1969] 1 Q.B. 349 (see above, p. 285); and *Woodward v. Hutchins* [1977] 1 W.L.R. 760.

[87] *Fraser v. Evans*, above.

[88] *Harakas v. Baltic Mercantile and Shipping Exchange Ltd.* [1982] 1 W.L.R. 958, where a body concerned to stop maritime fraud suggested to potential charterers that they be asked to give privileged information concerning a shipping company.

[89] *Fraser v. Evans*, above.

[90] *Re X* [1975] Fam. 47. See above, p. 351.

[91] *Wallersteiner v. Moir* [1974] 1 W.L.R. 991, 1004–1005. See *The Due Process of Law*, pp. 49–51 and 182–183. Dr. Wallersteiner's mode of conducting business did not have Lord Denning's approval. See also *Bryanston Finance Ltd.* v. *de Vries* [1975] All E.R. 609, 620. See above, p. 308, n. 55.

[92] *Att.-Gen.* v. *Times Newspapers Ltd.* [1973] 2 W.L.R. 452, 460, reversed [1974] A.C. 273. Lord Denning's attitude was adopted by the European Court of Human Rights (*Sunday Times Case*, 26.4.79, 18 Intl. Leg. Mat. 931) and is reflected in the Contempt of Court Act 1981.

[93] *Att.-Gen.* v. *B.B.C.* [1981] A.C. 303, 312 citing his own contempt cases. See below.

[94] *Ibid.* p. 316.

pending their application to a valuation court could not be contempt.[95] As already indicated, the Contempt of Court Act 1981, designed to clarify contempt law, was restrictively interpreted by Lord Denning so as not to allow blanket orders against publication at the outset of proceedings and the creation of new contempts.[96]

He was equally reluctant to allow individuals to invoke statutory provisions to restrain television transmissions. He refused to permit a private individual, relying on section 6 of the Race Relations Act 1965, to seek an injunction prohibiting the intentional stirring up of racial hatred by B.B.C. transmission of "anti-German" programmes.[97] Although prosecution required the Attorney-General's consent, arguably proceedings for an injunction could be brought without this. His ruling that the section gives no right to the individual to take action against a public corporation transmitting a programme instigating racial hatred (assuming that to be factually the case) is in spirit contrary to the cumulative effect of Article 20 (racial hatred to be prohibited by law) read with Articles 2(3)(a) (effective remedy) and 26 (equality before the law and equal protection of the law), and illustrates the conflict between freedom of speech and other rights.

Subsequently, taking the novel step of allowing an individual to initiate proceedings for an injunction to enforce a public right without the consent of the Attorney-General,[98] Lord Denning, putting aside his dislike of the subject matter, upheld a discretionary decision by the I.B.A. to transmit a film on Andy Warhol.[99] It will be remembered that Lord Denning, with one exception, made no order against publication of pornographic material.[1]

Nor was he prepared to permit a candidate, who had refused to appear on an election television programme because of participation by a National Front candidate, to block transmission of a programme of public interest. Section 9 of the Representation of the People Act 1969 gave candidates who "took part" in a programme a right of veto to ensure against improper editing and unfairness, but Lord Denning ruled that this did not cover "being shown" on a programme, so that film taken of the candidate while conducting his campaign could be transmitted.[2] Again, he would not permit trade unionists to interfere with freedom of the Press, seeking to deny them immunity under the Trade Union and Industrial Relations Act.[3] Even after the House of Lords' reversals of his secondary blacking decisions, if a trade union does not twist the issue into one affecting conditions of service, it will not be immune should it black copy or transmission of television films either as protest or because of contents, since this will be an interference with freedom of the Press, in aid of which an injunction will be granted,[4] and will not be in furtherance of a trade dispute.

[95] On this point his judgment was upheld in the Lords.
[96] *R.* v. *Horsham JJ., ex p. Farquharson* [1982] 2 W.L.R. 430. See above, pp. 348–349.
[97] *Thorne* v. *B.B.C.* [1967] 1 W.L.R. 1104.
[98] His attempt to establish an *actio popularis* in *Gouriet* v. *U.P.O.W.* [1977] 2 W.L.R. 310 proved abortive, being rejected by the Lords ([1978] A.C. 435).
[99] *Att.-Gen., ex rel. McWhirter* v. *I.B.A.* [1973] 1 Q.B. 629. See above p. 351.
[1] The exception related to the G.L.C.'s wrong test in licencing the exhibition of films grossly indecent at common law: *R.* v. *G.L.C. ex p. Blackburn* [1976] 1 W.L.R. 550. It must be said that Lord Denning had little occasion to make such orders, sitting as he did on the civil side.
[2] *Marshall* v. *B.B.C.* [1979] 1 W.L.R. 1071.
[3] *B.B.C.* v. *Hearn* [1977] 1 W.L.R. 1004; *Associated Newspapers Ltd.* v. *Wade* [1979] 1 W.L.R. 697; and *Hadmor Productions Ltd.* v. *Hamilton* [1981] 3 W.L.R. 139.
[4] *B.B.C.* v. *Hearn*, above.

Only where there is a "pressing social need" for restraint of publication of highly confidential information on moral, social or industrial grounds with a substantial risk of grave injustice and such as to outweigh the public right to know would Lord Denning concede that an injunction could be given in advance.[5] He did not in practice have to decide such cases, but from his other decisions it appears that he would have treated national security, and threatened publication of discovered documents on high-level policy as coming under this exception. Furthermore, the Attorney-General would be able to move for an injunction if there would be a serious contempt should publication not be restrained,[6] although any such application would be considered in the light of the preceding test.

In all contexts he was opposed to injunctions restraining freedom of expression. This was manifested in *Hubbard* v. *Pitt*[7] a case also involving freedom of association. An interlocutory injunction was sought against social workers conducting a tenants' campaign against a firm of Islington estate agents believed by them to be improperly assisting developers by harassing tenants. Lord Denning, in a dissent, pointed out that an important aspect of freedom of speech was the right of protest, and that the defendants, who were carrying placards and picketing on the pavement outside the estate agents' offices, claimed that the matter on the placards was true and of public concern. As an alleged libel it could not be restrained until after trial of the issue. Even if the picketing constituted a public or private nuisance or conspiracy, an interlocutory injunction should not be given because

> "It will virtually decide the whole action in favour of the plaintiffs: because the defendants will be restrained until the trial (which may mean two years or more) from picketing the plaintiffs' premises, by which time the campaign will be over."[8]

Lord Denning emphasised that "the right to demonstrate and the right to protest" by way of "the right of assembly, to meet together, to go in procession, to demonstrate, and to protest on matters of public concern" were exercisable without any impediment "so long as no wrongful act is done." Once the rights were not exercised peaceably and in good order, or there were threats or incitement to violence or obstruction to traffic, assembly could be prohibited. If violence broke out "it should be firmly handled and severely punished."[9]

Once wrongful acts were committed in the protest he would not countenance their continuance. He armed university authorities with an effective weapon against student sit-ins. The whole court accepted that the University of Warwick had taken all reasonable steps to identify the persons in possession of the Senate House and telephone exchange and not named in the summons: "the names of the ringleaders are enough." He went on, alone, to say: "People who defy the law cannot be allowed to avoid it by putting up technical objections."[10] A non-technical approach was also taken

---

[5] *Schering Chemicals Ltd.* v. *Falkman*, at pp. 864–866.
[6] *Att.-Gen.* v. *Times Newspapers Ltd.*, above, and *Att.-Gen.* v. *B.B.C.*, above.
[7] [1976] 1 Q.B. 142.
[8] *Ibid.* p. 178.
[9] *Ibid.* p. 178–179.
[10] *Warwick University* v. *de Graaf* [1975] 1 W.L.R. 1126, 1130.

to service of writs on redundant workers staging a sit-in.[11] The possibility of
passive resisters and sitters-in effectively nullifying legal proceedings against
them by reliance on the service requirements of R.S.C. Order 113 was thus
ended.

His decision in *R.* v. *Chief Constable of Devon and Cornwall, ex parte Central
Electricity Generating Board*[12] was consistent with this approach. For six
months environmentalists, anti-nuclear protesters and some local inhabitants had obstructed the C.E.G.B.'s employees and their use of plant in
attempting to survey a site in Cornwall for a possible nuclear power station.
The protest had been non-violent with the Board not using its powers of
self-help forcibly to eject protesters, or the police intervening, but there had
been one near-accident and drilling had had to be stopped because of
dangerous interference with drilling rigs. With references to rights of forcible
self-help, police assistance, breach of injunctions, inability to avoid the law
by bringing in fresh unidentified demonstrators, breach of the peace,
criminal conspiracy, unlawful assembly, police preventive powers and
recognisances for good behaviour he gave a "definitive legal mandate" that
would enable the police to be used to clear the obstructors off the site or at
any rate to assist the Board in so doing. His general ruling was important in
limiting future protest of such a kind, wherever it might occur, and in the
maintenance of order. His remarks are significant:

> "In deciding whether there is a breach of the peace or the apprehension
> of it, the law does not go into the rights or wrongs of the matter, or
> whether it is justified by self-help or not. Suffice it that the peace is
> broken or is likely to be broken by one or another of those present. With
> the result that any citizen can, and certainly any police officer can,
> intervene to stop breaches. If I were wrong on this point, if there was
> here no breach of the peace or apprehension of it, it would give a licence
> to every obstructor and every passive resister in the land. He would be
> able to cock a snook at the law as these groups have done. Public works
> of the greatest national importance could be held up indefinitely. This
> cannot be. The rule of law must prevail."[13]

Post-Publication

Lord Denning extended the protections accorded freedom of expression once
it had been exercised.

The justification of publication of information in the public interest was
his invention, whether raised in an action for damages, an application for an
injunction, or in a libel suit.[14]

[11] *Crosfield Electronics* v. *Baginsky and Others* [1975] 1 W.L.R. 1135.
[12] [1982] Q.B. 458.
[13] *Ibid.* p. 471. Even if Lord Denning would authorise the use of all legal machinery to end
protest just when it became effective, he would in case of environmental damage and loss of
amenity at least monetarily compensate the local inhabitants: at p. 466. But these were
sentiments rather than law in view of their Lordships' decision in *Allen* v. *Gulf Oil* [1981] A.C.
1001.
[14] *Initial Services Ltd.* v. *Putterill* (damages); *Fraser* v. *Evans* (libel and injunction); *Hubbard* v.
Vosper (libel); *Woodward* v. *Hutchins*, (injunction); and *Att.-Gen.* v. *B.B.C.* (injunction). See
above, pp. 285 and 308–309. It is implicit in *Granada*, that, apart from any effect that having
acted "irresponsibly" may have had, Granada would not have been liable for having made
use of converted documents for a programme of public interest.

Protection against disclosure of sources of information whether in answer to questions by a judge, or in discovery, was reasserted by Lord Denning, and, had it not been for *Granada's* "irresponsibility," he would not have ordered disclosure.[15] A degree of protection was also given television journalists and cameramen against being forced to reveal all film footage, something which would have risked their being treated at demonstrations as "camera spies."[16]

The scope and application of the law of contempt of court was, long before the reforms of the Contempt of Court Act 1981, narrowed by Lord Denning, with the Press being the major beneficiary of such limitations. In a series of judgments he sought to establish that, since contempt was a criminal offence, the ordinary principles of criminal law applied, so that intent, requiring knowledge, was necessary, even when the contempt was interference with the course of justice.[17] His confining the applicability of contempt to courts proper was in the short run important before the 1981 Act.[18] His balancing approach now prevails statutorily in deciding whether a contempt will be committed if a journalist declines to answer a question as to his sources.[19] He also ruled that outspoken, even erroneous, comment came within the concept of fair comment on a matter of public interest, and that the courts must uphold the right to criticise "to the uttermost," exercising jurisidiction in respect of scandalising the court sparingly.[20]

The limits of Lord Denning's tolerance in regard to contempt law, as in all areas, were reached if he perceived an abuse of process. Had he wished to apply general criminal law principles in *Harman*, he might well have characterised Miss Harman's belief, that the documents having been read out in court were no longer confidential and could be shown to a journalist, as a mistake of fact.[21]

Just as he would not permit abuse of process by "the advocates of open government," so equally would he nullify or sanction any perceived abuse by persons seeking to restrain freedom of expression. In *Goldsmith* v. *Sperrings Ltd.*,[22] in a dissent, Lord Denning would have taken the exceptional step of staying proceedings taken on a massive scale against *Private Eye's* wholesalers and retail outlets, the plaintiff, having, in addition to suing the magazine, which had been conducting a defamatory campaign against him, sued distributors and accepted settlements from those who undertook not to distribute future issues. Lord Denning considered such actions to be the equivalent of an interlocutory injunction doing *Private Eye* irremediable damage by way of "frightening writs" closing the lifeline by which it reached

---

[15] *Att.-Gen.* v. *Mulholland*; *Georgius*; and *B.S.C.* v. *Granada*. See above, pp. 337, 339 and 346.

[16] *Senior* v. *Holdsworth, ex p. I.T.N.* [1976] Q.B. 23. Above, p. 333.

[17] He was seeking to limit the interpretation given *Odham's Press Ltd., ex p. Att.-Gen.* [1957] 1 Q.B. 73. See *Attorney-General* v. *Butterworth*, at p. 722 ("actuating motive"); *Churchman* v. *Joint Shop Stewards Committee*; *Heatons Transport* v. *T.G.W.U.*; *Balogh* v. *St. Alban's Crown Court*; and *Re F.* See above p. 323. Several of these contempts arose in civil proceedings and hit at freedom of expression by way of continued picketing.

[18] *Att.-Gen.* v. *B.B.C.* See above, pp. 353–354.

[19] *Att.-Gen.* v. *Mullholland* and *B.S.C.* v. *Granada*. Above, pp. 333 and 346.

[20] *R.* v. *Metropolitan Police Commissioner, ex p. Blackburn (No. 2.)* [1968] 2 All E.R. 319, 320. See above, p. 330. Criteria for future contempts have fortuitously been liberalised because the contemnor was the then Mr. Quintin Hogg P.C., Q.C., M.P., publishing in *Punch*.

[21] It transpired to be a mistake of law, but that would not have bothered Lord Denning had he wished to decide otherwise.

[22] [1977] 1 W.L.R. 478.

its paying public. The majority of the Court of Appeal however held that no collateral advantage beyond that allowed by law had been proven, the plaintiff having sworn that his motive was not to stifle further publication. Unless satisfied that such an ulterior motive was present, for the court to stay proceedings would be an injustice to the plaintiff seeking relief to which the law entitled him. The differing judgments pose an extreme dilemma of choice: either the publication's continued freedom of expression and even existence were put at risk, or a defiant defamatory campaign could get a licence to commit (and funds to pay for) yet further wrongs to the plaintiff's reputation.

Restrictions on Freedom of Expression Necessary for Respect for the Rights or Reputations of Others

The restrictions thought necessary by English law for protecting the rights and reputations of others against exercise of the freedom of expression are marked out by the law of libel, slander, malicious falsehood and malicious prosecution and the law of criminal libel. Lord Denning contributed to libel law—not so greatly as other contemporaries such as Lord Devlin. However, in so doing, apart from two unsuccessful attempts at generalising and developing the law to facilitate "lawful criticism"[23] and the running of company businesses[24] he had to confine himself to narrow issues. Nonetheless, a general pattern emerges of leaning towards individual and Press freedom of expression, except in contexts where he perceived abuse of power or misbehaviour.[25]

Had he succeeded in introducing a distinction between "lawful criticism" and libel, he would have transformed the law. He had contended that libel was personal and subjective, and lawful criticism impersonal and objective, and to be treated as if malicious falsehood were in issue, thus placing on the plaintiff the burden of proving both malice and falsehood.[26] This would have liberated scientific criticism (in that case of the special anaesthetic techniques of a dental surgeon criticised in a B.M.A. article) and all technical, engineering, economic and academic publications from risks of libel suits. The rule would have been capable of extension so as to replace libel, and to permit far greater freedom of speech.

Lord Denning disapproved of the precedents on "secondary meanings" and on various kinds of innuendo,[27] matters which cause newspapers great problems by "accidental" defamation. To avoid the rule in *Cassidy* v. *Daily Mirror*,[28] imposing liability only because extrinsic facts unconnected with the publication might cause those knowing such facts to give an unnatural and unusual meaning to the words, thereby rendering them defamatory, Lord Denning unsuccessfully urged adoption of a new test whether the plaintiff

---

[23] *Drummond-Jackson* v. *B.M.A.* [1970] 1 W.L.R. 688, a dissent.
[24] *Riddick* v. *Thames Board Mills* [1977] Q.B. 881, a dissent. See also *Bryanston Finance Ltd.* v. *de Vries* [1975] Q.B. 703, a majority judgment.
[25] I have cursorily analysed major reported cases. A libel specialist using unreported judgments would doubtless find exceptions.
[26] *Drummond-Jackson* v. *B.M.A.*, above.
[27] *What Next in the Law*, p. 179.
[28] [1929] 2 K.B. 331.

had been identified, namely if ordinary sensible people, proved to have such special knowledge of the facts, might reasonably believe that the statement referred to the plaintiff.[29]

In a series of cases dealing with pleadings, innuendoes and particulars, Lord Denning, disapproving of fanciful meanings being attached to found liability and limit expression, took a very strict view of the necessity of pleading any meanings attached and precisely how words were alleged to refer to the plaintiff.[30] If a serious matter, requiring ventilation in the courts in order to do justice between the parties, arose, he would exercise discretion to allow late amendment of pleadings, adding a plea of justification.[31] He was strict in striking out pleadings if no cause of action was shown, and would not countenance an attempt to extend liability for slander by the addition of an alleged conspiracy so as to avoid the rule regarding the necessity for showing special damage.[32]

His wholly negative attitude to interim relief by way of interlocutory injunction has already been commented upon: there would be no prior restraint and prejudicing of the defences of fair comment and justification.[33]

Although he was reluctant to see the defence of absolute privilege extended,[34] or the privilege of Parliament extended,[35] thereby seeking to force M.P.'s to rely on the defence of qualified privilege, he wished to confer absolute privilege in proceedings for malicious prosecution against a solicitor who had given evidence leading to a bench warrant.[36]

In contrast he was willing to extend or generously to interpret the defence of qualified privilege. An important extension was effected by his majority judgment in *Bryanston Finance*[37] where he held dictation to a secretary as part of conducting a business is privileged. Subsequently, his dissent in *Riddick*[38] sought to take the approach further, although on a technically different basis, by holding that there was no publication when reports on fellow servants were made within a company. Lord Denning's desire to see collectivities operate within the defence of qualified privilege was also shown in his ruling that the innocent secretary of a committee would not be liable should he have written a letter on an occasion which would, had it not been for malice of the committee or some members, have been privileged.[39] He

---

[29] *Morgan* v. *Odhams Press* [1970] 1 W.L.R. 820, reversed [1971] 1 W.L.R. 1239 (3–2).

[30] *Lord* v. *Sunday Telegraph* [1970] 3 W.L.R. 754; *S. and K. Holdings Ltd.* v. *Throgmorton Publications* [1972] 1 W.L.R. 1036; *Allsop* v. *Church of England Newspaper Ltd.* [1972] 2 W.L.R. 600; *D.D.S.A. Pharmaceuticals Ltd.* v. *Times Newspapers Ltd.* [1972] 3 W.L.R. 582; *London Computer Operators Training Ltd.* v. *B.B.C.* [1973] 1 W.L.R. 424; *Fullam* v. *Newcastle Chronicle and Journal Ltd.* [1977] 1 W.L.R. 651; and *Grappelli* v. *Derek Block (Holdings)* [1981] 1 W.L.R. 822.

[31] *Associated Leisure Ltd.* v. *Associated Newspapers Ltd.* [1970] 3 W.L.R. 1001, where it was alleged that a takeover bid was designed to secure the Mafia a substantial interest in gaming and leisure undertakings.

[32] *Ward* v. *Lewis* [1955] 1 W.L.R. 9. The plaintiff was Mr. Stephen Ward, osteopath, later to become the object of Lord Denning's attention in the Profumo Report.

[33] Above, p. 353.

[34] *Merricks* v. *Nott-Bower* [1965] 1 Q.B. 57 and *Richards* v. *Naum* [1967] 1 Q.B. 620.

[35] See *The Family Story*, pp. 192–194, which discloses his dissenting views on the Strauss case, but which were not permitted to be added to the Privy Council advice.

[36] *Roy* v. *Prior* [1970] 1 Q.B. 283 reversed [1970] 2 All E.R. 729. See above, pp. 316–317 as to Lord Denning's negative attitude to allegations of malicious prosecution.

[37] [1975] Q.B. 703.

[38] [1977] Q.B. 881.

[39] *Egger* v. *Viscount Chelmsford* [1965] 1 Q.B. 248.

would not restrictively interpret the defence of qualified privilege given the Press and television by section 7 of the Defamation Act 1952, with the harsh result on individuals that radio and television publicity to police announcements about suspects, which are understood to refer to innocent persons, will be protected as being of public concern and for the public benefit.[40] A wide view of freedom of speech was taken, permitting angry, unwarranted, prejudiced comment and remarks, prompted even by gross and unreasoning prejudice, on occasions carrying qualified privilege, provided the speaker honestly believed what he said to be true: in the council chamber local authority members could speak openly on matters of public interest so long as they were not actuated by malice.[41] However, political candidates in elections could not, Lord Denning held, after section 10 of the 1952 Act, assert qualified privilege for their election speeches or literature as being made on a privileged occasion.[42] Journalists' qualified privilege at common law to give a fair and accurate report of proceedings in either House of Parliament was extended to a fair newspaper "sketch" of the day's proceedings, thereby giving important protection to satirical and subjective reporting, so long as the reporter fairly gives his impression of the debate as a whole, and does not deal only with one side.[43]

Lord Denning gave newspapers important guidance as to the defence of fair comment on a matter of public interest, even suggesting that, so long as the facts were correct and the opinion honestly held, it mattered not that it was wrong, exaggerated or prejudiced.[44] However, it seems that he cut down the breadth of this protection (which almost equated fair comment with qualified privilege) by emphasising in a later case that there must be a proper basis of fact.[45]

Since fair comment is related to the defendant's mind at the time he exercised his freedom of expression, affording him protection if he believed certain facts, a defendant cannot justify his comment by subsequent events, *i.e.* facts not in existence at that time.[46] Conversely, if at the time of publication a statement was not defamatory it will not be made defamatory by virtue of a subsequent statement.[47] This ruling was later distinguished to permit a plaintiff to claim that a second article linked him with a first article on the Scott Affair, where the first article was defamatory. He was thus identified and defamed by both articles read together.[48] Journalists may not escape liability by using asterisks, blanks or other devices if they intend to refer to the plaintiff.[49]

---

[40] *Boston* v. *W.S. Bagshaw and Sons* [1966] 1 W.L.R. 1126.

[41] *Horrocks* v. *Lowe* [1972] 1 W.L.R. 1625, affirmed [1975] A.C. 135.

[42] *Plummer* v. *Charman* [1962] 1 W.L.R. 1469.

[43] *Cook* v. *Alexander* [1974] Q.B. 279.

[44] *Slim* v. *Daily Telegraph* [1968] 2 Q.B. 157.

[45] *London Artists* v. *Littler* [1969] 2 W.L.R. 409, 418E.

[46] *Cohen* v. *Daily Telegraph* [1968] 1 W.L.R. 916.

[47] *Grappelli* v. *Derek Block (Holdings) Ltd.* [1981] 1 W.L.R. 822. Lord Denning was probably too busy writing judgments to realise how the music-going public reacts to cancellation of performances. He should have asked Lord Scarman about opera-goers' reactions. The judgment was probably dictated by Lord Denning's dislike of innuendoes based on extrinsic facts.

[48] *Hayward* v. *Thompson* [1981] 3 W.L.R. 470. He took a poor view of the journalist involved, who had written, together with his newspaper, a sensational story, had lost his notebook so it could not be disclosed, and would not reveal his sources. See p. 482.

[49] *Ibid.* p. 479.

Lord Denning was not prepared to extend liability to cover new heads of damage. Thus, for injurious falsehood there could be no damages for injured feelings, and in libel, if evidence of probable pecuniary loss was absent, damages were greatly reduced.[50] A claim that a libel had resulted in injury to health would not in England, according to Lord Denning, succeed, such a claim never having succeeded.[51] However, grieviously wounded feelings were a factor in assessing damages.[52] Once he thought that there was any question of taking "a poor view of the conduct by any of the defendants—be it journalist, sub-editor, editor or proprietor" the jury could fix whatever sum they think fit in aggravation of damages "so long as they do not wander off into the forbidden territory of exemplary damages."[53] Damages were not to be cut down on appeal unless there was such a misdirection as plainly to lead to a substantial miscarriage of justice. Lord Denning was here returning to his battle with the House of Lords and Lord Devlin[54] about exemplary damages, which he thought should be awarded as a deterrent where a newspaper had behaved intentionally and inexcusably, abusing its power or distorting information or publishing it scandalously.[55]

Newspapers could not add garnish, spice and embellishment, lose their privilege, and then seek to put in mitigation evidence that a reputation was tarnished by reason of privileged reports.[56] Nor were they allowed to bring up specific incidents in a man's career as opposed to his reputation,[57] although newspapers could adduce evidence of previous convictions in mitigation of damages.[58]

Once the jury had given its verdict Lord Denning ruled that it could not be asked questions,[59] and once discharged the court would not entertain evidence of what took place in the jury room to allow explanation of verdicts or of misunderstandings.[60]

Lord Denning was, in sum, a champion of freedom of expression. He insisted that the public had a right to be informed on matters of public interest. He was opposed to prior restraint. He cut down the scope of contempt law. He stopped gagging injunctions. He protected the Press against revelation of sources. He strictly limited the law of libel and

---

[50] *Fielding* v. *Variety Inc.* [1967] 2 Q.B. 841.

[51] *Wheeler* v. *Somerfield* [1966] 2 Q.B. 94.

[52] *Fielding* v. *Variety Inc.*, above.

[53] *Hayward* v. *Thompson*, above, at p. 482. Normally all co-defendants must misconduct themselves so as to justify an award of aggravated damages, but this does not apply to newspapers. An opposite rule, resulting from the fact that one set of facts gives rise to liability, does however benefit them: a payment into court need not be severed and defendants will be protected if the sum covers the damages however awarded in respect of each cause of action: *Pedley* v. *Cambridge Newspapers Ltd.* [1964] 1 W.L.R. 988.

[54] *Broome* v. *Cassell and Co.* [1971] 2 Q.B. 354, reversed [1972] A.C. 1027 concerning *Rookes* v. *Barnard* [1964] A.C. 1129.

[55] *What Next in the Law*, pp. 171 and 214.

[56] *Dingle* v. *Associated Newspapers Ltd.* [1964] A.C. 371. Rumours could not be permitted in mitigation. Either there must be justification or evidence of general reputation once privilege was not available as a defence.

[57] *Plato Films* v. *Speidel* [1961] A.C. 1090. All their Lordships seem to have been affected psychologically because the plaintiff was a military man and the period of reconciliation with Germany was beginning.

[58] *Goody* v. *Odhams Press Ltd.* [1967] 1 Q.B. 333.

[59] *Gould* v. *Hill* [1967] 1 Q.B. 579.

[60] *Boston* v. *W.S. Bagshaw and Sons* [1967] 2 All E.R. 87. See above, p. 329.

extended the defences. Yet he was at the same time an upholder of law and order, and where there was conflict between speech and order, order would prevail. He was, as throughout the law, reactive to any hint of abuse of process or power, therefore non-suiting libel plaintiffs with fanciful claims and sanctioning the Press in damages should they engage in sensationalism or "irresponsibility." The Press did extremely well at his hands, so that when they turned on him after *Granada*, Lord Denning, who was never a moral coward and would say bluntly what others thought but did not voice publicly, answered them forthrightly. He told them plainly (without exaggeration):

> "to see that they have always in mind their duty to act responsibly. If they should repeat their irresponsible conduct, they will find that curbs will be put upon their freedom. I have throughout my career upheld the freedom of the press, and of the media, and it is only out of regard for it that I would urge that it be not misused."[61]

The Rights to Peaceful Assembly and to Freedom of Association[62]

Lord Denning's assertion of the right to peaceful assembly, subject to limitation when unlawful acts or disorder occurs, has been dealt with above,[63] as has his assertion of freedom of association in connection with trade unions, where his emphasis was on the individual's right and on making this effective as against his association, rather than on the collective enforcement of individual rights by way of concerted trade union activity.[64]

The Right to Take Part in the Conduct of Public Affairs Directly and to Vote in Elections by Free and Equal Suffrage[65]

Two of Lord Denning's decisions in connection with elections were significant. His judgment in *Fox* v. *Stirk*[66] meant that in towns where there were large student populations in tertiary education, national election results would be affected if the town was a marginal constituency, and some local government wards would be quite changed in political character. Lord Denning held students living away from home had "residence" at their institutions as well as at their homes, could be registered at both places, and could vote, but only at one of the places where registered.

His second major decision interpreted the legislation requiring the ratio of the numbers of local government electors to the number of members to be elected to be "as nearly as may be" the same in every ward as permitting departure from the one man, one vote and votes of equal weight principle, something demanded by Article 25(*b*). Lord Denning held that by virtue of section 47 of the Act the Local Government Commission could affirm boundary changes appearing to the Commission desirable in the interests of effective and convenient local government.[67]

---

[61] The Dimbleby Lecture, November 20, 1980, reprinted in *What Next in the Law*, p. 329.
[62] Arts. 21 and 22.
[63] Above, pp. 355–356.
[64] Above, pp. 272–274 and see Davies and Freedland, Chap. 8.
[65] Art. 25.
[66] [1970] 3 W.L.R. 147.
[67] *Enfield L.B.C.* v. *Local Government Boundary Commission* [1979] 1 All E.R. 950.

That Lord Denning was not over-concerned with individual assertion of direct democratic rights appears from another local government decision where, in a majority decision, he held that a local government poll could not be demanded.[68] He gave a narrow interpretation to the section dealing with whether the conditions for a poll had been met. His view of the lack of merits of the plaintiff and his reliance on technicality doubtless dictated the outcome. Yet the plaintiff had substantial cause for complaint: the real issues had not been put in a previous poll but only a formal resolution—it was there that "technicality" had prevailed.

Lord Denning was reluctant that the courts should become embroiled in the internal struggles of the Labour Party. When a plaintiff (who was a voter seeking to give effect to his right to take part in the conduct of public affairs through freely chosen representatives and who had been running a campaign on these lines in his constituency party) was suspended by the National Executive, pending an inquiry into the disputes between different factions in the constituency, Lord Denning declined to apply the rules of natural justice to such suspension, which was a preliminary to a full inquiry, and held no ulterior purpose had on the facts been shown.[69]

Conclusions

How then does one assess Lord Denning's contribution? Others have written of him as lawyer and of his doctrinal developments, whereas this essay has concentrated on his attitudes and on the impact of his decisions. Nonetheless, it will be apparent from its content that, ironically, he will have strengthened the tendency to cite precedents, because his judgments, especially when the computerised information era arrives, will provide arguments for all: those arguing for civil rights will tend to rely on his dicta, and those arguing for public authorities will tend to rely on his ratios.[70] Well into the next century Denning principles will be provocative of legal development and relevant in reaching decisions.

His greatest case law achievement in human rights terms was the development of remedies and grounds for relief in litigation against the state and public authorities. At the same time he strengthened the position of the Press, essential for a society in which individual rights can flourish. The ordinary citizen was affected in his daily living by changes consequent on Denning decisions, in particular by alterations in economic rights strengthening the position of the consumer and those according married women property rights. In future Lord Denning's right to confidentiality and the right to work could burgeon in various directions.

Another aspect of his case law relevant to human rights was his support for the efficient functioning of the modern state. He would not permit the community interest to be impeded by reliance on property rights and

---

[68] *Bennett* v. *Chappell and Another* [1966] Ch.391, Winn L.J. *dubitante.*

[69] *Lewis* v. *Heffer* [1978] 1 W.L.R. 1061.

[70] Anxious to express his just general rule for the future, Lord Denning would, despite the demerits in his view of a litigant or the inapplicability of such rule by reason of the facts in the instant case, seize the opportunity of laying down a principle. It is little satisfaction to a litigant to hear a just general rule enunciated, when such rule is not applied in his circumstances—as in *Soblen*, in the first two leading discovery order cases, and in *Ashbridge Investments* v. *M.H.L.G.* [1965] 1 W.L.R. 1320.

freedom of contract to avoid controls on land use and property regulation, and he furthered the state's activities in funding itself by way of taxation. He even accepted judicial self-restraint in relation to the tribunal system and administration of social services. Finally, he was always an upholder of law and order powers and national security. It must be obvious to all that political problems are often twisted into legal issues and brought before the courts; that in such cases it will be issues on the margins which will require decision; and that there is likely to be controversy whichever way the decision goes. With Lord Denning's predilection for law and order it says a great deal for his support of freedom of expression and assembly that he decided as he did in *Hubbard* v. *Pitt*.[71]

It is appropriate here to emphasis the remarkable consistency and lack of contradiction in his approach over nearly four decades. Some have implied that his later decisions were affected by the length of his term of office and by his age changing his social and political perspective. This is not so, except to the extent that he may have become a little more outspoken and more impatient of having to play judicial games by wrapping his decisions in appropriate precedents for delectation of their Lordships. The reality is that he was always authoritarian: it was to illustrate this point that my essay began with the analysis of his pre-1968 cases.[72] Since at least 1949 he had been preoccupied with the themes of power, responsibility and abuse of power (including dishonourable conduct and exploitation of process)[73] whether by public authorities, groups or individuals. At the same time his overriding passion was individualised justice. He also abhorred technicality[74] and believed in common sense. In such circumstances his judgments against the convicted and those who abused their position were inevitable: they were not dictated by caprice, but by a consistent moral stance (with which observers may or may not agree).

In addition to possessing such ideas, Lord Denning was a man of action, occupying a position of power and willing to use it (even admitting to enjoying it as Pensions Appeals Judge). It was this willingness to use his power as Master of the Rolls which led to his clashes with the judicial hierarchy. If equine metaphors are to be used, one would say: no rider he of any unruly horse of policy: he was a great steed taking the bit between his teeth and thundering down the track to law reform and his just result, while all the other nags, observing the rules, never got out of the starting gate. In another age Lord Denning would have been a revolutionary general using in his ordnance the cannonballs fashioned by other artificers (such as Lords Goddard and Devlin) against the foes of injustice and the *ancien régime*. That Lord Denning was often a synthesiser of the ideas of others is no reproach: it is to his credit that he was prepared to push them from his powerful position.

Lord Denning's most significant contribution, in my opinion, has been re-emphasis of "justice," both in his judgments and in his extra-judicial

---

[71] [1976] 1 Q.B. 142.

[72] It is interesting to note that in 1968 Lord Gardiner asked Lord Denning to return to the House of Lords: *The Due Process of Law*, p. 188. The reasons for this request are not known.

[73] He was evenhanded: just as this attitude worked against plaintiffs by motivating the ending of civil jury trial in other than libel suits, and the adoption of a strict attitude to plaintiffs pleading innuendoes in libel suits, it worked against defendants, as in *Harman* and *Granada*.

[74] See, *e.g. Re Alsopp* [1967] 2 All E.R. 1056, 1059: "I care not how the result is reached." The other members of the Court read words into a will to reach the result.

writing. He has engraved the need for justice upon the conscience of at least two generations of practitioners and academics. Of course philosophers and lawyers have for over two thousand years theorised about justice, but it is Lord Denning's unique achievement (with the aid of modern communications "media" as well as the printed word) to have constructed a new social reality in the English legal profession. He can turn to his Marxist critics, saying that, rhetoric or not, he has reified justice, with the consequence that the profession now focuses upon it. Practising lawyers no longer deal with "the merits" merely as a matter of the particular facts in relation to any relevant law, but have serious concern for doing justice in any case.

Those who question whether Lord Denning has himself always done justice differ about whether justice has in fact been done, not about the necessity for doing it.[75] They are judging him by standards he has himself established. Lord Denning would like that.

In addition to his achievement in reasserting the sense of justice, he alerted English lawyers to the practicability, rather than the mere theoretical possibility, of mounting challenges to abuse of power from whatever quarter. Depending upon how the courts develop judicial review and discovery, future centuries may well perceive his potentialisation of remedies against the state as even more significant than his reminder that justice should always be done.

In summation, although others disagree, Lord Denning was both a great man and a great judge.[76] He was great in that he was pre-eminent in importance in his time, succeeding in stamping his character and some of his attitudes on the generations among which he lived.[77] He permanently affected certain important branches of human rights law, especially the property rights of women, the right to an effective remedy, the right to fairness and effectiveness in the administration of justice, the freedoms of expression and of the press, and the right that power be not abused—another way of stating a right to the rule of law. In other spheres he had a significant impact for change. In all spheres he left behind ideas for exploitation by future generations of lawyers. He was outstanding both in the magnitude of his achievements and in his moral attainments: integrity, courage, humanitarianism,[78] loftiness of purpose, and love of justice. He did

---

[75] Except for absolute moral relativists who discern only political or value choices unrelated to "fairness" or to any objectively verifiable value. They would consider "Has justice been done?" a non-question.

[76] J.A.G. Griffith (1979) 42 M.L.R. 350, reviewing *The Discipline of Law*, thought "At the end of the day it is impossible to put Lord Denning among the great names. His value as an innovator cannot be denied. And when his sympathies are roused he can be a formidable champion. But his view of justice is too personal, too idiosyncratic, too lacking in principle, for greatness. He may instruct, as he claims to do, in the principles of the law. But the grasp of political principle, the insight into the nature of the change that society is currently undergoing, for these he shows no special flair, no particular understanding." Peter Robson, in *Justice, Lord Denning and the Constitution*, pp. 60 *et seq.*, questions the very concept of a Great Judge. I use the notion of a great judge here not with a particular model of judicial role in mind, but in accordance with ordinary linguistic usage: *Compact Edition of the O.E.D. "Great,"* 15.b.

[77] Other judges were more liberal than Lord Denning (*e.g.* always Lord Salmon who has not received the recognition he deserves, sometimes Somervell L.J., and more modernly Lord Scarman), but they have never received the publicity Lord Denning attracted to himself by his office, his outspokenness and his willingness to have dealings with "the media."

[78] Many men would think his courageous and humane decision in *Starr*, affecting the welfare of thousands of ex-servicemen and their families, was a worthwhile achievement for a lifetime.

immense good to multitudes of persons who appeared before him or had the benefit of rulings made by him. This does not mean I adulate him, or am uncritical. He was a reformer, not a redeemer. Partaking of the characteristics sometimes found in reformers or judges, Lord Denning was authoritarian, could be opinionated and headstrong, appeared on occasions lacking in humility despite his courtesy, was ethnocentric and even prejudiced on certain issues, and from 1972, when passing his prime, became increasingly unsympathetic to organised labour and out of touch with large sections of political opinion in a rapidly polarising and changing society.

He was at times unlawyerlike in his handling of materials,[79] was disloyal to the conventions of judicial behaviour *inter se*, was careless of the constitutional proprieties of precedent, and, in flouting Parliament's wishes and taking an anti-trade union stance, was reckless of long term consequences in relation to perceptions by politicians and public of the judiciary. It is with compunction that I presumptuously write thus of so good and admirable a man: the duty to balance, and to ink in the warts when academically portraying a living subject is much akin to vivisection. However, Lord Denning knows his roughnesses, warts and pimples "perfectly well, and so does the House of Lords."[80] I am sure he would not wish to be cosmeticised. He knows that whatever strictures he may face, his will be a name great in the history of English Law.

[79] Perhaps the most delightful adversative comment was Russell L.J.'s dissent in *Indyka* v. *Indyka* [1967] P. 233 where, after pointing out that the judiciary was not unfettered by domestic legislation, he went on: "Further appeal is made to the views of the "common man," whose ancestors may be supposed to include both the man on the Clapham omnibus and the officious bystander. Are his supposed reactions a dependable guide through the necessarily complicated paths of a legal system? I doubt it."

[80] Lord Denning at his valedictory ceremony, *The Times*, July 31, 1982.

CHAPTER 8

Labour Law

PAUL DAVIES AND MARK FREEDLAND

Introduction

In one sense, the subject of this chapter needs no introduction. There is no need to demonstrate that Lord Denning is important to labour law. If one asked why that was, the answer spontaneously given in many quarters would be that he had devoted himself to controlling the excesses of trade unions—for a long time as the champion of the individual against the union and latterly as the chief architect of a structure of restraints upon the trade dispute immunities of trade union officials in organising industrial action. Indeed, Lord Denning sees his own contribution to labour law very substantially in these terms—as being directed against the abuse of group powers defined in those particular senses.[1] In other words he envisages his commitment as being the protection of certain particular types of interests viewed as essentially individual in nature. There is a temptation therefore when approaching this topic to treat Lord Denning simply as representing the high point of individualism in the judicial approach to labour law and to apply the already quite well developed critique of the individualist position.

We have chosen to take a rather different starting point for our discussion. An examination of Lord Denning as an individualist in labour law would tend to concentrate our attention very largely—almost exclusively—upon the common law. This is very much to restrict one's vision. For however much one may be conscious of the common law as a developing body of law, it is all too easy to view its development in relative isolation from the parallel changes in legislation and social and governmental policy. In labour law, Lord Denning's period of judicial activity has seen an enormous increase in the volume and extent of labour legislation and a number of highly significant transformations in the function of labour legislation. We think that one cannot adequately explain Lord Denning's labour law decisions except by identifying their often close and important relationship with these contemporary comparators. But there lies the nub of the issue. These transformations in the function of labour legislation have been far from technical exercises in "lawyers' law." On the contrary they have been the subject of bitterly fought political battles. Governments have been judged on their performance in the field of labour law, and at least one Government has called, and lost, an election during the course of a major strike on the issue of "who governs Britain?" How had Lord Denning reacted to and influenced these developments? It is precisely because Lord Denning is an avowedly creative judge, committed to the virtues of judicial legislation, that the question is, in the context of labour law, an interesting one. For the

---

[1] *The Discipline of Law* (1979), pp. 147–196.

history of legislative activity over the past 20 years, as recorded above, might
be thought to counsel even the most active judge that in this area of acute
political controversy, where the legislature is clearly engaged in the task of
seeking solutions, judicial restraint, even a dose of "substantive
formalism"[2] would be the wisest course, and be the way for the judge to
avoid allegations of constitutional impropriety by trespassing upon the
proper domain of Parliament.

That Lord Denning did not accept the counsel in the field of industrial
conflict law in the period after 1976 is well known, and his reputation as the
scourge of the unions dates largely from this period and from this area of law
(together with his decisions in the field of collective bargaining law).
However, a complete picture of Lord Denning's activities in relation to
labour law is much more complex and varied than this might suggest. In
order to illustrate this complexity and variety we shall look in turn at the
four traditional areas of labour law, beginning with trade union law and
then looking in turn at industrial conflict law, the law of collective
bargaining and individual employment law, and we shall attempt to display
the richness of the developing labour law of Lord Denning.

Lord Denning and Trade Union Law

Here we are concerned with the law governing the relationship between the
trade union and the member, the applicant for membership or the officer or
official of the union. The relations between the trade union and those
external to it are considered elsewhere in this chapter under the headings of
the law relating to industrial conflict and to collective bargaining. Lord
Denning would generally be viewed as having had a special concern for
trade union law in the sense we use that term here. He was indeed at his
most enterprising and experimental in leading the development of trade
union law, as we shall see, during the 1950s and 1960s. He came to view his
own decisions in the field in this light—so much is clear from his book, *The
Discipline of Law*,[3] where in the Part which deals with "Abuse of 'group
powers' " the powers of trade unions are those most strongly emphasised.[4]

But Lord Denning's activities in this area were not initially concentrated
solely upon trade unions. Initially at least he had a wider preoccupation
with the need to subject domestic tribunals to the controls appropriate to
public bodies. Domestic tribunals meant really the processes whereby
private associations exercised coercive powers against individuals—typically
but not exclusively disciplinary powers against their members; and it was by
virtue of those coercive powers that such associations acquired their duties,
as Lord Denning perceived them, to act as public bodies. From the starting
point of the late forties, this perception on his part could be realised only by
a combination of, on the one hand, a positive development of as yet rather
unformed doctrines of administrative law and, on the other hand, the
evolving of a structure of remedies for the individual against the association
by which to give effect to those doctrines in a relationship governed by
private law rather than public law, and rather exiguously governed at that.

[2] For a discussion of substantive formalism see R. Stevens, *Law and Politics* (1979), Part 3.
[3] Butterworths, London, 1979.
[4] See especially pp. 147–148.

When it came to trade unions, there would be still further obstacles posed by the tradition of legal abstention from regulation of the internal affairs of trade unions; but the starting point of this whole development occurs before those latter problems are reached.

Lord Denning says in *Discipline of Law* that he was first concerned with these matters in 1951.[5] Perhaps his historical perspective in 1978 was such as to emphasise that the starting point of this development lay broadly within the area of trade union law[6]; at all events we should prefer to locate the starting point in 1948 with his decision in *Russell* v. *Duke of Norfolk*[7] which concerned the withdrawal of a racehorse trainer's licence by the stewards of the Jockey Club. The majority of the Court of Appeal[8] took the view that, even assuming the relationship between the trainer and the Jockey Club to be a contractual one, they had no cause to imply any procedural limitation upon the stewards' power to withdraw a trainer's licence as a disciplinary measure. Lord Denning dissented from this view, holding that the principles of natural justice were applicable (though he agreed there was no evidence of their violation in this case). His reasoning foreshadows much subsequent development:

> "This penalty of disqualification is the most severe penalty that the stewards can inflict . . . . It disqualifies the trainer from taking any part in racing and thus takes aways his livelihood. Common justice requires that before a man is found guilty of an offence carrying such consequences, there should be an inquiry at which he has the opportunity of being heard . . . . It is very different from a mere dismissal of a servant or withdrawal of a licence or even expulsion from a club . . . ."[9]

The next case was *Abbott* v. *Sullivan*.[10] Lord Denning in *Discipline of Law* describes it as if it concerned a trade union.[11] In fact it concerned what we should now classify as a shop stewards' committee—the Cornporters Committee in the London Docks (though the committee was attended by a divisional officer of the Transport and General Workers Union who was the prime mover of the actions of which the plaintiff complained). The Committee maintained a register of cornporters and controlled employment in the trade, so that the removal of the plaintiff from the register resulted in his loss of employment as a cornporter. The members of the Court of Appeal were unanimously of the view that the Committee had acted outside its jurisdiction; but the majority[12] held that this gave rise to no claim to damages. Lord Denning dissented on the basis that there was an implied contract to stay within jurisdiction, the breach of which could give rise to damages; he justified his view on various levels of generality culminating in this important statement:

---

[5] *Ibid.* p. 150.
[6] The date of 1951 relates to the case of *Abbott* v. *Sullivan* [1952] 1 K.B. 189.
[7] [1949] 1 All E.R. 109.
[8] Tucker and Asquith L.JJ.
[9] *Ibid.* p. 119 E-G.
[10] [1952] 1 K.B. 189.
[11] p. 150.
[12] Evershed M.R., Morris L.J.

"The right of a man to work is just as important to him, if not more important, than his rights of property. We see in our day many powerful associations which exercise great powers over the rights of their members to work. They have a monopoly in important fields of human activity. A wrongful dismissal by them of a member from his livelihood is just as damaging, indeed more damaging, than a wrongful dismissal by an employer of his servant; and I see no reason why it should not give rise to a cause of action.[13]

In that case, Lord Denning, alone of the members of the Court of Appeal, was willing to adapt the remedial mechanisms of private law to the new demands of public law. In *Lee* v. *Showmen's Guild*[14] the whole Court of Appeal was willing to take that step—perhaps because it is more easily taken in relation to the relatively flexible remedy of injunction than in relation to the sacrosanct common law remedy of damages. The case concerned a body which we would today classify as a trade association of self-employed workers—travelling fairground showmen. The area committee of the Guild ruled against the plaintiff in a dispute between him and another member over the allocation of a site at a fair-ground, and he was expelled, with the consequence that he could not earn his living as a showman on fair-grounds in the United Kingdom controlled by the Guild. The Court of Appeal was unanimously of the view that an injunction lay to prevent the Guild from acting on a purported expulsion which was *ultra vires* and void because the plaintiff's conduct could not be brought within the rule on which the Guild purported to act. Lord Denning took the opportunity to attack the notions that the jurisdiction of the courts in these matters was confined to the protection of specifically proprietary rights, and that the courts had no control over the terms of the contract embodied in the rules of the association.[15] In so doing he was probably ahead of his Court of Appeal colleagues at that time; the result in the present case was sustainable on a narrower basis of strict contractual construction.

Down to this point, although Lord Denning's rhetoric is applicable to trade unions, he is not pre-eminently concerned with trade unions rather than with associations wielding coercive powers generally. With *Bonsor* v. *Musicians Union*,[16] the focus did settle upon trade unions and the closed shop. The decision is in two parts. The first part concerns the question whether the plaintiff was properly expelled by his union. This part of the decision is very like the decision in *Lee* v. *Showmen's Guild*; the Court of Appeal was unanimously of the view that the plaintiff had been improperly expelled by virtue of a purported but in fact *ultra vires* delegation of disciplinary powers from a branch committee to its secretary; Lord Denning made more ambitious claims than his fellow judges for the nature and extent of judicial control over trade union rules where there is a closed shop.[17] The second part of the decision—on cross-appeal by the union—concerned the question whether a trade union as such could be sued for damages for wrongful expulsion. The majority of the Court of Appeal held that it could not, on the

---

[13] *Ibid.* pp. 204–205.
[14] [1952] 2 Q.B. 329.
[15] *Ibid.* p. 343.
[16] [1954] 1 Ch. 479 (upheld by H.L., [1956] A.C. 104).
[17] [1954] 1 Ch. 479, 485–486.

basis of a decision of 1915[18] which denied legal entity to the trade union and held that the contract of membership was accordingly not with the union as such but with the rest of the members. Lord Denning dissented, and the view that the trade union could be sued as such was upheld by the House of Lords. Lord Denning's view that the trade union, being an entity distinct from its members in fact, should be so viewed in law, was again an assertion that the kind of wrong in question should not lack a remedy.[19]

The view of Lord Denning and the House of Lords represented a use of the common law to override the statutory framework for trade unions contained in the Trade Union Act 1871, for that Act, while legalising trade unions, refrained from according them corporate status almost certainly in order to minimise legal intervention into relations between trade unions and members. Lord Denning thought it appropriate to circumvent this, given the whole legal régime for trade unions as created by that Act and the Trade Disputes Act 1906:

> "In conclusion I would say that Parliament has legalised trade unions and has given them large immunities from the ordinary process of the law. It has exempted them from any liability for tort, and also from liability for certain contracts; but it has never exempted them from liability for wrongful exclusion of a member. Nowadays exclusion from membership means exclusion from his livelihood. No one in this country should be unlawfully excluded from his livelihood without having redress for the damage thereby done to him."[20]

His view that a trade union should be a competent party to a civil action has since been implemented by statute,[21] and has indeed ceased to be a matter of controversy.

Thus far, Lord Denning had seen his innovations tending to restrict the operation of the closed shop being in part accepted. A surprising reverse occurred in *Faramus* v. *Film Artistes Association*[22] which Lord Denning decided as the new Master of the Rolls. The plaintiff was excluded from membership of his trade union and therefore from employment in the film industry, after eight years of apparent membership, on the basis of a rule denying eligibility to anyone convicted of a criminal offence. The application of the rule in this case was harsh and distasteful in the extreme. Lord Denning took the view that the rule should be construed as directory, not imperative; that in any event it could be treated as in unlawful restraint of trade, and that section 3 of the Trade Union Act 1871 in protecting the purposes of a trade union from the restraint of trade doctrine did not protect specific rules such as this. He was in a minority in the Court of Appeal, and the majority was upheld by a unanimous House of Lords.[23] Again in a sense Denning can be seen as engaged in a kind of judicial review of the statutory regime for trade unions

[18] *Kelly* v. *NATSOPA* (1915) 31 T.L.R. 632.
[19] [1954] 1 Ch. 479 506–507.
[20] *Ibid.* p. 514.
[21] First by the Industrial Relations Act 1971 and currently under the Trade Union and Labour Relations Act 1974, s.2(1).
[22] [1963] 2 Q.B. 527.
[23] [1964] A.C. 925. The view of the majority of the Court of Appeal and of the House of Lords about the scope of statutory protection from the restraint of trade doctrine was later embodied in statute law by the Trade Union and Labour Relations Act 1974, s.2(5).

created by the Trade Union Act 1871. Moreover, although his ground of attack upon the union rule is specifically that of restraint of trade, he still clearly saw this as no more than one facet of a general control of trade union rules in terms of reasonableness as if they were by-laws.[24]

It would seem that the House of Lords was not willing to engage in this sort of judicial activism and was anxious to preserve the framework of legal abstention from control of the objects of trade unions. It is unsurprising that they should have accepted the closed shop in general as falling within the protection of that abstentionist framework; but it is slightly astonishing to find them validating an avowedly arbitrary[25] entry qualification as a necessary sacrifice to judicial restraint. This is especially ironical when the House of Lords was on the point of abandoning that restraint *vis-à-vis* the closed shop in the law of trade disputes,[26] an area in which Lord Denning was for some years to be more cautious than the House of Lords.[27] This diametrical opposition between Lord Denning and some of his appellate colleagues at that period, whereby he was innovative and aggressive in trade union law but conservative in trade dispute law while they were the opposite, is nicely illustrated in a decision almost exactly contemporary with *Faramus*, that of *Boulting* v. *A.C.T.A.T.*[28] Here the joint managing directors of a film production company sought relief against threatened industrial action to compel them to belong to the union which maintained a closed shop among film production workers. The majority of the Court of Appeal[29] treated the union's rule as to eligibility as unobjectionable in so far as it made managers eligible for membership; but they indicated that they took a narrow view of statutory trade dispute immunity which would have enabled them to circumvent the immunity if they had viewed the rule as unlawful. Lord Denning, dissenting, took the view that the rule should have been declared not to apply to managers as a matter of construction or alternatively unlawful so far as it did apply to managers for involving them in a conflict of interest and duty; on the other hand, he indicated a traditional broad approach to statutory trade dispute immunity which led him to regard it as extending to threatened action as much as to past action.[30] In terms of trade union law, he again stood alone in the interventionist stance he had taken in *Faramus*:

> "I take it to be clear that the rules of a trade union must be lawful. They are not a mere contract into which the union can insert any provision it likes without question by the courts. They are more like by-laws than a contract . . . . Just as with the by-laws of the old guilds, so with the rules of the modern trade union, they must even be 'subject to the general law of the realm as subordinate to it.' In particular they must not be repugnant to the general law. It seems to me that they are repugnant to

---

[24] [1963] 2 Q.B. 527, 539.

[25] [1964] A.C. 925, 942 (Lord Evershed).

[26] In *Rookes* v. *Barnard* [1964] A.C. 1129. See below, p. 382.

[27] See below, pp. 382–388.

[28] [1963] 2 Q.B. 606.

[29] Upjohn and Diplock L.JJ.

[30] The point was that the Trade Disputes Act 1906, s.4 conferred immunity on trade unions in respect of tortious acts "alleged to have been committed." Lord Denning's view that this extended to apprehended injury was later embodied in statute, see the Trade Union and Labour Relations Act 1974, s.14(1)(c).

the general law if they are so framed as to require their members to act inconsistently with a trust or duty imposed on them by law."[31]

Lord Denning's attempted full reconciliation of public law principles with private law remedies in the control of the closed shop was never to win full judicial acceptance in the period down to 1982, and he conceded defeat on this point extra-judicially in 1978:

> "I went too far in saying that a Rule may be invalidated simply because it is unreasonable. It is only invalid if it is in unreasonable restraint of trade."[32]

But Lord Denning's broad aims expressed in this series of cases were later to be realised in large measure by a combination of judicial development and statute.

In *Nagle* v. *Feilden*[33] Lord Denning had a unanimous Court of Appeal with him in a refusal to strike out a statement of claim seeking an injunction against the refusal by the stewards of the Jockey Club to grant a trainer's licence to a woman. His colleagues were, remarkably, prepared to accept an outcome arrived at by combining the public law notions of (1) injunction to restrain action upon a void decision and (2) invalidity of administrative action for arbitrariness or capriciousness with the private law notions of (3) public policy against restraint of trade and (4) intervention to protect the right to work as analogous with rights of property, and with the statutory notion of (5) illegality of sex discrimination.[34] Lord Denning, sustained by the preliminary nature of the proceedings, felt strong enough to be able to discard the contractual crutch on which he had hitherto limped ahead of his less daring colleagues:

> "All through the centuries courts have given themselves jurisdiction by means of fictions; but we are mature enough, I hope, to do away with them. The true ground of jurisdiction in all these cases is a man's right to work."[35]

Nagle v. *Feilden* concerned an association regulating access to an occupation, though not a trade union closed shop as such. Lord Denning was to reiterate his doctrine that the rules of such associations were controllable for unreasonableness where they affected the right to work in *Dickson* v. *Pharmaceutical Society*,[36] where a rule of conduct of the pharmacists' professional body restricting the sort of goods chemists could sell was held to be invalid for restraint of trade. In *Edwards* v. *SOGAT*,[37] Lord Denning had the opportunity to assert the doctrine in relation to a trade union running a pre-entry closed shop. The plaintiff complained that the union had purported to grant him purely temporary membership, and to rely on a rule providing for lapse of temporary membership when they were not entitled on

---

[31] [1963] 2 Q.B. 606, 627–628.
[32] *Discipline of Law*, p. 158.
[33] [1966] 2 Q.B. 633.
[34] As derived from the then still relatively rudimentary legislation against sex discrimination contained in the Sex Disqualification (Removal) Act 1919.
[35] [1966] 2 Q.B. 633, 646.
[36] [1967] 1 Ch. 708 (upheld by H.L., [1970] A.C. 403).
[37] [1971] 1 Ch. 354.

the facts so to do, and had then refused to re-admit him to membership so that he had lost employment. The Court of Appeal held unanimously that he was entitled to substantial damages for his loss of employment. Lord Denning with the support of Sachs L.J. held that the provision in the rules for temporary membership capable of arbitrary and capricious withdrawal was invalid,[38] and Lord Denning took the view that the automatic forfeiture rule for arrears of subscriptions was likewise invalid as giving the union an opportunity arbitrarily or capriciously to refuse to re-admit[39]—as they had done here, in his view.[40] In both judgments, the public law concept of action *ultra vires* and void for arbitrariness is fused with the private law remedy of damages—which did not in Lord Denning's view require a contractual basis. What is attacked in this decision is the union's power arbitrarily to *limit* membership as distinct from the power to expel from membership. The decision stresses the continuities between controlling expulsion and controlling exclusion; and between controlling rules and controlling their application.

For Lord Denning this marked the consummation of the application of public law controls to decisions of trade unions by which individual interests associated with the right to work were affected. In *Breen* v. *A.E.U.*[41] he applied these controls to the refusal by a trade union district committee to approve the plaintiff's election by his fellow members as a shop steward. So did the two other members of the Court of Appeal,[42] but they felt constrained to deny remedy on the basis of the finding by the trial judge that the decision of the committee had been arrived at in good faith and independently of an accusation made against the plaintiff in the past but subsequently shown to be false. So his colleagues maintained a stance which Lord Denning censured as an outdated one on the part of the judge at first instance:

> "The judge held that it was not open to the courts to review the decision of the district committee; because it was not exercising a judicial or quasi-judicial function. It was entirely a matter for discretion whether the plaintiff was approved or not. It would be vitiated if it was made in bad faith, but not otherwise. And he declined to find bad faith. In so holding, the judge was echoing views which were current some years ago. But there have been important developments in the last 22 years which have transformed the situation. It may truly now be said that we have a developed system of administrative law. These developments have been most marked in the review of decisions of statutory bodies; but they apply also to domestic bodies."[43]

---

[38] *Ibid.* p. 376 E-G.—"To call him a 'temporary' member is only a covert way of claiming to exclude him at their discretion: and, as such it cannot be allowed."

[39] *Ibid.* At p. 377A-C. "This rule (the automatic forfeiture rule) if valid, would put it into the power of the union as soon as a man was six weeks in arrears, either to enforce his exclusion, or to waive it, or to re-admit him. This could be as arbitrary or capricious as they pleased . . . . Such cannot be permitted."

[40] *Ibid.* p. 377 D-E—"Once he was excluded, the union treated his re-admission as a matter for their discretion . . . ." In this case, seeing that Mr. Edwards was wrongfully excluded in the first place, it was doubly wrong to refuse him re-admission.

[41] [1971] 2 Q.B. 175.

[42] Edmund Davies and Megaw L. JJ.

[43] *Ibid.* p. 189 G-H.

The 22 years presumably referred to *Russell* v. *Duke of Norfolk*[44] when Lord Denning had embarked on his often lonely journey along the road to public law control of domestic tribunals. So, in a way, with Lord Denning again in dissent in *Breen*, another wheel had come full circle.

But even if Lord Denning's doctrines are less than fully entrenched in the case-law, they are reflected in statute. From the beginning of the 1970s, it has been a matter of continued acceptance by Conservative administrations that there should be a right to complain to an industrial tribunal of arbitrary expulsion or exclusion from a trade union. Such a right was conferred by the Industrial Relations Act 1971[45] and retained by Conservative amendment to the Trade Union and Labour Relations Act 1974.[46] It was repealed by the Amendment Act of 1976 on the basis that a voluntary protection was provided by the T.U.C.'s Independent Review Committee; it was reintroduced by the Employment Act 1980.[47] Lord Denning acknowledged extra-judicially that, whilst the common law retained its significance, it was by statute that the protection he believed appropriate had been conferred.[48]

There is also a further sense in which there is a congruence between Lord Denning's approach to trade union law and the goals of successive Conservative governments of the 1970s and early 1980s expressed in their labour legislation. This consists in an increasingly clear identification of the individual right to work as imposing upon the trade union not only the duty to uphold the individual's freedom of association by not arbitrarily denying him membership, but also the duty to respect his freedom to dissociate by not imposing union membership upon him or impinging upon his access to work by reason of his unwillingness to belong. Lord Denning seems to have felt that even Conservative governments have not accepted this equation as fully as the situation demands.

This development in Lord Denning's thinking is fore-shadowed in *Boulting* v. *A.C.T.A.T.*[49] where he struggles unsuccessfully to adapt common law mechanisms to the point where they will enable individuals to complain of pressure put upon them to belong to trade unions. In *Langston* v. *A.U.E.W.*,[50] a car worker sought to assert that the freedom not to belong to a trade union which had been expressly conferred as against employers by the Industrial Relations Act 1971 should be available against trade unions putting pressure on employers. Lord Denning, and the Court of Appeal agreed with him, thought they had to recognise that the Act had refrained from giving the worker that direct recourse to the trade union in respect of his freedom to dissociate, so that the result they thought appropriate could be achieved only if the Act's general provisions about industrial disputes gave rise to liability (which the Court of Appeal found that they arguably did). Lord Denning clearly thought that the Act should have recognised Mr. Langston's claim in the terms in which he advanced it. He makes it clear what his basic equation is:

---

[44] [1949] 1 All E.R. 109, see above, p. 369.
[45] s.65.
[46] ss.5–6.
[47] ss.4–5.
[48] *Discipline of Law*, p. 174.
[49] [1963] 2 Q.B. 606, see above p. 372.
[50] [1974] I.C.R. 180 (see below in another context, p. 420).

"Joseph Langston is playing a lone hand. He is at odds with the other workers in the factory. He claims two rights of fundamental importance; first, the right not to be a member of a trade union or of an organisation of workers. Second, the right to work at his job. His fellow workers deny him these rights."[51]

For the remainder of the 1970s, despite the many upheavals in the legislation concerning the closed shop, Lord Denning does not have the opportunity for judicial pronouncement or action in relation to the closed shop. However, his several decisions concerning the construction of union rules can be seen as fairly uniformly concerned with maximising their provision for democratic decisions and effective voicing of viewpoints at variance with those of the executive or the prevailing majority of union activists. This is true of the decisions in *Losinska* v. *C.P.S.A.*,[52] *Equity* v. *Goring*,[53] *N.U.M. (Kent Area)* v. *Gormley*[54] and *Porter* v. *N.U.J.*[55]; and the latter two decisions in particular suggest that he would endorse another equation which underlies some of the policy formulations of recent Conservative administrations, namely that rank-and-file members' opinions are often, perhaps generally, more moderate and less militant than those of trade union leaderships.

In his last year on the bench, however, Lord Denning took the opportunity to display in its full colours his emergent view that the right to work gives rise to a freedom to dissociate from trade unions and a correlative duty on their part. In *Cheall* v. *APEX*[56] he, leading a majority in the Court of Appeal, summoned up the full rhetoric of the right to work against a trade union expulsion carried out in implementation of the Bridlington principles, which underlie the system by which TUC unions control mutual "poaching" of members.[57] Although the decision is immediately concerned with expulsion from a trade union, it is more fundamentally concerned with the prior fact that an expulsion carried out in implementation of Bridlington principles ultimately vindicates the claims of another union that the individual should belong to that union if he wishes access to particular employment.

Finally in *Taylor* v. *Co-operative Retail Services Ltd.*[58] Lord Denning examined a dismissal carried out in secondary implementation by the employer of a trade union expulsion again carried out in accordance with Bridlington principles and, being obliged to accept that the British legislation then in force provided no remedy as against the employer, suggested that the worker apply to the European Court of Human Rights for compensation against the United Kingdom Government, as had been successfully done in relation to the British Rail closed shop in *Young, James and Webster* v. *United Kingdom*.[59] This suggestion was parallel with proposals

[51] *Ibid.*p. 184B-C.
[52] [1976] I.C.R. 473.
[53] [1977] I.C.R. 393 (upheld by H.L., [1978] I.C.R. 79).
[54] *The Times*, October 21, 1977 (see Davies and Freedland, *Labour Law: Text and Materials* (1st ed., 1979), p. 569).
[55] [1979] I.R.L.R. 404.
[56] [1982] I.C.R. 543; reversed by H.L. [1983] I.C.R. 398.
[57] See Davies and Freedland, *op. cit.* (2nd edn., 1984) pp. 611–617.
[58] [1982] I.C.R. 600.
[59] [1978] I.R.L.R. 408.

then before Parliament and in the Employment Bill 1982,[60] and further indicates the similarity of policy which had come to exist in matters relating to trade unions between Lord Denning and the government of the day—a similarity which is the more striking for being neither conscious nor deliberate. It was presumably the sense of the dangers implicit in such a convergence of the executive and the judiciary in this field that led Lord Justice Donaldson as he then was, dissenting in *Cheall*, to reflect that judges must beware of confusing political policy with public policy, and that whether judges were better or less able than others to assess the merits and demerits of political policies was beside the point because that was not their function.[61]

Lord Denning and Trade Dispute Law

Introduction

Lord Denning came late to trade dispute cases. He delivered no judgments in this area as Denning J., as Denning L.J. or as Lord of Appeal in Ordinary. His first trade dispute judgment was as Lord Denning M.R. in *Stratford & Son Ltd.* v. *Lindley*,[62] and it was, as we shall see, a highly significant one from our point of view. From the standpoint of the late nineteen-fifties trade dispute law could be seen as an amalgam of common and statute law of which the main features had been determined in the period between 1898 and 1906. *Allen* v. *Flood*[63] stood for the principle that the intentional infliction of economic harm was not *per se* tortious. Although the contrary view had been accepted in the area of tortious conspiracy by the House of Lords in *Quinn* v. *Leathem*,[64] the provisions of section 1 of the Trade Disputes Act 1906 and the development at common law of a wide-ranging defence of justification for the tort of conspiracy had largely excluded simple conspiracy to inflict economic harm ("conspiracy to injure") from the area of trade disputes as well. However, where the intentional infliction of economic harm was accompanied by an additional element, it might nevertheless be tortious. Within the conceptual apparatus of the common law that additional element might be found either in interference with the plaintiff's existing legal rights (most obviously, but not exclusively, his contractual rights) or in the use by the defendant of independently unlawful means to inflict the economic harm.[65] The former line of reasoning led to the development of the tort of inducing breach of contract; the latter might suggest a tort of interference with economic interests by unlawful means.

However, whereas the tort of inducing breach of contract had been recognised at an early stage in *Lumley* v. *Gye*[66] and its application to trade disputes had been confirmed by the House of Lords in *South Wales Miners' Federation* v. *Glamorgan Coal Co. Ltd.*,[67] a general tort of interference with

[60] Proposals now embodied in section 1 of the Employment Act 1982 for compensation by the Government of individuals who could have recovered compensation from their employers for unfair dismissal for refusing to belong to a union between 1974 and 1980 had the law then been as it was from 1980 onwards.
[61] [1982] I.C.R. 543.
[62] [1965] A.C. 269.
[63] [1898] A.C. 1.
[64] [1901] A.C. 495.
[65] See generally P. Elias and K. Ewing, "Economic Torts and Industrial Action: Old Principles and New Liabilities" [1982] C.L.J. 321.
[66] (1853) 2 E. & B. 216.   [67] [1905] A.C. 239.

business by unlawful means had received only shadowy support by the late 1950s. It was, in consequence, around the tort of inducing breach of contract that the boundaries between lawful and unlawful industrial action were mainly drawn when Lord Denning first came to consider these cases. Because of the failure of the common law to develop a legal concept of a right to strike to give effect to the widely accepted social right to strike, by the middle 1960s the predominant view was that an individual employee's absence from work as part of a collective withdrawal of labour constituted just as much a breach of contract on his part as unauthorised absence to watch a football match, and that many forms of industrial action short of a complete withdrawal (*e.g.* blacking of a particular class of work) would also be a breach of the employee's contractual obligations. Any union official, lay or full-time, who counselled industrial action was thus likely to commit the tort of inducing breach of contract. The significance of this development in the law of the contract of employment was redoubled when it was put beside the decision in the *Glamorgan Coal Co.* case, where the House of Lords had refused to countenance any defence of justification for the tort that would embrace legitimate trade union interests. However, in section 3 of the Trade Disputes Act 1906 Parliament had rendered "not actionable" the act of inducing breach of a contract of employment where that act was done in contemplation or furtherance of a trade dispute.

Section 3, however, gave no protection where the contract breach of which was induced was not a contract of employment (usually called a "commercial" contract), *e.g.* where as a consequence (perhaps intended) of strike action taken against an employer that employer was not able to fulfil his supply contracts. This potential limitation on the protection afforded by section 3 was not sought to be exploited by employers until after the Second World War. In *D.C. Thomson & Co. Ltd.* v. *Deakin*[68] the Court of Appeal confirmed the principle of liability for inducing breach of commercial contract in trade disputes (at least where it was the defendants' aim to break that contract), but hedged the liability about with so many qualifications that employers in practice do not seem to have perceived that any major new legal remedy was being made available to them. In this case the plaintiffs ran a non-union shop and dismissed a man who joined a union. The union sought to organise a boycott of the plaintiffs in pursuit of which employees of Bowaters Ltd., who supplied paper to the plaintiffs, told Bowaters that they might not be willing to supply Thomsons. The defendants were officials of the union to which the Bowaters' employees belonged. The employer's claim for an interlocutory injunction was dismissed by the Court of Appeal. In particular the court stressed the need for the plaintiff to demonstrate the defendants' knowledge of the existence of the commercial contract and of its terms and their intention to procure its breach, neither of which were held to be established on the facts of the instant case. Further, the court, whilst recognising that the tort could be committed either by directly persuading the employer to break the commercial contract or by indirectly procuring the breach by putting the employer in a position where he was willy nilly unable to perform the commercial contract (*e.g.* because of blacking imposed by his employees), nevertheless insisted, in the latter, indirect, form of the tort, upon the procurement being effected by independently unlawful means

---

[68] [1952] Ch. 646.

and upon the breach following as a necessary consequence from the use of the unlawful means. On the facts of the case it was found that Bowaters' employees had not broken their contracts of employment because Bowaters had never in fact put their attitude to the test by asking them to deliver to Thomsons. Thus, neither inducement of breach of contract of employment nor breach of contract of employment itself could be advanced as constituting the necessary unlawful means in the actual case; and the question of whether these acts would have been so regarded had they been committed was left somewhat in the air at the level of dictum. However, the court was clearly motivated by a desire not to render tortious "general exhortations issued in the course of a trade dispute, such as 'Stop supplies to X' . . . ."[69] In line with this policy the court was also unwilling to see the direct approaches which the defendant had made to Bowaters to explain what they were doing and which had accompanied the exhortations addressed to Bowaters' employees as turning the tort from the indirect into the direct form, so obviating from the plaintiff's point of view the need to show unlawful means.

1964–1971

These then were the main lines of the framework of trade dispute law that existed at the end of the 1950s. For Lord Denning it was a framework which, properly articulated, was capable of achieving the correct balance between the claims of employees to a right to strike and the protection of the public and uninvolved employers against the consequences of trade disputes. In particular, he seems to have viewed the distinction between inducing breach of contracts of employment (protected by section 3 of the 1906 Act) and inducing breach of commercial contracts (unprotected) in this light. From this perspective the Court of Appeal's earlier decision in *D.C. Thomson & Co. Ltd.* v. *Deakin* appeared to contain some unduly restrictive features and, after delivering an orthodox opinion on the inducing breach point in *Stratford & Son Ltd.* v. *Lindley,* he subsequently delivered two important judgments which did much to lower the obstacles to success by a plaintiff in a claim based upon the tort of inducing breach of a commercial contract. As he was later to put it extra-judicially, the "law about 'inducing a breach of contract' was extended . . . by stretching the 'knowingly' part of it . . . and by stretching the 'breach' part."[70] The first development occurred in *Emerald Construction* v. *Lowthian,* when he put the following view:

> " . . . If the officers of the trade union, knowing of the contract, deliberately sought to procure a breach of it, they would do wrong . . . . Even if they did not know of the actual terms of the contract, but had the means of knowledge—which they deliberately disregarded—that would be enough. Like the man who turns a blind eye. So here, if the officers deliberately sought to get this contract terminated, heedless of its terms, regardless whether it was terminated by breach or not, they would do wrong. For it is unlawful for a third person to procure a breach of contract knowingly, or recklessly, indifferent whether it is a breach or not."[71]

[69] *Ibid.* p. 698.
[70] *The Discipline of Law* (1979), pp. 178 and 179.
[71] [1966] 1 W.L.R. 691, 700–701.

In this case Lord Denning also floated the suggestion that interference with a contract falling short of breach might be tortious, and he made this the basis of his judgment in *Torquay Hotel Co. Ltd.* v. *Cousins*[72] in which the defendant officials of the T.G.W.U. had called upon their members employed by Esso not to deliver fuel oil to the Imperial Hotel with which the union had a dispute. The supply contract contained, however, a *force majeure* clause, but Lord Denning bluntly stated that "the principle of *Lumley* v. *Gye* extends not only to inducing breach of contract, but also to preventing the performance of it."[73] This was a major extension of the scope of the tort of inducing breach to give protection to contractual expectations as well as to contractual rights; it was in effect a restriction of the territory governed by the principle of *Allen* v. *Flood* and an extension of the domain of *Lumley* v. *Gye*. It is significant that neither of the two other judges in the *Torquay* case concurred in this view, but rather adopted the traditional English analysis of exemption clauses that they protect against liability but not against breach.

These two Court of Appeal decisions, coupled with the House of Lords' judgment in *Stratford* v. *Lindley*,[74] brought about a revolution in plaintiffs' perceptions of the utility of the tort of inducing breach of commercial contract in trade dispute claims, to the extent that it has subsequently become the most commonly asserted ground of liability in such cases. Judicial development of the tort was part, indeed a leading part, of a general abandonment by the judiciary of a non-interventionist stance towards trade disputes which had characterised the four decades after 1920, an abandonment which accompanied growing governmental concern in the 1960s with increasing levels of strike activity and higher rates of inflation. Lord Denning's decisions, noted above, thus chimed in with a general judicial tendency of the period, although in his case developments were proposed and executed with a characteristic boldness and flair. What is perhaps more significant is a consideration of those developments which he mooted but then abandoned and of those developments achieved in other courts with which he did not agree and indeed sought to limit. It will be suggested that these demonstrate his commitment to his view of what the 1906 Act had laid down and his unwillingness to develop the common law in ways which rendered nugatory the protection conferred upon defendants in particular by section 3 of that Act. In short, his commitment to extending defendants' liability for inducing breach of commercial contract was accompanied by a commitment to preserve the "right to strike" in so far as that was expressed only through inducement of breaches of contracts of employment. From this perspective the distinction between inducing breach of contracts of employment and inducing breach of commercial contracts can be seen as the English way of making a distinction between primary industrial action (which would be lawful) and secondary industrial action (unlawful).

In *Daily Mirror Newspapers Ltd.* v. *Gardner*[75] (not a trade dispute case but it raised analogous issues) Lord Denning considered the legitimacy of the important distinction drawn in the *D.C. Thomson* case between direct and indirect inducement of breach of contract and the need for independently

---

[72] [1969] 2 Ch. 106.
[73] *Ibid.* p. 137.
[74] [1965] A.C. 269.
[75] [1968] 2 Q.B. 762.

unlawful means in the latter case, and suggested that liability could be founded upon indirect procurement even in the absence of unlawful means. The distinction was, he thought, "an undue restriction of the principle"[76] of liability for interference with contractual relations. In *Torquay Hotel Co. Ltd.* v. *Cousins*, decided only nine months later, he repudiated this view when its consequences for trade dispute cases proper became apparent. "I went too far when I said in *Daily Mirror Newspapers Ltd.* v. *Gardner* that there was no difference between direct and indirect interference . . . . This distinction must be maintained, else we should take away the right to strike altogether."[77] It is interesting that the example he gave of how his *Daily Mirror* views would unduly restrict the right to strike was not an example of secondary action as normally understood, but of primary action which would be rendered unlawful through its secondary consequences. "A trade union official, who calls a strike on proper notice, may well know that it will prevent the employers from performing their contracts to deliver goods, but he is not liable in damages for calling it . . . . A trade union official is only in the wrong when he procures a contracting party *directly* to break the contract, or when he does it indirectly *by unlawful means*."[78] However, the trade union official's protection in Lord Denning's example would then depend crucially upon how unlawful means were defined, which was the issue left undecided in *D.C. Thomson & Co.* v. *Deakin*. On this point Lord Denning was clear that the act of inducing a breach of a contract of employment which had been declared "not actionable" by section 3 of the 1906 Act could not be prayed in aid as constituting the necessary unlawful means, for "the act of inducing breach of contract of employment is a lawful act which is not actionable *at the suit of anyone* . . . ."[79] He here repeated a view he had expressed in *Morgan* v. *Fry*,[80] which had been decided earlier in the same year. From this analysis he also drew the conclusion, following *Thomson* v. *Deakin*, that for the defendants to tell Esso of the blacking their employees were imposing did not have the effect of turning their tort from the indirect into the direct form. "Seeing that the act is lawful, it must, I think, be lawful for the trade union official to tell the employers and their customers about it."[81] On both these last two points Lord Denning was disagreeing with views expressed by some of their lordships in the House of Lords in *Stratford* v. *Lindley*. There Lord Pearce had expressed the view that section 3 protected the official only from action by the employer (*e.g.* Esso) and not from actions by a third party (*e.g.* the owners of the Imperial Hotel), and two of their lordships had decided that the information the defendant officials had given to the employers' association about their intended embargo had in fact turned the defendant's actions into the direct form of the tort.

However, the development in the common law of the economic torts of this period that most caught the attention of lawyers, employers and trade unionists alike did not concern the tort of inducing breach of contract, but the tort of intimidation. This tort was resuscitated and extended by the

[76] *Ibid.* p. 781.
[77] [1969] 2 Ch. 106, 138.
[78] *Ibid.* pp. 138–139.
[79] *Ibid.* p. 139 (emphasis added).
[80] [1968] 2 Q.B. 710.
[81] [1969] 2 Ch. 106, 139.

House of Lords in *Rookes* v. *Barnard*[82] (Lord Denning did not sit at any level in this case) and it was both a much bolder extension of the conceptual basis of the economic torts than even Lord Denning's judgment in the *Torquay Hotel* case and a more dramatic demonstration of the view of the senior judiciary that the 1906 Act should no longer be regarded as giving a complete or even a broadly-based immunity to those acting in trade disputes, than any other case of this period, if only because it was the first since the 1900s unequivocally to signal this view. In *Rookes* the defendants were two shop stewards, employees of B.O.A.C., and a full-time union official (thus employed by his union and not B.O.A.C.) who threatened to call a strike against B.O.A.C. unless the employer dismissed the plaintiff, a former active member of the union who had subsequently left it. B.O.A.C. submitted to the threat and lawfully terminated the plaintiff's employment. The old cases supported the proposition that, if A threatens an unlawful action against B unless B (lawfully) acts to the disadvantage of C, A has committed a tort against C; but the old cases had found the necessary unlawful means only in threats of violence. The novelty of the House of Lords' decision was that it equated a threat to break a contract of employment with a threat of violence. The threatened strike was found to be a threatened breach of the contracts of employment of the employees of B.O.A.C., partly because of the general analysis of strikes as being breaches of contract (noted above) but mainly because of the concession by defendants' counsel in this case that a "no-strike" clause contained in the relevant collective agreement had been incorporated into the contracts of employment of B.O.A.C.'s employees. Having much extended the tort of intimidation beyond what had existed in 1906, their lordships then found that the defendants were not protected by any of the provisions of the 1906 Act, a perhaps not unsurprising conclusion from an historical point of view, although in fact one provision of the 1906 Act could quite easily have been extended to cover the new extension of the common law, had their lordships wished to do so.

The decision was a shattering blow to the structure of immunity created by the 1906 Act. Professor Kahn-Freund called it "a frontal attack upon the right to strike."[83] Clearly this was so, especially as some of their lordships were prepared to envisage the application of the tort to a "two-party situation," *i.e.* where the employer under threat of strike action in breach of contract acted to his own disadvantage. Could the employer seek an injunction to restrain the threatened strike or claim damages from the defendants for any concessions made to his employees under threat of such a strike?[84] It was difficult to see why not, and in 1965 Parliament moved to pass the Trade Disputes Act of that year, whilst at the same time appointing the Donovan Commission to carry out a more general review. The Act provided that a threat to break a contract of employment or to induce another to do so should not be actionable when done in contemplation or furtherance of a trade dispute. Lord Denning clearly shared the disquiet that the shift in the focus of illegality from acts to threats had totally undermined the 1906 Act, and it was characteristic of him that he should move judicially

---

[82] [1964] A.C. 1129.

[83] (1964) 14 *Federation News* 30.

[84] This issue has recently re-surfaced under the technical guise of duress: *Universe Tankships Inc. of Monrovia* v. *I.T.F.* [1982] 2 All E.R. 67.

to counter the *Rookes* decision even though Parliamentary change was in the offing and did in fact materialise. In two cases, *Stratford* v. *Lindley* and *Morgan* v.*Fry* —the latter decided on facts occurring before the passing of the 1965 Act—he attempted to limit the principle of *Rookes* v. *Barnard* and so maintain the integrity of the 1906 Act.

In *Stratford* the defendants, two full-time officials of a union, threatened to instruct their members, in breach of contract, not to handle barges owned by the plaintiff. Was this capable of amounting to intimidation? It had been rather unclear what the basis was upon which the union official had been held liable in *Rookes* since he had no contract with B.O.A.C. which he could threaten to break. It seems likely that he was regarded as liable as a conspirator with the other defendants who had threatened to break their contracts. In *Stratford* Lord Denning simply brushed aside the view that the officials could be seen as conspirators with the plaintiffs' employees and instead saw the threat they had made solely in terms of a threat to induce a breach of contracts of employment. Since, however, it was liability for that very act of inducement that section 3 of the 1906 Act protected defendants against, it followed that it could not be actionable to threaten to induce such a breach.

> "I must decline, therefore, to extend *Rookes* v. *Barnard* beyond its own particular circumstances: for if we did, we should greatly diminish the right to strike in this country. Nearly every strike notice would be unlawful as being intimidation. It would mean that an employer who, under threat of a strike, raised the wages would be entitled to recover damages from the trade union officers on the ground that the increase was extorted by intimidation. No one has ever supposed that any such action would lie. It has always been thought that section 3 covered it."[85]

Lord Denning's attack upon the principle of intimidation seems to have been successful at least to the extent that the House of Lords on appeal in that case chose to deal with it as a case of inducing breach of commercial contract rather than as one of intimidation, although the decision went against the defendants. However, the line drawn between union officials as conspirators with their members in threats to break their contracts of employment and union officials as threatening to induce breaches of contracts of employment was perhaps no more than a semantic one, and Lord Denning considered more fundamental ways of resolving the problem. One was to classify the nature of the threat to break the contract of employment in *Rookes* as a very special one because of the presence of the "no-strike" clause. "I can see a great difference between *Rookes* v. *Barnard* and the ordinary run of cases. In the ordinary case the right to strike—or rather the non-actionability of a strike—is guaranteed by section 3 of the Trade Disputes Act 1906. Whereas in *Rookes* v. *Barnard* that right was expressly bargained away."[86] However, since at this stage Lord Denning endorsed the recent analysis of the strike as a breach of the contract of employment whether or not there was an express "no strike" clause in the contract, the viability of his classification of *Rookes* as a special case was doubtful. This he himself recognised, for in *Morgan* v. *Fry*, where he was

---

[86] *Ibid.* p. 286.   [85] [1965] A.C. 269, 285–286.

faced with a virtual replica of the *Rookes* case except that there was no "no-strike" clause in the contracts, he sought to distinguish *Rookes* not on this basis but at a more fundamental level. Because of the "no-strike" clause *Rookes* was a "flagrant case," but "if *Rookes* v. *Barnard* is carried to its logical conclusion, it applies not only to the threat of a flagrant breach of contract . . . but also to the threat of any breach of contract."[87] Consequently, there must be something wrong in the analysis of the strike as breach of contract. "It is difficult to see the logical flaw in that argument; but there must be something wrong with it; for if that argument were correct, it would do away with the right to strike in this country."[88] His solution was to say that, where the strike was preceded by notice of a length equivalent to that needed to terminate the contract, then although the strike notice should still not be seen as notice to terminate the contracts, nevertheless it should operate as notice to suspend them rather than as notice of intended breach. This implied term as to suspension was "an implication read into the contract by the modern law as to trade disputes."[89]

1971–1976

The theory of suspension of the contract of employment by strike notice of an appropriate length was a characteristically bold Denning stroke. The notion did not commend itself to the other members of the court, who found other ways of protecting the defendants, nor to the Donovan Commission[90] nor to later courts.[91] Nevertheless, it is a notable example of Lord Denning's desire to protect section 3 of the 1906 Act from destruction and of his commitment to achieving this result through the resources of the common law. How Lord Denning might further have developed this line of argument one can only speculate, for the Industrial Relations Act 1971 radically changed the legal context of trade disputes, by replacing the common law torts by statutory unfair industrial practices within the area of "industrial disputes" (defined rather more narrowly than "trade dispute" had been in the 1906 Act) and, outside the area of industrial disputes, by removing the statutory protections against the economic torts entirely. Nevertheless, one of Lord Denning's decisions during the period of the Industrial Relations Act harked back to the earlier debates about *Rookes* v. *Barnard*. *Cory Lighterage* v. *Transport and General Workers' Union*[92] was a re-run of *Morgan* v. *Fry*, but in the new legal context and in an action brought by the employer rather than the individual. Lord Denning held the dispute not to be an industrial dispute, so that the defendant no longer had any statutory protection against the economic torts, but went on to suggest, as the basis for refusing an interlocutory injunction, that if the defendants had acted to secure the dismissal of a "troublemaker" there would be available at common law a defence of justification to the torts of conspiracy and intimidation. Since the conspiracy alleged was conspiracy to use unlawful means by inducing breaches of contracts of employment, this suggestion seemed contrary to the

---

[87] [1968] 2 Q.B. 710, 724.
[88] *Ibid.* p. 725.
[89] *Ibid.* p. 728.
[90] *Report*, Cmnd. 3623, 1968, paras. 936–952.
[91] See *Simmons* v. *Hoover Ltd.* [1977] I.C.R. 61.
[92] [1973] I.C.R. 339.

House of Lords' decision in the *Glamorgan Coal Co.* case, and in *Rookes* the House had seemed not to contemplate a defence of justification to the tort of intimidation. Nor did the other two members of the court rest their concurring decisions on this ground, but Lord Denning's judgment in this case further demonstrates his attachment to the lines of policy developed in *Morgan* v. *Fry.*

The majority of industrial conflict cases under the 1971 Act fell within the definition of industrial dispute and thus were dealt with by reference to the statutory unfair industrial practices and were heard at first instance by the National Industrial Relations Court, which had also been created by the Act and which, although treated as part of the High Court, occupied separate premises. Only five appeals of any significance came from the N.I.R.C. to the Court of Appeal during the short period of operation of the Act (it was repealed in 1974 and had become increasingly infrequently used from 1973 onwards in relation to industrial conflict) and so the latter court never had the opportunity to develop an overall view of the new Act. What can be said is that the Court of Appeal, unlike the N.I.R.C. which decided some 40 industrial conflict cases during the period 1971 to 1974, never became identified in the public mind with the aims and techniques of the 1971 Act in the way that the N.I.R.C. under the presidency of Sir John Donaldson did. Indeed, there were signs of a certain strain between the N.I.R.C. and the Court of Appeal when in *Churchman* v. *Joint Shop Stewards' Committee of the Workers of the Port of London*[93] the Court of Appeal, on the appeal of the Official Solicitor, overturned orders of the N.I.R.C. committing certain employees to prison for contempt of court on the grounds that disobedience to the N.I.R.C.'s orders had not been properly proved before that court. "In exercising those powers to punish for contempt and particularly those which concern the liberty of the subject, I would hold, and this court would hold, that any breach giving rise to punishment must be proved in the Industrial Court with the same strictness as would be required by the High Court here in this building."[94]

However, it would be wrong to conclude from this episode that Lord Denning was opposed to the policies that underlay the 1971 Act. Indeed, it seems likely that he positively welcomed some parts of the Act. As long ago as 1955 he had stressed the element of hardship for uninvolved parties that strikes could cause:

> "Anyone who looks about him today can see that disputes are not so often between employers and workmen but more frequently between one trade union and another trade union, or between a group of men and the union to which they belong. Strikes are frequent, both official and unofficial. As a result of these disputes many innocent people are injured. Many lose work and wages without any fault on their part. Others are put to great hardship and inconvenience. The whole community is struck at. It is all very well to talk of the right to strike, but I know of no law which gives any man or any group of men the right to strike at the community at large. It is nothing more nor less than a claim to a right to inflict suffering on innocent persons in order to gain

[93] [1972] I.C.R. 222.
[94] *Ibid.* p. 226.

your own ends. That is a state of affairs which cannot be tolerated in a civilised community."[95]

At this stage his proposal was the somewhat utopian one in a British context for some form of compulsory arbitration on the substantive merits of the dispute. His acceptance of the right to strike was conditional upon the absence of such machinery. "So long as there is no impartial tribunal available, there may be no alternative."[96] In the "national emergency" procedures of the 1971 Act the Secretary of State had powers in certain cases to order a temporary pause in the organisation of industrial action in order for further negotiations or a ballot of the employees to be held. In *Secretary of State for Employment* v. *ASLEF* [97] Lord Denning had to consider the application of these procedures to a national overtime ban and work-to-rule on the railways, by which "hundreds of thousands of commuters have been, and will be, put to misery, discomfort and loss; goods services have been, and will be, gravely disrupted and may break down altogether; supplies to power stations and coke ovens will soon be much reduced, so that they may have to cut down their services."[98] In the face of this Lord Denning was prepared to make considerable departures from his usual approach in administrative law issues of close supervision of executive action and to hold that the Minister had acted reasonably even though he had given no reasons for his view, that a ballot should be held because of doubts about the degree of support among the workers for the action called by the union.[99] In the subsequent ballot 85 per cent. of those voting voted in favour of industrial action.

However, by way of contrast, in what was undoubtedly the single most important piece of litigation to arise out of the 1972 Act the Court of Appeal, unlike both N.I.R.C. and House of Lords, refused to repair an omission in the drafting of the 1971 Act which threatened the whole structure of industrial conflict rules contained in it. The 1971 Act created a range of unfair industrial practices within the area of industrial disputes, but in operation the most important ones turned out to be the general liabilities contained in Part V of the Act. In particular, section 96 of the Act created an unfair industrial practice which was, in effect, the common law tort of inducing breach of contract and section 98 created an unfair industrial practice which was modelled upon the tort of inducing breach of a commercial contract. Unlike the 1906 Act, which had provided trade unions as such with a virtually complete protection from liability in tort in section 4, the 1971 Act equated the position of individuals (*e.g.* union officials) and trade unions, so that both unions and union officials could be sued for commission of the unfair industrial practices. Under the scheme of the Act, however, a distinction was made between unions which chose to register (which involved, *inter alia*, the obligation to have a rule-book which complied with the statutory model) and those which did not. Among the advantages of

---

[95] *The Road to Justice* (1955), p. 104.
[96] *Ibid.*
[97] [1972] I.C.R. 19.
[98] *Ibid.* p. 53.
[99] Sir Dennis Barnes, a senior official in the Department of Employment, subsequently commented that: "The provision in the Act, conceived to operate in a situation where industrial relations were unaffected by government policy on wages, was being used as a device for supporting what remained of the government wages policy:" D. Barnes and E. Reid, *Government and Trade Unions* (1980), p. 160.

registration was that a registered trade union was not liable for the section 96 unfair industrial practice nor was any person acting "within the scope of his authority on behalf of" a registered trade union, though the unfair industrial practice in section 98 still applied. Thus, for registered trade unions and those acting on their behalf a result was produced that was akin to that which had applied to non-union defendants by virtue of section 3 of the 1906 Act (*i.e.* protection against liability for inducing breaches of contracts of employment). For everyone else the result was akin to the law as it had been immediately before the passing of section 3, *i.e.* a general liability for inducing breaches of contract.

Contrary to the government's expectations only a handful of unions affiliated to the T.U.C. registered under the 1971 Act. In the dispute about job losses in the docks as a result of "containerisation," which flared up in early 1972 and proved to be a decisive test of the Act, plaintiffs in the London area brought actions against individual shop stewards, no doubt because the stewards were seen as acting without the official endorsement of their union. Injunctions were obtained and disobeyed and, after a pause imposed by the Court of Appeal in the *Churchman* case, the shop stewards were ordered to be gaoled on July 21,[1] an event which precipitated widespread industrial action by other workers and a threat by the T.U.C. to call a general strike. Slightly earlier, employers concerned with the industrial action at the ports of Liverpool and Hull had commenced actions against the Transport and General Workers' Union itself, holding it liable for the unofficial action of its stewards at those ports. The N.I.R.C. found the union liable and, indeed, in contempt of its orders to take steps to end the industrial action, but the union appealed to the Court of Appeal.[2] The legal problem concerned the extent to which an unregistered union could incur liability under section 96 of the Act for the unofficial acts of its stewards. Because the draftsman of the Act had expected unions to register, he had omitted to deal with the issue of unregistered unions' vicarious liability. Admittedly, the Act said nothing about the vicarious liability of registered unions either, but such unions were required to specify in their rules who was entitled to authorise industrial action on behalf of the union. To Lord Denning this suggested that Parliament must have intended in relation to unregistered unions also to make unions liable only for acts done within an authority conferred upon the stewards by the rules of the union or one of its official committees or senior officials. In this light he developed his famous analysis of the "dual role" of the shop steward, as in part a representative of the work group which elected him and in part the representative of the union. He concluded:

> "If this trade union had been registered under the Act, it would undoubtedly have gone clear. Its rules would have provided expressly—as, in my opinion, these do impliedly—that the shop stewards have no authority to call for industrial action on their own initiative. If registered, the shop stewards would be guilty of unfair industrial practices, but the union would not: see section 96(1)(*a*). Why then should the union be mulcted in heavy fines and large compensation, simply because it was not registered? If the legislature had intended

---

[1] For a chronology of these events see Davies, Note, (1973) 36 M.L.R. 78.
[2] *Heaton's Transport (St. Helens) Ltd.* v. *T.G.W.U.* [1972] I.C.R. 308.

that an unregistered union should be so penalised, it should have said so in terms. It should have said that an unregistered union—in contrast to a registered union—is to be liable for the actions of its shop stewards, whether authorised or not. For that is what it comes to. But Parliament has not said so. By keeping silent on its liability for shop stewards, Parliament has left it to the courts to decide. And we must decide it according to law, not influenced in the least by any political considerations. Was it not Lord Mansfield who said, in *Rex* v. *Wilkes* (1770) 4 Burr. 2527, 2561–2562:

> 'The constitution does not allow reasons of state to influence our judgments: God forbid it should! We must not regard *political consequences*; how formidable soever they might be: if rebellion was the certain consequence, we are bound to say *Fiat justitia, ruat coelum.*'

According to the law as I believe it to be, a union, registered or unregistered, is not responsible for the conduct of its shop stewards when they call for industrial action, if in so doing those shop stewards are acting outside the scope of their authority. On the evidence in this case I hold that the shop stewards at Liverpool and Hull were acting on behalf of their own work groups and not on behalf of the union. They were acting outside the scope of their authority from the union. They are undoubtedly liable themselves, but the union is not."[3]

The judgment of the Court of Appeal was delivered on June 13, *i.e.* before the London dockers were eventually gaoled but when it was already clear that this was the likely consequence of the actions against them (the *Churchman* case was decided by the N.I.R.C. on June 14 and by the Court of Appeal on June 19). The House of Lords heard an expedited appeal from the Court of Appeal's decision on July 10 to July 19, and on July 26 delivered a single, unanimous judgment holding the union liable, rejecting Lord Denning's theory of the dual role of shop stewards, and developing the theory of authority conferred upon shop stewards "from below," *i.e.* from the membership as a whole and not just "from above," *i.e.* by the official institutions of the union.[4] On the basis of this judgment the Official Solicitor applied for the release of the London dockers without their request to do so and obtained it after they had spent only six days in gaol and had given the court no apology for their conduct, on the grounds that in future the proper defendant in such actions was the union itself. The timing certainly but also to some extent the content of their lordships' judgments were widely thought to have been influenced by the events consequent upon the gaoling of the dockers. However, Lord Denning had the satisfaction of seeing the House of Lords in *General Aviation Services* v. *T.G.W.U.*[5] in fact decided after the Act had been repealed, then adopting views nearer to his own in *Heatons*, which views indeed he repeated, if less forcefully, in that case.

1977–1979

Thus, by 1974 Lord Denning's position on trade dispute law was not to be located at the most restrictive end of the judicial spectrum. No doubt it

---

[3] *Ibid.* p. 344–345.
[4] [1972] I.C.R. 222, 387.
[5] [1976] I.R.L.R. 224.

would be an exaggeration to say that in any general sense his position was a non-interventionist one, for it was, after all, he who had played the major role in developing the tort of inducing breach of commercial contract which had rendered the taking of secondary industrial action fraught with legal problems. Nevertheless, he clearly had a developed notion of an at least limited "right to strike" which was associated with the protection in section 3 of the 1906 Act against liability for inducing breach of contracts of employment, and he had not become closely associated with the restrictive provisions of the 1971 Act. By 1981, however, the public perception of Lord Denning's view on trade dispute law had entirely changed. Whether that view was approved of or not, few people would have dissented from the proposition that he had played a leading part in attempting to restrict the statutory provisions enacted by the Labour Government between 1974 and 1976. Some statistics, no doubt crude, highlight the point and raise the issue that needs to be explored. In the years from 1965 to 1976 Lord Denning decided 13 reported trade dispute cases, of which eight were decisions in favour of the persons taking industrial action and five were against. From 1977 to the end of 1981 he decided 10 such cases and in only one of them did he deliver a judgment in favour of those taking industrial action. What, then, was the nature of the trade dispute provisions enacted from 1974 onwards which seem to have produced such an abrupt change in Lord Denning's outlook?

It was a foregone conclusion that the Labour administration elected at the beginning of 1974 would repeal the Industrial Relations Act 1971. However, the repeal of the 1971 Act did not automatically revive the 1906 Act, which the 1971 Act had itself repealed. The policy of the Government, it became clear, was not simply to re-enact the *ipsissima verba* of the 1906 Act but, whilst adopting the non-interventionist policy of that Act, to put a modernised version of it on the statute book. As Lord Scarman later put it in *N.W.L.* v. *Woods*[6]: "So far as the Act of 1974 is concerned, the legislative purpose is clear: to sweep away not only the structure of industrial relations created by the Industrial Relations Act 1971, which it was passed to repeal, but also the restraints of judicial review which the courts had been fashioning one way or another since the enactment of the Trade Disputes Act 1906." However, the Labour government elected at the first general election of 1974 was a minority government and it found itself able only partially to implement its policy in the Trade Union and Labour Relations Act 1974. Section 14 of that Act restored the virtually complete immunity of trade unions as such. Section 13(1), applying to all other defendants, as enacted, protected persons acting in contemplation or furtherance of a trade dispute from liability for inducing a breach of a contract of employment or for threatening to induce such a breach or threatening that a contract of employment would be broken. This subsection, introduced by the opposition in place of the Government's original clause, was an exact repeat of the combined effect of section 3 of the Trade Disputes Act 1906 and the Trade Disputes Act 1965. The subsection thus overruled the decision in *Rookes* v. *Barnard*, but did not deal with any of the other common law developments since in the 1906 Act, notably the extesion of liability for inducing breach of a commercial contract.

[6] [1979] I.C.R. 867, 886.

Section 13(3) of the Act, which was not amended by the Opposition, did, however, carry matters somewhat further forward. This provided that an act declared to be "not actionable" by section 13(1) or a breach of contract in contemplation or furtherance of a trade dispute "shall not be regarded as the doing of an unlawful act or as the use of unlawful means for the purposes of establishing liability in tort." This dealt with the problem discussed by Lord Denning in the *Torquay Hotel* case and in *Morgan* v. *Fry* as to whether inducing breach of contract of employment could constitute unlawful means in a trade dispute for the purposes of liability for indirectly inducing a breach of a commercial contract, and the negative answer of the statute was in line with his views as then expressed. The subsection would equally prevent liability arising for the tort of conspiracy to use unlawful means, again thus producing a result in line with Lord Denning's views in the *Cory Lighterage* case. Perhaps most important of all, however, the subsection would materially reduce the scope of the tort of interference with business by unlawful means in the area of trade disputes. As we saw, such a general tort based on unlawful means was not clearly established in the 1950s, but two subsequent judgments of the Court of Appeal under Lord Denning—*Daily Mirror Newspapers* v. *Gardner* (1968) and *Acrow (Automation) Ltd.* v. *Rex Chainbelt Inc.*[7]—had done much to create it. The indirect form of the tort of inducing breach of contract, conspiracy to use unlawful means and intimidation could be seen as merely instances of this more general tort. Lord Denning had developed the tort, not in trade dispute cases but as a common law way of controlling businessmen's cartels, but the tort's continued exclusion from trade disputes could not be guaranteed without specific statutory provision. Hence section 13(3).

The Government secured the passage of its original version of section 13(1) only in 1976, by which time it had an overall majority in the House of Commons, with the enactment of the Trade Union and Labour Relations (Amendment) Act 1976. The new section 13(1) provided protection in respect of all types of contract (and so not just contracts of employment) and also covered interference with such contracts falling short of actual breach. Although section 13(3) was not in terms amended, its scope was much expanded because of the expansion of the scope of section 13(1). The protection provided by the new section 13(1) was, thus, not to be undermined by the reappearance of illegality in terms of the use of unlawful means. The effect was to exclude the common law developments of the nineteen-sixties of the tort of inducing breach of commercial contract, which had been associated particularly with Lord Denning's judgments. By the fortuitous results of the changing composition of Parliament the Government's necessarily two-stage programme of altering the trade dispute law could be seen in its first (1974) stage as confirming Lord Denning's position as developed in the 1960s, but in its second (1976) stage as directly contradicting it.

Lord Denning's response to the 1976 Act was rapid and decisive. In *B.B.C.* v. *Hearn*,[8] the first case to come before the Court of Appeal after the Amendment Act, he said:

"It is not necessary today to go through all the legislation which we

[7] [1971] 1 W.L.R. 1676.
[8] [1977] I.C.R. 685, 690–691.

have had relating to trade unions. I would only say that in three recent Acts, the Trade Union and Labour Relations Act 1974, the Employment Protection Act 1975, and the Trade Union and Labour Relations (Amendment) Act 1976, Parliament has conferred more freedom from restraint on trade unions than has ever been known to the law before. All legal restraints have been lifted so that they can now do as they will. Trade unions and their officers—and, indeed, groups of workmen, official or unofficial—are entitled to induce others to break their contracts—not only contracts of employment but other contracts as well—they are entitled to interfere and prevent the performance of contracts by others—all with impunity. Any such inducement or interference is not only not actionable at law. It is specifically declared to be "not unlawful." It is therefore proclaimed to be lawful, provided always this (and this is the one limit to the exemption which is conferred): it must be 'in contemplation or furtherance of a trade dispute.' "

If one takes the view that in context the phrase, "all legal restraints have been lifted," is to be read as applying only to liability for the economic torts,[9] although it is no doubt symptomatic of Lord Denning's reaction to the legislation that he permitted himself this ambiguity, then at one level his view that "Parliament has conferred more freedom from restraint upon trade unions (*sic*) than has ever been known to the law before" is correct. The new section 13(1) of Trade Union and Labour Relations Act did provide greater protection than had been laid down in the Acts of 1906 and 1965. But at a deeper level the issue was more complicated. It was argued in Government circles that the reason for the greater range of statutory protections in the 1974 and 1976 Acts was that a greater range of common law liabilities had been developed since 1906. After all, protection against interference with contractual liabilities falling short of breach would not have been necessary before Lord Denning's declaration in the *Torquay Hotel* case that: "The time has come when the principle should be further *extended* to cover 'deliberate and direct interference with the execution of a contract without causing any breach.' "[10]

The position with regard to section 3 of the 1906 Act was more complicated. That section was certainly confined, unlike section 13 of Trade Union and Labour Relations Act after 1976, to breaches of contracts of employment, but at least one thing is clear from the confused circumstances[11] in which that Act, and especially section 3 of it, were passed, namely that Parliament was not in 1906 drawing a conscious and principled distinction between contracts of employment and other contracts. The Donovan Commission in its Report of 1968 devoted some attention to the issue and concluded that "it is not possible at this distance of time to say why the protection afforded by section 3 was confined to breaches of

---

[9] Thus, section 15 of the 1974 Act, unamended in 1976 and in fact not significantly different from its predecessor in the 1906 Act, conferred little protection upon pickets against the criminal law. See *Broome* v. *D.P.P.* [1974] I.C.R. 84. Even in relation to tort liability section 13 contained an extensive, but by no means comprehensive, coverage, as Lord Denning himself was later to recognise.

[10] [1969] 2 Ch. 106, 138 (our italics).

[11] See generally R. Kidner, "Lessons in trade union law reform: the origins and passage of the Trade Disputes Act 1906" (1982) 2 L.S. 34.

contracts of employment," but it was prepared to hazard the view that "it may . . . have seemed . . . at the time that this was the situation which called for some immediate action and that there was no present need to go further."[12] Certainly, there is evidence that some of the important participants in the debate on section 3 thought that it and the other sections of the Act provided a complete immunity against the economic torts recognised at that time[13] and we have seen that it was in fact not until the 1960s that the significance of the limitation of section 3 to contracts of employment became apparent with the general development of the tort of inducing breach. Whilst the verbal formulae employed in section 13 (after 1976) were broader than those of section 3, the policy of the 1974–1976 legislation would have been perfectly familiar to the legislators of 1906. "Parliament has conferred more freedom from restraint on the trade unions than has ever been known to the law before" is a statement whose cogency depends very much upon whether the period of the implied contrast is that of the Industrial Relations Act, that of the late 1960s after all the common law developments of that decade, or the decade of the 1950s when the theory of collective laissez-faire was the accepted orthodoxy and when Professor Kahn-Freund could write that "it is in connection with trade disputes that the retreat of the courts from the scene of industrial relations can be most clearly seen."[14] None of these complexities, however, inform Lord Denning's categorical characterisation of the legislation as conferring unprecedented legal freedom upon employees taking industrial action.

No doubt, one can argue that the purely historical argument is not the crucial matter: whether those who supported the 1974 version of section 13 or those who supported the 1976 version can claim to be the true heirs of the 1906 Act may be a question that was properly raised during the political debates of 1974 to 1976, but how far is that a relevant consideration for the Court of Appeal in interpreting the legislation that Parliament in the end adopted? The arguments *pro* and *con* the 1976 Bill were well aired in Parliament. The C.B.I. had stated the essence of the argument *con* to the Donovan Commission, when it said that "if the protection given by section 3 were extended to persons who in contemplation or furtherance of a trade dispute induced the breach of a commercial contract, an employer in dispute with his workpeople might find the sources of supply of materials, or his outlet for sales, cut off by breach of such contracts so induced, and be without redress."[15] The argument *pro* the 1976 Bill and that, of course, ultimately accepted by Parliament was later well summarised by Lord Scarman as being "to exclude 'trade disputes' . . . from judicial review by the courts . . . . There is substituted for judicial review of trade disputes an advisory, conciliation and arbitration process with ACAS as the statutory body to operate it."[16] This was the old policy of collective laissez-faire with regard to trade disputes which, for good or ill, Parliament laid down in 1976 for the courts to implement.

For Lord Denning, however, the consequence of his analysis in *Hearn* of

---

[12] *Report*, Cmnd. 3623, 1968, para. 887.
[13] Wedderburn, "Industrial Relations and the Courts" (1980) 9 I.L.J., 78–79.
[14] O. Kahn-Freund, *Selected Writings* (1978), p. 21 (an essay originally published in 1959).
[15] *Op. cit.* para. 885.
[16] [1979] I.C.R. 867, 886.

the expansion of the immunities conferred by statute was that the statutory words should be narrowly construed. In this context there is no echo of his well-known general statements about the correct judicial approach to statutory interpretation: "We do not sit here to pull the language of Parliament and of Ministers to pieces and make nonsense of it . . . we sit here to find out the intention of Parliament and of Ministers and carry it out . . . ."[17] The stress in the industrial conflict cases is not upon the identification and implementation of Parliamentary intention, but upon the restriction of Parliamentary intention in order to protect the rights of "innocent parties." The tension between the right to strike and the need to protect non-disputants, which he had identified in 1955,[18] is increasingly resolved in favour of the latter as a counterweight to what Lord Denning clearly saw as undue Parliamentary protection of the former. In *Express Newspapers* v. *McShane*[19] he said:

> "I would also draw attention to the fact that, when Parliament granted immunities to the leaders of trade unions, it did not give them any *rights*. It did not give them a *right* to break the law or to do wrong by inducing people to break contracts. It only gave them immunity if they did. In construing this immunity, the correct approach was shown 70 years ago by the House of Lords in *Conway* v. *Wade* [1909] A.C. 506. The House then showed that the words of the statute are not to be construed widely so as to give unlimited immunity to law-breakers. They are to be construed with due limitations so as to keep the immunity within reasonable bounds. Otherwise the freedom of ordinary individuals—to go about their business in peace would be intruded upon beyond all reason."

As so often with Lord Denning, the terminology is as important as the substance of the passage. Gone are the acknowledgments to be found in the 1960s cases that the statutory immunities against the common law torts are the British way of giving effect to the "right to strike." Now the contrast between rights and immunities is stressed and trade unionists become "law-breakers" upon whom special protections are conferred by Parliament.

It is in this period also that Lord Denning makes a strong link between the closed shop and a union's effectiveness in industrial action. His concern with individuals unreasonably excluded or expelled from trade unions is a long-standing one, dating back at least until the early nineteen-fifties, but in the past he seemed to have drawn a sharp line between trade union law and industrial conflict cases. Thus, both *Morgan* v. *Fry* and the *Cory Lighterage* case were instances of Lord Denning's upholding the legal freedom of employees to take industrial action in a closed-shop situation to compel an individual either to re-join the union or to be dismissed. His general view of how the line between legality and illegality should be drawn in respect of industrial action was not apparently influenced by whether the industrial context was that of a closed shop or not. But in the period 1974 to 1976 the closed shop issue had proved to be as controversial as the formulation of section 13(1), as the Labour administration sought to retain the general

---

[17] *Magor & St. Mellons R.D.C.* v. *Newport Corp.* [1950] 2 All E.R. 1226, 1236.
[18] *The Road to Justice* (1955), pp. 104–105.
[19] [1979] I.C.R. 210, 218. See also *Associated Newspapers Group Ltd.* v. *Wade* [1979] I.C.R. 664, 694C.

unfair dismissal protections from the 1971 Act whilst protecting employers from liability for dismissing non-unionists where a closed shop was in operation. Again, the Government needed two attempts and fully achieved its legislative goal only with the Amendment Act of 1976. In 1978 Lord Denning saw the existence of a closed shop as an additional reason for construing the trade dispute immunities narrowly.

> "I draw attention to those rules [of the union] to show the quandary in which they place a member who is employed by the "Daily Express." Suppose he disagrees with the "blacking" and wants to go on working normally. He wants to keep to the law and fulfil his contract with his employers. The leaders of the union order him to break it. He then has no option. His freedom is taken away. He must obey the union instead of obeying the law. If he fails to obey the union, he is automatically guilty of conduct detrimental to the interests of the union: and for such conduct he can be expelled from the union and then lose his job, because it is a 'closed shop': and he may never be re-admitted to it or any other 'closed shop' in the trade. In short he can be turned out of his calling—the only calling he knows. That is a tremendous coercive power vested in the leaders of the union. So tremendous indeed, that its officers must be careful to keep themselves within the immunities given to them by Parliament. If they should overstep the mark, it is the duty of the courts to intervene so as to protect—so far as they can—the freedom of the individual under the law—his freedom to choose for himself what he should do—to say: 'I wish to do my duty by my employers.' "[20]

Again, strikers and those taking industrial action appear as law breakers rather than as the exercisers of rights, and the member's contractual obligations towards the union, in contrast to his obligation under the contract of employment, receive no mention; rather it is the member's freedom to disobey the union's instructions that is stressed.

When one turns to examine how this generally restrictive approach to the legislation expressed itself on particular issues, one finds that in his judgments Lord Denning came to emphasise one particular question above all, whilst giving some attention to two subsidiary[21] issues. His main concern

---

[20] [1979] I.C.R. 210, 217–218. See also *Associated Newspapers Group Ltd.* v. *Wade* [1979] I.C.R. 664, 686F.

[21] The two subsidiary areas, which space forbids discussion of here, were the principles for granting interlocutory injunctions and the nascent liabilities for inducing or procuring breaches of statutory duty. As to the former, a similar change of view as with the meaning of trade dispute can be detected. In *Fellowes & Sons* v. *Fisher* [1976] Q.B. 122 and *Hubbard* v. *Pitt* [1975] I.C.R. 308, Lord Denning can be found resisting the lowering of the legal hurdles for plaintiffs seeking interlocutory injunctions, which had been effected by the House of Lords in a patents case, *American Cyanamid Co.* v. *Ethicon Ltd.* [1975] A.C. 396, on the grounds that this approach was inappropriate in trade dispute cases where the issue is so often settled for good at the interlocutory stage. Yet in *Beaverbrook Newspapers* v. *Keys* [1978] I.C.R. 582 he was urging the public interest as a factor swinging the balance of convenience even more decisively in favour of plaintiff employers. However, it must be said that Lord Denning's views on the trade dispute issue were usually so firm even at the interlocutory stage that he rarely, unlike his more hesitant brethren in the Court of Appeal, sought refuge in the balance of convenience. As to the latter issue, the cases of *Meade* v. *Haringey L.B.C.* [1979] I.C.R. 494 and *Associated Newspapers Group* v. *Wade* [1979] I.C.R. 664 contain powerful dicta which may well bear fruit in the future. In them Lord Denning in effect identifies employees in the public sector as subject to additional restriction upon their right to strike, which was, no doubt, in part a reaction to the events of the winter of 1978/79, but may also turn out to be a prescient isolation of a major theme for public debate and perhaps legislation in the 1980s.

was with the interpretation of the phrase "in contemplation or furtherance of a trade dispute," which was a necessary pre-condition for immunity under section 13 as it had been under the 1906 Act. Here his approach was in sharp contrast to his approach before 1977. In *Stratford* v. *Lindley* he had found a trade dispute to exist in the context of a recognition dispute in spite of an element of inter-union rivalry which subsequently caused the House of Lords to find there was no dispute. In *Camden Exhibition and Display Ltd.* v. *Lynott*[22] he held that an overtime ban organised by an unofficial group of shop stewards in opposition to the official union policy was something done in furtherance of a trade dispute and not a "mere cover for disruptive or subversive elements." Certainly, in *Torquay Hotel* he took a narrower view and in *Cory Lighterage* gave full effect to the 1971 Act's removal of "worker and worker" disputes from the statutory definition of a trade dispute, but equally in *Sherard* v. *A.U.E.W.*[23] and *General Aviation Services* v. *T.G.W.U.*[24] he did not allow a political element to take a dispute outside the statutory definition. At the least it can be said that his policy was not at this time uniformly restrictionist. By 1978, however, his view in *Associated Newspapers Group* v. *Wade*[25] was: "It has repeatedly been said that these words 'in furtherance of' must be limited in some way. Else they would give trade unions a power to inflict tremendous injury on entirely innocent persons without any redress whatever." In only one of the cases decided by Lord Denning after 1976 did he decide that the employee defendants could bring themselves within the trade dispute definition. This set of results was achieved by Lord Denning even though, as a complement to the drafting of section 13, the definition of "trade dispute" in section 29 had been expanded and modernised as compared with the provisions of section 5 of the 1906 Act,[26] again in order to "sweep away . . . the restraints of judicial review which the courts have been fashioning one way or another since the enactment of the Trade Disputes Act 1906."[27]

Because neither section 13 nor section 29 of Trade Union and Labour Relations Act offered any very obvious way of limiting the phrase "in furtherance of a trade dispute" the cases decided by Lord Denning after 1976 demonstrate a degree of experimentation in the search for an appropriate restrictive device. In *Star Sea Transport Corp. of Monrovia* v. *Slater*[28] and again in *P.B.D.S.* (*National Carriers*) *Ltd.* v. *Filkins*[29] he suggested that "the correct principle is that officers of a trade union may take themselves outside their statutory immunity if they make demands which are wholly extortionate or utterly unreasonable or quite impossible to fulfil."[30] Here judicial disapproval of the objective of the exercise of industrial power renders the action unlawful, just as it had under the conspiracy doctrines before the reforms of 1906. An alternative, apparently

[22] [1966] 1 Q.B. 555.
[23] [1973] I.C.R. 421.
[24] [1975] I.C.R. 276.
[25] [1979] I.C.R. 664, 694.
[26] See generally R.C. Simpson, "Trade Dispute and Industrial Dispute in British Labour Law" (1977) 40 M.L.R. 16.
[27] See note 16, above.
[28] [1979] 1 Lloyd's Rep. 26.
[29] [1979] I.R.L.R. 356.
[30] *Ibid.* p. 360.

Labour Law

more acceptable but factually implausible, way of putting the same point was to say that, if the defendants' trade demand appeared to the court to be unacceptable, then this raised a strong inference that the defendants had an unprotected, non-trade motive in putting forward the demand. The *P.B.D.S.* case is particularly notable because there Lord Denning used these arguments to render unprotected primary industrial action organised by an unofficial group of employees contrary to the declared policy of the union at national level. The decision is, thus, in striking contrast with Lord Denning's decision in 1965 in the *Camden Exhibition* case.

The most creative of Lord Denning's restrictions, and certainly the ones to have had the most long-lasting impact on the law, referred more directly to the context of secondary action, *i.e.* industrial action taken against an employer other than the one with whom the original dispute arose. This was precisely the situation in which before 1971 the tort of inducing breach of commercial contract would very likely have provided the secondary employer with a legal remedy, but after 1976 this result could be achieved only if the immunity contained in section 13(1) could be removed.[31] In *Express Newspapers Ltd.* v. *Keys*[32] there was a strike by journalists, members of the National Union of Journalists, at the *Daily Mirror* and the defendant officials of the union SOGAT ordered their members employed at the *Daily Express* not to handle any additional output during the *Daily Mirror* strike, lest a permanent diminution of the *Mirror's* market share should occur to the detriment of the striking journalists and SOGAT members at the *Mirror*. This was held to be unprotected action by virtue of the introduction of a notion of "direct furtherance."

> "To return to the question. Can it fairly be said that the acts done by Mr. Keys [general secretary of SOGAT] were in 'furtherance' of the 'Daily Mirror' dispute? To my mind it cannot. The acts done were a consequence of a trade dispute, but not in 'furtherance' of it. As I read the statute, in order that an act should be done in furtherance of a trade dispute, it must be *directly* in furtherance of fit. You cannot chase consequence after consequence in a long chain and say everything that follows a trade dispute is in 'furtherance' of it.
>
> Whenever there is a strike which injuriously affects the public, everyone tries to mitigate the effect of it. When trains stop, people go by car. When one airline stops, they go by another airline. An so on. Everything that the general public does to try and stave off the effects of a strike is in consequence of it, but not in furtherance of it. So it seems to me that the action taken by the 'Daily Express' in handling and distributing the extra copies was not in furtherance of a trade dispute. It was a consequence of it. So the next step—of Mr. Keys telling SOGAT members not to distribute the extra copies—was not in furtherance of a

[31] Of course, if the immunity were removed by a finding that the defendants had not acted in furtherance of a trade dispute, none of the protections of section 13(1) would apply. Consequently, when making such an argument employers needed, and generally sought, to show only inducement of breaches of contracts of employment. But the point remains that Lord Denning seemed most concerned to restrict the notion of furtherance in cases of secondary action.

[32] [1978] I.C.R. 582.

trade dispute. It was a consequence of a consequence. It is far too remote to be protected by the statute."[33]

Clearly the *Daily Express* management's motivations were entirely commercial, but no explanation was offered by Lord Denning for the view that SOGAT's action, in seeking to prevent the *Daily Express* plans, could not be in furtherance of the Mirror dispute by removing a source of pressure upon the Mirror journalists to settle quickly. One suspects that the true rationale of the case is to be found in Lord Denning's desire, strongly expressed in the case, to protect the public deprived of their newspaper and the retail system of newspaper distribution: "The consequence of SOGAT's action . . . was much injury to the trade and to the public."[34]

Perhaps because Lord Denning came to realise that the notion of "directness" did not very well articulate the essence of his objection to trade union action in these cases, which was the imbalance, as he saw it, between the gains to the union in furthering the primary dispute and the harm suffered by the secondary employer and the public as a result, in *Express Newspapers Ltd.* v. *McShane*[35] Lord Denning developed a different formulation of his test. Here the primary dispute was between the National Union of Journalists and the provincial newspaper proprietors. In furtherance of this dispute the union called upon its members employed by the Press Association, which provided copy to both provincial and national newspapers, to come out on strike. The response of the union members at the Press Association was not whole-hearted, and in order to boost the morale of the striking Press Association members the union called upon its members employed by the national newspapers to black copy from the Press Association which the non-striking employees of that organisation were still managing to produce. The issue before the court was the legality of the blacking. In holding it to be illegal Lord Denning developed a distinction between the subjective and objective approaches to the notion of furtherance.

"It is said on behalf of the trade union leaders that 'furtherance' depended on their state of mind. If they genuinely and honestly *believed* that the 'blacking' would advance the cause of the provincial journalists, then their acts were done 'in furtherance of' the dispute. The judge did not accept that submission. Nor do I. 'Furtherance' is not a merely subjective concept. There is an objective element in it. The *Shorter Oxford English Dictionary*, defines 'furtherance' as 'the fact or state of being helped forward.' It seems to me that, for an act to be done 'in furtherance of' a trade dispute, it must be reasonably capable of doing so, or have a reasonable prospect of it in this way, that it must help one side or the other to the dispute in a *practical* way by giving support to the one or bringing pressure to bear on the other. Such as in the common case where men, who are in dispute with their employer, withdraw their labour, or 'black' materials coming to his factory, or are supported by pickets outside his gates. Those are practical measures which have an impact in *fact* on the employer. They directly damage the employer's business. Such acts have a different quality from those which do not

[33] *Ibid.* p. 586.
[34] *Ibid.* p. 586A.
[35] [1979] I.C.R. 210.

directly damage the employer's business but serve only to improve the
morale of the strikers or promote their confidence or encourage them in
their efforts, or damage innocent people not parties to the dispute. If
this is all they do, they are not 'in furtherance' of the dispute. In
ordinary speech we draw a distinction between giving moral support to
a cause and practical support to it. To be 'in furtherance of' a dispute,
an act must give practical support to one side or the other and not
merely moral support."[36]

In this passage Lord Denning not only rejects a subjective test of
"furtherance," but also adopts a strong version of the objective test, namely,
one requiring "practical effects" to flow from the secondary action, and,
further, rejects the proposition that improvement of the strikers' morale
could qualify as a practical effect. His approach is, thus, considerably more
restrictive than a simple rejection of the subjective approach might imply.
Nevertheless, the implication of this argument was not that all secondary
action was illegal, but that the court would draw a distinction between
legitimate and illegitimate forms of secondary action by reference to an
analysis of the "practical effects" of the secondary action in furthering the
primary action. That point was made more concrete in the next secondary
action case before the Court of Appeal, *Associated Newspapers Group* v. *Wade*[37]
and, significantly, it was a point expressly developed in the context of the
extension of statutory protection beyond contracts of employment in 1976.

"Mr. Alexander [counsel for plaintiffs] put it in more practical terms,
which again are worth recording. He said that the Trade Disputes Act
1906 was confined to inducing 'breaches of contracts of employment.' It
gave immunity when workers were induced to come out on strike
against their own employers: but not when a supplier was induced to
break his contract to supply goods to the employer. Lord Donovan's
Royal Commission on Trade Unions and Employers' Associations
1965–1968 (1968) (Cmnd. 3623) recommended that it be extended to
cover such a supplier: see pp. 234–235, paragraphs 891–893: and this
was done by the Trade Union and Labour Relations (Amendment) Act
1976, by extending immunity to acts done in order to induce 'breaches
of a contract.' So immunity is given now when pressure is brought upon
a first supplier so as to induce him not to supply goods to the
employer—and likewise a first customer. But Mr. Alexander submitted
that the immunity should not be given any further down the chain of
supply. It should not be granted, he suggested, to interfere with
supplies by the second supplier to the first supplier. Least of all by the
third supplier to the second supplier or lower down the chain . . . .
   Mr. Goldblatt [counsel for defendants] very fairly acknowledged that
these submissions were fairly close to the right answer. I agree. But I
would put it simply on the question of remoteness. Some acts are so
remote from the trade dispute that they cannot properly be said to be
'in furtherance' of it."[38]

[36] *Ibid.* p. 218.
[37] [1979] I.C.R. 664.
[38] *Ibid.* pp. 694–695.

The *Associated Newspapers* case is also important because at last Lord Denning brought himself around to what might be thought to have been from the outset the most important question: what did Parliament intend when it enacted the 1976 Act? The suggestion in that case was that Parliament intended only to protect action taken against a "first supplier" or "first customer," and thus the Court of Appeal was effectuating, not contradicting, Parliamentary intention. But this is difficult to accept. It is true that the example the Donovan Commission seemed mainly to have in mind when discussing the operation of section 3 of the 1906 Act was that of a commercial contract between disputing employer and supplier,[39] but their recommendation was for a general extension of the protection to commercial contracts (though a majority of the Commission did propose a different restriction, namely that only those acting on behalf of a registered trade union should be protected). The 1976 Act, of course, contained no express restriction to either listed trade unions or to commercial contracts to which the disputing employer was a party. The interpolation of the words into section 13(1), "except commercial contracts to which the disputing employer is not a party," would seem an act grossly exceeding the accepted British conventions of how judges must approach statutory interpretation. This perhaps explains why Lord Denning, having floated the notion in the guise of counsel's argument and having stated his agreement with it, then retreats into the safer, if more general, ground of "remoteness."

1979–1980

At this point two developments occurred which could be expected to have an impact upon the steady flow of Court of Appeal decisions adverse to trade unionists taking industrial action. In May 1979 (*i.e.* in the month following the decision in the *Associated Newspapers Group* v. *Wade*) a general election was held in which a Conservative administration was elected pledged to review the structure of trade dispute law contained in the 1974 to 1976 Acts. The Conservative Party's manifesto for that election had specifically mentioned the need to amend the 1976 Act in order to "ensure that the protection of the law is available to those not concerned in the dispute but who at present can suffer severely from secondary action (picketing, blacking and blockading)." In a "working paper for consultations on proposed industrial relations legislation" issued in July 1979 the Government proposed immediate legislation to restrict the statutory immunities for pickets to, in general, those picketing at their own place of work. Secondary picketing had been a particular feature of industrial action and topic of public debate during the winter of 1978/1979 and the Government wanted immediate action on this front, although, as we have seen, this social fact had not been reflected in the cases before the Court of Appeal, which had tended to raise the issue of the legality of secondary blacking. Indeed, it was precisely because such secondary action seemed to have had its legality restricted by the Court of Appeal that the working paper of July 1979 did not take a firm line as to whether more general legislation on secondary action (beyond picketing) was desirable, and the Employment Bill printed on December 6, 1979 did not in fact contain any more general provisions.

The second development was that the House of Lords heard appeals from

---

[39] See, *e.g.* para. 892 of the Commissions's Report.

decisions of the Court of Appeal in the trade dispute cases. Their lordships decided initially two cases, the second of which, *Express Newspapers Ltd.* v. *McShane*,[40] in which Lord Denning had developed the objective interpretation of the phrase "in furtherance of a trade dispute," was seen as particularly significant for the development of Government policy. As the Government later put it: "There were some hopes, particularly following the decision of the Court of Appeal in the MacShane (*sic*) case, that this development might afford a basis for consensus on the extent of immunity, provided that the immunity for secondary picketing was statutorily restricted because of its special connotations for public order. Since the Government would much prefer to proceed in these matters by consensus it was felt that further consideration must wait the decision of the House of Lords in the case of MacShane."[41] Perhaps taking the view that the production of "consensus" was the task of Parliament, the House of Lords had in fact turned to the more traditional legal question of what it was Parliament had intended to achieve when it passed the Acts of 1974 and 1976. Their lordships rejected (with Lord Wilberforce dissenting) the objective test developed by the Court of Appeal. In the other case, in fact the consolidated appeals from two Court of Appeal decisions arising out of the same facts, *N.W.L.* v. *Nelson* and *N.W.L.* v. *Woods*,[42] their lordships rejected the various versions of the "impossibility" doctrine, which the Court of Appeal had first developed in the *Star Sea* case and which, indeed, the Court of Appeal itself in the *N.W.L.*[43] cases had sought to restrict, perhaps because the "impossibility" test was seen as too limited and artificial a restriction and the objective test as a more satisfactory way of confining the 1974 to 1976 Acts.

Of more interest for present purposes than the technical arguments in the two cases is the contrast between the general approaches of the House of Lords and of the Court of Appeal to the interpretation of the Acts. Lord Scarman in *N.W.L.* stated his view of the policy behind the Acts which we have quoted above and added, referring to the *Star Sea* case: "The basic error, which is to be found in all three judgments of the Court of Appeal, is in the proposition, which the court accepted . . . that 'not every dispute connected with terms or conditions of employment . . . was necessarily a trade dispute' and that 'some limitation of those statutory words was necessary.' The legislative purpose of the Act is such that no limitation upon the ordinary meaning of the simple English words used by the statute is permissible . . . The Court of Appeal erred in [the *Star Sea* case] in holding that it was necessary to place 'some limitation' upon the words of section 29(1). None is needed, none was intended by Parliament."[44] In *Express Newspapers* Lord Scarman rejected the objective test in similar language but also made clear his satisfaction with this result: "It would be a strange and embarrassing task for a judge to be called upon to review the tactics of a party to a trade dispute and to determine whether in the view of the court the tactic employed was likely to further, or advance, that party's side of the dispute."[45] On this further point Lord Scarman was on his own. The

[40] [1980] I.C.R. 42.
[41] Department of Employment, *Working Paper on Secondary Industrial Action* (1981), para. 9.
[42] [1979] I.C.R. 867.
[43] *N.W.L.* v. *Woods* [1979] I.C.R. 744; *N.W.L.* v. *Nelson* [1979] I.C.R. 755.
[44] [1979] I.C.R. 867, 888–889. [45] [1980] I.C.R. 42, 65.

majority of the judges in *Express Newspapers*, whilst stressing the impropriety of the Court of Appeal's approach, clearly indicated their dislike of the law as passed in 1976 and invited the new Parliament to change it. Thus, Lord Diplock said:

> "My Lords, during the past two years there has been a series of judgments in the Court of Appeal given upon applications for interlocutory injunctions against trade union officials. These have the effect of imposing on the expression 'An act done by a person in contemplation or furtherance of a trade dispute,' for which immunity from civil actions for specified kinds of torts is conferred by section 13(1) of the Trade Union and Labour Relations Act 1974 (as now amended), an interpretation restrictive of what, in common with the majority of your Lordships, I believe to be its plain and unambiguous meaning. The terms in which the limitations upon the ambit of the expression have been stated are not identical in the various judgments, but at the root of them there appears to lie an assumption that Parliament cannot really have intended to give so wide an immunity from the common law of tort as the words of sections 13 and 29 would, on the face of them, appear to grant to everyone who engaged in any form of what is popularly known as industrial action.
>
> My Lords, I do not think that this is a legitimate assumption on which to approach the construction of the Act, notwithstanding that the training and traditions of anyone whose life has been spent in the practice of the law and the administration of justice in the courts must make such an assumption instinctively attractive to him. But the manifest policy of the Act was to strengthen the role of recognised trade unions in collective bargaining, so far as possible to confine the bargaining function to them, and, as my noble and learned friend, Lord Scarman, recently pointed out in *N.W.L.* v. *Woods*, to exclude trade disputes from judicial review by the courts. Parliament, as it was constituted when the Act and the subsequent amendments to it were passed, may well have felt so confident that trade unions could be relied upon always to act 'responsibly' in trade disputes that any need for legal sanctions against their failure to do so could be obviated."[46]

Similar views were expressed by Lords Keith and Salmon. Indeed, the latter devoted a part of his short judgment to discussion of a recent strike at the Charing Cross Hospital, evidence of which was presumably not before the House, and concluded that those taking the industrial action may well have been immune, "but if this is the law, surely the time has come for it to be altered."[47] Only Lord Wilberforce argued for an objective interpretation of "in furtherance," but he was careful to distinguish this interpretation from a judicial assumption that the words of the Act must be cut down. Even he, moreover, rejected the objective formulation of Lord Denning, adopted the less restrictive objective formulation of Lawton and Brandon L.JJ., and held, contrary to Lord Denning, that "morale is a vital factor in all confrontations, whether at Alamein or in Fleet Street . . . [and] here the

---

[46] *Ibid.* p. 56.
[47] *Ibid.* p. 61.

evidence goes beyond morale well into capability of practical effect . . . ."[48]

A judge more respectful than Lord Denning of the authority of the House of Lords or less committed than he to demonstrating the ability of the judges to bring about reforms without Parliamentary aid or less anxious than he to do what he saw as justice in the particular case might have regarded the decisions in *N.W.L.* and *Express Newspapers* as the end of the road for restrictive interpretation of the 1974 to 1976 Acts. After all, the effects of the Court of Appeal's decisions from 1977 onwards had been that the intended results of the 1976 Amendment Act had not achieved full effect before a general election had brought in a new administration which was ready to review those Acts. The House of Lords had firmly rejected Lord Denning's judicial approach, but most of their lordships shared his views as to what the law ought to be and had commended these views to Parliament. One can only speculate whether Lord Denning's judicial decisions would have achieved acceptance by the House had the Parliamentary balance of power at the end of 1979 been a different one. Lord Denning, however, had not yet shot his bolt. Their lordships delivered their judgments in the *Express Newspapers* case on December 13, 1979. On January 26, 1980 Lord Denning delivered the main judgment in *Duport Steels Ltd.* v. *Sirs*,[49] in which the Court of Appeal held the defendants were not protected by the 1974 to 1976 Acts.

The case arose out of a national strike in the public sector of the steel industry over a wage dispute between the unions and the British Steel Corporation. It was the first major dispute of the new administration's period of office and an important test of the Government's resolve on wage matters. All the judicial decisions considered below were given whilst the dispute continued. The withdrawal of labour in the public sector was virtually complete, but its impact was less than the unions had anticipated. The unions consequently decided to call out their members employed in the private sector of the industry, in order to increase the amount of economic disruption and to put pressure on the Government, which was rightly seen as having a major influence upon the wages policies of the Corporation. The unions had no dispute with the private sector employers. The private sector employers sought an interlocutory injunction against the defendant union officials. This was refused by Kenneth Jones J. on Friday, January 25, but granted by the Court of Appeal at a special sitting on Saturday, January 26.[50] Lord Denning found three arguments in the plaintiffs' favour. First, the dispute in the private sector was a dispute between the unions and the Government and so not a trade dispute, which was defined as a dispute between employers and workers (or between workers and workers). Second, and implausibly, he held that the defendants' acts in the private sector were too remote to be in furtherance of the dispute with the Corporation. This was the old argument all over again, as most recently expressed in *Associated Newspapers Group* v. *Wade*. This case, he managed to persuade himself, quoting only Lord Wilberforce from *Express Newspapers,* had not been overruled by the House of Lords. "The House did not say that that case was

[48] *Ibid.* p. 55.
[49] [1980] I.C.R. 161.
[50] Kenneth Jones J. remarked, rather plaintively, at the beginning of his judgment: "I am told [by counsel] that the immediate sequel of a refusal to grant an injunction will be an appeal to the Court of Appeal. Bearing that in mind, it seems unnecessary for me to give a lengthy judgment here . . . " *Ibid.* p. 166.

wrongly decided."[51] Thirdly, the public interest swung the balance of convenience in favour of granting the injunction. Lawton and Ackner L.JJ. delivered short concurring judgments and the Court then in a final bizarre step refused leave to appeal to the House of Lords.

However, on January 31 the Appeal Committee of the House of Lords gave leave to appeal and argument was heard on February 1, at the conclusion of which it was announced that the appeal was allowed. All three of Lord Denning's arguments received short shrift. Of the "two-disputes" argument Lord Diplock said it: "originated from a suggestion proferred from the bench[52] during the hearing in the Court of Appeal; not unnaturally in the haste of a Saturday morning hearing counsel for the private sector companies was reluctant to reject it. Further reflection, however, prior to the hearing in this House had led him to the conclusion that the 'two-disputes' argument cannot rationally be supported; he has not sought to uphold the judgments of the Court of Appeal upon this ground."[53] The point was simply that, even if the private sector dispute was correctly to be seen as one between unions and Government, nevertheless the calling out of the private sector employees was clearly an act done in furtherance of the dispute with the Corporation. As to the remoteness test, Lord Diplock said: "Among the three tests rejected as wrong in law was the test of remoteness the authorship of which was specifically ascribed in my own speech to Lord Denning. Recognising this, counsel for the respondents has not felt able to support the judgment of the Court of Appeal on this ground either."[54] As to the balance of convenience, the damage being suffered by the private sector companies was not enough to outweigh the virtual certainty that at a full trial the defendants would succeed on the trade dispute defence. The other law lords agreed with Lord Diplock.

Behind these detailed arguments, however, the House saw more fundamental constitutional issues, concerning the proper place of the Court of Appeal in the hierarchy of courts and the proper limitations upon the creative role of the judges, observance of which by the judges was necessary if the impartiality of the judiciary was to be preserved. Both Lord Diplock and Lord Scarman spelled these points out at length, the latter saying:

" . . . My Lords, this appeal raises two specific questions as to the interpretation of a statute, the Trade Union and Labour Relations Act 1974, as amended. But below the surface of the legal argument lurk some profound questions as to the proper relationship in our society between the courts, the government, and Parliament. The technical questions of law pose (or should pose) no problems. The more fundamental questions are, however, very disturbing; nevertheless it is upon my answer to them that I would allow the appeal. My basic criticism of all three judgments in the Court of Appeal is that in their desire to do justice the court failed to do justice according to law. When one is considering law in the hands of the judges, law means the body of rules and guidelines within which society requires its judges to

---

[51] *Ibid.* p. 172.
[52] Not apparently by Lord Denning, although he adopted the argument in his judgment.
[53] [1980] I.C.R. 161, 182.
[54] *Ibid.*

administer justice. Legal systems differ in the width of the discretionary power granted to judges: but in developed societies limits are invariably set, beyond which the judges may not go. Justice in such societies is not left to the unguided, even if experienced, sage sitting under the spreading oak tree.

In our society the judges have in some aspects of their work a discretionary power to do justice so wide that they may be regarded as law-makers. The common law and equity, both of them in essence systems of private law, are fields where, subject to the increasing intrusion of statute law, society has been content to allow the judges to formulate and develop the law. The judges, even in this, their very own field of creative endeavour, have accepted, in the interests of certainty, the self-denying ordinance of "stare decisis," the doctrine of binding precedent: and no doubt this judicially imposed limitation on judicial law-making has helped to maintain confidence in the certainty and evenhandedness of the law.

But in the field of statute law the judge must be obedient to the will of Parliament as expressed in its enactments. In this field Parliament makes, and un-makes, the law: the judge's duty is to interpret and to apply the law, not to change it to meet the judge's idea of what justice requires. Interpretation does, of course, imply in the interpreter a power of choice where differing constructions are possible. But our law requires the judge to choose the construction which in his judgment best meets the legislative purpose of the enactment. If the result be unjust but inevitable, the judge may say so and invite Parliament to reconsider its provision. But he must not deny the statute. Unpalatable statute law may not be disregarded or rejected, merely because it is unpalatable. Only if a just result can be achieved without violating the legislative purpose of the statute may the judge select the construction which best suits his idea of what justice requires. Further, in our system the rule "stare decisis" applies as firmly to statute law as it does to the formulation of common law and equitable principles. And the keystone of "stare decisis" is loyalty throughout the system to the decisions of the Court of Appeal and this House. The Court of Appeal may not overrule a House of Lords decision: and only in the exceptional circumstances set out in the practice statement of July 1, 1966 (*Practice Statement* (*Judicial Precedent*)[1966] 1 W.L.R. 1234), will this House refuse to follow its own previous decisions.

Within these limits, which cannot be said in a free society possessing elective legislative institutions to be narrow or constrained, judges, as the remarkable judicial career of Lord Denning himself shows, have a genuine creative role. Great judges are in their different ways judicial activists. But the constitution's separation of powers, or more accurately functions, must be observed if judicial independence is not to be put at risk. For, if people and Parliament come to think that the judicial power is to be confined by nothing other than the judge's sense of what is right (or, as Selden put it, by the length of the Chancellor's foot), confidence in the judicial system will be replaced by fear of it becoming uncertain and arbitrary in its application. Society will then be ready for Parliament to cut the power of the judges. Their power to do justice will become more restricted by law than it need be, or is today.

In the present case the Court of Appeal failed to construe or apply the statute in the way in which this House had plainly said it was to be construed and applied."[55]

1980–1981

When considered within the conventions of judicial discourse about other judges, this passage of Lord Scarman represented a major rebuke to Lord Denning, one perhaps more powerful, because more measured, than that delivered by Lord Simonds in 1951[56] and more notable because Lord Scarman represented a judicial tradition very different from the "substantive formalism" of Lord Simonds[57] and because it was an attack delivered by a judge who was, in terms at least of age and judicial experience, Lord Denning's junior. The words of Lord Diplock, also a judicial activist but in a rather different way and Lord Denning's junior, did not spare the Master of the Rolls either,[58] although Lord Diplock was again careful to distance himself from the policy which he reaffirmed the 1974 to 1976 Acts to contain. His conclusion as to the meaning of the Acts he described as "intrinsically repugnant to anyone who has spent his life in the practice of the law or the administration of justice."[59] Whether Lord Denning felt the sting of these rebukes one cannot know, but less than two weeks after the House of Lords' judgments in the *Duport Steels* case were delivered, Lord Denning would have had the satisfaction of reading in *The Times* the text of a Government working paper on secondary industrial action, which referred with approval to the Court of Appeal's decisions in the period 1977 to 1979, noted their overturn by the House of Lords, and proposed to restore the effect of those decisions by the addition of a clause to the Employment Bill which was then before Parliament.

---

[55] *Ibid.* pp. 189–190.
[56] *Magor & St. Mellons R.D.C.* v. *Newport Corp.* [1952] A.C. 189, 191.
[57] On Lord Simonds see R. Stevens, *Law and Politics* (1979), pp. 341–354.
[58] Lord Diplock said:

> "It endangers continued public confidence in the political impartiality of the judiciary, which is essential to the continuance of the rule of law, if judges, under the guise of interpretation, provide their own preferred amendments to statutes which experience of their operation has shown to have had consequences that members of the court before whom the matter comes consider to be injurious to the public interest. The frequency with which controversial legislation is amended by Parliament itself (as witness the Act of 1974 which was amended in 1975 as well as in 1976) indicates that legislation, after it has come into operaton, may fail to have the beneficial effects which Parliament expected or may produce injurious results that Parliament did not anticipate. But, except by private or hybrid Bills, Parliament does not legislate for individual cases. Public Acts of Parliament are general in their application; they govern all cases falling within categories of which the definitions are to be found in the wording of the statute. So in relation to section 13(1) of the acts of 1974 and 1976, for a judge (who is always dealing with an individual case) to pose himself the question: 'Can Parliament really have intended that the acts that were done in this particular case should have the benefit of the immunity?' is to risk straying beyond his constitutional role as interpreter of the enacted law and assuming a power to decide at his own discretion whether or not to apply the general law to a particular case. The legitimate questions for a judge in his role as interpreter of the enacted law are: 'How has Parliament, by the words that it has used in the statute to express its intentions, defined the category of acts that are entitled to immunity? Do the acts done in this particular case fall within that description?" [1980] I.C.R. 161, 177–178.

[59] *Ibid.* p. 177.

Referring to the Court of Appeal's decisions the working paper noted that as a result of them "action 'in furtherance' had to be reasonably closely related to the original dispute and the way the tests were applied by the Court of Appeal in the cases which came before them suggested that, although the immunity would extend to action taken to interfere with performance of a contract by the first supplier or customer of the party in dispute, it would not go far beyond that."[60] This view of the Court's decisions, especially no doubt the decision in *Associated Newspaper Group* v. *Wade*, the working paper now proposed to embody in statute law, and this was done in what became section 17 of the Employment Act 1980. The aim of the new section was described in the working paper as follows:

> "Where the inducement to break or interfere with any commercial contract arose in connexion with industrial action taken in furtherance of a trade dispute by employees of the employer in dispute, the person inducing the breach or interference would continue to have immunity under section 13. In the case of such 'primary action,' no one else whose commercial contracts suffered as a result would be able to obtain redress in the courts.
>
> Exactly the same position would hold in the case of secondary industrial action in furtherance of that trade dispute by employees of those first suppliers or customers of the employer in dispute who were not themselves party to the dispute . . . .
>
> But there the immunity for secondary action which interfered with commercial contracts would end. So if a person were, in furtherance of the original trade dispute, to induce a breach of or interfere with any commercial contract through secondary action, threatened or actual, taken by employees of anyone who was neither a party to that dispute nor a first supplier or customer . . . of such a party . . . . then the immunities contained in section 13(1) of TULRA would not apply."[61]

As a matter of drafting technique this result was achieved in section 17 of the 1980 Act, not by amendment of the definition of trade dispute contained in the 1974 to 1976 Acts, but by a description of a set of circumstances in which section 13(1) was not to apply. Put in a simplified way, section 13(1) was not to apply where breach of a commercial contract was induced as a result of secondary action, which was defined as the inducement of employees not employed by a party to the dispute to break their contracts of employment (section 17(1) and (2)). Had the section stopped there it would not have given effect to the "first supplier, first customer" exception because it would have removed immunity from all forms of secondary action resulting in breaches of commercial contracts. Consequently, section 17(3) restored the immunity provided by section 13 of the Trade Union and Labour Relations Act where the purpose of the secondary action was directly to disrupt the supply of goods and services between the employer in dispute and the secondary employer. Sections 17(4) and (5) provided two more limited exceptions, which complemented section 17(3); and sections 17(6) and (7)

---

[60] Department of Employment, *Working Paper on Secondary Industrial Action* (1980), para. 8.

[61] *Ibid.* paras. 17–19. These were the principles embodied in section 17 of the 1980 Act, although the precise way of doing this was not ultimately quite that suggested in the working paper.

contained important definitions. Finally, and this was to prove of great significance for Lord Denning, section 17(8) repealed for all purposes section 13(3) of the Trade Union and Labour Relations Act.

One might have thought that section 17 would signal the end of Lord Denning's creativity in the field of trade dispute law, at least so far as secondary action was concerned. Although it is true that section 17 is less restrictive of secondary action than a simple return to the formula of the 1906 Act would have been, for that Act conferred no protection for inducing breaches of commercial contracts, nevertheless Parliament had considered the issues raised in the Court of Appeal's decisions on "in furtherance" and had legislated to draw a line between acceptable and unacceptable forms of secondary action. In those circumstances what role was left for the judge but loyally to implement the new restrictions upon section 13(1)? In *Hadmor Productions Ltd.* v. *Hamilton*[62] Lord Denning demonstrated that he did not take this view. Relying upon arguments derived from the combined effect of the repeal of section 13(3) and the development of the tort of interference with business by unlawful means, he rendered unlawful primary industrial action because of its secondary consequences. This, of course was *precisely* the result he had wished to avoid in *Torquay Hotel Co. Ltd.* v. *Cousins*, and it had led him to restore in that case the distinction between direct and indirect inducement of breach of contract which he had recently doubted in the *Daily Mirror* case. Moreover, the means he used to achieve the desired result in *Hadmor* involved precisely the technique he had so vigorously rejected in *Torquay Hotel* and in *Morgan* v. *Fry*, namely the employment of acts declared by statute to be "not actionable" as unlawful means in order to establish liability in tort. Lord Denning's commitment from the 1960s to preserving at least a limited right to strike attached to the concept of primary industrial action, which can already be seen to be wavering in the period 1977 to 1979 when some of his decisions had the effect of rendering certain types of primary action unlawful, seems by 1981 to have become subjugated to a commitment to protect the interests of persons not parties to the dispute. In 1969 he had acknowledged that to render primary industrial action unlawful because of its secondary consequences would render the right to strike illusory. "Nearly every trade union official who calls a strike—even on due notice . . . —knows that it may prevent the employers from performing their contracts. He may be taken even to intend it. Yet no one has supposed hitherto that it was unlawful; and we should not render it unlawful today."[63] No such appreciation of the consequences of the decision is to be found in Lord Denning's judgment in *Hadmor*. However, his decision in *Hadmor* indicates not merely that Lord Denning had changed his mind. To render primary action unlawful because of its secondary consequences was to undermine entirely the carefully wrought structure of section 17 of the 1980 Act, by which all primary action and some forms of secondary action were to be lawful. The conclusion suggests itself that Lord Denning's policy of restriction of the legality of industrial action now operated independently of Parliamentary decision in the area.

The facts of *Hadmor Productions Ltd.* v. *Hamilton* presented a classic example of the tort of intimidation. The defendants, a full-time union official and a

---

[62] [1981] I.C.R. 690.
[63] *Torquay Hotel Co. Ltd.* v. *Cousins* [1969] 2 Ch. 106, 138.

shop steward employed by Thames Television, threatened to black the screening by Thames of a series of programmes made by the plaintiff company, an independent "facility" company which produced programmes for television, unless Thames agreed not to show the programmes. The defendants were thus threatening to break their contracts of employment or (and in the case of the union official only) to induce others to do so, unless Thames acted to the commercial disadvantage of Hadmor (though not unlawfully as between Thames and Hadmor since Thames was under no contractual obligation to show Hadmor's programmes). It will be recalled that in *Stratford* v. *Lindley* Lord Denning had sought to preserve a similar case from the impact of the decision in *Rookes* v. *Barnard* by analysing the defendants' acts in terms of threats to induce breach of contract rather than of threats to break contracts. That was, no doubt, a rather artificial distinction, but it indicates Lord Denning's approach at that time and points up the contrast with 1981. More significant is the fact that intimidation consisting of threats to break or induce breaches of contracts of employment was rendered non-actionable by the Trade Disputes Act 1965, which protection was restored by the first version of the Trade Union and Labour Relations Act in 1974 (*i.e.* by virtue of the clause substituted by the then Opposition), and which protection the Government in 1980 had not intended to take away in section 17 since the action threatened was to be taken by employees of the employer with whom the employees had a dispute.[64]

In short, the defendants seemed to be fully protected by section 13(1) of the 1974 Act, unless either there was no furtherance of a trade dispute or the defendants' acts could be analysed in terms of some tort other than that of intimidation which would not be protected by section 13. Lord Denning adopted both methods of attack. As to the first point, "the dispute was not a trade dispute at all . . . . It was an attempt to dictate to Thames Television the way in which they should conduct their business."[65] In support of this view he cited *B.B.C.* v. *Hearn*, his first restrictive decision after 1976 and the only one to have been approved by the House of Lords in 1979 and 1980, in which a threatened blacking of television transmissions to South Africa was held not to arise out of a trade dispute as defined in section 29 of Trade Union and Labour Relations Act because the dispute was not connected with any of the matters listed in that section. In *Hadmor*, however, as Lord Diplock, subsequently delivering a judgment in the House of Lords in which all the other members of the House concurred, had no difficulty in showing, "the evidence is all one way . . . that A.C.T.T. members employed by Thames on production of material for transmission feared that if programmes produced by facility companies were transmitted instead of programmes which Thames was capable of producing itself, this might lead to redundancies at the Hanworth and Teddington studios."[66] That fear of future redundancies was enough to bring the dispute within the area of trade disputes was shown by previous decisions, notably the judgment of Lord Denning himself at Court of Appeal level in *General Aviation Services* v. *T.G.W.U.*,[67] a case with "significant parallels" at a factual level with

[64] See para. 17 of the working paper on secondary industrial action, quoted above at n. 61.
[65] [1981] I.C.R. 706.
[66] [1982] I.C.R. 114, 123.
[67] [1975] I.C.R. 276.

Hadmor. There the Court of Appeal had had no difficulty in finding a trade dispute to exist though the relevant definition in the Industrial Relations Act 1971 was significantly narrower than that in operation in 1981. No element of fear of redundancies was present in the *B.B.C.* case, which was "clearly distinguishable."[68]

Lord Denning's second line of argument, logically necessary only if there was a trade dispute, was to show that the defendants had committed the tort of interference with business by unlawful means, the unlawful means being the intimidatory threats to break or induce breaches of the contracts of employment. He arrived at this result by construing one particular subsection of the 1980 Act (s.17(8)) as having revoked trade dispute immunity for secondary action generally. How was this view to be reconciled with the fact that the rest of section 17 contained a set of rules for distinguishing between protected and unprotected secondary action, to which section 17(8) was no more than a consequential tail-piece to avoid conflict with existing legislation? Lord Denning contented himself with dismissing the detailed provisions of section 17 as incomprehensible, and therefore in some way irrelevant to the effect of the section as a whole:

> "On reading through the Employment Act 1980, and especially section 17 on secondary action, I confess to a sense of bewilderment. It is the most tortuous section I have ever come across. After a careful re-reading, I think I can discern the general legislative purpose of section 17. It is to retain the statutory immunity for primary action, but to remove the immunity for secondary action. It means that trade union officials who call out men in a dispute with their employer are not liable for acts directed against the employer (primary action), but they are liable for acts directed against his customers or suppliers or other traders (secondary action). Some species of secondary action are given immunity by subsections (3), (4) and (5), but these are so confusing that I cannot attempt to summarise them. Suffice it to say that the general legislative purpose is to make secondary action unlawful and actionable when it directly interferes with the business of any customer or supplier or other trader—not party to the dispute—who suffers by it."[69]

Matters have surely come to a pretty pass when a judge feels free in effect to strike out parts of a statute as being void for uncertainty, and the House of Lords, speaking through the single opinion of Lord Diplock, had again wearily to assert the necessity of giving effect to statutes rather than to an imaginary preferred version of them. Lord Diplock said:

> "Lord Denning M.R. looked at subsection (8) of section 17 of the Employment Act 1980 in isolation, divorced from all the other provisions of the section of which it formed a part . . . My Lords, it seems to me, with great respect, that such a conclusion [as to the significance of the repeal of section 13(3) of TULRA] could never be reached by applying any of the accepted principles of statutory construction, even if section 17(8) had stood alone as a separate section

[68] [1982] I.C.R. 114, 124.
[69] [1981] I.C.R. 710–711. It is in any case doubtful whether *Hadmor* presented an example of secondary action as defined by section 17, since the industrial action was being threatened by employees of an employer with whom the employees were effectively in dispute.

of the Employment Act 1980. Standing as it does as the last of eight subsections in a section dealing with a selective withdrawal of immunity from certain kinds of secondary action which satisfy the carefully defined requirements of subsections (3), (4), or (5), it seems to me to be quite impossible to ascribe to subsection (8) a meaning which, in the way the earlier subsections are drafted, would make them wholly ineffectual; since it would impose liability in tort for all secondary action as defined in subsection (3), including secondary action which satisfied the requirements of subsections (3), (4), or (5)."[70]

Since the *Hadmor* decision, Lord Denning has made it quite clear in his extra-judicial pronouncements that he thinks that the placing of limits on the powers of trade unions to cause injury by industrial action is a self-evidently paramount policy against which the judges should be free to assess the adequacy of parliamentary legislation. In his book, *What Next in the Law*[71] he says:

"I wish, too, that we had had some doctrine—authorising judicial review of statutes—when we had the recent spate of cases on the Trade Union Acts of 1974 and 1976,"[72]

and indicates that he regards the 1980 Act as an insufficient response to the House of Lords trilogy:

"The decision of the House of Lords provoked much comment. It showed that the statutes gave the trade unions such considerable immunity that they could damage great industries—and destroy the nation itself—on the plea that they intended to further a trade dispute. In consequence, Parliament passed a statute, the Employment Protection Act 1980 (*sic*), to limit the immunities given to the trade unions. This went some way but not very far."[73]

Those responsible for the 1980 Act may well feel some sense of injustice at this disparagement of their efforts, since they had taken pains, as we have noted above,[74] to embody in statute law what they had seen as the burden of the Court of Appeal's decisions in the period 1976 to 1979. Lord Denning then goes on to vindicate his claim to have identified the true policy of the 1980 Act in *Hadmor*, only to be reversed in this by the House of Lords, and finally implies that the Employment Bill 1982 was needed to put right the damage done by the House of Lords in *Hadmor*:

"Now there is another bill before Parliament designed to put fetters on unfair actions by trade unions. Will it be passed into law? If it is, will it succeed? Time will show?"[75]

---

[70] [1982] I.C.R. 114, 130. Their lordships' displeasure was increased by the fact that Lord Denning had referred to *Hansard* to bolster his conclusions as to the significance of the repeal of section 13(3), a point on which he had already recently been repudiated by the House in *Davis* v. *Johnson* [1979] A.C. 264, and had compounded his error by referring only to the speeches of the Opposition, which suggested that the repeal of section 13(3) endangered the legality of primary industrial action, and had not mentioned the speeches of the Government side, which stated that no such result was intended or achieved.

[71] Butterworths, London, 1982.

[72] p. 321 (quoting apparently from his Dimbleby lecture of 1980).

[73] pp. 321–322.

[74] p. 406.

[75] *Op. cit.* p. 322.

It seems somehow appropriate to conclude this analysis with Lord Denning's own statement in these words of his view of the proper direction of the law in this field. One might otherwise have hesitated to attribute such a position to him.

Lord Denning and the Law of Collective Bargaining

This is a small chapter in the account of Lord Denning's activities in the field of labour law, but it is nevertheless an interesting one for the light it sheds on his attitudes towards the legislation passed between 1974 and 1976. The chapter is a small one because, as is well known to students of labour law, the widespread development of collective bargaining in Britain in the century after 1850 was achieved without the active support of the law, although public policy by and large was in favour of collective bargaining from the First World War onwards. Only in the wake of the Report of the Donovan Commission of 1968 was legislation to this end introduced, and yet so rapidly has the pendulum swung that in 1980 the centre-piece of this type of legislation, the statutory recognition procedure, was repealed. It was primarily in relation to the statutory recognition procedure introduced in 1975 that Lord Denning's views in this area were articulated and it is upon the decisions concerning it that we must concentrate. But the Employment Protection Act 1975 did not contain the first statutory procedure. That was to be found in the Industrial Relations Act 1971.

In the Act of 1971 the recognition machinery operated under the general supervision of the National Industrial Relations Court.[76] Applications arising out of recognition disputes were first to be referred to the N.I.R.C., which, after carrying out a screening process, would refer them to the Commission on Industrial Relations for investigation. Some attempt was made in the statute through definitions of "bargaining unit" and "bargaining agent" to provide criteria external to the C.I.R. as to how it should exercise its discretion. Any recommendation of the C.I.R. in favour of recognition could be enforced by a reference to compulsory unilateral arbitration if the employer did not bargain with the union, but only if the recommendation had been approved in a ballot ordered by the N.I.R.C. by a majority of the workers covered by the recommendation. During the period of the reference industrial action over the dispute was illegal, as was such action subsequently which was designed to undermine the C.I.R.'s recommendations.

Given the central position of the N.I.R.C. in this process litigation was inevitable, as were appeals to the Court of Appeal. The latter court heard two such appeals in recognition cases, one of which was to be significant as a pointer to later disagreements. In *T.S.A.* v. *Post Office*[77] the broad issue was raised as to how far recognition was seen as a way of promoting good industrial relations (as opposed to being an end in itself) and how far as a right conferred upon groups of workers (or even individual workers) to be represented by the union of their choice. In a simple recognition dispute,

---

[76] Industrial Relations Act 1971, ss. 44–54.
[77] [1974] I.C.R. 97. The other case heard by the Court of Appeal was *N.U.B.E.* v. *Mitsubishi Bank* [1974] I.C.R. 200 where the matter turned in Lord Denning's view on the issue of the legal enforceability of the agreement between union and employer.

where on the one hand there is an employer who refuses to recognise any union at all and, on the other, a single union with membership amongst the relevant employees, the divergence between the two views does not manifest itself to any great extent. Where, however, the employer's objection is not one to the principle of collective bargaining but is that the particular union in question is not appropriate and the basis of the lack of appropriateness in the employer's view is something other than the level of support that the union has, then the two views can lead to very difficult results. It only adds poignancy to the situation if the union being thus excluded is a small union not affiliated to the T.U.C., whilst the main beneficiary of the exclusion is a large T.U.C. affiliate.

The *T.S.A.* case in fact stemmed from an act of withdrawal of recognition by an employer. Because of the tendency of civil service employees to form separate unions for each separate grade of employee, the Post Office in the early years of the century had recognised a large number of unions—65 by 1920—and had then spent much of the period after 1944 trying to reverse the results of this initial thoughtlessness. By 1970 about 10 unions were recognised, one of the largest of which was the Union of Post Office Workers, which was affiliated to the T.U.C. The Telecommunications Staff Association, not affiliated to the T.U.C., had been formed as a breakaway union from the U.P.W. in 1928 by disgruntled male telephonists (female telephonists were mainly in the U.P.W.) and the Post Office had recognised it for bargaining purposes, although the U.P.W. had secured the T.S.A.'s exclusion from the Council of Post Office Unions, a joint negotiating body. In 1951 an independent committee recommended that the U.P.W. and the T.S.A. should amalgamate and that if this did not occur the Post Office should re-examine its policy of dual recognition. In 1970 the amalgamation movement broke down when on the point of apparent success; the Post Office at the request of the U.P.W. withdrew recognition from the T.S.A.; the T.S.A. applied under the 1971 Act for sole bargaining rights in respect of all telephonists; and the N.I.R.C. refused to refer the issue to the C.I.R. on the grounds that it was inconceivable the C.I.R. would do other than confirm the recently created status quo. Both the Court of Appeal and the House of Lords[78] overruled the N.I.R.C. on the grounds that the Court was prejudging the findings of the C.I.R. and was attempting to make the Court's screening process a more elaborate one than Parliament had intended. For Lord Denning, however, the matter was clearly of greater significance than a question of the proper distribution of functions between court and agency. Referring to litigation earlier in the year between the union and the Post Office arising under a different section of the Act but out of the same facts, he said: "This is another round in the struggle between a small trade union . . . and a big organisation of workers . . . ." In that earlier litigation he had said that "this case reminds me of the story of David and Goliath, with a difference. Goliath is winning all along the line."[79] In particular Lord Denning saw the withdrawal of recognition from the T.S.A. as the result of the rivalry between the T.S.A. and the U.P.W. and of the pressure put by the U.P.W. on the Post Office, and he seemed to ignore the evidence that management policy also was to reduce the number of unions

---

[78] [1974] I.C.R. 658.
[79] *Post Office* v. *Crouch* [1973] I.C.R. 366. 375.

with which the Post Office bargained. He was particularly anxious to reject as a legitimate element in the N.I.R.C.'s reasoning the fact that the U.P.W had said it would not bargain jointly with the T.S.A., a statement no doubt aimed at forestalling a C.I.R. recommendation to that effect. Such a threat amounted to "the use by a big organisation of workers of a big stick."[80]

If Lord Denning had fears that the recognition procedure contained in the 1971 Act could be used to entrench the position of big unions at the expense of small ones and that big unions could use their industrial power to undermine what was seen as the impartiality and rationality of the statutory process for deciding upon recognition claims, then these fears were likely to be increased in respect of the recognition procedure contained in the Employment Protection Act 1975, which replaced that of the 1971 Act. The element of judicial supervision was removed entirely. Recognition issues, which could now be raised only by trade unions and not, as under the 1971 Act, by employers and the Secretary of State as well, were to be raised directly with the Advisory, Conciliation and Arbitration Service, the administrative agency which replaced the C.I.R. ACAS, unlike the C.I.R., which had been run by commissioners who were appointed as experts, was under the control of a tripartite Council, whose members were only in part appointed as experts and were in the majority representatives of either T.U.C. or C.B.I. ACAS was to carry out enquiries and make recommendations much in the manner of the C.I.R., but ACAS was given virtually no statutory guidance on the criteria for recognition but was rather expected to develop these itself with the help, no doubt, of the C.I.R.'s experience. Recommendations by ACAS in favour of recognition attracted the sanction of compulsory arbitration without the need for any intervening ballot, and there were no special restrictions upon the use of industrial action over recognition claims.[81] This procedure was clearly very different from that of the 1971 Act, but, with the possible exception of the tripartite Council, was very much along the lines recommended by the Donovan Commission.

The Commission had remarked that its proposals avoided "the difficulty of detailed intervention by the courts in the processes of industrial relations which appears to us to be a consequence of enforcing recognition by law as in the U.S.A."[82] This was to prove a sanguine analysis of the extent to which the courts could be excluded. No direct appeal was provided from the recommendations of ACAS, but the courts did intervene on the basis of their general powers of review, to the extent that ACAS was at one stage moved to comment as follows: "To reconcile the conflicting approaches of the two sides of industry to a matter like trade union recognition the Service has to find ways in which compromises can be reached. This essential discretion is now seen, as a result of judicial decisions, to be much narrower than the Service originally understood was Parliament's intention."[83] This remark was made in the aftermath of two Court of Appeal decisions in particular, *U.K.A.P.E.* v. *ACAS*[84] and *E.M.A.* v. *ACAS*,[85] both of which were later

---

[80] [1974] I.C.R. 97, 108.
[81] Employment Protection Act 1975, ss. 11–16.
[82] *Op. cit.* para. 256.
[83] Letter from Chairman of ACAS to the Secretary of State for Employment, June 29, 1979, reprinted in ACAS, *Annual Report 1979*, Appendix C.
[84] [1979] I.C.R. 303.
[85] [1979] I.C.R. 637.

overruled by the House of Lords in early 1980[86] (at about the same time as
the House was overruling the Court of Appeal's decisions in the trade
dispute cases). These two cases allowed Lord Denning to articulate most
clearly his attitude towards the 1975 procedure, but his attitudes were
already becoming clear in the first, and most controversial, of the
recognition cases, *Grunwick Processing Laboratories* v. *ACAS*,[87] in which the
House upheld the Court of Appeal.

The *Grunwick* case, although the most publicly controversial, was perhaps
the least interesting legally and least restrictive of ACAS of the three cases.
Some of the employees of Grunwick had gone on strike, been dismissed and
had joined a trade union, APEX, which, *inter alia*, made an application to
ACAS for recognition in respect of the relevant classes of worker (both
striker and non-striker). ACAS distributed a questionnaire to the strikers,
whose names and addresses were supplied by the union, to ascertain their
attitude towards recognition but failed to persuade the employer to provide
the names and addresses of the non-strikers, who accordingly could not be
circulated. Both Court of Appeal and House of Lords held the subsequent
ACAS recommendation in favour of recognition void on the grounds that
ACAS had not discharged its statutory duty to "ascertain the opinions of the
workers to whom the issue relates,"[88] even though this failure stemmed from
the refusal of the employer to co-operate with ACAS. Lord Denning rejected
in terms the argument that the statute should be given a liberal construction
so as to forward the policy of the statute which was to encourage collective
bargaining and trade union recognition.

> "In all cases of statutory interpretation I am in favour of a liberal
> construction. But 'liberal' can be used both ways. Not only in
> construing powers, but also in construing safeguards. This statute
> makes great powers available to trade unions. By means of it they can
> bring immense pressure on an employer who does not wish to recognise
> a trade union and on his workers who do not wish to join a trade union.
> The union can go to ACAS and get a recommendation for recognition
> and thence to the committee and get an award. By that award there can
> be inserted in every man's contract terms and conditions to which
> neither he nor his employers have agreed. Such an interference of
> individual liberty could hardly be tolerated in a free society unless there
> were safeguards against abuse. So I would construe these safeguards in
> favour of the individual and not in favour of the trade union."[89]

The *Grunwick* case exposed a weakness in the Employment Protection Act
that it did not require employers to co-operate with ACAS's enquiries, but
the courts' decisions went only to the means ACAS should employ in
carrying out its enquiries and did not purport to specify the criteria ACAS
should use in deciding whether to grant or refuse recognition. That,
however, was the result of the Court of Appeal's decision in *U.K.A.P.E.* v.
ACAS and the decision thus constituted a much greater fetter upon ACAS's
activities. In that case the United Kingdom Association of Professional
Engineers, a small trade union not affiliated to the T.U.C., which aimed to

[86] [1980] I.C.R. 201 and 215.
[87] [1978] I.C.R. 231.
[88] Employment Protection Act 1975, s.14(1).
[89] [1978] I.C.R. 231, 237.

recruit senior engineers and adopted moderate policies as far as the use of industrial action was concerned, had recruited a number of such employees in the employ of W.H. Allen Ltd. and an ACAS questionnaire revealed that nearly four fifths of these employees wished to be represented in collective bargaining by U.K.A.P.E. The employers, however, refused to recognise that union on the grounds that, through their membership of the Engineering Employers' Federation, they were parties to a national recognition agreement for the industry concluded with the Confederation of Shipbuilding and Engineering Unions, a grouping of T.U.C. unions. Under the national agreement, TASS, a T.U.C. affiliate, had been granted recognition in respect of grades including professional engineers, although it was a minimal form of recognition falling short of recognition for the purposes of collective bargaining. Only 10 per cent. of the professional engineers at W.H. Allen wished to be represented by TASS and TASS was not in fact recognised by the employer for collective bargaining in respect of the professional engineers.

The issue was obviously a difficult one for ACAS, forcing it to choose between its general and particular statutory duties as described in section 1 of the 1975 Act. "The Service shall be charged with the general duty of promoting the improvement of industrial relations, and in particular of encouraging the extension of collective bargaining . . . ." Not to recommend in favour of U.K.A.P.E. would be to leave the professional engineers in effect unrepresented; to recommend in favour would probably have a deleterious effect upon industrial relations, both at W.H. Allen because of the predictable response by TASS (which was recognised in respect of lower-level technicians) and in the industry in general, because it would undermine the purpose of the E.E.F./C.S.E.U. agreement, which was to reduce the number of unions recognised in the industry and the consequent problems of overlapping and fragmented trade unionism. To Lord Denning this latter conclusion was unacceptable. His judgment gave no credence to the view that the choice of result was one Parliament had intended ACAS to make. Instead he plunged straight into the merits of the case, which he found to lie wholly with U.K.A.P.E. It was, he said, "another story of David and Goliath. By which I mean a small trade union pitted against a giant one. . . ."[90] The desires of the "big battalions" (both TASS and the employers) should not be able to override the wishes of the employees at W.H. Allen, and especially not by threats of industrial action. For ACAS to take account of threats of industrial action was to make it "the tool of the powerful trade unions. It would cease to be an independent and impartial tribunal as it ought to be. It would become the lackey—to grant or refuse recognition—as the powerful trade unions decreed."[91] ACAS had ignored "the rights of the individual members of U.K.A.P.E."[92] which, in a remarkable flight of fancy, were seen to include, on the basis of the right of association contained in article 11 of the European Convention on Human Rights, the right to have the union of their choice recognised by the

---

[90] [1979] I.C.R. 303, 310.
[91] *Ibid.* p. 314.
[92] *Ibid.* p. 316.

employer.[93] Consequently, of the two duties mentioned in section 1 of the
Act the particular should prevail over the general.

The strong thread of emotion running through Lord Denning's judgment,
equalled in labour law cases perhaps only in his judgment in *A.N.G.* v.
Wade,[94] which was delivered three months later, was in strong contrast with
the measured prose of their lordships in the House of Lords who, routinely
as it seemed at the time, overruled the Court of Appeal's decision when it
came before them for consideration in early 1980, at a time when the
Government had already published its proposals to abolish the statutory
recognition procedure. Delivering the leading judgment Lord Scarman
reasserted the view that Parliament had intended ACAS as the expert body
to make the decisions on industrial relations issues, and the limits of judicial
review must be set with that overriding fact in mind.

> "The purpose of Part I of the Act being to promote the improvement of
> industrial relations, Parliament has selected machinery which consists
> of an independent, expert, advisory service, ACAS, and an arbitral
> body, the Central Arbitration Committee. The courts have no part to
> play other than to exercise their function of judicial reviiew in the event
> of a challenge to the legality of any act or omission on the part of the
> bodies entrusted by statute with the duty of promoting the improve-
> ment of industrial relations. Since the Act makes no provision for
> appeal to the courts in the event of a party's dissatisfaction with an
> ACAS report, it is plain that it is Parliament's intention that
> recognition issues are for ACAS and the Central Arbitration Commit-
> tee. It is their discretion, their judgment, which is to determine such
> issues.
>
> Of course, it does not follow that the courts have no role to play.
> Judicial review of the lawfulness of the actions of the two statutory
> bodies is available to an aggrieved party or person . . . But the Courts
> will not tell a statutory body how it is to conduct its business or what
> decision, report or recommendation it is to make. They will invalidate
> the exercise of a statutory body's judgment or discretion only if satisfied
> that no reasonable person charged with the body's responsibilities
> under the statute could have exercised its power in the way that it did.
> Applying the principle to this case, the courts will not invalidate the
> ACAS report unless satisfied that no reasonable advisory, conciliation
> and arbitration service, with a due appreciation of its statutory duties
> and responsibilities, could have reported as it did."[95]

Similar issues were raised in *E.M.A.* v. *ACAS*, which also involved TASS
and which provoked Lord Denning to quote Magna Carta: "To none will we
sell, to no one will we delay or deny right or justice."[96] Again the House of

---

[93] The right to have the union of one's choice recognised goes, of course, far beyond the right to
join the union of one's choice, and even the latter principle is controversial. See *Young, James
and Webster* v. *U.K.* [1981] I.R.L.R. 408 (European Court of Human Rights), *Cheall* v. *APEX*
[1983] I.C.R. 398, and above, p. 376. Lord Denning would probably not have extended this
right to have a trade union recognised so far as to embrace ineffective unions. See his narrow
interpretation of "independence" as applied to trade unions in *Squibb U.K. Staff Association* v.
Certification Officer [1978] I.C.R. 115.

[94] [1979] I.C.R. 664.

[95] [1980] I.C.R. 210–211.

[96] [1979] I.C.R. 652.

Lords reasserted ACAS's discretion, but this time only by a majority held that ACAS had not abused its discretion by excessive delay.

Although the Employment Act 1980 repealed the statutory recognition procedure, the history of Lord Denning's recognition decisions has an interesting tail-piece. Nationalised industries have long been under specific obligations in their constitutive statutes to bargain with appropriate trade unions, and in 1980, as an issue under the Post Office Act 1969, the Post Office's policy of reducing the number of unions it bargained with returned to the Court of Appeal for judicial scrutiny in *R.* v. *Post Office, ex parte A.S.T.M.S.*[97] One of the many small unions recognised by the Post Office early in the century had been the Telephone Contracts Officers' Association, with some 1000 members. Again the Post Office proposed amalgamation, with a union that was a member of the Council of Post Office Unions, as a solution to its problems. This time, unlike with the T.S.A., amalgamation occurred, but, to everyone's surprise, not with the post office union but with A.S.T.M.S., a big T.U.C. affiliate but not a member of the Council. As Lord Denning put it, "out of the blue a big outside union came in."[98] The Post Office refused to recognise A.S.T.M.S. as the representative of the contracts officers and the Council refused to admit it to membership. Lord Denning rejected A.S.T.M.S.'s complaint. No longer was there any stress on the rights of the individual employees or upon any improper pressure applied by the Council unions. Now the emphasis was upon management's need to reduce the number of unions it bargained with. A.S.T.M.S. was not the carrier of individual rights but an "outside body."

> " . . . The Post Office say that far more efficiency can be obtained when there are only a few unions within the Post Office, which are members of the Council of Post Office Unions. That council can negotiate on one level with the Post Office without the intrusion of an outside body like the A.S.T.M.S. The Post Office pointed out that, if they were to recognise this section of the A.S.T.M.S., in future they would have to negotiate with two sets of people. On the one hand the Council of Post Office Unions: and on the other hand with this section of A.S.T.M.S. separately: because this section is not a member of the council. If they had to have separate negotiations, there would be a danger of disagreement, and a danger of 'leap-frogging.' As soon as one grade arrived at a settlement, another grade would say: 'We ought to go higher,' and the like. The Post Office, in these circumstances, say: 'If we are to reach pay settlements sensibly; if we are to achieve the restructuring of grading sensibly; and if we are to carry out the objectives of recognition, we should consult with the Council of Post Office Unions and not have the intrusion of an outside body. This section—although nominally independent—will be under the umbrella of the A.S.T.M.S.; and they will bring undesirable pressures to bear on our negotiations with our own people.' That seems to me an approach which cannot be faulted."[99]

No doubt it would be too cynical to attribute this very different approach

[97] [1981] I.C.R. 76.
[98] *Ibid.* p. 79.
[99] *Ibid.* p. 80.

solely to a reluctance on Lord Denning's part to cast A.S.T.M.S. in the role of David. Nevertheless, it is notable that policies and considerations that had been held to be unconvincing when prayed in aid by an administrative agency were without fault when used by an employer to discharge an obligation imposed directly upon it to consider which unions it was appropriate for it to recognise. At this point one seems to have crossed the boundary between public and private law and to be back in the latter area, where the starting point for analysis is the overarching fact of managerial prerogative.

Lord Denning and Individual Employment Law

Over the years a good deal of attention has been lavished upon Lord Denning's activity in certain aspects of Labour Law. His efforts on behalf of the individual *vis-à-vis* the trade union are well known.[1] Latterly, his activities in the area of trade disputes have attracted some attention.[2] His decisions in the area of trade union recognition dominated the discussion of that topic in the late 1970s.[3] In the area of individual employment law he is not so generally perceived to have a particular stance. But in some ways it is in that area that his whole approach to Labour Law is most roundly contained and fully expressed. That important fact is rather obscured from the perspective of the present-day academic[4] labour lawyer. Our view of individual employment law is dominated by its statutory element—the statutory "floor" of individual employment rights. From that perspective, Lord Denning's approach is apt to seem casuistic and to lack any very obvious dominating patterns. But it is very different if one takes a longer view encompassing the whole of his legal career. One then sees a powerful unifying theme running through his decisions and writings in this area. It becomes clear that he is a great protagonist of the common law of the contract of employment—as some say,[5] of the common law of master and servant. In recent years we have for the most part regarded that body of law as notable for its archaism and for its failure to match the realistic and reasonable social expectations of workers at large, especially in the matter of remedies for dismissal.[6] For Lord Denning, however, the common law of master and servant figured as a much more vigorous and significant body of law than such an analysis would suggest. In order to understand why and in what sense that is so, we need to examine his decisions and writings in this area. They span a whole era.

The involvement with the common law of the contract of employment began during Lord Denning's early days at the Bar. During that time he acted as one of the editors of *Smith's Leading Cases*, taking an active part in the

---

[1] See above, pp. 368–377.
[2] See above, pp. 388–411.
[3] See above, pp. 411–418.
[4] It is hoped that the juxtaposition in "The Family Story" is purely coincidental between the statements "Moral—Despise not your Enemy" (p. 98) and "Moral for Judges: Don't Despise the Academics." (p. 197).
[5] It is a terminology to which Lord Denning himself often reverts, especially as to "servant." Thus, (significantly as we shall see) in *Western Excavating (E.C.C.) Ltd.* v. *Sharp* [1978] I.C.R. 221, 224F—"Until recently, an ordinary servant had no security of tenure."
[6] *Cf.* Clarke (1969) 32 M.L.R. 532.

preparation of the thirteenth and last edition, which appeared in 1929.[7] We know that he was personally concerned[8] with the annotation to the master and servant case of *Cutter* v. *Powell*[9] (which concerned the recoverability of a seaman's wages where he died before completion of the voyage). Comparison with the previous edition shows that he developed and brought into prominence in the annotation the principle that the right to wages depends upon whether the consideration has been performed. This principle provided a rationale for denial of wages by reference to the servant's misconduct or his absence due to sickness in certain instances.[10] It also provides a reconciliation between cases to that effect and other older cases establishing that the relationship of master and servant continues during sickness and that the master remains responsible for the maintenance of the servant during such periods,[11] a paternalist view of the employment relationship derived particularly from domestic and agricultural service, to which Lord Denning would in general terms subscribe. It was a theme to which he returned in a casenote in the *Law Quarterly Review* in 1939[12] in order to provide a refutation of the proposition appearing to emerge from *Marrison* v. *Bell*[13] that wages were generally presumed to continue during sickness. The principle as developed by Lord Denning there and elsewhere permits the legal expression of a notion of moral entitlement to wages and of limits on that moral entitlement which is a recurring theme in his judgments—a legal version of the idea of a fair day's work for a fair day's pay. In *Secretary of State for Employment* v. *ASLEF (No. 2)*[14] he deduces from this general idea the proposition that "Wages are to be paid for services rendered not for producing deliberate chaos" and that accordingly wilful disruption of the work of the undertaking by means of a work-to-rule is a breach of contract going to the whole of the consideration. In *Chappell* v. *Times Newspapers Ltd.*[15] he advances readiness and willingness to work on the employee's part as a pre-condition for equitable relief against an employer's threat to treat employment as at an end, so that employees threatening future industrial action were debarred from such relief. In each case he refers the proposition back to his notes to *Cutter* v. *Powell*.[16]

Comparable with Lord Denning's use of these doctrines of consideration

---

[7] "Sir Thomas Willes' duty was to edit a new edition—the 13th. He asked two of us young men—Cyril Harvey and me—we had each taken Firsts at Oxford—to help him. It was an immense task—involving much research. But it taught me most of the law I ever knew." *The Family Story*, p. 94.

[8] "I was bold enough to be drastic in some of my notes—rewriting them and suggesting new principles—especially those in the leading cases of *Lampleigh* v. *Braithwaite, Cutter* v. *Powell* and *Taylor* v. *Caldwell.*" *ibid.*

[9] (1795) 6 T.R. 320.

[10] S.L.C., Vol. II, pp. 48–50.

[11] See *loc. cit.* p. 49.

[12] (1939) 55 L.Q.R. 353 "At first I was short of silk's work. I wrote an article or two for *The Law Quarterly Review*" (*Family Story*, p. 101).

[13] [1939] 2 K.B. 187. Lord Denning's case-note was influential—see Freedland, *The Contract of Employment*, pp. 110–111—and its arguments were recently adopted in *Mears* v. *Safecar Security Ltd.* [1981] I.C.R. 409, 418B (where the case-note is incorrectly cited).

[14] [1972] I.C.R. 19, 56B-F.

[15] [1975] I.C.R. 145, 174 B-H.

[16] [1972] I.C.R. 19, 56D, [1975] I.C.R. 145, 174D. The principle has recently been invoked by other judges in the Court of Appeal as the basis of denial of wages to employees engaged in a work-to-rule—*Henthorn and Taylor* v. *C.E.G.B.* [1980] I.R.L.R. 361.

and mutual conditionality of obligations as a means of doing justice between employer and employee has been his preparedness to associate implied contracts and restitutionary obligations with the master and servant relationship as a means of achieving just results. Indeed, as in other aspects of contract law,[17] Lord Denning implicitly asserts the same continuity between contract, implied contract and quasi-contract as typified the common law before the advent of the Victorian emphasis on express promise as the basis of obligation.[18] A major instance of his development of restitutionary principles occurred in *Reading* v. *The King*[19] where Lord Denning, at that time a puisne judge, declared at first instance:

> "There are many cases in the books where a master has been held entitled to the unauthorised gains of his servant or agent . . . . The master's claim in those cases does not rest in contract or in tort, but in the third category known as restitution . . . ."[20]

Lord Denning's technical creativeness in this penumbra of contract was further illustrated in two of his early decisions in the Court of Appeal in *James* v. *Thomas Kent Ltd.*,[21] and in *Powell* v. *Braun*.[22]

Moreover, the decisions of the 1940s, 1950s and early 1960s show that Lord Denning was not without a moral stance (or perhaps a series of moral stances) in this area of law. His decisions reflected a distinctly patriarchal and paternalistic outlook upon the employment relationship. He adopts what is to some extent a pre-industrial model of the relationship in which mutual social obligation is emphasised. In this he is following a long-standing judicial tradition[23] which tends primarily to emphasise the employee's obligations and especially to view him as subject to a general obligation of fidelity. As Denning J. he made a resounding declaration to that effect in *Reading* v. *The King*[24]—note how the opening words mark the personal identification with this rule:

---

[17] See Atiyah, Chap. 2.

[18] See Atiyah, *The Rise and Fall of Freedom of Contract* (1979), pp. 149–152.

[19] [1948] 2 K.B. 268 upheld on appeal, ultimately to the House of Lords, *sub nom. Reading* v. *Att.-Gen.* [1951] A.C. 507.

[20] [1948] 2 K.B. 268, 275.

[21] [1951] 1 K.B. 551. The employed director of a small company which ran a garage was enabled to sue for wrongful dismissal despite technicalities arising out of the Statute of Frauds—technicalities which had formed the subject of what is believed to be Denning's first published legal writing, an article in the *Law Quarterly Review* (1925) 41 L.Q.R. 79, and his first contribution to the law of master and servant.

[22] [1954] 1 W.L.R. 401.

[23] He typifies the pattern of development of the common law as a whole in relation to the contract of employment, as described by Alan Fox (*Beyond Contract: Work, Power, and Trust Relations* (1974), pp. 186–190). Fox points out how this picture of attitudes towards the employment relation is complicated by another strand—the ethic of work as a redemptive activity (*ibid.* p. 188). Compare Lord Denning in *Langston* v. *A.U.E.W.* [1974] I.C.R. 180, 190C-F—"A skilled man takes a pride in his work. He does not do it merely to earn money. He does it so as to make his contribution to the well-being of all. He does it so as to keep himself busy and not idle. To use his skill and to improve it to have the satisfaction which comes of a task well done. Such as Longfellow attributed to *The Village Blacksmith*:
> 'Something attempted, something done,
> has earned a night's repose . . . '
To my mind, therefore, it is arguable that in these days a man has, by reason of an implication in the contract, a right to work."

[24] [1948] 2 K.B. 268, 275.

"In my judgment, it is a principle of law that if a servant, in violation of his duty of honesty and good faith, takes advantage of his service to make a profit for himself in this sense, that the assets of which he has control, or the facilities which he enjoys, or the position which he occupies, are the real cause of his obtaining the money, as distinct from being the mere opportunity for getting it, that is to say, if they play the predominant part in his obtaining the money, then he is accountable for it to the master."

Lord Denning was to return to the theme of the employee's duty of fidelity in *Secretary of State for Employment* v. *ASLEF (No. 2)*[25] where he developed the notion of the implied duty not wilfully to defeat the aims of the contract.[26] But in the 1950s and early 1960s he was mainly concerned with the obligations imposed on the employer by the traditional paternalistic principles of master and servant law. This concern appears in a series of cases, mainly as a preoccupation with ensuring that insurers standing in the shoes of employers did not try to shed the social liabilities which employers should bear in return for the subordination of the employee to them by master and servant law. Thus in *Jones* v. *Manchester Corporation*[27] a hospital authority, presumably at the instance of their insurers, sought an indemnity from an inexperienced young woman doctor who had administered an anaesthetic negligently. Denning L.J. denied the existence of an implied right of indemnity and remarked rather acidly that

"[A]t one time masters used to insure their servants against liability. This case seems to show we are approaching a time when servants will have to insure their masters."[28]

He reiterated the principle even more strongly in *Romford Ice and Cold Storage Co. Ltd.* v. *Lister*[29] where the reproach to insurers for not respecting the traditional restraints is made very clear:

"Many a master has been made responsible for the mistakes of his servants, but never has he sought to get contribution or indemnity from his servants. One obvious reason is that it is not worth while . . . . The other reason is no doubt the reluctance of a good master to visit the risk of accidents on to his servants . . . . It seems that these reasons no longer commend themselves to employers or rather to their insurers."[30]

A further indication of Lord Denning's traditional paternalistic stance occurred in his famous partial dissent in *Close* v. *Steel Company of Wales*[31] where he held that the fencing provision of section 14 of the Factories Act 1937 imposed an obligation to fence the dangerous machine and parts in, as well as to fence the worker out. He said of the earlier cases to that effect that

[25] [1972] I.C.R. 19.
[26] [1972] I.C.R. 19, 55F–56G.
[27] [1952] 2 Q.B. 852.
[28] [1952] 2 Q.B. 872.
[29] [1956] 2 Q.B. 180, reversed [1957] A.C. 555. *sub nom. Lister* v. *Romford, etc.*
[30] [1956] 2 Q.B. 180, 186. The same point was made again by him in *Morris* v. *Ford Motor Co.* [1973] Q.B. 792, 798.
[31] [1962] A.C. 367. According to Robert Stevens, this partial dissent was the basis of his reputation as the champion of the workers. (*Law and Politics* (1979) p. 496). See the criticism of that reputation as "not entirely deserved" at note 313 on that page.

"By so holding they have given a protection to the workman which the common law *itself* does not give."[32] [emphasis added].

There is an implication here that in imposing health and safety obligations the Factories Act was doing no more than pursuing the aims of the common law. In fact the common law largely abandoned the paternalist approach to the employment relationship in relation to industrial accidents, and the Factories Acts were necessary to remedy a severe deficiency in this respect. But although historically somewhat tendentious, Denning's statement is a good indication of what he viewed as the proper goal of the common law in this area.

This all goes to show why Lord Denning, however much of a radical thinker he may be in contract law generally, is very much of a traditionalist in relation to the contract of employment. It is important for the purpose of our subsequent discussion to realise that this is pre-eminently true of his approach to the termination of the contract of employment. Here it would seem that Lord Denning has some sympathy with the idea of a full and unfettered freedom, so far at least as the common law is concerned, to limit the duration of the employment relationship by contract, and to dismiss the employee for misconduct within that duration. Even by 1977 his position in this respect was equivocal. In *Western Excavating (E.C.C.) Ltd.* v. *Sharp*[33] he sounds initially somewhat critical of the common law position:

"Until recently, an ordinary servant had no security of tenure. He could be dismissed on a month's notice or a month's salary in lieu of notice, although he might have served his master faithfully for years."[34]

But then a few sentences later we get what is surely a defence of the common law position:

"So, whereas at common law an employer could dismiss a man on a month's notice or a month's wages in lieu, nowadays an employer cannot dismiss a man even on good notice, except at the risk of having to pay him a large sum should the industrial tribunal find that the dismissal was unfair."[35]

Lord Denning did not at any stage seek to challenge that basic common law position. One might think of *Barnard* v. *National Dock Labour Board*[36] as an exception. There he was in the vanguard of the movement to subject the powers of a disciplinary tribunal—here the London Dock Labour Board having powers of suspension and dismissal over registered dock workers—to judicial control. But it was clear that his willingness so to hold was dependent not on his identifying the problem as one of security of tenure for the employee, but, on the contrary, on his being able to *distinguish* between this case and the ordinary employment situation.

This remained Lord Denning's stance in relation to the termination of ordinary contracts of employment, and in the years immediately preceding the advent of unfair dismissal legislation he gave more than one decision in

---

[32] [1962] A.C. 367, 388.
[33] [1978] I.C.R. 221.
[34] [1978] I.C.R. 221, 223F.
[35] [1978] I.C.R. 221, 224G.
[36] [1953] 2 Q.B. 18.

that vein. Thus in *Richardson* v. *Koefod*[37] he refused to associate tenure with
the ordinary contract of employment by applying the old notion of an
implied yearly hiring, and in *Graves* v. *Whitby U.D.C.*[38] he refused to treat a
chief officer in public employment as anything other than an ordinary
employee although the relevant nationally agreed conditions of service
treated even a subordinate officer as entitled to procedural safeguards in
relation to dismissal. Moreover, in *Cowling* v. *Matbro Ltd.*[39] he showed
himself fully committed to the common law position whereby an employer is
free to justify a dismissal by reference to misconduct on the employee's part
not known to the employer at the time of the dismissal and therefore not
acted upon when dismissing:

> "I have no doubt that if an employer, after the trial, discovers that the
> servant was guilty of other misconduct—other than that of which he has
> been acquitted—this court may, in its discretion, grant a new trial and
> allow the employers to plead and prove this freshly discovered
> misconduct, rather than let the servant retain a judgment contrary to
> the justice of the case."[40]

It is more than slightly daunting to find Lord Denning in 1969 dealing with
a procedural point in an employee's *civil* action for wrongful dismissal in
terms heavy with overtones of criminality on the employee's part ("trial",
"guilty" "acquitted" "freshly discovered misconduct," etc.) It is somewhat
redolent of the Victorian combination of, on the one hand, the master's
freedom of contract to hire and fire as he chooses and, on the other hand, a
treatment of the employee's misconduct as the criminal violation of social
obligations under the Master and Servant laws.[41] Let us consider in light of
all this how Lord Denning responded to the creation from the mid-1960s
onwards of the statutory floor of individual employment rights which was
placed beneath the common law structure we have described.

Lord Denning in fact reacted to the new legislation very much as a
traditionalist and an exponent of master and servant law. This is not to say
that he simply set his face against the new statutory framework. His
reactions were much more complex than that. They were responses to
particular aspects of the new statutory structure rather than to its existence
as a whole. The touchstone was and remained the common law of master
and servant. The underlying question for Lord Denning was whether the
aims and effects of the legislation could be seen as broadly consistent with
those of the common law. If so, he would be ingenious in its support. If not,
he would keep it within narrow bounds. This meant that he generally took a
cautious approach towards the legislation, especially where the legislation
seemed to him to threaten that freedom of action that the common law of

---

[37] [1969] 1 W.L.R. 1812.
[38] [1970] 1 Lloyd's Rep. 517.
[39] [1969] 1 W.L.R. 598.
[40] [1969] 1 W.L.R. 598, 601. It was precisely this position that the House of Lords was later to
vindicate in *Devis (W.) & Sons Ltd.* v. *Atkins* [1977] I.C.R. 662 where the unfair dismissal
legislation was regarded as a "rogues' charter" in so far as it was inconsistent with this
position, (see *per* Lord Diplock at p. 672F).
[41] For details of the master and servant laws see Freedland, *The Contract of Employment*, pp.
137–139, 144–145.

master and servant accorded to the master. He accepted that the statutes constrained employers not to abuse their powers but was reluctant to see those powers fundamentally curtailed.

This approach has one particular aspect of great significance for the judicial role generally. Since 1971, successive governments have accepted the necessity for a specialist court of appeal of High Court status from industrial tribunals (which are the tribunals of first instance for the application of individual employment legislation). From 1971 to 1974 there was the National Industrial Relations Court. From 1975 to 1976 there were particular judges in the Queen's Bench Division who specialised in employment cases. Since then we have had the Employment Appeal Tribunal. Successive Presidents first of the N.I.R.C.[42] and then of the E.A.T.[43] have each developed a distinctive approach to individual employment legislation and have maintained a considerable degree of commitment to the aims of the legislation as each of them has viewed those aims. They have in effect taken a series of internal perspectives upon the legislation. The picture is very different when individual employment cases go from the specialised appellate tribunal to the Court of Appeal and the House of Lords. In the House of Lords there is a certain sense of remoteness from the policies of the legislation[44] verging at times upon an open lack of comprehension.[45] In Lord Denning's Court of Appeal there was more of a distinct external perspective upon the legislation—there was in a sense a concern to integrate its results into a common-law pattern. It is worth examining the consequences of this approach in relation to the major items of individual employment legislation.

The first such statute to be the subject of Lord Denning's decisions was the Redundancy Payments Act 1965. In the early years at least Lord Denning showed some sympathy with the policy of requiring employers to pay lump sums to employees being made redundant. He viewed it as compensation for long service.[46] It did not restrict the employer's freedom of action, especially as the payments were partly rebatable[47] from the state redundancy fund. There were what seemed to him adequate controls upon unreasonable claims by employees. He said in the first redundancy payments case to come before the Court of Appeal, *O'Brien* v. *Associated Fire Alarms Ltd.*[48]

> "The scheme of the Act is this: If a man has served his employer for two years or more and is then dismissed because they have no work for him, he is entitled to be paid a redundancy payment: but if he is dismissed because of his own conduct he is not entitled to a redundancy payment. Nor is he so entitled if the employer offers him suitable alternative employment which he unreasonably refuses."

[42] Sir John Donaldson, P.
[43] Sir Raymond Phillips, P. (1976–1978), Sir Gordon Slynn, P. (1978–1981), Sir Nicolas Browne-Wilkinson, P. (1981–1983).
[44] *Cf. Devis (W.) & Sons Ltd.* v. *Atkins* [1977] I.C.R. 662.
[45] *Cf. De Rosa* v. *John Barrie Ltd.* [1974] I.C.R. 480.
[46] See *Lloyd* v. *Brassey* [1969] 2 Q.B. 98, 102: "It is in a real sense compensation for long service. No man gets it unless he has been employed for at least two years by the employer, and then the amount of it depends solely upon his age and length of service."
[47] *Ibid.* p. 104G. "Bridge J. thought that might be hard on the [new employer] but that is the policy of the Act. After all, most of the payment is borne by the Redundancy Fund."
[48] *O'Brien* v. *Associated Fire Alarms Ltd.* [1968] 1 W.L.R. 1916, 1922.

On the other hand, it was offensive to Lord Denning that employees should receive redundancy payments on merely technical grounds if their jobs had not really disappeared. This seemed to him to be the position where a farmer sold his farm and the purchaser took over the farmworkers. In *Lloyd* v. *Brassey*[49] he applied an inclusive approach to the concept of "transfer of a business" to produce the result that there was no liability to redundancy payments on such a transfer. Lord Denning was clearly irritated that the statutory formulation suggested an analysis at variance with the ordinary result as it would appear to a common lawyer:

> "[The claimant] was not dismissed at all—let alone dismissed by reason of redundancy. He remained in the same job doing the same work as before but at an increased wage. It would seem absurd to suggest that he is entitled to redundancy payment. But the Divisional Court have held that he is entitled to it. It is all because of some 'deeming' provisions in the Act whereby a thing is deemed to be that which it is not."[50]

Equally for Lord Denning it was not for the employer to produce subjective criticisms of the employee as a way of denying him a redundancy payment to which he was in substance entitled. In *Hindle* v. *Percival Boats Ltd.*[51] he dissented to this effect in the case of a carpenter who was dismissed by a firm of boat builders during a process of changeover from wood to fibreglass boats. Lord Denning gave full effect to the statutory presumption of redundancy in those circumstances, and vindicated the loyalty that he sees a good employer as owing to his long-serving employees.[52]

Again in *Marriott* v. *Oxford Co-op Society Ltd. (No. 2)*[53] Lord Denning clearly felt that it was not right for an employer to deny the employee a redundancy payment by imposing a less desirable job on the employee and then taking technical advantage of the employee's having tried the new job for a short time before finally leaving. The statute did not make proper provision for trial periods. This had eventually to be done by a later statute.[54] There was also a trap for the unwary employee in that the legislation seemed to require him to leave *without notice* if he was to treat the employer's imposition of a change of terms as a dismissal.[55] Lord Denning was prepared to overcome both these problems in favour of the employee by a manipulation of the common law of the contract of employment which he later admitted was rather extreme.[56] The merits of the case were clear enough to him to justify this.[57]

The *Marriott* case represented the high point of Lord Denning's preparedness to stretch individual employment legislation in favour of employees. There followed a couple of minor decisions on the Redundancy

---

[49] [1969] 2 Q.B. 98.
[50] *Ibid.* pp. 102G-H.
[51] [1969] 1 W.L.R. 174.
[52] *Ibid.* pp. 181A-B.
[53] [1970] 1 Q.B. 186.
[54] Employment Protection Act 1975, Sched. 16, Pt. I (see now Employment Protection (Consolidation) Act 1978, s.84).
[55] This was the so-called "no-notice trap" resulting from the terms of s.3(1)(*c*) of the Redundancy Payments Act 1965. It was also eliminated by the Employment Protection Act 1975; see now Employment Protection (Consolidation) Act 1978, s.83(2)(*c*).
[56] *Western Excavating (E.C.C.) Ltd.* v. *Sharp* [1978] I.C.R. 221, 227 A-C.
[57] [1970] 1 Q.B. 186, 192B-C.

Payments Act in which his tone is sympathetic to the worker's case but his construction of the Act is essentially cautious.[58] The note of caution became sharper in *Woodhouse* v. *Peter Brotherhood Ltd.*[59] where it was held, against the employee, that there was no continuity of employment where an employee was transferred on the sale of a factory, because the new owner had put the factory to a different use. This narrow view was not what one might have expected after *Lloyd* v. *Brassey*[60]; but in this case Lord Denning seems to have been at pains to restrain rash innovation on the part of the newly founded Industrial Court, whose President, Donaldson J., had ruled, in favour of the employee, that continuity was preserved if the working environment of the employees was not affected by the transfer. Lord Denning specifically overruled this approach.[61] One feels that in so holding, Lord Denning was refusing to construe the legislation from the perspective of the employee and was refusing also to allow the Industrial Court a free hand to develop a specialised approach to the interpretation of labour legislation. There is a sharp contrast with his own willingness to be innovative when using the techniques of the common law of the contract of employment.

There then followed a group of decisions in which Lord Denning set about placing what he regarded as due restrictions on the use that could be made of the redundancy payments legislation, restrictions directed particularly against the use of that legislation to protect working practices maintained by trade unions against the interests of employers. In this group of cases there are two major themes, the first concerned with overtime working and the second concerned with employees' resistance to unilateral variations in terms and conditions carried out by employers to save labour costs in the, by then, developing conditions of recession. Thus, firstly, in *Tarmac Roadstone Holdings* v. *Peacock*[62] and in *Gascol Conversions* v. *Mercer*[63] he brought about the exclusion in most situations[64] of overtime hours from the calculation of the week's pay for the purposes of redundancy payments. He insisted that for industrial workers the formal contract of employment, typically incorporating[65] the basic working week collectively agreed at national level, should be the determinant of "normal working hours." He made the reasons for so holding very clear:

> "[I]t is a very great advantage to the men to have short working hours of 40 hours a week—on basic rates—with considerable overtime work—on overtime rates . . . . No doubt the union feel that the advantages outweigh the disadvantage. The men cannot have it both ways. Having committed themselves by written agreement to normal working hours of 40, they cannot go back on it."[66]

---

[58] *Hetherington* v. *Dependable Products Ltd.* (1970) 9 K.I.R. 183; *Lee* v. *Barry High Ltd.* [1970] 1 W.L.R. 1549.

[59] [1972] I.C.R. 185.

[60] [1969] 2 Q.B. 98, see above, p. 425.

[61] [1972] I.C.R. 186, 203F-G.

[62] [1973] I.C.R. 273.

[63] [1974] I.C.R. 420.

[64] Specifically, from the *Tarmac* case, in all cases except where it is contractually obligatory upon the employer to provide the overtime concerned and upon the employee to work it.

[65] The incorporation was by virtue of a statutory statement of terms and conditions of employment, treated on the facts of the *Gascol* case as amounting to a written contract of employment as such.

[66] [1974] I.C.R. 420, 426G-H.

The second and more important theme of this group of cases was that there was no liability for redundancy payment where an employer changed the terms and conditions of employment by way of a reorganisation in the interests of efficiency. This was applied first in *Chapman* v. *Goonvean & Rostowrack China Clay Co. Ltd.*[67] to a case where an employer's withdrawal of a free transport service to and from work made it impossible for certain workers to continue in their jobs. Then it was applied in *Johnson* v. *Nottinghamshire Combined Police Authority*[68] to a case where two women clerks at a police station were dismissed when they refused for domestic reasons to change from normal hours and a five-day week to a shift system and a six-day week. Finally it was applied in *Lesney Products Ltd.* v. *Nolan*[69] to a case where nine machine setters at a toy factory refused to accept a change from one day shift with much overtime to a system of two shorter day shifts.

This line of cases creates a very significant restriction on the right to redundancy payments. It is sharply at variance with Lord Denning's habitual concern with the law of the contract of employment, for it differentiates between the employee's job and his terms and conditions of employment. He was clearly much impressed with the need to avoid a repetition of two cases in the late 1960s[70] where employees had obtained redundancy payments despite—indeed by means of—their refusal to abandon restrictive or inefficient working practices. Lord Denning, in equating the problem in *Chapman* with problems of that kind, displayed a new attitude to the role of redundancy payments which is not typical of his earlier judgments: "It is very desirable in the interests of efficiency, that employers should be able to propose changes in the terms of a man's employment for such reasons as these: so as to get rid of restrictive practices; or to induce higher output by piece work; or to cease to provide free transport at an excessive cost."[71] It is rather as if, as his judgment in *Gascol* suggests, he came to view the redundancy payments legislation as a battleground on which collective conflicts between management and unions were being fought out. In that situation one finds him concerned to vindicate the principles of the law of the contract of employment, and in particular the freedom of the employer, having given due notice to terminate the contract of employment, then to offer further employment on such terms as he may decide.

Presumably after the *Chapman* and *Johnson* decisions he felt that sufficient had been done to indicate the proper bounds of redundancy payments liability,[72] for his subsequent decisions in this area are free of that pre-occupation and display a greater willingness to view the issues from the perspective of the individual employee.[73] Indeed in both *Evenden* v. *Guildford*

---

[67] [1973] I.C.R. 310.
[68] [1974] I.C.R. 170.
[69] [1977] I.C.R. 235.
[70] *Dutton* v. *Bailey Ltd.* (1968) 3 I.T.R. 355; *Line* v. *White & Co.* (1969) 4 I.T.R. 336.
[71] [1973] I.C.R. 310, 315E.
[72] By the time of the *Lesney* case, for example, Lord Denning is clearly less convinced of the policy pursued in the *Chapman* case and refers to the decision as a very difficult one: [1977] I.C.R. 235, 237B, 239F.
[73] See, in addition to the *Evenden, Ioannou* and *Globe Elastic* cases (below), *Wood* v. *York City Council* [1978] I.C.R. 840.

City Football Club[74] and *B.B.C.* v. *Ioannou*,[75] the law of the contract of employment is deployed to operate in the worker's favour. They are decisions protective of, even paternalistic towards, the employee in the manner of the *O'Brien*[76] *Hindle*[77] and *Marriott*[78] cases. In the *Evenden*[79] case, the doctrine of promissory estoppel and the statutory presumption of continuity were used to sidestep the statutory provisions that had been strictly construed in *Woodhouse* v. *Peter Brotherhood*[80]; the employer was held to his moral obligations in the traditional Denning manner:

> "Mr. Evenden entered into his employment with the football club on the faith of the representation that he would not be prejudiced and that his employment should be regarded as a continuous employment. Acting upon it, he has lost any right against the supporters club. The football club cannot be allowed to go back on it."[81]

In the *Ioannou* case,[82] the employee is protected by the placing of careful limits upon the statutory provisions enabling the employee to waive in advance his rights to redundancy payments and under the unfair dismissal legislation.

Hence, if one accepts an analysis which sees Lord Denning as concerned with a balance of collective interests in his redundancy payments decisions in the early seventies, it would seem then that he had ceased to feel that was a central concern by the mid-seventies so far as redundancy payments were concerned. It is, after all, important to remember that he had no general hostility to the policy of the redundancy payments legislation though he does on the other hand seem to have had his own conception, based on the law of the contract of employment, of the proper parameters within which the legislation should operate. It may well be that he felt that the particular issues raised by the cases of the early 1970s challenged those limits, in a way that the claims made in the later cases did not. There may also have been some feeling by the mid-1970s that it was in the area of unfair dismissal legislation that the balance of collective interests had to be located, and it is to the consideration of his decisions on that topic that we now turn.

Within the period 1972 (when the unfair dismissal provisions of the Industrial Relations Act 1971 came into force[83]) to the end of 1981, Lord Denning took part in 26 Court of Appeal decisions on the law of unfair dismissal. In many ways, Lord Denning's reactions to the unfair dismissal

---

[74] [1975] I.C.R. 367; (employing football club estopped from denying continuity of employment between themselves and supporters' club); applied by Lord Denning in Court of Appeal in *Secretary of State for Employment* v. *Globe Elastic Thread Co.* [1978] I.C.R. 104, but overruled by H.L. in that case; [1979] I.C.R. 706.

[75] [1975] I.C.R. 267; (definition of "fixed-term contract"—partially overruled by Lord Denning's Court of Appeal in the unfair dismissal case of *Dixon* v. *B.B.C.* [1979] I.C.R. 281).

[76] See above, p. 424.

[77] See above, p. 425.

[78] See above, p. 425.

[79] See above, n. 74.

[80] [1972] I.C.R. 186; see above, p. 426.

[81] [1975] I.C.R. 367, 374 C-D.

[82] See above, n. 75.

[83] On February 28, 1972. The case for the making of legislation about unfair dismissal had been developed in Ch. 9 of the Donovan Commission Report (1968) (Cmnd. 3623).

legislation as expressed in these decisions are closely parallel to his reactions
to the redundancy payments legislation. The two sets of reactions were not
contemporaneous; there is a time lag very roughly corresponding to the six
years by which unfair dismissal legislation followed after redundancy
payments legislation. It is important indeed to avoid too mechanistic a view
of this parallel; each of the two sets of developments was influenced by the
other, by other developments in Labour Law and by changes in industrial
society at large. Nevertheless, one can detect a pattern comparable with the
one we have already examined in relation to redundancy payments whereby
Lord Denning accorded a positive reception to the legislation in its early
years; then became more cautious in relation to it; and then set about
restricting it to what he regarded as its proper sphere of operation. Even
more directly than in relation to the redundancy payments legislation, Lord
Denning's touchstone throughout was the common law of master and
servant, both as a source of principles and value judgments and as a source
of regulatory techniques. Again it is necessary to trace this pattern
chronologically through the cases.

Rather curiously, Lord Denning's first reaction to the new legislation
appeared in a case decided before it came into force. In *Hill* v. *C.A. Parsons
Co. Ltd.*[84] a member of the United Kingdom Association of Professional
Engineers successfully sought an injunction against his purported dismissal,
which had taken place at the instance of the Draughtsmen's and Allied
Technicians Association by way of an attempt by that union to achieve a
closed shop in the company.[85] The Court of Appeal held that it was
appropriate to depart from the normal rule against enforcement *in specie* of
contracts of employment, in order to maintain the *status quo* until the unfair
dismissal provisions came into effect. In this context, Lord Denning spoke of
the new provisions approvingly as conferring "important rights on workers
in respect of membership of trade unions"[86] and emphasised the power they
conferred to recommend re-engagement as well as that of awarding
compensation.[87] It is a case where both the values and the techniques of the
common law of the contract of employment are seen by Lord Denning as
available in support of the new legislation. An injunction, in his view, both
could and should be granted because this was not a case where the mutual
confidence between employer and employee had broken down.

Once the legislation came into effect, the issues that came before Lord
Denning's Court of Appeal were more individual than collective in nature;
and his approach, although equally as approving as in *Hill* v. *Parsons Ltd.*,
becomes different. He seems in that first period to have viewed the unfair
dismissal legislation as a kind of broadening out of the redundancy
payments legislation—as a process of making sure that long and faithful

---

[84] [1972] Ch. 305.

[85] This was not to be the last judicial intervention into the dispute with U.K.A.P.E. at Parsons
Ltd.—see *Parsons Ltd.* v. *A.U.E.W. (TASS)* [1972] I.C.R. 151 (N.I.R.C.)—nor Lord
Denning's last visit to the dispute between DATA (which became TASS) and U.K.A.P.E.—
see *U.K.A.P.E.* v. *ACAS* [1979] I.C.R. 303, above p. 414.

[86] [1972] Ch. 305, 315C.

[87] *Ibid.* p. 315F. The Trade Union and Labour Relations Act 1974 added a power to
recommend *reinstatement* as well as re-engagement (Sched. I, para. 17(1)) and the
Employment Protection Act 1975 turned these into powers to *order* rather than to recommend
(s.71). (See now Employment Protection (Consolidation) Act 1978, s.69). But these have
proved purely nominal changes.

service does not go unrewarded in appropriate cases, which may not be confined to redundancy cases. He made this very clear in the first such case, that of *Smith Cabinets Ltd.* v. *Brindle*.[88] Note how the legislation is now seen entirely in terms of compensation; the reference to re-engagement in *Hill* v. *Parsons Ltd.*[89] has gone (rarely to recur):

> "At common law [the employee] could have been dismissed on reasonable notice. I should have thought she would have been entitled to three months notice. She would not have been entitled to any compensation for her long service or for loss of office. Just three months notice. No more. Now the Act of 1971 made a great difference. An employer is not allowed to dismiss a servant unfairly without compensation. The Act gives an employee a right in his job which is akin to a right of property. The employer can no longer give the legal notice and say: 'Out you go, without compensation.' "[90]

In that case[91] therefore, Lord Denning led the Court of Appeal in holding that where notice of dismissal was given before the Act came in, to expire after the Act came in, the employer could not escape the Act by wrongfully in breach of contract refusing to let the employee work out her notice. The employer could not invoke the common law to defeat the statute in relation to the so-called "straddling notice."

To very comparable effect was another "straddling notice" case, that of *Lees* v. *Arthur Greaves Ltd.*[92] where the Court of Appeal again rejected a preliminary objection taken on behalf of the employer, this time that the employee in accepting payment in lieu of part of his notice had terminated this employment by agreement with his employer and so had not been dismissed. Lord Denning said stoutly, "I decline to infer any agreement by him when it would mean that he would be deprived of any compensation,"[93] and he took the point that the employer's argument would, if accepted, defeat not only straddling notice cases but cases of notices given after the Act came into force.[94] In another case of payment in lieu of notice decided at more or less the same time, *Dedman* v. *British Building Appliances Ltd.*,[95] the problem was that the employee seemed to fall outside the then prevailing limitation period of four weeks.[96] Lord Denning's Court of Appeal, while intent on finding for the employee, declined to do so by means of a notional extension of the period of employment and preferred to achieve the result by means of a liberal interpretation of the "practicability" criterion for the limitation period. One has the impression that Lord Denning would not have been reluctant to use contractual techniques, but was positively concerned to provide relief against the over-short limitation period: "seeing

[88] [1973] I.C.R. 12.
[89] [1972] 2 Ch. 305, 315F.
[90] [1973] I.C.R. 12, 21A-C.
[91] Where the employee, a secretary who had been in the employment of a furniture company for 26 years, was dismissed three months after it was taken over by a merchant banker, the judgment states, without experience in the trade. (See *ibid*. 20B-E).
[92] [1974] I.C.R. 501.
[93] *Ibid*. p. 505D-E.
[94] *Ibid*. p. 505E-F.
[95] [1974] I.C.R. 53.
[96] Extended to three months by the Trade Union and Labour Relations Act 1974 (see now Employment Protection (Consolidation) Act 1978, s.67(1)). *Cf. Walls Meat Co. Ltd.* v. *Khan* [1979] I.C.R. 52.

that the time limit is so strict, it is a comfort to find that there is an 'escape clause.' "[97]

Then a note of caution crept in in *Abernethy* v. *Mott Hay and Anderson*[98] which concerned an argument about whether it was fair to dismiss a civil engineer ostensibly for redundancy but in fact for inflexibility and lack of suitability for promotion. Lord Denning seems to have felt that where an industrial tribunal had adjudged the dismissal fair, the appellate courts should not lend themselves to legalistic arguments of unfairness. The employer had acknowledged a liability for redundancy payment of some £850 (a further reason for grounding the dismissal in redundancy) and had offered an *ex gratia* payment of £750. So there had been compensation for long service. Lord Denning who had hitherto stressed that *contractual* questions were matters of law for the appellate courts,[99] remarked sharply that, "It must be remembered in all those cases that the appeal from the tribunal is only on law. There is no appeal on fact."[1]

A cautious attitude towards the legislation again made itself felt in *Hare* v. *Murphy Brothers Ltd.*,[2] where the issue was whether a foreman could claim that his employment subsisted during eight months' imprisonment for unlawful wounding, so that he could treat as a dismissal the employer's refusal to take him back when he was released from prison. Lord Denning, in reacting sharply against a doctrine propounded in the Industrial Court, took a distinctly restrictive position against the type of claim being advanced on behalf of the employee.[3] One wonders whether Lord Denning felt that the legislation, which he had come to view very much as being about compensation rather than about re-engagement, was being too readily invoked to seek over-large compensation from employers who had already acknowledged some responsibility to compensate for dismissal as in the *Abernethy* case.[4] Thus he says here, with more than a trace of reproach:

> "[The employers] did make him an *ex gratia* payment of £150 which eventually he cashed. So he has had that. But he now seeks further compensation."[5]

From then onwards Lord Denning did not take part in any decisions on the law of unfair dismissal until 1977, with the exception of *B.B.C.* v. *Ioannou*,[6] a decision on contracting-out of both redundancy payments and unfair dismissal legislation in which he leant against employers seeking to contract out.

But, towards the end of 1977, Lord Denning within the space of one month delivered five judgments on the law of unfair dismissal which were all of great general significance. Between them these decisions seem to represent a decisive attempt on Lord Denning's part to set up the appropriate

---

[97] [1974] I.C.R. 53, 600.
[98] [1974] I.C.R. 323.
[99] *e.g. Lees* v. *Arthur Greaves Ltd.* [1974] I.C.R. 501, 504H.
[1] [1974] I.C.R. 323, 327C-D.
[2] [1974] I.C.R. 603.
[3] There is a distinct analogy in this respect with the decision in the redundancy payments case of *Woodhouse* v. *Peter Brotherhood Ltd.* [1972] I.C.R. 186 (see above, p. 426).
[4] [1974] I.C.R. 323.
[5] [1974] I.C.R. 603, 606C.
[6] [1975] I.C.R. 267.

guidelines for the interpretation of the unfair dismissal legislation; in fact to place it on a common-sense basis which had the common law as its principal starting-point.

In *Retarded Children's Aid Society* v. *Day*[7] the Industrial Tribunal had held it to be fair but the Employment Appeal Tribunal had held it to be unfair to have dismissed a house-father of a home for mentally retarded people, run by a registered charity, for pursuing more severe methods towards the residents than those of which the charity approved. Lord Denning stressed that procedural objections to the fairness of the dismissal should not normally be treated as grounds for appeal (confined to points of law) from industrial tribunals.[8]

His judgment was a corrective, in fact and one suspects in intention, to the emphasis on fair procedure according to the Industrial Relations Code of Practice[9] which the Industrial Court had created and which the Employment Appeal Tribunal had started to renew.[10] It represents some degree of tacit working back to the common law position in which procedural objections cannot be advanced against a dismissal in the "ordinary case of master and servant"[11]; here, procedural considerations are being downgraded, though by no means totally excluded.

The process was taken a stage further very shortly afterwards in *Alidair Ltd.* v. *Taylor*[12] where an airline pilot had been dismissed following an inquiry held by the airline into a faulty landing apparently attributable to the pilot's error of judgment. The industrial tribunal found that the dismissal was rendered unfair by defects in the inquiry procedure. So Lord Denning could not as in the previous case validate the dismissal by reference to the wisdom and experience of the industrial tribunal. Instead he drew a distinction the full import of which has perhaps not been appreciated.[13] He said that the industrial tribunal had been wrong to assess whether the decision to dismiss had been reasonable as a function of whether the inquiry had been properly conducted; instead they should have considered simply whether it was reasonable to dismiss the pilot for flying his plane badly, bearing in mind that the employer was entitled to the benefit of a subjective test.[14]

This is a far cry indeed from the days of *Hindle* v. *Percival Boats Ltd.*[15] where he dissented from that very position in relation to redundancy payments. It seems to reflect a feeling on Lord Denning's part that the unfair dismissal

---

[7] [1978] I.C.R. 437.

[8] *Ibid.* p. 443C-G.

[9] Issued by the Secretary of State for Employment under the Industrial Relations Act 1971; superseded in this context by ACAS Code of Practice No. 1, Disciplinary Practice and Procedures in Employment (1977), to which "Highway Code" status is attached in industrial tribunal proceedings by s.6(11) of the Employment Protection Act 1975.

[10] A valuable account of this development down to 1978 is to be found in Anderman, *The Law of Unfair Dismissal* (1978), pp. 81–99.

[11] *Cf.* Lord Reid in *Ridge* v. *Baldwin* [1964] A.C. 40, 65.

[12] [1977] I.C.R. 445.

[13] Perhaps because Lord Denning was not alone among the appellate court judges in wishing to restrict the ambit of procedural objections to dismissal, and indeed was not up till that time the most prominent of the judges in that respect, because of the decision and dicta of the Court of Appeal and of the House of Lords in *Devis (W.) & Sons Ltd.* v. *Atkins* [1977] I.C.R. 662 in which, perhaps significantly, he had played no part.

[14] [1978] I.C.R. 445, 450C-F.

[15] [1969] 1 W.L.R. 174. See above, p. 425.

legislation had created too broad an area of challenge to decisions to dismiss, which it was now for the courts to reduce to proper proportions.

The next case in this group, that of *Nothman* v. *Barnet Borough Council*[16] was the occasion for some purposive[17] construction of the unfair dismissal legislation to prevent it from discriminating against a woman teacher by excluding her from remedies for unfair dismissal over the age of 60 where a man could have claimed up to the age of 65.

The two remaining cases in this group of five reflect clearly a sense that Denning was concerned to keep the law of unfair dismissal within the appropriate bounds. In *Massey* v. *Crown Life Insurance Co.*[18] the manager of an insurance company branch office had for five years before his dismissal opted to be treated as self-employed for tax purposes and had so agreed with the company. It was held that he could not in these circumstances claim remedies for unfair dismissal. Lord Denning said bluntly that

> "Having made his bed as being self-employed, he must lie on it,"[18a]

and he made it clear that he thought this would generally be the right approach to the building workers working on "the lump." It is a view of the correct sphere of the statute which is dominated by the contractual perspective on the employment relationship.

The same is pre-eminently true of the last in this group of cases, *Western Excavating Ltd.* v. *Sharp*[19] where the issue was whether constructive dismissal (*i.e.* exclusionary conduct by the employer entitling the employee to treat himself as dismissed) was to be tested by a broad concept of reasonableness or a more precise concept of contractual repudiation. In preferring the contractual test the Court of Appeal as a whole and Lord Denning in particular clearly saw the common law as a means of defence against extravagant development of the statutory framework:

> "The new test of 'unreasonable conduct' of the employer is too indefinite by far. It has led to acute difference of opinion between the members of tribunals. Often there are majority opinions. It has led to findings of 'constructive dismissal' on the most whimsical grounds. The Employment Appeal Tribunal tells us so. It is better to have the contract test of the common law. It is more certain; as it can well be understood by intelligent laymen under the direction of a legal chairman."[20]

The decision represents the triumph of Lord Denning's vindication of the principles of the common law in relation to the new statutory structure of individual employment law.

The common law of contract was seen by him as providing the basis for overturning the decision of the industrial tribunal; which comes somewhat strangely from one who had so recently, in the *Retarded Children's Aid Society* case,[21] insisted on the paramountcy of the industrial tribunal as the right judge of the facts in these cases.

---

[16] [1978] I.C.R. 336; upheld by H.L., [1979] I.C.R. 111.
[17] See *per* Lord Denning, [1978] I.C.R. 336, 344E. Lord Diplock, to whom Lord Denning ascribes the description of the "purposive approach," deals tartly enough with its use in this case—see [1979] I.C.R. 111, 113C.
[18] [1978] I.C.R. 590.   [18a] *Ibid.* p. 596D.
[19] [1978] I.C.R. 221.   [20] *Ibid.* p. 227F-G.
[21] [1978] I.C.R. 437, 443; see above, p. 432.

After that period of intense activity in the field, Lord Denning was involved in a number of further decisions in the following five years but their impact is more diffuse.

Two individual cases may be singled out for mention. More important of the two for its practical consequences was *Hollister* v. *National Farmers Union*[22] where the N.F.U. had reorganised its insurance business in Cornwall with consequential changes in the terms and conditions of its group secretaries in that area which the employee found unacceptable; he was dismissed as a result. Lord Denning's court held, with the industrial tribunal, and against the Employment Appeal Tribunal, that a reorganisation of this kind fell within the category of "some other substantial reason" (other, that is, than misconduct, redundancy and the other listed reasons)[23] capable of justifying dismissal; and that the failure of the employer to consult or negotiate with the group secretaries did not vitiate the fairness of the dismissal in its particular circumstances.

The tenor of his judgement is to the effect that necessary business decisions cannot be deflected either substantively or procedurally by the employees of the business. In this, there is an important continuity with the decision of Lord Denning's court in the redundancy payments case, earlier discussed, of *Chapman* v. *Goonvean & Rostowrack China Clay Co.*,[24] and the composite effect is to confer an extensive protection upon employers in carrying out reorganisations of their enterprises, in terms both of redundancy payments and of liability for unfair dismissal. By this, the freedom of action conferred by the common law of the contract of employment is extensively re-asserted.

The other judgment of Lord Denning for consideration is, by contrast with that in *Hollister,* more significant for the attitude it expresses than for its practical consequences. In *London Transport Executive* v. *Clarke*[25] an industrial tribunal had concluded, and had been upheld by the E.A.T in holding, that a bus mechanic had been unfairly dismissed after "taking off" for seven weeks absence without leave to Jamacia. The main argument against the employee was that he had dismissed himself by this absence and so could not claim to have been dismissed by his employer. The majority of Lord Denning's court rejected this doctrine of "self-dismissal," though they held the finding of unfairness to be perverse. But Lord Denning insisted that there were cases which fell to be classified as self-dismissal; justice and balance required it.[26]

The whole judgment is a vindication of the common law as a safeguard against the unacceptable consequences of the uncontrolled operation of the statute. Lord Denning emphasises the autonomy of the industrial tribunals and (with a trace of disingenuousness, perhaps) invokes his own assertion of that autonomy in the *Retarded Children's Aid Society* case[27] to show how perverse decisions on the part of tribunals can be controlled only by so defining dismissal as to deny them jurisdiction in the first place.[28] He says as much, in these terms:

[22] [1979] I.C.R. 542.
[23] *Ibid.* p. 547G.
[24] [1973] I.C.R. 50, see above p. 427.
[25] [1981] I.C.R. 355.
[26] *Ibid.* p. 364F-G.
[27] [1978] I.C.R. 437, 443, see above, p. 432.
[28] [1981] I.C.R. 355, 365H-366B.

"In the circumstances of this case, all members of this court think that this man should not be awarded thousands of pounds compensation— or any compensation. I think that, the only legitimate way of achieving this result is to hold that the man dismissed himself."[29]

So the common law is the *deus ex machina*; and who better to act as the high priest of that deity? Again Lord Denning's own words cannot be bettered:

"It is over 50 years ago now that I studied in depth the common law relating to the discharge of contract by breach or by incapacity or by repudiation. The result is to be found in *Smith's Leading Cases* (13th ed., 1929) Vol. II, pp. 46–56. I adhere to what I then said. All I would say is that nowadays some people seem to think that a contract is never discharged by a breach—no matter how fundamental unless it is accepted by the other side. That is a great mistake."[30]

So the answer lies not only in the common law, but in the true old common law. The wheel has come full circle from the time when Denning the young barrister took an especial interest in the common law of master and servant.[31]

By the 1980s, Lord Denning's rhetoric in unfair dismissal cases expresses a greater adherence to traditional master and servant law than most of his fellow judges would be prepared to admit to—thus in his Parthian shot in this field in *Woods* v. *W.M. Car Services Ltd.* [32] he expressed the implied term relating to mutual trust and confidence as being to the effect that "just as the servant must be good and faithful so an employer must be good and considerate [to his servants]."[33] But if by the 1980s Lord Denning seemed in unfair dismissal cases to be isolated by the form of his discourse, it should nevertheless be appreciated that the Court of Appeal as a whole fully vindicated the underlying substance of his judgments. It is clear in retrospect that the retrenchment upon the unfair dismissal legislation in which his Court of Appeal engaged in the *Western Excavating,*[34] *Alidair*[35] and *Retarded Children's Aid Society*[36-7] cases turned out to have set the pattern for the late 1970s. Moreover, in *Wass Ltd.* v.*Binns* [38] one sees the Court of Appeal taking a restrictive approach to procedural unfairness which carries this process of retrenchment even further than one thinks Lord Denning himself would have been prepared to do. So in the end Lord Denning turns out to have led the way both in the positive and the negative aspects of judicial reception of the new wave of individual employment legislation. Not only have we seen this to be the case with the redundancy payments and unfair dismissal legislation, but this would also seem to be true of his decisions in the area of legislation concerned with equal pay and discrimination in

[29] *Ibid.* at p. 366C.
[30] *Ibid.* at p. 362B-C.
[31] See above, p. 419. See his article, "Quantum Meruit" (1925) 41 L.Q.R. 79.
[32] [1982] I.C.R. 693.
[33] *Ibid.* p. 698E.
[34] [1978] I.C.R. 221, see above, p. 433.
[35] [1978] I.C.R. 445, see above, p. 432.
[36-7] [1978] I.C.R. 437, see above, p. 432.
[38] [1982] I.C.R. 486.

employment generally, of which considerations of space preclude more than a passing mention here.[39]

Conclusion—what is special about Lord Denning in relation to labour law?

Have we in this chapter done more than describe a commonplace position at great length? After all, there does exist independently of what we have written a well-developed critique of Lord Denning's judicial activities generally, not least in the other chapters of this book. And there is no shortage of articulate examination of his contribution to Labour Law—some of its choicest expressions being found in Law Lords' judgments. So can we claim to have done more than echo the voices that have already proclaimed Lord Denning as in general the arch-activist of his judicial era and in Labour Law the leading protagonist of laissez-faire anti-collectivism towards trade unions?

We think it may be possible to suggest some conclusions from what has gone before which may help to redeem it from these strictures. We have been conscious of a danger in what we have written that Lord Denning may have been viewed by us in excessive isolation from his fellow judges; in particular, that his usually concurring colleagues in the Court of Appeal may have been accorded too mute and inglorious a role by us. It is, it must be admitted, hard not to find his judgments, whatever their imperfections, more interesting than those of other judges.

It is, then, important to locate Lord Denning's labour law judgments in relation to those of the other appellate judges who decided the cases in question. This is fairly straightforward to do. There is on the whole a broad concurrence between Lord Denning and his colleagues in terms of the values and attitudes applicable to labour law issues, subject to a divergence about the proper role of the judiciary and the necessity for judicial restraint, the latter being on the whole more strongly felt in the House of Lords. We may seem again to be singing the old favourite tunes; but there is something to be gained by singing them in counterpoint with each other. For neither in the question of the proper role of the judiciary nor in the sphere of Labour Law has time stood still since Lord Denning became a judge in 1944. His judicial career has spanned an era which has seen very significant movements on both fronts, and he has often been at the centre of those developments. It is the interaction of these two aspects of his decisions which is so singularly

---

[39] Although Lord Denning's initial reaction to the equality legislation in *Peake* v. *Automotive Products* [1977] I.C.R. 968 was cautious, even questioning of its aims ("the natural differences of sex must be regarded even in the interpretation of an Act of Parliament") he later recanted from that view (*Ministry of Defence* v. *Jeremiah* [1980] I.C.R. 13) and gave the equal pay legislation especially a broad interpretation (*Shields* v. *E. Coomes (Holdings) Ltd.* [1978] I.C.R. 1159; *Clay Cross (Quarry Services) Ltd.* v. *Fletcher* [1979] I.C.R. 1). He was in part influenced by his desire to integrate fully into English law the provisions of the Treaty of Rome and of the directives made under it (see, *e.g.* his dissent in *Macarthys Ltd.* v. *Smith* [1979] I.C.R. 785). It is interesting, however, to note the limits to his broad approach. These were reached when the legislation seemed to stand in the way of the employer's freedom to reward his employees according to their merits (*National Vulcan Engineering Insurance Group Ltd.* v. *Wade* [1978] I.C.R. 800) or when it seemed to confer upon a governmental agency too great powers to obtain normally confidential information (*Science Research Council* v. *Nassé* [1978] I.C.R. 1124). See further on issues of equality legislation Chapters 4 and 7.

interesting, and which gives rise to so significant a process of comparison and contrast between him and his fellow-judges.

In, we hope briefly, developing this theme, it is useful to separate Lord Denning's decisions in, on the one hand collective labour law—trade dispute law, trade union law and the law concerning collective bargaining—and, on the other hand, in individual employment law, the law concerning the individual worker and his employer. This is a rudimentary and imperfect classification but nonetheless useful for present purposes. It gives labour lawyers a special frisson of anxiety to admit to such a distinction because it threatens a particular kind of fragmentation of our subject that we are in general terms committed to resisting. But with that disclaimer we shall use it here.

To begin, then, with the law of trade unions, trade disputes and collective bargaining. It has been here that Lord Denning's judicial activism has been relatively notorious, and also here that the values he applies correspond most closely to a stereotype of the role of the judiciary in labour law. But the very activism which ultimately drives a wedge between Lord Denning and many of his appellate colleagues, especially in the House of Lords, has its own particular roots and impulses which serve also to differentiate his stance towards labour law quite significantly from theirs. As we have seen, the area in which Lord Denning was first active among these three was that of trade union law. In terms of labour law, he was applying values about the autocracy and arbitrariness of trade union action towards some individuals that would not in themselves have been challenged by his colleagues. But he was often in dissent from them because the particular judicial activism embodied in his judgments was not acceptable to them. There are several aspects to this. Firstly, this mostly occurred when substantive formalism was in the ascendant. Lord Denning was later to establish a degree of personal judicial ascendancy which counteracted this, and judicial style was to some extent to swing towards a more activist position under his tuition. Secondly, it was an activism which grew from public law roots—indeed we have seen how it originated in relation to domestic tribunals generally and not just trade unions—and it was in that area that the substantive formalism of the 1940s and 1950s imposed some of the most powerful constraints.

By the end of the 1960s, however, there had been a sufficiently extensive development of administrative law to encompass the area of control of domestic tribunals and generally to meet Denning's concerns in that area. Thenceforth his decisions in the field of trade union law ceased to display the unity of purpose and crusader zeal they had shown earlier on. But in a sense—and here there is a development singular to Lord Denning himself—he comes during the 1970s to see trade dispute law and the law relating to collective bargaining as representing another front on which the same battle has to be fought. As his writings show, he envisages a real continuity between the abuse of trade union power in internal relations with which he was concerned in trade union law and the abuse of trade union power in external relations, the control of which he comes increasingly to view as the role of trade dispute law, and of the law relating to collective bargaining. Although he carries the Court of Appeal with him in this development, he encounters in the House of Lords a resistance to this new species of judicial activism—a resistance to the mounting of a major challenge to the Parliamentary determination of the appropriate regime for a highly politicised area of activity. This has some parallels with the original resistance to the public law challenge to executive discretion, which gave rise to his frequent isolation in the domestic tribunal cases of the 1940s and 1950s. This particular development is, of course, quite unique to Lord Denning and to labour law.

At some risk of avoiding the commonplace only at the cost of over-ingenuity, one can point to an interesting and again uniquely personal relationship between Lord Denning's development in collective labour law and his development in individual employment law. If his preoccupations in the area of collective labour law are essentially of a public law origin, his concerns in the area of individual employment are pre-eminently of a private law character. From the 1940s to the 1960s the existing framework of master and servant law comfortably accommodates his lively but underlyingly traditionalist approach to the issues that he confronts. For Lord Denning, the common law governing this essentially private law relationship is as fertile as the public law concerning domestic tribunals is barren; so far from challenging its limits, he works at the centre of its tradition.

But whereas in the area of trade union law, his initially *outré* propositions were by the 1970s largely co-opted by judicial and statutory developments, his traditionalist position in individual employment law was by that time in his eyes increasingly challenged by the development of a statutory framework of individual employment law. Although initially he felt there to be a continuity between the aims of master and servant law and the provisions of the new employment protection legislation, from the era of the National Industrial Relations Court onwards he came increasingly to view it as appropriate to deploy the common law of contract of employment as a means of curbing the excesses of individual employment legislation rather than as a means of furthering its ends. His fellow-judges in the Court of Appeal, while concurring in his decisions and for the most part agreeing with the value judgments involved, do not on the whole display the same fervour as he does in vindicating the positions of the common law of the contract of employment, just as they, during that period, concurred with his decisions but without his degree of activism in the area of collective labour law. Ultimately, by the close of the Seventies and the beginning of the Eighties this was to leave him in some degree of spiritual isolation from his appellate colleagues in relation to individual employment law, an isolation admittedly less marked than his more confrontational isolation in collective labour law, but in its own way just as much a product of his singularly personal history as a judge and law-maker.

PART II
LORD DENNING AND THE WIDER
WORLD OF LAW

CHAPTER 9

Lord Denning as Jurist

A.W.B. SIMPSON

The editors have given me a brief which, at first sight, must be rejected. It would clearly be quite inappropriate and presumptuous for me to attempt to *assess* Lord Denning as jurist. Such matters have to be left to history and to those informal mechanisms whereby opinion is formed. But I must, in the spirit of my subject, make sense and not nonsense of my instructions,[1] adopting a purposive and flexible approach. So I take it that I should write about the context in which such an assessment must be made, and about the place of jurists in legal development today.

I

What is a jurist anyway? *The Shorter Oxford Dictionary* is unhelpful—"one who practises the law," "one versed in the science of the law: a legal writer," "a student of the law, or one who takes a degree in law." The second sense is of some assistance, since it relates jurists to legal science. But something more is surely involved: the title is not simply descriptive but also honorific. But "jurist" is not an honorific title for a judge as such; being a judge, even an excellent judge, does not make a jurist. Across the Channel in France there are many judges but neither they nor anyone else regards any of them as jurists.[2] They are not regarded as having a significant role in the development of the law; their function is that of being the self-effacing servants and instruments of the law. In our system, too, where the major class of judges are laymen,[3] most judges are not viewed as potential let alone actual jurists. This point may perhaps be made more apparent if we remind ourselves of some of the moral and social qualities which seem essential to making a man or woman a good judge, qualities quite distinct from the essentially intellectual qualities associated with the idea of a jurist. Some of the judicial virtues—patience, good manners, gravity without pomposity—are in reality no more than social graces. Others are moral, and related to the concept of honour: for example, incorruptibility and fearlessness. These we rather take for granted, not being familiar with social conditions in which judicial corruption is common, and in which judges who wish to be upright require to be brave. Yet without them judicial decisions are hardly possible. Excellence as a judge requires more, and the virtue required has traditionally been called wisdom. What seems to be involved is the capacity

---

[1] See *Magor and St. Mellons R.D.C.* v. *Newport Corpn.* [1952] A.C. 189 and *Seaford Court Estates Ltd.* v. *Asher* [1949] 2 K.B. 481.
[2] See, *e.g.* J.H. Merryman, *The Civil Law Tradition* (Stanford, 1949), Chap. VI and Chap. IX; Merryman uses the term "scholars" where I use "jurist."
[3] *i.e.* the lay magistrates, who both outnumber the professional judges and deal with the vast mass of criminal business.

to present the decision in a manner which makes it acceptable and legitimate to all concerned. An individual may possess the required qualities and earn the respect which derives from them without being much of a lawyer, or even a lawyer at all. In *The Family Story*,[4] Lord Denning himself has a lot to say about being a good judge, and about the qualities required, for example:

> "One thing a judge must never do. He must never lose his temper. However sorely tried . . . .

This illustrates the point that good judges do not need to be experts—self-control is not an expert's skill. So any assessment of Lord Denning's merits and achievements as a judge will only be peripherally relevant, if relevant at all, to his standing as a jurist, as too will be his obvious desire to do justice to the particular litigants before him.

Jurists are, however, essentially and primarily experts, and they belong to eras in the development of the law in which a special class of experts exercise a predominant influence upon the evolution of the law. The term also carries with it an air of commendation and respect—unless it is used merely sarcastically. Jurists as an institution originated in the ancient world, and were a Roman invention; the Greeks never had any jurists at all, notwithstanding their enthusiasm for legal philosophy. The Roman jurists were not judges, and their involvement in adjudication was very indirect. The judges who actually decided litigation were laymen, and like the lay magistrates and jurymen of the common law who, between them, decided the vast majority of cases in the great days of the common law, they have left no memorial. The jurists, who have, were individuals of high social rank who devoted themselves to the study, exposition and analysis of private law, and who, during the great period of its development, exercised a decisive influence upon its content, form, and structure. Their typical activity was that of giving legal opinions in answer to questions (*respondere*), and these opinions could then be used by the laymen who actually operated the system. The analogy between this function and that of the common law judge directing a jury is an obvious one. The service provided by the jurists was not directly remunerated, though jurists were in fact rewarded by the enormous honour and respect accorded to them in Roman society. Though jurists were not uncommonly men who had played their part in the *cursus honorum* of Roman political life, their status did not depend upon office-holding or appointment. Their authority was personal and dependent upon an acquired reputation for skill, knowledge and wisdom. No doubt it would be an exaggeration to claim that today when the term jurist is employed, any very precise comparison with the ancient world is normally intended. With the decline in the study of Roman law, knowledge of the work and function of the Roman jurists has in any event become rarer than it once was. But it nevertheless remains true that the conception is Roman in derivation, and if it is to carry with it anything more than a sense of vague commendation it must suggest some special status in the legal system and one loosely similar to that enjoyed by such men as Ulpian and Paul—the status of an acknowledged expert, possessing to a marked degree personal authority, and through it a capacity to mould and develop substantive law.

---

[4] See pp. 206 *et seq.* and pp. 161 *et seq.*

Also involved is a quality of historical greatness which is peculiarly difficult to define. But certain figures in the history of the common law are supposed as legal experts in private law to have exercised a major influence upon the system through their writings and legal opinions; short lists will of course differ, but Littleton, Coke, Blackstone and Blackburn may serve as uncontroversial examples. Thus to rank a contemporary judge or legal writer as a jurist suggests that he belongs to a very select club indeed, admission to which depends upon the judgment of history.

II

Jurists then are associated with periods of legal evolution in which individual legal experts, who lay claim to some special skill or wisdom in the analysis and solution of legal problems, are able to exercise a predominant influence upon the development of the law. Not all societies have produced or maintained the conditions in which juristic development is possible. Thus the rise of the bureaucratic state ended the great days of the Roman jurists, and one cannot but wonder whether the world we now live in is one in which jurists are still possible. In the ancient world, the activities of the jurists in relation to abstract, substantive law was in part made possible by a system of procedure which facilitated the perception of a distinction between fact and law.[5] There also existed intellectual conditions which were as essential.[6] It was thought that private law, regulating the relationships between individuals or small groups in an essentially static world, was an institution of predominant importance, and that a principal function of government was to enable this regulation to be performed. But the justice which it was the business of government to administer was not man made, much less a product of legislative choice; it was in some sense objective and hence an object of expert study; there was a belief in the science of law or justice. By expert study and reflection could be achieved the discovery and formulation of those analytical categories into which the problems and conflicts of the world could be sorted and appropriate solutions discovered. Jurists who engaged themselves in the prestigious work of discovery required of course practical wisdom, and the leading Roman jurists appear to have been persons with their feet firmly on the ground; some possessed extensive political or military experience. In their legal work they were however distanced from immediate involvement in cases, and able, on the basis of the theories of the time, to be moderately speculative, and express the law in terms of *general* categories, rules and principles, so essential to the intellectual development of the law.

It is clear that we no longer live in the sort of world in which jurists in Europe first evolved. It is possible to go further than this and argue that the changes which have taken place are so fundamental that there no longer exists in our society any juristic role at all. Such an argument might be developed along the following lines. First it might be said that the idea of a body of expert's law regulating society belongs to an age in which both law

---

[5] See generally W. Kunkel, *An Introduction to Roman Legal and Constitutional History*, (trans. J.M. Kelly, Oxford, 1973, Chap. 7).

[6] The best account is A.M. Honoré's in *Tribonian*, (London 1978), pp. 30 *et seq.*

and society are conceived of in static terms. Yet today we have come so far as to think that society can be deliberately changed, by changing law. Second it might be said that the whole significance of private law in the scheme of government has changed so radically that the experts associated with it are no longer of much significance. Since the days of the late eighteenth century when the business of the Home Office could be conducted from three rooms, the scale of governmental intervention has increased immeasurably, and in the process the main body of the law has passed under the control of the higher civil service—virtually none of whom are or have been in modern times schooled in the world of private law.[7] Furthermore, this main body of law, being departmental legislation, has perverted the whole conception of law, for it principally functions by conferring powers to act outside the law.[8] Third, the old belief in a legal science, originally hardly distinguished from ethics, has faded. Today there are competing theories of ethics, and no consensus; in the absence of consensus, how can there be belief in objective justice? Fourth, the general acceptance of ideas derived from Marxism has destroyed any legitimacy in the construction of law by an elite group. No doubt other factors could be prayed in aid, but a powerful case can be put forward along these lines for scepticism as to the role of jurists in our time.

Paradoxically, however, the changes in society which could be instanced as constituting nails in the coffins of jurists seem typically nineteenth century. Yet the nineteenth century was a period which is particularly associated with the English judge as jurist. The great leading cases of that century seem to be the high point of juristic development in the common law, when the legal experts evolved those impressive bodies of abstract legal principle to be used by the lay jurors who decided the disputes. A sceptic might however reply that the destruction of the autonomy of the common law by the extension of Civil Service powers took a long time, and that when such cases as *Rylands* v. *Fletcher*[9] or *Indermaur* v. *Dames*[10] or *Prince*[11] were decided the politicians and civil servants of the time were quite ready to leave such arcane questions to the legal experts; in more modern times this has ceased to be true. Thus today after a lapidary decision such as *D.P.P.* v. *Morgan*[12] the politicians and civil servants at once set up a bizarre little group[13] (containing no jurists) to decide if it was "right." The route to legal evolution and development seems today to be through legislative mechanisms, through committees and commissions, through political action but not through the methods of Paul or Ulpian or Coke or Blackburn. There seems today to be no field of private law left which is regarded as immune from departmental and legislative interference, and any legal issue which is thought to be of genuine social importance is also thought to lie within the political field. Hence, judges who aspire to be jurists by playing an active role in the evolution of the law are perpetually at risk of being accused of

---

[7] This is a peculiar feature of English government in this century, which sharply distinguishes it from, for example, American government.
[8] The thrust of the *ultra vires* doctrine is to set external bounds to this unregulated area.
[9] (1868) L.R. 3 H.L. 330.
[10] (1866) L.R. 1 C.P. 274, 2 C.P. 311.
[11] (1875) L.R. 2 C.C.R. 154.
[12] [1976] A.C. 192.
[13] Called "The Advisory Group on the Law of Rape" in order to pretend it was not a committee, treading on the toes of the Criminal Law Revision Committee.

political activity, an accusation which tends to undermine the value and legitimacy of their work, and of themselves being the victims of political activity.

III

A powerful case can, therefore, be made for the view that we no longer live in a period in which the activity of jurists remains a significant mechanism for the development of the law. This is an age of legislation, and it is those who can directly or indirectly control the form of legislation who are the law makers today. It is against the background of such an argument that Lord Denning's long career on the bench will fall to be considered. Are the days of the great judge, the judge as jurist, really now over?[14] Are the senior judges destined to become, or are they indeed in course of becoming, mere functionaries? To this last question it is clear that Lord Denning's own answer would be an emphatic negative. From his writings and opinions it is clear that be believes both in the continued importance of the common law as an autonomous system, and in the existence of a special role in the state for the senior judges. Though he does not put the matter in this way, he thinks that there is still a jurist's job to do. What then is it?

For an answer we must turn to his writings, which are in one respect most unusual. Hardly any of those many hundreds of forgotten and curiously anonymous men who have held high judicial office in the common law system have left us even the briefest statements of their judical philosophies. Indeed, so far as most of them are concerned, there is no reason to suppose that they possessed one in any self-conscious or articulate sense. Just as plumbers may plumb for a lifetime without perplexing themselves as to what it is all about, so too may judges judge, and most do. But from time to time there have been exceptions, and Lord Denning is one. He stands in good company. The great Lord Coke, a notable reinterpreter of ancient precedents, made frequent and sometimes cheerfully inconsistent remarks about the judicial function, of which the most revealing was the contention that "out of the old bottles must come the new wine,"[15] a sentiment with which I suspect Lord Denning would find himself in agreement. Sir Mathew Hale, another great judge, writing in the mid-seventeenth century, set out a fairly comprehensive statement of what he supposed to be the nature of judicial decision in a passage on which later commentators have fathered the declaratory theory of precedents.[16] But the classic statement of the function of the judge as jurist is that of James Parke in *Mirehouse* v. *Rennell*,[17] by when the notion of legal science, with the jurist as scientist, had become fashionable:

> "Our Common Law system consists in the applying to new combina-
> tions of circumstances those rules of law which we derive from legal
> principles and judicial precedents; and for the sake of attaining

[14] Louis L. Jaffe's book, *English and American Judges as Lawmakers* (Oxford, 1969) opens with a chapter entitled "Is the Great Judge Obsolete?"

[15] This aphorism is an elegant variation of St. Mathew IX 17.

[16] *The History of the Common Law of England* (ed. C.N. Gray, Chicago and London Universities 1971), Chap. IV.

[17] (1833) 1 Cl. & F. 527, 546.

uniformity, consistency and certainty, we must apply those rules, where they are not plainly unreasonable and inconvenient, to all cases which arise; and we are not at liberty to reject them, and to abandon all analogy to them, in those to which they have not yet been judicially applied, because we think that the rules are not as convenient and reasonable as we ourselves could have devised. It appears to me to be of great importance to keep this principle of decision steadily in view, not merely for the determination of the particular case, but for the interests of law as a science."

Lord Denning's own views are scattered about his writings, and are particularly related to the modern judicial hierarchy, established by the late nineteenth century Judicature Acts, which imposed two tiers of appellate judges on the backs of the trial judges. He conceives of the appellate judges as having a special responsibility[18] for the development of the law, and his view of what this is can best be viewed as a reaction to what other writers have said about the judicial function in modern society.

For there exists today a voluminous and expanding literature concerned not only with the judicial function generally (especially in America) but more particularly with the achievements in modern times of the English judiciary. Both the superior judges and the lay judges in the magistrates' courts have been passed in review—professional judges of intermediate status have, so far, escaped. Much of the literature has been debunking or otherwise hostile in tone; this is particularly true of writings influenced by sociology or Marxism (or some combination of the two). Disenchantment with traditional authoritarian structures is of course widespread, and debunking literature, linked loosely by a pessimistic view of Britain in decline, is today a growth industry. Understandably, the judges have not found all this comfortable, and have at times reacted irritably. An example is Lord Radcliffe's haughty review of L. Blom-Cooper's study of the House of Lords,[19] or Lord Simon of Glaisdale's remarkable recent letter to the *Sunday Times* cautioning the public against the wild radicals of the ponderous *Modern Law Review*. Other reactions have been more urbane, such as the writings, half a century ago, of Benjamin Cardozo, which began the modern judicial literature of self-revelation. Cardozo's writings were themselves in part a response to ideas which were to become linked by the realist movement—itself debunking in character. His *The Nature of the Judicial Process* (1921) offered a judicial philosophy which attempted to reconcile his belief in the legitimacy of judicial innovation with his respect for the rule of law, not of judges, and involved a rejection of the more iconoclastic notions then embryonic in some of the leading law schools.

In England the impetus which has driven judges to the pen has been different. Realism in its more extreme forms has never been taken seriously; the late C.K. Allen even sneered at it as "jazz jurisprudence."[20] It was essentially a movement in the law schools, and when the movement was at

---

[18] Perhaps the clearest development of Lord Denning's ideas here are to be found in his Romanes Lecture, but this deals only with the special function of the judges of the House of Lords.

[19] (1973) 36 M.L.R. 555.

[20] C.K. Allen, *Law in the Making* (4th ed. 1946), p. 45. The remark was excised from later editions. See generally W. Twining, *Karl Llewellyn and the Realist Movement* (London, 1973).

its height in America, English law schools were such shabby institutions that nobody took them (as opposed to a few individual professors) at all seriously. The stimulus came from the state, and the first sizeable judicial contribution not so much to the theory of judicial decision but to the place of the common law and its traditional values in the constitutional structure was Lord Chief Justice Hewart's outburst, *The New Despotism* (1929). Although no-one would today regard this book—once very widely read—as a sophisticated contribution to political theory, it did perceptively, if somewhat belatedly, identify The Enemy as the growing and lawless bureaucracy of the collectivist state, which has continued to flourish quite independently of the political persuasion of the government in power. The bureaucracy, continually extending its empire by legal mechanisms (typically conferring discretion, non-accountability and secrecy) has in the process dramatically reduced the status of the high priests of the traditional common law, and the process has continued. Recent judicial writing in England which deals in self-examination—notably the writings of Lords Denning and Devlin[21]—must be understood in part as responding to this change in the distribution of power, in which the common law judges have declined in importance. The reactions have been different—Lord Devlin essentially accepting the change as inevitable, and in consequence adopting a modest view of the place of the judiciary in government: Lord Denning rather more inclined to fight back and even reclaim lost territory. Such judicial writings can also be regarded as responding to another body of literature, the literature of judicial activism, and indeed as belonging to it. This body of writing is specifically directed towards examining the success or failure of modern English appellate judges in discharging responsibilities for the condition of the law which some, including Lord Denning himself, would cast upon them.

The leading writer in this school is Robert Stevens, and his attitudes to the English judges have been profoundly influenced by comparison with the state of affairs in the United States of America, where the constitution provides a special position for law which is not obviously mirrored in arrangements on this side of the Atlantic. His massive study of the Lord Chancellors and the Law Lords in *Law and Politics* (1979) continuously evaluates judicial achievement in terms of a contrast between the creative judge, whose conception of the judicial role is the desirable one, and the narrow minded formalist who, at least as an appellate judge, simply fails to earn his pay. The creative judge's starting point is a belief in a changing or evolving society, in which there is a continuous need for the law to be modified so as to bring it back into touch with social needs. Unlike the economic determinists who appear to think that this just happens automatically, the devotees of judicial activism go on to claim that the job cannot be left to the legislature (or civil service); the judges must play an active part in the process through judicial decisions. The call to the judges to make law is often combined with the assertion that they do this anyway, and might as well make a virtue of necessity. The good judge is the bold innovator, the self-conscious judicial law maker; the bad judge (of whom there have been too many in England) is the conservative formalist, with his mechanical vision of the judicial process.

[21] *The Judge* (Oxford, 1979).

The influence of comparison between the achievements of the American Supreme Court on the one hand and the English House of Lords on the other is most clearly seen in Louis L. Jaffe's *English and American Judges as Law Makers* (1969), which opens with the assertion:

> "The great judge was great because when the occasion cried out for new law he dared to make it. He was great because he was aware that the law is a living organism, its vitality dependent upon renewal."

Such thinking is often associated with a nostalgia, and looks back with envy to the great names of the past; Jaffe's own list contains Coke, Bacon (rather oddly),[22] Holt, Mansfield and Willes. Things in England are not what they were, and the place of law and lawyers in English society insignificant beside their American counterparts.[23]

To what extent Lord Denning's own views have been influenced by such writings as have been mentioned, I do not know. Certain judges—Lord Devlin is an obvious example—have a taste for academic and scholarly writing about law, and appear, from their writings, speeches and legal opinions, to be familiar with some of this critical material. But it seems very unlikely that Lord Denning's own view on the role and responsibility of an appellate judge has been more than trivially influenced by critical legal literature. He has himself admitted to a dislike of legal theory, acquired during his university days under the direction of "The Tutor Who Knew No Law"—the awful Segar of Magdalen.

> "Jurisprudence was too abstract a subject for my liking. All about ideologies, legal norms, and basic norms, 'ought' and 'is', realism and behaviourism, and goodness knows what else. The jargon of the philosophers of law has always been beyond me."[24]

Anti-intellectualism amongst English lawyers can be a pose, but this surely comes from the heart. Whatever ideas he has formed on the function of the judge have developed out of his long years at the bar, and, since 1944, on the bench; they represent the interaction between his upbringing and character on the one hand, and his experience on the other. As a judicial activist, his work and writings belong to a movement but are not a product of it.

Nevertheless, Lord Denning has come to see himself in terms of categories he did not himself define, accepting such labels as "activist" or "iconoclast" from others. His well known lecture "The Way of an Iconoclast," delivered in Oxford back in 1959 to a meeting of the Society of Public Teachers of Law, took its title from remarks made earlier by Professor Walker at a degree ceremony in the University of Glasgow. Lord Denning has indeed welcomed the mantle of the progressive judge, and in one of his recent books has stated clearly and, one need hardly add, succinctly, his own judicial philosophy:

> "My root belief is that the proper role of the judge is to do justice between the parties before him. If there is any rule of law which impairs the doing of justice, then it is the province of the judge to do all that he

---

[22] Bacon's contribution to the evolution of equity is obscure but surely not very significant.

[23] The American Constitution of course ensures to the judiciary an autonomous role which, if it exists in our system, is less surely based.

[24] See *The Family Story*, p. 38. Tales of the unhappy Robert Segar were still told when I was an undergraduate in 1951–1954. *Cf.* the similarly unhappy experiences of Gibbon.

legitimately can to avoid that rule—or even to change it—so as to do justice in the instant case before him. *He need not wait for legislation to intervene*: because that can never be of any help in the instant case. I would emphasise, however, the word 'legitimately': the judge is himself subject to the law and must abide by it."[25]

The italics are mine, inserted to emphasise the fact that what is involved is lawyer's law reform by judicial decision. Much of Lord Denning's energies have been directed to this end, and his campaign against *stare decisis*, made very public in his Romanes Lecture "From Precedent to Precedent" (1959) has been principally directed to facilitating the work. So, too, in part has been his advocacy of a less literal and more purposive approach to statutory interpretation, which would give the courts a limited but significant role in modifying the impact of legislation.

While the reform of substantive lawyer's law through judicial decision has been one constant theme throughout Lord Denning's career, the other has been the attempt to reassert the independent authority of the common law as a control over the organs of the collectivist state and other quasi-public bodies who have acquired a legally privileged position in it. As an independent arm of government, the judiciary in England do not possess any clearly defined constitutional position, and there has long been extreme difficulty in marrying the conception of the rule of law to the doctrine of Parliamentary sovereignty: poor Dicey tied himself in knots over the problem. Lord Denning's work here has largely centred upon the idea—first clearly stated some 30 years ago in his Hamlyn lectures—that the inadequacies of the law in its control of official power have lain principally in the procedures involved; he then argued that whereas the procedures for securing personal freedom were efficient, those for controlling power were not. In *The Discipline of Law* he returned to this subject, and a considerable part of the book is concerned to review the judicial decisions in which he has tried to improve the position of the individual in conflict with group or state power. Lord Denning's involvement here falls easily into a tradition traceable back to the thirties, to the days of *The New Despotism*, the writings of C.K. Allen, and the *Committee on Ministers' Powers*; amongst the judges, his forbear was Lord Atkin.

IV

Lord Denning's achievements as a jurist must rest ultimately upon an assessment of the permanence and effectiveness of his work in these two principle areas with which he has been concerned—the reform of lawyers' law and the control of state or group power. Permanence here can lie in the survival of particular modifications in the law, or in the general redirection of the development of the system. So far as the former area is concerned, the individual decisions and doctrinal modifications—the "High Trees" doctrine, the deserted wife's equity or promissory estoppel, negligent misstatement—all these have been exhaustively reviewed both elsewhere and in this book; some have flourished, others have died quietly or been ritually

[25] *The Family Story*, p. 174.

murdered. But the high level of controversy[26] amongst professional lawyers
which has surrounded Lord Denning's work in this area, and which has
surfaced both in other judicial opinions and in extra judicial commentary,
cannot but cast some doubt upon the scope for the judge as jurist in the
reform of private law. The difficulty does not lie simply in the existence of a
legislature and the underpinnings of Law Commissions, Royal Commissions, Departmental Committees, etc., for most of the work of these bodies in
private law simply accumulates dust. Waiting for legislation is a little like
waiting for Godot. The problem is, instead, an intellectual one, and it has
made it difficult for Lord Denning to secure any general consensus within
the profession for the legitimacy of law reform through judicial decision. The
essence of the problem lies in the apparent conflict within the notion that a
judge, who is bound by law, may change the law. Lord Denning's
detractors, both on and off the bench, have said strong things about what
appears to them to be the manipulation of the law which is involved in law
reform through judicial decision. A recent example is Paul Watchman's
"Palm Tree Justice and the Lord Chancellor's Foot," an article which does
no more than make explicit what many lawyers have been saying privately
for years.[27] A belief, whether well based or not, that judges as jurists are
bound to engage in devious behaviour is not favourable to this work. One
obstacle to progress has been removed, partly no doubt in response to Lord
Denning's own advocacy; the House of Lords is no longer absolutely bound
by its own decisions. But for Lord Denning, down in the Court of Appeal,
this proved a hollow victory.

   Historically, of course, the law has changed and evolved, and intellectual
mechanisms for legitimising this have existed; the problem is to present
judicial activism in an acceptable guise. Lord Denning has toyed with the
idea of "a new equity,"[28] but the suggestion has not caught on. He has also
hinted from time to time at the notion of deep structure, now fashionable in
linguistic circles, and once in legal ones.[29] Here the law is conceived of as
consisting in deep fundamental principles, and it is to these that the judge
owes allegiance, not to the mass of illustrative and at times misguided
decisions based upon them. Whether such a theory will become acceptable
again is difficult to predict, but it seems at least doubtful. Such a theory is
more likely to flourish in a small, homogeneous judiciary which expresses
itself in a more oracular fashion than is the custom today. Matters here
could, of course, change. The incessant conversion of questions of fact into
questions of law, which has been encouraged by the disappearance of the
civil jury and the over-provision of appeals, has gone hand in hand with the
spread of the rambling and excessively detached judicial opinion. Such
opinions eventually degrade their own importance, and in all probability the
individual judicial opinion will decline in significance, as has happened in
the United States. There (and the process has begun here) the on line
computer systems serve to dredge up as much as one can use on any topic,
and the more there is the less notice is taken of it. As they say in the world of

---

[26] I refer not simply to the published material but to the private arguments which all lawyers
   must have heard or joined.
[27] In *Justice, Lord Denning and the Constitution* (ed. P. Robson and P. Watchman, Westmead,
   1981). Lord Denning's most hostile judicial critic was surely the late Lord Simonds.
[28] In a lecture published in *Current Legal Problems*, (1952), Vol. 5.
[29] *e.g.* in *The Discipline of the Law*, pp. 287 *et seq.*

computers—garbage in, garbage out. Precedent becomes less and less important, and other theories of judicial decision replace *stare decisis*.

But I suspect that Lord Denning's contribution to the reform of lawyers' law may well not prove to be his most significant achievement. In the reform of the law there may well be a job for jurists to do, but the judgment seat is not a position from which jurists can easily operate. In the absence of civil juries to decide the case, the judge is too much affected by impressions of the individual merits of the dispute; the range of material he can consult is absurdly limited by the outmoded conventions of the bar, and the random presentation of disconnected problems makes any systematic development impossible. Furthermore, the undisciplined individualism of English appellate judges, and their complete lack of any collegiate spirit, reduces much of their work to mere confusion. It no longer seems possible for a single judge, be he Master of the Rolls, Lord Chancellor or Lord of Appeal, to dominate the system as once Lord Mansfield did. Law reform seems all much better done through the more disciplined and systematic institution of the committee. If I am right in my prognosis, then Lord Denning's stature as a jurist must depend on some other aspect of his work, and one which is not continuously at risk of being taken over by Parliamentary legislation, or sabotaged by his colleagues.

Formally, under the orthodox doctrine of the English constitution, there is no such area; according to the principle of parliamentary sovereignty, nothing lies outside the competence of Parliament, which in reality means the cabinet and civil service. But as a description of the position in practice, this is unrealistic. There are what seem like logical limits—legislation must be applied and interpreted—but these are perhaps not particularly significant, since the administration and interpretation of the law can readily be transferred to other agencies than the regular courts. More significant are limits set politically or by opinion, whether generally or by particular interest groups. No government has yet succeeded in controlling police malpractice, or significantly reduced secrecy in government. No government could wholly abolish the doctrine of *mens rea*, or jury trial for the more serious offences. The judge as jurist is likely to find his chief scope in those very areas where, for some reason or another, Parliament fears to tread. But not all such areas are appropriate—only those in which the maintenance and development of the traditional values of the rule of law have sufficient appeal to public opinion to make of the judiciary an independent political force in government. Lord Denning's work in the development of remedies restraining the abuse of power and in the protection of individual rights lies in this area, where it is idle to expect much good from legislation; government has too deep an interest in the expansion of discretionary power, in the restriction and abnegation of individual rights in the name of the public good, and in the paying off of interest groups. Consequently, any significant developments by judicial decision will normally bring courts and government into some degree of conflict. Back in 1949 in *Freedom Under the Law* Lord Denning committed himself to the values of individual freedom and the restraint of the abuse of power, and recently in *The Family Story*[30] he returned to the theme:

"The law itself should provide adequate and efficient remedies for

[30] p. 179.

abuse or misuse of power from whatever quarter it may come. No matter who it is—who is guilty of the abuse or misuse. Be it government, national or local. Be it trade unions. Be it the press. Be it management . . . To my mind it is fundamental to our society to see that powers are not abused or misused. If they come into conflict with the freedom of the individual—or with any other of our fundamental freedoms—then it is the province of the judge to hold the balance between the competing interests."

Very many of the notable legal decisions in which Lord Denning has been involved, and almost all of the most controversial, have lain in this province.

V

Inevitably, juristic activity here is a form of political activity, being concerned with the relative distribution of power in society, and the judge as politician has in recent times been the subject of much critical writing. To those pessimistic writers who develop or reflect the doctrines of Marxism there is no good to be had out of the ideology of the rule of law or the achievements of a supposedly independent judiciary, now or at any other time. Judges are essentially collaborators in a sinister conspiracy of the governors against the governed. The business in which they are engaged is essentially evil, and the supposed virtues of legalism mere shams, devices which serve to legitimise the activities of the judiciary in the maintenance of class domination and the exploitation integral to it. The most notable application of these gloomy notions to the common law is to be found in a historical article—Douglas Hay's *Property, Authority and the Criminal Law*, the opening piece in *Albion's Fatal Tree*. The tone of what is now a cult book is set by the use, on the cover, of a detail from Hogarth's ferocious painting "The Bench," in which the lecherous Chief Justice Sir John Willes presides over his repulsive sleeping colleagues in the Court of Common Pleas. To such writers, judges as jurists are mere confidence tricksters, and the analogies, if valid, would apply as well to Lord Denning as to his forbears on the bench. Less committed writers, of whom Professor Griffith is the most notable example since Laski, lack the fervent hostility exuded by *Albion's Fatal Tree*; perhaps the tone has softened since judges no longer have people killed. His *Politics of the Judiciary*[31] is a curiously vacillating work, its conclusions hedged and compromised. Judicial neutrality, we are assured, is a myth; the judiciary is ultimately subservient to government, and

> "it is demonstrable that on every major social issue which has come before the courts in the last 30 years—concerning industrial relations, government secrecy, police powers, moral behaviour—the judges have supported the conventional, established, and settled interests."[32]

Yet we are told also that "the idea of the rule of law is not wholly illusory,"[33] that judicial independence of government is a great virtue, and that in spite of the class analysis scattered through the book, matters are

[31] 1977. (Fontana Paperbacks, 2nd ed. 1981). References are to the 2nd edition.
[32] pp. 239–240.
[33] pp. 232.

ordered much the same under non-capitalist régimes. Confronted with the need to reach some sort of conclusion, Griffith at one point relapses into utopianism:

"I am not sure what would be the attitude of judges in the ideal society. Perhaps they would not be needed because conflict between Government and the Governed would have been removed."[34]

But if there is a message it is that judges in modern society need to be a little more socially progressive, a little more on the side of those who challenge authority—indeed, a little more like the American judges, who get a pat on the back for their occasional "positive assertions of fundamental values."[35] So, at the end of the day, Griffith's position is not fundamentally different from Lord Denning—there *is* a special role here for the courts. Engagement in it will, inevitably, involve political decision, but unless judicial intervention is based upon some general juristic theory which differentiates it from mere support of one interest group against another, then it is unlikely to command the public support which is essential to its permanence.

Lord Denning has, as we have seen, claimed to be no legal philosopher, but this is too modest. He is in fact a utilitarian, whose aim in cases involving supposed abuse of power is to strike a balance between private individual right and public convenience. This was very clearly set out in *Freedom Under the Law:*

"The moral of it all is that a true balance must be kept between personal freedom on the one hand and social security on the other."[36]

Lord Denning is not in any way unique in adopting this philosophy of rights; it is probably typical of judicial thinking, and has recently been used to provide a theoretical basis for the *Report of the Royal Commission on Criminal Procedure*,[37] where its status and pedigree are shortly but usefully discussed. It may be contrasted on the one hand with systems of thought in which individual rights play no part, and on the other with systems in which rights are treated as fundamental in the sense that they are non-negotiable and in that sense absolute—though there may remain areas of dispute as to the precise extension of rights. The "fair balance" theory has the obvious attractions of the middle way; it has affinities with the common law's reasonable man. But it also embodies three disadvantages as a basis for juristic as contrasted with legislative activity. The first is that the solution of legal problems is presented in terms more apt for political negotiation—if law is thought to involve the impartial application of rules, it is difficult to see how the rules can settle the outcome of a balancing act. The second is that it can easily degenerate into the view that individuals only have rights to the extent to which they cause no inconvenience to authority. Rights are thus lost when most needed. The third is that the theory appears to confer on the judges the same unbridled discretion which they are committed to restrain in others. *Quis custodiet custodies?* Lord Denning's ultimate stature as a jurist may turn on whether in the eyes of posterity his intuitive sense of justice has enabled him in his judicial decisions to locate the fair balance correctly.

[34] p. 241.
[35] p. 241.
[36] See the passages quoted in *The Family Story*, pp. 178–179.
[37] Cmnd. 8092, paras. 1.11–1.35.

CHAPTER 10

Lord Denning: A Commonwealth Perspective

S. WADDAMS

Lord Denning is very popular with Canadian law students. The casebook method of teaching brings them into contact with somewhat more judicial prose than their English counterparts, and Lord Denning's distinctive and very readable style comes as a welcome contrast to most of what they have to contend with. It is not only the prose style that is attractive, but also Lord Denning's clear statement of the facts of his cases, his ability to distil the essence of the questions to be debated, and his clear and bold expression of his own views.

The extent of Lord Denning's influence on Anglo-Canadian law can be judged by the frequent references to his decisions in the recent series of special lectures given by the Law Society of Upper Canada.[1] The topic was "Remedies" and Lord Denning's decisions were central to the discussion of almost every field of private law remedies. The discussion of injunctions revolved almost entirely around his recent decisions.[2]

The law of restitution which is becoming increasingly important in Canada also owes much to Lord Denning's influence. The Supreme Court of Canada recently held that a "de facto" wife was entitled to a share in a man's business assets.[3] The conclusion was based on unjust enrichment, and the principal judgment included the following phrases:

> "The principle of unjust enrichment lies at the heart of the constructive trust. 'Unjust enrichment' has played a role in Anglo-American legal writing for centuries. Lord Mansfield, . . . put the matter in these words: ' . . . the gist of this kind of action is that the defendant, upon the circumstances of the case, is obliged by the ties of natural justice and equity to refund the money.' It would be undesirable, and indeed impossible, to attempt to define all the circumstances in which an unjust enrichment might arise . . . . The great advantage of ancient principles of equity is their flexibility: the judiciary is thus able to shape these malleable principles so as to accommodate the changing needs and mores of society, in order to achieve justice. The constructive trust has proven to be a useful tool in the judicial armoury. . . . "[4]

Hussey v. *Palmer*[5] though dealing also with domestic property-sharing

[1] Law Society of Upper Canada March Special Lecture Series (1981).
[2] Particularly *Mareva Compania Naviera S.A. of Panama* v. *International Bulk Carriers S.A.* [1975] 2 Lloyd's Rep. 509, and *Fellowes & Son* v. *Fisher* [1976] Q.B. 122.
[3] *Pettkus* v. *Becker* (1980) 117 D.L.R. (3d) 257.
[4] *Ibid.* at p. 273.
[5] [1972] 1 W.L.R. 1286.

Lord Denning: A Commonwealth Perspective

problems was not cited by the court. But the echoes of Lord Denning's judgment in that case are unmistakable:

> "It [a constructive trust] is a trust imposed by law whenever justice and good conscience require it. It is a liberal process, founded on large principles of equity, to be applied in cases where the defendant cannot conscientiously keep the property for himself alone, but ought to allow another to have the property or a share in it . . . . It is an equitable remedy by which the court can enable an aggrieved party to obtain restitution. It is comparable to the legal remedy of money had and received which, as Lord Mansfield said, is very beneficial, and, therefore, much encouraged."[6]

The unacknowledged pervasive effect of Lord Denning's views may be taken as more eloquent testimony of his influence than a string of overt references to his cases.

But it is in the law of contracts that his major contribution is to be found. To say that Lord Denning has influenced the law of contracts is rather like saying that the study of physics owes something to Newton. Almost every significant area of contract law centres on one or more decisions of Lord Denning's. One cannot discuss the law of offer and acceptance without considering *Storer* v. *Manchester City Council*[7]; or consideration without taking account of *Central London Property Trust Ltd.* v. *High Trees House Ltd.*[8]; or intention without *Merritt* v. *Merritt*[9]; or unilateral contracts without *Errington* v. *Errington*[10]; or third party beneficiaries without *Beswick* v. *Beswick*[11]; or incorporation of written documents without *Thornton* v. *British Crane Hire Ltd.*[12]; or exemption clauses without *Karsales (Harrow) Ltd.* v. *Wallis*[13]; *Levison* v. *Patent Steam Carpet Cleaning Co. Ltd.*[14] and *Photo Production Ltd.* v. *Securicor Ltd.*[15]; or the parol evidence rule without *Mendelssohn* v. *Normand Ltd.*,[16] *Jaques* v. *Lloyd D. George and Partners Ltd.*,[17] and the bold assertion that "we do not allow printed forms to be made a trap for the unwary"[18]; or mistake and third parties without *Lewis* v. *Averay*[19]; or mistaken assumptions without *Solle* v. *Butcher*[20] and *Magee* v. *Pennine Insurance Co.*[21]; or *non est factum* without *Gallie* v. *Lee*[22]; or unconscionability without *Lloyd's Bank* v. *Bundy*[23]; or performance and breach without *Cehave N.V.* v. *Bremer Handelsgesellschaft mbH*[24]; or

---

[6] *Ibid.* at pp. 1289–1290.
[7] [1974] 1 W.L.R. 1403.
[8] [1947] 1 K.B. 130.
[9] [1970] 1 W.L.R. 1211.
[10] [1952] 1 K.B. 290.
[11] [1966] Ch. 538, affirmed [1968] A.C. 70.
[12] [1971] 2 Q.B. 163.
[13] [1956] 1 W.L.R. 936.
[14] [1978] Q.B. 69.
[15] [1978] 1 W.L.R. 856, reversed [1980] A.C. 827.
[16] [1970] 1 Q.B. 177.
[17] [1968] 1 W.L.R. 625.
[18] *Neuchatel Asphalte Co.* v. *Barnett* [1957] 1 W.L.R. 356, 360.
[19] [1972] 1 Q.B. 198.
[20] [1950] 1 K.B. 671.
[21] [1969] 2 Q.B. 507.
[22] [1979] 2 Ch. 17, affirmed [1971] A.C. 1004.
[23] [1975] Q.B. 326.
[24] [1976] Q.B. 44.

misrepresentation without *Leaf* v. *International Galleries*[25]; and *Esso Petroleum Co. Ltd.* v. *Mardon*[26]; or specific performance without *Hill* v. *C. A. Parsons Ltd.*[27]; or damages without *Jarvis* v. *Swan's Tours Ltd.*[28] and *Anglia Television Ltd.* v. *Reed*[29] and *Schorsch Meier GmbH* v. *Hennin*[30]; or penalties and forfeitures without *Stockloser* v. *Johnson*[31]; or illegality without *Kiriri Cotton Ltd.* v. *Ranchhoddas Keshavjai Dewani*[32] and *Ashmore, Benson Pease & Co. Ltd.* v. *A.V. Dawson Ltd.*[33]

Lord Denning's greatest influence in Canada is certainly in the law of contracts. The reasons for this are worth considering. There is the fact that Lord Denning's political views, for which he has been much criticised in England, are rarely associated with contract cases. There is the consideration that many areas of Commonwealth law are now quite distinct from English law, particularly, in Canada, family law, labour law and administrative law, whereas contract law is still quite uniform. But, most important of all, I think, is the fact that contract law is just entering a period of rapid change, and in the last 10 years concepts unchallenged since the nineteenth century have been subjected to radical re-evaluation. Lord Denning has been in the vanguard of the re-evaluation. Other areas of law have changed too, but in contract law Lord Denning has been able frequently to hit upon a persuasive formulation of principles to which other courts were already beginning to give shape.

Law students, especially first year law students, are inclined to regard the doctrine of precedent as more closely analogous to a mill-stone—or at best an anchor, than to a chart or compass. They constantly find the views they are learning to favour, rejected, apparently on the ground of binding precedent. Eventually they learn that the doctrine of precedent is more malleable than it seems at first to be, but there is no doubt of the attraction of Lord Denning's bold approach to recalcitrant authority. The phrases are characteristic of his style: "Notwithstanding earlier cases which might suggest the contrary, it is now settled that . . . "[34]; "I think that those limitations are out of date"[35]; "but those cases may have to be reconsidered."[36]

To congratulate a judge on his bold approach to precedent might be taken as a rather mixed compliment, like a reference in a school report to an imaginative approach to spelling, or a creative use of the multiplication tables. I should say at once, therefore, that Lord Denning's approach to precedent is not always as bold as the foregoing dicta seem to indicate, for Lord Denning's approach to the development of common law rules generally reveals sophistication and historical understanding, combined with effective advocacy. This is illustrated by the rule of contract law—sometimes called the doctrine of privity—that a person cannot sue on a contract made

[25] [1950] 2 K.B. 86.
[26] [1976] Q.B. 801.
[27] [1972] 1 Ch. 305.
[28] [1973] 1 Q.B. 233.
[29] [1972] 1 Q.B. 60.
[30] [1975] Q.B. 416.
[31] [1954] 1 Q.B. 476.
[32] [1960] A.C. 192 (P.C.).
[33] [1973] 1 W.L.R. 828.
[34] *Karsales (Harrow) Ltd.* v. *Wallis* [1956] 1 W.L.R. 940.
[35] *Jarvis* v. *Swan's Tours* [1973] 1 Q.B. 233, 237.
[36] *Heywood* v. *Wellers* [1976] Q.B. 446, 459.

Lord Denning: A Commonwealth Perspective

between two other persons for his benefit. It is easy to point to cases, real and hypothetical, where this rule leads to injustice. The ordinary lawyer or law teacher would perhaps stop at that point, regretting the rule and calling upon the legislature or the House of Lords or the Supreme Court of Canada to alter it. The scholar, however, or the truly learned practitioner, goes further. He asks how the rule in its present form arose, what arguments supported it, whether the arguments still carry weight, whether the law was always so, whether in earlier times there were devices for evading the rule, and, if so, whether they can be regarded as part of the present law. This is what Corbin did in his article in the *Law Quarterly Review* in 1930[37] where he established that the courts of equity before the Judicature Act had frequently enforced contracts for the benefit of third parties by the device of finding the promisee to be a trustee for the third party. He argued that this device was available to the unified High Court after the Judicature Act, and was a perfectly proper and desirable use of the trust concept fully in keeping with the historic role of equity. Unfortunately, however, his argument has not so far found very much favour with the English and Canadian courts.[38]

In *Beswick* v. *Beswick*[39] Lord Denning mounted a full scale attack on the rule of privity by attempting to undermine the case of *Tweddle* v. *Atkinson*[40] on which the modern law had been built. Going back to a case decided two hundred years earlier[41] Lord Denning asserted that *Tweddle* v. *Atkinson* was wrongly decided on the law as it then stood, and that in any event the result could be justified on a quite different ground. Contracts could be enforced, he said, at common law by the device of the third party's bringing his action in the name of the promisee.

There were several other arguments canvassed in the case. In the end, the House of Lords found in favour of the third party beneficiary on one of these, and rejected Lord Denning's views.[42] But Lord Denning's judgment influences the way everyone now thinks about the problem. What was formerly thought to be an unshakeable rule of English law—indeed a necessity of the doctrine of consideration—becomes a nineteenth century innovation of doubtful ancestry. Lord Reid in *Beswick* v. *Beswick* said:

> "Lord Denning's view, expressed in this case not for the first time, is that [where A contracts with B for the benefit of X] X could enforce this obligation. But the view more commonly held in recent times has been that such a contract confers no right on X . . . . It is true that a strong Law Revision Committee recommended so long ago as 1937 . . . ; 'that where a contract by its express terms purports to confer a benefit directly on a third party it shall be enforceable by the third party in his own name . . . .' And if one had to contemplate a further long period of Parliamentary procrastination this House might find it necessary to deal with this matter. But if legislation is probable at an early date I would not deal with it in a case where that is not essential."[43]

---

[37] "Contracts for the Benefit of Third Persons" (1930) 46 L.Q.R. 12.
[38] See *Re Schebsman* [1944] Ch. 83 (C.A.), *Greenwood Shopping Plaza Ltd.* v. *Beattie* (1980) 111 D.L.R. (3d) 257 (S.C.C.).
[39] Above, n. 11.
[40] (1861) 1 B. & S. 393.
[41] *Dutton* v. *Poole* (1678) 2 Lev. 210.
[42] [1968] A.C. 70.
[43] *Ibid.* at p. 72.

Lord Reid spoke in the expectation that the Law Commissions were about to codify the whole law of contracts, but his words make it clear that he did not regard judicial law reform on the point as out of the question. Twelve years later Lord Scarman said:

"I respectfully agree with Lord Reid that the denial by English law of a jus quaesitum tertio calls for reconsideration. In *Beswick* v. *Beswick* . . . Lord Reid, after referring to the Law Committee's recommendation in 1937 . . . that the third party should be able to enforce a contractual promise taken by another for his benefit, observed: 'And if one had to contemplate a further long period of Parliamentary procrastination this House might find it necessary to deal with this matter.' The Committee reported in 1937: *Beswick* v. *Beswick* was decided in 1967: it is now 1979 but nothing has been done. If the opportunity arises I hope the House will reconsider *Tweddle* v. *Atkinson* . . . and the other cases which stand guard over this unjust rule."[44]

Yet it was only five years before *Beswick* v. *Beswick* that Viscount Simonds had asserted, for the majority of the House of Lords,

"a principle which is, I suppose, as well established as any in our law, a 'fundamental' principle, as Lord Haldane called it in *Dunlop Pneumatic Tyre Company Limited* v. *Selfridge and Company Limited* . . . an 'elementary' principle as it has been called times without number, that only a person who is a party to a contract can sue upon it. Our law, said Lord Haldane, knows nothing of a jus quaesitum tertio arising by way of contract. Learned counsel . . . claimed that this was the orthodox view and asked your Lordships to reject any proposition that impinged upon it. To that invitation I readily respond. For to me heterodoxy, or, as some might say, heresy, is not the more attractive because it is dignified by the name of reform. Nor will I easily be led by an undiscerning zeal for some abstract kind of justice to ignore our first duty which is to administer justice according to law, the law which is established for us by Act of Parliament or the binding authority of precedent. The law is developed by the application of old principles to new circumstances. Therein lies its genius. Its reform by the abrogation of those principles is the task not of the courts of law but of Parliament.[45]

The change in the approach of the House of Lords to judicial law reform since 1962 is not attributable solely to Lord Denning. But I think it is fair to say that he has contributed more than any other single judge to a more flexible approach. The law in relation to third party beneficiaries is not yet fully established as Lord Denning would wish it. But he did not abandon the fight[46] after *Beswick* v. *Beswick*, and his view will surely prevail in the end.

The main point that I seek to illustrate from this discussion of third party beneficiaries is that Lord Denning is not only a judge but also an advocate, and a very effective one. He might, having failed to persuade his fellow Law Lords in *Midland Silicones*, and moving shortly afterwards to the Court of

---

[44] *Woodar Investments Development Ltd.* v. *Wimpey Construction U.K. Ltd.* [1980] 1 W.L.R. 277, 300.

[45] *Midland Silicones Ltd.* v. *Scruttons Ltd.* [1962] A.C. 446, 467–8.

[46] See *Jackson* v. *Horizon Holidays Ltd.* [1975] 1 W.L.R. 1468.

Appeal, simply have continued to assert his own views. This would have led to perpetual dissents in his own court and to a serious loss of prestige with the House of Lords, the profession, and the public. On the other hand he might have simply applied the law as Viscount Simonds had declared it to be. Few could have faulted him for this course but it would have been inconsistent with Lord Denning's own concept of justice. Instead, he explored other arguments than those directly rejected in *Midland Silicones*— not just theoretical arguments, but practically useful arguments that might actually persuade his fellow judges. Law teachers, faced with the problem of reconciling their wish to describe the law as it ought to be with their duty to teach the law as it is seek a solution by blurring the line: persuasive arguments can and do make new law. This is why Lord Denning is an attractive figure to law teachers as well as to students. His judgments illustrate that a persuasive argument can alter the law.

Some of Lord Denning's critics describe him as an irresponsible judicial maverick, and speak in the next breath of the harm he has done to the law. Surely they cannot be right on both points. Lord Denning has no power to act alone, and could hardly do much serious harm to the law with dissenting judgments. Although Lord Denning is known for his dissents, far more often he carries one or more of his fellow judges with him: in many Court of Appeal cases including very recent cases the second and third judgments have commenced "I agree . . . " and "I also agree . . . ." Although his decisions have been often overruled and reversed, they have been more often left undisturbed or upheld and even when reversed have been influential. These are not the signs of a maverick—nor of a judge whose powers declined with age—but rather of a skilful advocate who, although he does not win all his cases, can effectively bridge the gap between the law as (in his view) it ought to be and the law as (he can persuade other judges that) it is.

Lord Denning's powers of advocacy are nowhere better illustrated than by the case of *Gallie* v. *Lee*.[47] There, Mrs. Gallie, a 78-year-old widow, placed complete trust in her nephew, Parkin, who was her chief adviser, her closest relative, and the beneficiary of her will. Mrs. Gallie had a leasehold interest in her house, which she was willing to give to Parkin, provided that she could continue to live in the house. Parkin, who wished to raise money for the use of his friend Lee, arranged to have a document drawn up evidencing a sale by Mrs. Gallie to Lee, and Mrs. Gallie, who had broken her glasses and could not read the document, signed it believing it to be a deed of gift to Parkin. Parkin was present at the time and witnessed her signature. Lee borrowed money from a building society securing his promise to repay a mortgage of his leasehold interest as evidenced by the document. Three years later Mrs. Gallie brought an action against Lee and the building society to set aside the sale and to invalidate the mortgage.

The law relating to mistake in signed documents was then as follows: a signer who had been deceived by misrepresentation about the nature of a document was entitled to assert a defence of *non est factum*, which had the effect of making the document void against everyone, if the document was of a different class or character from what the signer believed. Negligence on the part of the signer did not normally preclude the assertion of the defence,

---

[47] Above, n. 22.

a Court of Appeal decision of 1911[48] having held that the signer owed no duty to any third party who might later rely on the document.

Stamp J., applying this law, held that Mrs. Gallie was entitled to assert the defence and that in consequence the sale and the mortgage were void.[49] Indeed Stamp J. extended the scope of the defence slightly by holding, contrary to one possible interpretation of an earlier case,[50] that Mrs. Gallie's knowledge that the document in fact related to her house was insufficient to preclude the defence. The nine pages of the judgment discuss the leading cases, but leave the impression that the judge had no real doubt in his mind about the result, either on the application of the law or on considerations of justice. The strongest form in which the building society's argument appears is that Mrs. Gallie would have been just as badly off if the document *had* been a deed of gift to Parkin, as she believed, for he might then have sold or mortgaged the lease and given the proceeds to Lee. Put like this the argument does not look very strong, and Stamp J. had no hesitation in dismissing it:

> "[This argument] in my mind confused what she intended to do with her object in doing it . . . the submissions on this part of the case advanced on behalf of the defendants are dangerously like a submission that it made no difference to her whether her signature was obtained by a trick, or whether Mr. Parkin having obtained a deed of gift, was subsequently tricked by Mr. Lee."[51]

Throughout, the result is influenced by the very name of the case, *Gallie* v. *Lee*. It looks like a dispute between Mrs. Gallie and Mr. Lee and the merits of that dispute are obviously all on the side of Mrs. Gallie. The real defendant, the building society, is not named in the style of cause. The tendency (and this was just the defect of the then existing law) is to assimilate the position of the two defendants. It is also assumed throughout Stamp J.'s judgment that Mrs. Gallie is the real plaintiff. Nowhere is there a hint of awareness that the real party to gain from the decision would not be Mrs. Gallie but her estate, and that behind the estate and behind the litigation stood Parkin, the very person who was primarily responsible for the deception.

The casual reader would not find anything remarkable in Stamp J.'s decision. Most would have called it a perfectly ordinary decision and a straightforward application of the principle of *non est factum*. No doubt this was the view of the note editors of the *Law Quarterly Review* and the *Modern Law Review*. The case was selected for reporting in the *All England Reports*[52] but only for volume one of the *Weekly Law Reports*, not for the *Law Reports*. If the defendant had not been a wealthy financial institution that could afford to litigate a matter of principle, one supposes that an appeal would not have been recommended.

The *Cambridge Law Journal* did include a comment on the decision of Stamp J.[53] in which the writer, while welcoming the logic of not foreclosing the defence simply because the signer knew that the document related to

---

[48] *Carlisle & Cumberland Banking Co.* v. *Bragg* [1911] 1 K.B. 489.
[49] [1968] 1 W.L.R. 1190.
[50] *Howatson* v. *Webb* [1908] 1 Ch. 1.
[51] [1968] 1 W.L.R. 1199.
[52] [1968] 2 All E.R. 322.
[53] [1968] C.L.J. 187 (C.C. Turpin).

particular land, mildy regretted, in moderate academic language, that the courts had no power to apportion losses in cases where one of two innocent parties had to suffer by the fraud of a third. The commentator said:

> "In conclusion, it may be remarked that it seems regrettable that the court must in every case of this kind cause the whole loss to fall on one or other of two innocent parties. It would surely be better for the courts to have power to apportion the loss between the parties upon an analysis of all the circumstances of the case, including the negligence of either party, the relative experience of each, the relationship between each party and the author of the fraud and the nature of the document the signatory thought he was signing and of that upon which the third party thought he was relying. The present rule of *non est factum* operates in an arbitrary way with results that are often unfair."[54]

No criticism is here intended of the editors of the *Law Reports*, or the *Law Quarterly Review* and the *Modern Law Review*, still less of the commentary in the *Cambridge Law Journal*. Ninety-nine out of 100 lawyers would have reacted in the same way. At least 80 out of the 100 would have recommended against an appeal, and probably the full 99 would have thought it adverse to the building society's interests to appeal to a court presided over by the Master of the Rolls. Lord Denning's sympathy for the individual against corporate power of all sorts is legendary. One could hardly concoct a case suggesting greater sympathy for the signer than one of an old lady of 78 (now 84) who had broken her spectacles, been deceived by her trusted nephew, and having won at trial, was now being dragged into the Court of Appeal by a wealthy financial institution seeking to foreclose her interest in her own home.

But these predictions would have been totally erroneous. It is far too crude a classification of Lord Denning's views to say that he is always on the side of the weak against the strong; he would certainly say that the poor and wealthy alike are entitled to justice. But more significantly, Lord Denning's judgment in the Court of Appeal entirely changes the reader's view of the problem. Once Lord Denning has spoken it is as though a kaleidoscope has been turned and it becomes impossible ever again to see the problem as it appeared to Stamp J. All seven judges in the Court of Appeal and House of Lords who consider the case subsequently cannot help seeing it in the way in which Lord Denning presents it. Lord Denning does not gain their support by haranguing them or browbeating them, but by presenting the case in such a way that they cannot avoid coming to the conclusion he favours. This is the skill of the great advocate: not to overwhelm his adversary by simple argumentive force—not even necessarily to achieve success on every point he argues—but to present the case in such a way that his hearers cannot prevent themselves from being carried along to the desired destination. So Lord Denning seems to influence the other judges in this case. They all disagree with him, some strenuously, and on points that seem to be and really are important, but there is never any room for the slightest doubt about their actual conclusion.

The key to Lord Denning's view of the case is that the real dispute is not between Gallie and Lee but between Parkin (the presumed beneficiary of Mrs. Gallie's estate) and the building society. The building society had very

[54] *Ibid.* at p. 190.

wisely given an undertaking not to enforce the mortgage during Mrs. Gallie's lifetime, so this removed any possibility of actually evicting the old lady. Lord Denning in presenting the facts emphasises the present age of Mrs. Gallie ("an old lady of 84 years of age") the interest of Parkin ("she has made a will leaving everything to him") and his involvement in the litigation ("the plaintiff and Mr. Parkin saw solicitors"). He also included a reference absent in Stamp J.'s judgment to the fact that Parkin witnessed Mrs. Gallie's signature. Lord Denning put the case as follows:

> "On these facts the judge found that the assignment was not her deed: and that she was entitled to the property free of any mortgage or charge. I must say at once that, as the case then stood, this would lead to a most unjust result. The one person to benefit would be Mr. Parkin. He would get the house under his aunt's will, free of any mortgage or charge . . . ."[55]

This would be sufficient to jolt most readers out of their complacent acceptance of the result reached at the trial. Parkin, the very person responsible for the deception, is to be the gainer. But Lord Denning adds another point:

> "He would get the house . . . on the footing that the deed of assignment *was not her deed*: yet he was the very person who witnessed her signature to the assignment and thus vouched that it *was* her deed."[56]

This point has the elegance of the solution to a good chess problem. Once you see it it is obvious. Yet the majority of lawyers would have discussed *non est factum* without thinking of its English meaning or of its relevance to the function of a witness, proving again that Latin phrases in the law are often a source of obscurity rather than of illumination.[57]

Lord Denning's marshalling of the facts made it seem obvious that justice required the reversal of Stamp J.'s decision. Salmon L.J., in agreeing with the result, said:

> "I confess that I reach this conclusion with no regret. The action was brought by Mrs. Gallie at her nephew's instigation for the sole purpose of enabling him to enjoy the lease on her death free from encumbrance, or perhaps to raise another loan on it from another building society during her life. It would indeed be unjust if her nephew knowing all the material facts save that Lee intended to cheat him, and being an active participant in the scheme for putting forward a document (which he himself had witnessed) for the purpose of inducing the defendant building society to lend money on the security of the house, could now deprive the building society of that security and let it whistle for its money. The building society's only prospect of recovering the money due to it is by realising its security; Lee is not worth powder and shot."[58]

It is with a twinge of regret that one reads at the end of the case in the law reports a statement by counsel that Mrs. Gallie had in fact altered her will

---

[55] [1969] 2 Ch. 17, 30.
[56] *Ibid.*
[57] See *per* Lord Shaw of Dunfermline in *Ballard* v. *North British Railway Co.* [1923] S.C. 43, t p. 56 (H.L. Sc.): "The day for canonizing Latin phrases has gone past."
[58] [1969] 2 Ch. 47.

between trial and appeal and that Parkin was no longer the beneficiary after all! The members of the Court are reported to have replied simply that they had reached their judgments on the basis of the materials available to them at the relevant time.[59] It is an oddity that the most powerful arguments turn out to be have been based on an error of fact. Yet this error does not in the least detract from the court's decision. The validity of the document could hardly be held to vary according to the actual provisions of Mrs. Gallie's will, still less according to future alterations in her will. It is sufficient to make the point that Parkin *might* have benefitted from the outcome. But the point obviously carried much more force with a court that believed that he actually had benefited.

The occurrence of this error, however, points up one of the dangers of a judge taking over the role of advocate. Counsel for the building society could not have made the arguments in the form adopted by Lord Denning, because he knew them to be based on an error of fact or, if he did not know, Mrs. Gallie's counsel would soon have set him right. Lord Denning's ability to persuade depended in part upon his ignorance, and it might be thought wrong that Mrs. Gallie's counsel was deprived of the opportunity of correcting the misapprehension before the court rendered judgment.

By the time the case reached the House of Lords,[60] Lord Denning's implied prediction had been fulfilled. Mrs. Gallie had died and was represented by an executrix. Lee, who had not been represented in the Court of Appeal, disappears altogether from the case. For once the practice of changing the style of cause to name only the actual litigants in the House of Lords serves a useful purpose, for the understanding that the dispute is between Saunders (executrix) and the Anglia Building Society, instead of between Gallie and Lee is the key to its resolution. All five law lords delivered speeches, heeding Lord Reid's warning of the dangers of a single speech ("some latitude should be left for future developments"[61]—a remark that itself reflects Lord Denning's view of the element of flexibility to be desired in the common law process). None of the Lords agreed precisely with everything Lord Denning said. Yet his influence pervades every speech, and the final result was a very drastic reduction in the scope of the plea of *non est factum* as against third parties. The plea is now only available where there is a fundamental mistake in the nature of the document signed *and* the signer shows that he was not negligent.

In Canada the effect of *Gallie* v. *Lee* is not yet clear. Canadian jurisdictions face a difficulty that is becoming increasingly common with the greater flexibility of the common law in the English courts. The English Court of Appeal case holding that the signer's negligence did not defeat a plea of *non est factum* (*Carlisle & Cumberland Banking Co.* v. *Bragg*[62]) had been followed by the Supreme Court of Canada in 1956 in *Prudential Trust Co. Ltd.* v. *Cugnet*,[63] the majority simply saying that the 1911 case established the law. Now that the case has been overruled by the House of Lords, lower Canadian courts face a difficult problem. If they follow the House of Lords they are departing from a decision of the Supreme Court of Canada, normally binding. On the

---

[59] *Ibid.* at pp. 49–50.
[60] *Sub nom. Saunders* v. *Anglia Building Society* [1971] A.C. 1004.
[61] *Ibid.* at p. 1015.
[62] Above, n. 48.
[63] [1956] S.C.R. 914.

other hand if the lower Canadian courts adhere to the Supreme Court of Canada decision, the position would be that a rule, based on an English Court of Appeal case of 1911, everywhere agreed to be undesirable, and abandoned in England and the rest of the common law world, might continue in force in Canada for decades until the Supreme Court of Canada found a suitable case in which to deal with it. This last point is particularly forceful as the Supreme Court of Canada has much else besides private law to occupy its time. Of course Canadian courts are bound by the Supreme Court of Canada and not by the House of Lords. No-one in Canada could advocate slavish adherence to the decisions of the English courts. But is not the alternative (following the 1956 Supreme Court of Canada decision) an even more slavish adherence, *i.e.* to an obsolete English Court of Appeal case decided over 70 years ago, without even the merits of justice and logic to support it? Either route raises difficulties. On the question of *non est factum* Grange J. recently held that he was bound by the 1956 decision of the Supreme Court of Canada to follow *Carlisle & Cumberland Banking Co.* v. *Bragg*, even though overruled in England, and (Grange J. considered) rightly overruled. He said:

> "I say with great respect that the reasoning and conclusion of [the dissenting judgment in *Prudential Trust Co. Ltd.* v. *Cugnet*] appeals to me; the signer has it within his power to prevent the fraud which the third party does not. To adopt the reasoning of the majority would seem always to condemn a third party to an investigation of the circumstances of the signing of the document which is regular on its face. But it is the majority judgment . . . that is the law of the land . . . . I appreciate that the House of Lords in *Saunders* (*executrix of the will of Rose Maude Gallie, deceased*) v. *Anglia Building Society* . . . has overruled *Carlisle & Cumberland Banking Company* v. *Bragg* . . . but neither the *Saunders* case nor any of the Canadian cases which refer to it . . . can lessen the binding effect on me of *Prudential Trust Co. Ltd.* v. *Cugnet.*"[64]

The Ontario Court of Appeal dismissed an appeal saying:

> "Like Grange J. we are bound by the judgment in *Prudential Trust Co. Ltd.* v. *Cugnet.*"[65]

However, the alternative route was taken by another Ontario trial judge,[66] also upheld by the Court of Appeal, in an exactly analogous situation also springing from a change in English law instituted by Lord Denning. The issue here concerned obligations owed in foreign currency. Until 1974 the law was that the English courts could give judgment only in sterling, and that the conversion of a foreign debt to sterling was to be calculated at the date of breach, not at the date of judgment. In *Schorsch Meier GmbH* v. *Hennin*[67] Lord Denning gave strong reasons for departing from these rules which were ultimately accepted by the House of Lords in *Miliangos* v. *George Frank Textiles Ltd.*[68]

---

[64] *Marvco Color Research Ltd.* v. *Harris* (1980) 27 O.R. (2d) 686 (H.C.).

[65] 29 O.R. 162. Since this chapter was drafted, the Supreme Court of Canada reversed the *Marvco* case, overruling *Prudential Trust Co. Ltd.* v. *Cugent*. See 141 D.L.R. (3d) 577.

[66] Carruthers J., in *Batavia Times Publishing Co.* v. *Davis* (1978) 20 O.R. (2d) 868 (H.C.).

[67] Above, n. 30.

[68] [1976] A.C. 443.

The effect of the *Miliangos* case was that an English court could actually give judgment in a foreign currency. The power of a Canadian court to give judgment in foreign currency is complicated by a statutory provision which has been interpreted to require judgments to be in Canadian money.[69] However, the statute does not settle the question of whether the conversion of the foreign obligation into Canadian money should take place at the date of breach or at the date of judgment. In the case of a steadily declining dollar, all the arguments that supported the conclusion in *Schorsch Meier*, and *Miliangos* support also the choice of the later date for currency conversion. Naturally the earlier English "breach date" rule had been applied by the Supreme Court of Canada in earlier Canadian cases.[70] However, Carruthers J. considered himself free to adopt the judgment date rule. He said:

> "The decision of the House of Lords in *Miliangos* has reversed the English cases, and in particular, the rule of law upon which the Canadian cases, including those of the Supreme Court of Canada to which I have referred, have proceeded. Although strictly speaking *Miliangos* has not overruled those decisions of the Supreme Court of Canada, including the decision of the Judicial Committee of the Privy Council in *Owners of Steamship Celia* v. *Owners of Steamship Volturno* and they therefore remain today as authorities binding upon the lower courts of Canada, I find it difficult to accept that those cases should now be applied by the lower court. Apart from the fact that the 'breach day' rule which they applied no longer exists in England, when I consider that justice requires that a creditor should not suffer by reason of a depreciation of the value of currency between the due date on which the debtor met his obligation and the date when the creditor was eventually able to obtain judgment, I think what Lord Wilberforce had to say . . . is most pertinent."[71]

Carruthers J. then applied the judgment date rule for conversion of the foreign obligation. The Ontario Court of Appeal, in affirming the decision, did not comment on the problem of binding precedent.[72]

The close association between Canadian and English law led in earlier times to a generally unquestioned assumption that the common law in England was also the law of Canadian jurisdictions. The assumption was also that legal rules were static. Canadian common law has diverged in several instances from English law, and no-one denies that a conscious choice by the Supreme Court of Canada to reject modern English authority binds the lower courts. But where the Supreme Court of Canada has 25 years ago followed an English case without discussion, and the case is subsequently overruled by the House of Lords after careful argument and with persuasive reasons, it seems an unduly rigid application of stare decisis to hold the lower courts bound by the Supreme Court of Canada decision, when the latter rests so clearly on assumptions that have subsequently

---

[69] Currency and Exchange Act R.S.C. 1970 (c. C–39), s.11.
[70] *Custodian of Enemy Property* v. *Blucher* [1927] S.C.R. 420; *Gatineau Power Co.* v. *Crown Life Insurance Co.* [1945] S.C.R. 655.
[71] (1978) 20 O.R. (2d) 447.
[72] See 26 O.R. (2d) 800.

proved false (*i.e.* that the law of England is as was stated and that the common law was not expected to change). Whichever route the Canadian courts take they can be accused of slavishly following English cases; if they cannot avoid this opprobrium they might at least feel free, I would suggest, to follow the more recent and the more persuasive of the English cases. This problem of the force of English decisions in Commonwealth jurisdictions has become acute largely because of the increasing flexibility of which Lord Denning has been such an effective advocate. There can surely be little doubt of the view that Lord Denning himself would take in such cases if he were a Commonwealth judge.

Even where Lord Denning's views have not been accepted by the House of Lords they are often important. Examples could be given of cases where Lord Denning's views, though rejected by the House of Lords, have influenced subsequent legislation,[73] or, in a well known instance, have been vindicated by the European Court of Human Rights.[74] But even where there is no such express vindication, Lord Denning's views have often been influential. A recent example, in the field of damages for personal injuries, is *Lim Poh Choo* v. *Camden and Islington Area Health Authority*.[75] The case concerned the vexed problem of the permanently insentient patient, in that particular case a 33 year-old physician who suffered severe and permanent brain damage because of the defendant's negligence. Lord Denning suggested, and his suggestion is original so far as I know, that a permanently insentient plaintiff should not be entitled to recover loss of future earnings as such. This proposition, though rejected by the majority of the Court of Appeal and by the House of Lords, is worth serious attention. Lord Denning said:

> "In my opinion where a plaintiff is rendered unconscious or insensible, fair compensation should not include an item for loss of earnings as such, but instead it should include an item for pecuniary loss suffered by the dependants of the injured man by reason of his accident. After all, if that is the compensation regarded as fair by the legislature in case of his natural death, it may be justly regarded as fair in case of his living death—provided also that full compensation is also given for every expense that may be incurred on his behalf and every service that may be rendered to him by relatives and friends. The cost of keeping the plaintiff for the rest of his days will exceed by far the salary or wages that he would have earned if he never had been injured. It is not fair to the defendants to make them pay both."[76]

The House of Lords rejected this view, partly because the House had just felt compelled to decide in another case where life had been shortened and there were dependants, that full compensation for loss of earning capacity should be available to an injured plaintiff whether he lived to enjoy the

---

[73] The concept of the "deserted wife's equity" introduced by Lord Denning in *Bendall* v. *McWhirter* [1952] 2 Q.B. 466, rejected by the House of Lords in *National Provincial Bank Ltd.* v. *Hastings Car Mart Ltd.* [1965] A.C. 1175, finds a place in matrimonial property legislation all over the Commonwealth. See, for example, Family Law Reform Act Stat. Ont. 1978 (c. 2), ss.38–49.

[74] The *Sunday Times* case, 22 Y.B. 402 applying Article 10 of the European Convention on Human Rights. See *Attorney-General* v. *Times Newspapers Ltd.* [1973] Q.B. 710, reversed H.L. [1974] A.C. 273.

[75] [1979] Q.B. 196, varied [1980] A.C. 174.

[76] [1979] Q.B. 196, 218–219.

compensation or not.[77] If this were right in the case of a plaintiff whose life had been shortened, it seemed to follow that it must be right too in the case of a plaintiff who was to survive insentient.

But the academic and judicial debate on these questions will certainly continue, and Lord Denning's original and vigorous views will be influential. In a recent article in the *Canadian Bar Review* by B. M. McLachlin, Lord Denning's views in *Lim Poh Choo* are in substance adopted.[78] The writer, a law teacher subsequently appointed to the Bench, takes the view that recovery of lost future earnings should depend on the use to be made of the award by the plaintiff.

The influence of Lord Denning's judgments has not always been beneficial. It would be astonishing if in praising a judge for his bold innovations, a commentator found no decisions to criticise. The very qualities that are most admirable in Lord Denning—an ability to see a legal problem from a new point of view and the boldness to express that point of view with clarity and conviction—carry their own inevitable risks.

A contrast can be drawn to illustrate this point between two decisions of Lord Denning's, both on the question of economic loss in tort law. Lord Denning's dissenting judgment in *Candler* v. *Crane, Christmas & Co.*[79] in 1951 is everywhere cited as a leading judgment on the question of liability for negligent misstatement causing economic loss. Lord Denning's view presents an argument in favour of liability that is forceful, but at the same time thoughtful. All the major questions that need to be considered are addressed, and as is well known, his arguments eventually prevailed in the House of Lords[80] and have been followed throughout the Commonwealth.[81]

The contrasting case is *Spartan Steel and Alloys Ltd.* v. *Martin & Co. (Contractors) Ltd.*,[82] a case on the difficult problem of economic loss caused by negligent activities. In the *Spartan Steel* case the defendant had caused an interruption of power to a factory by negligently severing an electric cable. Lord Denning rejected the arguments put in favour of recovery.

> "[Counsel for the plaintiff] . . . said that if there was any limitation on the recovery of economic loss, it was to be found by restricting the sphere of duty not by limiting the type of damages recoverable. In the present case, he said, the defendants admittedly were under a duty to the plaintiffs and had broken it. The damages by way of economic loss were foreseeable, and, therefore, they should be recoverable. He cited several statements from the books in support of his submission, including some by myself. At bottom, I think the question of recovering economic loss is one of policy . . . . The more I think about these cases, the more difficult I find it to put each into its proper pigeonhole. Sometimes I say 'there was no duty.' In others I say 'the damage was too remote.' So much so that I think the time has come to discard those

---

[77] *Pickett* v. *British Rail Engineering Co.* [1980] A.C. 136.
[78] "What Price Disability? A perspective on the Law of Damages for Personal Injury," (1981) 59 Can. Bar Rev. 1.
[79] [1951] 2 K.B. 164. Fleming calls it a "classical dissent," *Law of Torts* (5th ed.), p. 637.
[80] *Hedley Byrne & Co. Ltd.* v. *Heller & Partners Ltd.* [1964] A.C. 465.
[81] See *Mutual Life and Citizens' Assurance Co.* v. *Evatt* [1971] A.C. 793, *Haig* v. *Bamford* [1977] 1 S.C.R. 466.
[82] [1973] Q.B. 27.

tests which have proved so elusive. It seems to me better to consider the particular relationship in hand, and see whether or not, as a matter of policy, economic loss should be recoverable."[83]

Lord Denning suggests five considerations. These are the law relating to public utilities which have not been held liable for economic losses, the fact that power cuts are generally endured without thought of litigation, the possibility of fraudulent claims, the desirability of spreading the loss, and the assertion that a person suffering physical damage is more deserving of compensation than one suffering economic loss only. But one only needs to read these considerations to see that they do not supply very convincing reasons for a rule of law excluding recovery of economic loss in all cases. An even moderately rigorous analysis would show that the considerations beg important questions and rest on untenable assumptions. One can easily envisage Lord Denning himself, if he favoured extension of liability, giving short shrift to cases that had denied liability on such grounds. It is not surprising, therefore, that on this particular question the *Spartan Steel* case has not been followed in the Commonwealth outside England.[84]

The reasoning is superficially attractive. Lord Denning seems to be inviting his readers to throw off the fetters of precedent and to look at the question realistically. Who can object to discarding the artificial and elusive legal tests of the past (the ill-reputed pigeonholes filled with black letter law) and looking at the question as one of "policy"? But if we are to destroy the legal doctrine of the past we must have something better to put in its place. *Spartan Steel* seems to have been a case of premature and even indiscriminate destruction. Subsequent attempts in Canada, New Zealand and Australia to elaborate rational principles in this area of law show that Lord Denning's views have not here been found to be helpful.[85]

The decision that first brought Lord Denning into prominence as a judge, *Central London Property Trusts* v. *High Trees House Ltd.*[86] cannot be reckoned, either, as one of his most successful judgments. Few would now dispute the need for reform and development of the criteria for enforcement of promises. The English law of consideration had made bargain the "be all and end all" of enforceability. The American Law Institute had pointed the way to a more flexible test by providing that in some circumstances subsequent reliance on a promise could justify enforcement.[87] In the *High Trees* case Lord Denning, sitting as a trial judge, asserted that "a promise intended to be binding, intended to be acted upon, and in fact acted upon is bindng . . . ."[88] This assertion, it seemed, dispensed not only with the need for a bargain, but with the need for reliance also, for it seems that Lord Denning did not intend by the phrase "in fact acted upon" to introduce a requirement of substantial change of position on the part of the promisee. This was surely too wide, and in *Combe* v. *Combe*[89] Lord Denning, by then in the Court of

---

[83] *Ibid.* at p. 36–37.
[84] See *Rivtow Marine Ltd.* v. *Washington Iron Works* (1973) 40 D.L.R. (3d) 530, *Caltex Oil (Australian) Pty. Ltd.* v. *The Dredger "Willemstad"* (1977) 11 A.L.R. 227 (H.C.), *Bowen* v. *Paramount Builders Ltd.* [1977] 1 N.Z.L.R. 394 (C.A.).
[85] See cases cited in n. 84, above.
[86] [1947] 1 K.B. 130.
[87] American Law Institute, *Restatement of Contracts*, s.90.
[88] [1947] 1 K.B. 130, 136.
[89] [1951] 2 K.B. 215.

Appeal, was compelled to retreat, which he did by stating that the principle of the *High Trees* case "does not create new causes of action";

> "Seeing that the principle never stands alone as giving a cause of action in itself, it can never do away with the necessity of consideration where that is an essential part of the cause of action. The doctrine of consideration is too firmly fixed to be overthrown by a side wind. Its ill effects have been largely mitigated of late, but it still remains a critical necessity of the formation of a contract, although not of its modification or discharge. I fear that it was my failure to make this clear in *Central London Property Trust Ltd.* v. *High Trees House Ltd.* which misled [the trial judge] in the present case."[90]

The consequence of this retreat has been the creation of a distinction between cases where the promise in question has been sought to be enforced by a plaintiff ("as a sword") and by a defendant ("as a shield"),[91] a distinction that often does not answer to the merits of the case. It may be suggested that a sounder development would have been to draw upon American experience and to develop the law, more modestly, in the direction of protecting reliance with the possibility of limiting enforcement to the extent of the promisee's reliance.

Another doctrine of contract law developed by Lord Denning which some would consider unsound, a doctrine perhaps applied more often in Canada than any of his other contributions in any area of the law, is fundamental breach. Lord Denning developed this doctrine in order to prevent suppliers of goods from taking unfair advantage of exemption clauses, and it was enthusiastically taken up both in England and Canada. The effect of the doctrine was summarised in *Karsales (Harrow) Ltd.* v. *Wallis*[92]:

> "The law about exempting clauses, however, has been much developed in recent years, at any rate about printed exempting clauses, which so often pass unread. Notwithstanding earlier cases which might suggest the contrary, it is now settled that exempting clauses of this kind, no matter how widely they are expressed, only avail the party when he is carrying out his contract in its essential respects. He is not allowed to use them as a cover for misconduct or indifference or to enable him to turn a blind eye to his obligations. They do not avail him when he is guilty of a breach which goes to the root of the contract. It is necessary to look at the contract apart from the exempting clauses and see what are the terms express or implied, which impose an obligation on the party. If he has been guilty of breach of those obligations in a respect which goes to the very root of the contract, he cannot rely on the exempting clauses."[93]

In *Suisse Atlantique Societe d'Armement Maritime S.A.* v. *N.V. Rotterdamsche Kolen Centrale*[94] (the facts of which had nothing to do with unfair exemption

---

[90] *Ibid.* at p. 220.
[91] See, for example, *Gilbert Steel Ltd.* v. *University Construction Ltd.* (1976) 67 D.L.R. (3d) 606, 610 (Ont. C.A.).
[92] [1956] 1 W.L.R. 936.
[93] *Ibid.* at p. 940.
[94] [1967] 1 A.C. 361.

clauses) the House of Lords held, contrary to Lord Denning's view, that there was no rule of law that prevented parties from contracting as they thought fit. Lord Reid plainly recognised a need to control the unfair use of exemption clauses, but thought that the means of control had to be given by Parliament.

The result of the *Suisse Atlantique* case was rather unsatisfactory for Parliament did not act immediately, and so a potential gap appeared in the law. In *Harbutt's Plasticine Ltd.* v. *Wayne Tank and Pump Co. Ltd.*[95] the Court of Appeal held the supplier of plastic pipe liable for the loss of a factory by fire, despite an exemption clause purporting to exclude such liability, *Suisse Atlantique* being distinguished on rather thin grounds. The decision has been subjected to much criticism, and it must be conceded, I think, that Lord Denning was somewhat too eager to re-establish the doctrine of fundamental breach. Unfortunately, the case in which he chose to do so was not nearly as suitable a case as that in which the doctrine had first been developed, (*Karsales (Harrow) Ltd.* v. *Wallis* involved a consumer sale of an automobile), for the justice of the case seemed rather on the side of the supplier of the pipe than of the factory owner or his insurer who was the real plaintiff.

Subsequently Lord Denning developed the view that the true test of enforcement of exemption clauses was unconscionability.[96] The development of unconscionability suggests that he might not have decided *Harbutt's Plasticine* as he did had he considered the case from that point of view, for it seems that there was nothing unreasonable or unfair in the exclusion.

However, it is difficult to speak with confidence on this point, because in *Photo Production Ltd.* v. *Securicor Transport Ltd.*[97] Lord Denning again struck down an exemption clause in a business contract. The case involved a clause excluding the liability of a security firm for the wrongdoing of its employees. The plaintiff's factory was destroyed by a fire set by one of the defendant's employees. Ironically, the trial judge had accepted Lord Denning's view, as expressed in several recent cases, that the test of enforceability should be unconsionability, and then had decided that the clause was perfectly fair and reasonable, being an allocation of an insurable risk between business parties of equal bargaining power. Lord Denning in the Court of Appeal said that the right test had been applied, but the wrong conclusion reached, thus unfortunately confirming the fears of those who say that the doctrine of unconscionability will set contract law afloat without chart or compass. Lord Denning thought it unfair that the security company should exclude its liability for fires set by its employees. But he gives no satisfactory reason why an insurable risk should not be allocated by agreement between two large business corporations.

In the House of Lords the doctrine of fundamental breach as developed by Lord Denning was firmly overruled, this conclusion being strengthened by reference to the recent enactment of the Unfair Contract Terms Act 1977. But Lord Wilberforce was, on the whole, not critical of the doctrine, pointing out that it had served a useful and indeed a necessary purpose:

"The doctrine of fundamental breach in spite of its imperfections and

---

[95] [1970] 1 Q.B. 447.
[96] See *Gillespie Bros. & Co. Ltd.* v. *Roy Bowles Transport Ltd.* [1973] Q.B. 400, *Levison* v. *Patent Steam Carpet Cleaning Co. Ltd.* [1978] Q.B. 69.
[97] (1978) 1 W.L.R. 856, reversed H.L. [1980] A.C. 827.

doubtful parentage has served a useful purpose. There were a large number of problems, productive of injustice, in which it was worse than unsatisfactory to leave exemption clauses to operate. Lord Reid referred to these in the *Suisse Atlantique* case, pointing out at the same time that the doctrine of fundamental breach was a dubious specific. But since then Parliament has taken a hand: it has passed the Unfair Contracts Terms Act 1977 . . . . After this Act in commercial matters generally, where the parties are not of unequal bargaining power, and where risks are normally borne by insurance, not only is the case for judicial intervention undemonstrated, but there is everything to be said . . . for leaving the parties free to apportion the risks as they think fit and for respecting their decision."[98]

It is not a bad epitaph for the doctrine of fundamental breach, unsound though it may be, to say that it has served a useful purpose, that it has avoided injustice and that the alternative would have been worse than unsatisfactory.

In Canada the position is again unclear. The doctrine of fundamental breach was at first enthusiastically adopted. After *Suisse Atlantique* the courts paid lip service to the principle of construction, but continued to strike down exemption clauses nominally on the basis of construction but without any explanation suggesting a genuine attempt to construe. The Supreme Court of Canada has approved the *Photo Production* case[99] but as in the very case in which approval was announced the clause in question was struck down without an explanation consistent with principles of construction, it seems likely that the position will remain as before. So the doctrine of fundamental breach, though abolished in England, seems likely to live on in Canada (where there is no legislation comparable to the Unfair Contract Terms Act) in the guise of a rule of construction.

Much criticism has been directed against Lord Denning in England for his decisions on questions of public policy and labour law and for his expressions of opinion on other matters of political controversy. These are little known in Canada, where Lord Denning's reputation is based on his judgments, particularly in private law areas. The prevailing image of Lord Denning is shown by the design of the "Lord Denning T-shirt" produced by students at the University of Toronto depicting Lord Denning surmounted by the word "Equity." A few years ago I had occasion to quote to my contract law students Lord Denning's dictum about the allegedly unruly horse of public policy:

> "With a good man in the saddle the unruly horse can be kept in control. It can jump over obstacles. It can leap the fences put up by fictions and come down on the side of justice."[1]

A friend of one of the students drew a cartoon showing Lord Denning in the saddle of the horse of public policy leaping over the fictitious fences towards the green pastures of justice. The card was sent to Lord Denning with greetings on his seventy-ninth birthday, and he must have been pleased with it, for he wrote back a letter of thanks (with which the students were

---

[98] [1978] A.C. 834, 843.
[99] *Beaufort Realties (1964) Inc.* v. *Chomedey Aluminum Co. Ltd.* (1980) 116 D.L.R. (3d) 193.
[1] *Enderby Town Football Club Ltd.* v. *The Football Association Ltd.* [1971] Ch. 591, 606.

delighted) adding a wish that they should all become good horsemen and horsewomen, and he published the cartoon in his book "The Discipline of Law."[2]

I have dwelt on Lord Denning's contribution to private law because it is there that his reputation among Canadian lawyers rests, and I think it is there that his reputation will continue into the future. Long after his views on trade unions, immigration, and sexual immorality have been forgotten, students throughout the Commonwealth will be reading his decisions in contract cases. The style and substance of Lord Denning's judgments guarantees that many will be selected by future casebook editors and will be read with pleasure and excitement by students. Indeed I believe that it is true to say that Lord Denning's influence on Canadian law is in a state of growth, for it is recent graduates who have read the greatest number of Lord Denning's judgments, and these graduates have still to make their own influence felt in the profession.

[2] See p. 173.

Farewell to Lord Denning

July 30, 1982

THE LORD HIGH CHANCELLOR: LORD HAILSHAM OF ST. MARYLEBONE

Mr. Attorney,

It is given to few men to become a legend in their lifetime. There would be few in this country who would deny that Lord Denning is one of these few. From the numbers and standing of his own fraternity of the law assembled here today to do him honour we can readily infer that he has been and is a golden legend.

The law in England has its periods of growth and creativity. It has also enjoyed periods of quiescence and consolidation. Each period has its value, and, to a large extent, the values are complementary. When I was called to the Bar in 1932, Lord Denning had already been a barrister for nine years. He had six years to go before he donned the silk gown. The law, at least in my opinion, was in one of its periods of quiescence. It seemed almost as if Our Lady of the Common Law had gone into a decline, and had handed over her power of development to the sovereignty of Parliament, which, however, in those pre-war days was not over ready to accept the baton. True, there were landmark decisions, like *Donoghue* v. *Stevenson*, and even dissenting opinions such as that of Lord Atkin in *Liversidge* v. *Anderson*. I put this period of quiescence down as ending somewhere about 1945 after *Liversidge* v. *Anderson* and *Duncan* v. *Cammell, Laird*.

In 1945 Lord Denning had been a puisne judge for one year. It thus happens that his career spans the next period of about 35 years, say from *High Trees* to *Gouriet*, and it so happens, partly by chance, but partly also more than coincidentally, that during those 35 years Our Lady of the Common Law awoke from her slumbers and entered upon a period of renewed creativity, generated no doubt by the vast social and legislative changes which have overtaken us, and inspired by a desire to do right to all manner of people without fear or favour, affection or ill will, in the changed circumstances of the post-war world.

To this period we owe the revival and extension of that sleeping beauty, natural justice, the vast development of administrative law and judicial review, the renewed assertion by the courts of their independence of the executive, and their belief in the rule of law.

It would by wholly unjust to ascribe all of these changes to the Master of the Rolls who is now at length to doff his wig and lay aside the silk and golden robes. But it would be equally wrong in his presence and in this company not to acknowledge the vast debt which this revival of the common law owes to his deep learning, his powerful legal intellect, and even to his telling and pungent English style.

English Law derives from statute and the common law. It is the function of the courts to interpret the one and evolve the other. From its dual source English law derives at once its vitality and its inspiration.

The Court of Appeal remains the focal point of modern English jurisprudence. It is not infallible, and, unless it becomes so, there will always be a humble purpose left for the Appellate Committee of the House of Lords. But the Court of Appeal remains the mainspring of innovation, and, to abandon my metaphor, for 20 years Lord Denning has presided over the Civil Division of the Court of Appeal.

Without him, things will never be quite the same again. I like to think that notwithstanding his retirement our period of creativity will not quite come to an end, still less relapse once more into quiescence. But, Master of the Rolls, we shall miss you. We shall miss your passion for justice, your independence and quality of thought, your liberal mind, your geniality, your unfailing courtesy to colleagues, to counsel, and to litigants in person who, like the poor, are always with us, particularly in the Court of Appeal. Above all, we shall miss you and your gift of friendship, your sturdy independence, and your unflagging and effervescent enthusiasm. Now you belong to history. But here you see around you a company of admirers and friends. We wish you well, both you and Lady Denning. Come and see us often. Wherever lawyers are gathered together they will always rejoice to see you in their midst.

Bibliography

Books

Smith's Leading Cases (13th ed., 1929).
Bullen & Leake's Precedents of Pleadings in Actions in the King's Bench Division of the High Court. With notes (9th ed., 1935).
Freedom under the Law (1949).
The Changing Law (1953). Reprinted 1954.
The Freehold and the Law in Hunter (Leslies). Bishop of Sheffield. Two views on the Parsons Freehold.
The Road to Justice (1955) (essays).
The Discipline of Law (1979).
The Due Process of Law (1980).
The Family Story (1981).
What Next in the Law (1982).
The Closing Chapter (1983).
Landmarks in the Law (1984).

Official Reports

Committee on procedure in Matrimonial Cases and two interim reports, Cmd. 6881, 6945, 7024 (1946).
Committee on Legal Education for Students from Africa, Cmnd. 12, 55 (1961).
Profumo Affair—Lord Denning's Report, Cmnd. 2152.
Legal Records 1963–66, Cmnd. 3084 (1900).
Report of the Secretary to the Commissioners 1969–76.
Royal Commission on Historical Manuscripts.

Case Notes

(1939) 55 L.Q.R. 343–345, 353–357.

Articles

"Quantum Meruit and the Statute of Frauds" (1925) 41 L.Q.R. 79.
"Re-entry for Forfeiture" (1927) 43 L.Q.R. 53.
"Quantum Meruit: The Case of Craven–Ellis v. Canons Ltd." (1939) 55 L.Q.R. 54.
"Meaning of Ecclesiastic Law" (1944) 60 L.Q.R. 235.
"Presumptions and Burdens" (1945) 61 L.Q.R. 379.
"Matrimonial Problems in the Magistrates Court" (1949) 113 J.P.N. 643; (1950) 28 N.Z.L.R. 416.
"Recovery of Money" (1949) 65 L.Q.R. 37.
"Universities and Law Reform" (1949) 1 *Society of Public Teachers of the Law* 258.
"The Restatement of the Law: its Place in the English Courts" (1951) 37 A.B.A.J. 329; 404.
"Spirit of the British Constitution" (1951) 29 Can. Bar Rev. 1180.
"English Law and the Moral Law" (1954) February 25, *The Listener*.
"Courts and Tribunals" 1 B.J.A.L. 107. (Based on a lecture to the Royal Institute of Public Administrators.)
"Way of the Iconoclast" (1959) 5 J.S.P.T.L. 77 (1960) 3 Sydney L. Rev. 209.
"Legal Education in Africa: Sharing our Heritage" (1961) 56 L.S. Gaz. 147. (An article based on the lecture to the Law Christian Fellowship, held January 26, 1961.)
Speech at the opening ceremony of Third Australian Legal Convention (1967) 41 A.L.J. 224.
"Let Justice be Done," Fifth Wilfred Fullager Memorial Lecture: Revision with same title delivered: Tenth Annual Manitoba Law School foundation lecture (1975) 2 Manitoba L.R. 3; (1975) 6 Man. L.J. 227.
"The Freedom of the Individual Today" (1977) 45 Medico-Legal Journal. (Based on an address to the Medico-Legal Society in 1977.)
"Misuse of Power" (1980) 55 A.L.J. 720. (Edited lecture of the Richard Dimbleby Lecture in 1980.)

Lectures

"The Divorce Laws," King's College London. 1947.

"The Equality of Women," Annual Conference of the National Guidance Council. 1950.

"The Independence of the Judges." The presidential address of the Rt. Hon. Lord Justice Denning, President of the Holdsworth Club of the students of the Faculty of Law, University of Birmingham (1949–50). 1950. Published in Harvey (ed.), *The Lawyer and Justice* (1978).

"The Need for a New Equity." Address to the Bentham Club by its president. (1952) Current Legal Problems 1.

"The Influence of Religion on Law." Earl Grey Memorial Lecture No. 33. 1953.

"Notes on a Lecture on the Changing Law." 1953.

"The Rule of Law in the Welfare State." Birbeck College London, Haldane Memorial Lecture, No. 20. 1953.

"The Christian Approach to the Welfare State," Shaftesbury Lecture No. 17. 1954.

"The Equality of Women," Eleanor Rathbone Memorial Lecture. 1959.

"From Precedent to Precedent." The Romanes Lecture delivered in the Sheldonian Theatre, Oxford University. 1959.

"Responsibility before the Law," Lionel Cohen Lectures Ser 7. 1961—Hebrew University of Jerusalem.

"Borrowing from Scotland," 28th David Murray Foundation Lecture, University of Glasgow. 1961.

"Independence and Impartiality of Judges." Lecture at Witwatersrand University. First in series August–September, 1954, Nuffield Foundation (1954) 71 S.A.L.J. 345.

"The Traditions of the Bar." Lecture at Witwatersrand University. Second in series, 1954. (1955) 72 S.A.L.J. 43.

"The Price of Freedom: We Must be Vigilant Within the Law." Lecture to A.B.A. August 1955. (1955) 41 A.B.A.J. 1011, 1059.

"The Right Standards of Conduct." Lecture to the Law Society. (1957) 54 L.S. Gaz. 609.

"The Individual, the State and the Law." Lecture in Justice Riblitt Hall, Inner Temple. (1963) 6 *Lawyer* 35.

"Recent Changes in the Law." Address to 13th Dominion Legal Conference, Dunedin, April 13, 1966. (1966) N.Z.L.J. 167.

"Law and Life in Our Times." Turner Memorial Lecture, 1967. (1967) 2 *Tasmania University L. Rev.* 349.

"Giving Life to the Law." (1976) 1 Malaya L. Rev.

"Gems in Ermine." English Association Presidential address. 1964.

"Let Justice be Done." An oration at Birkbeck College on the 151th Anniversary of its foundation. 1974.

"Restraining the Misuse of Power." Jubilee Presidential address Holdsworth Club, University of Birmingham. 1978.

"Jubilee Lectures," celebrating the foundation of the Faculty of Law of the University of Birmingham. (Ed. I. R. Scott.)

"Misuse of Power." Dimbleby Lecture, 1980.

Book Reviews

Cheshire, *Law of Contract* (1945). (1946) 62 L.Q.R. 190.

Salmond, *Principles of the Law of Contract* (1945). (1946) 62 L.Q.R. 190.

Winfield, *A Text Book on the Law of Torts* (3rd ed., 1949). (1949) 63 L.Q.R. 516.

Williams, *Joint Obligations* (1949). (1950) 66 L.Q.R. 253.

Seavey, *Cogitations on Tort* (1954). 68 Harv. L. Rev. 564 (1955).

Winfield, *A Text Book on the Law of Tort* (6th ed., 1954). (1955) Camb. L.J. 113.

Jackson, *Supreme Court in the American System of Government* (1955). (1956) 72 L.Q.R. 418.

Vanderbilt, *Challenge of Law Reform* (1955). (1956) 72 L.Q.R. 418.

Goff and Jones, *Law of Restitution* (1966) (1967) 83 L.Q.R. 277. L.Q. Rev. 83: 277 Ap' '67.

Griswold, *Law and Lawyers in the United States* (1964). 80 Harv. L. Rev. 916 (1967).

Index of Judges

479

Index

481